Lecture Notes in Artificial Intelligence　11298

Subseries of Lecture Notes in Computer Science

More information about this series at http://www.springer.com/series/1244

Chiara Ghidini · Bernardo Magnini
Andrea Passerini · Paolo Traverso (Eds.)

AI*IA 2018 – Advances in Artificial Intelligence

XVIIth International Conference
of the Italian Association for Artificial Intelligence
Trento, Italy, November 20–23, 2018
Proceedings

Springer

Editors
Chiara Ghidini ⓘ
Fondazione Bruno Kessler
Povo (TN), Italy

Andrea Passerini
University of Trento
Povo (TN), Italy

Bernardo Magnini
Fondazione Bruno Kessler
Povo (TN), Italy

Paolo Traverso
Fondazione Bruno Kessler
Povo (TN), Italy

ISSN 0302-9743   ISSN 1611-3349 (electronic)
Lecture Notes in Artificial Intelligence
ISBN 978-3-030-03839-7   ISBN 978-3-030-03840-3 (eBook)
https://doi.org/10.1007/978-3-030-03840-3

Library of Congress Control Number: 2018960440

LNCS Sublibrary: SL7 – Artificial Intelligence

This Springer imprint is published by the registered company Springer Nature Switzerland AG
The registered company address is: Gewerbestrasse 11, 6330 Cham, Switzerland

Preface

This volume collects the contributions presented at the XVII Conference of the Italian Association for Artificial Intelligence (AI*IA 2018). The conference was held in Trento, Italy, during November 20–23, 2018. The conference is organized by AI*IA (the Italian Association for Artificial Intelligence), and it is held annually.

The conference received 67 submissions. Each paper was carefully reviewed by at least three members of the Program Committee, and finally 41 papers were accepted for publication in these proceedings.

AI*IA 2018 featured exciting keynotes by Lise Getoor, Professor of Computer Science and Director of the D3 Data Science Research Center at University of California Santa Cruz, and Malik Ghallab, Emeritus Research Director at LAAS CNRS in Toulouse. The rest of the conference program included short presentations of the accepted papers followed by poster sessions, the Doctoral Consortium, a broad choice of workshops, tutorials, panel sessions, and an open event. The list of workshops comprised the 7th Italian Workshop on Machine Learning and Data Mining (MLDM), the Second Workshop on Advances in Argumentation in Artificial Intelligence (AI^3), the Workshop on Multi-Agent Systems and Social Network (MAS & SN), the R.i.C.e. R.c.A - RCRA Incontri E Confronti Workshop (RiCeRcA), the 4th Italian Workshop on Artificial Intelligence for Ambient Assisted Living (AI*AAL), the 5th Italian Workshop on Artificial Intelligence and Robotics (AIRO), and the Second Workshop on Natural Language for Artificial Intelligence (NL4AI). This edition featured for the first time a set of high-quality tutorials covering a broad spectrum of topics, namely, "Timeline-Based Planning and Execution: Theory and Practice," "Novel Developments in Ontology-Based Data Access and Integration," "Formal Ontological Analysis and Knowledge Representation," "Adversarial Machine Learning and Probabilistic Knowledge Representation in Machine Learning." Another novelty of this year's edition was the assignment of a best paper award, assigned to "A Generalized Framework for Ontology-Based Data Access" by Elena Botoeva, Diego Calvanese, Benjamin Cogrel, Julien Corman, and Guohui Xiao, and of a best student paper award, assigned to "The Role of Coherence in Facial Expression Recognition" by Lisa Graziani, Stefano Melacci, and Marco Gori. In accordance with the practice of the last AI*IA conferences, the program was complemented by an open event targeted at the general public concerning the impact of artificial intelligence on society. Within this event, titled "Angeli e Demoni dell'Intelligenza Artificiale: evoluzioni possibili e impatti sulla nostra vita," expert panelists, including Carlo Casonato, Michela Milano, François Pachet, Piero Poccianti, and Francesco Profumo, discussed what is happening in the artificial intelligence field, with particular emphasis on the opportunities, challenges, potential threats, and national and international strategies it is generating in different sectors of society.

The chairs wish to thank the Program Committee members and the reviewers for their invaluable work in reviewing the contributions, and the organizers of all

workshops, tutorials, panels and of the Doctoral Consortium for contributing to the
success of the conference. Special thanks go to the Organizing Committee for
managing this event in a very competent and professional way. Last by not least, we
would like to thank the proceedings chair, Paolo Dragone, for putting these proceedings together.

November 2018

Chiara Ghidini
Bernardo Magnini
Andrea Passerini
Paolo Traverso

Organization

Executive Committee

General Chair

Paolo Traverso   Fondazione Bruno Kessler, Italy

Program Chairs

Chiara Ghidini   Fondazione Bruno Kessler, Italy
Bernardo Magnini   Fondazione Bruno Kessler, Italy
Andrea Passerini   DISI, University of Trento, Italy

Workshop and Tutorial Chairs

Stefano Borgo   CNR-ISTC, Italy
Mauro Dragoni   Fondazione Bruno Kessler, Italy

Doctoral Consortium Chairs

Marco Rospocher   Fondazione Bruno Kessler, Italy
Luciano Serafini   Fondazione Bruno Kessler, Italy
Sara Tonelli   Fondazione Bruno Kessler, Italy

Industry Liason and Sponsorship Chair

Marco Guerini   Fondazione Bruno Kessler, Italy

Publicity and Web Manager

Mauro Dragoni   Fondazione Bruno Kessler, Italy

Proceedings Chair

Paolo Dragone   DISI, University of Trento, Italy

Local Organization

Annalisa Armani   Fondazione Bruno Kessler, Italy
Silvia Malesardi   Fondazione Bruno Kessler, Italy
Chiara Ghidini   Fondazione Bruno Kessler, Italy
Bernardo Magnini   Fondazione Bruno Kessler, Italy
Andrea Passerini   DISI, University of Trento, Italy
Mauro Dragoni   Fondazione Bruno Kessler, Italy

Program Committee

Fabio Aiolli	University of Padua, Italy
Davide Bacciu	University of Pisa, Italy
Matteo Baldoni	University of Turin, Italy
Stefania Bandini	University of Milan-Bicocca, Italy
Nicola Basilico	University of Milan, Italy
Federico Bergenti	University of Parma, Italy
Tarek Richard Besold	City, University of London, UK
Stefano Bistarelli	University of Perugia, Italy
Andrea Burattin	Technical University of Denmark, Denmark
Elena Cabrio	Universitè Côte d'Azur, CNRS, Inria, France
Stefano Cagnoni	University of Parma, Italy
Diego Calvanese	Free University of Bozen-Bolzano, Italy
Luigia Carlucci Aiello	Sapienza University of Rome, Italy
Amedeo Cesta	ISTC-CNR, Italy
Federico Chesani	University of Bologna, Italy
Francesco Corcoglioniti	University of Trento, Italy
Gabriella Cortellessa	ISTC-CNR, Italy
Stefania Costantini	University of L'Aquila, Italy
Riccardo De Masellis	Stockholm University, Sweden
Dario Della Monica	University of Naples Federico II, Italy
Claudio Di Ciccio	Vienna University of Economics and Business, Austria
Tommaso Di Noia	Politecnico di Bari, Italy
Michelangelo Diligenti	University of Siena, Italy
Michele Donini	Amazon, USA
Agostino Dovier	Unversity of Udine, Italy
Aldo Franco Dragoni	Polytechnic University of Marche, Italy
Floriana Esposito	University of Bari, Italy
Stefano Ferilli	University of Bari, Italy
Alberto Finzi	University of Naples Federico II, Italy
Salvatore Gaglio	University of Palermo, Italy
Marco Gavanelli	University of Ferrara, Italy
Massimiliano Giacomin	University of Brescia, Italy
Claudio Giuliano	Fondazione Bruno Kessler, Italy
Floriana Grasso	University of Liverpool, UK
Nicola Guarino	ISTC-CNR, Italy
Giuseppe Jurman	Fondazione Bruno Kessler, Italy
Evelina Lamma	University of Ferrara, Italy
Nicola Leone	University of Calabria, Italy
Antonio Lieto	University of Turin, Italy
Marco Lippi	University of Modena and Reggio Emilia, Italy
Francesca Alessandra Lisi	University of Bari, Italy
Fabrizio Maria Maggi	University of Tartu, Estonia
Marco Maratea	University of Genoa, Italy
Simone Marinai	University of Florence, Italy

Andrea Marrella	Sapienza University of Rome, Italy
Viviana Mascardi	University of Genoa, Italy
Fulvio Mastrogiovanni	University of Genoa, Italy
Alessandro Mazzei	University of Turin, Italy
Stefano Melacci	University of Siena, Italy
Paola Mello	University of Bologna, Italy
Alessio Micheli	University of Pisa, Italy
Alfredo Milani	University of Perugia, Italy
Stefania Montani	University of Piemonte Orientale, Italy
Angelo Oddi	ISTC-CNR, Italy
Francesco Orsini	University of Florence, Italy
Matteo Palmonari	University of Milan Bicocca, Italy
Viviana Patti	University of Turin, Italy
Maria Teresa Pazienza	University of Rome, Tor Vergata, Italy
Ruggero G. Pensa	University of Turin, Italy
Roberto Pirrone	University of Palermo, Italy
Simone Paolo Ponzetto	University of Mannheim, Germany
Daniele Porello	Free University of Bozen-Bolzano, Italy
Gian Luca Pozzato	University of Turin, Italy
Francesco Ricca	University of Calabria, Italy
Fabrizio Riguzzi	University of Ferrara, Italy
Andrea Roli	University of Bologna, Italy
Silvia Rossi	University of Naples Federico II, Italy
Salvatore Ruggieri	University of Pisa, Italy
Fabio Sartori	University of Milan-Bicocca, Italy
Marco Schaerf	Sapienza University of Rome, Italy
Giovanni Semeraro	University of Bari, Italy
Luciano Serafini	Fondazione Bruno Kessler, Italy
Carlo Strapparava	Fondazione Bruno Kessler, Italy
Stefano Teso	Katholieke Universiteit Leuven, Belgium
Daniele Theseider Dupré	University of Piemonte Orientale, Italy
Olga Uryupina	University of Trento, Italy
Eloisa Vargiu	Eurecat Technology Center, Spain
Marco Villani	University of Modena and Reggio Emilia, Italy
Serena Villata	CNRS, France
Giuseppe Vizzari	University of Milan-Bicocca, Italy

Contents

Machine Learning

Natural Language Processing

Planning and Scheduling

Recommendation Systems and Decision Making

Agents and Multi-Agent Systems

An Introduction to the Major Features of a Scripting Language for JADE Agents

Giuseppe Petrosino[✉] and Federico Bergenti

Dipartimento di Scienze Matematiche, Fisiche e Informatiche,
Università degli Studi di Parma, 43124 Parma, Italy
giuseppe.petrosino@studenti.unipr.it, federico.bergenti@unipr.it

Abstract. This paper presents a concise description of the major features of the Jadescript language for agent-oriented programming. First, the need for a programming language intended explicitly to support the design and implementation of agents and multi-agent systems based on JADE is motivated. Then, core features which characterise the language as an agent-oriented programming language, namely, those meant to support message passing and event-driven programming, are briefly described. The description of core features uses an illustrative example to show how the language can be concretely used to program multi-agent systems, at least in simple, but significant, cases.

1 Introduction and Motivation

Among the significant number of innovations that the research on agents and multi-agent systems have popularised, *Agent-Oriented Programming* (*AOP*) [19] plays a singular role for the interest that it is gaining also outside of the agent community, e.g., to support model-driven development [11]. Usually, AOP is described as a programming paradigm explicitly designed with the intent to assist programmers in the concrete implementation of agents and multi-agent systems. In this sense, AOP is a way to interface the knowledge level, as introduced by Newell in [16], and put it into practice. More generally, AOP is not only related to the abstractions which programmers use for the construction of agents and multi-agent systems, but it is also related to the concrete syntax that programmers adopt to manage such abstractions. Therefore, it is not surprising that the first public appearance of the acronym is in a paper by Shoham [18], which proposes a new programming language, namely Agent-0, to introduce a whole new syntax and semantics to support the concrete implementation of software agents.

The fact that AOP has to do equally with agent-specific abstractions and with the syntax and the semantics of programming languages has been put aside in the last twenty years by the strong opinion, shared by a significant number of researchers, that the abstractions that AOP helped to identify could be effectively used in the scope of mainstream programming technologies. The widespread adoption of agent platforms like JADE [1] had the effect of shifting the focus from the syntax and the semantics of programming languages

© Springer Nature Switzerland AG 2018
C. Ghidini et al. (Eds.): AI*IA 2018, LNAI 11298, pp. 3–14, 2018.
https://doi.org/10.1007/978-3-030-03840-3_1

to the provision of platform-level abstractions accessible from mainstream programming technologies. Actually, since its initial conception, JADE and similar platforms (e.g., [11] for a survey) have been intended primarily to offer support to Java programmers, and the decision to support developers of multi-agent systems with a Java framework, rather than with a specific language, is part of the basic ideas that originated those platforms. The fact that JADE and similar platforms were so intimately linked with Java can be justified by the characteristics of the programming technologies available at the time when agent platforms were popularised. Java was an emerging technology, and it was common opinion that it would have changed radically the way software was built. Programmers wanted to use it, if nothing else, for their professional growth, and high-profile decision makers were happy with it because it was the technology that marked the growth of the Web. Today, the professional practice of programming is significantly different, and a dynamic landscape of programming technologies is in use, with each programming technology designed to target specific scenarios.

Mentioned motivations are some of the reasons why, after a decennial experience with the use of JADE in a wide span of scenarios ranging from highly dynamic industrial applications [13] to high-profile management services [5], we came to the conclusion that a specific programming technology is needed to assist the programmer in the development of complex functionality, and to promote the effective use of the beneficial features of agent technology for *Agent-Oriented Software Engineering* (*AOSE*) [6]. We first experimented a smooth depart from Java by introducing JADEL [3,7], an AOP language which uses a dialect of Java called Xtend [8] to support the procedural subset of the language. JADEL has been under constant development since four years, and the experiments in the use of the language emphasised that the adoption of a Java dialect has two important drawbacks related to the fact that Java is today a commodity that most programmers master. First, programmers would have preferred the immediate use of Java, and they do not seem to find added value in the use of a dialect whose major differences from Java are related to syntactic sugar. Second, programmers tend to prefer the direct use of JADE from Xtend, rather than the use of the agent-oriented, and more abstract, features that JADEL provides. This is partially justified by the fact that the large body of documentation available for JADE easily translates to procedural code written in Xtend.

The two important drawbacks just mentioned, which are ultimately caused by the very basic design choice of grounding JADEL on a dialect of Java, suggested to rework the ideas that originated JADEL to further loose the tight with Java. A descendant of JADEL called Jadescript has been recently conceived to provide support for the construction of agents and multi-agent systems on top of JADE with no direct use of Java, but still preserving interoperability with JADE agents and multi-agent systems. This paper briefly describes the major features of Jadescript, and it is organised as follows. Section 2 shows a brief overview of the language using an illustrative example and giving emphasis on supported agent-oriented abstractions. Section 3 concludes the paper and discusses planned future developments of the language and of its support tools.

2 Overview of Jadescript

Jadescript is an AOP language intended to support the implementation of agents using an event-driven style of programming with explicit emphasis on the possibility for agents to exchange messages. The major abstractions that Jadescript supports are (communication) ontologies [20], (agent) behaviours, and agents. JADE programmers are familiar with such abstractions, and Jadescript keeps them exactly as JADE programmers would expect (e.g., [2] for a detailed description of such abstractions). In addition, Jadescript is a scripting language which tries to reduce the gap between an agent-oriented source code and a semantically equivalent pseudocode. For this reason, Jadescript shares some resemblances with popular scripting languages like Python, e.g., in the use of semantically relevant indentation. In brief, the main objectives of Jadescript are all related to the goal of raising the level of abstractions that programmers use in all programming tasks related to the construction of agents and multi-agent systems. Such goals can be summarized as follows:

1. To provide programmers with high-level, agent-oriented abstractions;
2. To assure that the high level of abstraction of the language does not force to accept major methodological or computational compromises; and
3. To ensure that available agent technology is used effectively.

Such objectives are common to many AOP languages that have been recently proposed (e.g., [7] for a survey), even if there is not yet an agreement on how they should be concretised in a specific programming language. Note that Jadescript shares a lot with its direct ancestor JADEL, but its marked depart from Java makes it closer to pseudocode. In addition, the use of concepts defined in ontologies (see Subsect. 2.2) as structured data types, which is not directly supported by JADEL, ensures that the abstract view of manipulated data that ontologies provide can also be used in the construction of agents.

Even if Jadescript is designed to enable the effective implementation of JADE agents and multi-agent systems, Jadescript is not an object-oriented language. However, the close relationship with Java is still actual in the compilation process that is assumed for Jadescript source files. A Jadescript source file, if valid, is primarily intended to be compiled to one or more Java source files. Such files are then compiled to Java bytecode using one of the available Java compilers, and resulting Java bytecode is eventually executed by a *Java Virtual Machine* (*JVM*) with the help of JADE. This approach is not new, and it has been proven effective, e.g., by JADEL, SARL [17], and other proposals. The choice of compiling Jadescript source files to Java source files was taken for the following reasons. First, the adopted approach grants interoperability with Java and JADE, thus extending the potential of Jadescript and promoting code reuse. Note that the minimal interface to Java which is still present in Jadescript to support the integration with the features of the underlying JVM is considered low-level its use is discouraged. Second, off-the-shelf Java compilers emit Java bytecode using a rich set of well-tested and decade-proven checks and optimizations, which would be pointless to try to recreate for a Jadescript to bytecode compiler. Third, the semantics of Jadescript can be designed in terms of the underlying semantics of Java, which eases the process of designing the semantics of the language and it also helps ordinary JADE and Java programmers to appreciate, and possibly adopt, Jadescript. Finally, the availability of powerful tools for the construction of this type of compilers in the Eclipse ecosystem supports the effective provision of professional tools to programmers, which seems to be essential to propose Jadescript to the programmers that appreciate and already use JADE in high-profile projects (e.g., [12] for recent a survey).

The current implementation of the Jadescript compiler uses the tools of the Xtext suite [9] to ensure a smooth integration with Eclipse. Actually, Jadescript is currently supported by a rich set of tools packed as an Eclipse plug-in, and the current version of the tools and of related documentation is available upon request from authors. Note that an open-source distribution is planned for the near future, and it is expected as soon as the bundle could contain sufficient documentation and, at least, one complete tutorial.

The remaining of this section describes the features that can be included in a Jadescript source file. Note that the overview of Jadescript discussed in this section is by far not exhaustive. Only a selected set of features is presented, and interested readers are directed to the documentation that comes bundled with the distribution of Jadescript tools for further discussions. In order to ease the descriptions of the features of the language, an illustrative example is discussed throughout this section. The selected example is well-known to JADE programmers because the JADE implementation of a very similar multi-agent system is presented in one of the most popular tutorials on JADE. The considered example assumes that a multi-agent system contains a group of seller agents, each of which manages a music shop which sells two types of items, books and DVDs. Each item for sale has a unique title and a price. In addition, each DVD has a specific list of tracks. Finally, each track has a title and a duration. Seller agents own items and they sell them to other agents, which play the role of buyer agents in the considered scenario. The scenario starts when a buyer agent asks all seller agents about the availability of a specific item. In the likely case that the item is available at the shops managed by some of the seller agents, the buyer would request to one of them to actually buy the item. In detail, the scenario starts when a buyer agent sends call-for-proposal messages to all known seller agents to ask them if a specific item is available at their respective shops. Seller agents can quote the requested item, by responding with a propose message, or they can quit the protocol by returning a refuse message. Once the buyer agent receives a satisfactory proposal from a seller agent, it issues a request message to ask the seller agent to actually sell the item. Therefore, the discussed scenario implements an contract net protocol [10], even if the protocol is not explicitly identified. Note that the presented Jadescript implementation of the scenario is not intended to be interoperable with the corresponding implementation which uses JADE. Technically, the loss of interoperability is caused by the fact that JADE misses some checks that are needed to fully comply with the semantics of IEEE FIPA messaging, while Jadescript provides them.

2.1 Procedural Features

The structure of a Jadescript source file is fixed, and it starts with the mandatory declaration of the module where all features declared in the source file are contained, using the keyword **module**. For the time being, modules are simply named groups of features, each of which can be public or private to the module. Imported features from other modules are enumerated using the keyword **import**. The list of imported features from other modules follows the mandatory module declaration. Finally, every Jadescript source code is completed with a list of declarations related to the major features supported by the language, i.e., ontologies, behaviours, and agents. Such features are discussed in the following after a brief description on the procedural features of the language.

Jadescript is a statically typed language, and the types of all features referenced in a source code are known at compile time. In particular, Jadescript provides no ways to synthesise new types at run time. The Jadescript type system is based on five groups of types: primitive types, ontology types, collection types, behaviour types, and agent types. Primitive types are **boolean, double, float, integer**, and **text** (strings of characters), and they match the corresponding Java types. The common structured types of procedural languages are called ontology types in Jadescript because they are accessed in terms of concepts, propositions, predicates and actions declared in ontologies (see Subsect. 2.2). Jadescript also offers collection types for lists and maps. Examples of valid declarations for lists and maps are **list of integer** and **map of integer : text**. Finally, behaviour types and agent types are provided to manage behaviours (see Subsect. 2.3) and agents (see Subsect. 2.4), respectively. Every behaviour definition or agent definition implicitly defines a new data type, whose use is restricted with respect to other data types. In particular, Jadescript provides specific constructs for the manipulation of behaviours and of agents to ensure that such abstractions are given first-class support in the language.

Jadescript is an agent-oriented language and it provides common statements and expressions of procedural languages to let agents properly handle events using behaviours. The following is a summary of the subset of supported statements and expressions that are not specific to AOP.

In the tradition of programming languages derived from the C language, function calls can be used as statements in Jadescript. In addition, the **do-nothing** statement can be used to write empty blocks of code, which is necessary because the delimitation of blocks in Jadescript is based on indentation.

Jadescript provides a single statement to assign a value to a variable, an element of an ontology type, an element of a collection type, or a property of an agent or a behaviour. The same statement can also be used to declare the name of a variable, and the common = operator is provided for such tasks. Declarations are distinguished from assignments because the compiler tracks names, and when a new name is found, the = operator is assumed to refer to a declaration. In order to relieve the programmer from the burden of explicitly declaring the types of variables, the Jadescript compiler infers automatically the types of variables from mandatory initialisation expressions. Therefore, there is no need to explicitly declare variables in Jadescript. Note that the type inference that Jadescript provides is limited with respect to other languages, and the types of some elements of a Jadescript source code, e.g., the types of formal parameters in function declarations, need to be explicitly stated. Finally, note that Jadescript provides the `create` statement to create instances of collection and ontology types, and to assign them to variables. After the keyword `create`, the first required term is the type of which the instance is being created; right after that, an identifier is required, which determines the name of the new variable that will refer to the newly created value. If needed, a comma-separated list of named arguments is provided after the keyword `with`.

Jadescript provides ordinary control statements. The classic `if` statement can be used to express conditional statements. Like in most procedural languages, the `if` statement can also have multiple `if-else` branches and an optional `else` branch at the end. After every condition, a new block of code is opened by increasing the indentation level in a new line. Jadescript also provides two forms of iterative statements in terms of the common `while-do` statement, and of the `for-in-do` statement. In particular, iteration over collections is supported with the `for-in-do` statement, which can be used to iterate over the elements of lists or over the keys of maps. At each iteration, an element from the collection which follows the keyword `in` is extracted and, before the body of the statement is executed, the element is assigned to a variable whose name is declared after the keyword `for`. For both types of iterative statement, indentation is used to create the blocks of statements that are iterated. Finally, the `return` statement can be used to terminate the execution of a function and possibly return a value to the caller. Note that the `return` statement can also be used to terminate the execution of an event handler (see Subsect. 2.3).

Jadescript provides a specific set of statements to work with collections. In particular, `add-to`, `remove-from`, and `clear` statements are used to manipulate the contents of lists. Note that `add-to` and `remove-from` can possibly specify an optional index to work on an element different from the last element of the list. Similarly, `remove-from` and `clear` are available for maps. Other common operations on collections, e.g., access to a specific element, are made available using expressions (see below), possibly in conjunction with the = operator.

Besides statements, Jadescript offers a system of expressions, and a limited subset of them can also be used at the left side of the = operator. Every expression computes a value and the type of computed value is evaluated and statically checked by the compiler. Expressions often contain prefix and infix operators, and common precedence and associativity rules are used to disambiguate the order of evaluation. Ordinary Boolean expressions are formed in Jadescript using the keywords `and`, `or`, and `not`. Boolean operations follow a lazy evaluation scheme: if the value of the whole operation can be deducted from the evaluation of the first operand, then the second operand is not evaluated. In addition, ordinary comparison operators with the common semantics are provided. Finally, arithmetic expressions are supported in Jadescript using ordinary operators for addition, subtraction, multiplication, division, and modulo.

Jadescript provides operators to work on collections and on their elements. Ordinary square brackets are available to access the elements of lists and maps. When applied to lists, they require a nonnegative integer to be used as an index in the list. When applied to maps, they require a value compatible with the type of the keys to access the corresponding value in the map. Note that square brackets can also be used at the left side of the = operator to modify lists and maps. In addition, the `size-of` operator can be used to retrieve the number of elements of lists and maps. The `contains` operator has the function to check if the collection returned by the evaluation of the left-side operand contains the element returned by the evaluation of the right-side operand. It can work on lists and on the keys of maps. Finally, Jadescript offers a concise way to instantiate lists and maps by declaring theirs elements. A list literal is written as a comma-separated list of values between square brackets. The type of the elements contained in the list is computed by finding the closest common ancestor of the types of enumerated elements. Similarly, Jadescript offers a way to quickly instantiate a map by enumerating a set of key-value pairs. A map literal is written as a comma-separated list of key-value pairs between curly brackets, where keys are separated from values by colons. The type of the keys of the map is computed by finding the closest common ancestor of the types of enumerated keys. The type of the values of the map is computed by finding the closest common ancestor of the types of enumerated values.

Type casting is supported in Jadescript using the `as` operator, which forces the type of the result of the evaluation of the expression on its left side to the type specified on its right side, if types are actually compatible. Type inspection is supported in Jadescript by means of the `is` operator, which has the function to check if the type of the value returned by its left operand is compatible with the type specified as right operand.

2.2 Ontologies

Ontologies are used by agents to share descriptions of concepts, actions, predicates, and propositions, and to refer to them in messages. Concepts are structured entities used to describe the world where agents execute. In Jadescript, a concept is defined by stating its name, its elements, and if it is an extension of another concept. Actions are structured entities used to refer to the actions that agents can be requested to perform. An action is stated in Jadescript by identifying its name, its formal parameters, and if it can be considered an extension of another action. Predicates are structured entities used to state logical facts about the world where agents execute. In Jadescript, a predicate is stated by identifying its name, its formal parameters, and whether or not it can be considered an extension of another predicate. Similarly to predicates, propositions are used to state logical facts: they perform the same function as predicates, but they have no formal parameters. Finally, besides the declaration of concepts, actions, predicates and propositions, an ontology is characterised by a unique name in its module and by an optional base ontology that it extends. Figure 1 shows an example of the ontology declaration used to implement the music shop example

```
1   ontology MusicShop
2     concept item(title as text, price as double)
3     concept track(duration as integer)
4     concept book extends item
5     concept DVD(tracks as list of track) extends item
6
7     predicate owns(title as text)
8     predicate quote(buyer as text, good as item)
9
10    action sell(buyer as text, title as text)
```

Fig. 1. Example of an ontology written in Jadescript.

described earlier in this section. The ontology shown in Fig. 1 is an example of an ontology which includes three concepts, two predicates, and an action.

With the exception of propositions, all features declared in an ontology can be used to create structured values, whose elements can be accessed using the of operator, also at the right side of the = operator. The of operator mimics the way English expresses the intention to access properties of a concept. Note that the of operator is not limited to the features declared in ontologies, and it can also be used to access the properties of behaviours (see Subsect. 2.3) and of agents (see Subsect. 2.4).

2.3 Behaviours

Behaviours are used to define how agents operate in the multi-agent system during their lifetime. In Jadescript, these are built upon JADE behaviours and they are characterised by the peculiar scheduling mechanisms of JADE behaviours (e.g., [2] for details). The keyword behaviour can be used to define new Jadescript behaviours. A minimal behaviour is declared by stating its name, which must be unique in the module, and its type, which can be cyclic or one shot. More complex types of behaviours, as supported by JADE, are planned for future versions of the language. The declaration of a behaviour can restrict the types of agents that can adopt the behaviour using the keywords for agent, and it can link the behaviour to an ontology with the keywords uses ontology. Finally, the declaration of a behaviour is completed with a list of optional features to be used to implement the behaviour. Those are properties, functions, procedures, actions and (event) handlers. Note that, whenever an expression can be used in the definition of one of such features, the keyword agent can be used to refer to the agent which is currently linked with the behaviour.

A property of a behaviour is a part of the run-time state of the behaviour. It is distinguished by a name, unique in the declaration of the behaviour, an optional type, and a mandatory initializer expression. The type is deduced from the type of the initializer expression by the compiler, so it is not explicitly stated. Properties can be accessed from all other features of the behaviour, and from other agents and behaviours, using the of operator, which mimics the use of *of* preposition of possession in English to enhance readability.

Functions and procedures can be declared in behaviours. This allows programmers to define parameterised blocks of code to perform tasks. The declarations of functions must specify the type of the values that they return. Functions and procedures can have zero or more arguments, and the names and the types of such arguments must be specified with a list of formal parameters. Finally, functions and procedures have bodies expressed in terms of sequences of statements. Note that indentation is used to delimit the bodies of functions and procedures.

Actions are the primary features used to describe how behaviours perform their tasks. When a behaviour is selected for execution, its action is immediately executed. Note that actions declared in behaviours are conceptually different from actions declared in ontologies. The former are executable pieces of code scheduled for execution with the behaviour, while the latter are descriptions of the actions that agents can be requested to perform, and they are primarily intended to support communication among agents.

Various forms of on constructs can be used to declare (event) handlers in the scope of behaviours. Handlers are used to identify the blocks of code that are supposed to be executed when interesting events occur. For the time being, the most important type of event handler available in behaviours is intended to support the reception of messages. Handlers of this type assign a name to the messages being received and specify a condition that interesting messages are demanded to satisfy to be processed.

Behaviours can be made active by using the `activate-behaviour` statement, which can be used inside the actions of agents and behaviours. This statement creates a new behaviour and it marks the behaviour as active, so that it can be actually scheduled for execution by the agent that issued the statement. Some behaviours need a set of arguments in order to be initialized, and such arguments are passed to the behaviour by using the keyword `with` in the scope of the `activate-behaviour` statement. It is evident that, together with receiving messages, sending messages is a central activity to support agent communication. This task is performed in Jadescript using the keyword `send`. There are two syntactical forms available in the language to use this keyword. The most expressive form can be used if an instance of the concept which represents the message to be sent is already available. This form allows accessing all the features of IEEE FIPA messages [10] because concepts representing messages need to be explicitly created. On the contrary, the use of the simplified form allows to send messages in a more concise manner. The simplified form creates a message and sends it immediately, but only the performative, the list of receivers, the content, and, implicitly, the ontology can be specified.

Figure 2 shows a behaviour used to implement the music shop example described earlier in this section. The `WaitForRequests` behaviour is scheduled by seller agents to wait for incoming call-for-proposal messages. When one of such messages is received, the behaviour is used to check if the requested item is available in the shop, and to reply accordingly.

```
1  cyclic behaviour WaitForRequests for agent Seller uses
2    ontology MusicShop
3    on message m when
4      performative of m is cfp and
5      content is owns do
6      catalogue = catalogue of agent
7
8      content = content of m as owns
9
10     title = title of content
11
12     buyer = sender of m
13
14     if catalogue contains title do
15       good = catalogue[title]
16
17       send propose quote(buyer, good) to buyer
18     else do
19       send refuse sell(buyer, title) to buyer
```

Fig. 2. Jadescript behaviours used in the music shop example.

2.4 Agents

Jadescript agents are the core abstraction used to build Jadescript multi-agent systems. They are basically JADE agents and they can be defined using the keyword **agent**. Agents are structured in terms of the following features: properties,

```
1  agent Buyer uses ontology MusicShop
2    on create with args as list of text do
3      title = args[0]
4
5      create list of text sellers
6
7      skip = true
8
9      for a in args do
10       if skip do
11         skip = false
12       else do
13         add a to sellers
14
15     activate behaviour SendCFPs with sellers = sellers,
16       title = title
17
18     activate behaviour WaitForResponses
```

Fig. 3. Jadescript buyer agents used in the music shop example.

functions, procedures, and (event) handlers. Properties, functions and propositions are the same features available in the declaration of behaviours. Handlers are restricted forms of the handlers available in behaviours because they can be used only to react to events regarding the lifecycle state of agents. One of such events is captured with the `on-create` handler, which is activated just before the agent becomes available in the agent platform. Similarly, the `on-destroy` handler is triggered just before the agent is removed from the agent platform. Interested readers should consult JADE documentation [2] for a description of the possible lifecycle states of an agent. Figure 3 shows the source code of buyer agents used to implement the music shop example discussed in this section.

3 Conclusion

This paper provides a concise description of the major features of Jadescript, a scripting language for AOP. Jadescript follows the path traced by other proposals (e.g., [7] for a survey), which ultimately share the goal to try to increase the level of abstraction perceived by programmers. The long-term vision of the project is to allow programmers to easily implement distributed and decentralised systems by designing interactions among agents in terms of message exchanges, which can be readily translated into Jadescript agents and behaviours. The first step taken towards this long-term vision is to completely abandon Java and its dialects, which were still present in JADEL, to provide programmers with a scripting language designed explicitly to promote readability.

Among the numerous envisioned developments of the language, the generalisation of message handlers to more general event handlers seems particularly significant. Such a possibility would enable agents to sense the environments where they execute, and to react to changes that occur in it, and it would ultimately enable the use of Jadescript in situations where agents are immersed in dynamic environments, e.g., the industrial environments discussed in [14, 15], or the highly dynamic environments discussed in [4]. The support for generic types of events in the language would require syntactic enhancements to let programmers describe interesting events. In addition, it would also require to design a framework to let event sources push events to agents.

References

1. Bellifemine, F., Bergenti, F., Caire, G., Poggi, A.: JADE - a Java agent development framework. Multi-Agent Programming. MASA, vol. 15, pp. 125–147. Springer, Boston (2005). https://doi.org/10.1007/0-387-26350-0_5
2. Bellifemine, F., Caire, G., Greenwood, D.: Developing multi-agent systems with JADE. Wiley Series in Agent Technology. John Wiley & Sons, Hoboken (2007)
3. Bergenti, F.: An introduction to the JADEL programming language. In: Proceedings of IEEE 26th International Conference on Tools with Artificial Intelligence (ICTAI), pp. 974–978. IEEE Press (2014)

4. Bergenti, F., Caire, G., Gotta, D.: An overview of the AMUSE social gaming platform. In: Proceedings of Workshop "From Objects to Agents". CEUR Workshop Proceedings, vol. 1099 (2013)
5. Bergenti, F., Caire, G., Gotta, D.: Large-scale network and service management with WANTS. In: Industrial Agents: Emerging Applications of Software Agents in Industry, pp. 231–246. Elsevier (2015)
6. Bergent, F., Huhns, M.N.: On the use of agents as components of software systems. Methodologies and Software Engineering for Agent Systems. MASA, vol. 11, pp. 19–31. Springer, Boston (2004). https://doi.org/10.1007/1-4020-8058-1_3
7. Bergenti, F., Iotti, E., Monica, S., Poggi, A.: Agent-oriented model-driven development for JADE with the JADEL programming language. Comput. Lang. Syst. Struct. 50, 142–158 (2017)
8. Bettini, L.: Implementing Domain-Specific Languages with Xtext and Xtend. Packt Publishing, Birmingham (2013)
9. Eysholdt, M., Behrens, H.: Xtext: Implement your language faster than the quick and dirty way. In: Proceedings ACM International Conference on Object Oriented Programming Systems Languages and Applications (OOPSLA 2010), pp. 307–309. ACM (2010)
10. Foundation for Intelligent Physical Agents: FIPA specifications (2002). http://www.fipa.org/specifications
11. Kardas, G.: Model-driven development of multiagent systems: a survey and evaluation. Knowl. Eng. Rev. 28(4), 479–503 (2013)
12. Kravari, K., Bassiliades, N.: A survey of agent platforms. J. Artif. Soc. Soc. Simul. 18(1), 11 (2015)
13. Monica, S., Bergenti, F.: A comparison of accurate indoor localization of static targets via WiFi and UWB Ranging. Trends in Practical Applications of Scalable Multi-Agent Systems, the PAAMS Collection. AISC, vol. 473, pp. 111–123. Springer, Cham (2016). https://doi.org/10.1007/978-3-319-40159-1_9
14. Monica, S., Ferrari, G.: Particle swarm optimization for auto-localization of nodes in wireless sensor networks. In: Tomassini, M., Antonioni, A., Daolio, F., Buesser, P. (eds.) ICANNGA 2013. LNCS, vol. 7824, pp. 456–465. Springer, Heidelberg (2013). https://doi.org/10.1007/978-3-642-37213-1_47
15. Monica, S., Ferrari, G.: Accurate indoor localization with UWB wireless sensor networks. In: Proceedings of 23rd IEEE International Conference on Enabling Technologies: Infrastructure for Collaborative Enterprises (WETICE 2014), pp. 287–289. IEEE Press (2014)
16. Newell, A.: The knowledge level. Artif. Intell. 18, 87–127 (1982)
17. Rodriguez, S., Gaud, N., Galland, S.: SARL: A general-purpose agent-oriented programming language. In: 2014 IEEE/WIC/ACM International Conference on Intelligent Agent Technology. IEEE Computer Society Press, Warsaw, Poland (2014)
18. Shoham, Y.: AGENT-0: A simple agent language and its interpreter. In: Proceedings of 9th National Conference on Artificial Intelligence (AAAI 1991). vol. 91, pp. 704–709 (1991)
19. Shoham, Y.: An overview of agent-oriented programming. In: Bradshaw, J. (ed.) Software Agents. vol. 4, pp. 271–290. MIT Press (1997)
20. Tomaiuolo, M., Turci, P., Bergenti, F., Poggi, A.: An ontology support for semantic aware agents. In: Kolp, M., Bresciani, P., Henderson-Sellers, B., Winikoff, M. (eds.) AOIS -2005. LNCS (LNAI), vol. 3529, pp. 140–153. Springer, Heidelberg (2006). https://doi.org/10.1007/11916291_10

Timed Memory in Resource-Bounded Agents

Stefania Costantini[1], Andrea Formisano[2]([✉]), and Valentina Pitoni[1]

[1] DISIM – Università di L'Aquila, L'Aquila, Italy
[2] GNCS-INdAM and DMI – Università di Perugia, Perugia, Italy
andrea.formisano@unipg.it

Abstract. In intelligent agents memory plays a crucial role in the choice of future course of action, as it is progressively formed by means of agent's interactions with the external environment. Previous work exists in logic concerning formalization of reasoning on the formation of beliefs in non-omniscient agents. We address an aspect which has been hardly considered so far, i.e., the notion of "explicit time", by introducing timed beliefs, timed inferences, by means of temporal logic operator on time intervals.

1 Introduction

The interaction between an agent and its environment plays an important role in constructing the agent's "memory" and affects its future behavior. In fact, through memory an agent is potentially able to recall and to learn from experiences so that its beliefs and its future course of action are grounded in these experiences. The exploitation of "memories" requires the interaction among different memory components. Such correlation can be obtained in various ways, e.g., via neural networks, via mathematical models or via logical deduction. Memorization mechanisms in agent architectures have typically been inspired by models of human memory developed in cognitive science, that postulated the existence of two distinct though interacting memory components: short-term memory and long-term memory (cf., e.g., [1–3] and the references therein).

In computational logic, [4] introduces DLEK (Dynamic Logic of Explicit beliefs and Knowledge) as a logical characterization for representing reasoning about the formation of beliefs through perception and inference in non-omniscient resource-bounded agents. They consider perception, short-term memory (also called "working memory"), long-term memory (also called "background knowledge") and their interaction. DLEK is grounded in previous work about awareness (cf. [5–7] and the references therein). DLEK is a logic that consists of a static part called LEK, which is an epistemic logic, and a dynamic component, which extends the static one with "mental operations". Resource-boundedness in DLEK is modeled via the assumption that beliefs are kept in the short-term memory, while implications that allow reasoning to be performed are kept in the long-term memory. New beliefs can be formed in DLEK either from perception,

C. Ghidini et al. (Eds.): AI*IA 2018, LNAI 11298, pp. 15–29, 2018.
https://doi.org/10.1007/978-3-030-03840-3_2

or from previous beliefs in short-term memories and rules in the background knowledge. Inferences that add new beliefs are performed one step at a time via an interaction between short- and long-term memories in consequence of an explicit "mental operation" that will occur whenever an agent deems it necessary and can allot the needed time [8,9]. Beliefs are represented via an explicit modal "B" operator and knowledge (implications) via an explicit "K" operator. The DLEK logic has in our opinion great relevance because it provides a logical formalization of short and long-term memories which has the merit to abstract away from procedural aspects so as to be potentially at the basis of any kind of implementation, even encompassing non-symbolic components. In fact, DLEK has been demonstrated to be suitable for modeling the SOAR memory mechanism [10]. DLEK has however no notion of explicit time, while agents' actual perceptions are inherently timed and so are many of the inferences drawn from such perceptions. In this paper we present an extension of DLEK to TDLEK ("Timed DLEK") obtained by introducing explicit time, timed beliefs, and timed inferences, the latter by means of temporal logic operators on time intervals. We also extend the logic by introducing conditional removal or restructuring of beliefs in the working memory. The issue of time in agents has been coped with in several other works, (see, e.g., among many, [11–14]), where however the objective is that of dealing with time in communication and coordination among agents; thus, our attempt to deal with time in memory management is a novelty in the literature.

In the rest of the paper, Sects. 2 and 4 present syntax, semantics of the extended logic, the axiomatization, and the canonical model. Section 3 describes an example scenario. In Sect. 5 we propose a brief discussion on complexity and conclude.

2   Temporalizing DLEK Logic: TDLEK

We introduce TDLEK starting from LEK and DLEK. We will illustrate the new logic by difference from LEK and DLEK while emphasizing the aspects that we modify/extend.

We may notice that most of the time-based logics follow the seminal work of [15]. In Metric Temporal Logic (MTL) [16] the modalities of LTL are augmented with timing constraints; thus, expressions of the form $\Box_I$ and $\Diamond_I$ are introduced, where I is a *time interval* which, under the *Pointwise Semantics*, can either be finite or diverge to infinity. The works of [17,18] cope with time intervals by introducing modalities for every possible relationships among intervals and also among points and intervals. In this work we consider MTL under pointwise semantics and time points expressed as natural numbers, which is known to admit decidable versions where satisfiability and model-checking have been proved to be EXPTIME-complete [19,20].

2.1 TLEK and TDLEK

We consider an underlying discrete linear model of time and identify time instants with natural numbers and time intervals with intervals in $\mathbb{N}$. More in general, we consider any arithmetic expression e over natural numbers, with value $v_e \in \mathbb{N}$, as denoting the time instant v_e. For simplicity, in what follows, we identify each expression e with its value v_e. A "time-interval" is a closed finite interval $[\ell, u]$ or an infinite interval $[\ell, \infty)$ (considered open on the upper bound), for any expressions/values ℓ, u such that $0 \le \ell \le u$. Given $I_1 = [t_1, t_2]$ and $I_2 = [t_3, t_4]$ (where both t_2 and t_4 can be ∞) we indicate as $I_1 \uplus I_2$ the unique smallest interval including both I_1 and I_2. We write $I_1 \le I_2$ meaning that I_1 is "before" I_2, with a possible non-empty intersection.

As it is customary in logic programming, we assume some signature specifying (countable) sets of *predicate, function,* and *constant* symbols. From constant and function symbols, compound terms are built as usual. The *Herbrand universe* is the collection of all such terms (which includes constant symbols). We assume that the integer numbers and the symbol ∞ are included among the constant symbols and that the arithmetic operators are included among the function symbols. Consequently, arithmetic expressions are terms of the signature. Atoms have the form $pred(\tau_1, \ldots, \tau_n)$ where $pred$ is a predicate symbol, n its arity and $\tau_1, \ldots, \tau_n$ are terms. We denote by $Atmg$ the countable set of atoms of the signature (i.e., the *Herbrand base*).

A *time-stamped* (or, briefly, *timed*) atom p_t is an atom p annotated with a time instant, called *time-stamp*, t. We denote by $Atmtg$ the set of all atoms and time-stamped atoms (note that $Atmg \subseteq Atmtg$). For an atom p, by p_I with $I = [\ell, u]$, we mean the conjunction $p_\ell \wedge p_{\ell+1} \wedge \cdots \wedge p_u$. In this frame of mind, we will often denote the time-stamped atom p_t as p_{I_t} with $I_t = [t, t]$. A plain atom p stands for $p_{[0, \infty)}$.

Below is the definition of the formulas of the language $\mathcal{L}_{TLEK}$. With a slight abuse, in this grammar we use J_1, J_2, I, I_1, I_2, and $I_1 \uplus I_2$ as terminal symbols standing for time intervals (possibly specified through arithmetic expressions, as said earlier)

$$\Phi_{J_1} := p_{J_1} \mid \neg \Phi_I \mid \Box_I \Phi_{I_1} \mid B_i \Phi_I \mid K_i \Phi_I$$
$$\Phi_{J_2} := \Phi_{I_1} \vee \Phi_{I_2} \mid \Phi_{I_1} \wedge \Phi_{I_2} \mid \Phi_{I_1} \to \Phi_{I_2}$$

with the restrictions that $I_1 \subseteq I \subseteq J_1$ in the first production and $I_1 \uplus I_2 \subseteq J_2$ in the second one. (Others Boolean connectives $\top, \bot, \leftrightarrow$ are defined from $\neg$ and $\wedge$ as usual.) Notice that, by the mentioned restriction (and the fact that $I_1, I_2 \subseteq I_1 \uplus I_2$), any formula $\Phi_t = \Phi_{[t,t]}$ is entirely composed of atoms having t as time-stamp.

For simplicity, considering the previous grammar rules, in writing a compound formula Φ whose annotating interval J_1 (resp., J_2) coincides with I (resp., with $I_1 \uplus I_2$) we will often omit such interval. Hence, for example, we write simply $\neg \Phi_I$ in place of $(\neg \Phi_I)_I$ and we write $\Phi_{I_1} \to \Phi_{I_2}$ in place of $(\Phi_{I_1} \to \Phi_{I_2})_{I_1 \uplus I_2}$.

In the formula $\Box_I \Phi_{I_1}$ the MTL Interval "always" operator is applied to a timed formula. Both I and I_1 can be $[0, \infty)$ and $\Box_{[0, \infty)}$ will sometimes be written simply as $\Box$. The operator B_i is intended to denote belief and the operator K_i to denote knowledge. Both referred to agent i with respect to a finite set $Ag = \{1, \ldots, k\}$ of agents.

Terms/atoms/formulas as defined so far are *ground*, namely there are no variables occurring therein. We introduce variables and use them in formulas in a restricted manner, as usual for example in answer set programming. Variables can occur in formulas in any place constants can occur and are intended as placeholders for elements of the Herbrand universe. More specifically, a ground *instance* of a term/atom/formula involving variables is obtained by uniformly substituting ground terms to all variables (*grounding* step), with the restriction that any variable occurring in an arithmetic expression (i.e., specifying a time instant) can be replaced by a (ground) arithmetic expressions only. Consequently, a non-ground term/atom/formula represents the possibly infinite set of its ground instances, namely, its *grounding*. As it is customary in logic programming, variable symbols are indicated with an initial uppercase letter whereas constants/functions/predicates symbols are indicated with an initial lowercase letter. We denote by *Atm* and *Atmt* the collections of all non-ground atoms and non-ground time-stamped atoms, respectively. In the rest of the paper, unless differently specified, we deal with ground terms/atoms/formulas.

Example 1: An example of a non-ground TLEK formula is:
$$K_i(\Box_{[t_1,t_2]} (send\_registration\_form_T \rightarrow \Box_{[T,T+14]} send\_payment_{T_1})),$$
where we suppose that an agent knows that it is possible to register to a certain conference in the period $[t_1, t_2]$ and that, after sending the registration form, the payment must be sent within fourteen days (still staying within the interval $[t_1, t_2]$). Since, by the restrictions on formulas stated earlier, it must be the case that $T_1 \in [T, T + 14]$ and both T, $T + 14$ must be in $[t_1, t_2]$, only a finite set of ground instances of this formula can be formed by substituting natural numbers to the variables T, T_1 (specifically, the maximum number of ground instances is $t_2 - t_1 - 14 + 1$ assuming to pay on the last day t_2). In case one would consider the more general formula
$$K_i(\Box_{[t_1,t_2]} (send\_registration\_form(X)_T \rightarrow \Box_{[T,T+14]} send\_payment(X)_{T_1})),$$
where X represents a member of some department, i.e., *department_member*(X) holds for some ground instance of X, then the set of ground instances would grow, as a different instance should be generated for each department member (i.e., for each ground term replacing X). In practice, however, ground instances need not to be formed a priori, but rather they can be generated upon need when applying a rule; in the example, just one ground instance should be generated when some member of the department intends to register to that conference at a certain time $T = \hat{t}$. ∎

Rules of the form $K_i(\Box_I(\varphi_{I_1} \rightarrow \psi_{I_2}))$ are a key feature of LEK and TLEK; they are supposed to be kept in the long-term memory and, as seen below, allow other beliefs to be derived from former ones. This derivation is performed in the working memory, which is where beliefs are kept. In the above example, if the agent believes to have sent a registration form, via the $K_i(\ldots)$ rule it will consequently infer to believe to have to send the payment within due time.

Remark 1: We allow projection of knowledge, belief, and necessity from larger to smaller intervals via the following axioms that we anticipate here to simplify the presentation and the understanding of what follows.

1. $B_i\,\varphi_{I_1}{\to}B_i\,\varphi_{I_2}$, $K_i\,\varphi_{I_1}{\to}K_i\,\varphi_{I_2}$, and $\Box_I\,\varphi_{I_1}{\to}\Box_I\varphi_{I_2}$, for all $I_2 \subseteq I_1$ and $i \in Ag$.
2. $\Box_{I_1}\,\varphi_{I_3} \to \Box_{I_2}\,\varphi_{I_3}\ \forall I_2 \subseteq I_1$ such that $I_3 \subseteq I_2$;
3. $(\Box_I\,\varphi_{I_1} \to \psi_{I_2}) \to (\Box_{I_3}\,\varphi_{I_5} \to \psi_{I_6})$ where $I_3 \subseteq I$ and $I_5 \subseteq I_1$ and $I_6 \subseteq I_2$. ∎

Interaction between long-term and short-term memories and thus derivation of new beliefs is not automatic, it is rather performed by an agent whenever deemed necessary, by means of invocation of an explicit, we might say "conscious", mental operator.

The language $\mathcal{L}_{TDLEK}$ of Temporalized DLEK (TDLEK) is obtained by augmenting $\mathcal{L}_{TLEK}$ with the expression $[\alpha]\,\psi_I$, where ψ_I is a ground timed formula. Such expression reads (cf., [4]) "ψ holds [in our setting, in the interval I], after the mental operation (or mental action) α is publicly performed by all agents". The mental operations that we consider are the same as in [4], though applied to ground timed formulas. Notice that the rational of considering ground formulas is that they represent perceptions (either new or already recorded in agent's memory) coming in general from the external world (we say "in general" as, in fact, in some of the aforementioned agent-oriented frameworks perceptions can also result from *internal events*, i.e., from an agent's observations of its own internal activities). We assume that an agent has "time accurate" perceptions, for instance $rain_{[t_1,t_2]}$ is perceived with precise time instants rather than considering $rain_{[T_1,T_2]}$ which might signify that the agent perceived rain in an unspecified interval. The cases of imprecision because an agent might "not remember" or might have been told a vague fact by someone else are not considered here.

These are the four mental operations of interest:

- $+\varphi_I$: the mental operation that serves to form a new belief from a perception φ_I. A perception may become a belief whenever an agent becomes "aware" of the perception and takes it into explicit consideration. Notice that there is no restriction for φ_I to be a positive atom. In fact, perceptions may concern facts that hold (e.g., 'it rains') or do not hold ('it does not rain'). So, φ_I might well be a negated atom/formula.
- $\vdash(\varphi_{I_1}, \psi_{I_2})$ with $I_1 \leq I_2$: an agent, believing that φ is true in I_1 and having in its long-term memory that φ_{I_3} implies ψ_{I_4}, where $I_1 \subseteq I_3$, $I_2 \subseteq I_4$ and $I_3 \leq I_4$, starts believing that ψ is true in I_2. Thus, as seen in detail below, in order to perform this operation it is necessary to retrieve from the long-term memory and then use a rule of the form $K_i(\Box_I(\varphi_{I_3} \to \psi_{I_4}))$ for some wider I.
- $\cap(\varphi_{I_1}, \psi_{I_2})$: believing both φ_{I_1} and ψ_{I_2}, she starts believing their conjunction.

Note that we do not consider the mental operation $-\varphi$ as formulated in [4], which represents arbitrary "forgetting", i.e., removing a belief. In fact, we assume that simple forgetting can be performed, e.g., based upon the time-stamps. We substituted it with this mental operation:

- $\dashv(\varphi_{I_1}, \psi_{I_2})$ with $I_2 \leq I_1$ and where both φ_{I_1} and ψ_{I_2} are atoms: an agent, believing φ_{I_1} and having in the long-term memory that φ_{I_3} implies $\neg\psi_{I_4}$, where $I_1 \subseteq I_3$, $I_2 \subseteq I_4$ and $I_4 \leq I_3$, removes the belief ψ_{I_2}.

2.2   TLEK and TDLEK Semantics

Semantics of DLEK and TDLEK are both based on a set W of worlds. But whereas in DLEK a valuation function $V : W \to 2^{Atm}$ is used, in TDLEK we define the valuation function on the sets of ground time-stamped atoms: $V : W \to 2^{Atmtg}$. For a world w, let t_1 the minimum time-stamp of atom $p_{t_1} \in V(w)$ and let t_2 be the supremum (we can have $t_2 = \infty$) among all time-stamps of atoms in $V(w)$. Then, we can denote w as w_I where $I = [t_1, t_2]$. Moreover, we refer to $V_t(w)$ as the set of atoms in $V(w)$ having t as time-stamp. Similarly, $V_J(w)$ is the set of atoms with time-stamps in the interval J. The notion of LEK/TLEK model does not consider mental operations, discussed later.

Definition: A *TLEK model* is a tuple $M = \langle W; N; \{R_i\}_{i \in Ag}; V \rangle$ where:

- W is the set of worlds;
- $R_i \subseteq W \times W$ is the accessibility relation; for $i \in Ag$ and $w_I \in W$ we have $R_i(w_I) = \{v_{I_1} \in W \mid w_I R_i v_{I_1} \text{ with } I \cap I_1 \neq \varnothing\}$ called *epistemic state of i in w_I*, indicating all the situations that agent i considers possible in the world w_I or, equivalently any situation the agent can retrieve from long-term memory based on what it knows in world w_I. R_i is an equivalence relation so as to model omniscience in the background knowledge. Notice that, since indistinguishable worlds must have the same time span, this means that an agent always knows the time interval she is in; this is in accordance with omniscience in the long-term memory and is usually the case in practical agent systems that we aim to model, where all events are time-stamped.
- $N : Ag \times W \to 2^{2^W}$ is a *"neighbourhood"* function. $\forall i \in Ag$ and $\forall w_I \in W$, $N(i, w_I)$ defines, in terms of sets of worlds, what agent i is allowed to explicitly *believe* in the world w_I; $\forall i \in Ag$, $w_I, v_I \in W$, and $X \subseteq W$:
  1. if $X \in N(i, w_I)$ then $X \subseteq R_i(w_I)$: each element of the neighbourhood is a set composed of reachable worlds; i.e., agent i may have among its beliefs only those which are compatible with the current epistemic state;
  2. if $w_I R_i v_{I_1}$ with $I \subseteq I_1$ then $N(i, w_I) \subseteq N(i, v_{I_1})$: if the world v_{I_1} is compliant with the epistemic state of world w_I, then agent i in the world w_I should have a subset of beliefs of the world v_{I_1}.
- $V : W \to 2^{Atmtg}$ is the valuation function.

Truth conditions for ground TDLEK formulas are defined inductively as follows, where the difference from [4] consists in: (i) the entailment of timed atoms (timed formulas follow in consequences), (ii) considering the $\Box_I$ operator on timed formulas, (iii) introducing extended definitions for mental operations.

We first consider ground TDLEK formulas. Let $M = \langle W, N, \{R_i\}_{i \in Ag}, V \rangle$ a $TLEK$ model; then we have, for every $w_I \in W$: $M, w_I \models \Phi_J$ if $J \subseteq I$ and one of the following conditions holds:

- $\Phi_J = p_J$ iff $\forall t \in J$, $p_t \in V_t(w_I)$;
- $\Phi_J = (\neg \varphi_{I_1})_J$ with $I_1 \subseteq J$ iff $M, w_I \nvDash \varphi_{I_1}$;
- $\Phi_J = (\Box_{I_1} \varphi_{I_2})_J$ with $I_2 \subseteq I_1 \subseteq J$ iff for all $v_{I_3} \in R_i(w_I)$, $M, v_{I_3} \vDash \varphi_{I_2}$;
- $\Phi_J = (K_i \varphi_{I_1})_J$ with $I_1 \subseteq J$ iff $M, v_{I_3} \vDash \varphi_{I_1}$ for all $v_{I_3} \in R_i(w_I)$;
- $\Phi_J = (B_i \varphi_{I_1})_J$ with $I_1 \subseteq J$ iff $\parallel \varphi_{I_1} \parallel_{i, w_I}^M \in N(i, w_I)$ where $\parallel \varphi_{I_1} \parallel_{i, w_I}^M = \{v_I \in W \mid M, v_I \vDash \varphi_{I_1}$ with $I_1 \subseteq I\} \cap R_i(w_I)$. Namely, if the set $\parallel \varphi_{I_1} \parallel_{i, w_I}^M$ of worlds reachable from w_I which entail φ in the very same model M belongs to the *neighbourhood* $N(i, w_I)$ of w_I. Hence, knowledge pertains to formulas entailed in model M in every reachable world, while beliefs pertain to formulas entailed only in some set of them, where this set must however belong to the neighbourhood and so it must be composed of reachable worlds. Thus, an agent is seen as omniscient with respect to knowledge, but not with respect to beliefs.
- $\Phi_J = (\varphi_{I_1} \wedge \psi_{I_2})_J$ with $I_1 \uplus I_2 \subseteq J$ iff $M, w_I \vDash \varphi_{I_1}$ and $M, w_I \vDash \psi_{I_2}$;
- $\Phi_J = (\varphi_{I_1} \vee \psi_{I_2})_J$ with $I_1 \uplus I_2 \subseteq J$ iff $M, w_I \vDash \varphi_{I_1}$ or $M, w_I \vDash \psi_{I_2}$;
- $\Phi_J = (\varphi_{I_1} \to \psi_{I_2})_J$ with $I_1 \uplus I_2 \subseteq J$ iff $M, w_I \vDash \neg \varphi_{I_1}$ or $M, w_I \vDash \psi_{I_2}$;

Concerning a mental operation α performed by any agent i, we have: $M, w_I \vDash [\alpha] \varphi_{I_1}$ iff $M^\alpha, w_I \vDash \varphi_{I_1}$ with $I_1 \subseteq I$ and $M^\alpha = \langle W; N^\alpha(i, w_I); \{R_i\}_{i \in Ag}; V \rangle$ Here α represents a mental operation affecting the sets of beliefs. In particular, such operation can add new beliefs by direct perception, by means of one inference step, or as a conjunction of previous beliefs. When introducing new beliefs, the neighbourhood must be extended accordingly, as seen below; in particular, the new neighbourhood $N^\alpha(i, w_I)$ is defined for each of the mental operations as follows.

- $N^{+\psi_{I_1}}(i, w_I) = N(i, w_I) \cup \parallel \psi_{I_1} \parallel_{i, w_I}^M$ with $I_1 \subseteq I$: the agent i adds to its beliefs event/perception ψ perceived at a time in I_1; the neighbourhood is expanded to as to include the set composed of all the reachable worlds which entail ψ_{I_1} in M.
- $N^{\vdash(\psi_{I_1}, \chi_{I_2})}(i, w_I) =$
$$\begin{cases} N(i, w_I) \cup \parallel \chi_{I_2} \parallel_{i, w_I}^M & \text{if } M, w_I \vDash B_i(\psi_{I_1}) \wedge K_i(\Box_{I_3}(\psi_{I_1} \to \chi_{I_2})) \\ N(i, w_I) & \text{otherwise} \end{cases}$$
namely, the agent i adds χ_{I_2} as a belief in its short-term memory if it has ψ_{I_1} among its previous beliefs and has in its background knowledge $K_i(\Box_{I_3}(\psi_{I_1} \to \chi_{I_2}))$, where $I_3 \subseteq I$; otherwise, if the intervals do not match then the operation does not succeed and thus the set of beliefs remains unchanged. If the operation succeeds then the neighbourhood is by adding χ_{I_2} as a new belief, as seen before.
- $N^{\cap(\psi_{I_1}, \chi_{I_2})}(i, w_I) =$
$$\begin{cases} N(i, w_I) \cup \parallel \psi_{I_1} \wedge \chi_{I_2} \parallel_{i, w_I}^M & \text{if } M, w_I \vDash B_i(\psi_{I_1}) \wedge B_i(\chi_{I_2}) \\ N(i, w_I) & \text{otherwise} \end{cases}$$
namely, the agent i adds $\psi_{I_1} \wedge \chi_{I_2}$ as a belief if it has among its previous beliefs both ψ_{I_1} and χ_{I_2} with $I_1, I_2 \subseteq I$; otherwise the set of beliefs remain unchanged. The neighbourhood is expanded, if the operation succeeds, with those sets of reachable worlds where both formulas are entailed in M.

We write $\models_{TDLEK} \varphi_{I_1}$ to denote that φ_{I_1} is true in all worlds w_I, $I_1 \subseteq I$, of every *TLEK* model M.

As concerns non-ground formulas, we extend the semantics by putting $M, w_I \models \Phi$ iff $M, w_I \models \hat{\Phi}$ for all ground instance $\hat{\Phi}$ of Φ. (Recall that the $\hat{\Phi}$'s are obtained from Φ by substituting all variables, with constants or expressions/values in all possible ways).

Remark 2: We adopt expressions like $K_i \Box_{I_1} \varphi_{I_2}$, where in particular φ_{I_2} can be an implication, in order to represent knowledge in the long-term memory wherever applicability of such knowledge is time-dependent. The role of the $\Box$ operator, that from the above-stated truth conditions may seem superfluous, becomes apparent whenever interval extremes are defined by means of expressions over time instants; such correlations indicate that a certain implication makes sense only within a certain interval.   ∎

Remark 3: For the mental operations considered previously we have the following:

- $\models_{TDLEK} (K_i(\Box_{I_3}(\varphi_{I_1} \to \psi_{I_2})) \land B_i \varphi_{I_1}) \to [\vdash(\varphi_{I_1}, \psi_{I_2})] B_i \psi_{I_2}$.
  Namely, if an agent i has φ_{I_1} as one of its beliefs and has $K_i(\Box_{I_3}(\varphi_{I_1} \to \psi_{I_2}))$ in its background knowledge, then as a consequence of the mental operation $\vdash(\varphi_{I_1}, \psi_{I_2})$ the agent i starts believing ψ_{I_2};
- $\models_{TDLEK} (B_i\varphi_{I_1} \land B_i\psi_{I_2}) \to [\cap(\varphi_{I_1}, \psi_{I_2})]B_i(\varphi_{I_1} \land \psi_{I_2})$.
  Namely, if an agent i has φ_{I_1} and ψ_{I_2} as beliefs, then as a consequence of the mental operation $\cap(\varphi_{I_1}, \psi_{I_2})$ the agent i starts believing $\varphi_{I_1} \land \psi_{I_2}$;
- $\models_{TDLEK_t} [+\varphi_{I_1}]B_i\varphi_{I_1}$. Namely, as a consequence of the operation $+\varphi_{I_1}$ (thus after the perception of φ at a time included in I_1) the agent i adds φ_{I_1} to its beliefs.   ∎

We propose a substantial modification to the definition of the operation $-\varphi$ of [4]; there, a belief was just arbitrarily removed. Here instead, we introduce the negative correspondent to the operation $\vdash(\varphi_{I_1}, \psi_{I_2})$, namely, $\dashv(\varphi_{I_1}, \psi_{I_2})$ where φ_{I_1} and ψ_{I_2} are atoms. Via this operation, an agent believing φ_{I_1} and having in the long-term memory a rule $K_i(\Box_I(\varphi_{I_1} \to \neg\psi_{I_2}))$ removes the belief ψ_{I_2}. Notice that, should ψ be believed in a wider interval I_3 such that $I_2 \subseteq I_3$, the belief ψ is removed concerning interval I_2 but is left for the remaining sub-intervals (so, its is "restructured"). Therefore, our extension to DLEK and TDLEK makes beliefs *defeasible*: a belief can be seen as a default which represents the current state of affairs in the agent's "world", that might be invalidated (entirely or in a sub-interval) by further perceptions.

Remark 4: Application of the new operation may, e.g., concern beliefs of the form $\psi_{[t,\infty)}$, that often signify that ψ will hold either indefinitely or "until" terminated by an other belief. For instance, $student_{[t,\infty)}$ or $married_{[t,\infty)}$ mean that one, after enrolling to a school or after marrying, will remain in the consequent state for an indefinite time; however, if graduating or, respectively, divorcing at time t_1, previous beliefs must be replaced by $student_{[t,t_1-1]}$ or $married_{[t,t_1-1]}$.

Also, ψ may represent in many cases the "opposite" of φ; e.g., if we have $\varphi = door\text{-}open$ then ψ can be $door\text{-}closed$. Rules of above form in the long-term memory can also represent exceptions, e.g., a person is at home ($\psi = at\text{-}home$) for the whole day (I_2) and she is thus believed to be there; however, if it is also later on believed that she went out $\varphi = go\text{-}out$ in I_1, then the belief of her being at home remains before and after, but does not hold in I_1. ∎

Let us consider the example of a door open or closed, where only agent i can perform the *action* to open or close the door. Let us assume that performed actions are recorded among an agent's perceptions, with the due time stamp. For reader's convenience, actions are denoted using a suffix "A". For simplicity, actions are supposed to always succeed and to produce an effect within one time instant. Let us consider the following rules (kept in long-term memory):

$$K_i(\Box(open\text{-}doorA_T \rightarrow door\text{-}open_{[T+1,\infty]}))$$
$$K_i(\Box(close\text{-}doorA_T \rightarrow door\text{-}closed_{[T+1,\infty]})).$$

Let us now assume that the agent closes the door, e.g., at time 5; then, a belief will be formed of the door been closed from time 6 on; however, if the agent later opens the door, e.g., at time 8, as a consequence the door will result to be open from time 9 on. It can be seen that the application of previous rules in consequence of an agent's action of opening/closing the door determines some "belief restructuring" in the short-term memory of the agent. In absence of other rules concerning doors, we intend that a door cannot be believed to be simultaneously open and closed. The related belief update is determined by the following rules:

$$K_i(\Box(door\text{-}open_{[T,\infty]} \rightarrow \neg door\text{-}closed_{[T,\infty]}))$$
$$K_i(\Box(door\text{-}closed_{[T,\infty]} \rightarrow \neg door\text{-}open_{[T,\infty]}))$$

With the above timing, the result of their application is that the belief formed at time 5, i.e., $door\text{-}closed_{[6,\infty]}$ will be replaced by $door\text{-}closed_{[6,8]}$ plus $door\text{-}open_{[9,\infty]}$.

Below we extend TDLEK truth conditions so as to encompass the new mental operation $\dashv(\varphi_{I_1}, \psi_{I_2})$. As before, $M, w_I \models [\alpha]\varphi_{I_1}$ iff $M^\alpha, w_I \models \varphi_{I_1}$ with $M^\alpha = \langle W; N^\alpha(i, w_I); \{R_i\}_{i \in Ag}; V \rangle$. Here, α represents $\dashv(\varphi_{I_1}, \psi_{I_2})$, with $I_2 \leq I_1$ and φ_{I_1} and ψ_{I_2} are atoms, affecting the sets of beliefs. Assume that in the long-term memory we have $K_i(\Box_{I_3}(\varphi_{I_1} \rightarrow \neg\psi_{I_2}), I_3 \subseteq I$. The new neighbourhood $N^{\dashv(\varphi_{I_1}, \psi_{I_2})}(i, w_I)$ is defined as follows:
$N^{\dashv(\varphi_{I_1}, \psi_{I_2})}(i, w_I) =$

$$\begin{cases} (N(i, w_I) \setminus \parallel \psi_{I_1} \parallel_{i,w_I}^M) \cup \parallel \psi_{I_2 \setminus I_1} \parallel_{i,w_I}^M & \text{if } M, w_I \models B_i(\varphi_{I_1}) \wedge B_i(\psi_{I_2}) \wedge \\ & \qquad K_i(\Box_{I_3}(\varphi_{I_1} \rightarrow \neg\psi_{I_2})) \\ N(i, w_I) & \text{otherwise} \end{cases}$$

Hence, after the perception of φ in I_1, the agent i replaces previous belief ψ_{I_2} in the short-term memory with $\psi_{I_2 \setminus I_1}$; otherwise, if the intervals do not match, the operation does not succeed and the set of beliefs remains unchanged.

Note that, to simplify the description, we applied some abuse in notation concerning the formula $\psi_{I_2 \setminus I_1}$, because the set $I_2 \setminus I_1$ is not necessarily an interval. Namely, the subtraction $I_2 \setminus I_1$ can produce two different results:

- if $I_1 \subseteq I_2$, $I_1 = [t_0, t_1]$, and $I_2 = [t_2, t_3]$, then $I_2 \setminus I_1 = [t_2, t_0 - 1] \cup [t_1 + 1, t_3]$. Thus, ψ_{I_2} is replaced by $\psi_{[t_2, t_0 - 1]}$ and $\psi_{[t_1 + 1, t_3]}$ (and similarly if $t_3 = \infty$). Hence, the notation $\psi_{I_2 \setminus I_1}$ has to be intended as the conjunction of $\psi_{[t_2, t_0 - 1]}$ and $\psi_{[t_1 + 1, t_3]}$.
- Otherwise, $I_1 = [t_0, t_1]$, $I_2 = [t_2, t_3]$ with $t_3 \leq t_1$. Is this case $I_2 \setminus I_1 = [t_2, \min(t_3, t_0 - 1)]$ and ψ_{I_2} is replaced by $\psi_{[t_2, \min(t_3, t_0 - 1)]}$ (and similarly if $t_3 = \infty$).

We have the following property: $\models_{TDLEK} (K_i(\Box_{I_3}(\varphi_{I_1} \rightarrow \neg\psi_{I_2})) \wedge B_i \varphi_{I_1} \wedge B_i \psi_{I_2}) \rightarrow [\dashv(\varphi_{I_1}, \psi_{I_2})](B_i \psi_{I_2 \setminus I_1})$ which means: if an agent i has ψ_{I_2} as one of its beliefs, perceives φ in I_1, and has $K_i(\Box_{I_3}(\varphi_{I_1} \rightarrow \neg\psi_{I_2}))$ in its background knowledge, then after the mental operation $\dashv(\varphi_{I_1}, \psi_{I_2})$ the agent i starts believing $\psi_{I_2 \setminus I_1}$.

3 Example

Let us consider the following scenario: the Program Committee of some Conference solicits submission of AI papers for the main track of the Conference. We have an agent (Author) who is of course a resource bounded one, in the sense that she has a certain background knowledge and explicit timed beliefs and forms new explicit timed beliefs by means of the mental operations illustrated before. Our agent i (author) has in her long-term memory the following rules:

1. $K_i(\Box(read\text{-}guidelines \wedge submission\text{-}respect \rightarrow fullPaper\text{-}ready))$.
   This rule indicates that if the author read the submission guidelines and her paper fulfills them, then she can consider her paper ready. Such rule does not have an explicit time constraints (the implicit interval of each sub-formula is $[0, \infty]$) and the formula describes something that is always true.
2. $K_i(\Box_{[t_0, t_1]}(abstract\text{-}ready_t \rightarrow \Box_{[t+1, t_1]} submit\text{-}abstract_{t_a}))$.
   This rule indicates that if the author has the paper's abstract ready at any moment $t \in [t_0, t_1]$ then at the next moment until t_1 she can submit the abstract.
3. $K_i(\Box_{[t_0, t_2]}((fullPaper\text{-}ready_{t_c} \wedge \Box_{[t_0, t_1]} submit\text{-}abstract_{t_b}) \rightarrow$
   $$\Box_{[t_c + 1, t_2]} submit\text{-}fullPaper_{t_d}))$$
   The meaning of this rule is that it is always true within the interval $[t_0, t_2]$ that, if the agent has the full paper ready at some moment in time $t_c \in [t_0, t_2]$ and had already submitted the abstract at $t_b \in [t_0, t_1]$, then from the next moment of time $t_c + 1$ she can submit the full paper (such that $t_b \leq t_c + 1$);
4. $K_i(\Box_{[t_0, t_4]}(\Box_{[t_0, t_2]} submit\text{-}fullPaper_{t_e} \rightarrow \Box_{[t_2 + 1, t_4]} receive\text{-}reviews_{t_f}))$.
   This rule indicates that if the author submitted the paper to the Conference during the required interval of time $[t_0, t_2]$ then she will receive a notification of acceptance or rejection before time t_4;

5. $K_i(\Box_{[t_2+1,t_5]}(\Box_{[t_2+1,t_4]}receive\text{-}reviews_{t_g} \rightarrow \Box_{[t_4,t_5]}send\text{-}rebuttal_{t_h}))$.
This rule indicates that if the author receives reviews during the interval $[t_2, t_4]$ then she can respond at any moment during the interval $[t_4, t_5]$;

6. $K_i(\Box_{[t_4,t_6]}((\Box_{[t_4,t_5]}send\text{-}rebuttal_{t_h} \wedge \Box_{[t_4,t_3]}receive\text{-}acceptNote_{t_j}) \rightarrow$
$$\Box_{[t_3,t_6]}send\text{-}final\text{-}version_{t_v}))$$
This rule indicates that if the agent receives an acceptance notification during the interval $[t_4, t_3]$ and she remembers that she sent the rebuttal in $[t_4, t_5]$ then she has to send the final version of the paper until t_6;

7. $K_i(\Box(paper\text{-}rejected_{t_s} \rightarrow \neg assume\text{-}paper\text{-}accepted_{t_y}))$.
This rule indicates that if an agent assumes that her paper is accepted and at a certain point she receives a reject notification, she has to change her belief.

Let us now consider one of our authors (agents) A_1, who has decided to prepare a submission to this Conference. She writes an abstract for her paper and believes that it is ready at moment t_x. So, she has in her short-term memory the belief $B_{A_1}(abstract\text{-}ready_{t_x})$, where of course $t_x \in [t_0, t_1]$. She can infer from the second rule, by performing the mental operation $\vdash (abstract\text{-}ready_{t_x}, submit\text{-}abstract_{t_a})$ that at any moment t, such that $t_x + 1 \leq t \leq t_1$ the abstract can be submitted. Let us assume now that our author has submitted the abstract successfully at time $t_x + 1 \leq t_y \leq t_1$. Then, she adds to her beliefs $B_{A_1}(submit\text{-}abstract_{t_y})$. After that, she starts preparing the full paper; she completes it after some time and so believes that it is ready at time $t_z \leq t_2$: therefore, $B_{A_1}(fullPaper\text{-}ready_{t_z})$ it is added to her beliefs. At this point, our author has the new belief $B_{A_1}(fullPaper\text{-}ready_{t_z})$ and retrieves from her memory the belief $B_{A_1}(submit\text{-}abstract_{t_y})$ then by performing the mental operation $\cap(submit\text{-}abstract_{t_y}, fullPaper\text{-}ready_{t_z})$ she can start believing that $B_{A_1}(submit\text{-}abstract_{t_y} \wedge fullPaper\text{-}ready_{t_z})$ is true where $t_y \in I_1$, $t_z \in [t_0, t_2]$ and $t_y \leq t_z$). Then, according to the third rule at the next moment in time $t_d \in [t_z + 1, t_2]$ she can submit the full paper. Finally, assuming that our agent submitted her paper successfully at time t_d she adds $B_{A_1}(submit\text{-}fullPaper_{t_d})$ to the short-term memory and waits for notification from the Conference Chairs.

To illustrate the effect of the performed actions on the agent's beliefs change, let us consider the case of an optimistic agent A_2 which, after submission, assumes the paper to be accepted and so forms the belief $B_{A_2}(assume\text{-}paper\text{-}accepted_{[t_a,\infty)})$ with $t_a \geq t_2$. If the Program Chairs will send notification of acceptance then as a consequence the paper will be believed to be accepted and, vice versa, if there is a rejection. If at time t_3 agent A_2 received a rejection note, she starts believing $B_{A_2}(paper\text{-}rejected_{[t_3,\infty)})$; therefore, via the mental operation $\dashv (paper\text{-}rejected_{[t_3,\infty)}, assume\text{-}paper\text{-}accepted_{[t_a,\infty)})$ and since $t_3 > t_a$, she can replace the timed atom $assume\text{-}paper\text{-}accepted_{[t_a,\infty)}$ with the more limited $assume\text{-}paper\text{-}accepted_{[t_a,t_3-1]}$ which indicates the actual interval where the belief has remained in the short-term memory without being contradicted.

4   Axiomatization and Canonical Models

The logic TDLEK can be axiomatized as an extension of the axiomatization of DLEK as follows. As seen before, knowledge/belief on an interval allow one to draw inferences in intervals included therein, while upward and downward reflection (corresponding to properties of the operator K_i) preserve the interval. We implicitly assume modus ponens, standard axioms for classical propositional logic, and the necessitation rule for each K_i. The TLEK axioms are:

1. $K_i(\Box_{I_1}\varphi_{I_2}) \wedge K_i(\Box_{I_3}(\varphi_{I_2} \rightarrow \psi_{I_4})) \rightarrow K_i(\Box_{I_3}\psi_{I_4})$ with $I_1 \uplus I_4 \subseteq I_3$ and $I_1 \subseteq I_3$;
2. $K_i(\Box_{I_1}\varphi_{I_2}) \rightarrow \Box_{I_1}\varphi_{I_2}$;
3. $K_i(\Box_{I_1}\varphi_{I_2}) \rightarrow K_i K_i(\Box_{I_1}\varphi_{I_2})$;
4. $\neg K_i(\Box_{I_1}\varphi_{I_2}) \rightarrow K_i \neg K_i(\Box_{I_1}\varphi_{I_2})$;
5. $B_i\varphi_{I_1} \wedge K_i(\Box_{I_2}(\varphi_{I_1} \leftrightarrow \psi_{I_1})) \rightarrow B_i\psi_{I_1}$.

The axiomatization of TDLEK as extension of DLEK is:

1. $[\alpha]f \leftrightarrow f$ where $f = p$ or $f = p_t$ or $f = p_I$;
2. $[\alpha]\neg\varphi_{I_1} \leftrightarrow \neg[\alpha]\varphi_{I_1}$;
3. $[\alpha](\varphi_{I_1} \wedge \psi_{I_2}) \leftrightarrow [\alpha]\varphi_{I_1} \wedge [\alpha]\psi_{I_2}$;
4. $[\alpha]K_i(\Box_{I_1}\varphi_{I_2}) \leftrightarrow K_i([\alpha](\Box_{I_1}\varphi_{I_2}))$;
5. $[+\varphi_{I_1}]B_i\psi_{I_1} \leftrightarrow (B_i([+\varphi_{I_1}]\psi_{I_1}) \vee K_i(\Box_{I_2}([+\varphi_{I_1}]\psi_{I_1} \leftrightarrow \varphi_{I_1})))$;
6. $[\vdash(\varphi_{I_1}, \psi_{I_2})]B_i\chi_{I_2} \leftrightarrow (B_i([\vdash(\varphi_{I_1}, \psi_{I_2})]\chi_{I_2}) \vee$
   $((B_i\varphi_{I_1} \wedge K_i(\Box_{I_3}(\varphi_{I_1} \rightarrow \psi_{I_2})) \wedge K_i(\Box_{I_3}[\vdash(\varphi_{I_1}, \psi_{I_2})]\chi_{I_2} \leftrightarrow \psi_{I_2})))$;
7. $[\dashv(\varphi_{I_1}, \psi_{I_2})]B_i\chi_{I_2} \leftrightarrow (B_i([\dashv(\varphi_{I_1}, \psi_{I_2})]\chi_{I_2}) \vee$
   $((B_i\varphi_{I_1} \wedge K_i(\Box_{I_3}(\varphi_{I_1} \rightarrow \neg\psi_{I_2})) \wedge K_i(\Box_{I_3}[\dashv(\varphi_{I_1}, \psi_{I_2})]\chi_{I_2} \leftrightarrow \neg\psi_{I_2})))$;
8. $[\cap(\varphi_{I_1}, \psi_{I_2})]B_i\chi_{I_3} \leftrightarrow (B_i([\cap(\varphi_{I_1}, \psi_{I_2})]\chi_{I_3}) \vee$
   $((B_i\varphi_{I_1} \wedge B_i\psi_{I_2}) \wedge K_i(\Box_{I_4}([\cap(\varphi_{I_1}, \psi_{I_2})]\chi_{I_3} \leftrightarrow (\varphi_{I_1} \wedge \psi_{I_2})))))$
   where $I_3 = I_1 \uplus I_2$;
9. $\dfrac{\psi_I \leftrightarrow \chi_I}{\varphi_I \leftrightarrow \varphi_I[\psi_I/\chi_I]}$.

We write TDLEK $\vdash \varphi_{I_1}$ which signifies that φ_{I_1} is a theorem of TDLEK. Both logics TLEK and TDLEK are sound for the class of *TLEK* models. The proof that TDLEK is strongly complete can be achieved by using a standard canonical model argument.

The *canonical TLEK model* is a tuple $M_c = \langle W_c; N_c; \{R_{c_i}\}_{i \in Ag}; V_c \rangle$ where:

- W_c is the set of all maximal consistent subsets of $\mathcal{L}_{TLEK}$; so, as in [4], canonical models are constructed from worlds which are sets of syntactically correct formulas of the underlying language and are in particular the largest consistent ones. As before, each $w \in W_c$ can be conveniently indicated as w_I.
- For every $w_I \in W$ and $i \in Ag$, $w_I R_{c_i} v_{I_1}$ if and only if $K_i\Box_{I_2}\varphi_{I_3} \in w_I$ iff $K_i\Box_{I_2}\varphi_{I_3} \in v_{I_1}$; i.e., R_{c_i} is an equivalence relation on knowledge; as before, we define $R_{c_i}(w_I) = \{v_{I_1} \in W \mid w_I R_{c_i} v_{I_1}$ with $I \cap I_1 \neq \varnothing\}$. Thus, we cope with our extension from knowledge of formulas to knowledge of timed formulas.
- Analogously to [4], for $w_I \in W$, $\Phi_I \in \mathcal{L}_{TLEK}$ and $i \in Ag$, we define $A_{\Phi_I}(i, w_I) = \{v_I \in R_{c_i}(w_I) \mid \Phi_I \in v_I\}$. Then, we put $N_c(i, w_I) = \{A_{\Phi_I}(i, w_I) \mid B_i\Phi_I \in w_I\}$.

- V_c is a valuation function defined as before.

As stated in Lemma 2 of [4], there are the following immediate consequences of the above definition: if $w_I \in W_c$ and $i \in \text{Ag}$, then

- given $\Phi = \Box_{I_1} \varphi_{I_2}$ with $I_1 \subseteq I$ and $\varphi_{I_2} \in \mathcal{L}_{TLEK}$, it holds that $K_i \Box_{I_1} \varphi_{I_2} \in w_I$ iff $\forall v_{I_3} \in W$ such that $w_I R_{c_i} v_{I_3}$ we have $\Box_{I_1} \varphi_{I_2} \in v_{I_3}$;
- for $\Phi_{I_1} \in \mathcal{L}_{TLEK}$ with $I_1 \subseteq I$, if $B_i \Phi_{I_1} \in w_I$ and $w_I R_{c_i} v_{I_2}$ then $B_i \Phi_{I_1} \in v_{I_2}$.

Thus, while R_{c_i}-related worlds have the same knowledge and N_c-related worlds have the same beliefs, as stated in Lemma 3 of [4] there can be R_{c_i}-related worlds with different beliefs. The above properties can be used analogously to what is done in [4] to prove that, by construction, the following results hold:

Lemma 1: $\forall w_I \in W_c$ and $B_i \Phi_{I_1}, B_i \Psi_{I_2} \in \mathcal{L}_{TLEK}$ where $I_1, I_2 \subseteq I$, if $B_i \Phi_{I_1} \in w_I$ but $B_i \Psi_{I_2} \notin w_I$, it follows that there exists $v_{I_3} \in R_{c_i}(w_I)$ such that either $\Phi_{I_1} \in v_{I_3}$ but $\neg \Psi_{I_2} \in v_{I_3}$, or $\neg \Phi_{I_1} \in v_{I_3}$ but $\Psi_{I_2} \in v_{I_3}$. ∎

Lemma 2: $\forall \Phi_I \in \mathcal{L}_{TLEK}$ and $\forall w_I \in W_c$, $\Phi_{I_1} \in w_I$ iff $M_c, w_I \vDash \Phi_{I_1}$ where $I_1 \subseteq I$. ∎

Lemma 3: If $\Phi_{I_1} \in \mathcal{L}_{TDLEK}$ then there exists $\tilde{\Phi}_{I_1} \in \mathcal{L}_{TLEK}$ such that $TDLEK \vdash \varphi_{I_1} \leftrightarrow \tilde{\Phi}_{I_1}$. ∎

Under the assumption that in every formula $\Box_I \varphi_{I_1}$ the interval I is finite, the previous lemmas allow us to prove the following theorems (whose proofs are analogous to those in [4]). The limitation to finite intervals is not related to features of the proposed approach, but to well-known paradoxes of temporal logics on infinite intervals.

Theorem 1: TLEK is strongly complete for the class of *TLEK* models. ∎

Theorem 2: TDLEK is strongly complete for the class of *TLEK* models. ∎

5   Concluding Remarks

In this work we extended an existing approach to the logical modeling of short- and long-term memories in Intelligent Resource-Bounded Agents by introducing explicit time instants and time intervals in formulas. We considered not just adding new beliefs, rather we introduced a new mental operation not provided in DLEK, to allow for removing/restructuring existing beliefs. The resulting TDLEK logic shares similarities in the underlying principles with hybrid logics (cf., e.g., [21]) and with temporal epistemic logic (cf., e.g., [22]); as concerns the differences, the former has time instants but no time intervals, and the latter has neither time instants nor time intervals.

With regard to complexity, for DLEK it has been proved that the satisfiability problem is decidable and it has been conjectured to be in PSPACE. It is easy to believe that our extensions cannot spoil decidability. In fact, on the one hand we employ metric temporal logic, which admits fragments having widely differing complexities and can easily become undecidable [20,23]. On the other hand however, in TDLEK metric temporal logic is actually used only for *controlling* inferences, checking whether perceptions and pre-existing beliefs fit into the specified intervals. Inference steps to derive new beliefs are analogous to DLEK: just one modal rule at a time is used and a sharp separation is postulated between the working memory, where inference is performed, and the long-term memory. Future developments include a careful evaluation of the complexity of the TLEK/TDLEK approach, the temporalization of B_i and K_i.

References

1. Logie, R.H.: Visuo-Spatial Working Memory. Essays in Cognitive Psychology. Psychology Press, Hove (1994)
2. Pearson, D., Logie, R.H.: Effect of stimulus modality and working memory load on menthal synthesis performance. Imagin. Cogn. Pers. **23**(2–3), 183–191 (2004)
3. Gero, J.S., Peng, W.: Understanding behaviors of a constructive memory agent: a Markov chain analysis. Knowl.-Based Syst. **22**(8), 610–621 (2009)
4. Balbiani, P., Fernández-Duque, D., Lorini, E.: A logical theory of belief dynamics for resource-bounded agents. In: Proceedings of AAMAS 2016, pp. 644–652. ACM (2016)
5. Fagin, R., Halpern, J.Y.: Belief, awareness, and limited reasoning. Artif. Intell. **34**(1), 39–76 (1987)
6. Ågotnes, T., Alechina, N.: A logic for reasoning about knowledge of unawareness. J. Log. Lang. Inf. **23**(2), 197–217 (2014)
7. van Ditmarsch, H., French, T.: Semantics for knowledge and change of awareness. J. Log., Lang. Inf. **23**(2), 169–195 (2014)
8. Alechina, N., Logan, B., Whitsey, M.: A complete and decidable logic for resource-bounded agents. In: Proceedings of AAMAS 2004, pp. 606–613. IEEE Computer Society (2004)
9. Grant, J., Kraus, S., Perlis, D.: A logic for characterizing multiple bounded agents. Auton. Agents Multi-Agent Syst. **3**(4), 351–387 (2000)
10. Laird, J.E., Lebiere, C., Rosenbloom, P.S.: A standard model of the mind: toward a common computational framework across artificial intelligence, cognitive science, neuroscience, and robotics. AI Mag. **38**(4), 13–26 (2017)
11. Bansal, A.K., Ramohanarao, K., Rao, A.: Distributed storage of replicated beliefs to facilitate recovery of distributed intelligent agents. In: Singh, M.P., Rao, A., Wooldridge, M.J. (eds.) ATAL 1997. LNCS, vol. 1365, pp. 77–91. Springer, Heidelberg (1997). https://doi.org/10.1007/BFb0026751
12. Omicini, A., Ricci, A., Viroli, M.: Timed environment for web agents. Web Intell. Agent Syst. **5**(2), 161–175 (2007)
13. Micucci, D., Oldani, M., Tisato, F.: Time-aware multi agent systems. In: Weyns, D., Holvoet, T. (eds.) Multiagent Systems and Software Architecture, Proceedings of the Special Track at Net. ObjectDays, pp. 71–78. Katholieke Universiteit Leuven, Belgium (2006)
14. Chesani, F., Mello, P., Montali, M., Torroni, P.: Monitoring time-aware commitments within agent-based simulation environments. Cybern. Syst. **42**(7), 546–566 (2011)

15. van Benthem, J.: The Logic of Time - A Model-theoretic Investigation into the Varieties of Temporal Ontology and Temporal Discourse, vol. 156. Synthese library and Kluwer, Boston (1991)
16. Koymans, R.: Specifying real-time properties with metric temporal logic. Real-Time Syst. **2**(4), 255–299 (1990)
17. Halpern, J.Y., Shoham, Y.: A propositional modal logic of time intervals. J. ACM **38**(4), 935–962 (1991)
18. Balbiani, P., Goranko, V., Sciavicco, G.: Two-sorted point-interval temporal logics. Electr. Notes Theor. Comput. Sci. **278**, 31–45 (2011)
19. Henzinger, T.A., Manna, Z., Pnueli, A.: What good are digital clocks? In: Kuich, W. (ed.) ICALP 1992. LNCS, vol. 623, pp. 545–558. Springer, Heidelberg (1992). https://doi.org/10.1007/3-540-55719-9_103
20. Ouaknine, J., Worrell, J.: Some recent results in metric temporal logic. In: Cassez, F., Jard, C. (eds.) FORMATS 2008. LNCS, vol. 5215, pp. 1–13. Springer, Heidelberg (2008). https://doi.org/10.1007/978-3-540-85778-5_1
21. Areces, C., Blackburn, P., Marx, M.: Hybrid logics: characterization, interpolation and complexity. J. Symb. Log. **66**(3), 977–1010 (2001)
22. Engelfriet, J.: Minimal temporal epistemic logic. Notre Dame J. Form. Log. **37**(2), 233–259 (1996)
23. Hirshfeld, Y., Rabinovich, A.M.: Logics for real time: decidability and complexity. Fundam. Inform. **62**(1), 1–28 (2004)

An Information Model for Computing Accountabilities

Matteo Baldoni(✉), Cristina Baroglio, Katherine M. May,
Roberto Micalizio, and Stefano Tedeschi

Dipartimento di Informatica, Università degli Studi di Torino,
c.so Svizzera 185, 10149 Torino, Italy
{matteo.baldoni,cristina.baroglio,katherine.may,roberto.micalizio,
stefano.tedeschi}@unito.it

Abstract. We propose an information model that describes which data should be available, together with their relationships, in order to identify accountabilities in a group of interacting parties. The model is intended for use in multi-agent systems, and is expressed by means of Object-Role Modeling, due to the relational nature of the concepts involved.

Keywords: Accountability · Responsibility · ORM
Information model

1 Introduction

Many contexts, both in the human world and in software, are characterized by the distribution of activities through a group of interacting parties: each member in the group takes care of a part of the activity, and the desired overall result is achieved only when each member behaves properly, and properly interacts with the others. This happens both in human organizations, and in distributed systems like multi-agent systems (MAS). Such contexts often resort to the concept of *responsibility* to refer to the assignment of a task (or a duty) to a member in the group, e.g. [11,14,16,17]. Despite the centrality of the notion of responsibility, and despite the many discussions and models proposed in philosophy, psychology, law, etc. (among which the well-known triangle model of responsibility by Schlenker *et al.* [30]), there is a lack of computational support to the specification and the use of responsibilities inside information systems (that are thought for the business world), as well as in MAS. Even widely used tools like RBAC (role-based access control) or widely adopted agent organization platforms (like JaCaMo [7]) do not provide an understanding of the concept.

A particularly relevant exception in this landscape is the ReMMo conceptual model by Feltus [17], which proposes a conceptualization of how responsibility is structured. Interestingly, this is also the first proposal in its field that brings into the picture the notion of accountability: ReMMo, in fact, defines responsibility as "a charge assigned to a unique actor to signify its accountabilities concerning

C. Ghidini et al. (Eds.): AI*IA 2018, LNAI 11298, pp. 30–44, 2018.
https://doi.org/10.1007/978-3-030-03840-3_3

a unique business task". Accountability is considered a central concept in many fields that study human interaction. In sociology (e.g., [15,18,25]) it is well-known that social order, i.e. the functioning of a group of individuals, depends on often complex relationships between the parties, relationships that the parties accept, and that bring about expectations on each other's behavior. From the seminal work in [18], many studies identify in *accountability* the key notion on top of which interaction is built. In political sciences, e.g. [1], accountability is seen as a major driving force of individuals when it comes to decide about their own behavior. Psychologists provide evidence that accountability increases the salience of goals [27]. Ethnomethodologists postulate that social behavior is configured by relying on the same mechanisms through which it is explained, which indeed give meaning to social action, e.g. [18]. Management studies, e.g. [29], consider it a framework for managing expectations. So, ReMMO is surely an important proposal but still it leaves questions to be answered. In particular, it does not provide an information model that ties the concepts to the environment, capturing constraints on how data evolves. Such a layer is necessary both for attributing responsibilities and, given a situation of interest, for identifying those who answer for it (forward and backward responsibility, according to [26]).

This paper pursues three research aims. First, it refines the characterization of accountability traced in [2,3]. In particular, relying on a wide literature on accountability (including but not limited to [1,9,18,22,27,29,32]) we identify the main concepts that come into play in the process of accountability determination, such as *expectation* and *control*, as well as the relationships between them. Second, the paper proposes an *information model for accountability*, that is, it describes which data need to be available to develop systems that, in any situation of interest arising in a group of interacting agents, allow the identification of responsibilities. The model, that we provide in Object-Role Modeling (ORM[1]) due to the relational nature of the represented concepts, contributes to the development of systems that support the governance of a group of interacting parties. Third, the paper sets the ground for the development of approaches to MAS programming where interaction, coordination, and exception handling will rely on the sibling notions of responsibility and accountability.

The paper is organized as follows. Section 2 characterizes the concept of accountability we rely upon. Section 3 outlines the main requirements that a model of accountability should satisfy and, then, presents the accountability model. Section 4 compares the proposal to other proposals for accountability. Discussions end the paper.

2   Accountability and Responsibility

Responsibility, accountability, answerability, liability, causation, sanction are all related terms, sometimes used as synonyms, some other times used to capture different shades of meaning. A thorough ontological analysis of the term is not in

---

[1] For an introduction to ORM, please check http://www.orm.net/pdf/ ORMwhitePaper.pdf.

the scope of this work. We will provide just a minimal characterization, sufficient to understand those facets of the notions, on which we rely. In essence, we understand *accountability* as representing the deceivingly simple concept of one principal holding another to account for his/her actions, both "good" and "bad". From this definition, we identify two integral pieces to accountability: (1) a relationship between two entities in which one feels a liability to account for his/her actions to the other; and (2) a process of accounting in which actions are declared, evaluated, and scored. The mechanism of accountability contains two sides that we call *positive* or *negative accountability*. Positive accountability means that a principal is expected to act in a certain way and will be held to account for that expectation's fulfillment. Negative accountability, on the other hand, means that a principal is expected to not impede social progress and negatively impact others. The model that we propose captures the information necessary to positive accountability.

Concerning *responsibility*, Feltus [17] sees it as a charge assigned to an agent, which is always linked at least to one accountability. This view is compatible with the triangle model [30]², according to which the term bears two main understandings, each of which investigated at depth by philosophers: one amounting to causation (who did it?), the other to answerability (who deserves positive or negative treatment because of the event?). Schlenke *et al.* explain how responsibility, as individuals perceive it, depends on the strength of three linkages, each of which involves two out of three basic elements, that are prescriptions, events, and identities. Prescriptions come from regulative knowledge and (broadly speaking) concern what should be done or avoided. Events simply occur in the environment. Identities include but are not limited to roles of the individual that are relevant in the context. The three linkages, thus, respectively capture whether and to which extent: a prescription is considered to concern an event, an event is considered relevant for an identity, a prescription is considered to concern an identity.

Accountability has distinctive traits which do not allow making it a special kind of responsibility. First of all it involves two agents, the one who gives the account and the one who takes the account [9, 22, 27, 30]. Indeed, following [30], accountability is a pyramid, that comes into being when an accredited public watches a responsibility triangle. The account taker can only be someone who has some kind of authority on the account giver [12, 29]. The origin of such an authority may be various; for instance, it may be due to a principal-agent relationship, or to a delegation. The account taker is sometimes called the *forum* [9]. Following ReMMO, accountability is in relationship with responsibility (it concerns a responsibility), and a responsibility may be subject to many accountabilities. Accountability may also involve a sanction, as a social consequence of the account giver's achievement or non-achievement of what expected, and of its providing or not providing an account.

---

² A psychological model by Schlenke *et al.* which is widely used in the context of human resource management.

All such considerations yield that, in order to properly tackle accountability in a computational system, it is necessary to identify those data that are specific to accountability and their relationships. We now summarize the key aspects of accountability, that we rely upon in drawing the model, reporting also the reference literature:

(a) *Accountability implies agency.* If a principal does not possess the qualities to act "autonomously, interactively and adaptively", i.e. with agency, there is no reason to speak of accountability, for the agent would be but a tool, and a tool cannot be held accountable [31].

(b) *Accountability requires but is not limited to causal significance.* The plain physical causation (also called scientific causation in [30]), that does not involve awareness or choice, does not even create a responsibility, let aside accountability. This view is supported also by [9,10].

(c) *Accountability does not hinder autonomy.* Indeed, accountability makes sense because of autonomy in deliberation [1,10,30,32].

(d) *Accountability requires observability.* In order to make correct judgments, a forum must be able to observe the necessary relevant information. However, in order to maintain modularity, a forum should not observe beyond its scope. For example, if a principal buys a product and the product is faulty, that principal holds the factory as a whole accountable. The factory, in turn, holds one of its members accountable for shoddy production. In other words, accountability determination is strictly related to a precise context. In each context, the forum must be able to observe events and/or actions strictly contained in its scope and decipher accountability accordingly. As context changes, accountability will change accordingly. For this reason, a mechanism to compose different contexts and decide accountability comprehensively is essential.

(e) *Accountability requires control.* Without control decisions cannot be enacted, the agent does not have an impact on the situation. It will be ineffectual. In [21], control is defined as the capability, possibly distributed among agents, of bringing about events. Due to our focus on positive accountability, i.e. on bringing about a situation of interest, we follow this proposal and interpret omissions (not acting) as non-achievements. [13] gives a slightly different definition of control as the ability of an agent to maintain the truth value of a given state of affairs. Alternatives where control amounts to interference or constraint can be devised but are related to negative accountability.

(f) *Accountability requires a mutually held expectation.* Accountability is a directed social relationship concerning a behavior, that serves the purposes of sense-making and coordination in a group of interacting parties, sharing an agreement on how things should be done [18]. The role of expectation is widely recognized [1,18,32]. Both parties must be aware of such a relationship for it to have value (the account-taker to know when it has the right to ask for an account, the account giver to know when towards whom it is liable in case of request).

(g) *Accountability is rights-driven.* One is held accountable by another who, in the context, has the claim-right to ask for the account. Particularly relevant on this aspect the understanding of accountability that is drawn in tort law [12], where the account-taker is the only recognized authority who can ask for an account, and the account-giver has a liability towards the account-taker (to explain when requested). Further analysis is carried out in [19].

3   Modeling Accountability with ORM

We have seen that accountability describes a relationship-centric approach, as it is fundamentally defined through relationships that permit one principal to take to account another. Without that relationship-permitting accounting, accountability would be reduced to a hybrid of traceability and blame-giving. To aid the modeling endeavor, use of ORM becomes a natural choice because of its built-in language advantage that places relationships at the center of its expressive power [20]. Throughout the process of modeling, we made use of both ORM and OWL (https://www.w3.org/TR/owl2-syntax/) to experiment with different tools and found that our instrument of choice, ORM, allowed us a more easily comprehensible description of accountability than OWL. We found the centrality of the relationship, rather than the entity, to be particularly apt at expressing our desired concepts in ORM. In particular, the possibility to place constraints on role groups in relationships proved invaluable for describing how relationships interact with and depend on one another. We recall that in this paper we focus on positive accountability, that is when principals do not act as they should (rather than act as they shouldn't in the case of negative accountability). In other words, we are dealing with the *regulation of task completion* rather than task interference.

3.1   Accountability Requirements

For accountability to function, there must be a *base relationship* because of which a principal feels an obligation to account for his/her actions. The relationship entails a nuanced approach to unexpected outcomes or actions. For instance, a buyer may expect a seller to provide some goods and hold him/her to account should the seller not do so, but *not* in absence of payment. In other words, an unexpected action does not necessarily implicate wrongdoing, thanks to *mitigating circumstances* which circumscribe the scope of the accountability relationship – lack of payment is a mitigating circumstance. A straightforward case without mitigating circumstances would be a principal who acts with full understanding of his/her action effects and expected social role, that clearly caused the outcome/action in question, and could have chosen to act otherwise (i.e. has control over the given state of affairs). Thus, a forum would look for, among other qualities, *causation* as well as *autonomy* and *understanding* in action.

Due to the focus on positive accountability, a forum's interest lies in assessing possibility to act, that is, if a principal had complete potential and autonomy as author of the outcome. We can also say he/she effectively caused the outcome through inaction contrary to social expectations (e.g. a merchant who refuses to provide goods that were paid as agreed). A forum must also determine a principal's *situational knowledge* of his/her expected agreed-upon role (e.g. the merchant must be aware the client expects him/her to ship the purchased items). Therefore, a model of positive accountability must respect the following requirements:

[R1] *Identify relationships of account giving between principals for certain outcomes;*
[R2] *Account for mitigating circumstances;*
[R3] *Establish a principal's qualities of:*
   .1 *Agency*
   .2 *Causal contribution to outcome;*
   .3 *Possibility/opportunity to act;*
[R4] *Allow for the passing of judgment.*

Requirement [R1] expresses the simplest: we must place in *relationship* two principals (who are not necessarily individuals but may, for instance, amount to organizations like a shipping company or an office) along with agreed *expected outcomes*. Note that for us accountability relationships are always the result of an act that was explicitly, deliberately, and voluntarily performed by the account giver, and that amount either to the creation of the accountability relationship by itself or to the acceptance some "rules of the game" – e.g. when enacting some role.

[R2] refines the base relationship through *context*. Context contains a series of conditions that stipulate when there are no mitigating circumstances. We reiterate that we speak in the absence of negative accountability, and can consequently discount interference from other system actors. Context, therefore, represents a kind of precondition to outcome's realization to be specified by the principal on who the expectations lie. The specialized context also protects the principal by disallowing unattainable obligations. The accountability relationship consequently takes the form as described in [10].

[R3] presents us with a more complex modeling problem. For agency, we adopt the definition given in [8], "The person is an autonomous, intentional, and planning agent who is capable of distinguishing right and wrong and good and bad". A principal, arguably autonomous by design, satisfies the first part of the agency condition when s/he stipulates the ability to bring about an expectation from a context, that is, execute a plan, whether that be his/her own plan or a plan to hold another accountable. In order to know "good" from "bad", a principal must have foreknowledge of his/her social expectations, whose completion for all intents and purposes are "good" and "right", and, in absence of negative accountability, whose non-completion are the only "bad" and "wrong" actions.

Likewise, for causal contribution, in absence of negative accountability and by declaring *control* over a *context* and *expectation*, a principal recognizes that one leads to another thanks to some intermediate action on her/his part. As a consequence, given context, the declared principal effectively *causes* either the outcome in question or its absence. Though a principal can subcontract out his/her plan, meaning another principal could be the "cause" of the first principal's outcome, from a modular viewpoint the first retains his/her causal relevance for the outermost outcome as the "manager".

The possibility/opportunity to act condition completes a concept already covered by the previously discussed requirements. Thanks to a principal's *control* in a specified *context*, if that context comes about, that principal can *freely choose* to act or not act and bring about the desired *outcome*. Again, without negative accountability, through his/her control, that principal has the possibility and opportunity to act.

We choose to leave out the sanctioning piece, that is often yielded by accountability, to the requirement [R4], the passing of judgment, for future implementations of accountability. Our primary concern consists, indeed, in identifying the information that is needed to *support* the passing of judgement and the possible consequent sanction.

3.2   A Model Takes Shape

The accountability model is reported in Fig. 1 as an ORM model. Concerning ORM, we report a little information for those who are not familiar with this notation; for details about ORM notation, please see [20]. In ORM all elements with the same name are the same entity/relationship. Entities/relationships can play identifiable (often named, e.g., *account-giver* or *subgoal*) roles inside relationships, that are explicitly depicted in the model. Part (or all) of the roles that make the relationship can be related to groups of roles inside another relationship by a constraint. For instance, in Fig. 1 we use inclusion and exclusive or. Relationships represent facts. They are denoted by a reading that gives an intuition of the relationship, and can be characterized in many ways, for instance by graphically denoting reflexivity, a-/anti-/simmetry, commutativity (e.g. *contains* is asymmetric).

Central to the model lies the relationship of accountability (accountability requirement [R1]) which contains two principals, one (account-giver) who is accountable to the other (account-taker), for an achievement (... *is accountable to ... for ...*). An achievement is a pair that is made of a context and an outcome, meaning that the interest in the outcome raises in a specific context –thus, the context limits accountability for an outcome. An Achievement can be structured into subgoals. The asymmetric relation *contains* represents such structure. The accountability relationship is further constrained so that a principal who is accountable must be in control and that there must be a mutually held expectation on that principal to act. The idea of contextual control is then further specified by its two types: control that comes from one's own efforts, and control that comes from one's ability to hold another accountable.

Based on the identified requirements, we identify the following key nouns, which will take the shape of objects. *Principal* partially satisfies the agency requirement [R3] by representing an autonomous individual or organization who might potentially be thought of in legal terms as a persona juris. *Context* and *Outcome* both represent sets of facts that characterize some states of interest. They are always associated with one another in the model but the meaning of such association depends on further information. An outcome represents a condition to achieve, i.e. a set of facts that should be brought about and that can be

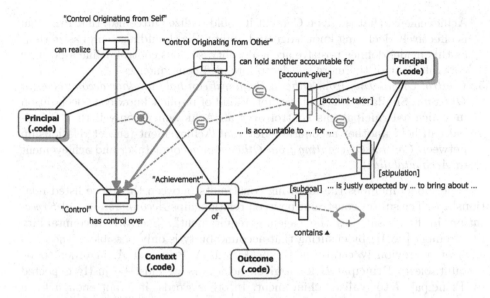

Fig. 1. ORM model for the accountability relationship.

verified. Context corresponds either to mitigating circumstances (accountability requirement [R2]), or to some preconditions under which a principal has the possibility to pursue an outcome, or the conditions under which an expectation that some outcome will be achieved is activated. The relationships between such objects, based on the requirements that are explained in Sect. 3.1, are as follows:

1. *Accountability: Principal is accountable to Principal for Achievement.* Represents the actual atomic accountability relationship in which the first Principal can be held to account to the second about Achievement. It has three roles and is constrained by the presence of some of those elements both in a relationship of expectation (outgoing arrow towards *... is justly expected by ... to bring about ...*), and in one of control (outgoing arrow towards *... has control over ...*). This fact type satisfies both [R1] (relationship) and [R2] (mitigating circumstances) requirements.

2. *Expectation: Principal is justly expected by Principal to bring about Stipulation.* Partially satisfies the foreknowledge requirement of the agency condition in order to distinguish right from wrong. By this relationship, the principal recognizes that if given the opportunity, realizing the achievement is good and not doing so is bad. With the word justly, we require that both principals are in agreement over the expectation.

3. *Control: Principal has Control over Achievement.* Control expresses contextual autonomy in that a Principal can effectively decide whether or not to realize an Achievement. Control is then divided into two types of control: Control from Self and Control from Other.

4. *Control Originating from Self: Principal can realize Achievement.* This type of control represents a modularization of knowledge. If a Principal could realize

Achievement (that is, given Context it could realize Outcome), that Principal is effectively declaring knowledge and ability. We should also emphasize that, as this model defines positive accountability, so does control define a positive control. Control therefore speaks to intended consequences.

5. *Control Originating from Others: Principal can hold another accountable for Outcome.* Similarly we can interpret a kind of implicit knowledge declaration in which a Principal has control over an Achievement only if that Principal can hold another accountable for that Achievement (subset relationship between *Control Originating from Other* and account-taker and achievement in *Accountability*).

The model includes the following constraints between the above listed relationships. The subset constraint between relationships *Accountability* and *Expectation* in Fig. 1 satisfies the "agency requirement" (Sect. 3.1, accountability requirement [R3.1]) by ensuring that accountability is only possible in the presence of a previously established expectation. A Principal A, in order to be accountable to Principal B for a given achievement, must be justly expected by Principal B to realize achievement. In other words, it is not enough for a Principal to exert autonomy, there must also be a socially established agreement of expectation. Simply put, in order to be accountable, a Principal must not only exert situational autonomy, but must also be expected to do so.

Subset constraint between account-giver and achievement in *Accountability*, on one side, with *Control*, on the other side, instead satisfies both the "causal" as well as the "possibility/opportunity" condition ([R3.2] and [R3.3]), as well as links mitigating circumstances to a principal-specified context. The constraint expresses in words that a Principal can be accountable for an Achievement only if that same Principal also has control over that Achievement, which means over an Outcome in same given Context. That is, in order to be accountable for an Outcome, a Principal must exhibit causal relevance over, and have possibility to realize, that Outcome and, thus, be a crucial influence in the truth value result of Outcome in Context.

4   Comparison and Discussion

The 2002 December Report of the Auditor General of Canada [23] recognizes accountability as a critical element of representative democratic government, and proposes a well-known (and widely accepted) definition of accountability, that takes recent developments in public management and governance into account. Here, accountability is defined as "a relationship based on obligations to demonstrate, review, and take responsibility for performance, both the results achieved in light of agreed expectations and the means used". All the elements of the definition are explained in Exhibit 9.1 [24]. The model we propose captures this understanding of accountability in a straightforward way. Of particular importance is the notion of *agreed expectation* stemming *from either a formal or informal agreement* as a key part of accountability. As underlined in our model, the creation of a just expectation relationship requires an agreement between the parties; an internal expectation, generated from one's opinions, is not enough to hold another accountable. Another important point is that the key focus of accountability is on results accomplished or not accomplished, i.e. on outcomes, for which principals explicitly take responsibility. Exhibit 9.2 explains that performance should be clearly linked with each party's capacity (e.g., skills) to deliver. This is what we capture by control. Exhibit 9.2 also explains that besides the accomplishments expected, also the operating constraints to be respected should be explicit, understood, and agreed upon. Operating constraints amount to those mitigating circumstances which, in our model, are explicitly captured by the context and agreed upon by the principals involved.

In [10], the concept of accountability requirement is defined as a directed relationship between two principals (account-giver and account-taker), an antecedent, and a consequent, which together constitute the mutual and conditional expectation between two parties. Should the antecedent become true, account-giver becomes accountable for the expected consequent with account-taker. An organization serves as a context for the accountability requirements. Principals enter the organization by playing some of its roles. Accountability requirements include commitments, authorizations, prohibitions, and empowerment. All the foreseen declinations of the accountability requirement only implicitly entail a notion of control.

[2–4] propose a protocol to ensure accountability as a design property in an organizational setting. The authors distill five principles for supporting accountability, which make use of the same concepts from the definition of multi-agent organizations (role, goal, power). A commitment-based protocol is, then, defined with the aim of guaranteeing the aforementioned principles, both in the construction of the organization and, through an enhanced monitoring functionality, while it operates. The ORM model we proposed here is more general: it does not explicitly include concepts like organization and role, but those concepts are still derivable. Principle one states that *all the collaborations subject to considerations of accountability among principals occur within a single scope called organization*. Naturally, in order to properly identify relationships of accountability, all agreements, including expectations and declarations of control, must belong to the same scope to satisfy the subset constraints for accountability. The second and third principles concern the process of enrollment of an agent into an organization. Specifically, *a principal can enroll in an organization only by playing a role that is defined inside the organization* and *a principal willing to play a role in an organization must be aware of all the powers associated with such a role before adopting it*. As for [6], the ability to affect the institutional state is provided by the acquisition of some powers associated with the role itself at enactment time. The definition of a role delimits the range of actions an agent, who plays that role, can perform (i.e. its powers) inside the organization, thereby encoding the outcomes over which it has control. From the point of view of the ORM model, a role is essentially a set of outcomes and contexts that are grouped together with a purpose of organizing work. Playing a role, therefore, means having control (through powers) over a set of outcomes associated with it, and being aware of the fact that there could be a social expectation related to their realization. The forth principle states that *a principal is accountable, towards the organization or another agent, for those goals s/he has explicitly accepted to bring about.* From the declaration of just (i.e. mutually agreed) expectation, in conjunction with the subset constraint from accountability, we can conclude that an agent must agree to a goal (through the expectation relationship) before that agent can be considered accountable. Finally, the fifth principle states that *a principal must have the leeway for putting before the organization the provisions s/he needs for achieving the goal to which s/he is committing. The organization has the capability of reasoning on the requested provisions and can accept or reject them.* By specifying control, a principal stipulates contextual conditions under which s/he can realize an outcome. Without a principal's declaration of control, s/he cannot be held accountable thanks to the subset constraint and will not be considered committed to an outcome.

5   Conclusions

In the proposed information model of accountability, just expectation is a key concept, because for an accountability relationship to hold, there must be a fact stating an active and agreed expectation between two principals about an outcome. The way in which this fact is determined is outside the scope of the proposal. For a discussion of expectations and their use in practical reasoning see, for instance [28].

The relationships, which in the model tie accountability, expectation, and control, are versatile and can be used in many ways. The availability of accountability facts influences the behavior of the whole group of interacting agents, both those who play the role of account-givers and those who play the role of account-takers. For instance, a principal, knowing that another principal is accountable for some achievement, and knowing that the account-giver is justly expected to bring about the achievement, will draw expectations on the behavior of that principal, and on the control exercised by that principal, and it will orient its own behavior consequently. Another principal, knowing to be accountable for an achievement, will likely take the outcome into account as a goal when the related context holds. It will be possible for the principal to pursue the achievement because, through one of the inclusion constraints, in order for an accountability fact to hold, there is a control fact stating the principal has control over the achievement. In case control of the outcome is *from self*, it will perform some skill or power of its own. If, instead, its control is *from other*, the principal actually depends on accountability relationships involving some party. This recursive view of accountability, through control from other, accommodates hierarchies of authorities. For instace, a head of office is accountable over the office procedures not because s/he realizes them directly, but because of the accountability relationships his/her employees have towards him/her. These examples explain how accountability facts have an impact on future actions because in general they will increase awareness, thus accommodating the views in [1,27]. Moreover, we discuss in [5], by relying on a practical example, how the proposed model overcomes some weaknesses in tackling goal distribution in business processes. In that context, the choice of a language, for expressing achievements, that allows for temporal expressions, introduces requirements on the way in which conditions are brought about, and shows how through the language it is possible to account also for the means used.

Taking a different perspective, the model tells which information is to be collected in order to support the identification of the responsibilities that are involved in the realization of a state of interest. Here, we give to the term responsibility the already discussed meaning provided by [17]. Recall that in that model each responsibility has associated a number of accountabilities. Suppose that the information conforms to our model and that its creation and evolution is collected by some monitoring framework. When a situation of interest arises (in particular, when some achievement is not satisfied), the availability of accountabilities makes it possible to identify the involved principals; not only those trivially involved in the last step that brought to the condition under scrutiny, but also those who, with their choices and actions, drove the execution towards its end. For instance, suppose the sellers in a shop share a view of the available items, and that it is their responsibility to timely inform the other sellers when some item is sold out. Seller Bob forgets to inform seller Alice that the last TV set was sold. Alice is, then, asked by a client about the availability of TV sets. She answers "yes" but when at some point of the sale she looks for the item, it turns out there is none and the sale fails. Accountability will help to identify Bob as the one who should answer. In this simple case only one is responsible and nothing can be done to fix the situation. In other cases it will, instead, be possible to activate compensation processes or to refine the executed processes, based on collected evidence. In fact, the principals, that are connected by the accountability and control relationships, are the executors of a network of related activities, and each will possibly contribute to the understanding of the situation under scrutiny. Note that if we think of each principal as corresponding to a different process, such an understanding will be built across processes, by exploiting the links that are captured by the accountability relationships.

On the other hand, the absence of a just-expectation fact will help to conclude the principal is not liable. For instance, consider a company where help-desk requests are a responsibility of some principal. A system administrator has access to and can operate on what is recorded in the database –thus also on help-desk requests, that are there stored– but is not expected to answer to such requests, so if a request is not attended the administrator will not be held to account. Similarly, a principal who is justly expected to satisfy some achievement, but who has no control over that achievement will not be asked to account for the achievement –for instance, a new help-desk operator who does not have the proper access rights yet.

The availability of knowledge about the internal structure of an organization would support the realization of mechanisms to reason about accountability at different levels of granularities, as hoped for in Sect. 2. In other words, the model allows for modularity. So, for instance, a whole organization, acting as a principal, can be accountable for an outcome. That same organization, however, can have internal accountability relationships to add further nuance. Along these lines, it would also be interesting to combine the accountability model with a representation of *compensations*, e.g. [33], that should be executed when an outcome is not achieved. Related to these aims, further nuance could be added by taking into account role power differences in collective accountability. For instance, we might say that the director of the organization should assume more accountability than individual parts because that individual pulls more weight and has more decision power in the organization. We could then assign accountability weights to the various roles in the organization with values that reflect power differences in order to keep accountability proportional to one's pull in the organization.

References

1. Anderson, P.A.: Justifications and precedents as constraints in foreign policy decision- making. Am. J. Polit. Sci. **25**(4), 738–761 (1981)
2. Baldoni, M., Baroglio, C., May, K.M., Micalizio, R., Tedeschi, S.: ADOPT JaCaMo: accountability-driven organization programming technique for JaCaMo. In: An, B., Bazzan, A., Leite, J., Villata, S., van der Torre, L. (eds.) PRIMA 2017. LNCS (LNAI), vol. 10621, pp. 295–312. Springer, Cham (2017). https://doi.org/10.1007/978-3-319-69131-2_18
3. Baldoni, M., Baroglio, C., May, K.M., Micalizio, R., Tedeschi, S.: Supporting organizational accountability inside multiagent systems. In: Esposito, F., Basili, R., Ferilli, S., Lisi, F. (eds.) AI*IA 2017. LNCS, vol. 10640, pp. 403–417. Springer, Cham (2017). https://doi.org/10.1007/978-3-319-70169-1_30
4. Baldoni, M., Baroglio, C., May, K.M., Micalizio, R., Tedeschi, S.: Computational accountability in MAS organizations with ADOPT. J. Appl. Sci. **8**(4), 489 (2018). Special issue "Multi-Agent Systems"
5. Baldoni, M., Baroglio, C., Micalizio, R.: Goal distribution in business process models. In: Ghidini, C., et al. (eds.) AI*IA 2018. LNCS, vol. 11298, pp. 252–265. Springer, Cham (2018)
6. Boella, G., van der Torre, L.W.N.: The ontological properties of social roles in multi-agent systems: definitional dependence, powers and roles playing roles. Artif. Intell. Law **15**(3), 201–221 (2007)
7. Boissier, O., Bordini, R.H., Hübner, J.F., Ricci, A., Santi, A.: Multi-agent oriented programming with JaCaMo. Sci. Comput. Program. **78**(6), 747–761 (2013). https://doi.org/10.1016/j.scico.2011.10.004
8. Braham, M., van Hees, M.: An anatomy of moral responsibility. Mind **121**(483), 601–634 (2012)
9. Hulstijn, J., Burgemeestre, B.: Design for the values of accountability and transparency. In: van den Hoven, J., Vermaas, P.E., van de Poel, I. (eds.) Handbook of Ethics, Values, and Technological Design, pp. 303–333. Springer, Dordrecht (2015). https://doi.org/10.1007/978-94-007-6970-0_12
10. Chopra, A.K., Singh, M.P.: The thing itself speaks: accountability as a foundation for requirements in sociotechnical systems. In: IEEE 7th International Workshop RELAW. IEEE Computer Society (2014). https://doi.org/10.1109/RELAW.2014.6893477

11. Conte, R., Paolucci, M.: Responsibility for societies of agents. J. Artif. Soc. Soc. Simul. **7**(4), 1–2 (2004)
12. Darwall, S.: Civil Recourse as mutual accountability. In: Morality, Authority, and Law: Essays in Second- Personal Ethics I. Oxford University Press (2013)
13. Dastani, M., Lorini, E., Meyer, J.C., Pankov, A.: Other-condemning anger = blaming accountable agents for unattainable desires. In: Proceedings of AAMAS. ACM (2017)
14. Yazdanpanah, V., Dastani, M.: distant group responsibility in multi-agent systems. In: Baldoni, M., Chopra, A.K., Son, T.C., Hirayama, K., Torroni, P. (eds.) PRIMA 2016. LNCS (LNAI), vol. 9862, pp. 261–278. Springer, Cham (2016). https://doi. org/10.1007/978-3-319-44832-9_16
15. Durkheim, E.: De la division du travail social. PUF (1893)
16. Eshleman, A.: Moral responsibility. The Stanford Encyclopedia of Philosophy (2014)
17. Feltus, C.: Aligning access rights to governance needs with the responsability Meta-Model (ReMMo) in the frame of enterprise architecture. Ph.D. thesis, University of Namur, Belgium, March 2014
18. Garfinkel, H.: Studies in Ethnomethodology. Prentice-Hall Inc., Englewood Cliffs (1967)
19. Grant, R.W., Keohane, R.O.: Accountability and abuses of power in world politics. Am. Polit. Sci. Rev. **99**(1), 29–43 (2005)
20. Halpin, T., Morgan, T.: Information Modeling and Relational Databases. Morgan Kaufmann Publishers, Burlington (2008)
21. Marengo, E., Baldoni, M., Baroglio, C., Chopra, A., Patti, V., Singh, M.: Commitments with regulations: reasoning about safety and control in REGULA. In: AAMAS 2011, vol. 2, pp. 467–474. IFAAMAS (2011)
22. Nissenbaum, H.: Accountability in a computerized society. Sci. Eng. Ethics **2**(1), 25–42 (1996)
23. Office of the Auditor General of Canada: 2002 December Report of the Auditor General of Canada: Chapter 9 (2002). http://www.oag-bvg.gc.ca/internet/ English/parl_oag_200212_09_e_12403.html
24. Office of the Auditor General of Canada: Exhibit 9.1 The elements of accountability (2002). http://www.oag-bvg.gc.ca/internet/English/att_20021209xe01_e_ 12282.html
25. Parsons, T.: The Structure of Social Action. Collier-Macmillan, London (1968)
26. van de Poel, I.: The Relation Between Forward-Looking and Backward-Looking Responsibility. In: Vincent, N., van de Poel, I., van den Hoven, J. (eds.) Moral Responsibility. LOET, vol. 27, pp. 37–52. Springer, Heidelberg (2011). https:// doi.org/10.1007/978-94-007-1878-4_3
27. Quinn, A., Schlenker, B.R.: Can accountability produce independence? Goals as determinants of the impact of accountability on conformity. Pers. Soc. Psychol. Bull. **28**(4), 472–483 (2002)
28. Ranathunga, S., Cranefield, S., Purvis, M.: Integrating expectation monitoring into BDI agents. In: Dennis, L., Boissier, O., Bordini, R.H. (eds.) ProMAS 2011. LNCS (LNAI), vol. 7217, pp. 74–91. Springer, Heidelberg (2012). https://doi.org/ 10.1007/978-3-642-31915-0_5
29. Romzek, B.S., Dubnick, M.J.: Accountability in the public sector: lessons from the challenger tragedy. Public Adm. Rev. **47**(3), 227–238 (1987)
30. Schlenker, B.R., Britt, T.W., Pennington, J., Rodolfo, M., Doherty, K.: The triangle model of responsibility. Psychol. Rev. **101**(4), 632–652 (1994)

31. Simon, J.: Distributed epistemic responsibility in a hyperconnected era. In: Floridi, L. (ed.) The Online Manifesto: Being Human in a Hyperconnected Era, pp. 145–159. Springer, Cham (2015). https://doi.org/10.1007/978-3-319-04093-6_17
32. Suchman, L.: Centers of coordination: a case and some themes. In: Resnick, L.B., Säljö, R., Pontecorvo, C., Burge, B. (eds.) Discourse, Tools, and Reasoning: Essays on Situated Cognition, pp. 41–62. Springer, Heidelberg (1997). https://doi.org/10.1007/978-3-662-03362-3_3
33. Unruh, A., Bailey, J., Ramamohanarao, K.: A framework for goal-based semantic compensation in agent systems. In: Barley, M., Mouratidis, H., Unruh, A., Spears, D., Scerri, P., Massacci, F. (eds.) Safety and Security in Multiagent Systems. LNCS (LNAI), vol. 4324, pp. 130–146. Springer, Heidelberg (2009). https://doi.org/10.1007/978-3-642-04879-1_10

Applications of AI

From Semantically Abstracted Traces to Process Mining and Process Model Comparison

Giorgio Leonardi[1], Manuel Striani[2], Silvana Quaglini[3], Anna Cavallini[4], and Stefania Montani[1(✉)]

[1] DISIT, Computer Science Institute, University of Piemonte Orientale,
Alessandria, Italy
stefania.montani@uniupo.it
[2] Department of Computer Science, University of Torino, Turin, Italy
[3] Department of Electrical, Computer and Biomedical Engineering,
University of Pavia, Pavia, Italy
[4] Istituto di Ricovero e Cura a Carattere Scientifico Fondazione "C. Mondino"
- on behalf of the Stroke Unit Network (SUN) Collaborating Centers, Pavia, Italy

Abstract. Process model comparison can be exploited to assess the quality of organizational procedures, to identify non-conformances with respect to given standards, and to highlight critical situations. Sometimes, however, it is difficult to make sense of large and complex process models, while a more abstract view of the process would be sufficient for the comparison task. In this paper, we show how process traces, abstracted on the basis of domain knowledge, can be provided as an input to process mining, and how abstract models (i.e., models mined from abstracted traces) can then be compared and ranked, by adopting a similarity metric able to take into account penalties collected during the abstraction phase. The overall framework has been tested in the field of stroke management, where we were able to rank abstract process models more similarly to the ordering provided by a domain expert, with respect to what could be obtained when working on non-abstract ones.

1 Introduction

Nowadays, many information systems adopted by organizations and companies record data about the executed business process instances in an *event log* [15], which stores the sequences (*traces* [15] henceforth) of activities that have been completed at the organization, typically together with key execution parameters, such as times, costs and resources. Event logs can be provided as an input to *process mining* [15] algorithms, a family of a-posteriori analysis techniques able to extract non-trivial knowledge from these historic data; within process mining, *process model discovery* algorithms, in particular, take as input the log traces and build a process model, focusing on its control flow constructs. Classical process mining algorithms, however, provide a purely syntactical analysis, where

© Springer Nature Switzerland AG 2018
C. Ghidini et al. (Eds.): AI*IA 2018, LNAI 11298, pp. 47–59, 2018.
https://doi.org/10.1007/978-3-030-03840-3_4

activities in the traces are processed only referring to their names. Activity names are strings without any semantics, so that identical activities, labeled by synonyms, will be considered as different, or activities that are special cases of other activities will be processed as unrelated. On the other hand, the capability of relating *semantic structures* such as ontologies to activities in the log can enable process mining techniques to work at *different levels of abstraction* (i.e., at the level of instances or concepts) and, therefore, to mask irrelevant details, to promote reuse, and, in general, to make process analysis much more flexible and reliable. Interestingly, *semantic process mining*, defined as the combination of semantic processing capabilities and classical process mining techniques, has been recently proposed in the literature, and the area is rather active (see Sect. 6). However *semantic process model discovery*, in particular, needs to be further investigated.

Following these considerations, we propose a **trace abstraction mechanism**, able to map activities in the log traces to terms in an ontology, so that they can be converted into higher-level concepts by navigating a hierarchy, up to the desired level. Consecutive activities that abstract as the same concept are also merged into the same abstracted *macro-activity*, properly managing delays and other activities in-between. Abstracted traces are then given as an input to **process mining**: in particular, we rely on classical algorithms embedded in the open source framework ProM [16].

Once the process model of a given organization has been obtained, it is useful to compare it to other organizations' ones, as well as to existing standards. In the medical field, for instance, the analysis of the patient management processes actually implemented in practice supports quality of service evaluation. Evaluating the provided service is a key task in a competitive healthcare market, where hospitals have to focus on ways to deliver high quality care while at the same time reducing costs. Specifically, the actual process model, mined from the organization event log, can be compared to the reference clinical guideline, to verify the existence and the entity of changes, possibly due to local resource constraints, or sometimes to medical errors. Moreover, a ranking of different hospitals' process models can support audit activities and resource assignment. Sometimes, however, it is difficult to make sense of large and complex process models, while a more abstract view of the processes themselves would be sufficient for the comparison task. In order to address both the need for process model comparison and the need for abstraction, we have then *extended a similarity metric* we defined in our previous work [12], in order to allow for comparison and ranking of *models mined from abstracted traces* as well. We also report on our experimental work in the field of stroke care, where we were able to rank abstract process models (i.e., models mined from abstracted traces) more similarly to the ordering provided by a domain expert, with respect to what could be obtained when working on non-abstract ones.

2   Semantic Trace Abstraction

In our framework, semantic trace abstraction has been realized as a multi-step procedure. The following subsections describe the various steps.

2.1   Ontology Mapping

The first step relies on ontology mapping. The **ontology**, which has been formalized by using the Protégé editor, is partially depicted in Fig. 1, and comprises:

- a *goal taxonomy*, composed by a set of classes, representing the main goals in stroke management, namely: "(Secondary) Prevention", "Pathogenetic Mechanism Identification", "Brain Damage Reduction" and "Causes Identification". Moreover, the class "Administrative Actions" collects procedures related to the administrative aspects of health care, such as admission, discharge, transfer, and so forth. These main goals can be further specialized into subclasses, according to more specific goals (relation "is-a"; e.g., "Early Relapse Prevention" is a subgoal of "Prevention");
- an *activity taxonomy*, composed by all the activities that can be logged in stroke management traces (in "is-a" relation with the general class "Activity"); activities are the atomic steps of stroke management, and do not need further specialization;
- a set of "aimsTo" relations, which formalize that an activity can be executed to implement a (sub)goal. Multiple "aimsTo" relations could connect a given activity to different goals (e.g., CAT (Computer Aided Tomography) can implement "Monitoring" or "Timing" even within the same guideline).

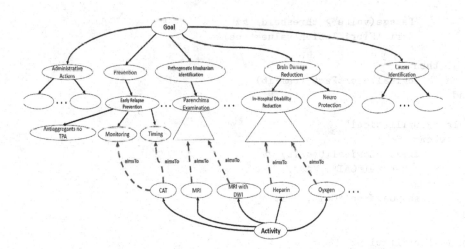

Fig. 1. An excerpt from the stroke domain ontology

In the case of multiple "aimsTo" relations, the proper goal to be used to abstract a given activity will be selected by a rule base, described in the following subsection.

2.2   Rule-Based Reasoning for Disambiguation

As a second step in the trace abstraction mechanism, a **rule base** is exploited, in order to identify which of the multiple goals of an activity in the ontology should be considered for abstracting the activity itself. Rules cover therefore a disambiguation task. Contextual information (i.e., the activities that have been already executed on the patient at hand, and/or her/his specific clinical conditions) is used to activate the correct rules. The rule base has been formalized in Drools [10].

As an example, referring to the CAT activity mentioned above, the rules reported below apply to patients who have experienced a severe brain damage and suffer from atrial fibrillation. These patients must undergo a therapy that starts with ASA (a class of anti-inflammatory drugs), and continues with daily AC (anti-coagulant drug) administration. Before the first AC, a CAT is required, to assess AC starting time, which could be delayed in case CAT detects a hemorrhagic transformation. After a few days of AC administration, another CAT is needed, to monitor therapeutic results. Therefore, depending on the context, CAT can implement the "Timing" or the "Monitoring" goal (see Fig. 1).

Forward chaining on the rules below (showed as a simplified pseudocode with respect to the system internal representation, for the sake of simplicity) allows to determine the correct goal for the CAT activity.

```
rule "SevereDamage"
    when
      (
          Damage(value > threshold) &&
          AtrialFibrillation(value=true)
      )
    then
        logicalInsertFact (DamFib);
end

rule "Fibrillation1"
    when
        existInLogical(DamFib) &&
        isBefore("CAT", "AC")
    then
        setGoalName("CAT", "Timing");
end

rule "Fibrillation2"
    when
        existInLogical(DamFib) &&
        isAfter("CAT", "AC")
```

```
    then
        setGoalName("CAT", "Monitoring");
end
```

2.3 Trace Abstraction

Once the correct goal of every activity has been identified, trace abstraction can be completed. The level in the ontology to be chosen for abstraction (e.g., a very general goal, such as "Prevention", or a more specific one, such as "Early Relapse Prevention"), has to be specified as an input by the user.

In this last step, when a set of consecutive activities on the trace abstract as the same goal, they have to be merged into the same abstracted **_macro-activity_**, labeled as the common goal at hand. A macro-activity is an abstracted activity that covers the whole time span of multiple activities, and is labeled as their common goal in the ontology, at the specified abstraction level. As a special case, the macro-activity can abstract a single activity as its goal.

This procedure requires a proper treatment of _delays_ (i.e., of time intervals between two activities logged in the trace, within which no other activity takes place), and of activities in-between that implement a different goal (_interleaved activities_ henceforth).

Specifically, the procedure to abstract a trace operates as follows:

- for every activity i in the trace:
  - i is abstracted as the goal it implements (at the ontology level selected by the user); the macro-activity m_i, labeled as the identified goal, is created;
  - for every element j following i in the trace:
    * if j is a delay, its length is added to a variable $tot - delay$, that stores the total delay duration accumulated so far during the creation of m_i;
    * if j is an interleaved activity, its length is added to a variable $tot - inter$, that stores the total interleaved activities durations accumulated so far during the creation of m_i;
    * if j is an activity that, according to domain knowledge, abstracts as the same goal as i, m_i is extended to include j, provided that $tot - delay$ and $tot - inter$ do not exceed domain-defined thresholds. j is then removed from the activities in the trace that could start a new macro-activity, since it has already been incorporated into an existing one, and will be skipped in the following iterations;
  - the macro-activity m_i is appended to the output abstracted trace which, in the end, will contain the list of all the macro-activities that have been created by the procedure.

The variables $tot - delay$ and $tot - inter$, accumulated during abstraction, are also provided as an output attribute of each macro-activity. As discussed in Sect. 4, they will be used as a penalty in abstracted process model similarity calculation.

3   Process Mining

In our approach, process mining is implemented resorting to the well-known tool ProM, extensively described in [16]. ProM (and specifically its newest version ProM 6) is a platform-independent open source framework that supports a wide variety of process mining and data mining techniques, and can be extended by adding new functionalities in the form of plug-ins.

For the work described in this paper, we have exploited ProM's Heuristic Miner [17]. Heuristic Miner is a plug-in for process model discovery, able to mine process models from logs. It receives as input the log, and considers the order of the activities within every single trace. It can mine the presence of short-distance and long-distance dependencies (i.e., direct or indirect sequence of activities), with a certain degree of reliability. The output of the mining process can be visualized as a graph with two types of nodes: activity nodes and gateway nodes - these last ones representing AND/XOR join/fork points.

Currently, we have chosen to rely on Heuristics Miner, because it is known to be tolerant to noise, a problem that may affect medical logs (e.g., sometimes the logging may be incomplete). Anyway, testing of other mining algorithms available in ProM 6 is foreseen in our future work.

4   Process Model Comparison

In our framework, we have extended a metric we described in [12], which worked on models mined from non-abstracted traces, in order to permit the comparison of models mined from abstracted traces as well.

In the following, for the sake of completeness, we will first summarize the initial contribution [12] details, and then illustrate the extensions.

4.1   Initial Contribution

Since mined process models are represented in the form of graphs, we have defined a distance that extends the notion of graph edit distance [2]. Such a notion calculates the minimal cost of transforming one graph into another by applying edit operations, i.e., insertions/deletions and substitutions of nodes, and insertions/deletions and substitutions of edges. While string edit distance looks for an *alignment* that minimizes the cost of transforming one string into another by means of edit operations, in graph edit distance we have to look for a *mapping*. A mapping is a function that matches (possibly by substituting) nodes to nodes, and edges to edges. Unmatched nodes/edges have to be deleted (or, dually, inserted in the other graph). Among all possible mappings, we will select the one that leads to the minimal cost, having properly quantified the cost of every type of edit operation. In particular, when considering node mapping, activity nodes will only be mapped to activity nodes, while gateway nodes will be mapped to gateway nodes.

Formally, let $G1 = (N1, E1)$ and $G2 = (N2, E2)$ be two graphs, where Ei and Ni represent the sets of edges and nodes of graph Gi. Let $|Ni|$ and $|Ei|$ be the number of nodes and edges of graph Gi. Let M be a partial injective mapping (see [6]) that maps nodes in $N1$ to nodes in $N2$ and let $subn$, $sube$, $skipn$ and $skipe$ be the sets of substituted nodes, substituted edges, inserted or deleted nodes and inserted or deleted edges with respect to M. In particular, a substituted edge connects a pair of substituted nodes in M.

In our approach, the fraction of inserted/deleted nodes, denoted $fskipn$, the fraction of inserted/deleted edges, denoted $fskipe$, and the average distance of substituted nodes, denoted $fsubn$, are defined as follows:

$$fskipn = \frac{|skipn|}{|N1| + |N2|}$$

where $|skipn|$ is the number of inserted or deleted nodes;

$$fskipe = \frac{|skipe|}{|E1| + |E2|}$$

where $|skipe|$ is the number of inserted or deleted edges;

$$fsubn = \frac{2 * \left(\sum_{n,m \in M_A} dt(n,m) + \sum_{x,y \in M_G} dg(x,y) \right)}{|subn|}$$

where M_A represents the set of mapped activity nodes in the mapping M, M_G represents the set of mapped gateway nodes in M; $dt(n,m)$ is the distance between two activity nodes m and n in M_A, and $dg(x,y)$ is the distance between two gateway nodes x and y in M_G; $|subn|$ is the number of substituted nodes.

In detail, $dt(n,m)$ is a proper knowledge-intensive distance definition, to be chosen on the basis of the available knowledge representation formalism in the domain at hand. Currently, we are adopting Palmer's distance [13].

To calculate $dg(x,y)$ we proceed as follows:

1. if x and y are nodes of different types (i.e., a XOR and an AND), their distance is set to 1;
2. if x and y are of the same type (e.g., two ANDs), we have to calculate the difference between their incoming/outgoing activity nodes. The distance between a pair of activity nodes is still calculated exploiting Palmer's distance [13]. Further details can be found in [12].

Finally, the average distance of substituted edges $fsube$ is defined as follows:

$$fsube = \frac{2 * \sum_{(n1,n2),(m1,m2) \in M} (|r(e1) - r(e2)| + |p(e1) - p(e2)| + |m(e1) - m(e2)| + |s(e1) - s(e2)|)}{4 * |sube|}$$

where edge $e1$ (connecting node $n1$ to node $m1$) and edge $e2$ (connecting node $n2$ to node $m2$) are two substituted edges in M; $|sube|$ is the number of substituted edges; $r(ei)$ is the reliability of edge ei [17]; $p(ei)$ is the percentage of traces that crossed edge ei; $m(ei)$ and $s(ei)$ are statistical values (mean and standard deviation of the elapsed times) calculated over all the occurrences of the $ni->$ mi pattern (i.e., ni directly followed by mi) in the traces, and normalized in $[0, 1]$ dividing by the duration of the longest $ni->mi$ pattern in the log. If one of these parameters is unavailable (e.g., reliability is unavailable because Heuristic Miner was not used), its contribution is simply set to 0. Different/additional parameters learned by a miner could be considered as well in $fsube$ in the future.

The extended graph edit distance induced by the mapping M is:

$$ext_{edit}(M) = \frac{wskipn * fskipn + wskipe * fskipe + wsubn * fsubn + wsube * fsube}{wskipn + wskipe + wsubn + wsube}$$

where $wsubn$, $wsube$, $wskipn$ and $wskipe$ are proper weights $\in [0, 1]$.

The extended graph edit distance of two graphs is the minimal possible distance induced by any mapping between these graphs. To find the mapping that leads to the minimal distance we resort to a greedy approach, in order to limit computational costs. It can be shown that the algorithm works in cubic time on the number of nodes of the larger graph [6].

4.2   Extensions

The novel extensions we present in this paper basically lead to substitute $fsubn$ with a more complete definition, where average abstraction penalties are also summed up when considering the mapping of two activity nodes (which, in this new version, more properly represent macro-activity nodes). We introduce the following definitions:

Delay Penalty. Let n and m be two macro-activities, that have been matched in the mapping. Let $average_{delay_n} = \frac{\sum_{i=1}^{k} length(i)}{numtraces}$ be the sum of the lengths of all the k delays that have been incorporated into n in the abstraction phase, divided by the number of abstracted traces that include n (and let $average_{delay_m}$ be analogously defined). Let $maxdelay$ be the maximum, over all the abstracted traces, of the sum of the lengths of the delays incorporated in a macro-activity. The Delay Penalty $delay_p(n, m)$ between n and m is defined as:

$$delay_p(n, m) = \frac{|average_{delay_n} - average_{delay_m}|}{maxdelay}$$

As for interleaved activities penalty, we operate analogously to delay penalty, by considering the average lengths of the interleaved activities that have been incorporated within the involved macro-activities in the abstraction phase.

Interleaving Length Penalty. Let n and m be two macro-activities, that have been matched in the mapping. Let $average_{inter_n} = \frac{\sum_{i=1}^{k} length(i)}{numtraces}$ be the sum of the lengths of all the k interleaved activities that have been incorporated into n in the abstraction phase, divided by the number of abstracted traces that include n (and let $average_{inter_m}$ be analogously defined). Let $maxinter$ be the maximum, over all the abstracted traces, of the sum of the lengths of the interleaved activities incorporated in a macro-activity. The Interleaving Length Penalty $interL_p(n, m)$ between n and m is defined as:

$$interL_p(n, m) = \frac{|average_{inter_n} - average_{inter_m}|}{maxinter}$$

Then, formally, $fsubn$ becomes

$$fsubn = \frac{2 * \left(\sum_{n,m \in M_A} \varphi(n.m) + \sum_{x,y \in M_G} dg(x, y)\right)}{|subn|}$$

where

$$\varphi(n, m) = \frac{dt(n, m) + delay_p(n, m) + interL_p(n, m)}{3}$$

Notably, the abstraction penalty contributions might also be weighted differently from $dt(n, m)$, if the domain expert suggests to give more/less importance to Palmer's distance between macro-activities with respect to abstraction penalties themselves.

5 Experimental Results

In this section, we describe the experimental results we have obtained, in the application domain of stroke care. The available event log was composed of more than 15000 traces, collected at the Stroke Unit Network (SUN) collaborating centers of the Lombardia region, Italy. The number of traces in the different Stroke Units (SUs) of the network varied from 266 to 1149. Traces were composed of 13 activities on average. For our validation study, we asked a SUN stroke management expert to provide a ranking of some SUs (see Table 1, column 1), on the basis of the quality of service they provide, with respect to the top level SU. Such a ranking was based on her personal knowledge of the SUs human and instrumental resource availability (not on the process models); therefore, it was qualitative, and *coarse-grained*, in the sense that more than one SU could obtain the same qualitative evaluation. The top level SU will be referred as H0 in the experiments. The expert identified 6 SUs (H1-H6) with a high similarity level with respect to H0; 5 SUs (H7-H11) with a medium similarity level with respect to H0; and 4 SUs (H12-H15) with a low similarity level with respect to H0. The ordering of the SUs within one specific similarity level is not relevant, since, as observed, the expert's ranking is coarse-grained. It is instead important to distinguish between different similarity levels. We then mined the process models of the 16 SUs by using Heuristic Miner, both working on non-abstracted traces, and working on abstracted traces. We ordered the two available process model sets with respect to H0, resorting to the extended similarity metric presented in Sect. 4.2, globally obtaining two rankings. In the experiments, we set all the weights (see Sect. 4) to 1, except for *wskipn* and *wskipe*, which were set to 2. Indeed, the domain expert suggested to strongly penalize missing macro-activities or missing connections, with respect to substitutions. Moreover, in $fsubn$ abstraction penalty contributions were weighted 20% of $dt(n, m)$ (abstraction penalties were simply set to zero when comparing models mined from non-abstracted traces). As regards abstraction thresholds (see Sect. 2.3), on the other hand, they were common to all traces in the log, and set on the basis of medical knowledge. Results are shown in Table 1. Column 1 shows the expert's qualitative evaluation (similarity with respect to the reference SU H0), and lists the corresponding SUs names; columns 2 and 3 show the ranking obtained by relying on our distance definition, mining the process models on non-abstracted and abstracted traces, respectively. In particular, abstraction was conducted at level 2 in the ontology (where level 0 is "Goal"). When working on models mined from non-abstracted traces, we correctly rate two process models in the high similarity group (33%), zero process models in the medium similarity group (0%), and one process model in the low similarity group (25%, column 2). When working on models mined from abstracted traces, on the other hand, we correctly rate three process models in the high similarity group (50%), three process models in the medium similarity group (60%), and one process model in the low similarity group (25%, column 3). In summary, when working on abstracted traces, our extended distance definition, able to properly consider abstraction penalties as well, leads to rankings that are closer to the qualitative ranking provided by the human expert, and therefore allows to better classify the quality of service provided to patients by the different SUs.

6   Related Works

The use of semantics in business process management, with the aim of operating at different levels of abstractions in process discovery and/or analysis, is a relatively young area of research, where much is still unexplored.

One of the first contributions in this field can be found in [4], which introduces a process data warehouse, where taxonomies are exploited to add semantics to process execution data, in order to provide more intelligent reports. The topic was also studied in the SUPER project [14], within which several ontologies were created, such as the process mining ontology and the event ontology; these ontologies define core terminologies of business process management, usable by machines for task automation. However, the authors did not present any concrete implementations of semantic process mining or analysis. The work in [5] focuses on the use of semantics in business process monitoring, an activity that allows to detect or predict process deviations and special situations, to diagnose their causes, and possibly to resolve problems by applying corrective actions. Detection, diagnosis and resolution present interesting challenges that, on the authors' opinion, can strongly benefit from knowledge-based techniques. In [5] the idea to explicitly relate (or annotate) elements in the log with the concepts they represent, linking these elements to concepts in ontologies, is addressed. However, the management of interleaved activities or delays is not addressed, and multiple concept inheritance is not considered. Referring to medical applications, the work

Table 1. Ordering of 15 SUs, with respect to a given query model. Correct positions in the rankings with respect to the expert's qualitative similarity levels are highlighted in bold.

Qual. similarity - medical expert	Non-abstract	Abstract
High - H1	**H2**	**H5**
High - H2	H9	**H2**
High - H3	H7	H12
High - H4	H8	**H3**
High - H5	H13	H8
High - H6	**H6**	H13
Medium - H7	H15	**H7**
Medium - H8	H5	H6
Medium - H9	H1	**H11**
Medium - H10	H12	**H10**
Medium - H11	H4	H15
Low - H12	H3	**H14**
Low - H13	H11	H1
Low - H14	H10	H4
Low - H15	**H14**	H9

in [7] proposes an approach, based on semantic process mining, to verify the compliance of a Computer Interpretable Guideline with medical recommendations. In this case, however, semantic process mining refers to conformance checking rather than to process discovery. More recently, an ontology-based approach has been used to extract the event log from legacy systems [3]. Another research direction adopts abstraction as a way to establish a relationship between the events typically recorded in the log by the information system, and the high-level activities which are of interest when mining business process models [1]. However, in our work we assume that traces are sequences of activities (i.e., with respect to event traces, they have already been pre-processed). Therefore, both lines of research are only loosely related to ours.

As regards process model comparison, our approach extends the one in [12], which is based on the notion of graph edit distance [2]. Within the same area of research, it is worth citing the work in [11], which makes use of a normalized version of the graph edit distance. The approach is used to support workflow modification in an agile workflow system, and takes into account control flow information as well as activity information. However, [11] only makes use of syntactical information in the definition of the edit operation costs. Closer works to our approach are described in [6] and [9]. With respect to [6], we have moved towards semantics in activity node substitutions, by allowing for the exploitation of domain knowledge: the work in [6], in fact, just relies on the edit distance between activity node names; moreover, it does not consider the cost of edge substitutions. With respect to the contribution in [9], that extends [6] by dealing with gateway nodes, we explicitly use domain knowledge in this phase of distance calculation as well, while [9] only calculates the fraction of the incoming/outgoing activity nodes that were mapped. Finally, the novel extensions described in this paper allow to deal with models mined from abstracted traces as well; to the best of our knowledge, this issue has never been considered before in the literature.

7   Conclusions

In this paper, we have described a framework able to semantically abstract traces, and provide them as an input to process mining. Models mined from abstracted traces can then be compared and ranked, by adopting an extended process model similarity metric, which can take into account abstraction phase penalties as well. In the experiments, we mined the process models of some SUs by using Heuristic Miner, both working on non-abstracted traces, and working on abstracted ones. We then ordered the two available process model sets with respect to the model of the best equipped SU in the SUN network, resorting to the extended metric. We verified that, when working on abstracted traces, distance calculation leads to a ranking that is closer to the qualitative one provided by a domain expert, thus better classifying the quality of service provided to patients by the different SUs. In the future, we plan to test the approach in different application domains as well, after having acquired the corresponding domain knowledge. In those domains, different aspects such as, e.g., the role of the actors implementing the activities, may be considered as well, and exploited in the similarity metric, which is easily extendable, given its modularity. Finally, an abstraction mechanism directly operating on process models (i.e., on the graph, instead of the log), may be considered, possibly along the lines described in [8], and abstraction results will be compared to the ones currently enabled by our framework.

References

1. Baier, T., Di Ciccio, C., Mendling, J., Weske, M.: Matching events and activities by integrating behavioral aspects and label analysis. Softw. Syst. Model. **17**(2), 573–598 (2018)
2. Bunke, H.: On a relation between graph edit distance and maximum common subgraph. Pattern Recognit. Lett. **18**(8), 689–694 (1997)
3. Calvanese, D., Kalayci, T.E., Montali, M., Santoso, A.: The onprom toolchain for extracting business process logs using ontology-based data access. In: Clarisó, R., (eds.) Proceedings of the BPM Demo Track and BPM Dissertation Award co-located with 15th International Conference on Business Process Modeling (BPM 2017), Barcelona, Spain, 13 September 2017, CEUR Workshop Proceedings, vol. 1920. CEUR-WS.org (2017)
4. Casati, F., Shan, M.-C.: Semantic analysis of business process executions. In: Jensen, C.S., et al. (eds.) EDBT 2002. LNCS, vol. 2287, pp. 287–296. Springer, Heidelberg (2002). https://doi.org/10.1007/3-540-45876-X_19

5. de Medeiros, A.K.A., et al.: An outlook on semantic business process mining and monitoring. In: Meersman, R., Tari, Z., Herrero, P. (eds.) OTM 2007 Part II. LNCS, vol. 4806, pp. 1244–1255. Springer, Heidelberg (2007). https://doi.org/10.1007/978-3-540-76890-6_52

6. Dijkman, R., Dumas, M., García-Bañuelos, L.: Graph matching algorithms for business process model similarity search. In: Dayal, U., Eder, J., Koehler, J., Reijers, H.A. (eds.) BPM 2009. LNCS, vol. 5701, pp. 48–63. Springer, Heidelberg (2009). https://doi.org/10.1007/978-3-642-03848-8_5

7. Grando, M.A., Schonenberg, M.H., van der Aalst, W.M.P.: Semantic process mining for the verification of medical recommendations. In: Traver, V., Fred, A.L.N., Filipe, J., Gamboa, H. (eds.) HEALTHINF 2011 - Proceedings of the International Conference on Health Informatics, Rome, Italy, 26–29 January, 2011, pp. 5–16. SciTePress (2011)

8. Günther, C.W., van der Aalst, W.M.P.: Fuzzy mining – adaptive process simplification based on multi-perspective metrics. In: Alonso, G., Dadam, P., Rosemann, M. (eds.) BPM 2007. LNCS, vol. 4714, pp. 328–343. Springer, Heidelberg (2007). https://doi.org/10.1007/978-3-540-75183-0_24

9. LaRosa, M., Dumas, M., Uba, R., Dijkman, R.: Business process model merging: an approach to business process consolidation. ACM Trans. Softw. Eng. Methodol. **22**(2), 11 (2013)

10. De Maio, M.N., Salatino, M., Aliverti, E.: Mastering JBoss Drools 6 for Developers. Packt Publishing, Birmingham (2016)

11. Minor, M., Tartakovski, A., Schmalen, D., Bergmann, R.: Agile workflow technology and case-based change reuse for long-term processes. Int. J. Intell. Inf. Technol. **4**(1), 80–98 (2008)

12. Montani, S., Leonardi, G., Quaglini, S., Cavallini, A., Micieli, G.: A knowledge-intensive approach to process similarity calculation. Expert Syst. Appl. **42**(9), 4207–4215 (2015)

13. Palmer, M., Wu, Z.: Verb semantics for english-chinese translation. Mach. Transl. **10**, 59–92 (1995)

14. Pedrinaci, C., Domingue, J., Brelage, C., van Lessen, T., Karastoyanova, D., Leymann, F.: Semantic business process management: scaling up the management of business processes. In: Proceedings of the 2th IEEE International Conference on Semantic Computing (ICSC 2008), 4–7 August 2008, Santa Clara, California, USA, pp. 546–553. IEEE Computer Society (2008)

15. van der Aalst, W.: Process Mining: Data Science in Action. Springer, Heidelberg (2016). https://doi.org/10.1007/978-3-662-49851-4

16. van Dongen, B., Alves De Medeiros, A., Verbeek, H., Weijters, A., van der Aalst, W.: The proM framework: a new era in process mining tool support. In: Ciardo, G., Darondeau, P. (eds.) ICATPN 2005. LNCS, vol. 3536, pp. 444–454. Springer, Berlin (2005). https://doi.org/10.1007/11494744_25

17. Weijters, A., van der Aalst, W., Alves de Medeiros, A.: Process Mining with the Heuristic Miner Algorithm, WP 166. Eindhoven University of Technology, Eindhoven (2006)

Using CNNs for Designing and Implementing an Automatic Vascular Segmentation Method of Biomedical Images

Pierangela Bruno[1]([✉])[iD], Paolo Zaffino[2][iD], Salvatore Scaramuzzino[2], Salvatore De Rosa[3], Ciro Indolfi[3], Francesco Calimeri[1][iD], and Maria Francesca Spadea[2][iD]

[1] Department of Mathematics and Computer Science, University of Calabria, Rende, Italy
{bruno,calimeri}@mat.unical.it
[2] Department of Experimental and Clinical Medicine, University of Catanzaro, Catanzaro, Italy
{p.zaffino,s.scaramuzzino,mfspadea}@unicz.it
[3] Division of Cardiology, Department of Medical and Surgical Sciences, University of Catanzaro, Catanzaro, Italy
{saderosa,indolfi}@unicz.it

Abstract. The assessment of vascular complexity in the lower limbs provides important information about peripheral artery diseases, with a relevant impact on both therapeutic decisions and on prognostic estimation. Currently, the evaluation is carried out by visual inspection of cine-angiograms, which is largely operator-dependent. An automatic image analysis could offer a fast and more reliable technique to support physicians with the clinical management of these patients. In this work, we introduce a new method to automatically segment the vascular tree from cine-angiography images, in order to improve the clinical interpretation of the complexity of vascular collaterals in Peripheral Arterial Occlusive Disease (PAOD) patients. The approach is based on: (1) a feature-detection method to convert the video into a static image with lager Field Of View (FOV) and (2) a custom Convolutional Neural Network (CNN) for the segmentation of vascular structure. Experimental evaluations over a set of clinical cases confirm the viability of the approach: accuracy is assessed in terms of area under the ROC curve, where an average value of 0.988 ± 0.006 is measured.

Keywords: Segmentation · Convolutional Neural Networks
Feature detection · Cine-angiography · Bioinformatics
Biomedical imaging

S. Scaramuzzino at the time of the study

C. Ghidini et al. (Eds.): AI*IA 2018, LNAI 11298, pp. 60–70, 2018.
https://doi.org/10.1007/978-3-030-03840-3_5

1   Context and Motivation

The assessment of vascular complexity in the lower limbs provides relevant information about peripheral artery diseases; in fact, vascular collaterals act as a sort of natural bypass system, sustaining tissue perfusion downward of vascular occlusion [1]. Intuitively, they can exert a protective impact on limb ischemia, thus reducing symptoms and improving the outcome in patients with Peripheral Arterial Occlusive Disease (PAOD) [2]. This is why assessing the collateral vascular network in patients with PAOD has a significant impact on both therapeutic decisions and on prognostic estimation.

Different clinical studies for the estimation of vascular collateral growth in PAOD patients resulted in conflicting results, mostly because of the technical difficulties in the quantification of vascular network and its flow capability. Such an evaluation is currently carried out by human operators via visual inspection of cine-angiograms, resulting in scorings that are largely operator-dependent. The task is particularly hard not only because of the intrinsic difficulty, for human operators, in obtaining objectively measurements, but also because of some significant technical issues: (*i*) the vascular system, consisting of vessels of highly variable shape and size, irregularly fills a 3-D Euclidean space; (*ii*) the information is obtained from a sequence of image frames, each one covering a fraction of the anatomical district, while the scoring must refer to the whole scanned area; (*iii*) the Field Of View (FOV) might include external objects, such as surgical instruments and tools, electrode cables, catheters, etc.

In this work we define a new methodology for automatic vessel tree identification, with the goal of fostering more reliable clinical assessments in the described scenario. In particular, we aim at making use of Convolutional Neural Networks (CNNs) for the segmentation of the vascular tree over a single image encompassing the whole FOV and obtained by stitching each contiguous frame of the cine-angiogram. Interestingly, to the best of our knowledge, this is one of the first attempts to segment vessels in the ilio-femoral district on 2-D projective images. In fact, the method presents several challenges: (i) non-trivial image pre-processing operations and feature detection are needed in order to elaborate and convert the cine-angiography video into a whole static image with a larger FOV; (ii) fine-tuning of CNN parameters in each layer, in order to reach high segmentation accuracy.

The remainder of the paper is structured as follows. In Sect. 2, we provide a detailed description of our approach. Section 3 presents our experimental analysis and evaluation of results. Eventually, in Sect. 4 we draw our conclusion.

2   Proposed Approach

The main goal of this work is to provide a new approach for automatic vessel segmentation from cine-angiography images. The workflow of the proposed framework, illustrated in Fig. 1, can be divided into two steps: (*i*) a feature-detection method is used to build a static image with lager FOV, by stitching

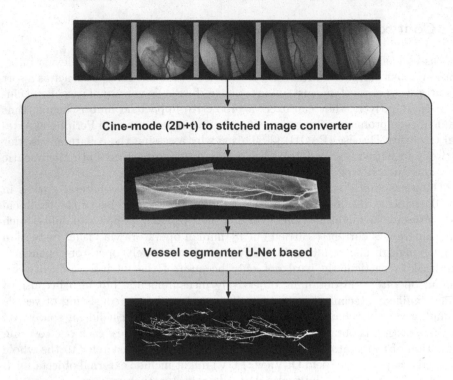

Fig. 1. Workflow of the proposed framework.

contiguous frames of cine-angiography videos and minimizing the overlapping error, and (*ii*) an adaptation of U-Net [3] fully convolutional deep neural network architecture is used to segment the vascular tree from the stitched image.

In the following, we briefly describe the background techniques and methods, and provide further details on the proposed approach.

2.1   Image Stitching

In order to have a single image on which the vessel tree segmentation can be performed, frames belonging to each cine-angiography are stitched together; as a result, a single static image inducing a larger FOV is obtained. To accomplish such a task, in the preprocessing phase the 2-D images acquired over time are extracted from the video file (in DICOM format) and adaptive histogram equalization is performed on the negative of each image; then, each frame t is geometrically aligned with the frame $t + 1$ by matching corresponding fiducial points extracted from each image. This strategy is iterated over all the available frames and, finally, the stitched image is smoothed by a median convolution filter with a 3×3 kernel size. More in detail Speeded Up Robust Features (SURF) [4], Maximally Stable Extremal Regions (MSER) [5] and corner features are used to identify fiducial points. Once corresponding points between consecutive frames are found, in order to stitch the images together, the rigid geometrical transformation that makes the corresponding points overlapping is applied. In this context, the amount of points used to compute the transformation represents a crucial aspect for the accuracy of the alignment and the resulting images that will compose the training dataset for the vessel segmentation. Then, we performed several experimental tests with the aim to discover a better combination of preprocessing operations to maximize the amount of fiducial points detected for each frame. Therefore, the matching features are computed on images preprocessed by the following workflow:

1. negative image computation
2. adaptive histogram equalization
3. non-uniform illumination estimation
4. edge-detection using Canny filter [6].

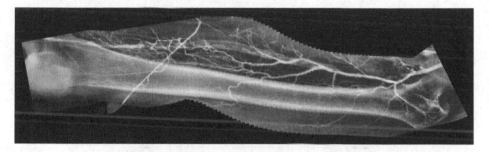

Fig. 2. Example of stitched image obtained by merging a sequence of cine-angiography frames.

The entire algorithm is written in Matlab; an example of a stitched image obtained by means of the methodology described above is depicted in Fig. 2. The quality of the image is pretty high, except for some artifacts derived from the stitching process that interested mostly small vessels. Being the first study of automatic segmentation of the vascular tree on cineangiography, it is not possible to precisely quantify the impact of such artifacts on the diagnosis outcome. However, usually small vessels are ignored by visual inspection. So, the proposed method is at least comparable with the current clinical practice.

2.2 Network Description

Several studies investigated neural-network based methods for automatic vessel segmentation of medical images [7,8], especially for retina segmentation [9,10]; state-of-the-art solutions are capable to provide accurate segmentation of the structure of interest over static and well-contrasted images. Nevertheless, to the best of our knowledge, no work investigated, to date, the problem of segmenting vascular tree on 2-D projective images acquired over time (e.g., cineangiography). In this work, we decided to make use of the U-Net model; this network structure outperformed other existing methods in binary segmentation applications, such as satellite image analysis [11], medical image analysis [12], and other [13].

The U-Net model is a fully convolutional network with symmetrical structure, composed of a contracting and an up-sampling part. The contracting path consists of the repeated application of two 3 × 3 convolutions and a 2 × 2 maxpooling operation with stride 2 for downsampling. The expansive path consists of an upsampling of the feature map followed by a two 3 × 3 convolutions. In the final layer, a 1 × 1 convolution is used to map all 64 component feature vectors to the desired number of classes [3]. All layers use Rectified Linear Unit (ReLU) [14], except for the last layer, where Softmax [15] is used in order to select the best scoring category; hence, for each pixel it returns the probability to be part of a vessel or not.

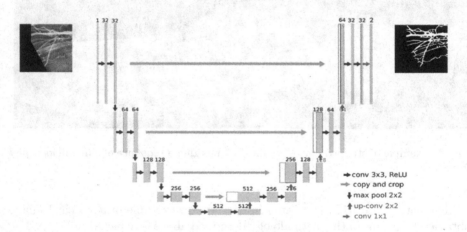

Fig. 3. U-Net architecture adapted from [3].

In order to adapt the basic U-Net architecture to the requirements of our setting, we introduced several modifications (Fig. 3):

1. the output segmentation layer is expanded from 1 to 2 feature maps to enable multi-class segmentation;
2. dropout [16] of 0.5 is used after each convolutional layer for addressing the overfitting problem;
3. batch normalization [17] is used in all layers to improve learning;
4. the number of feature maps in all layers is reduced in order to accelerate deep network training.

The network has been trained with the categorical cross-entropy loss function [18], which is defined as follow:

$$L = -\frac{1}{N} \sum_{i=1}^{N} [y_i log(\hat{y}_i) + (1 - y_i)log(1 - \hat{y}_i)] \tag{1}$$

where y_i are true labels, $\hat{y}_i$ are predicted labels and N is the number of classes.

3 Experimental Analysis

In the literature, automatic segmentation performance is commonly scored against ground truth (GT) manual segmentation, carried out by an expert clinician [19]. In this paper, our approach is evaluated by means of two common metrics: (i) Receiver Operating Characteristic (ROC) analysis [20]; (ii) Dice Similarity Coefficient (DSC) [21].

Table 1. Confusion matrix for vessel classification.

	Vessel present	Vessel absent
Vessel detected	TRUE POSITIVE (TP)	FALSE POSITIVE (FP)
Vessel not detected	FALSE NEGATIVE (FN)	True NEGATIVE (TN)

Taking Table 1 into account, a ROC curve is a plot of true positive fractions ($S_e = \frac{TP}{TP+FN}$) versus false positive fractions ($S_p = 1 - \frac{TN}{TN+FP}$) by varying the threshold on the probability map. The closer a curve approaches the top left corner, the better the performance of the system. The Area Under the Curve (AUC), which is 1 for a perfect system, is a single measure to quantify this behavior [22]. DSC measures the overlap and similarity between Ground Truth (GT) and Automatic Segmentation (AS) by means of the formula $2\frac{|GT \cap AS|}{|GT|+|AS|}$. Results can range from 0 to 1, with 0 indicating no overlap and 1 indicating complete overlap [23].

Dataset. The proposed approach is tested on a dataset including 30 cine-angiographies acquired at the Interventional Cardiology Units of Magna Graecia University Hospital (Catanzaro, Italy) and at Federico II University Hospital (Naples, Italy); patients have previously given explicit informed consent to the use of their anonymized data for research purpose. For each cine-angiography, a stitched image is generated according to 2.1. The resulting images represent the entire ilio-femoral district for each patient. The vessel-to-background contrast is jeopardized by the presence of catheters, surgical tools, screws and other anatomical structures, especially bone; furthermore, the acquisition method reduces the quality of images that are characterized of various lighting effects and motion blur.

Table 2. Results in terms of ROC and AUC for 12 subjects.

	DSC	AUC
Case 0	0.591	0.984
Case 1	0.645	0.991
Case 2	0.646	0.986
Case 3	0.633	0.992
Case 4	0.726	0.997
Case 5	0.627	0.992
Case 6	0.561	0.974
Case 7	0.648	0.987
Case 8	0.737	0.992
Case 9	0.494	0.990
Case 10	0.686	0.986
Case 11	0.601	0.987
Mean	0.633	0.988
Standard deviation	0.067	0.006

GT segmentations of the input images are manually drawn by an expert clinician on the large field of view image generated by the stitching step. The entire dataset is split in training set (80%) and testing (20%); in particular, the 20% of the training set is used as validation set in order to monitor the training process and prevent overfitting. We also train and evaluate U-Net model using four-fold cross-validation (folds are split into disjoint sets of patients).

Training Phase. The input image and their corresponding segmentation maps are used to train the network. Since images are defined on a grayscale, the framework is used with the grayscale parameter enabled, so that only one input channel was used during the operation. The network is implemented in Tensor-Flow [24] using the Keras [25] wrapper and trained for 800 epochs, using the Adadelta [26] optimizer with default parameters. In order to match the input shape of the network, the training/validation images are subdivided into 30600 tiles with a resolution of 128×128 pixels. For the network training we us only 24480 tiles (80%), while the remaining 6120 (20%) are used for validation.

All experiments are performed on a machine equipped with a 12 x86_64 Intel(R) Core(TM) CPUs @ 3.50 GHz, running GNU/Linux Debian 7 and using CUDA compilation tools, release 7.5, V7.5.17 NVIDIA Corporation GM204 on GeForce GTX 970.

3.1   Results and Discussion

The experimental results from the test set are presented in Table 2. For each of the 12 subjects selected for testing on the given database, DSC and AUC are

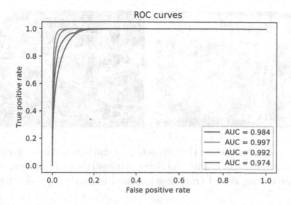

Fig. 4. ROC curve for the two best and the two worst results according to Table 2

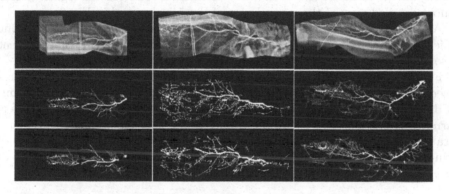

Fig. 5. Results produced by U-Net. The picture shows (from top to bottom) anatomical images, ground truth, automatic segmentations.

computed and are used as a measures of the performance. It is worth noting that, in order to improve visual inspection, post-processing is applied with the aim of removing small objects of size less than 400 pixel representing the 1×10^{-4} of the entire image from obtained results; this operation does not cause significant changes in terms of accuracy. The herein proposed approach achieves a DSC mean value of 0.633 ± 0.067 and an AUC mean value of 0.988 ± 0.006. Taking into account the two best and worst results obtained (i.e., AUC values of 0.997, 0.992 and 0.984, 0.974, respectively), Fig. 4 shows ROC graphs in terms of True Positive Rate (TPR) on Y axis and False Positive Rate (FPR) on X axis. ROC curve is close to the top-left corner, and it implies that the model agrees very well with the GT.

Illustrative segmentation results, along with the manual segmentations and anatomical images, are shown in Fig. 5. Results show that the network is able to distinguish between catheter and vessel with high precision, confirming the overall positive performance. In order to highlight the similarity between the

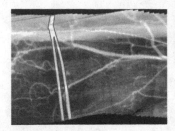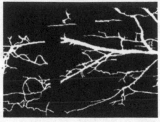

Fig. 6. Example image featuring the presence of catheters (left) and the associated automatic segmentation (right). The red line circumscribes the catheters which appearance is very similar to the vessel (not marked in this image). (Color figure online)

vessels and the catheters and to show the correctness of automated segmentation, a more detailed view of the central case of Fig. 5 is depicted in Fig. 6.

Although very good ROC results are obtained, visual inspection shows some typical errors; in particular, false detection of noise and other artifacts are present close to bones or in areas with excessive brightness.

Furthermore, besides the high segmentation accuracy obtained by the proposed methodology, it is worth to underline robustness regarding the anatomical district and the type of images. This allows a potential interesting transfer-learning applications. Indeed, even if trained on the cine-angiography ilio-femoral database, its application to the DRIVE database [27] (composed of pictures of retina) results in an high score among all experiments (mean AUC equals to 0.97).

4   Conclusion

In this work we presented a novel ilio-femoral vessel segmentation approach, which is based on the conversion of cine-angiographies into images with large field of view and the subsequent application of a properly improved U-Net for the detection of details and hard examples in the segmentation tasks. We presented the results of an experimental activity aimed at assessing the effectiveness of our proposal, which turns out to be comparable to current state-of-the-art methods; it proved to be effective and robust, and the resulting automated vessel segmentation approach can be a suitable tool to be integrated into a complete prescreening system for PAOD assessment.

As future work is concerned, we plan to improve the quality of the approach in order to obtain segmentations even closer to manual ones; to this aim, a combination of multiple human-generated segmentations will be necessary in order to establish a ground truth and avoid, or further limit, human errors [28]. Furthermore, it is worth noting that our approach currently takes into account only information that is local to each pixel; one might think of including, in the training phase, useful information from shapes and structures present in the entire image. The automated vessel segmentation from ilio-femoral district provides the basis for automated assessment of pathological condition. Resulting segmentation images of the vessel pattern can be mathematically analyzed via nonlinear methods, such as fractal analysis [29], in order to provide quantitative indicators of the extent of neo-vascularization.

Acknowledgments. The authors gratefully acknowledge the support of NVIDIA Corporation with the donation of GPUs that were used in this research.

References

1. Prior, B.M., et al.: Time course of changes in collateral blood flow and isolated vessel size and gene expression after femoral artery occlusion in rats. Am. J. Physiol.-Hear. Circ. Physiol. **287**(6), H2434–H2447 (2004)
2. McDermott, M.M., et al.: Superficial femoral artery plaque and functional performance in peripheral arterial disease: walking and leg circulation study (WALCS III). JACC: Cardiovasc. Imaging **4**(7), 730–739 (2011)
3. Ronneberger, O., Fischer, P., Brox, T.: U-Net: convolutional networks for biomedical image segmentation. In: Navab, N., Hornegger, J., Wells, W.M., Frangi, A.F. (eds.) MICCAI 2015. LNCS, vol. 9351, pp. 234–241. Springer, Cham (2015). https://doi.org/10.1007/978-3-319-24574-4_28
4. Bay, H., Tuytelaars, T., Van Gool, L.: SURF: speeded up robust features. In: Leonardis, A., Bischof, H., Pinz, A. (eds.) ECCV 2006. LNCS, vol. 3951, pp. 404–417. Springer, Heidelberg (2006). https://doi.org/10.1007/11744023_32
5. Matas, J., Chum, O., Urban, M., Pajdla, T.: Robust wide-baseline stereo from maximally stable extremal regions. Image Vis. Comput. **22**(10), 761–767 (2004)
6. Canny J.: A computational approach to edge detection. In: Readings in Computer Vision, pp. 184–203 (1987)
7. Yang, S., Yang, J., Wang, Y., Yang, Q., Ai, D., Wang, Y.: Automatic coronary artery segmentation in X-ray angiograms by multiple convolutional neural networks. In: Proceedings of the 3rd International Conference on Multimedia and Image Processing, pp. 31–35 (2018)
8. Moccia, S., De Momi, E., El Hadji, S., Mattos, L.S.: Blood vessel segmentation algorithms - review of methods, datasets and evaluation metrics. Comput. Methods Programs Biomed. **158**, 71–91 (2018)
9. Hu, K., et al.: Retinal vessel segmentation of color fundus images using multiscale convolutional neural network with an improved cross-entropy loss function. Neurocomputing **309**, 179–191 (2018)
10. Alonso-Caneiro, D., Read, S.A., Hamwood, J., Vincent, S.J., Collins, M.J.: Use of convolutional neural networks for the automatic segmentation of total retinal and choroidal thickness in OCT images (2018)
11. Iglovikov, V., Mushinskiy, S., Osin, V.: Satellite imagery feature detection using deep convolutional neural network: a kaggle competition. arXiv preprint arXiv:1706.06169 (2017)
12. Iglovikov, V., Rakhlin, A., Kalinin, A., Shvets, A.: Pediatric bone age assessment using deep convolutional neural networks. arXiv preprint arXiv: 1712.05053 (2017)
13. Hrkac, T., Brkic, K., Kalafatic, Z.: Multi-class U-Net for segmentation of non-biometric identifiers
14. Dahl, G.E., Sainath, T.N., Hinton, G.E.: Improving deep neural networks for LVCSR using rectified linear units and dropout. In: IEEE International Conference, pp. 8609–8613 (2013)

15. Gold, S., Rangarajan, A.: Softmax to softassign: neural network algorithms for combinatorial optimization. J. Artif. Neural Netw. **2**(4), 381–399 (1996)
16. Srivastava, N., et al.: Dropout: a simple way to prevent neural networks from overfitting. J. Mach. Learn. Res. **15**(1), 1929–1958 (2014)
17. Ioffe, S., Szegedy, C.: Batch normalization: accelerating deep network training by reducing internal covariate shift. arXiv preprint arXiv. 1502.03167 (2015)
18. Kroese, D.P., Rubinstein, R.Y., Cohen, I., Porotsky, S., Taimre, T.: Cross-entropy method. In: Gass, S.I., Fu, M.C. (eds.) Encyclopedia of Operations Research and Management Science. Springer, Boston (2013). https://doi.org/10.1007/978-1-4419-1153-7_131
19. Fenster, A., Chiu, B.: Evaluation of segmentation algorithms for medical imaging. In: Engineering in Medicine and Biology Society, pp. 7186–7189 (2005)
20. Bradley, A.P.: The use of the area under the ROC curve in the evaluation of machine learning algorithms. Pattern Recognit. **30**(7), 1145–1159 (1997)
21. Dice, L.R.: Measures of the amount of ecologic association between species. Ecology **26**(3), 297–302 (1945)
22. Marín, D., Aquino, A., Gegúndez-Arias, M.E., Bravo, J.M.: A new supervised method for blood vessel segmentation in retinal images by using gray-level and moment invariants-based features. IEEE Trans. Med. Imaging **30**(1), 146–158 (2011)
23. Crum, W.R., Camara, O., Hill, D.L.: Generalized overlap measures for evaluation and validation in medical image analysis. IEEE Trans. Med. Imaging **25**(11), 1451–1461 (2006)
24. Abadi, M., et al.: TensorFlow: a system for large-scale machine learning. OSDI **16**, 265–283 (2016)
25. Chollet, F., et al.: Keras (2015)
26. Zeiler, M.D.: ADADELTA: an adaptive learning rate method. arXiv preprint arXiv:1212.5701 (2012)
27. Niemeijer, M., Staal, J., van Ginneken, B., Loog, M., Abramoff, M.D.: Comparative study of retinal vessel segmentation methods on a new publicly available database. In: Medical Imaging 2004: Image Processing, vol. 5370, pp. 648–657 (2004)
28. Fritzsche, K., et al.: Automated model based segmentation, tracing and analysis of retinal vasculature from digital fundus images. In: State-of-The-Art Angiography, Applications and Plaque Imaging Using MR, CT, Ultrasound and X-rays, pp. 225–298 (2003)
29. Novianto, S., Suzuki, Y., Maeda, J.: Near optimum estimation of local fractal dimension for image segmentation. Pattern Recognit. Lett. **24**(1–3), 365–374 (2003)

Identification and Characterization of Lanes in Pedestrian Flows Through a Clustering Approach

Luca Crociani[1(✉)], Giuseppe Vizzari[1], Andrea Gorrini[1], and Stefania Bandini[1,2]

[1] Complex Systems and Artificial Intelligence Research Center, Department of Computer Science, Systems and Communication, University of Milano-Bicocca, Milan, Italy
{luca.crociani,giuseppe.vizzari,andrea.gorrini, stefania.bandini}@unimib.it
[2] Research Center for Advanced Science and Technology, The University of Tokyo, Tokyo, Japan

Abstract. Pedestrian behavioral dynamics have been growingly investigated by means of (semi)automated computing techniques for almost two decades, exploiting advancements on computing power, sensor accuracy and availability, computer vision algorithms. This has led to a unique consensus on the existence of significant difference between uni-directional and bi-directional flows of pedestrians, where the phenomenon of lane formation seems to play a major role. This collective behavior emerges in condition of variable density and due to a self-organization dynamics, for which pedestrians are induced to walk following preceding persons to avoid and minimize conflictual situations. Although the formation of lanes is a well-known phenomenon in this field of study, there is still a lack of methods offering the possibility to provide an (even semi-)automatic identification and a quantitative characterization. In this context, the paper proposes an unsupervised learning approach for an automatic detection of lanes in multi-directional pedestrian flows, based on the DBSCAN clustering algorithm. The reliability of the approach is evaluated through a inter-agreement test between a human expert coder and the results of the automated analysis.

Keywords: Pedestrian dynamics · Lane formation · Analysis Clustering

1 Introduction

Pedestrian dynamics have been growingly investigated by means of (semi)automated computing techniques for almost two decades, exploiting advancements on computing power, expressiveness of languages and models, sensor accuracy and availability, computer vision advances. We are witnessing a

© Springer Nature Switzerland AG 2018
C. Ghidini et al. (Eds.): AI*IA 2018, LNAI 11298, pp. 71–82, 2018.
https://doi.org/10.1007/978-3-030-03840-3_6

transition from time-consuming manual counting and/or post-processing tasks (e.g. [6,13]) to computer supported analyses involving automated tracking algorithms such as [1], characterization of the pedestrian population (e.g. group identification [15]), identification of typical trajectories for the definition of origin/destination matrices [10].

A relevant example of useful outcomes of this kind of analyses is represented by [17], which deeply discusses the physics of bi-directional flows of pedestrians in corridor settings: in particular, it is quantitatively observed that the dynamics significantly differ for uni- and bi-directional flows at least for densities between 1 and 2 ped/m^2, in contrast with previous studies. While this experiment brings relevant findings about the bi-directional dynamics, it does not fully explain how the lane formation phenomenon emerges, how it can converge to a stable state and whether the dynamics differ at a very microscopic level depending on, e.g., the lane width. The dynamism of the phenomenon, on the other hand, increases the difficulty of defining tools or formulas for its analysis. Counter-flow movements represent thus one of the situations that can be further fruitfully investigated by means of computer supported analyses.

Currently, besides intuitive characterizations of the lane formation phenomenon, some mathematical formulations for aggregated analysis of lane formation have already been defined in the literature [14]. A well-known criterion is described by the order parameter [3], which is achieved by superimposing a discrete representation of the observed environment to aggregate the number of pedestrians moving in each direction for each row of the grid (overall direction of movements are supposed to be parallel to the x axis of the grid). Values of this observable close to 0 indicate overall chaotic dynamics in the analyzed time window. Vice-versa, an order parameter equal to 1 means that the dynamics is perfectly ordered and each row of the grid only contains pedestrians moving in the same direction. This metric, however, is of limited applicability due to the need of discretising the analyzed environment and assuming that lanes and flows are perfectly aligned with the corridor.

Another kind of analysis of the lane formation phenomenon is based on the notion of rotation, or turbulence of trajectories in a given time interval [5]. This aggregate observable increases its value with the number of changes in direction of tracked pedestrians and it can be considered an aggregated indicator of the quantity of head-on conflicts in the observation.

These mathematical formulations, on one hand, are already able to quantitatively describe the dynamics observed in controlled situations (e.g. bidirectional flows in straight corridors), but they provide aggregated indicators not actually very informative on the number of lanes and their relevant features, such as width, number of included pedestrians, duration. This kind of more detailed characterization can be employed as an additional element for the validation of simulation models.

A more generally applicable approach, based on a technique from the machine learning area, has been proposed in [9]. In the paper, authors describe performed experimental observations and analyses employing a clustering algorithm to support the identification of pedestrian lanes in the video. The approach is a simple customization of the well-know DBSCAN algorithm [4] (Density Based Clustering Analysis) and it aggregates the instantaneous information about the position and velocity of pedestrians to form the clusters. Although results are preliminary, the adoption of an unsupervised machine learning technique seems particularly suited to this kind of problem. Moreover, a similar approach providing an automatic characterization of the flows in the scene is proposed in [10]. The described algorithm is capable of aggregating positions and velocity vectors of pedestrians and identify origins and destinations of main pedestrian flows in the scene, but the scope of the analysis is not as microscopic as to characterize the possible pedestrian lanes.

The present paper builds on these results trying to provide both a general method for the analysis of the lane formation phenomenon as well as an approach to evaluate its effectiveness. To estimate the precision and reliability of the proposed algorithm for the automated characterization of lanes, we use the video and tracking results collected during the execution of controlled experiments focused on pedestrian counter flows dynamics described in [2,7]. More precisely, we tested the level of inter-rater agreement between the results achieved by the automated tool and by an expert human coder through a series of Cohen's Kappa statistical analysis [11].

The paper breaks down as following. Section 2 described the methodology and the clustering algorithm, with details on the two steps of the process; Sect. 3 presents an overview of results, and describes reliability test procedure. The paper concludes with final remarks and future works.

2   A Clustering Algorithm to Characterize Lane Formation

In the vein of [9], we propose a novel clustering-based approach able to identify lanes in arbitrary settings. The algorithm is based on a hierarchical two-steps application of DBSCAN, with distance metrics and respective parameters specifically tailored to deal with this problem. The aim is to achieve clusters that are in tune with the intuitive conception of the lane formation phenomenon.

We briefly introduce the main concepts of DBSCAN to enable the reader grasping the main concepts of the proposed approach. The algorithm identifies an arbitrary number of clusters of any given shape in the data-set (also concave, which are generally not suitable for simpler algorithm as, e.g., K-means). While the fact that the number of lanes and therefore clusters is unknown could be managed by applying iteratively K-means increasing K and evaluating the silhouette index [12] to select the best value, the domain of application makes the presence of potentially concave shapes of lanes quite plausible.

The adopted approach is aimed at identifying "dense" and well separated zones according to three elements:

– the assumed distance metric $\phi(\overrightarrow{x_i}, \overrightarrow{x_j})$ between two vectors;

- a threshold θ of distance to define the neighborhood;
- the minimum size of a cluster $minPoints$.

While the first element relates to the choice of a function to compute distance between pair of points, the other two are the actual parameter of the algorithm for the final identification of clusters. For the computation of the output, DBSCAN assigns a label to each point specifying whether the point is of type noise, border or core. The first label is assigned to points which do not have enough neighbors (less than minPoints) and which are not neighbors of a core point. Otherwise, a point is labeled as border point if it is neighbor of a core point but that does not have enough neighbors. A point is labeled as core, then, if it has at least $minPoints$ neighbors and, thus, defines a dense area of the data-set. Finally, according to DBSCAN a cluster is composed with the set of all neighbor core points, plus their neighbor border points.

In the customization of DBSCAN proposed in this paper, the characterization of the lane formation phenomena is computed with a hierarchical approach in which two distinct distance metrics are applied with different thresholds. For the context of application, we assume that the parameter $minPoints$ is shared in the two procedures. Furthermore, this parameter is set to 3 to allow the characterization of lane for a situation in which three persons walk in a river-like pattern, that we consider as the simplest case of lane. The choice of a hierarchical approach is mainly motivated by the need of knowing the average flow direction for the final identification of lanes: this information is eventually used to identify clusters which describe queuing pedestrians in the observed scenario.

A intuitive description of the two-steps of the algorithm is shown in Fig. 1. In the first step velocity vectors from the input raw data are used to identify big clusters associated to the main directions of flow, using a distance function which accounts for the *angular distance* between vectors. A second step of DBSCAN is further performed on the output clusters, considering the global average velocity of pedestrians within the cluster and the coordinates of pedestrians to finally characterize the lanes. In this second step, the distance metric is more complicated, since it must consider additional information, and it will be formally described in Sect. 2.2, but it basically considers pedestrians' positions with respect to the positions of neighboring members of the same flow-cluster.

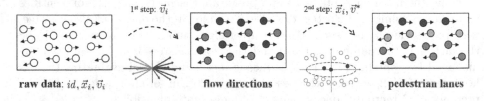

Fig. 1. Workflow of the hierarchical clustering algorithm to characterize the lane formation.

The algorithm works on almost instantaneous data, potentially allowing the implementation on real-time systems: by means of an aggregation with mobile average, mean positions and velocity vectors of pedestrians related to short time windows (less than half second) are calculated. The two sequential procedures will be now discussed in the following subsections.

2.1 Recognition of Main Directions of Movement

Predominant directions of flow are recognized to identify the potential counter-flow situation and also to achieve relevant information for the second step of the procedure, where the average velocity of pedestrians walking in the same direction is relevant for the computation of distance.

This process takes as input the set of velocity vectors $\vec{v_i}$ of observed pedestrians in the current frame and analyze the differences in their orientation. The magnitude of the vector is not influencing the result in this case: the emergence of locally higher densities in counter-flow situations, in fact, can lead to sensible differences among the speeds of pedestrians, and then to errors in the clustering process. To avoid this bias, the distance metric ϕ for a pair of velocity vectors $(\vec{v_i}, \vec{v_j})$ is defined as:

$$\theta(\vec{v_i}, \vec{v_j}) = arccos\left(\frac{\vec{v_i} \cdot \vec{v_j}}{\|\vec{v_i}\| \cdot \|\vec{v_j}\|}\right) \tag{1}$$

where the numerator denotes the dot-product between the two vectors. This distance describes the inner (i.e. minimum) angle between $\vec{v_i}$ and $\vec{v_j}$ and a unique threshold $\theta_v \in [0, 180]$ is introduced to calibrate the range of neighborhood. In the results presented in the next section, θ_v is configured to about 50°.

While this could be considered as a rather high value, two considerations must be introduced. On one hand, given the hierarchical structure of the process we prefer a looser definition of neighborhood at this stage and refining the output in the next task. Secondly, a thorough calibration on the parameters of the algorithm is still an ongoing work and the results later presented are referred to a calibration that was chosen because it generated visually stable and plausible results (fact that is also endorsed with the Kappa analysis shown in Fig. 4). As shown in Fig. 1, this process outputs clusters describing pedestrians headed towards the same direction of movement.

2.2 Characterization of Lane Formation

The second step works sequentially on the individual clusters identified with the previous task, by performing density-based clustering using only their points. It takes as input the actual positions of pedestrians $\vec{x_i}$ and the average velocity vector of the clustered pedestrians $\vec{v^*}$ which is used for the computation of distance. The aim is the final identification of pedestrian lanes in the given frame, and this objective is pursued with the definition of a particularly tailored distance metric to compose clusters describing pedestrians which are not only relatively close, but also in an arrangement that can be associated to a form of queuing situation. With this purpose, in fact, a function able to differentiate distances according to the movement direction of the pedestrian is required. We then configure a function ϕ_l for a pair of points $(\overrightarrow{x_i}, \overrightarrow{x_j})$ as to compute distance values asymmetric with respect to the axis of the representation of the analyzed environment; the rational is that this measure grows more substantially along one of the axis of the 2-dimensional space (we consider the y-axis by assumption):

$$\phi_l(\overrightarrow{x_i}, \overrightarrow{x_j}) = \sqrt{\left(\frac{\hat{x}_{ij}}{\xi_l}\right)^2 + (\hat{y}_{ij})^2} \tag{2}$$

where $\hat{x}_{ij}$ and $\hat{y}_{ij}$ are the x- and y-coordinates of the relative position of pedestrian j with respect to i (the evaluated point), after being rotated according to the average velocity $\overrightarrow{v^*}$ of clustered pedestrians at the first step. ξ_l is the calibration parameter of this function. The vector rotation is performed to align pedestrian positions according to the average direction of movement, for which the distance grows slower in order to aggregate positions describing queuing pedestrians. Formally, it is described with the following equation:

$$(\hat{x}_{ij}, \hat{y}_{ij}) = \bigodot \left(\overrightarrow{x_j} - \overrightarrow{x_i}, \ -\measuredangle\left(\overrightarrow{v^*}, (1,0)\right)\right) \tag{3}$$

$\bigodot$ is an operator that rotates in counter-clockwise direction the vector according to the given angle. $\measuredangle$ is a function computing the counter-clockwise angle between two vectors and $(1, 0)$ is a unit vector introduced to align the orientation of the movement direction $\overrightarrow{v^*}$ along the x-axis, by rotating neighbor points accordingly: in this way, relative positions of pedestrians are rotated in order to change the reference system to the trivial case in which the average direction of movement is along the x-axis (this is achieved using the negative angle in the second part of Eq. 3) and the ellipse is described as in Fig. 2.

The functioning of this part of the algorithm is also graphically exemplified in Fig. 2. The function ϕ_l defines the neighborhood of points with an elliptical shape, whose long side is aligned toward the average direction of movement $\overrightarrow{v^*}$: this allows pedestrians that are walking in a river-like formation to be considered as members of the same lane although there is a certain distance between them, whereas if they walk in a line-abreast formation the same distance might be considered more relevant. The dimensions of the ellipse are provided by the threshold θ_l and the parameter ξ_l, which acts as a multiplier to define the proportion of the long side. In this way the algorithm provides clusters with a shape that follows the direction $\overrightarrow{v^*}$ and aggregate points referring to queuing pedestrians.

3   Reliability Test of the Clustering Algorithm

In order to validate the reliability (i.e. *internal validity*) of the above described tool for the automated characterization of lanes, we use the video and tracking results collected during the execution of controlled experiments focused on

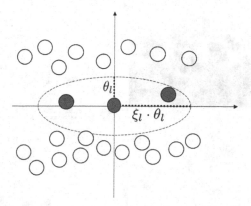

Fig. 2. Example of neighbourhood of a pedestrian according to the distance metric ϕ_l. The limits of the neighbourhood are indicated by the drawn ellipse, configurable with parameters θ_l and ξ_l as described. For simplicity, it is assumed that the direction of flow is $(1, 0)$.

pedestrian counter flows dynamics, thoroughly described in [2, 7]. In particular, we focused on one of the performed experiments, based on the analysis of fully-balanced bidirectional pedestrian flows. Moreover, we execute a cross-checking analysis between the results achieved through a preliminary calibration of the algorithm[1] and the results achieved by a human coder, expert in the field of pedestrian crowd dynamics.

Although the formation of lanes is a well-known phenomenon in this field of study, there is still a lack of formal definition for its quantitative characterization. Thus, we started from drafting a common-sense definition of the lane formation phenomenon for sake of human coder analysis, as follow: "*a pedestrian lane is a group of three or more pedestrians, walking in the same direction with a river-like spatial arrangement, avoiding collision with counter flows*".

Then, the human coder was asked to analyze the video images of the experiments, comparing them with a video-clip composed of No.570 frames related to the trajectories of pedestrians (see Fig. 3): the video clip has been prepared with the trajectories of the tracked pedestrians participating the above described experiments, annotated with a numerical identifier to allow human coder to identify pedestrians walking in lanes. To facilitate manual annotation procedure of ID_lane, the coder was asked to analyses the images of the two synchronized videos starting from the bottom-right part of the screen. To more thoroughly evaluate all these indicators the coder was asked to rewind the video and take the necessary time to characterize pedestrian lanes.

According to the above described methodology, the video of one experimental procedure (fully-balanced bidirectional flows) was analyzed by annotating the situation one frame every 30 and by describing the lane formation phenomenon

---

[1] Results are achieved with parameters $\theta_v = 25°$, $\theta_l = 0.6\,\mathrm{m}$, $\xi_l \cdot \theta_l = 2.4\,\mathrm{m}$, $minPoints = 2$.

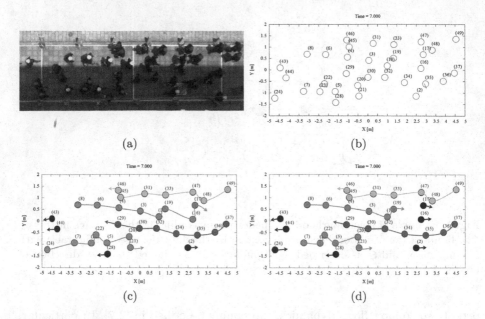

Fig. 3. (a) A frame of the video images of the experiment. (b) Numerical identifiers and positions of pedestrians after the tracking process. Granular classification of lanes by our algorithm (c) and by the human coder (d) in the particular frame (arrows indicating the movement direction have been added afterwards).

observed in the last second. Pedestrians have been classified with a numerical identifier considering:

- their condition of "walking out of any lane" or "walking in a lane" (i.e. *gross classification*);
- their belonging to a certain lane (i.e. *granular classification*).

More in details, the coder was asked to annotate the following information for each second of the video: (*i*) time of the video; (*ii*) numerical identifier of pedestrian; (iii) numerical identifier of lane. The conventional value -1 was assigned to identify the condition of "walking out of any lane" while greater or equal to 0 were used to assign the ID of the lane the pedestrian belonged to in that time frame.

The described data analysis procedure had the objective to cross-check the results about lane formation phenomenon achieved through the clustering algorithm and the support of a human coder, aiming at measuring the level of reliability of the tool. To do so, we tested the level of inter-rater agreement between the two rating methods by means of a series of Cohen's Kappa statistical analysis [11]. The Kappa statistics measures the level of inter-rater agreement between two raters in classifying a certain object/subject by using categorical variables. It has a maximum value of 1, when agreement is perfect, 0 when agreement is no better than chance. Other values can be roughly interpreted as:

- $0.00 < K \leq 0.20$ - *poor agreement*;
- $0.20 < K \leq 0.40$ - *fair agreement*;
- $0.40 < K \leq 0.60$ - *moderate agreement*;
- $0.60 < K \leq 0.80$ - *good agreement*;
- $0.80 < K \leq 1.00$ - *high agreement*.

Results (see Figs. 4 and 5) showed an average high inter-rater agreement between the two independent coding methods in both gross classification ($K = 0.837$, SD 0.144) and granular classification ($K = 0.841$, SD 0.139), confirming the consistency of results and empirically corroborating the reliability of the automated clustering algorithm.

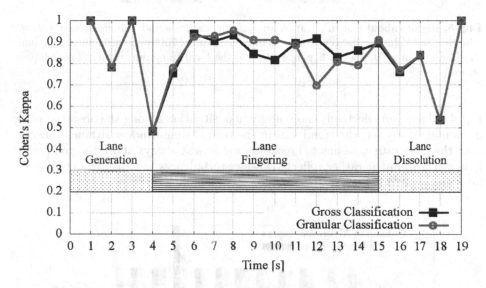

Fig. 4. Level of agreement between the algorithm and the human rater in gross classification (black line) and granular classification (red line). The chart illustrates also the three phases of the observed lane formation phenomenon. (Color figure online)

As introduced by other works in the literature, the lane formation phenomena can be characterized into different phases [5,8]. In this work, we analyzed the observed pedestrian counter flow situations as subdivided into three phases:

1. *lane generation*: from the first frame in which pedestrians are separated according to their movement direction, to the moment in which the two flows physically interact and lanes start to emerge;
2. *lane fingering*: bidirectional flow characterized by the consolidation of the emerged lanes;
3. *lane dissolution*: lanes are being dissolved.

According to this consideration, Cohen's Kappa show a lower level of inter-rater agreement in case of lane generation and lane dissolution situations (see

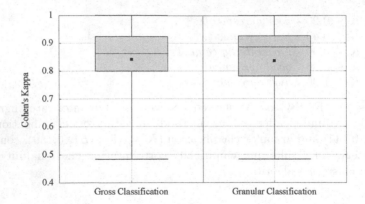

Fig. 5. Results about Cohen's Kappa analysis among *gross* and *granular classification*. The Box and Whisker plot reports: local maximum value, 75th percentile, mean, median (highlighted in red), the 25th percentile and the local minimum value. (Color figure online)

Fig. 4), due to an effectively more ambiguous situation among the observed phenomenon. Moreover, the trend within the central time window although always over the moderate agreement threshold (and almost always above the good one) is not stable, but it rather reflect transient turbulences in which the number of lane and their positions in the corridor was changing.

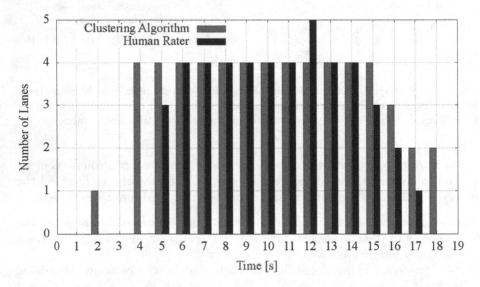

Fig. 6. A comparison between the number of lanes identified per second by the clustering algorithm and by the human coder.

To more fruitfully evaluate the level of reliability of the automated clustering tool, we performed also a paired sample t-test comparing the number of lanes identified per second by the clustering algorithm and by the human rater. Results (see Fig. 6) showed a slight significant difference between the two rating methods, $t(18) = -2.137$, $p = 0.047$, in situation of *lane generation* and *lane dissolution*. This seems reasonable, since these transient situations represent a sort of phase change between more stable configurations, that the human coder can foresee, also being able to rewind and look back at the past, a situation similar to automated trackers taking a global perspective on the analyzed video compared to those based on a limited-temporal-locality assumption [16].

4   Conclusions

The paper presented an unsupervised learning approach for an automatic detection of lanes in multi-directional pedestrian flows, based on the DBSCAN clustering algorithm. We also presented a method for the evaluation of its reliability employing an inter-rater agreement test between a human expert coder and the results of the automated analysis. Achieved results are promising and they will support a further calibration of the overall work-flow, that will also consider additional data-sets from the literature and potentially consider multiple human coders.

Event though there are many future works in this line of research (first of all, the impact of the presence of groups on the overall phenomenon, which is considered a potentially relevant factor [2]), the central goal is to achieve a characterization of lanes throughout the whole analyzed video and time frame, whereas the current approach only considers relatively small time windows. The basic idea to aggregate current results into a global description of identified lanes is to connect local lanes within different time windows whenever the Jaccard distance among them (considering them as sets of pedestrians identifiers) is greater than a certain threshold. This will allow us to have a more comprehensive characterization of a lane, granting the possibility to evaluate its persistence in time, average cardinality, length, and potentially other aggregated measures.

Acknowledgement. The authors thank Prof. Katsuhiro Nishinari, Prof. Daichi Yanagisawa and Dr. Claudio Feliciani for their contribution in the design and execution of the experiments referred in this paper. The authors thank also Dr. Yiping Zeng for his contribution in the implementation of the algorithm.

References

1. Boltes, M., Seyfried, A.: Collecting pedestrian trajectories. Neurocomputing **100**, 127–133 (2013)
2. Crociani, L., Gorrini, A., Feliciani, C., Vizzari, G., Nishinari, K., Bandini, S.: Micro and macro pedestrian dynamics in counterflow: the impact of social groups. arXiv preprint arXiv:1711.08225 (2017)

3. Dzubiella, J., Hoffmann, G., Löwen, H.: Lane formation in colloidal mixtures driven by an external field. Phys. Rev. E **65**(2), 021402 (2002)
4. Ester, M., Kriegel, H.P., Sander, J., Xu, X., et al.: A density-based algorithm for discovering clusters in large spatial databases with noise. In: KDD, vol. 96, pp. 226–231 (1996)
5. Feliciani, C., Nishinari, K.: Empirical analysis of the lane formation process in bidirectional pedestrian flow. Phys. Rev. E **94**(3), 032304 (2016)
6. Fruin, J.J.: Pedestrian Planning and Design. Metropolitan Association of Urban Designers and Environmental Planners Inc., New York (1971)
7. Gorrini, A., Crociani, L., Feliciani, C., Zhao, P., Nishinari, K., Bandini, S.: Social groups and pedestrian crowds: experiment on dyads in a counter flow scenario. arXiv preprint arXiv:1610.08325 (2016)
8. Helbing, D., Molnár, P., Farkas, I.J., Bolay, K.: Self-organizing pedestrian movement. Environ. Plan. B: Plan. Des. **28**(3), 361–383 (2001)
9. Hoogendoorn, S., Daamen, W.: Self-organization in pedestrian flow. In: Hoogendoorn, S.P., Luding, S., Bovy, P.H.L., Schreckenberg, M., Wolf, D.E. (eds.) Traffic and Granular Flow '03, pp. 373–382. Springer, Berlin (2005). https://doi.org/10.1007/3-540-28091-X_36
10. Khan, S.D., Bandini, S., Basalamah, S., Vizzari, G.: Analyzing crowd behavior in naturalistic conditions: identifying sources and sinks and characterizing main flows. Neurocomputing **177**, 543–563 (2016)
11. Landis, J.R., Koch, G.G.: The measurement of observer agreement for categorical data. Biometrics **33**, 159–174 (1977)
12. Liu, Y., Li, Z., Xiong, H., Gao, X., Wu, J.: Understanding of internal clustering validation measures. In: 2010 IEEE International Conference on Data Mining, pp. 911–916, December 2010. https://doi.org/10.1109/ICDM.2010.35
13. Older, S.: Movement of pedestrians on footways in shopping streets. Traffic eng. control **10**(4), 160–163 (1968)
14. Schadschneider, A., Klingsch, W., Klüpfel, H., Kretz, T., Rogsch, C., Seyfried, A.: Evacuation dynamics: empirical results, modeling and applications. In: Meyers, R. (ed.) Encyclopedia of Complexity And Systems Science, pp. 3142–3176. Springer, New York (2009). https://doi.org/10.1007/978-0-387-30440-3
15. Solera, F., Calderara, S., Cucchiara, R.: Socially constrained structural learning for groups detection in crowd. IEEE Trans. Pattern Anal. Mach. Intell. **38**(5), 995–1008 (2016)
16. Roshan Zamir, A., Dehghan, A., Shah, M.: GMCP-Tracker: global multi-object tracking using generalized minimum clique graphs. In: Fitzgibbon, A., Lazebnik, S., Perona, P., Sato, Y., Schmid, C. (eds.) ECCV 2012. LNCS, pp. 343–356. Springer, Heidelberg (2012). https://doi.org/10.1007/978-3-642-33709-3_25
17. Zhang, J., Klingsch, W., Schadschneider, A., Seyfried, A.: Ordering in bidirectional pedestrian flows and its influence on the fundamental diagram. J. Stat. Mech.: Theory Exp. **2012**(02), P02002 (2012)

Arianna[+]: Scalable Human Activity Recognition by Reasoning with a Network of Ontologies

Syed Yusha Kareem[1(✉)], Luca Buoncompagni[1], and Fulvio Mastrogiovanni[1,2]

[1] Department of Informatics, Bioengineering, Robotics and Systems Engineering, University of Genoa, Via Opera Pia 13, 16145 Genoa, Italy
kareem.syed.yusha@dibris.unige.it
[2] Teseo srl, Piazza Montano 2a, Genoa, Italy

Abstract. Aging population ratios are rising significantly. Meanwhile, smart home based health monitoring services are evolving rapidly to become a viable alternative to traditional healthcare solutions. Such services can augment qualitative analyses done by gerontologists with quantitative data. Hence, the recognition of Activities of Daily Living (ADL) has become an active domain of research in recent times. For a system to perform human activity recognition in a real-world environment, multiple requirements exist, such as scalability, robustness, ability to deal with uncertainty (e.g., missing sensor data), to operate with multi-occupants and to take into account their privacy and security. This paper attempts to address the requirements of scalability and robustness, by describing a reasoning mechanism based on modular spatial and/or temporal context models as a network of ontologies. The reasoning mechanism has been implemented in a smart home system referred to as Arianna[+]. The paper presents and discusses a use case, and experiments are performed on a simulated dataset, to showcase Arianna[+]'s modularity feature, internal working, and computational performance. Results indicate scalability and robustness for human activity recognition processes.

Keywords: Activities of Daily Living · Ontology network
In-home healthcare

1 Introduction

In recent times, there is a rise in population of elderly individuals, as it is estimated that approximately 20% of the world's population will be age 60 or older by 2050 [8]. This motivates the research community and technology companies to provide, at home, healthcare services for the elderly, such that they can live safely and independently for longer periods of time. The ability to perform Activities of Daily Living (ADL) without assistance from other people can be considered as a reference for the estimation of the independent living level of the elderly individuals [12]. Nowadays, geriatrists judge the well being of elderly individuals

© Springer Nature Switzerland AG 2018
C. Ghidini et al. (Eds.): AI*IA 2018, LNAI 11298, pp. 83–95, 2018.
https://doi.org/10.1007/978-3-030-03840-3_7

by observing them while they perform ADL, such as *walking* and *dressing*. When possible, they measure variations in both space and time domains, needed to perform particular ADL. This is done in sessions at certain time intervals, e.g., each year, to make quantitative judgments. But for some ADL, e.g., *eating*, they rely on qualitative judgments of how the activity is performed, based on questionnaires. Instrumental ADL (IADL) are taken into account as well, with similar qualitative observations, since they require a certain level of planning capabilities and social skills, such as *housekeeping*, *cleaning*, and *cooking*.

A quantitative assessment of such qualitative data can be provided by a smart home specialized for elderly care, as it can recognize activities performed throughout the day and report to geriatrists. This would enable accurate health assessments based on continuous evaluations. As presented in [5,13], depending on the kind of sensors employed in the smart home, activity recognition (AR) can be performed using data originating from vision, inertial, distributed sensors or a combination of them. However, AR is enabled by *a priori* AR modeling, and for this the approaches used in the literature are mostly of two types, one being data-driven, and the other being knowledge-driven. A discriminative (e.g., Support Vector Machines and Artificial Neural Networks) type, data-driven approach is used when complex, multi-modal data streams are involved, e.g., data originating from cameras [17] and accelerometers [3], for posture recognition and fall detection. When simpler data are involved (e.g., while using distributed sensors) either a generative (e.g., Hidden Markov Models and Dynamic Bayesian Networks) type, data-driven approach is taken [9], or a knowledge-driven approach is adopted [6,16]. Although some sensors (e.g., cameras) provide high accuracy for monitoring individuals; due to privacy issues, simpler sensors (e.g., Passive Infrared (PIR), light, and Radio-Frequency Identification (RFID)) are largely used.

Learning (or development) of AR models, in data-driven approaches, happens by training over datasets, whereas in knowledge-driven approaches it is done by explicitly encoding knowledge, typically in the form of set of axioms, used for AR based on sensor data. In terms of modularity with activity models, the former approach is not friendly since, if a new activity is to be introduced into the system, a new dataset has to be collected and the entire training process has to be performed. Whereas the latter approach is modularity friendly as a new activity model's knowledge can simply be added as a set of axioms and rules.

In this paper, we describe a knowledge-based approach for domain modeling (i.e., of context/activity) and reasoning (i.e., context/activity recognition), which is currently part of our Arianna$^+$ smart home framework. The approach adopts: (1) Ontology Web Language (OWL), based on description logics (DL) [4], which is a fragment of first order predicate logic, designed to be as expressive as possible while retaining decidability. It allows to describe a given domain by defining relevant concepts (in the terminological box or TBox), and by asserting properties of individuals that are instances of those concepts (in the assertional box or ABox). Reasoners can then be used to derive facts, i.e., make implicit knowledge explicit, by reasoning mechanism [10] based on *subsumption* of concepts and *instance checking*. (2) Rules based on the Semantic Web Rule Language (SWRL) [11], which allow the system to perform query and manipulations as a unique operation based on logic conjunctions.

Due to issues of language expressivity, OWL-DL reasoners do not perform temporal reasoning. Nevertheless, the idea of using OWL for AR can be found in the literature and [14] highlights that when ontological techniques are extended with even simple forms of temporal reasoning, their effectiveness increases. Moreover, symbolic temporal concepts have been used for AR [7], and this is usually done using Allen's algebra [2], which allows DL reasoners to consider instances of time belonging to particular intervals. In the literature, some attempts [6,16] at ontology-based AR take temporal reasoning into account but accumulate temporal instances. Hence, their search space grows exponentially [15] with respect to the number of axioms in the ontology, which is an issue for large-scale, real-time applications. In this paper, we take basic temporal aspects for AR into account, without accumulating time instances within ontologies.

In a real-world environment, we argue that AR systems must carefully guarantee *scalability* and *robustness* requirements. On the one hand, scalability can be achieved when (i) the system is *modular* with respect to activity models and (ii) types of sensors, as well as, (iii) is able to manage computational resources and memory. On the other hand, robustness, which is a more strict requirement to be achieved, strongly depends on the *design* of the activity models. We also argue that a redundancy of models, with which we can assess the same activity, can increase the overall system's robustness. The above-listed requirements lead respectively, to the issues of: (i) designing modular activity models as part of an ontology network, which is able to infer activities based on the occurrence of events, (ii) designing a system's architecture that incorporates distributed sensors data, and (iii) designing the activity models such that they represent the context over time, and evaluate them with the most suitable behavior (e.g., with a scheduled frequency).

This paper extends the work presented in [6], wherein we propose to use a hierarchy of ontologies, that decouple logic operations for semantically describing the context and support modular composition of reasoning behaviors for online activity recognition. Here, we present an AR-enabled smart home system from a software architecture perspective, and an implementation of a relevant use case, which is tested based on simulated data from distributed sensors. Furthermore, we address the issues presented above and highlight the modularity features and performance of Arianna$^+$, while reasoning over an ontology network.

The paper is organized as follows. Section 2 discusses the modular ontology network. Arianna$^+$'s architecture is presented in Sect. 3, whereas Sect. 4 discusses an implementation of a use case. Finally, conclusions follow.

2   Activity Detection

2.1   Dynamic Ontology Networks

In [6], an ontology network is defined as a graph G, wherein the set of *nodes* N are ontologies (each with an independent DL reasoner) containing *statements* of the form (1), i.e., having a Boolean state s and a generation timestamp t:

$$\texttt{Statement} \sqsubseteq_{=1} \texttt{hasState}(s) \sqcap_{=1} \texttt{hasTime}(t) \tag{1}$$

and are used to describe a specific part of the *context*, while the set of directed *edges* E are communication channels used for sharing statements between the nodes. Hence G is of the form:

$$G = \{N, E\} \tag{2}$$

where, $N = n_1, n_2, \ldots, n_n$, such that each node specializes in reasoning within a particular context, and $E = e_{12}, e_{13}, \ldots, e_{1n}, e_{21}, e_{23}, \ldots, e_{2n}, \ldots, e_{mn}$, such that the index of each edge signifies the direction of flow of statements, e.g., in e_{12} statements flow from n_1 to n_2. Consider an *event*, indicating that water is flowing from the sink in the kitchen. It can have different interpretations for a system aimed at recognizing activities such as cooking or cleaning. Instead of recognizing them actively from the same representation, with an ontology network it is possible to decouple their models in order to reason upon them based on an event or set of occurring events. Where, an event occurs based on rules that aggregate statements by logical conjunction. We show in the following Sections that this approach enforces system's modularity with respect to activity models, and if the network is such that it evaluates only the models related to a specific part of the overall context, then it also decreases the computation time.

The system checks the statements in the network with a given frequency and, when an event is detected, specific external *procedures* are executed in order to: (i) *move* statements from one node to another via edges, and (ii) evaluate models for activity recognition. For instance, statements could be generated from distributed sensors (e.g., detecting that Adam is in the kitchen at 8:00 am), then the system aggregates this information with prior knowledge to detect events (e.g., Adam is in the kitchen in the morning). When such an event occurs, the model for detecting that Adam is having breakfast gets evaluated by checking statements and their temporal relations within the model.

Moreover, activity models can generate statements, e.g., indicating that Adam had (or did not have) breakfast at a certain time, and hence can trigger new events, which can further be used to describe the context and evaluate models via procedure executions. A formal algebra of statements, used for defining events that execute procedures based on the context, has been proposed in [6].

2.2   A Network of Activity Detectors

For the sake of description, we consider a simplified ontology network $\mathcal{O}$ as shown in Fig. 1. In it there are 6 nodes; n_1 is a location-based contextual-

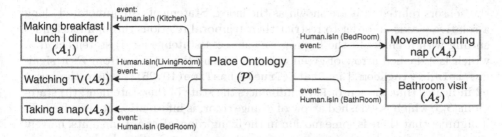

Fig. 1. A simplified ontology network $\mathcal{O}$.

izing model called *Place Ontology* $\mathcal{P}$ and $n_2, \ldots, n_6$ are called *activity models* $\mathcal{A}_i$, where $i = 1, \ldots, 5$ respectively. Nodes are designed such that statements within $\mathcal{P}$ take into account the spatial aspect, and statements within $\mathcal{A}_i$ take into account the spatial and temporal aspects of AR. $\mathcal{A}_i$ are listening for particular events that $\mathcal{P}$ generates, and the edges that link them are the following $E = e_{12}, e_{13}, e_{14}, e_{15}, e_{16}$. The nodes communicate and statements flow between them via edges, such that, $\mathcal{A}_i$ get activated and then evaluated by their independent reasoners, when a particular event occurs, as depicted by the graph in Fig. 1. If the evaluation of an activity model gets satisfied, its procedure generates a new statement to notify the recognition of an activity, e.g., `WatchingTV.{hasState(True), hasTime(19:28)}`.

Within activity models, particular statements and temporal relations, must get satisfied for successful activity recognition. These are shown for $\mathcal{A}_2$, which recognizes the activity *WatchingTV*, in Fig. 2. In it, statements are vertical arrows pointing upwards to indicate a *True* state and downwards for *False*. These statements are either transferred from another node (e.g., dashed arrows represent statements coming from $\mathcal{P}$), or are generated by this node (e.g., solid arrows are the statements generated by $\mathcal{A}_2$) and are indicated along with a name and an index or a range of indexes. A name is denoted by a capital letter and

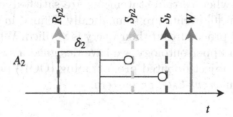

Fig. 2. Visual representation of statements that make up the $\mathcal{A}_2$ model: statements are shown as vertical arrows where dashed arrows indicate information from $\mathcal{P}$, and solid arrows indicate statements generated by this model. Statement indexes indicate sensors influencing the state of that statement, while the temporal restrictions are shown as black lines. (Color figure online)

the sensors related to it are shown as the index. Statements are annotated along a relative x-axis, in order to restrict their temporal relations through black lines ending with a circle. In the Figure, we can see 4 statements: (i) statement R_{p2}, which is a dashed arrow of green color, is information coming from $\mathcal{P}$; it signifies isIn_LivingRoom.{hasState(True), hasTime(19:25)}, where the index $p2$ indicates that the sensor PIR2 influences the state of this statement; (ii) statement S_{p2}, which is a dashed arrow of orange color, is information coming from $\mathcal{P}$; it signifies that there is some motion in the living room after δ_2 time units, naively representing the idea that, if Adam is sitting on the sofa then he is not sitting still; this statement can be replaced by a much robust statement, for instance, sitting.{hasState(True), hasTime(19:26)}, given that there may be other sensors in the system (e.g., wearable sensors, pressure sensors in the sofa); (iii) statement S_b, which is a dashed arrow of blue color, is information coming from $\mathcal{P}$; it signifies highBrightnessTV.{hasState(True), hasTime(19:28)}, where the indexes b indicates that brightness sensor influences the state of this statement; (iv) statement W, which is a solid arrow of red color, is generated when the overall model is satisfied, it signifies WatchingTV.{hasState(True), hasTime(19:28)}; this happens when statements S_{p2} and S_b are generated after δ_2 time units with respect to the R_{p2} statement.

With respect to the AR system presented in [6], the difference in the implementation of Arianna$^+$ is two-fold. Firstly, in [6] time-related instances get accumulated in the models for the purpose of temporal reasoning, and after an activity is recognized, the statements are removed to reduce the increasing complexity of the ontologies. In Arianna$^+$, when $\mathcal{A}_i$ receive statements from $\mathcal{P}$ the values of old instances get updated, if they are available. This has the effect of not accumulating statements in $\mathcal{A}_i$, i.e, the procedure related to it is in charge of updating and evaluating it, without accumulating time-related instances. Such a procedure performs temporal reasoning using both symbolic relations (inferred by the DL reasoner) and numerical/logical operations on the timestamps (inferred externally). This approach of using an external reasoner has the affect of overcoming DL limitation, such as the issue of finding the minimum value in a set of numbers under the open world assumption. Secondly, events are queries that return Boolean value when certain statements are satisfied, or not, in an ontology of the network. In [6] events are semantically defined in an upper-ontology that schedules related procedures if their query is verified. Whereas in Arianna$^+$ rather than having an upper-ontology, we have designed a system's architecture that incorporates the object-oriented programming (OOP) paradigm to execute $\mathcal{A}_i$ procedures with an *event-listener* pattern.

3   Arianna$^+$'s Architecture

3.1   From Sensing to Context Awareness

Figure 3 shows the system's architecture. It recognizes activities with $\mathcal{O}$ as described above; it comprises of the *sensing, aggregation, reasoning* and *application* layers. In this Section, we focus on the interfaces between those layers,

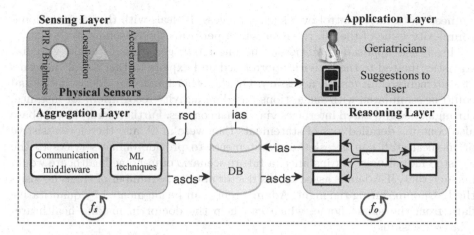

Fig. 3. Arianna$^+$'s architecture where the link *rsd* signifies the flow of raw sensor data, *asds* signifies the flow of aggregated sensor data in the form of statements, *ias* signifies inferred activity statements and *f* signifies frequency.

which enable the modular features of Arianna$^+$ as highlighted in Sect. 2. Firstly, in the reasoning layer, $\mathcal{O}$ is used over time for recognizing activities based on data taken from the database (DB), which is getting accumulated with the latest sensor values and timestamps by the aggregation layer, which in turn is connected to the physical sensory layer. Finally, the application layer is used to easily interface geriatricians, other medical staff, assisted people and their relatives with Arianna$^+$'s services.

The *reasoning layer* is Arianna$^+$'s core. It is made up of $\mathcal{O}$ and its internal working is as described in Sect. 2.2. There are two components in the working of this layer. The first is the initialization of $\mathcal{O}$ (i.e, TBox of ontologies are defined as nodes. While procedures and events are defined as edges). The second is the frequency f_o with which, in $\mathcal{O}$, the procedure of $\mathcal{P}$ takes in aggregated sensor data statements (link *asds*) from the database, updates the ABox, reasons (spatially) with knowledge within $\mathcal{P}$, and declares occurrence of an event, if any. If the declared event is being listened for by one or many $\mathcal{A}_i$, then their procedures get activated. Once an activity model's procedure is active, it takes in statements from $\mathcal{P}$ and updates its own ABox, then reasons (spatially and temporally) with knowledge within the model and declares the recognition of a user activity. This completes a chain of reasoning processes (i.e., $\mathcal{P}$ *plus* an activity model), and if an activity is recognized in the process, then the procedure associated with the model saves the inferred activity statement (link *ias*) back in the database. As the reasoning process has not negligible computational time, if it is simply performed every time new sensor data statements arrive in the database, and if the frequency with which the new data arrives is faster than the reasoning process, then the system would not meet the near real-time constraint. Hence, we need f_o to have control over such a process. It deals with the computational complexity issue of the DL reasoner which performs the reasoning in $\mathcal{O}$.

From the *application layer*, on the one hand, geriatricians could visualize statistics related to the activities performed and explore further details in terms of statements (link *ias*), if necessary. On the other hand, the elderly individual could be stimulated with suggestions based on activity recognition, for instance, through dialogue-based interfaces via virtual coaches. Furthermore, the database also contains detailed logs of statements that were in $\mathcal{O}$, and therefore assistive or medical staff can access those statements to provide online services to the assisted individuals. For instance, a future scenario of in-home healthcare would be such that, if Adam is asked by his doctor about the number of times he visits the bathroom during the night, Adam's reply can be augmented by quantitative data from the smart home, which can help the doctor in making healthcare-related decisions.

The *aggregation layer* takes raw sensor data (link *rsd*) from heterogeneous sensors in the *sensing layer* and by using dedicated perception modules, processes the raw data to generate statements of the form (1). Then, it stores aggregated sensor data statements (link *asds*) in the database. This layer relies on a communication middleware module to channel all the Boolean data the sensors generate, and stores them in the database, if simple distributed sensors are considered. Furthermore, it relies on classification modules (e.g., obtained via machine learning approaches) that can provide statements with semantics (e.g., *sitting down*, *lying down*, etc), and stores them in the database, i.e, if sensors generating more complex data streams are considered. Remarkably, having a formal structure for a statement not only assures a modular evaluation of activity models, but also enables the overall AR system to take heterogeneous sensors into account. Statements are stored in the database at a frequency f_s, and moreover each perception module in this layer can have its own frequency at which it processes the raw sensor data to generate statements and store them in the database.

It is noteworthy that the frequencies f_s and f_o are independent of each other, such that, (i) the aggregation layer stores latest aggregated sensor data statements in the database at a frequency f_s, which can be unique for different perception modules, and (ii) the reasoning layer reasons based on the latest statements that are available to it from the database, with a frequency f_o.

4   Use Case Setup

4.1   Activity Models and Simulation Setup

The use case considered in this paper utilizes all $\mathcal{A}_i$ in $\mathcal{O}$, as shown in Fig. 1. Their description is as follows. $\mathcal{A}_1$ infers *Making breakfast, lunch or dinner*. It is listening for the event $\exists$ Human.isIn(Kitchen). It generates one of the statements, Making breakfast or Making lunch or Making dinner, when the assisted person uses furniture (e.g., the kitchen cabinet), after being present in the kitchen for a minimum time period of 60 s, and if that time period is inside one of the *a priori* defined intervals of the day, i.e., morning, afternoon or evening. $\mathcal{A}_2$ infers *Watching TV*. It is listening for the event ∃ Human.isIn(LivingRoom). It generates the statement Watching TV when the occupant uses furniture (e.g., the TV), after being present in the living room for a minimum time period of 60 s, during any time of the day. $\mathcal{A}_3$ infers *Taking a nap in morning, afternoon or evening*. It is listening for the event ∃ Human.isIn(BedRoom). It generates one of the statements Taking a nap in morning or Taking a nap in afternoon or Taking a nap in evening, when the assisted person uses furniture (e.g., the bed), after being present in the bedroom for a minimum time period of 60 s, and if that time period is inside one of the intervals of the day, i.e., morning, afternoon or evening. $\mathcal{A}_4$ infers *Movement during nap*. It is listening for the event ∃ Human.isIn(BedRoom). It generates the statement Movement during nap when the person uses furniture (e.g., the bed) and the PIR associated with the bed remains active even after 60 have passed on the bed, during any time of the day. $\mathcal{A}_5$ infers *Bathroom visit in morning, afternoon, evening or night*. It is listening for the event ∃ Human.isIn(BathRoom). It generates one of the statements Bathroom visit in morning or Bathroom visit in afternoon or Bathroom visit in evening or Bathroom visit in night, when the assisted person uses furniture (e.g., the toilet seat), after being present in the bathroom for a minimum time period of 60 and if that time period is inside one of the intervals of the day, i.e., morning, afternoon, evening or night.

The use case is implemented by generating a simulated dataset with values and timestamps of a set of PIR sensors and a brightness sensor. It depicts a scenario where an assisted person performs stereotypical activities that are held for eight minutes. The dataset is kept small so as to do extensive in-depth performance testing. The simulation is performed by updating the database with simulated sensor data in the form of statements (mimicking the link *asds* connecting the aggregation layer and the database). As shown in Fig. 4, Adam enters the kitchen, and after spending a minute in the kitchen, he opens the door of

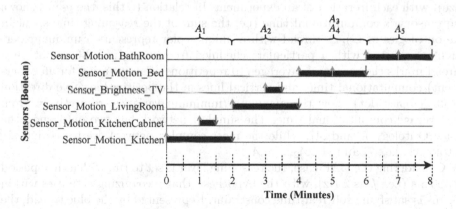

Fig. 4. The simulated dataset used in implementation of the use case.

the kitchen cabinet and then closes it. He is in the kitchen for a total duration of 2 min. Next, he goes to the living room. After a minute in the living room, he switches on the TV and then switches it off after 30 s. He is in the living room for a total duration of 2 min. Next, he goes to the bedroom and simulates sleeping on the bed. He does not stay still in the bed, rather is constantly in motion. He is in the bedroom for a total duration of 2 min. Finally, the person goes to the bathroom. He is in the bathroom for a total duration of 2 min.

Among open source ontology reasoners that exist, e.g., Fact++, Pellet, Hermit and ELK. We use Pellet as it has more features in comparison [1] and is able to pinpoint the root contradiction or clash when inconsistency occurs. Experiments have been performed on a workstation with the following configuration: Intel® Core® $i7$ 2.6 GHz processor and 8 GB of memory. For assessing the system's performance, two types of evaluations are performed and compared. The first is the Contextualized Activity Evaluation (CAE), and the second is the Parallel Activity Evaluation (PAE). The CAE case represents the working of $\mathcal{O}$ as described in Sect. 2.2, where $\mathcal{P}$ behaves as a contextualizer such that an activity model gets activated based on the context. In the PAE case, $\mathcal{P}$ is no longer made to behave as a contextualizer, hence $\mathcal{A}_i$ are active in all contexts.

An evaluation (CAE or PAE) is performed as an experiment by setting a particular frequency f_o (of the reasoning layer). An experiment is performed with 5 iterations, with each iteration an extra activity model is added to $\mathcal{O}$ to increase the system's complexity. Each iteration is repeated 10 times to assess the reasoner's average computational time, and the maximum and minimum variance, from among 10 values. In total four experiments are performed, their process and results are described in the following Section.

4.2 Performance Assessment

Performance results are shown in Fig. 5, where x-axis shows the increasing number of ontologies in $\mathcal{O}$ (i.e., the number of activities Arianna+ attempts to recognize), with each iteration of an experiment. In relation to this, the y-axis shows the reasoner's computational time (i.e, the sum of the reasoning time spent in the ontologies of $\mathcal{O}$). A thread with a unique color represents a unique experiment conducted with a particular scheduled frequency f_o. A black dot on a thread marks the reasoner's average (10 repetitions of an iteration for an experiment) computational time, and vertical lines in the positive/negative direction (from a black dot) show the maximum/minimum variance, respectively, from the average computational time. The simplest network has two ontologies, the Place Ontology $\mathcal{P}$ and $\mathcal{A}_1$, while the most complex network we tested has six ontologies, i.e., $\mathcal{P}$ and $\mathcal{A}_1, \mathcal{A}_2, \ldots, \mathcal{A}_5$.

Considering the CAE case, the reasoning layer is set to run with a time period of 500 ms (i.e., f_o is 2 Hz), with the hypothesis that recognizing activities within 500 ms is satisfying soft real-time constraint. Represented by the blue thread, the reasoner's computational time is high and increases linearly with the increase in system's complexity. Following the success of the previous test, and considering the PAE case, f_o is kept the same, i.e, 2 Hz. However, this case is not represented

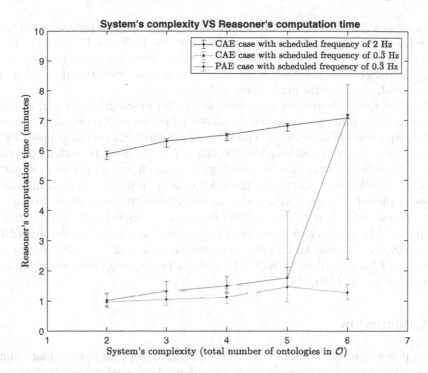

Fig. 5. System's complexity *versus* reasoner's computation time. On x-axis are the number of ontologies, where 2 means $(\mathcal{P} + \mathcal{A}_1)$, 3 means $(\mathcal{P} + \mathcal{A}_1 + \mathcal{A}_2)$, etc. (Color figure online)

by any thread, as an undefined amount of time was being taken by the reasoner to finish the reasoning process. Following the drawback in the previous case, and considering the same case, i.e., PAE, the reasoning layer is set to run with a higher time period of 3000 ms (i.e, f_o is $0.\bar{3}$ Hz), to make sure that the reasoning process completes within the frequency f_o, a condition which is satisfied with that time period. Represented by the red thread, the reasoner's computational time is initially low but then behaves exponentially, with the increase in system's complexity. Finally, following the success of the previous case, and considering the CAE case, f_o is kept the same, i.e, $0.\bar{3}$ Hz. Represented by the green thread, the reasoner's computational time is initially low and remains low, as it increases linearly with the increase in complexity of the system.

More in the discussion of the results:

1. Comparing the two CAE cases with frequencies 2 and $0.\bar{3}$ Hz, respectively, against each other, and against the PAE case with frequency at 2 Hz, we see that, with the approach described in Sect. 2.2 (i.e., represented by the CAE cases), it is possible to have activity recognition with a high frequency. This shows Arianna+'s ability to serve near real-time applications.

2. In case of PAE, when there are 6 ontologies in $\mathcal{O}$, a high variance is seen with the reasoner's average computational time on the higher end, thus confirming an exponential behavior. In case of CAE when there are 5 ontologies in $\mathcal{O}$, a high variance is seen with the reasoner's average computational time on the lower end, thus confirming a linear behavior.

3. The PAE case (wherein, even if multiple smaller ontologies are used, all their reasoners are running in parallel), represented by the red thread; shows an evident exponential behavior and can be compared to using one large ontology in the system. As We know from the literature that (see Sect. 1), with an increase in the number of axioms in an ontology the search space increases exponentially. Therefore in comparison, the CAE case, with its linear behavior, shows clearly the advantage of Arianna$^+$'s modularity feature with respect to activity models and their contextualized evaluation. Furthermore, such claim is supported by the fact that our system does not accumulate instances within ontologies as it uses an external reasoner to deal with temporal aspects of reasoning (as described in Sect. 2.2) and stores the recognized activities in a database (as mentioned in Sect. 3).

5   Conclusion

In this paper, we present the activity recognition structure of our smart home framework Arianna$^+$, whose core is a reasoning layer based on an ontology network, which is grounded on ontology models, statements, procedures, and events-listeners, for which we provide general-purpose definitions. A use case scenario comprising of 5 activity models was implemented and experimentally evaluated for assessing its behavior and computational performance. Results (with CAE) indicate that an AR system which exploits the modularity feature of a network of ontologies in a contextualized manner, and in which temporal instances are not accumulated, has near real-time AR capability and it addresses the scalability and robustness requirement. Limitations of the presented use case are that it considers a single occupant in the environment and although extensively, it is tested with a simulated dataset. Hence, future work involves testing with data from a real distributed sensor scenario and incorporating perception modules in the aggregation layer, such that the network of ontologies can take statements related to human gestures and postures. Nevertheless, this paper provides a general-purpose discussion about ontology networks for AR. While the full evaluation of this approach awaits further investigation and user feedback, our initial results provide a base for building real-world use cases.

References

1. Abburu, S.: A survey on ontology reasoners and comparison. Int. J. Comput. Appl. **57**(17), 37 (2012)
2. Allen, J.F.: Maintaining knowledge about temporal intervals. In: Readings in Qualitative Reasoning about Physical Systems, pp. 361–372. Elsevier (1990)

3. Atallah, L., Lo, B., Ali, R., King, R., Yang, G.Z.: Real-time activity classification using ambient and wearable sensors. IEEE Trans. Inf. Technol. Biomed. **13**(6), 1031–1039 (2009)
4. Baader, F., Horrocks, I., Sattler, U.: Description logics as ontology languages for the semantic web. In: Hutter, D., Stephan, W. (eds.) Mechanizing Mathematical Reasoning. LNCS (LNAI), vol. 2605, pp. 228–248. Springer, Heidelberg (2005). https://doi.org/10.1007/978-3-540-32254-2_14
5. Bruno, B., et al.: Multi-modal sensing for human activity recognition. In: Proceedings of 24th IEEE International Symposium on Robot and Human Interactive Communication (RO-MAN), pp. 594–600. Kobe, Japan (2015)
6. Buoncompagni, L., Bruno, B., Giuni, A., Mastrogiovanni, F., Zaccaria, R.: Arianna: towards a new paradigm for assistive technology at home. In: Proceedings of 8th Italian Forum on Ambient Assisted Living - ForItAAL, Genova, Italy (2015)
7. Chen, L., Nugent, C.D., Wang, H.: A knowledge-driven approach to activity recognition in smart homes. IEEE Trans. Knowl. Data Eng. **24**(6), 961–974 (2012)
8. Cohen, J.E.: Human population: the next half century. In: Science, **302**, 1172–1175 (2003)
9. Cook, D.J., Krishnan, N.C., Rashidi, P.: Activity discovery and activity recognition: a new partnership. IEEE Trans. Cybern. **43**(3), 820–828 (2013)
10. Donini, F.M., Lenzerini, M., Nardi, D., Schaerf, A.: Deduction in concept languages: from subsumption to instance checking. J. Log. Comput. **4**(4), 423–452 (1994)
11. Horrocks, I., et al.: SWRL: a semantic web rule language combining OWL and RuleML. W3C Memb. Submiss. **21**, 79 (2004)
12. Liu, L., Stroulia, E., Nikolaidis, I., Miguel-Cruz, A., Rincon, A.R.: Smart homes and home health monitoring technologies for older adults: a systematic review. Int. J. Med. Informatics **91**, 44–59 (2016)
13. Mshali, H., Lemlouma, T., Moloney, M., Magoni, D.: A survey on health monitoring systems for health smart homes. Int. J. Ind. Ergon. **66**, 26–56 (2018)
14. Riboni, D., Pareschi, L., Radaelli, L., Bettini, C.: Is ontology-based activity recognition really effective? In: 2011 IEEE International Conference on Pervasive Computing and Communications Workshops (PERCOM Workshops), pp. 427–431. IEEE (2011)
15. Salguero, A.G., Espinilla, M., Delatorre, P., Medina, J.: Using ontologies for the online recognition of activities of daily living. Sensors **18**(4), 1202 (2018)
16. Scalmato, A., Sgorbissa, A., Zaccaria, R.: Describing and recognizing patterns of events in smart environments with description logic. IEEE Trans. Cybern. **43**(6), 1882–1897 (2013)
17. Veeraraghavan, A., Roy-Chowdhury, A.K., Chellappa, R.: Matching shape sequences in video with applications in human movement analysis. IEEE Trans. Pattern Anal. Mach. Intell. **27**(12), 1896–1909 (2005)

A Scalable Architecture to Design Multi-modal Interactions for Qualitative Robot Navigation

Luca Buoncompagni(✉), Suman Ghosh, Mateus Moura,
and Fulvio Mastrogiovanni

Department of Informatics, Bioengineering, Robotics and Systems Engineering,
University of Genoa, Via Opera Pia 13, 16145 Genoa, Italy
luca.buoncompagni@edu.unige.it

Abstract. The paper discusses an approach for teleoperating a mobile robot based on qualitative spatial relations, which are instructed through speech-based and deictic commands. Given a workspace containing a robot, a user and some objects, we exploit fuzzy reasoning criteria to describe the pertinence map between the locations in the workspace and qualitative commands incrementally acquired. We discuss the modularity features of the used reasoning technique through some use cases addressing a conjunction of spatial kernels. In particular, we address the problem of finding a suitable target location from a set of qualitative spatial relations based on symbolic reasoning and Monte Carlo simulations. Our architecture is analyzed in a scenario considering simple kernels and an almost-perfect perception of the environment. Nevertheless, the presented approach is modular and scalable, and it could be also exploited to design application where multi-modal qualitative interactions are considered.

Keywords: Robot teleoperation · Fuzzy spatial relations
Multi-modal robot interaction

1 Introduction

Nowadays, robots are being deployed in daily-life environments with health-care and assistive purposes. Those applications usually exploit distributed environmental sensors, which provide information about a user's state and activities for experts that evaluate the well-being of a person. In some scenarios, caregivers might use telepresence robots to communicate with the person and ask for assessments that sensors do not provide. Those robots are required to interface smoothly with persons, especially elderly adults, taking into account social

L. Buoncompagni, S. Ghosh and M. Moura—These authors contributed equally to this work.

© Springer Nature Switzerland AG 2018
C. Ghidini et al. (Eds.): AI*IA 2018, LNAI 11298, pp. 96–109, 2018.
https://doi.org/10.1007/978-3-030-03840-3_8

and spatial cognition. In other similar scenarios, pet-like robots, such as Miro [12] have been developed as companions for a long-term motivation of users with interaction and mobility difficulties. For both scenarios, the navigation of the robot should allow different degrees of autonomy to meet different users' needs [11]. In this paper, we address the issue of locating a mobile robot with a high degree of autonomy, controlled through qualitative incremental commands.

In these scenarios, robots should be able to navigate in an environment shared with humans, who might like to naturally issue commands that drive the robot to specific areas of the room, with no high precision requirements. For instance, if a child stays in the bedroom for a long time during a sunny day playing with his or her pet-like robot, the mother could ask the robot to go *close to the exit door*, trying to motivate the child to play in the garden. On the other hand, if an older adult is on the sofa and receives a call from the doctor; he or she might ask a telepresence robot to locate itself in a comfortable position, for instance, *in front of the television and on the right-hand side of the table*. Generally, we consider the teleoperation based on qualitative commands all the times that a user cannot give either geometrical or velocity references.

Robot teleoperation is a largely investigated problem in the literature, especially for exploration and manipulation tasks, where a certain precision is required. Several types of systems exploit different interfacing devices such as joysticks, smartphones, Leap Motions, smartwatches, eye-tracking technology, etc. Different applications lead to different approaches; for instance, a reacting control is suitable for low-level interacting behaviors. Instead, a high-level interaction usually requires that the user provides additionally informations; typically, velocity or geometrical references, e.g., *go slower*, *go forward*, etc. Remarkably, while the user is issuing those commands, he or she is required to continuously operate the robot, since its behavior also depends on the states it had at previous instances of time. In other words, the robot has a memory, and the users operate it by giving differential references, which could be based on previous positions or speeds.

We designed an interaction pattern that relies on a robot having in memory a set of commands that restrict the possible target position in space. These restrictions are described qualitatively concerning the robot and generic objects, seen from the user's viewpoint. The perception of such knowledge from visual and auditory channels is an extremely challenging problem, especially for general-purpose systems. Due to a large number of uncontrolled variables influencing the experiments, human-robot interaction applications are typically designed through the *iterative developing* process based on the (*i*) developing, (*ii*) testing, and (*iii*) evaluating phases, which are performed in an iterative manner. During *ii* and *iii*, some measurement of the interaction, as used in [9], can guide further developments to be undertaken during the *i* phase of the next iteration. Remarkably, to do not bias experiments outcomes with developers beliefs, it is suggested that the *i* phase tries to improve the system with minor changes, i.e., the evaluation frequency should be high.

If verbal commands are used to guide the robot to a target position, symbolic representations are required to understand the user's sentences and find a target pose suitable for the given commands. Typically, in such cases, systems exploit a map between geometrical positions (or velocities) and symbols, for each known location, based on the user's inputs [10, 13]. During verbal interaction, users also communicate through other modalities, such as deictic gestures. In many works multi-modal robot interaction is investigated – for instance, [5] proposes to use Reinforcement Learning and applied associative memories – for fusing audio and gestures, and instruct the robot on qualitative commands for picking and place tasks. For merging such interaction modalities, a Markov Decision Process in [8], Recurrent Neural Networks in [1], and a Dynamic Bayesian Network in [7], have been used. Remarkably, not only do such methods allow dealing with uncertainties, but they can also be used for *learning* behaviors in a data-driven manner. However, the models generated by these techniques are typically not modular, since the introduction of a new behavior might affect the probability distribution of all the other states). Thus, the system can not always scale among iterative development steps.

Fuzzy logic formalism, mainly developed to be used with natural language, can be used for representing the robot position with respect to shape, position and orientation of general objects. In particular, [15] proposes a mapping function between sentences (containing spatial relations) and a fuzzy membership value associated with a physical location, while [14] uses fuzzy membership functions for fusing gestures and natural language. Moreover, [3] proposes mathematical morphology for describing north, south, east and west points of objects or rooms. Fuzzy morphology has also been developed for image processing. [6] presents a kernel-based approach for classifying spatial relationships between hand-drawn symbols, where such kernels are generated through a data-driven approach based on Support Vector Machines.

In this work, we developed a system that allows symbolic teleoperation of a mobile robot based on fuzzy spatial relations between objects issued through multi-modal commands. Our main contribution is a software architecture defining the required components and interfaces to be used during the steps undertaken in an iterative development process. Our objective is to start designing and testing a modular and scalable reasoning technique that can be used in dynamic environments and with a broad set of qualitative commands, possibly customized for each user and scenario. We present our architecture through a preliminary implementation suitable for the i phase of the first iteration (i.e., concerning a simplified, but real use case shown in Fig. 1), and we discuss its scalability and modality features achieved through fuzzy reasoning and Monte Carlo simulations.

In particular, we address the problem of representing qualitative spatial references and finding a suitable target position that the robot should reach. In this scenario, we assumed a robot that perfectly knows its location, the locations of referenced objects and their *identifiers*. Also, it can perfectly translate the user's voice in text, and detect his or her pointing gestures. Moreover, in the presented use case, the user interacts only though combinations of five spatial relations (i.e., in *front* of, *behind* of, on the *right* of, on the *left* of, and *near* to). Nevertheless, the paper shows how the architecture can accommodate and merge different spatial relation models, based also on some different input modalities, in a modular manner.

Fig. 1. The referencing scenario.

Section 2 gives an overview of our system, while in Sect. 3 we introduce the user interfacing pattern for the referenced use case. In Sect. 4 we present a fuzzy spatial reasoner based on fuzzy kernels, which are further detailed in Sect. 5. Section 6 presents our experimental evaluation and discusses preliminary results. Conclusion follows in Sect. 7.

2   Software Architecture

Figure 2 presents the proposed interaction patterns from a Component-Based Software Engineering (CBSE) perspective, graphically shown through a structural Unified Modeling Language (UML) diagram. In the Figure, boxes represent software *components*, which provide and require *interfaces* to operate. The latter are graphically identified with the ball-socket notation. All interfaces are described by a specific *message* defining the data type exchanged among components through *ports* (i.e., data communication channels). We specify the proposed components for the widely adopted Robot Operating System (ROS) framework. Therefore, we assume a component to be a *node* or a *service*, the former characterized by a *spinning rate*, while the latter provides services on demand.

Within an area monitored by a motion capture system, the Rigid Body Detector component provides to the robot the position of all the elements of our referencing scenario. The robot process inputs coming from the Speech Processor component, that parses sentences to providing semantic tags for specific words, which are used for identifying qualitative regions in space that contain the target position.

When the user says a sentence containing a valid command (i.e., meaningful semantic tags are found in the text translation of the person's voice), and eventually performs a deictic gesture, the relative inputs are provided to the Command Logic component, implemented as a finite state machine. In particular, the robot is initially in a (*i*) *ready* state and when a command is issued, to the Command Logic goes to a (*ii*) *listening* state. It can lead to an (*iii*) *invalid* state if the command is not understood, or to a (*iv*) *computing* state, which holds until a suitable target position is found. When this occurs, the robot starts moving and returns to the ready state; otherwise an (*v*) *inconsistent* state emerges, and the spatial beliefs of the robot are erased.

The Command Logic maintains in the memory the user's instructions that the robot should take into account for finding a suitable target point. Such a memory is implemented as a buffer that contains all the vocal and gesture commands of the user until either the target position is found, or an inconsistent state is reached, or the user explicitly asks for a new interaction pattern. In all those cases the buffer is cleaned and the interaction restarts.

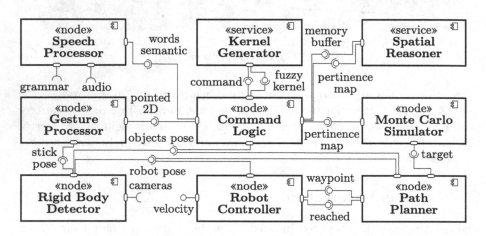

Fig. 2. The ROS-based software architecture.

Each element of the memory buffer is a representation of the suitable positions that respect a single command, i.e., a fuzzy kernel, provided by the Kernel Generator component. The Spatial Reasoner component merges all representations in the buffer to find an overall fuzzy landscape, which describes the degree of pertinence of each location in the workspace with respect to the given commands. Since we design the system for accommodating commands based on generic spatial relations, we consider the fuzzy pertinence map to be a general function spanning in values between $[0, 1]$, where the higher the pertinence value represents the most suitable target candidate point.

The Monte Carlo Simulator component solves the problem of findings a suitable target in such a generic landscape. It evaluates the pertinence of randomized locations until certain conditions are met. As heuristic conditions, we posed (i) a very high threshold after which the simulations are terminated, (ii) upper and lower pertinence bounds for which the target position is generated, although the simulations continue looking for improvements, and (iii) a limit on the maximum number of simulations. When the Monte Carlo Simulator produces a target point with fuzzy pertinence value higher than in the previous simulation, the new target is provided to the Path Planner component, implemented using the Rapidly-Exploring Random Tree (RTT*) algorithm, which consequentially provides waypoints, used as references for the low-level Robot Controller.

This architecture allows a continuous interaction, since new commands are stored in a buffer and are evaluated as soon as previous computations ends, i.e., as soon as Monte Carlo simulation provides a suitable point. Therefore, while the robot is moving towards a target, the user can guide it reactively. In this paper, we evaluate such property through the estimation of the time spent in the computing state, especially as far as the complexity of the Kernel Generator and the Spatial Reasoner are concerned. However, it is important to highlight that for a real application the complexity of finding a path and perceiving the environment might introduce not negligible delays before the robot starts moving, and consequently affect user's reaction time.

3   Multi-modal Interface

In this section we show how a user can interface with the robot in our simplified scenario. In particular, he or she can instruct the robot using five types of spatial relations, each associated with a specific fuzzy kernel. We design an interaction pattern where the user mainly uses sentences to guide the robot. However, he can further enforce and enhance his command by pointing to a specific location.

We suppose that the commands are always between the robot and a well-defined object, e.g., *go in front of box number 1*. For understanding these types of sentences, we used the Concept-Action Grammar Generator (CAGG) [4] which, given a text resulting from the speech-to-text process, returns the semantics of the sentence through tags associated to specific keywords. Such association is based on rules encoded on a Backus-Naur Form (BNF) grammar of the form:

$$\texttt{<go> : <relation> <object>,} \tag{1}$$

where each identifier between angled brackets is associated to a specific set of keywords to be matched in a sentence for obtaining the related semantic tag (e.g., [front, 1]).

Moreover, through simple sentences is also possible to give other directives to the robot, such as to mark the task *done* (when the interaction is complete), and to *reset* the buffer (to clean the commands memory). These types of commands are recognized through a different grammar that allows changes of the Command

Logic state, as detailed:

$$\texttt{<directive>} : \texttt{<go>} \mid \texttt{<reset>} \mid \texttt{<done>}. \tag{2}$$

Therefore, for recognizing a user sentence we use a hierarchy of grammars, where Rule 2 is on the top layer and Rule 1 is evaluated only if the **go** directive is found.

Last but not the least, the motion caption system tracks the orientation of a stick that the user holds in his hand (Fig. 1) while performing deictic gestures. When the user performs a pointing gesture, we compute the intersection point of the line generated by the stick orientation and the ground plane containing the robot and objects. The robot is instructed to be *near* a point computed as above. It is to be noted that pointing is typically a not precise source of information, especially when the user is standing at a distance from the scene. We thus consider the identified point in the ground to be qualitative as an explicit spatial relation given through a spoken sentence (e.g., *go near box 2*). In other words, the *near* spatial relation generated by a pointing gesture accounts for non-negligible pointing errors by the user.

4   Spatial Reasoner

Within a workspace $W \subseteq \mathbb{R}^2$, we assign the robot goal position by maximizing the qualitative fuzzy values represented in the landscape of possible target positions. For our use case, we divided the workspace into discretized rectangles of equal size. For each unit rectangular element, we select the center point P as its location. Thus, we have a set of possible locations $\{P_i, \ \forall i \in [1, n]\} \subset W$. In this scenario, the fuzzy landscape $\mathcal{M} \subset \mathbb{R}^3$ is a pertinence map that assigns to each point in the workspace a fuzzy membership $\mathcal{M}(P_i) = \mu_i \in [0, 1]$, which represents how pertinent a location is with respect to all the spatial restrictions contained in the robot's memory. As we mentioned before, for each command issued by the user, the system computes a fuzzy spatial kernel $\mathcal{K} \subset \mathbb{R}^3$ which represents the fuzzy membership of each point of the workspace for just for a single command. Therefore, a generic kernel $\mathcal{K}_j$ embeds for each point of the workspace, a fuzzy membership value $\mathcal{K}_j(P_i) = \mu_{ji} \in [0, 1]$, that describes its pertinence for a single spatial relation, as shown in Fig. 3.

(a) $\mathcal{K}_1$: **behind** O_h. (b) $\mathcal{K}_2$: **left** O_h. (c) $\mathcal{K}_3$: **near** O_h. (d) $\mathcal{M}{=}\mathcal{K}_1{\otimes}\mathcal{K}_2{\otimes}\mathcal{K}_3$.

Fig. 3. Three fuzzy spatial kernels applied to the same object O_h (3b, 3a, and 3c) and their conjunction, i.e., the pertinence map (3d).

Given m commands in the robot memory, a set of $B = \{\mathcal{K}_j, \ \forall j \in [1, m]\}$ kernels are generated. The system then computes an overall pertinence map through fuzzy conjunctions considering the minimum value of the fuzzy membership among all kernels in B. This is done for each point P_i of the workspace. Formally,

$$\mathcal{M}(P_i) = \bigotimes_{j=1}^{m} \mathcal{K}_j(P_i) = \min_{j \in B}(\mu_{ji}), \tag{3}$$

represents the fuzzy pertinence of the i-th point to satisfy all the m commands.

For example, Fig. 3d shows the intersection between relations $(\mathcal{K}_1)$ left, $(\mathcal{K}_2)$ behind, and $(\mathcal{K}_3)$ near, applied to the same object O_h located in the center of the workspace. Brighter regions of the workspace indicate consistent locations of a target point that respects all three given commands. Remarkably, with this formalization, it is possible to see kernels as generic modules that represent the intersection of different spatial relations, applied in different contexts. From a general perspective, all kernels can (i) represent fuzzy membership values between 0 and 1, (ii) for each point of the workspace.

If we consider a robot that evaluates the pertinence map $\mathcal{M}^t(P_i)$ (containing fuzzy membership values μ_i^t) for each time instance t when a new command is issued, the computation of Eq. 3 can be simplified and evaluated as:

$$\mathcal{M}^{t+1}(P_i) = \mathcal{M}^t(P_i) \otimes \mathcal{K}_{m+1}(P_i) = \min(\mu_i^t, \ \mu_{m+1,i}), \tag{4}$$

which denotes a computation complexity of $\mathcal{O}(n)$ since it requires an element-to-element comparison between two sets of size n. This assures reasoning scalability because Eq. 4 computes the pertinence map in an incremental manner and its computation cost does not increase with the size of commands in the robot memory, but always remains constant if the workspace is fixed. Nevertheless, with this approach, we lose information concerning previous instances in time. Hence, backtracking to previous valid pertinence landscape (i.e., removing the effects of $\mathcal{K}_j$ from $\mathcal{M}^t$) remains an open issue.

In the pertinence landscape $\mathcal{M}$, we can define a target position $T*$ as a location with high fuzzy value, formally:

$$T^* = \operatorname*{argmax}_{P_i} \mathcal{M}(P_i) \equiv \{P_i : \mathcal{M}(P_i) = \mu_i \to 1\} \subset W. \tag{5}$$

Unfortunately, for generic kernels, this problem is not well-posed since there might exist many points with the same high pertinence value. Indeed, even if in the referenced scenario we used simple kernels based on heuristics (discussed in the next section), Fig. 3d shows more than one suitable target point with sufficiently high fuzzy pertinence.

To address this issue and choose a quantitative target position T with a fuzzy pertinence similar to T^*, we used the randomized Monte Carlo simulation approach introduced in Sect. 2. At the end of each q-th simulation, new randomized locations P_i are evaluated. Among them, the point with the best pertinence is elected the new target T^q, iff it represents a more pertinent solution than the one selected during the previous simulation, i.e., $\mathcal{M}(q^t) > \mathcal{M}(T^{q-1})$.

5   Spatial Kernel

Figure 3b and a show the kernels used for commands `left` and `behind` respectively. We adopt a simplification of the formalization proposed in [2], which defines fuzzy pertinence of spatial relations between objects with a general shape. In this work, we reason on the spatial relations in a scene having w point-like objects O_h, i.e., a set of occupied locations $\{O_h, \forall h \in [1, w]\} \subset W$. Through a command that satisfies Rule 1, the user specifies an `object` O_h and, if specific *relation* are used (i.e., *left*, *behind*, *right*, and *front*), he or she specifies also an orientation $\hat{u}$. Thus, we posed

$$\mathcal{K}_j(P_i) = \max\left(0, 1 - \frac{2}{\pi}\beta\right) \quad \text{where} \quad \beta = \arccos\frac{\overrightarrow{O_h P_i} \cdot \hat{u}}{||\overrightarrow{O_h P_i}||}, \tag{6}$$

where $\hat{u}$ represents a unit vector along direction of kernel orientation with respect to a global frame $\hat{x}\hat{y}$ fixed as in Fig. 1. Throughout the paper, our global $\hat{y}$ axis is always directed from south to north in the images of fuzzy landscapes.

The user orientation is fixed along the $\hat{y}$ axis. The $\hat{u}$ direction is initially fixed along the $\hat{x}$ axis. Figure 3a shows the kernel representing the `behind` relation, which is computed for $\hat{u}$ rotated anticlockwise by $\frac{\pi}{2}$ with respect to the $\hat{x}$ axis. Figure 3b shows the `left` relation, computed for $\hat{u}$ rotated by π. Consequently, inverse relations such as `front` and `right` are computed for $\hat{u}$ rotated by $\frac{2}{3}\pi$ and 0 respectively. Remarkably, while we consider spatial relations between point-like objects, we also describe their encompassing bounding box, and force all the kernels to have $\mu_{ji} = 0$ for all P_i points within the w boxes.

The above kernel formulation cannot be used for representing a relation such as `near`, since Eq. 6 does not take into account the distances between P_i and O_h, but only the orientation of the connecting vector $\overrightarrow{O_h P_i}$. For representing a spatial pertinence related to the distance between the object O_h and a possible target point P_i, we used a Gaussian kernel (Fig. 3c) defined as

$$\mathcal{K}_j(P_i) = e^{-\frac{A^2}{2\sigma^2}} \quad \text{where} \quad A = ||\overrightarrow{O_h P_i}||, \tag{7}$$

where σ has been set as the width of the workspace divided by four; if W is considered to represent a square space, $\sigma = \frac{\sqrt{n}}{4}$.

Notably, the `near` restriction is the only relation of the referenced use case associated with the pointing gesture. In particular, if the user pointed to a specific location $G \subset W$ in the ground, we merely apply the kernel in Eq. 7, centered in G instead of the center of an object, i.e., $O_h \equiv G$.

6   Use Case

Figure 1 shows the scenario in which we test the system using a Miro robot [12] that navigates in an squared workspace of $5.76m^2$ discretized into $n = 576$ unit blocks of size $0.01m^2$. Within the workspace, four objects (identified through

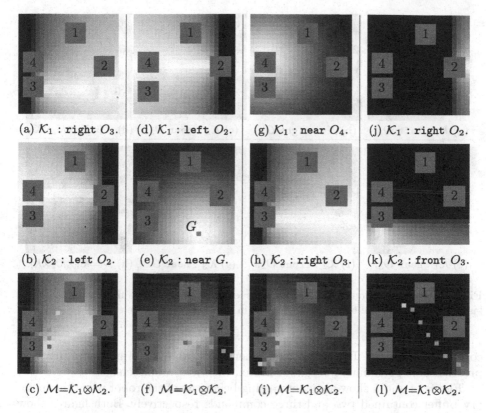

Fig. 4. Four different instructions based on two kernels (shown by columns), centered in an object (enumerated boxes) or in a pointed location (purple cells). The third row shows the initial and target position (yellow and red cells respectively), and the followed path (green cells). (Color figure online)

an enumeration) are statically located in such a way to have the center in a discretized position (i.e., $O_h \equiv P_j \ \forall h \in [1, w]$), and to occupy a given number of cells (Figs. 4 and 5). A user looks at the scene and instructs the robot using a microphone and a pointer. The global reference $\hat{x}\hat{y}$ is fixed from the user's orientation, as shown in the figure.

We design an experimental script divided into three parts. Initially, we explain to the user the types of sentences understood by the robot, and how to perform valid pointing gestures. During the second phase, the user decides a target point T^* (that we record) and begins instructing the robot to try to reach that position. The test is performed again with a different target point before moving on to the third phase, which is a repetition of the second phase, with the difference being that T^* is imposed on the user by us. The navigation ends when the user believes that the robot's target position T is qualitatively close enough to the intended location T^*; in this case, he is supposed to issue a **done**

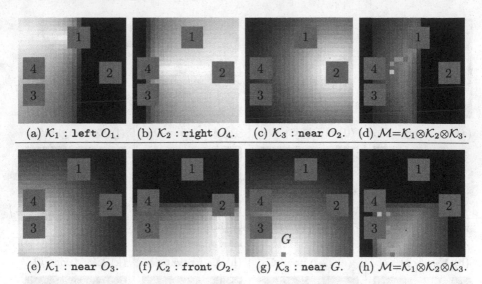

(a) $\mathcal{K}_1$: left O_1. (b) $\mathcal{K}_2$: right O_4. (c) $\mathcal{K}_3$: near O_2. (d) $\mathcal{M}=\mathcal{K}_1\otimes\mathcal{K}_2\otimes\mathcal{K}_3$.

(e) $\mathcal{K}_1$: near O_3. (f) $\mathcal{K}_2$: front O_2. (g) $\mathcal{K}_3$: near G. (h) $\mathcal{M}=\mathcal{K}_1\otimes\mathcal{K}_2\otimes\mathcal{K}_3$.

Fig. 5. Two instructions given through three commands (shown by rows), where the last column shows the robot navigation as in Fig. 4. (Color figure online)

command (Rule 2). The whole experiment took about half an hour. Here, we present some preliminary results collected with five volunteers.

Figures 4 and 5 show some interesting behaviors of the robot when the memory buffer contained two and three commands respectively. Both figures show the kernel independently, as well as their conjunction (i.e., the pertinence map), in which we superimpose the path traversed by the robot. Particularly, Fig. 4c shows the robot behavior in a case where the user said "Miro, go on the right of box 3" (Fig. 4a) "and on the left of box 2 please" (Fig. 4b). In the second column, Fig. 4f shows the robot's final location when the user said "go on the left of box 2" and pointed to G, while Fig. 4i shows a solution found if the robot is constrained to be on the right of O_3 and close to O_4. Figure 4l illustrates a case where the conjunction of the user's instructions was almost inconsistent. Similarly, Fig. 5d demonstrates a case where the user later decided to provide a relation concerning object O_2 to move the robot more towards it, while remaining on the left of O_1, and on the right-hand side of O_4. Finally, Fig. 5h presents a scene where a pointing gesture is used to correct an erroneous previous instruction (near O_3) given by the user which caused the robot to move to the north of O_3, while she actually intended to move the robot to the south of O_3 (i.e., *closer* from her viewpoint).

During all the experiments (performed with a processor Intel® Core™ i5-460M 2.53 GHz and 4 GB of memory), we compute Eq. 4 137 times with a buffer size spanning in $m \in [1, 9]$. For each times we compute the pertinence map the Spatial Reasoner spent 6 ± 2 ms, while the Monte Carlo simulator (which had an upper pertinence threshold of 0.95) spent 4 ± 2 ms for identifying a sufficiently high value. The generation of the navigation path is one of the most expensive tasks, which lasts for 4789 ± 1958 ms. In accord with Eq. 4, the computation where no affected by the number of commands and scales linearly with the number of point in the workspace.

During the third phase of our experiments, we propose to the user some target T^* complex enough to be described given the five supported relations and the objects' locations (such as the one perfectly reached in Fig. 5h). We observed that the user spent time thinking about the correct command to issue (in average 40 ± 36 s). During all the experiments the robot memory was reset 34 times, in average every 4 commands, and we computed $\mathcal{M}$ with $m = 1$ for 54 times, with m equal to 2, 3, 4 for 39, 24, 12 times respectively, and with $m \in [5, 9]$ less than 3 times. For all those maps, before to meet one of its terminating condition, the Monte Carlo simulations retrieved a fuzzy pertinence value of 0.82 ± 0.17. Particularly for the target points that the users tagged with a **done** command (T), we compute a distance of 0.080 ± 0.034 meters between that point and the initially intended target position T^*; reached with a fuzzy pertinence found by Monte Carlo of 0.78 ± 0.20.

7   Conclusions

We presented a preliminary evaluation of a mobile robot that can locate itself based on qualitative conjunctions of spatial relations concerning specific objects, issued through speech-based and deictic commands. Our architecture relies on fuzzy kernels that are used to represent a landscape indicating the pertinence of each point of the workspace to satisfy a set of the qualitative commands expressed by a user. We computed the robot position based on combinations of kernels and Monte Carlo simulations, and we observed a real robot navigate toward qualitative targets within a simplified scenario.

We described the scalability feature of our ROS-based architecture[1], as well as the modularity of its reasoning approach. We discussed the types of kernels that can be adopted and evaluated for more complex interaction semantics and modalities. In particular, we described its components and interfaces with the aim of reusing them during further iterative development steps, toward a natural interaction in real applications.

The current implementation is limited due to the fact that the representation of the pointing gestures, the verbal commands and the objects orientation might depend on the user interpretation. Moreover, similarly to navigation algorithms based on potential fields, our approach relies on a one-to-one spatial mapping between a fuzzy representation and the workspace. Therefore, the inclusion of information which is not directly mappable to spatial semantics (e.g., voice volume) is an open issue in the reasoning process. Nevertheless, other interaction modalities (e.g., based on gaze) can be supported by the adopted fuzzy reasoning technique.

---

[1] available at https://github.com/EmaroLab/mmodal_teleop.

Since the number of users is not adequate for evaluating the naturalness of the interactions, we are currently collecting further data through more structured experiments. From a preliminary interaction assessment, we noted that the presented kernels are not always exhaustive, especially if no other spatial relations are included in the reasoning process, e.g., *between, far*, etc. Our future objective is to design additional kernels and perception modules to be evaluated through experiments involving the presented architecture.

References

1. Antunes, A., Pizzuto, G., Cangelosi, A.: Communication with speech and gestures: applications of recurrent neural networks to robot language learning. In: Proceedings of GLU 2017 International Workshop on Grounding Language Understanding, pp. 4–7 (2017)
2. Bloch, I.: Fuzzy relative position between objects in image processing: a morphological approach. IEEE Trans. Pattern Anal. Mach. Intell. **21**(7), 657–664 (1999)
3. Bloch, I., Saffiotti, A.: Why robots should use fuzzy mathematical morphology. In: Proceedings of the 1st International ICSC-NAISO Congress on Neuro-Fuzzy Technologies, La Havana, Cuba (2002)
4. Buoncompagni, L., Mastrogiovanni, F.: An open framework to develop and validate techniques for speech analysis. In: Proceedings of the 3rd Italian Workshop on Artificial Intelligence and Robotics A workshop of the XV International Conference of the Italian Association for Artificial Intelligence (AI*IA 2016), vol. 1834, pp. 15–20. Genova, Italy, CEUR-WS (2016). http://ceur-ws.org/Vol-1834/
5. Cruz, F., Parisi, G.I., Twiefel, J., Wermter, S.: Multi-modal integration of dynamic audiovisual patterns for an interactive reinforcement learning scenario. In: Intelligent Robots and Systems (IROS), 2016 IEEE/RSJ International Conference on, pp. 759–766. IEEE (2016)
6. Delaye, A., Anquetil, E.: Learning of fuzzy spatial relations between handwritten patterns. Int. J. Data Min., Model. Manag. **6**(2), 127–147 (2014)
7. Huang, C.M., Mutlu, B.: Learning-based modeling of multimodal behaviors for humanlike robots. In: Proceedings of the 2014 ACM/IEEE International Conference on Human-robot Interaction, pp. 57–64. ACM (2014)
8. Lucignano, L., Cutugno, F., Rossi, S., Finzi, A.: A dialogue system for multimodal human-robot interaction. In: Proceedings of the 15th ACM on International Conference on Multimodal Interaction, pp. 197–204. ACM (2013)
9. Olsen, D.R., Goodrich, M.A.: Metrics for evaluating human-robot interactions. In: Proceedings of PERMIS. vol. 2003, p. 4 (2003)
10. Poncela, A., Gallardo-Estrella, L.: Command-based voice teleoperation of a mobile robot via a human-robot interface. Robotica **33**(1), 1–18 (2015)
11. Potenza, A., Kiselev, A., Loutfi, A., Saffiotti, A.: Towards sliding autonomy in mobile robotic telepresence: a position paper. In: ECCE 2017-European Conference on Cognitive Ergonomics, 20–22 September 2017, Umeå University, Sweden (2017)
12. Prescott, T.J., Mitchinson, B., Conran, S.: Miro: An animal-like companion robot with a biomimetic brain-based control system. In: Proceedings of the Companion of the 2017 ACM/IEEE International Conference on Human-Robot Interaction, pp. 50–51. ACM (2017)

13. Ross, R.J., Shi, H., Vierhuff, T., Krieg-Brückner, B., Bateman, J.: Towards dialogue based shared control of navigating robots. In: Freksa, C., Knauff, M., Krieg-Brückner, B., Nebel, B., Barkowsky, T. (eds.) Spatial Cognition 2004. LNCS (LNAI), vol. 3343, pp. 478–499. Springer, Heidelberg (2005). https://doi.org/10.1007/978-3-540-32255-9_26
14. Srimal, P.A.S., Muthugala, M.V.J., Jayasekara, A.B.P.: Deictic gesture enhanced fuzzy spatial relation grounding in natural language. In: 2017 IEEE International Conference on Fuzzy Systems (FUZZ-IEEE), pp. 1–8. IEEE (2017)
15. Tan, J., Ju, Z., Liu, H.: Grounding spatial relations in natural language by fuzzy representation for human-robot interaction. In: 2014 IEEE International Conference on Fuzzy Systems (FUZZ-IEEE), pp. 1743–1750. IEEE (2014)

CH1: A Conversational System to Calculate Carbohydrates in a Meal

Bernardo Magnini[1(✉)], Vevake Balaraman[1,2], Mauro Dragoni[1],
Marco Guerini[1], Simone Magnolini[1,3], and Valerio Piccioni[1,2]

[1] Fondazione Bruno Kessler, Via Sommarive 18, Povo, Trento, Italy
{magnini,balaraman,dragoni,guerini,magnolini,piccioni}@fbk.eu
[2] University of Trento, Trento, Italy
[3] AdeptMind Scholar, Toronto, Canada

Abstract. We present a conversational system that aims at calculating the amount of consumed carbohydrates in a meal by diabetic patients. Through a chat input, users can freely describe foods, which are first semantically interpreted and then matched against a nutritionist database for the final calculation of carbohydrates. Specific issues that have been addressed include: large-scale food recognition in Italian, without any restriction; interpretation of fuzzy quantities in relation to food (e.g. a portion of, a dish of, etc.); exploitation of dialogue strategies to revise system mis-interpretations and failures. CH1 integrates innovative neural approaches to language interpretation with rule-based approaches for ontology reasoning. In the paper we provide both experimental evaluations for the main components of the system, as well as qualitative user tests.

Keywords: Conversational agents · Utterance interpretation
Neural models

1 Introduction

There is now a high expectation for a new generation of conversational systems that are able to naturally interact and assist humans in a number of scenarios, including virtual coaches, personal assistants and automatic help desks. However, replicating human conversation abilities requires technological progresses which are still challenging. Recent research in this area addresses challenges that include the realization of full end-to-end approaches (e.g. [3]), the capacity to incorporate structured knowledge sources into neural architectures [7], the use of zero-shot learning techniques to mitigate effort of domain portability [4,14], and the use of transfer learning to exploit general knowledge for slot-filling approaches [2]. This paper investigates the application of state-of-art technologies to a concrete task-oriented conversational scenario, and evaluate their impact. We restrict our attention to scalable and portable approaches for the interpretation of textual utterances.

C. Ghidini et al. (Eds.): AI*IA 2018, LNAI 11298, pp. 110–122, 2018.
https://doi.org/10.1007/978-3-030-03840-3_9

The application scenario is provided by CH1, a conversational system that aims at calculating the amount of carbohydrates consumed in a meal by diabetic patients. Through a chat input, users can freely describe foods and the amount eaten for each of them. Both foods and quantities are first semantically interpreted and then matched against a nutritionist database for the final calculation of carbohydrates. An example of such interactions is provided in Table 1.

Table 1. An example of CH1 conversation.

CH1:	Cosa hai mangiato nel tuo ultimo pasto? (What did you eat in your last meal?)
USER:	Canederli in brodo (Soup with canederli)
CH1:	Hai mangiato: canederli in brodo. Consulto ora il database (You have eaten: soup with canederli. I am now consulting the database)
CH1:	Non conosco i valori nutrizionali di canederli in brodo. Quale dei seguenti cibi é il piú simile: canederli con pancetta, tortellini in brodo; canederli? (I do not know the nutrition values for soup with canederli. Which of the following foods are more similar: canederli with bacon; soup with tortellini; canederli?)
USER:	Canederli (Canederli)
CH1:	Quanti grammi di canederli hai mangiato? (How many grams of canederli did you eat?)
USER:	150
CH1:	Con il tuo pasto compósto da 150 g di canederli hai assunto un totale di 63.97 grammi di carboidrati (With your meal of 150 g of canederli you have assumed a total of 63.97 grams of carbohydrates)

CH1 aims at substituting the current procedure used by the patients, who, through their mobile phone, have to send a message with their meals to a medical doctor, who, in turn, has to calculate the amount of consumed carbohydrates.

2   The CH1 Conversational Agent

CH1 is a conversational agent based on OpenDial [5], an open-source, modular platform for building spoken dialogue systems implemented in Java. CH1 is based on four main components (see Fig. 1): (i) *utterance interpretation*, based on a neural model for entity recognition; (ii) a *dialogue manager*, which defines the behaviour of the system in response to certain user actions; (iii) an *ontology mapping* component, which provides a mapping among the entities expressed in the user utterance and the concepts of the domain Knowledge Base (e.g. food,

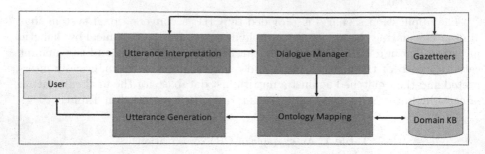

Fig. 1. CH1 architecture.

quantities, as well as the amount of carbohydrates for unit of food); and (iv) a component for *utterance generation*, based on templates.

Such components communicate among each others by accessing the content of four OpenDial primitives: the user's utterance, the user's action, the system's action, and the system's utterance. We now introduce the four components.

2.1   Utterance Interpretation

The Utterance Interpretation module is at the core of CH1, as it performs the semantic interpretation of user's utterance, recognizing entities and relations and allowing users to interact with CH1 in a natural way. The module casts utterance understanding as a sequence labelling task, identifying sequences of tokens corresponding to the following five domain entity types:

- *MEAL*: indicates the occasion of meal, like *breakfast, lunch*, etc.
- *FOOD*: indicates the name of a single food, like *smoked salmon, spaghetti carbonara*, etc.
- *QUANTITY*: indicates a quantity associated to a food, like *a dish of, 80 grams of*, etc.
- *DRESSING*: indicates the use of a dressing served for the food, like *olive oil, vinaigrette*, etc.
- *COURSE*: indicated the course of a dish, like *main course, appetizer*, etc.

Entity names are labeled using the IOB (Inside-Outside-Beginning) notation [12], as shown in Table 2. Lack of punctuation, improper use of grammars, lack of capitalization for proper names, make this task even more challenging. On top of this, in many cases quantities are not present for each food, and, even when they are present they tend to be described in a fuzzy way (e.g. *"un piatto abbondante di"*) that need a proper mapping onto precise weights.

Details about the neural model at the core of the CH1 approach, and about the gazetteers used in our experiments, are provided, respectively, in Sects. 3 and 5.1.

Table 2. IOB annotation of entities in a user utterance.

Pasta	al	pomodoro	e	grana	,	una	fetta	di	formaggio
B-FOOD	I-FOOD	I-FOOD	O	B-DRESS	O	B-QUANT	I-QUANT	O	B-FOOD

2.2 Dialogue Manager

CH1 is a task-oriented, mixed initiative, dialogue system. At each turn, the dialogue manager selects the appropriate dialogue state among those defined in the dialogue flow (see Fig. 4). The core user intent is to provide food and quantities for which CH1 has to calculate carbohydrates. Additional intents allow the user both to refine quantities, and to select candidate foods provided by the mapping algorithm. Intent recognition is based on pre-defined templates, a rather effective approach given the limited number of intents required by the CH1 dialogue. The coverage of the templates is increased by using techniques based on synthetic generation.

More details about the dialogue manager, as well as a complete dialogue schema, are provided in Sect. 4.

2.3 Ontology Mapping and Domain KB

Once foods and quantities have been recognized, they need to be mapped onto a food ontology for computing carbohydrates. Here, we briefly present the knowledge component underlying CH1, providing an overview of the HeLiS ontology. More details about the resolution of the mapping through dialogue are provided in Sect. 4.2.

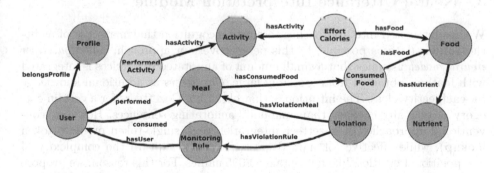

Fig. 2. The HeLiS ontology.

The main concepts of the HeLiS ontology are shown in Fig. 2 and are organized in four main branches: (i) Food, (ii) Activity, (iii) Monitoring, and (iv) User. Further details about the ontology are provided in [1] and online.[1]

---

[1] http://w3id.org/helis.

The Food branch is responsible for modeling the instances macro-grouped under the BasicFood and Recipe concepts. The former includes also Nutrients' information (carbohydrates, lipids, proteins, minerals, and vitamins). The latter is used to describe complex dishes composition (such as Lasagna) through a list of ⟨BasicFood, Quantity⟩ pairs. The *User* branch contains the conceptualization of user specific information. The goal is to enables the representation of users' events that might be relevant for the dialogue, for instance to record amounts of food consumed. Users' events are represented via the Meal and Consumed-Food concepts. The last concept is a reified relation, enriched with attributes for representing the fact that a user consumed a specific quantity of a food.

The HeLiS ontology has been integrated within CH1 with the aim of going beyond the mere access to the resource for informative purposes. So while CH1 can query the HeLiS ontology with ⟨Food, Quantity⟩ pairs to obtain the corresponding amount of carbohydrates, the User branch is also updated with the current food and quantities for future interactions (e.g. the mapping of a fuzzy quantity to a specific weight).

2.4   Utterance Generation

The utterance generation component is activated by the dialogue manager in order to compose textual messages to be presented to the user. The component makes use of a number of textual templates (instantiated using information maintained in the dialogue states) in order to construct appropriate system's utterances, e.g. instructions about how to proceed, answers to user clarification questions, greetings, etc.

3   Neural Utterance Interpretation Module

We are interested into approaches to entity recognition that make use of as little training data as possible. In this perspective, our approach, called *gazetteer neural model*, assumes that a small amount of annotated utterances is integrated with features obtained from, possibly large, *Gazetteers* as additional knowledge for each entity class. The intuition is that obtaining Gazetteers for a certain category is typically cheaper than manually annotating sentences. However, conventional approaches of gazetteer integration (e.g. single-token or multi-token lookup), while effective for named entities, do not capture the complexity of compositional entities, like for instance FOOD names. For this reason, we propose to integrate two neural models: the first model considers entities in their context of occurrence, and it is trained on traditional annotated data; the second model considers entities out of their context, and it is trained on gazetteers. Then, the second model, that we call NN_g, is used as a feature by the first model, and combined into a CRF layer (see Fig. 3). More specifically, the first model is based on the NeuroNLP2 model presented in [6], while the second model is based on the NN_g classifier presented in [4]. We call the combined approach NeuroNLP2 + NN_g.

The core of the NN_g classifier is a 3-layer bidirectional LSTM, with 128 units per layer and with a single dropout layer (with a dropout probability of 0.5), between the third BLSTM and the output layer (a softmax layer). We used the NN_g last layer BLSTM output as a feature to be integrated in the NeuroNLP2 system through a fully connected layer, in order for the main model to better learn how to use it. For NN_g, a fully connected layer with 32 nodes and a ReLU has been substituted to the original SoftMax layer (in red in Fig. 3).

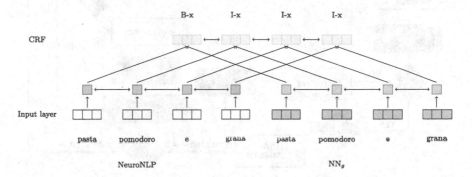

Fig. 3. NeuroNLP combined with NN_g.

4   Dialogue Structure

At every interaction turn the system tries to understand the user utterance, extracting all the information directly related to the question and also any contextual information that can be used in subsequent steps of the dialogue or to profile the user. For example, at the beginning of the conversation CH1 asks to the user *"What did you eat in your latest meal?"* The expected answer involves foods (the information needed to complete the task), but, as described in Sect. 3, CH1 extracts also quantities, meals, dressings and courses (that are additional information usable to profile the user or to have a more precise result).

Considering the schema in Fig. 4, we can see that when the user answers the first question (*"What did you eat in your latest meal?"*) CH1 performs several operations, including resolving *fuzzy quantities* and *food mismatches*

4.1   Resolving Fuzzy Quantities

Since the amount of carbohydrates intake defines the quantity of insulin that a diabetic user has to inject, a precise computation of the weight of each food eaten by the user is needed. Analyzing the DPD dataset (see Sect. 5.1), we found that in many cases users do not provide quantities for food, or, even when they are provided, they tend to be represented as fuzzy concepts (e.g. *"un piatto abbondante di"*). In order to properly query HeLiS, we need to map such quantities

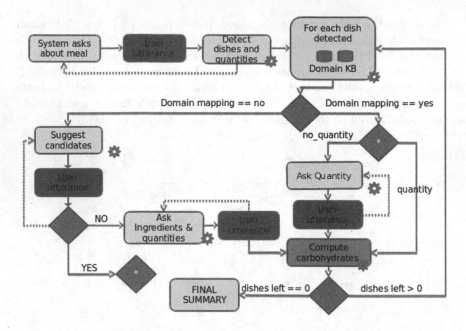

Fig. 4. The overall structure of the CH1 dialogue.

onto precise weights. One viable solution could be to map fuzzy quantities onto prototypical weights; still, in our scenario we need to map them to the meaning intended by each user (i.e. different users can have a different concept of *"piatto abbondante"*). So, whenever a fuzzy quantity is detected the system asks for the grams of that quantity. In order to enhance user experience, if the fuzzy quantity was already encountered in previous dialogues with that user, the system asks for the confirmation of the mapping that was already provided. In Table 3 we provide a dialogue excerpt on how CH1 deals with fuzzy quantities in case they where already used.

4.2   Resolving Food Mismatches

Food is a crucial type of entity to complete the CH1 task. However, recognizing food expressions in user's utterances and having a knowledge base entry for that

Table 3. A dialogue excerpt of CH1 handling a fuzzy quantity.

CH1:	Cosa hai mangiato nel tuo ultimo pasto?
USER:	un piatto abbondante di pasta al pomodoro
CH1:	Hai mangiato: pasta al pomodoro - un piatto abbondante. Consulto ora il database
CH1:	Posso considerare che 'piatto abbondante' corrisponda a 150 grammi, come al solito?
USER:	Sì
...	

food is not always possible. In fact, although the entity recognition algorithm can recognize a large variety of food expressions, these entities often are not represented in the food KB (only 30% of the food entities of the DPD dataset are present in the HeLiS ontology). As an example of the mapping problem, assuming that the entity *"pasta al ragù"* has been recognized by the Neural Semantic Interpretation, and that HeLiS contains the entity *"pasta alla bolognese"*, CH1 can not directly map the two entities and needs to find the best mapping for *"pasta al ragù"*.

This task is far from being trivial. We decided to use an approach based on semantic similarity, which selects the five most similar *HeLiS entities* to the *food entity* recognized. CH1 then uses dialogue templates to ask the user if some of them is similar to the *food entity* recognized. Although this strategy is reasonable in most of the cases, there are specific situations in which this assumption is not the best solution. For example the *vegetarian* version of a meat-based dish is semantically similar to it (e.g. *"pasta alla carbonara"* and *"pasta alla carbonara vegetariana"*), but from the nutrition point of view they differ significantly. To extract the most similar entities we calculate the average vector (centroid) of the vectors of the tokens that compose the *food entity*; in the same way we calculate the vectors of all the entities in HeLiS and we select the five with the higher cosine similarity with the *food entity* vector. Some preliminary experiments shows that using Glove [11] as word embedding performs slightly better than Word2Vec [8].

5   Experiments and Evaluation

In this Section we report and discuss the results obtained evaluating the CH1 utterance interpretation component on the DPD dataset.

5.1   Dataset

DPD – Diabetic Patients Diary[2] – is a data set in Italian, made of diary entries written by diabetic patients. Each day the patient has to annotate what s/he eats in order to keep track of his/her dietary behavior. In this dataset, all entities of type FOOD, MEAL, QUANTITY, DRESSING and COURSE have been manually annotated by two annotators (inter-annotator agreement is 96.75 dice coefficient). The dataset contains 1043 sentences, 4082 entities and 8878 tokens. Sentences in the dataset have a telegraphic style, e.g. the main verb is often missing, substantially resulting in a list of foods, often enriched with dressing and with quantities. Table 4 reports counts about the five entity types annotated in DPD.

Gazetteers – Independently from the DPD dataset, we created one gazetteers for each of the five entity types. In Table 5 we describe each gazetteer, reporting its size in terms of number of entity names, the average length of the names (in number of tokens), plus the length variability of such names (standard deviation,

---

[2] The DPD corpus is freely distributed under a CC-BY license at http://hlt-nlp.fbk.eu/technologies/dpd.

Table 4. Count of entities in DPD according to the entity type.

	#entities	#unique
MEAL	14	8
FOOD	3254	974
QUANTITY	741	164
DRESSING	68	21
COURSE	5	5

SD). We also report additional metrics that try to grasp the complexity of entity name in the gazetteer: (i) the normalized type-token ratio (TTR), as a rough measure of how much lexical diversity there is for the nominal entities in a gazetteer, see [13]; (ii) the ratio of $type_1$ tokens, i.e. tokens that can appear in the first position of an entity name but also in other positions, and $type_2$ tokens, i.e. tokens appearing at the end and elsewhere; (iii) the ratio of entities that contain another entity as sub-part of their name. With these measures we are able to partially quantify how difficult it is to recognize the length of an entity, how difficult is to individuate the boundaries of an entity (ratio of $type_1$ and $type_2$ tokens), how much compositionality there is starting from basic entities (i.e. how many new entities can be potentially constructed by adding new tokens).

Table 5. Description of the gazetteers used in the experiments.

Gazetteer	#entities	#tokens	length ± SD	TTR	type1 (%)	type2 (%)	sub-entity (%)
MEAL	14	17	1.21 ± 0.41	-	14.29	07.14	07.14
FOOD	23472	83264	3.55 ± 1.87	0.75	17.22	22.97	11.27
QUANTITY	173	230	1.33 ± 0.47	0.69	06.20	10.85	10.98
DRESSING	49	104	2.12 ± 1.32	0.49	04.00	24.00	28.57
COURSE	10	13	1.30 ± 0.45	-	11.11	33.33	20.00

5.2 Experiments

In order to assess the performances of our approach on entity recognition (i.e. the gazetteer neural model described in Sect. 3), we compared it with state of art approaches, which are listed in this section.

CRF + Multi-token Gazetteer. Conditional Random Field (CRF) has been proven to be among the more effective learning algorithm for sequence labelling. We use the following features of the current token in a sequence: (i) lowercase representation of the token, (ii) 3-characters prefix of the token, (iii) 3-characters suffix of the token, (iv) if the token is a digit, (v) if the token contains any digit, (vi) if the token is a punctuation character, (vii) a gazetteer specific label (if the consecutive tokens are present in two or more gazetteers, a new label is created in order to represent the membership of those gazetteers combined). If the token is not present in any of the gazetteers, a label representing the total exclusion is used, (viii) the *id* of the embedding cluster that contains the token embedding (the algorithm used is mini-batch K-mean searching for 500 clusters, the embeddings are created from an Italian Wikipedia dump with the Glove model).

NeuroNLP2 No Gazetteers. This is the last Pytorch [10] implementation of the Ma and Hovy [6] system.[3] NeuroNLP2 reaches near state of the art performance on named entity recognition for English. In this configuration, no gazetteer has been used.

NeuroNLP2 + Single-token Gazetteer. This is NeuroNLP2 with additional features considering the presence of a single token in the gazetteer, see for example [9]. To do that, we extract the gazetteer vocabulary and we provide a Boolean value to every token in the sentence, which indicates the presence or absence of the token in the gazetteer. If the number of gazetteers in the domain is n, corresponding to the number of entity classes, a single token takes a vector of n-dimensions: if the vocabularies of the different gazetteers do not overlap this is one-hot vector, otherwise we can have multiple positive dimensions.

NeuroNLP2 + Multi-token Gazetteer. The second approach uses the same feature space as the single-token method, but instead of checking the presence of a single token in the gazetteer, it looks for the longest entity name in the gazetteer contained in the sentence. If we consider the example in Table 2, "I would like to order a salami pizza and two mozzarella cheese sandwiches", and assume a gazetteer for the class FOOD composed by two entries: *mozzarella pizza, salami sandwiches*, with the multi-token approach none of the tokens would have the gazetteer feature equal to true, while with the single token approach both *mozzarella pizza, salami* and *sandwiches* would have the presence set to true. This technique provides more consistent usage of gazetteers, especially in case of noisy entity names, although a possible drawback is a lack of generalization.

NeuroNLP2 + NN$_g$ Gazetteer. This is our approach, based on the NN$_g$ gazetteer model integrated in NeuroNLP2, and described in Sect. 3.

In Table 6 we report the results on the DPD test-set after training the various approaches using the train and dev partitions of the dataset. The experiments are conducted using a 10-fold cross validation setup and the averaged results are reported for each method. Additionally, in Table 7 we report the intersection among entities in the various folds (i.e. how many entities in the test set can be found in the training set or the gazetteers). These percentages are a rough indicator of (i) how a perfect match baseline using gazetteers can perform, and (ii) how much the NeuroNLP2 system can take advantage of already seen entities during training phase.

---

[3] https://github.com/XuezheMax/NeuroNLP2.

Table 6. Results on DPD entity recognition. NN_g trained only to recognize FOOD labels. NeuroNLP2 + token and multi-token use gazetteer only for FOOD entities.

Approach	Accuracy	Precision	Recall	F-1
CRF + multi-token gazetteer	92.99	89.18	88.73	88.95
NeuroNLP2 no gazetteer	93.27	88.83	89.90	89.35
NeuroNLP2 + single token gazetteer	93.30	88.47	89.69	89.07
NeuroNLP2 + multi-token gazetteer	93.53	89.44	89.91	89.67
NeuroNLP2 + NN_g gazetteer	93.49	**89.68**	**89.94**	**89.80**

Table 7. Entities overlap between various sets averaged across 10-fold setup. The percentage refers to the count of entities in the test data set.

	Total Overlap		Unique overlap	
	Test ∩ Train	Test ∩ Gaz	Test ∩ Train	Test ∩ Gaz
All Entity Types	79.90	47.88	66.75	36.13
FOOD Entity Only	78.39	51.48	64.88	38.22

Interestingly, while NeuroNLP2 is able to outperform the CRF approach, adding the NN_g output to the former boosts its performances, indicating that the ability to represent the compositional nature of food names is fundamental for a better recognition and segmentation of user's input.

Finally, Table 8 shows the per category results of the NN_g approach, showing high robustness on the FOOD category.

Table 8. Results on DPD for NeuroNLP2+NN_g over the five categories.

Entities	Precision	Recall	F-1
MEAL	33.33	25.92	28.52
FOOD	88.85	89.97	89.40
QUANTITY	94.50	94.58	94.46
DRESSING	85.92	61.58	70.68
COURSE	00.00	00.00	00.00

6   Qualitative Evaluation

We also run a qualitative analysis of CH1 interactions with human users to get a broader understanding of its functioning and of the perceived quality of experience. This analysis was used both for improving the current version of the system and to get better insights on how to further develop it. The qualitative evaluation has been performed in two ways:

Overall evaluation, using a questionnaire administered to 6 users (volunteers that used CH1 for some interactions) with the following questions:

- Which are the most useful aspects of CH1?
- Which are the less useful/intuitive aspects of CH1?
- Which aspects you wish were present in CH1?

In-line evaluation, giving to another group of 6 volunteers the possibility to interact with CH1 and leave in-line comments (using a specific tag #COMMENT) during the interaction so to signal the *specific* point of interest (either something that was really appreciated or that was problematic according to the user).

With regard to the positive aspects, the answers pointed to *easiness and clarity* of the agent, *speed* (in obtaining the desired information), *precision* in the provided answers, the ability to remember previous foods/quantities provided by the user. The possibility to use fuzzy quantities when a precise weight was not known was also appreciated. Regarding problems that were signaled we found a consistent issue in coverage of the DB (3 out of 6 in the questionnaire and several in-line comments), and in general some suggestion to improve interaction. Among these we find: (i) the final y/n question should include also the possibility to directly input additional food, (ii) having an easier recovery strategy if a food is not correctly recognized, (iii) having a 'same food' strategy to save interaction turns (e.g. *"risotto ai funghi"* can be mapped to *"risotto coi funghi"* without asking for confirmation) (iv) the ability to handle more fuzzy quantities.

In general this qualitative analysis clearly indicates that the overall structure of the dialogue and the interaction is appreciated and that further work should include refinement of the resources (Helis and quantities DB).

7 Conclusion and Future Work

We described CH1, a conversational system that aims at calculating the amount of consumed carbohydrates in a meal by diabetic patients. Through a chat input, users can freely describe foods, which are first semantically interpreted and then matched against a nutritionist database for the final calculation of carbohydrates.

Experimental results on a corpus of real users utterances show that the neural approach with the use of gazetteers outperforms simpler models. More specifically, we showed that nominal entities (food names in the DPD corpus) recognition based on gazetteer features extracted by the NN_g classifier are more significant that conventional features based on presence-absence of tokens. As for future work, we plan to carry on deeper investigation and experiments on the entity mapping issue, trying to exploit linguistic features of entity names (e.g. the semantic head of a nominal phrase).

Acknowledgments. This work has been partially supported by the AdeptMind scholarship. The authors thank the anonymous reviewers for their help and suggestions.

References

1. Bailoni, T., Dragoni, M., Eccher, C., Guerini, M., Maimone, R.: Healthy lifestyle support: the PerKApp ontology. In: Dragoni, M., Poveda-Villalón, M., Jimenez-Ruiz, E. (eds.) OWLED/ORE -2016. LNCS, vol. 10161, pp. 15–23. Springer, Cham (2017). https://doi.org/10.1007/978-3-319-54627-8_2
2. Bapna, A., Tur, G., Hakkani-Tur, D., Heck, L.: Towards zero shot frame semantic parsing for domain scaling. In: Interspeech 2017 (2017)
3. Bordes, A., Boureau, Y.L., Weston, J.: Learning end-to-end goal-oriented dialog. arXiv preprint arXiv:1605.07683 (2016)
4. Guerini, M., Magnolini, S., Balaraman, V., Magnini, B.: Toward zero-shot entity recognition in task-oriented conversational agents. In: Proceedings of the 19th Annual SIGdial Meeting on Discourse and Dialogue, pp. 317–326. Association for Computational Linguistics (2018). http://aclweb.org/anthology/W18-5036
5. Lison, P., Kennington, C.: OpenDial: a toolkit for developing spoken dialogue systems with probabilistic rules. In: Proceedings of ACL 2016 System Demonstrations, pp. 67–72 (2016)
6. Ma, X., Hovy, E.: End-to-end sequence labeling via bi-directional LSTM-CNNs-CRF. In: Proceedings of the 54th Annual Meeting of the Association for Computational Linguistics (Volume 1: Long Papers), vol. 1, pp. 1064–1074 (2016)
7. Madotto, A., Wu, C.S., Fung, P.: Mem2Seq: effectively incorporating knowledge bases into end-to-end task-oriented dialog systems. arXiv preprint arXiv:1804.08217 (2018)
8. Mikolov, T., Sutskever, I., Chen, K., Corrado, G.S., Dean, J.: Distributed representations of words and phrases and their compositionality. In: Advances in Neural Information Processing Systems, pp. 3111–3119 (2013)
9. Park, G., Lee, H.G., Kim, H.: Named entity recognition model based on neural networks using parts of speech probability and gazetteer features. Adv. Sci. Lett. 23(10), 9530–9533 (2017)
10. Paszke, A., et al.: Automatic differentiation in PyTorch (2017)
11. Pennington, J., Socher, R., Manning, C.: Glove: global vectors for word representation. In: Proceedings of the 2014 Conference on Empirical Methods in Natural Language Processing (EMNLP), pp. 1532–1543 (2014)
12. Ramshaw, L.A., Marcus, M.P.: Text chunking using transformation-based learning. CoRR cmp-lg/9505040 (1995). http://arxiv.org/abs/cmp-lg/9505040
13. Richards, B.: Type/token ratios: what do they really tell us? J. Child Lang. 14(2), 201–209 (1987)
14. Xie, S., Wang, S., Yu, P.S.: Active zero-shot learning. In: Proceedings of the 25th ACM International on Conference on Information and Knowledge Management, CIKM 2016, pp. 1889–1892. ACM, New York (2016). https://doi.org/10.1145/2983323.2983866

Analyzing Microblogging Posts for Tracking Collective Emotional Trajectories

Corrado Loglisci[✉], Giuseppina Andresini, Angelo Impedovo,
and Donato Malerba

Department of Computer Science, University of Bari, Bari, Italy
{corrado.loglisci,giuseppina.andresini,
angelo.impedovo,donato.malerba}@uniba.it

Abstract. The technologies of communication, such as forums and instant messaging, available in the social media platforms open to the possibility to convey and express emotions and feelings, besides to facilitate interaction. Emotions and social relationships are often connected, indeed, emotions and feelings can make the users favorable or reluctant to socialize, as well, experiences of socialization can influence the behaviors. Being personal, emotions and feelings can be crucial in the dynamics of social communities, perhaps more than other elements, such as events and multimedia items, because the individuals tend to interact with the users with who have particular affinity or with who share sensations. In this paper we introduce the problem of tracking users who share emotional behavior with other users. The proposed method relies on a cyberspace based on emotional words extracted from social media posts. It builds emotional trajectories as sequences of points of the cyberspace characterized by highly similar emotions. We show the viability of the method on Twitter data and provide a quantitative evaluation and qualitative considerations.

1 Introduction

The widespread of social media has been one the main contributors to stimulate the formation of new forms of collectives. Individuals overcome the diffidence to establish face-to-face relationships with new modalities of interaction based on online boards, forums and chats. The communication language becomes essentially textual, but this does not obstacle the individuals to convey typical verbal expressions, feelings and emotions. Interactions and emotions are therefore interrelated and inherently variable. The emotional state of an individual can change because of the interaction with others, as well as personal sensations and experiences can limit the use of social media platforms and can even change the relationships with users with who there is already interaction. Relationships and emotions can be also co-active [7], in the sense that, at the same time, individuals can have affinity with someone and aversion with some others. Thus,

© Springer Nature Switzerland AG 2018
C. Ghidini et al. (Eds.): AI*IA 2018, LNAI 11298, pp. 123–135, 2018.
https://doi.org/10.1007/978-3-030-03840-3_10

it emerges that the study of the emotions and feelings can play a relevant role in the dynamics of the social communities, especially because, being personal and intimate, emotional affinities can guide the individuals in the choice of the users with who socialize and communities to follow. Technologies able to carry on this study can turn out to be useful in the development of online communities platforms, cyber-bullying monitoring systems and social media campaigns services.

In this paper, we introduce the problem of following the evolution of the emotions manifested by micro-blogging posts. However, studying the behavior of single individuals could not be particularly effective and not informative for the analysis of collectives, while it seems promising [6] to consider the collectives for first and then examine an individual in depth. Thus, we propose to track emotions expressed by the users over time and build collectives on the basis of similar emotions. To do that, we could group users with analogous emotional states, but this would disregard possible interactions, therefore, we consider the simplest form of interaction, that is, a pair of users. Thus, collectives are built by grouping pairs of users with similar changes of the emotional states. The analysis of the pairs may provide evidence of the existence of interactions, while the analysis of the pairwise changes may be evidence of the correlation between interactions and emotions.

The computational solution relies on a cyberspace in which the emotions of pair of users are moving around. The cyberspace is built by processing micro-blogging posts through natural language processing technologies. The emotional trajectories are determined as sequences of pairwise points of the cyberspace characterized by highly similar emotions. This perspective revises the idea of concrete objects (e.g., vehicles or pedestrians) that move in a physical space and form trajectories, which often are the subject of analysis of many studies in trajectory mining. We evaluate the viability of the method on Twitter messages in English and provide quantitative results and qualitative insights.

2   Basics

The notion of cyberspace follows the one of physical space, in which objects move around and produce sequences of geo-referenced positions. In this work, the cyberspace is structured in two levels, termed as *posting-space* and *feature-space*. The posting-space has three dimensions, two are associated to two main classes of emotions, *positive* emotions and *negative* emotions, respectively, while the third one corresponds to a discrete time axis. We denote as $p(u) : \langle (p_1, \tau_1), (p_2, \tau_2), \ldots, (p_m, \tau_m) \rangle$ a succession of points associated to the user u in the posting-space ($p_i \in \mathbf{R}^2$ is the emotional point at the time-instant τ_i of the user u). The posting-space describes only punctual information on the emotions, whilst we are interested in representing interactions and emotions. This is the reason why we introduce a level of cyberspace upon the posting-space. The feature-space has four dimensions, three dimensions are associated to three new features, while the fourth one correspond to interval-based time axis: each four-dimensional point refers to a pair of users observed in two consecutive time-instants. The three new features are specifically defined to capture the interactions and emotions of pairs of users and therefore describe the interaction of two users and emotions they express over two consecutive time-instants. In particular, a feature maps the points of two users u_r and u_s, observed at the time instants $\langle \tau_i, \tau_{i+1} \rangle$, into a numeric value z_l (formally $Fl|_{\langle \tau_i, \tau_{i+1} \rangle}(p(u_r), p(u_s)) \rightarrow z_l$). In the following, we report a description of the features:

- *Emotional Displacement.* This feature is introduced to describe the emotional variability of two users over time and, more precisely, denotes the quantity of emotional cyberspace covered by two users over the two time-instants $\langle \tau_i, \tau_{i+1} \rangle$. We determine it as the Euclidean distance computed on the two middle points that the users draw in two time-instants respectively (see Fig. 1(a)). The feature has values in the range $(0, \sqrt{2}]$. Intuitively, the larger the greater variation of the emotions of the pair, compared to the past.
- *Emotional Distance.* This feature is introduced to describe the emotional difference of two users u and v in the time-instants $\langle \tau_i, \tau_{i+1} \rangle$. We compute it as the distance between the two angles formed on the straight lines (each drawn on the two points of an user) and positive axis (see Fig. 1(b), Emotional Distance is θ_v-θ_u). The feature has vablues in the range $[0,90]$. Intuitively, the larger, the closer a user is to the positive (the other user is approaching the negative).
- *Emotional Ratio.* This feature is introduced to describe the divergence of two users and, more precisely, denotes the variation of the inter-distance over two time instants $\langle \tau_i, \tau_{i+1} \rangle$. We compute it as the ratio between the two inter-distances, that is, the Euclidean distance between the two points at the second time instant τ_{i+1}, divided by the Euclidean distance between the two points at the first time instant τ_i (see Fig. 1(c), Emotional Ratio δ_{i+1}/δ_i). The feature has values in the range $(0, +\infty)$. Intuitively, the larger the greater the divergence.

In the following, we introduce notions necessary to define the concept of emotional trajectory.

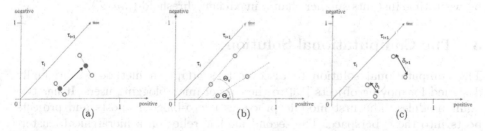

Fig. 1. Representation of the posting-space (positive, negative and time) and computation of the features.

A *Pair Set* $\mathcal{G} = \{(u_r, \mathcal{R}) \mid u_r \notin \mathcal{R}\}$ is a set of pairs that have one user in common (u_r).

Definition 1. *[Pair Cluster] Let $\mathcal{G}$ be a pair set, $[z_{l_{lower}}, z_{l_{upper}}]$ be a value range for the feature F_l, $\mathbb{1}(\cdot)$ be an indicator function which, when applied to F_l, returns true if the argument falls in $[z_{l_{lower}}, z_{l_{upper}}]$, false otherwise: $\mathcal{G}$ is a pair cluster iff there exist time-instants τ_i s.t. $\forall (u_r, u_s) \in \mathcal{G}$ the indicator function $\mathbb{1}(F_l|_{\langle \tau_i, \tau_{i+1}\rangle}(p(u_r), p(u_s)))$ returns true.*

Intuitively, a pair cluster (PC) comprises all the pairs for which the values of the feature F_l fall in the same range.

A pair cluster is refined by the concept of a *similarity-based pair cluster* (SPC) as follows:

Definition 2. *[Similarity-based Pair Cluster] Let $\mathcal{G}$ be a pair set, $[z_{l_{lower}}, z_{l_{upper}}]$ be a value range for the feature F_l, $\mathbb{1}(\cdot, \cdot)$ be an indicator function which, when applied to F_l, returns true if the two arguments fall in $[z_{l_{lower}}, z_{l_{upper}}]$, false otherwise: $\mathcal{G}$ is a similarity-based pair cluster iff there exists a sequence of time-instants $\langle \tau_i, \tau_{i+1}, \ldots, \tau_h, \tau_{h+1}\rangle$ s.t. $\forall (u_r, u_s), (u_r, u_t) \in \mathcal{G}$, the indicator function $\mathbb{1}\left(F_l|_{\langle \tau_j, \tau_{j+1}\rangle}(p(u_r), p(u_s)), F_l|_{\langle \tau_j, \tau_{j+1}\rangle}(p(u_r), p(u_t))\right)$ returns true ($\tau_j = \tau_i, \ldots, \tau_h$), for all the three features F_l.*

Intuitively, a similarity-based pair cluster (SPC) comprises all the pairs for which the values of the three features fall in three ranges respectively over a sequence of consecutive time-instants. It is worth of noting that a pair set cannot be involved in more than one SPC simultaneously, therefore the pairs of a SPC cannot have at the same time-instants different ranges of a feature, while a subset of the pair set can be involved in others SPCs since they can have different emotional behaviour with other users.

Definition 3. *[Emotional Trajectory] A collection $\mathcal{E}$ of similarity-based pair clusters is an emotional trajectory iff the relative pair sets are identical.*

An emotional trajectory (ET) is centered on one user (the user u_r of the pair set) and combines it with other users, resulting in a collective of pairs having similar emotional behaviors. Not all the ETs are interesting, but only those with a number of users greater than a minimum threshold ($minU$) and a distance between time-instants smaller than a maximum threshold ($maxT$).

3   The Computational Solution

The computational solution to discover ETs adapts a method we originally designed for moving objects [13] to the case of microblogging users. It has two main modules. The first module processes micro-blogging posts and projects posts into the cyberspace. The second module relies on a hierarchical clustering algorithm working on the points projected in the cyberspace. The clustering algorithm outputs similarity-based pair clusters, which are combined together to discover valid ETs.

3.1   Projection of Microblogging Posts into Cyberspace

As said, the cyberspace is the structured in two levels. The posting-space is used to account for the presence of positive and negative emotions in the micro-blogging posts. The distinction in positive and negative is not novel and has been encoded in the lexical database WordnetAffect [21], in which positive and negative are affective labels to which are associated *synsets* (sets of synonyms) respectively.

To recognize emotions two main alternatives can be found in the literature [11,20], *(i)* language processing approach and *(ii)* machine learning. The first approach relies on lexical resources and spots emotional key-words in the text, while the second approach asks for more, in that it needs a tagged corpus to derive a model, which is then used to classify an untagged corpus. The performance of such model strongly depends on the quality of the tagged corpus, indeed it should have well-formatted and correctly written sentences, which is a condition very·difficult to guarantee in the social textual corpora, such as micro-blogging posts, often characterized by typos and abbreviations. Moreover, the use of machine learning algorithms would force us to handle only qualitative-categorical information by overlooking that quantitative-numerical. Indeed, supervised classifiers address the emotion recognition by mapping a sentence into a categorical item, that is, a emotion label, which neglects the presence of multiple emotions in the same sentence or the will of an user to emphasize specific emotions (for instance, by repeating different emotional words). These are the reasons why we adopt a language processing approach.

In this work, we detect emotions by spotting emotional key-words associated to the *synsets* corresponding to the categories positive and negative in Word-netAffect. The mentions are then used to quantify the presence of emotions in the posts. More precisely, we consider the relative frequency of the positive (negative) emotions for an user and compute it as the number of the occurrences of the key-words out of the number of messages authored by the user and posted in a pre-determined time-interval. If a message has more emotional key-words, it is counted just as many. Procedurally, for each noun, verb, adverbs and adjective appearing in the text, we first search for the synsets in the database Word-netAffect by using the lemmatized form and pos-tagging annotation, then, we take the emotion category associated to the synset. In the case the word has more synsets, we consider the most frequent synset, according to the ordering computed in WordNet.

The first component of the proposal builds also the temporal dimension of the posting-space, in which the time-instants are equally spaced. In particular, it maps a time-interval (from the temporal dimension of the posts) into a time-instant of the posting-space. For instance, the time-intervals [Sept_9th_2012,Sept_11th_2012] and [Sept_12th_2012,Sept_14th_2012] are mapped into two consecutive time-instants τ_i and τ_{i+1}. This way, a point of the posting-space denotes an aggregation of the posts authored by an user and published in a time-interval.

Once the temporal dimension has been built and the relative frequencies of the emotions have been computed, the points of the posting-space are generated and mapped into the feature-space by using the features introduced in Sect. 2. The time-instants of the feature-space are not overlapped, that is, there are no points with a time-instant in common ($\langle \tau_i, \tau_{i+1} \rangle$ and $\langle \tau_{i+1}, \tau_{i+2} \rangle$).

3.2 Tracking Emotional Trajectories

The second module is in charge of discovering ETs from the fourth-dimensional points of the feature-space. It should be noted that those points depict the smallest form of interaction (two users) over the shortest time-interval (two consecutive time-instants). This gives us some hints on how designing the method for the second module. Starting from the consideration that a ET involves more than two users and that may cover more than two time-instants, the key idea is to consider the points of the feature-space as *building blocks* and build valid ETs by grouping the points and combining together these groups along the time axis. To do this, we first find out pair clusters (PCs), then generate similarity-based pair clusters (SPCs) and finally build the ETs from SPCs.

Clustering Pairs of Users. To find out PCs, we propose a hierarchical clustering algorithm that groups points based on the similarity of the three features. It does not rely on costly functions of distance, as instead many clustering algorithms do, but decides the membership of an element to a cluster by means of a test performed on the values of the features, which requires less computation. The algorithm resorts to the principle of decision trees, traditionally used for predictive tasks, and induces a tree-like structure from the points of the feature-space. In the following, we describe the structure of the tree, while later on we explain the procedure.

The nodes of the tree are associated to subsets of points: the points contained in the root have similarity with respect to one feature, while the points contained in the leaves have similarity with respect to all the three features. An internal node is characterized by *(i)* a feature, *(ii)* a pair cluster L (Definition 1), *(iii)* a threshold value c (whose range is included in the co-domain of the feature). Moreover, an internal node is connected to other nodes by means of two-way branches. A branch goes from a "starting node" to an "ending node" and encodes the clustering function through a test of the threshold value c against the values of the feature of the points contained in the starting node. More precisely, a branch guides a subset of the pairs of the PC of the starting node towards the ending node, that is, the set of the points that satisfy the test. Thus, the points of an ending node represent the pair of users (u_r, u_s) for which the indicator function $\mathbb{1}(\cdot, \cdot)$ is true for the associated feature. The feature we assign to a node is selected with a criteria based on the (dis)similarity of the points reaching the node. More precisely, we select the feature that maximizes the reduction between the dissimilarity computed on the points of the node and dissimilarity of two subsets, as formulated in the following

$$DissReduction = \sigma^2(L)_F - \frac{\sigma^2(left)_F * |left| + \sigma^2(right)_F * |right|}{|L|}, \qquad (1)$$

where $\sigma^2(L)_F$ ($\sigma^2(left)_F, \sigma^2(right)_F$) is the dissimilarity computed on the values of the feature F for the points of L ($left, right$), which is defined as $\sigma^2(L) = \sum_{i=1}^{n} p_i * (v_i - \bar{v})^2$, where, $v_i(i = 1 \ldots n)$ are the values of the feature F in the set L, p_i is the probability of observing v_i in L and $\bar{v}$ is the mean of the values $v_1, \ldots, v_n$.

Procedurally, the tree is built by means of an algorithm that recursively splits the initial set of the points into subsets of decreasing size. The algorithm starts from the root (which contains the complete set of the points) and, moving downwards, creates new (ending) nodes, to which assigns subsets of the points of the previously created (starting) node. The ending nodes of an execution of the algorithm become the starting nodes of next execution. More precisely, after having appended new nodes to the tree, the algorithm examines one node at a time. It builds two-by-two subsets of points for each feature, but takes only those that maximize the dissimilarity reduction $DissReduction$ (Eq. 1). The selected subsets are identified by a threshold value, which splits the values of the feature in two ranges. Thus, one subset covers one range and comprises the points whose values of the feature fall in that range (Definitions 1 and 2). The recursive procedure terminates when the initial dissimilarity (computed on the root) has been reduced for the features by a factor fixed by the user ($required\_reduction \in [0, 1]$) or when all the leaves have a number of pairs of users smaller than the square of $minU$. In the latter case, the tree might not have all the features.

Discovering Emotional Trajectories. To discover ETs we should use similarity-based pair clusters (Definition 3). These can be sought in the leaves of the tree before built. Indeed, by the effect of the dissimilarity reduction (Eq. 1), the features of the points of the leaves fall in the same value ranges, compared to the features of the points of the internal nodes. Procedurally, we search for SPCs in each leaf by gathering the three elements of an SPC, that is, (i) pair sets (pairwise users), (ii) ranges of the features $[z_{l_{lower}}, z_{l_{upper}}]$ and (iii) sequences of time-instants $\langle \tau_i, \tau_{i+1}, \ldots, \tau_h, \tau_{h+1} \rangle$. We first group the points of a leaf by pair sets (that is, pairs having an user in common) and then select the ranges of the features and sequences of the time-instants. The ranges are obtained from the tree by following the path from the leaf upwards the root and taking the list of the features and relative ranges. The sequences of time-instants are obtained by taking the time-instants associated to the points of the pair set. It is worth of noting that the SPCs are maximal, thus there are no two SPCs which are contained in each other and which contain the same points. The discovery of an ET is completed with an operation that takes SPCs, with the same pair set, from different leaves and sorts the corresponding time-instants by increasing order. Not all the SPCs are considered, but only those that satisfy the threshold of the minimum number of users $minU$ and maximal gap between consecutive time-instants $maxT$.

4 Experimental Evaluation

The proposed computational solution has been applied to microblogging posts of the Twitter platform. The original dataset concerns the 2012 U.S. Presidential Election and collects tweets posted between August 1, 2012 and November 6, 2012 that mention the words "Obama" and/or "Romney"[1]. We considered an excerpt that covers the period November 1, 2012 – November 5, 2012. For each tweet, we took the text of the tweet, time-stamp when the message was written and nickname of the author, then we removed URLs, emoticons and hash-tags, discarded messages that had only social tagging and no textual content. Finally, we kept the tweets that were longer than 35 chars. The working dataset has a daily average of almost 47000 tweets (standard deviation equal to 48461), comprises almost 236.000 tweets and almost 117.000 users.

Experiments were performed at the different widths of the time-intervals in which the posts were aggregated. Considering that the dataset covers a time-duration of 124 h we chose the values of 30, 60, 120, 240 min. The threshold $maxT$ was triple times the value of the time-interval width, therefore 90, 180, 360, 720 min, while the threshold $minU$ was manually tuned.

Empirical comparisons were conducted with the algorithm TRACLUS originally designed for clustering physical trajectories [9]. The algorithm partitions sequences of points into a set of line segments at characteristic points, and then, groups similar line segments in a dense region (cluster). Further details can be found in [9]. The specific parameters of TRACLUS were configured as indicated by the implementation available at the link http://dm.kaist.ac.kr/jaegil/# Publications. As to the comparison, we do not force TRACLUS to work on the feature-space, which would represent an environment different from its original one, but we applied it to the points of the posting-space, which, like those of the physical space, have two coordinates (positive and negative axis). The results of the two solutions were evaluated with a cluster-based validation measure, Silhouette index [19], which estimates the similarity of an object with respect to the objects of the same cluster compared to the objects of other clusters. In the case of the ETs, an object corresponds to an emotional trajectory, that is, points of a pair of users over the feature-space, while, for TRACLUS, an object corresponds to the points of an user over the posting-space. For the ETs, the Silhouette index was computed as average of the values on the SPCs used in the ETs.

---

[1] The corpora was downloaded on January 2018 from the link https://old.datahub. io/dataset/twitter-2012-presidential-election/resource/9bb14d78-9519-459a-9fad-e630e3e9a0a1.

In Fig. 2a, we report the plots representing the influence of the time-interval width on the number of ETs and on the number of users involved in the ETs. The first observation concerns the smaller set of ETs we have at lowest width (30 min). This can be mainly attributed to the sparseness of the occurrences of the emotional words and therefore to the sparseness of the points of the posting-space, which does not ease the construction of highly similar features. This may indicate an attitude of the users, in the context of the examined dataset, to convey emotions with a timing greater than half hour. On the contrary, we see a relatively larger number of ETs when the width is 60 and 120, which is reasonably due to a more dense distribution of emotional words, denoting a behaviour of the users to write posts with emotive content on a hourly/two hourly basis. This consideration is strengthened by the results of width 240 min, where the ETs decrease because the posting-space is not able to account for local frequencies and therefore the differences of the distribution of the positive and negative emotions are smaller, with the result to have less ETs but with more users, as compared to the previous cases. The values of the Silhouette index (Fig. 2b) confirm these considerations. We see highly cohesive ETs (high similarity of the features) especially at the width 60 and 120 min, while, there is a reduction at widest time-intervals, although the separability is generally good.

In Fig. 3a, we report the plots representing the influence of the minimum required number of users. The number of the ETs decrease when $minU$ grows because we require that a higher number of users keep similar features, which is more difficult to obtain compared to when $minU$ is smaller. It should be also noted that there are no substantial changes under the value of 200, while we see less ETs around to 400 users, which may be an indication of a phenomenon of concentration of the users around a set of fairly distinct emotional behaviours, each comprising at least 400 users.

The comparison with the clusters discovered by TRACLUS deserves some considerations. The number of ETs is smaller than the clusters by an algorithmic choice. The algorithm TRACLUS does not work on the temporal discontinuity, therefore, the clusters do not admit a temporal gap and cover uninterrupted sequences of time-instants, which generally are shorter than the sequences of the ETs. On the contrary, our proposal admits temporal discontinuity and generates sequences of time-instants that include temporal gaps and that, consequently, cover the temporal extent of the clusters of TRACLUS. The same reason explains the difference of the two algorithms, more evident in Fig. 3b. In terms of the Silhouette index values: although discovered in different time-intervals, the clusters of TRACLUS can have large similarity and consequently low separability, which leads to high variability of the emotional behaviors of the users and small significance of the results.

In Fig. 4, we report the plots representing the distribution of the ETs over the quartiles generated on the number of users, along the days of the dataset. We observe a quite uniform distribution of the ETs, especially in the first day, denoting the heterogeneity of the emotional behaviours of the users. On the contrary, on the last day, we observe the reduction of the ETs having few users and growth of the ETs having many users. This mirrors the concentration of emotional profiles in a few and well distinct trajectories.

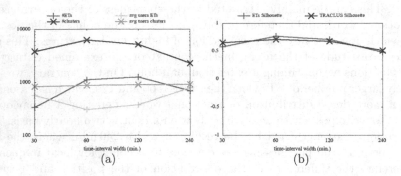

Fig. 2. Results produced at different values of the time-interval widths ($minU = 50$, $maxT = 3 *$ time-interval width). (a) Number of ETs compared to the number of clusters. (b) Evaluation of the ETs and clusters in terms of Silhouette index.

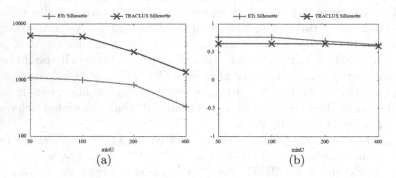

Fig. 3. Results produced at different values of minimum threshold of the users (width $= 60$, $maxT = 3 *$ time-interval width). (a) Number of ETs compared to the number of clusters. (b) Evaluation of the ETs and clusters in terms of Silhouette index.

5   Related Works

The studies of the emotions and of the interactions as reaction to the emotional factors find large literature in the Sociology and Psychology, but, with the spread of social media, they embrace also the interest of computer scientists [3,18]. A substantial research stream focuses on the correlation between emotions in micro-blogging and social events discussed on the microblogs [22], while the time-variability is an aspect of the emotions that only recently has attracted interests. The work proposed in [2] uses descriptive statistics for a temporal analysis aiming at quantifying the intensity of the basic emotions and recognizing

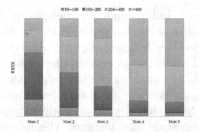

Fig. 4. Distribution of the ETs over the quartiles generated on the number of users.

different types of users. The study proposed in [6] investigates the reactivity of the users of instant messaging in comparison to persistent communication, in order to capture the real-time interactions between users. They provide an agent-based model of emotional interaction which works on the power-law distribution of the communication activity of the users. The agent recovers patterns based on user activity and emotions in chat rooms. However, this does not guarantee the identification of users with similar emotions, which is one of the purpose of the current work. In [5] the authors propose a simulation model used for predicting behaviours in online chat. They describe an agent-based simulation of the emotional interaction online of individuals by using automatic annotation of the affective content of exchanged messages. In [23] the method explores the correlation between emotion subjectivity and topics discussed in the posts. They first extract subjective corpora and then track the evolution of the emotions with respect to sub-topics. A similar problem is investigated in [24] through a time-aware topic modeling method. They combine two probabilistic models, one to represent the evolutions of the topics and the other one to represent the evolutions of the emotions in a state space. In [10], the authors use socialization measures to estimate the quantity the emotions expressed in the tweets posted from a geographic area, social connections and demographics. Similarly, in [8] there is a probabilistic model to capture semantically coherent regions where people post messages with similar topics. The model infers parameters used for an Expectation maximization algorithm finalized to discover sequences of such regions. The approach described in [1] represents one of the few studies on the evolution of the emotions on social media. It combines structured learning and lexicon acquisition to track the dynamics of sentiment-based lexicon on Twitter.

6   Conclusions

In this paper, we have introduced the novel problem to analyze the evolving nature of the emotions, which can be collocated at the intersection among sociology, psychology and computer science. We have proposed a method which sees emotions as collectors of individuals and which, consequently, attributes an evolving nature to such collectives. The collectives are not the representation of actual interactions happened in the social media, but indicate the presence of interactions on the basis of similar emotional behaviors. The proposed method first exploits a representational mechanism to elicit emotions from social media texts and then builds collectives by grouping individuals with similar evolutions. The application to the Twitter posts reveals the sensitivity of the method to the temporal basis used in the analysis: we have significant emotional behaviors when the analyze groups individuals on hourly basis rather than longer time-durations. Although we have considered two main categories of emotions, the use of a more fine-grained scale (for instance, the Ekman's model [4]) would require the adaptation of the posting-space only. Indeed, it should have a number of dimensions equal to the number of categories. No modification is instead necessary to the lexical resources (the database WordnetAffect has already a refined categorization of emotions), feature-space and algorithm of discovery of ETs. As future work, we intend to investigate different research directions: *(i)* extraction of emotion-based relationships between users [14,15], *(ii)* study of the temporal association/correlation among emotions [12,17] and *(iii)* detection of periodicities in the emotional states of the microblogging users [16].

Acknowledgments. This work fulfills the objectives the project "Computer-mediated collaboration in creative projects" (8GPS5R0) collocated in "Intervento cofinanziato dal Fondo di Sviluppo e Coesione 2007–2013 – APQ Ricerca Regione Puglia - Programma regionale a sostegno della specializzazione intelligente e della sostenibilita' sociale ed ambientale - FutureInResearch".

References

1. Castellucci, G., Croce, D., De Cao, D., Basili, R.: User mood tracking for opinion analysis on twitter. In: Adorni, G., Cagnoni, S., Gori, M., Maratea, M. (eds.) AI*IA 2016. LNCS (LNAI), vol. 10037, pp. 76–88. Springer, Cham (2016). https://doi.org/10.1007/978-3-319-49130-1_7
2. Chen, X., Sykora, M.D., Jackson, T.W., Elayan, S.: What about, mood swings: identifying depression on twitter with temporal measures of emotions. In: Companion Proceedings of the the Web Conference 2018, WWW 2018, pp. 1653–1660. International World Wide Web Conferences Steering Committee (2018)
3. Dini, L., Bittar, A.: Emotion analysis on twitter: the hidden challenge. In: Proceedings of the Tenth International Conference on Language Resources and Evaluation LREC 2016, Portorož, Slovenia, 23–28 May 2016 (2016)
4. Ekman, P.: Facial expression and emotion. **48**, 384–392 (1993)
5. Galik, M., Rank, S.: Modelling emotional trajectories of individuals in an online chat. In: Timm, I.J., Guttmann, C. (eds.) MATES 2012. LNCS (LNAI), vol. 7598, pp. 96–105. Springer, Heidelberg (2012). https://doi.org/10.1007/978-3-642-33690-4_10
6. Garas, A., Garcia, D., Skowron, M., Schweitzer, F.: Emotional persistence in online chatting communities. Sci. Rep. **2** (2012)
7. Keene, J.R., Lang, A.: Dynamic motivated processing of emotionaltrajectories in public service announcements. Commun. Monogr. **83**(4), 468–485 (2016)
8. Kim, Y., Han, J., Yuan, C.: TOPTRAC: topical trajectory pattern mining. In: Proceedings of the 21st ACM SIGKDD International Conference on Knowledge Discovery and Data Mining, Australia, pp. 587–596 (2015)

9. Lee, J., Han, J., Whang, K.: Trajectory clustering: a partition-and-group frame-work. In: Proceedings of the ACM SIGMOD International Conference on Management of Data, Beijing, China, 12–14 June 2007, pp. 593–604 (2007)
10. Lerman, K., Arora, M., Gallegos, L., Kumaraguru, P., Garcia, D.: Emotions, demographics and sociability in twitter interactions. In: Tenth International Conference on Web and Social Media, Cologne, Germany, pp. 201–210 (2016)
11. Liu, S., Lee, I.: Discovering sentiment sequence within email data through trajectory representation. Expert Syst. Appl. **99**, 1–11 (2018)
12. Loglisci, C.: Time-based discovery in biomedical literature: mining temporal links. IJDATS **5**(2), 148–174 (2013)
13. Loglisci, C.: Using interactions and dynamics for mining groups of moving objects from trajectory data. Int. J. Geogr. Inf. Sci. **32**(7), 1436–1468 (2018)
14. Loglisci, C., Ienco, D., Roche, M., Teisseire, M., Malerba, D.: Toward geographic information harvesting: extraction of spatial relational facts from web documents. In: Vreeken, J. (ed.) 12th IEEE International Conference on Data Mining Workshops, ICDM Workshops, Brussels, Belgium, 10 December 2012, pp. 789–796. IEEE Computer Society (2012)
15. Loglisci, C., Ienco, D., Roche, M., Teisseire, M., Malerba, D.: An unsupervised framework for topological relations extraction from geographic documents. In: Liddle, S.W., Schewe, K.-D., Tjoa, A.M., Zhou, X. (eds.) DEXA 2012. LNCS, vol. 7447, pp. 48–55. Springer, Heidelberg (2012). https://doi.org/10.1007/978-3-642-32597-7_5
16. Loglisci, C., Malerba, D.: Mining periodic changes in complex dynamic data through relational pattern discovery. In: Ceci, M., Loglisci, C., Manco, G., Masciari, E., Ras, Z.W. (eds.) NFMCP 2015. LNCS (LNAI), vol. 9607, pp. 76–90. Springer, Cham (2016). https://doi.org/10.1007/978-3-319-39315-5_6
17. Loglisci, C., Malerba, D.: Leveraging temporal autocorrelation of historical data for improving accuracy in network regression. Stat. Anal. Data Min. **10**(1), 40–53 (2017)
18. Roshanaei, M., Mishra, S.: Studying the attributes of users in twitter considering their emotional states. Soc. Netw. Anal. Min. **5**(1), 34;1–34;13 (2015)
19. Rousseeuw, P.J.: Silhouettes: a graphical aid to the interpretation and validation of cluster analysis. J. Comput. Appl. Math. **20**, 53–65 (1987)
20. Sailunaz, K., Dhaliwal, M., Rokne, J., Alhajj, R.: Emotion detection from text and speech: a survey. Soc. Netw. Anal. Min. **8**(1), 28 (2018)
21. Strapparava, C., Valitutti, A.: WordNet affect: an affective extension of WordNet. In: Proceedings of the Fourth International Conference on Language Resources and Evaluation, LREC 2004, Lisbon, Portugal, 26–28 May 2004. European Language Resources Association (2004)
22. Zhao, Y., Qin, B., Dong, Z., Chen, H., Liu, T.: What causes different emotion distributions of a hot event? A deep event-emotion analysis system on microblogs. In: Li, J., Ji, H., Zhao, D., Feng, Y. (eds.) NLPCC 2015. LNCS (LNAI), vol. 9362, pp. 453–464. Springer, Cham (2015). https://doi.org/10.1007/978-3-319-25207-0_42
23. Zhou, Q., Zhang, C.: Emotion evolutions of sub-topics about popular events on microblogs. Electron. Libr. **35**(4), 770–782 (2017)
24. Zhu, C., Zhu, H., Ge, Y., Chen, E., Liu, Q.: Tracking the evolution of social emotions: a time-aware topic modeling perspective. In: 2014 IEEE International Conference on Data Mining, ICDM 2014, Shenzhen, China, 14–17 December 2014, pp. 697–706 (2014)

Knowledge Engineering, Ontologies and the Semantic Web

On the Notion of Goal in Business Process Models

Greta Adamo[1,3(✉)], Stefano Borgo[2], Chiara Di Francescomarino[1],
Chiara Ghidini[1], and Nicola Guarino[2]

[1] FBK-IRST, Via Sommarive 18, 38050 Trento, Italy
{adamo,dfmchiara,ghidini}@fbk.eu
[2] ISTC-CNR Laboratory for Applied Ontology, Trento, Italy
{stefano.borgo,nicola.guarino}@cnr.it
[3] DIBRIS, University of Genova, via Dodecaneso 35, 16146 Genova, Italy

Abstract. Business process modelling languages allow to capture business processes by embracing different paradigms, emphasising different business process elements or characteristics and exploiting different graphical notations. In the literature, several definitions of business process have been proposed which define business processes in terms of (some of) their components and participants. While some of these components, for instance activities or data objects, have been analysed from different perspectives and play a relevant part in the graphical design of a business process model, other relevant components remain in a shadowy area as they do not typically appear in the graphical design of a business process model nor in the annexed documentation. Typical examples of these shadowy elements are business process *goals*. As a result, while it is extremely clear and well agreed that business processes realise a business goal, it is somehow more difficult to state exactly what this business goal is, or if this business goal is unique. In this paper, we carry on an analysis of business process goals tailored to propose a classification of different types of goals that pertain to a business process.

1 Introduction

Business process modelling (BPM) notations support the graphical representation of business process-relevant entities and their interplay by following different modelling paradigms (e.g., imperative vs declarative) at different levels of formality (descriptive vs precise formal semantics).

Despite the wide literature on execution semantics and on the comparison between graphical elements of different languages [13,16,18,26], and the numerous definitions of what a business process is (see e.g., [7,12,15,30]), the BPM community still lacks a robust ontological characterisation of the entities involved in process models[1] and, even more importantly, of the very notion of business process.

---

[1] We will interchangeably use the notions of "process model" and "process diagram".

© Springer Nature Switzerland AG 2018
C. Ghidini et al. (Eds.): AI*IA 2018, LNAI 11298, pp. 139–151, 2018.
https://doi.org/10.1007/978-3-030-03840-3_11

Acknowledging this lack of a robust ontological characterisation, some efforts have been devoted to fill this vacuum. For example, [24] provides an ontological analysis of BPMN activities and events. More recently, Adamo and colleagues [2] explored the "arrow" element in business process diagrams, illustrating the different types of ontological dependences between activities it can represent, besides the well known activity execution order within the process control flow. With the work described in [1] we have started enlarging the set of process models entities involved in the ontological investigation, in particular by including in the analysis not only the behavioural entities but also typical process participants such as data objects, actors, and so on.

In this paper we take a step forward by investigating a special notion in the definition of business processes, that is, the notion of (business) process *goal*. Differently from other notions typically mentioned in the definitions of business process, such as *activity*, *input/output*, or *organisation*, the notion of goal lacks a graphical representation in most of the popular business process modelling notations available to date.[2] As a consequence, the link between goals and business processes remains often implicit, with the risk of slipping into a paradoxical situation: on the one hand, it is said to be central to the definition of business processes; on the other hand, it is treated as external to the process itself, its reading and explanation. Thus, differently from what happens, e.g., in software development, where goal-oriented methodologies have heavily contributed to the development of the field of requirement engineering, goals rarely appear as first class citizens in business process modelling methodologies, while implicitly (and often heavily) influencing the way a process is designed.

The purpose of the paper is to tackle the above paradox by offering a first investigation of the notion (or the notions) of goal in the business process context, by providing a first classification of types of goals and their relationship with typical process participants that will hopefully contribute to the ontological foundations of BPM and to methodologies for business process design and modelling.

The paper is structured as follows. Section 2 presents a scenario that we use to ground the presentation. Section 3 reviews the definitions of business process and goal present in the literature, while Sect. 4 provides an analysis of the different types of goals and their relationship with typical process participants, which constitutes the main body of the paper. The paper ends with related works (Sect. 5) and concluding remarks (Sect. 6).

2   A Motivating Scenario

Consider the generation process of the fiscal code for a newborn in an Italian hospital. Regardless of *how* the process is carried out, we can say that the overall *primary* process goal, or the *reason to exist*, of this process is the generation and association of a unique fiscal code to each newborn (and no one else). Thus, the

---

[2] Exceptions can be found in some versions of EPC, the ARIS modelling language [25], and in the Guard-Stage Milestone (GSM) notation [14].

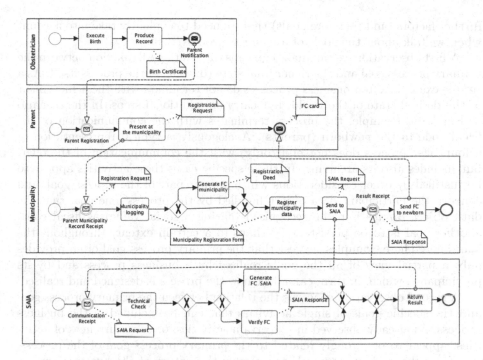

Fig. 1. Birth management process

process is characterised by a well defined input (the presence of a newborn in a hospital) and a well defined output (the state of the world in which this newborn is associated to a fiscal code).

The diagram of Fig. 1 shows the process model (represented in the BPMN 2.0 [21] notation) describing (a simplified[3] version of) the generation of a newborn's fiscal code in an Italian hospital. The process starts with the obstetrician producing a (required) birth certificate, which is given to the parents who present it at the municipality. The municipality registers the request, optionally generates a proposed fiscal code, and then sends the request (possibly with the tentative fiscal code) to the (national) SAIA information system managed by a specific branch of the Home Office. SAIA checks the request and generates or validates the fiscal code before returning it to the municipality which then generates the card for the newborn.

The diagram of Fig. 1 depicts a process that, given the expected initial state, leads to realise the goal expressed above. Indeed, it starts with a well defined input of an obstetrician delivering a newborn and describes how to bring about a state of the world in which this newborn is associated with a fiscal code. Nonetheless, the gap between the primary process goal and this (simplified, yet articulated) process representation is huge. Is the primary process goal depicted above the only motivation for the process to be organised in this way? Are there

---

[3] We omit here several variants such as the registration directly at the hospital.

further factors (and therefore goals) that we need to explicitly take into account when we talk about the goals of a business process?

A first observation we can make concerns the relation/distinction between the primary process goal and the richer final state (output) of the process itself. As a simple example, often business processes do not terminate with the achievement of the desired state of the world, but carry on additional steps. In the scenario of Fig. 1, for example, the process terminates with the communication of the fiscal code to the newborn (parents). Analogously, a typical representation of a loan offer process does not end (only) with the communication of the offer, but includes also its archiving. In these specific cases these activities appear to be justified by other considerations which are not part of the process goal, and concern the participant data object handled by the process: one goal that the data object *carries* is to be recognised (having a social value) as fiscal code, another goal is to be persistent (perhaps to a certain extent) throughout the loan offer. These examples suggest that the primary process goal often provides only a partial view of all the goals realised by a business process and by its participants, which, in turn, can affect how the process is designed and realised.

A second observation concerns the relation between the primary process goal and the specific goals of single activities that can be included in the business process. As already observed in [2] certain activities, or co-occurrences of activities, appear to be strongly related to the primary process goal of the process, and their change, e.g., removal, can modify the nature of the business process and even lead question whether it should still be considered the "same" process, while others seem to be merely related to how steps are performed. As an example the removal of any 'generate fiscal code' in our scenario would dramatically change the process meaning. On the contrary the removal of the 'generate fiscal code' at the municipality level alone would be considered just a process refactoring. Thus, the relationship between general (sub-)process goals and goals of specific activities, and similarly the relation/decomposition of goals in different sub-goals associated to different parts of the process are important levels at which goals need to be analysed in business processes if we want to understand why a process as a certain structure and not others.

Besides data objects, further participants whose specific goals can impact the way a process is designed are the organisational actors in which a process occur. Similarly to single activities, we note that the goals of some actors appear to be closer, and somehow fundamental, to the primary process goal, while others may be different, or even conflicting. These situations should be explicitly taken into account when designing a process. In our example, regardless of the way the process is designed we can intuitively understand that the goal of SAIA of maintaining a national registry is extremely relevant to the process at hand, while the goals of the obstetrician have a different reason and impact on it. Generally speaking, some specific (soft) goals are introduced in the process because of the participation of the obstetrician which clearly requires to take part in a very effective and speedy manner.

Yet another perspective is given by the viewpoint of process executions and of the technical environment as mentioned in the definition by Weske [30]. Indeed, one of the goals of this process is its repeatability over different newborns, the possibility of allowing multiple concurrent executions, the ability of being carried out by any specific municipality, and so on. These execution-oriented goals may have an impact on the way the process is designed affecting, e.g., qualities similar to the ones usually described by means of soft goals in requirement engineering.

As this short informal discussion shows, characterising the goals of a business process is not a trivial activity, due to the multitude of aspects and features that may be considered. In the rest of the paper we provide an analysis of some of the dimensions upon which goals may depend, focusing in particular on the business process control flow and its participants. A characterisation of the business process goals can then be used both in the process design phase (e.g., to take into account goals when modelling in a systematic manner) and in the process analysis phase (e.g., to explain processes discovered from data and, possibly refactor them in a way that is goal aware).

3 Background

This section aims to provide some background notions that are used throughout the paper. First, we provide a recap of well known definitions of what a business process is, then a brief introduction of the notion of goal and of its classifications is presented.

3.1 On the Definition of Business Process

Several definitions of business process have been proposed in literature. Davenport [7] sees a business process as *a structured, measured set of activities designed to produce a specific output for a particular customer or market. [. . .] A process is thus a specific ordering of work activities across time and space, with a beginning and an end, and clearly defined inputs and outputs.* Another definition is provided in Hamer and Champy [12] where business processes are *a collection of activities that takes one or more kinds of input and creates an output that is of value to the customer.* A similar perspective is taken by Johansson [15] who defines a business process as *a set of linked activities that take an input and transform it to create an output. Ideally, the transformation that occurs in the process should add value to the input.* Finally, a more modern and comprehensive definition is presented in Weske [30] where business processes are *a set of activities that are performed in coordination in an organizational and technical environment. These activities jointly realize a business goal. Each business process is enacted by a single organization, but it may interact with business processes performed by other organizations.*

By analysing these definitions we can divide them in two groups. The first three see a business process as composed by a set of (ordered) *activities* that aim to transform an *input* in an *output* which is of *value* for (or is desired by) a customer or market. The second, the more recent definition, replaces this notion of "output for someone" with the stronger notion of business *goal*, thus better empowering and taking into account also the goals of the organisation where the process is enacted together with the desires of the customer(s) and markets. Despite the wide acknowledgements of the importance of the definition of Weske, the BPM literature does not provide in depth explanations for what a process goal is, its connection with the process output, and with the several participants involved in the organisational and technical environment. Furthermore, no goal-oriented business process design and modelling methodologies are explicitly present in literature.

3.2   On the Definition of Goal and Its Classifications

In areas like multi-agent systems, philosophy, and psychology, goal is generally understood in terms of states that are desired by an agent. Rolf and Asada in [22] state that *the goal is a state of the world which satisfies some conditions posed by the agent (for whatever reason)*. There are different ways to understand this notion depending on whether the desired state is a setting of the world (a situation external to the agent) or is the agent's representation of it (e.g., an internal description like a list of values for state variables). The difference is that in the second case the goal indicates only the relevant features that the achieved state should satisfy. Practically, the goal corresponds to a class of world states.

The notion of goal plays also a crucial role in the area of planning systems. Indeed, as stated in [9] "planning concerns the computational deliberation capabilities that allow an artificial agent to reason about its actions, choose them, organize them purposefully, and act deliberately to achieve an objective" often referred to as a *goal*. Goals are therefore typically meant to be states or conditions that have to be reached by the system in order to solve a problem represented in term of initial condition (see e.g., [17]).

In software engineering, the notion of goal of a system has been investigated in the field of goal-based requirement engineering (GORE). Here goals are not defined in terms of states of the world but in terms of objectives: Van Lamsweerde defines a goal as *an objective the system under consideration should achieve. [...]*[29], while Anton states that goals are *high level objectives of the business, organization or system. They capture the reasons why a system is needed and guide decisions at various levels within the enterprise* [3]. Within this field several classifications of goals were developed, for instance the distinction between *functional* and *non-functional* goals [29]. The first denote the services that the system must achieve; the second refer to quality attributes and *constraints* of the system, such as security, usability, and reliability.[4] Another way to classify goals

---

[4] Functional and non-functional goals are linked with the notions of functional and non-functional requirements (NFR) [6]. Despite the overlaps/similarities between the terms *goal* and *requirement*, they should be treated separately: indeed goals are used to capture *why* (the motivation for which) the system needs to behave in a certain way, while requirements underly *how* the goal must be achieved [3].

is related to its temporal characteristics [29]: *achieve* goals specify the behaviour required by a system sometimes in the future, while *maintain* goals regulate the behaviour of a system in all possible states. Finally, an *optimize* goal is used to compare behaviours to select those which better meet some (soft) property. A further classification of goals is among *hard goals* and *soft goals* [29]. Hard goals are related to functional requirements and are well defined and measurable, while soft goals are defined as imprecise with a no clear cut sense, and they lay the basis for the non-functional requirements [6].

4   Business Processes and Their Goals

We present here a first investigation and categorisation of the notion(s) of goal(s) that can be found in business processes. We ground our investigation on the notion of *participant* so as to keep our analysis independent from the specific modelling approach or modelling language that can be used to represent business process models. In the BPM literature, actions (at the token level) refer to intentional transformations from some initial state (of the local world at stake) to some other state. Their participants are the entities that take part in the transformations. In the terminology of [4], action tokens are *events*, while their participants are (physical or non-physical) *objects*. Thus, typical participants of a business process are the entities denoted by means of the constructs for data or information objects (e.g., a document, or its content) as well as organisational objects (e.g., actors playing roles).

We have identified five categories of goals: (i) *primary goal* (reason to exist), (ii) *transaction goal*, (iii) *data and organization oriented goal* (actors and objects), (iv) *instantiation goal*, (v) *quality goal*.

The Primary Goal (Reason to Exist). The first, and possibly most important perspective upon which to explore the notion of goal in business process, is tied up to the process' "reason to exist". From an intuitive point of view most people would answer the question "why does the process in Sect. 2 exist?" with the answer "to generate a fiscal code for a newborn". Or to the question "why does a loan process exist?" with the answer "to handle requests and issue loan offers." Formulating this intuition in a precise definition is not easy. If we take seriously the investigation of the reason to exist of a business process, several other elements may need to be addressed. One may say that a loan process exists because banks exist and have the goal of making money, or because people are willing to borrow from banks in order to satisfy their personal goals. To narrow the investigation, recall that business processes need to have a well defined input, which constraints the state of the word in which the process starts, and also organisational boundaries, which informally demarcates some actors for which the goal is of value.

Thus, since the goal appears to be connected to an evolution of states of the world (or a fragment of it) for some actors/organisations, we can start from the definition of goal for an agent as expressed in [22] (see Sect. 2) and modify it as follows:

the goal of a business process is the realisation of a state of the world, starting from an initial condition, which is of value to one or more organisational participants (for whatever reason).

That is, the goal of a process is to bring about a state of the world, starting from some initial conditions, which is of interest to at least one participant organisation. Usually, one or more of these participant organisations is regarded as the process *owner*. For instance, the goal of the process in Sect. 2 is to generate a fiscal code for each newborn, and this is the goal of the municipality and of SAIA.

Transaction Goals. While the primary goal gives a high level perspective, it does not aim to explain why, at the end of the modelling process, the model layout is in this or that way. This organisational aspect is related to transaction goals (and sub-goals), that is, all those goals which are roughly represented and observable in the behavioural model of a business process, where the procedural aspects are explicit defined. If we take this perspective, a business process is conceived as a processable workflow (model) system composed of: (i) a set of activities, (ii) their transactions and relationships (control flow), (iii) the participants that perform the activities, as well as the data flow.

The elements characterised by the transaction goals, which are mostly present in the behavioural view of a business process (model) are: (i) the final state reached after the last transaction (e.g., the token in an *end* state in a Petri-net.); and (ii) the output (effects) of each activity/sub-process. The behavioural perspective focuses on the cumulative effects' of activities which participate in the process, and the effect of the final activity is assumed to be the final desired state of the process. Thus, from this perspective the goal of the process is given by the accumulation of activities' (desired) effects conceived as partial or intermediate goals. The accumulation leads to a final comprehensive effect taken as the desired goal of the process itself.

Compared to the primary goal, transaction goals constitute richer descriptions. A problem in focusing only on this perspective is the fact that not all activities which participate to the behavioural dimension are essential to achieve the primary goal of the process (think of a verification check which is not necessary to the process) neither to characterise the identity of the process itself. Also, as discussed in Sect. 2, it may be the case that accumulations of activities' effects already realise a state of the world that correspond to the primary goal even before the process' end. Thus an investigation between primary and transaction goals may be useful in order to isolate *representative* activities that are relevant to the identity of the process.

Data and Organization Oriented Goals. Among the different process participants, actors playing roles in organisations and objects in the data flow appear to be particularly important when describing process goals. Both participants are explicitly represented in certain modelling languages (e.g., BPMN or EPCs) together with their intuitive relation with the behavioral component. For instance, in BPMN 2.0 organisational actors and roles are captured by modelling elements such as pools and the lanes, whose intuitive meaning is to specify who, within the organisation, is in charge of executing a specific set of tasks. Similarly data objects are often depicted together with their relations with activities, and they can serve as a prerequisite of an activity or be something produced/updated by an activity.

As already illustrated in Sect. 2, organisational actors and data objects can have specific goals which do not necessarily coincide with those of the process. Some goals of actors/data objects appear to be closer, and somehow fundamental, to the overall goal of the process, while others may be different, or even conflicting, and this should be taken into account when designing a process. Another important characteristics of these participants is that often they act as carriers of the primary goal. This is what happens to the fiscal code in our example. This object, traveling along the data flow of the process changes its state such as registered, requested, generated, checked and so on. An object can also have goals attributed to it such as, for the fiscal code, being permanently stored somewhere or being revealed to the person it corresponds to. Besides these specific aspects, this object participates in a fundamental manner to the overall process goal.

Instantiation Goals. Although business processes are traditionally conceived as *types* at the diagram level, they assume a significance only because they are executable. The execution level concerns the *instantiation* of the process in so-called execution traces, or cases. A case, thus, assumes the form of a sequence of events (thought of as the executions of the activities at the diagram level), each of them paired with its execution time and, possibly, additional attributes concerning performers, data objects and so on. For example, the instantiation of the fiscal code process concerns the generation of a specific code x concerning a newborn y with parents z, in a specific municipality, each activity happening at a specific time.

The instantiation dimension can be another lens through which to observe business process goals. A first class of meta-goal that concerns all business processes is related to properties that are usually investigated in formal methods and verification under the umbrella of soundness properties [28]. Indeed processes have the goal of being sound, with no livelocks, deadlocks, and other anomalies which relate to the fact that they can be executed from start to end in any (or relevant) circumstances. Further goals, which are implicit and always valid at the instantiation level, are related to execution repeatability. The generation of the fiscal code must be executed (and in the same way) not only once, or twice, or ten times, but for all newborns until the goal of generating a fiscal code per newborns remains valid. Similarly, it has to allow the concurrent execution of several instances, a property that may be unwanted in other scenarios. While these goals may be rarely visible at an abstract representation level, such as the one of Fig. 1, they become determinant when refining the representation at a level closer to the technological one.

Quality Goals. Another orthogonal dimension in discussing goals of a business process is provided by the categories of *hard* and *soft* goals typical of requirement engineering. In this perspective, if the hard goals appear to be related to the primary goal of the process, the notion of soft goal appears to be related to all the organisational, decisional, and strategic assumptions that are expressed in term of business functions having an impact on the enterprise choices.

Consider, for instance, the process of *purchasing raw material to sell a product*. This process involves many functions and departments, such as acquisition, quality, marketing, and sale. All of them have activities to perform and goals to be achieved, and often the strategic and decision oriented dimensions of an organisation are captured by qualities the process must satisfy rater than procedures the process must perform (see [5]). These qualities of a process are rather close to the notion of soft goals proper of non-functional requirements. Typical examples that pertain to business processes are *performance, security, multidimensionality*, and *user-friendliness* goals with all their proper subgoals. For instance, security may be expanded in accuracy, traceability, availability, and so on. Quality goals are indeed present in our example: fiscal codes should be generated within a certain timeframe and stored in a reliable data store, just to mention two of them.

5   Related Work

We classify the literature related to this paper into three main groups: (i) works dealing with the analysis of business process model notations and their elements, and the enrichment of business process models; (ii) works centred on the ontological analysis of business process modelling notations and its elements; and, (iii) works investigating the definition of goal and its classification.

Numerous researches focus on the analysis of the *elements* involved in business processes and business process modelling languages. Many of their publications provide a comparison of different modelling notations [16,26] or develop meta-models of business process models across notations [13,18]. Other works use ontologies for semantically enriching business process models [10,19,23], while others provide upper-level ontologies for business processes [20]. The second category of related works is centred on ontological analysis addressing business process notations and business process model elements. Within this category, we can find works such as [1], using the ontological analysis of business process elements (e.g., participants) across notations. In [24] the authors offer an ontological analysis of BPMN 2.0 elements and choreography diagram elements, respectively. In the former work, the authors focus on the ontological characterisation of events and activities in BPMN. However, none of the research in these two groups deals specifically with the notion of business process goals.

Investigations of the notion of goals and on their classifications, and mainly concern research areas different from business process management constitute the third group of related works. The classification of goals presented in this paper has been stimulated by goal oriented requirements engineering papers such as [29], and [3], which are focused on defining and classifying goals, and where distinctions between hard vs soft goals, and functional vs non-functional goals are presented. Further relevant studies, for example [27] and [5], explore the notion of soft goal as in requirement engineering, also in the context of business processes. In addition, [31] presents a framework for business process redesign that takes into account also the element of goal. Despite these efforts a specific investigation, classification and foundational characterisation of the notion of goal in business processes is still lacking.

6   Concluding Remarks and Future Works

Surprisingly an analysis of the specific types of goals that characterise business processes is lacking in the literature even though business goals are explicitly isolated as core elements in the definition of business process and are arguably central in the design of business process models. This paper has investigated the notion of goal in business process and suggested to distinguish five types of goals in this area: primary goals, transaction goals, organisation and data oriented goals, instantiation goals, and finally quality goals.

With these distinctions at hand, one can start a goal-based analysis of business processes which amounts to look at the models from the perspective of the goals that justify their existence and layout as well as to analyse which parts of the processes are enforced by which types of goal, and which can be taken as goal-independent. For instance, we can say that for their nature primary goals pertain to all business processes since, as discussed, they provide the very reason for their existence. Similarly, any business process presents instantiation goals as the possibility to execute the process is a necessary condition for its consideration. Indeed the presence of primary goals and instantiation goals is somehow independent from the specific scenario of a business process and what it realises, and these goals can be considered an invariant type whose analysis should concern the design and documentation of all business processes. Transaction goals play a fundamental role in the phases of a process in which an entity (physical or information) changes state or qualities. The transaction goals guide the organisation of the control flow, and the relationships between the goals of the different activities and those of the overall process. Quality goals can then be used to track the changes in single participants while coordinated by the larger transition goals. Regarding organisational goals, we can say that they focus primarily on agentive actors and the study of a process based on organisation goals would allow to concentrate on responsibility and coordination.

These are just initial observations and the extent and exploitation of the goal-based analysis of processes is something we plan to investigate in the future, as well as the relationships between kinds of goals. In the future we also plan to extend and consolidate the analysis here presented in order to deepen the investigation on the role that goals can play in the definition of what constitutes a business process and in the relationships between goals and different process participants. In particular, it will be interesting to integrate this work with the analysis of the ontological dependences between process participants that we have started in [2]. This line of research contributes to the ontological foundation of business process models. In the long run, we also aim at transforming this, and other ontological analysis of business process models, in guidelines that can support business analysts in modelling better business processes and implement these guidelines in modelling tools such as MoKi [11].

References

1. Adamo, G., Borgo, S., Di Francescomarino, C., Ghidini, C., Guarino, N., San-filippo, E.M.: Business processes and their participants: an ontological perspective. In: Esposito, F., Basili, R., Ferilli, S., Lisi, F. (eds.) AI*IA 2017. LNCS, vol. 10640, pp. 215–228. Springer, Cham (2017). https://doi.org/10.1007/978-3-319-70169-1_16
2. Adamo, G., Borgo, S., Di Francescomarino, C., Ghidini, C., Guarino, N., San-filippo, E.M.: Business process activity relationships: is there anything beyond arrows? In: Weske, M., Montali, M., Weber, I., vom Brocke, J. (eds.) BPM 2018. LNBIP, vol. 329, pp. 53–70. Springer, Cham (2018). https://doi.org/10.1007/978-3-319-98651-7_4
3. Anton, A.I.: Goal-based requirements analysis. In: Proceedings of the 2nd International Conference on Requirements Engineering, ICRE 1996, pp. 136–144. IEEE Computer Society, Washington (1996)
4. Borgo, S., Masolo, C.: Foundational choices in DOLCE. In: Staab, S., Studer, R. (eds.) Handbook on Ontologies. INFOSYS, pp. 361–381. Springer, Heidelberg (2013). https://doi.org/10.1007/978-3-540-92673-3_16
5. Cardoso, E.C.S., Almeida, J.P.A., Guizzardi, R.S.S., Guizzardi, G.: A method for eliciting goals for business process models based on non-functional requirements catalogues. IJISMD **2**(2), 1–18 (2011)
6. Chung, L., do Prado Leite, J.C.S.: On non-functional requirements in software engineering. In: Borgida, A.T., Chaudhri, V.K., Giorgini, P., Yu, E.S. (eds.) Conceptual Modeling: Foundations and Applications. LNCS, vol. 5600, pp. 363–379. Springer, Heidelberg (2009). https://doi.org/10.1007/978-3-642-02463-4_19
7. Davenport, T.: Process Innovation: Reengineering Work Through Information Technology. Harvard Business School Press, Boston (1993)
8. Garbacz, P., Kutz, O. (eds.): Formal Ontology in Information Systems - Proceedings of the Eighth International Conference, FOIS 2014, 22–25 September 2014, Rio de Janeiro, Brazil, Frontiers in Artificial Intelligence and Applications, vol. 267. IOS Press, Amsterdam (2014)
9. Ghallab, M., Nau, D., Traverso, P.: Automated Planning and Acting. Cambridge University Press, Cambridge (2016)
10. Ghidini, C., Di Francescomarino, C., Rospocher, M., Tonella, P., Serafini, L.: Semantics-based aspect-oriented management of exceptional flows in business processes. IEEE Trans. Syst. Man Cybern. Part C (Appl. Rev.) **42**, 25–37 (2012)
11. Ghidini, C., Rospocher, M., Serafini, L.: Modeling in a Wiki with MoKi: reference architecture, implementation, and usages. Int. J. Adv. Life Sci. **4**(3&4), 111–124 (2012)
12. Hammer, M., Champy, J.: Reengineering the Corporation: A Manifesto for Business Revolution. Harper Business, New York (1993)
13. Heidari, F., Loucopoulos, P., Brazier, F.M.T., Barjis, J.: A meta-meta-model for seven business process modeling languages. In: IEEE 15th Conference on Business Informatics, CBI 2013, pp. 216–221. IEEE Computer Society (2013)

14. Hull, R., et al.: Introducing the guard-stage-milestone approach for specifying business entity lifecycles. In: Bravetti, M., Bultan, T. (eds.) WS-FM 2010. LNCS, vol. 6551, pp. 1–24. Springer, Heidelberg (2011). https://doi.org/10.1007/978-3-642-19589-1_1

15. Johansson, H.J., McHugh, P., Pendlebury, A.J., Wheeler, W.A.: Business Process Reengineering: Breakpoint Strategies for Market Dominance. Wiley, Hoboken (1993)

16. List, B., Korherr, B.: An evaluation of conceptual business process modelling languages. In: Proceedings of the 2006 ACM Symposium on Applied Computing, SAC 2006, pp. 1532–1539. ACM (2006)

17. Marrella, A., Lespérance, Y.: A planning approach to the automated synthesis of template-based process models. Serv. Oriented Comput. Appl. 11(4), 367–392 (2017)

18. Mili, H., Tremblay, G., Jaoude, G.B., Lefebvre, E., Elabed, L., Boussaidi, G.E.: Business process modeling languages: sorting through the alphabet soup. ACM Comput. Surv. 43(1), 4:1–4:56 (2010)

19. Natschläger, C.: Towards a BPMN 2.0 ontology. In: Dijkman, R., Hofstetter, J., Koehler, J. (eds.) BPMN 2011. LNBIP, vol. 95, pp. 1–15. Springer, Heidelberg (2011). https://doi.org/10.1007/978-3-642-25160-3_1

20. Nicola, A.D., Lezoche, M., Missikoff, M.: An ontological approach to business process modeling. In: Prasad, B. (ed.) Proceedings of the 3rd Indian International Conference on Artificial Intelligence, 17–19 December 2007, Pune, India, pp. 1794–1813. IICAI (2007)

21. Object Management Group (OMG): Business process model and notation (BPMN) version 2.0. Standard (2011)

22. Rolf, M., Asada, M.: What are goals? And if so, how many? In: 2015 Joint IEEE International Conference on Development and Learning and Epigenetic Robotics (ICDL-EpiRob), pp. 332–339. IEEE (2015)

23. Rospocher, M., Ghidini, C., Serafini, L.: An ontology for the business process modelling notation. In: Garbacz and Kutz [8], pp. 133–146 (2014)

24. Sanfilippo, E.M., Borgo, S., Masolo, C.: Events and activities: Is there an ontology behind BPMN? In: Garbacz and Kutz [8], pp. 147–156 (2014)

25. Scheer, A.: ARIS - vom Geschäftsprozess zum Anwendungssystem. Springer, Heidelberg (2002). https://doi.org/10.1007/978-3-642-56300-3. [u.a.], 4, durchges. aufl. edn

26. Söderström, E., Andersson, B., Johannesson, P., Perjons, E., Wangler, B.: Towards a framework for comparing process modelling languages. In: Pidduck, A.B., Ozsu, M.T., Mylopoulos, J., Woo, C.C. (eds.) CAiSE 2002. LNCS, vol. 2348, pp. 600–611. Springer, Heidelberg (2002). https://doi.org/10.1007/3-540-47961-9_41

27. Soffer, P., Wand, Y.: On the notion of soft-goals in business process modeling. Bus. Process Manag. J. 11(6), 663–679 (2005)

28. van der Aalst, W., et al.: Soundness of workflow nets: classification, decidability, and analysis. Formal Aspects Comput. 23(3), 333–363 (2010)

29. Van Lamsweerde, A.: Goal-oriented requirements engineering: a guided tour. In: Proceedings of Fifth IEEE International Symposium on Requirements Engineering, pp. 249–262. IEEE (2001)

30. Weske, M.: Business Process Management. Concepts, Languages, Architectures. Springer, Heidelberg (2012). https://doi.org/10.1007/978-3-642-28616-2

31. Yu, E.S.K., Mylopoulos, J.: Using goals, rules and methods to support reasoning in business process reengineering. Int. Syst. Acc. Financ. Manag. 5(1), 1–13 (1996)

Towards an Ontological Modelling
of Preference Relations

Daniele Porello$^{(\boxtimes)}$ and Giancarlo Guizzardi

Free University of Bozen-Bolzano, Bolzano, Italy
{daniele.porello,giancarlo.guizzardi}@unibz.it

Abstract. Preference relations are intensively studied in Economics, but they are also approached in AI, Knowledge Representation, and Conceptual Modelling, as they provide a key concept in a variety of domains of application. In this paper, we propose an ontological foundation of preference relations to formalise their essential aspects across domains. Firstly, we shall discuss what is the ontological status of the relata of a preference relation. Secondly, we investigate the place of preference relations within a rich taxonomy of relations (e.g. we ask whether they are internal or external, essential or contingent, descriptive or non-descriptive relations). Finally, we provide an ontological modelling of preference relation as a module of a foundational (or upper) ontology (viz. OntoUML).

The aim of this paper is to provide a sharable foundational theory of preference relation that foster interoperability across the heterogeneous domains of application of preference relations.

Keywords: Preference relations · Ontology of relations
Foundational ontology · Conceptual model · OntoUML

1 Introduction

Preference relations have been extensively studied in Economics as they provide an essential theory to formalise and possibly explain human economic behaviour. Preference relations are also ubiquitous in Computer Science, in particular in AI, Knowledge Representation, and Multiagent Systems, as they provide a key concept in domains such as planning, autonomous agents modellisation, recommender systems, and resource allocation. Moreover, the use of preference relations is very extensive in Conceptual Modelling, for instance in applications to domains such as business process, services, and economic exchange.

Although preference relations are an ubiquitous concept in many areas, a clear ontological foundation of them is still to be developed. In this paper, we start the program of providing an exhaustive ontological analysis of preference relations. In particular, we intend to provide an analysis of preference relations that integrates a theory of preference relations with a larger theory of the main ontological categories, by initiating the development of a module for

© Springer Nature Switzerland AG 2018
C. Ghidini et al. (Eds.): AI*IA 2018, LNAI 11298, pp. 152–165, 2018.
https://doi.org/10.1007/978-3-030-03840-3_12

preference relations to be integrated within a foundational (or upper) ontology (cf. [2,9]). A foundational ontology is a theory of the most general categories that are required in heterogeneous modelling tasks and whose principles hold across-domain. The foundational ontology program is a quite interdisciplinary endeavour that requires cognitive adequacy, philosophical awareness, as well as effective formalisations. Examples of such very general categories are object, event, property, relation, state, process, space, and time.

The mathematical treatment of preference relation is very well understood as well as their empirical foundation. Preference relations usually involve an agent who provides a ranking (a type of ordering) among the available options or alternatives.

An essential distinction between preference types is that between *ordinal* and *cardinal* preference. Ordinal preference are simply a (type of) ranking of the options, whereas cardinal preferences associate to each option a value that represents the level of satisfaction of the agent concerning that option. A formalisation of ordinal preference relation in terms of modern formal logic has been developed by the Nobel Prize for Economics Arrow [1], who was inspired by the axiomatic method of Tarski. Preference relations are modelled by means of binary relations that satisfy a number of axioms, usually related to the theory of orders (e.g. total, partial, or weak orders). That is, preference relations can be axiomatised within a first-order theory of orders.

The foundation of cardinal preference relation is traditionally referred to the work of von Neumann and Morgenstern about the theory of expected utility [29]. In general, cardinal preference relations are usually modelled by means of utility functions defined on a set of alternatives with values in a suitable set of numbers (usually, the real numbers).

Traditionally, preference relations are ultimately founded on the choice behaviour of an agent, see [10]. Cardinal preferences can be rationalised, under suitable conditions, by ordinal preference, and ordinal preferences can in turn be derived from choice functions that meet a number of suitable conditions. This type of foundation grounds a preference relation, which is allegedly something that is in the mind of an agent, in an observable behaviour, that is, the agents' actual observable choices. This operationalisation of the concept of preference relations was one of the most salient contributions of the economic foundation of preference, justifying the empirical elicitation of human agents' preferences. Another important distinction between preferences depends on whether they are ascribed to *individual agents* or to *collective agents*. Collective preferences are important when modelling preferences ascribed to societies, groups of agents, or sets of users (e.g. in recommender systems). The foundation in Economics of collective preference is essentially due to [1]. A discussion of the formalisation of collective preferences in terms of a first-order theory of ordering is proposed in [17].

A recent approach to the foundation of preference relations has been developed by Dietrich and List [4,5] and discussed in [15,19]. Here, preference relations are dependent on the properties of the alternatives at issue, whose salience depends on the views of the agent. This view brings us close to the approach of this paper in that the properties of the preferences are intended in an ontological sense. Thus the work of Dietrich and List is one of the closest related work to the present contribution.

Although the formalisation of preference relations is quite well established, a detailed ontological understanding is missing. We intend to fill this gap by initiating the investigation of the ontological foundation of preference relations.

The methodology of this paper is the following. We start by analysing the semantics of sentences of the form "agent i prefers a over b". That is, we look for those pieces of reality that are required in order to make the statements about preferences true. Specifically, we investigate what are the *truth-makers*, see for instance [12], of the statements about preferences. This view has been introduced for the ontological analysis of relations in [7]. This approach naturally leads to asking important ontological questions about which type of objects are related by a preference relation, to what extent preference relations depends on the ontological properties of the relata, which type of relations is the type of preference relation.

The contribution of this paper is twofold. Firstly, we informally analyse the type of preference relations by discussing their place within a taxonomy of relations. Secondly, we propose a formalisation of our analysis by means of an ontologically well-founded approach to conceptual modelling. In particular, we extend the methodology of OntoUML, which provides a solid ontologically deep approach to conceptual modelling [9], to provide a formal ontological understanding of preference relations. Our aim is to develop a module of OntoUML for preference relations that explicitly manifests the truth-makers of preferential statements and relates preference relations to the main general categories of a foundational ontology. Finally, we discuss how to model various types of preference relations by extending our proposed OntoUML module.

The remainder of this paper is organised as follows. Section 2 discusses an informative taxonomy of relations. Section 3 proposes how to place preference relations within the taxonomy of relations and discusses what may counts as a truth-maker of a relational sentence involving preferences. Section 4 proposes the modelling of preference relations in OntoUML and presents viable extensions. Section 5 concludes.

2   A Taxonomy of Relations

We summarise the discussion of the kinds of relations in terms of their truth-makers. To provide a fine-grained analysis of relations, we introduce three pairs of distinction that were traditionally at the core of important debates in analytical philosophy on the nature of relations: internal and external, essential and contingent, and descriptive and non-descriptive relations. We summarise the examples of this types of relations in Table 1.

Before proposing the definitions of those distinctions, we have to introduce a number of important concepts in ontology to categories properties. The choice of terminology we use in this paper is mainly due to [7]. A formalisation of the subsequent concepts in first-order logic is presented in [2,8,9,22].

An *individual quality*, or simply a *quality*, is a property of an object, usually used to make comparisons between objects along a certain dimension. We say that the quality *inhere* in its object, which is termed the *bearer* of the quality. The relations of inherence is a particular type of existential dependence, which has been formalised in [9]. Examples of qualities of an object are *the color of this rose* or *the weight of this laptop*. We say that the quality existentially depends on its bearer, in the sense that the color of a certain rose is always ontologically separated from the color of a different rose. To compare qualities of different objects, we make the distinction between the qualities of an objects and the values of those qualities, i.e. the *quality values* (or *qualia*). The quality values are abstract objects that are introduced for the purpose of explaining or measuring the similarity of two objects along a certain dimension (e.g. the color). Quality values are possibly organised into metric spaces with a distance function that captures the similarity judgments between quality values. Examples of such metric structures are Gärdernfors conceptual spaces, cf. [6].

Relational qualities (or *externally dependent modes* in [9]) are qualities whose existence depends (besides on the bearer of the quality) on an object which is ontologically separated to the object in which they inhere.[1] Examples of relational quality are *Mary's desire of buying a Ferrari* which existentially depends on Mary, but also on the object of the desire. In Sect. 4, we shall discuss quality values also for relational qualities.

We term a quality *intrinsic* of an object if and only if it does not depend on any other object besides its bearer. For instance, one may view the *color* of an object as a quality that only depends on the object.

An *essential property* of an object is an intrinsic property that depends on the mere existence of the object. For example, if one views that any existing object must have a mass, then the mass is an essential property of any object.

We move now to the definitions of types of relations. We start by recalling the distinction between *internal* and *external* relations. We use a first-order notation for relations, where $R(a_1, \ldots a_n)$ denotes an n-ary relation. We say that R is *internal* if and only if its truth-value only depends on the intrinsic properties of its relata; a relation is *external* if that is not the case.[2] For instance, the truth-value of "a is taller than b" depends on the height of a and b, which are intrinsic properties of a and b, whereas the truth-value of "a desires b" does not depend only on intrinsic properties of a and b, hence it is external.

---

[1] We do not have space here to provide an exhaustive view of the separation of objects. We simply say that two objects are separated if they are existentially independent, cf. [9].

[2] This is the definition provided by Russell [25]. A stronger definition is the one proposed by Moore [14], which views an internal relation as a relation the holds merely in virtue of the existence of the relata. This second view of internal relation is what we term here *essential*, following the terminology of [7].

A relation is *essential* if and only if its truth-value depends only on the existence of its relata; it is *contingent* otherwise. For instance, "*a* is taller than *b*" is not essential, since the height is not an essential property of the object, e.g. there may be moments in time where a person *b* is taller than a person *a*. By contrast, if one views that any object, in virtue of its mere existence, must have a mass, then "*a* is heavier than *b*" is an essential relation.

Finally, we introduce the distinction between descriptive and non-descriptive relations, which have been investigated in particular in [7].

A relation is *descriptive* if and only if its truth-value depends on at least one property of some of its relata which is existentially dependent on another distinct relata; it is *non-descriptive* otherwise. For instance, in a comparative relation between objects, as in the case of "*a* is taller than *b*", the height differential that makes *a* taller depends on *b* (that is, it is externally dependent on *b*), thus the relation is descriptive. By contrast, a comparative relation between mere quality values is non-descriptive: according to this view, that the number associated to the height of *a* is bigger or smaller than the number associated to the height of *b* only depends on the numbers themselves.

The following table summarises the examples of the types of relations that we have introduced. As the table shows, descriptive vs non-descriptive and internal vs external provides the two dimensions for analysing relations. Moreover, one may find essential relations in any possible combination of the previous criteria. For the relationship between this taxonomy of relations and the problem of reifications of relations, that is, the problem of discussing which type of relations deserves reification, we refer to [7].

In the next section, we shall discuss which is the suitable categorisation for preference relations.

Table 1. Types of relations

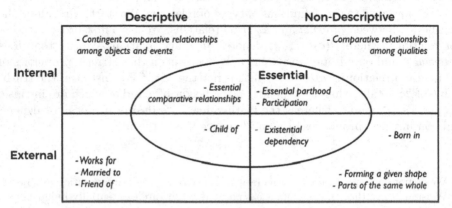

3   The Type of Preference Relations

We discuss now what is the placement of preference relations within the taxonomy of relations discussed in the previous section. At the end of this section, we apply the categorisation of preference relations in order to elicit the truth-makers of statements about preferences. We focus on sentences such as "i prefers a to b", where i is an agent and a and b are alternative options. In this section, we abstract from the type of preference relation, e.g. whether they are cardinal or ordinal preferences, or individual or collective preferences, and we aim to approach any preference relation.

Preference relations are in fact ternary relations, we denote them by means of the formula PREF(i, a, b). The first component of the preference relation i is an agent, thus the property of agency must be spelled our in order to provide an exhaustive ontological model of a preference relation. Here, we simply assume that the user, or the modeller, can endorse any vision of agency she or he may see fit (e.g. the belief-desire-intention model of agency [3,23]). In the case of collective preferences, that is where i is a collective agents or a community of agents, we need to choose a view of collective agency to complement the ontological model of preference, e.g. [11,20,21].

The type of the other two components of the preference relation is in fact quite general. Preference relations may be defined on very heterogeneous types of entities. For instance, an agent may have preferences over objects, candidates for elections, parties, vacation plans, evening events, services, loans or mortgages, stock options, and so on. Preference relation are indeed an ubiquitous concept in a variety of economic settings. Thus, in principle, we do not want to put any substantial restriction on the domain of the possible pairs of entities that may enter the second and the third component of the preference relation.

Concerning the ontological status of the truth-makers of a statement about preference, we notice that the qualities of the entities a and b are indeed not sufficient for assessing whether a is preferred to b or not. For instance, a blue car may be preferred to a red one by a certain agent, whereas the opposite may hold for another agent. Moreover, the preferences of an agent may evolve through time, may depend on what an agent already owns, may depend on the resources available to the agent. This examples shows that we have to access the view that the agent i has about the options a and b, in order to assess the truth-value of the preference relation.

To understand the relationship between the options involved in a preferential statement and the agent, we introduce the concepts of *value*, *value magnitude*, *value entity* (or *value bearer*), and *value beholder*, cf. [28].

A *value beholder* is a role that an agent plays *qua* agent who is making a choice, or assessing a preference, between two options.[3] The *value entity* is again a role, this time, it is the role that an option plays in the context of a preference assessment of an agent. The value entity is a role that depends on an agent i and on the option at issue. For simplicity here, we assume that the value entity of an

---

[3] For an ontological theory of roles, we refer to [9] and [13].

option for an agent is unique, thus we refer to it by the definite description "the value entity of a for i".[4] The category of *value* is intended here as a category of qualities that inhere in the value beholder. An element of this category represents the value of the value entity for the value beholder.

The *value magnitude* is an abstract category whose function is to enable comparisons between the values that agents associate to value entities.[5] We may assume here that this category as an abstract set of ordered points. In treating preference relation, we are assuming that relational qualities (such as the value of a value entity for a value beholder) have also quality values. In particular, the quality value of the value of an option for an agent i is an element of the category of value magnitude. To formalise this view, we may introduce a relation of *location* between the relational qualities (the category of value) involved in a preference statement and the space of values (the category of value magnitude).[6]

For instance, in the context of the statement "Mary prefers a Porsche to a Ferrari", Mary plays the role of the value beholder, the options Porsche and Ferrari are playing the role of the value entities of this context, the values of this value entities for Mary (as value beholder) are represented as elements of the category of values, and the quality values associated to those options are represented by means of elements of the category of value magnitude.

Applying the definitions of the previous section, we can categories the entities involved in a preferential context as follows. The value of an option a for an agent i is a *relational quality* that inheres in the value beholder (the role of i) and that depends on the option a (as value entity). Analogously, the value of an option b for i. What counts as a truth-maker of the preferential statement is whether for agent i the value magnitude associated to the value entity of a is greater than the value magnitude associated to the value entity of b (according to the scale provided by the category of value magnitudes).

On this ground, we can assess the placement of preference relations PREF(i, a, b) among the taxonomy of the previous section.

Firstly, we show that preference relations are not internal, thus they are external relations. Remind that in an internal relations, the individual qualities of the relata are sufficient to assess the value of the statement. In the case of preference relation, the qualities that are required to assess whether a is more valuable than b for i are external qualities that inhere in i.

---

[4] This simplification amounts to assuming that in a preference statement only one *dimension* of choice is involved [15, 19]. That is, the value of a for i does not depend on any further conditions. To extend this modelling, one may assume that the value of a for i may depend on a number of parameters; e.g. "the value of a for i given that i already has a certain amount of a" may capture the marginal value for i of getting a further a.

[5] A specification of this category, and what types of metric spaces is associated to it, is left for future work and for dedicated application of specific views of preferences. We shall also discuss this point in the next section, when we approach the distinction between cardinal and ordinal preferences.

[6] This is the way qualities and quality values are related for instance in DOLCE, cf. [2].

Secondly, preferences are descriptive relations. According to our previous definition, a relation is descriptive if the truth-value of the statement depends on at least one relational quality that depends on one of the other relata. In the case of preference relation, the value of a (or b) for agent i is indeed a relational quality of i that depends on one of the (other) relata of the preference relation, namely a (or b).

Finally, preference relations are contingent relations: the mere existence of the relata is not sufficient for assessing the truth-value of $\mathrm{PREF}(i, a, b)$. For instance, the mere existence of i, a and b does not make a or b valuable for her or him, as i may not be aware of their existence, or i never had to compare a and b.

Therefore, to conclude, preference relations are external, descriptive, and contingent relations.

3.1 The Truth-Makers of Statements About Preference Relations

In order to assess the truth-value of a statement about preferences, a number of entities must be presupposed. Firstly, we have to postulate the existence of an agent and two alternatives. Secondly, we have to presuppose the existence of a number of relational qualities that inhere in i and that existentially depend on a and b. We can define the truth-maker of the preferential statement $\mathrm{PREF}(i, a, b)$ as the (mereological) sum of the relational qualities that inhere in i and that existentially depend on a (the value of a for i) and of the relational quality that inhere i and depends on b (the value of b for i). That is, the truth-maker of $\mathrm{PREF}(i, a, b)$ is a complex relational quality that inheres in the agent i.

More specifically, we are here endorsing a *weak* version of truth-making, cf. [16]. In the *strong* version of truth-making t is a truth-maker of the sentence ϕ if the existence of t is sufficient to make ϕ true. By contrast, t is a *weak* truth-maker of ϕ if it makes the proposition ϕ true not just because of its existence, but because of the way t contingently is. The distinction between strong and weak truth-makers is crucial for investigating preference relation.

For $\mathrm{PREF}(i, a, b)$, the mere existence of the sum of the the relational qualities is not sufficient to determine the truth-value of $\mathrm{PREF}(i, a, b)$. One has to look at the *quality values*, in the category of value magnitude, of the relational qualities "the value of a for i" and "the value of b for i", and to check their relationship. There are in general four cases: i) the value magnitude of a is greater than the value magnitude of b, and in this case $\mathrm{PREF}(i, a, b)$ is true; ii) the value magnitude of b is greater than the value magnitude of b, and in that case $\mathrm{PREF}(i, b, a)$ is true; iii) they are equal (i.e. they are located in the same point of the category of value magnitude), and in that case both $\mathrm{PREF}(i, a, b)$ and $\mathrm{PREF}(i, b, a)$ hold, according to a weak version of preference (thus i is indifferent between a and b); iv) they are incomparable, and in that case neither $\mathrm{PREF}(i, a, b)$ or $\mathrm{PREF}(i, a, b)$ are true.

Thus, from an ontological perspective, the preference relation is an interesting type of external contingent non-descriptive relation whose truth-value depends on relational qualities as well as on a comparative relation between value magnitudes. We shall see this aspect in more detail by approaching, in the next section, the formalisation of this view in OntoUML.

4 An Ontology Module for Preference in OntoUML

We represent the previous view by starting the development of a module of OntoUML dedicated to preference relations. OntoUML [8,9] is an ontologically well-founded version of the UML 2.0 fragment of class diagrams, which has been extensively used for developing an ontologically sound methodology for conceptual modelling. Moreover, OntoUML has a denotational formal semantics and several operational semantics done by mappings to specific formal languages such as Alloy and Description Logics. To model preferences in OntoUML, we introduce the modelling elements that correspond to the previous analysis. The model is then depicted in Fig. 1.

We assume a type for agents AGENT, which classify the entities to which preference relations may be ascribed. AGENT is a *mixin* (non-sortal), i.e., a type that can classify things of different *kinds*, i.e., things that have different onto-logical natures [9]. For instance, in separating between individual and collective preferences, agents may include individual or collective agents, with their specific ontological differences [21].

Since we assume that agents (in the sense of entities with *intentionality*) are necessarily agents (in the modal sense), we stereotype the type AGENT as a *Category*, in OntoUML. In other words, a *Category* is a type that describes essential properties that are shared by entities of different *kinds*.

Agents can play the "role" of VALUE BEHOLDER in a *value ascription* rela-tion. Value Ascription is itself an extrinsic and descriptive relation, whose truth-maker is a *Value*. We represent the type VALUE BEHOLDER as a *role mixin* because: (i) it classifies entities only contingently, i.e., no value beholder is nec-essarily a value beholder; (ii) one is a value beholder due to a relational condition; (iii) it is a mixin, i.e., it can classify entities of multiple kinds.

A VALUE (the truth-maker of the value ascription relation[7]) is an example of a *mode* [9]. A mode is an existentially dependent entity that, as such, can only exist by inhering in some other individual. In particular, a value is a *relationally dependent mode*, i.e., a mode that inheres in an individual but which is also exter-nally dependent on a different individual. In this case, value is a sort of mental state inhering in the value beholder but which is also externally dependent on a VALUE ENTITY (also termed a Value Bearer). A value mode take a value in at least one (but possibly several) VALUE MAGNITUDE SPACES. These spaces have, in OntoUML, the semantics of the abstract conceptual spaces, delimiting the possible values an intrinsic property can be projected into [9].

A PREFERENCE is also a relational mode but a complex one (i.e., a complex mental state). In fact, a preference is a mode inhering a value beholder that

---

[7] The relation of *derivation* connects a descriptive relation with its truthmaker. In OntoUML, derivation is represented by a dashed line with a black circle in the end connected to the truthmaker type [9].

is essentially composed of exact two existing values, inhering in that very same value beholder. In other words, preference is a mereological sum of values and, in that sense, it is similar to the *relators* that are the truth-makers of comparative relations [7]. However, since in this case all the constituents of this sum inhere in the same bearer, preference is also an intrinsic dependent entity [9]. In any case, as a relational mode, preference is externally dependent on the value entities on which its constituent value modes depend on (thus, it is a *derived* relation).

PREFERENCE serves then as the truth-maker of the ternary relation *has preference*. This relation is itself a derived relation that supervenes on an *internal and non-descriptive comparative relation* between the VALUE MAGNITUDES of the value modes that constitute that preference. This, of course, constrains VALUE MAGNITUDE SPACES to be spaces structured by internal comparative relations (in the same manner that spaces such as Weight and Height afford that). Moreover, *has preference* is an external descriptive relation itself. It connects the rolemixin VALUE BEHOLDER with two other rolemixins PREFERRED ENTITY and DEPRECATED ENTITY[8]. The classification condition of VALUE ENTITIES into playing these "roles" is given by the result of the internal comparative relations between the modes constituting the preference and which are externally dependent on each of these value entities. To put it simply, the value bearer of the value mode that has the highest magnitude in this comparison then plays the role of PREFERRED ENTITY; the value bearer of the one with the lower magnitude then plays the role of DEPRECATED ENTITY. It should be clear by now to the reader why both PREFERRED ENTITY and DEPRECATED ENTITY are modelled as rolemixins: they both classify value entities contingently, in the scope of a (has preference) relation, and classify entities of multiple kinds.

4.1 Types of Preference Relations

The module of OntoUML that we have introduced can be extended to model a variety of types of preference relations that are used in application to specific domains. We mentioned already the distinction between individual and collective preference, that can be approached by refining the class of agents. An articulated analysis of the distinction between individual and collective preferences requires modelling the relationship between the individual and the collective attitude, by analysing how the individuals contributes to the formation of the collective preference, along the lines of the approach in [18,20]. We leave this aspect for a future dedicated work.

The distinction between ordinal and cardinal preferences can be approached by refining the value magnitude space. In the ordinal case, we need an ordering structure on the set of quality values representing the value magnitudes. The properties of the preference ordering that are required for capturing the intended

---

[8] Unfortunately, in English, there seems to be no exact term to refer to the non-preferred entity of a preference relation. In Portuguese, for instance, there exist in the lexicon both the term *Preferido* (to refer to the preferred entity) as well as the term *Preterido* (to refer to the non-preferred one).

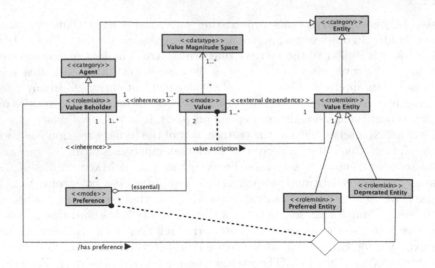

Fig. 1. OntoUML model for preference relations

view of preference can be derived from the ordering structure of the value magnitude space. For instance, if we admit transitive preferences (i.e. relations that satisfy the condition: if $\mathrm{PREF}(i, a, b)$ and $\mathrm{PREF}(i, b, c)$, then $\mathrm{PREF}(i, a, c)$), we need a transitive ordering on the value magnitude space.

The case of cardinal preferences requires the value magnitude space to be constructed as a set of numbers, that provide a measure of the value magnitudes (e.g. the real numbers). The choice of the space depends on the scale and on the granularity assumed to assess the comparisons of value magnitudes.

A further important aspect of preference relation in the economic literature is whether they are *comparable* or not, cf. [24]. Briefly, two agents' preference relations are comparable if there is common scale that allows for making sense of comparisons such as "the preference of agent i for a over b is more intense than the preference of agent j for c over d". Comparability is a fundamental concept in economics that allows for enabling a number of important solution concepts in voting, resource allocation, and mechanism design. In our module, comparability can be approached by assuming a local value magnitude space for each individual preference relation. The assumption of comparability would then entail that the value magnitude spaces of distinct individuals are comparable by means of a new relation.

Finally, an important aspect of (cardinal) preference relations and in particular of expected utility theory is the role of probability to model the likelihood of the event in which an agent obtains the objects involved in the preference relation. To include probabilities in our module, we have to provide a more complex construction of the value magnitude space where the value magnitude associated to a certain value also depends on the risk attitudes of the agent involved. We leave this aspect to a future dedicated ontological foundation of expected utility theory.

5   Conclusion

We have presented the basics of an ontological analysis of preference relations. After discussing the type of preference relations within a taxonomy of types of relations, we concluded that preferences are external, descriptive and contingent relations. We investigated the truth-makers of the sentences regarding preferences and we proposed to view them as complex relational qualities that inhere a value beholder. Prosaically, the preference is a complex mental state of an agent.

The type of preference relations is interesting from an ontological perspective because it requires a complex truth-making mechanism that involves both external and internal relations, the latter type enters in the comparisons of the value magnitudes associated to the value entities that are under comparison. Future work shall investigate this mechanism in general to understand which relations meet this pattern.

Then, we presented a formalisation of our view of preferences in OntoUML, providing the essential elements of a dedicated module. The motivation for using the OntoUML methodology is to provide an accessible and sharable modelling of preference relations that may be applied across domains to foster the interoperability and the mutual understanding among modellers. Future work regards the development of the OntoUML module to articulate specific types of preferences and the integration of the preference module with other module designed to treat important concepts in economics, e.g. economic competition [26] and risk [27]. Moreover, we are interested in providing a formalisation of this view of preference in a logic-based language to integrate it with foundational ontologies such as UFO or DOLCE [2,9] and to study reasoners for the preference module.

References

1. Arrow, K.: Social Choice and Individual Values. Cowles Foundation for Research in Economics at Yale University, Monograph 12. Yale University Press, New Haven (1963)
2. Borgo, S., Masolo, C.: Foundational choices in DOLCE. In: Staab, S., Studer, R. (eds.) Handbook on Ontologies. IHIS, pp. 361–381. Springer, Heidelberg (2009). https://doi.org/10.1007/978-3-540-92673-3_16
3. Bratman, M.: Intention, Plans, and Practical Reason. CSLI Publications, Stanford (1987)
4. Dietrich, F., List, C.: A reason-based theory of rational choice. Nous 47(1), 104–134 (2013)
5. Dietrich, F., List, C.: Where do preferences come from? Int. J. Game Theor. 42(3), 613–637 (2013)
6. Gärdenfors, P.: The geometry of Meaning: Semantics Based on Conceptual Spaces. MIT Press, Cambridge (2014)

7. Guarino, N., Guizzardi, G.: Relationships and events: towards a general theory of reification and truthmaking. In: Adorni, G., Cagnoni, S., Gori, M., Maratea, M. (eds.) AI*IA 2016. LNCS (LNAI), vol. 10037, pp. 237–249. Springer, Cham (2016). https://doi.org/10.1007/978-3-319-49130-1_18
8. Guizzardi, G., Fonseca, C., Benevides, A.B., Almeida, J., Porello, D., Sales, T.: Endurant types in ontology-driven conceptual modeling: towards OntoUML 2.0. In: Trujillo, J., et al. (eds.) ER 2018. LNCS, vol. 11157, pp. 136–150. Springer, Cham (2018). https://doi.org/10.1007/978-3-030-00847-5_12
9. Guizzardi, G.: Ontological foundations for structural conceptual models. Ph.D. thesis, CTIT, Centre for Telematics and Information Technology, Enschede (2005). http://doc.utwente.nl/50826/
10. Kreps, D.: Notes on the Theory of Choice. Underground Classics in Economics. Avalon Publishing, New York (1988). https://books.google.it/books?id=9D0Oljs5GrQC
11. List, C., Pettit, P.: Group Agency. The Possibility, Design, and Status of Corporate Agents. Oxford University Press, Oxford (2011)
12. MacBride, F.: Truthmakers. In: Zalta, E.N. (ed.) The Stanford Encyclopedia of Philosophy, fall 2016. Stanford University, Stanford (2016). Metaphysics Research Lab
13. Masolo, C., et al.: Social roles and their descriptions. In: Proceedings of the Ninth International Conference Principles of Knowledge Representation and Reasoning, KR2004, 2–5 June 2004, Whistler, Canada, pp. 267–277 (2004)
14. Moore, G.E.: External and internal relations. Proc. Aristot. Soc. 20, 40–62 (1919)
15. Ottonelli, V., Porello, D.: On the elusive notion of meta-agreement. Polit. Philos. Econ. 12(1), 68–92 (2013)
16. Parsons, J.: There is no truthmaker argument against nominalism. Australas. J. Philos. 77(3), 325–334 (1999)
17. Porello, D.: Ranking judgments in arrow's setting. Synthese 173(2), 199–210 (2010)
18. Porello, D.: A proof-theoretical view of collective rationality. In: Proceedings of the 23rd International Joint Conference on Artificial Intelligence, IJCAI 2013, 3–9 August 2013, Beijing, China (2013)
19. Porello, D.: Single-peakedness and semantic dimensions of preferences. Logic J. IGPL 24(4), 570–583 (2016)
20. Porello, D.: Logics for modelling collective attitudes. Fundam. Inform. 158(1–3), 239–275 (2018)
21. Porello, D., Bottazzi, E., Ferrario, R.: The ontology of group agency. In: Proceedings of the Eighth International Conference of Formal Ontology in Information Systems, FOIS 2014, 22–25 September 2014, Rio de Janeiro, Brazil, pp. 183–196 (2014)
22. Porello, D., Guizzardi, G.: Towards a first-order modal formalisation of the unified foundational ontology. In: Proceedings of the Joint Ontology Workshops 2017 Episode 3: The Tyrolean Autumn of Ontology, 21–23 September 2017, Bozen-Bolzano, Italy (2017)
23. Rao, A.S., Georgeff, M.P.: Modeling rational agents within a BDI-architecture. KR 91, 473–484 (1991)
24. Roemer, J.E.: Theories of Distributive Justice. Harvard University Press, Cambridge (1998)
25. Russell, B.: Philosophical Essays. Routledge, Abingdon (1910)
26. Sales, T., Porello, D., Guizzardi, G., Mylopoulos, J., Guarino, N.: Ontological foundations of competition. In: 10th International Conference on Formal Ontologies and Information Systems, FOIS 2018, Cape Town, South Africa (2018)

27. Sales, T.P., Baião, F., Guizzardi, G., Guarino, N., Mylopoulos, J.: The common ontology of value and risk. In: 37th International Conference on Conceptual Modeling (ER) (2018)
28. Sales, T.P., Guarino, N., Guizzardi, G., Mylopoulos, J.: An ontological analysis of value propositions. In: 21st IEEE International Enterprise Distributed Object Computing Conference, EDOC 2017, 10–13 October 2017, Quebec City, QC, Canada, pp. 184–193 (2017)
29. Von Neumann, J., Morgenstern, O.: Theory of Games and Economic Behavior. Princeton University Press, Princeton (1947)

A Generalized Framework
for Ontology-Based Data Access

Elena Botoeva, Diego Calvanese$^{(\boxtimes)}$, Benjamin Cogrel, Julien Corman,
and Guohui Xiao

Faculty of Computer Science, Free University of Bozen-Bolzano, Bolzano, Italy
{botoeva,calvanese,cogrel,corman,xiao}@inf.unibz.it

Abstract. The database (DB) landscape has been significantly diversified during the last decade, resulting in the emergence of a variety of non-relational (also called NoSQL) DBs, e.g., XML and JSON-document DBs, key-value stores, and graph DBs. To enable access to such data, we generalize the well-known ontology-based data access (OBDA) framework so as to allow for querying arbitrary data sources using SPARQL. We propose an architecture for a generalized OBDA system implementing the virtual approach. Then, to investigate feasibility of OBDA over non-relational DBs, we compare an implementation of an OBDA system over MongoDB, a popular JSON-document DB, with a triple store.

1   Introduction

The database (DB) landscape has been significantly diversified during the last decade to satisfy the needs of a wide variety of modern applications. Traditional relational DB management systems now coexist with the so-called *NoSQL* (not only SQL) DBs, which redefine the format of the stored data, and how it is queried. These *non-relational* DBs usually adopt one of the following four main data models: the column-family, key-value, document, or graph data model, and while some of them can be queried through well-known declarative query languages, such as SQL or SPARQL, others offer ad-hoc querying mechanisms (e.g., the aggregation framework of MongoDB), or even require writing JavaScript functions (e.g., in CouchDB[1]). This wider choice of DBMSs offers the possibility to match application needs more closely, allowing for instance for more flexible data schemas, or more efficient (though simple) queries.

As a result, accessing data using native query languages is getting more and more involved for users. In this paper, we propose a generalization of the *ontology-based data access* (OBDA) framework as a uniform solution to this problem. The OBDA paradigm [22] has emerged as a proposal to simplify access to relational data for end-users, by letting them formulate high-level queries over a conceptual representation of the domain of interest, provided in terms of an ontology. In the classical *virtual* OBDA approach, these queries are translated

---

[1] http://couchdb.apache.org/.

© Springer Nature Switzerland AG 2018
C. Ghidini et al. (Eds.): AI*IA 2018, LNAI 11298, pp. 166–180, 2018.
https://doi.org/10.1007/978-3-030-03840-3_13

automatically into lower-level ones that DB engines can handle. This is done by exploiting a declarative specification of the relationship between the ontology and the data at the sources, provided in terms of *mapping assertions*. This separation of concerns between query formulation at the conceptual level and query execution at the DB level has proven successful in practice, notably when data sources have a complex structure, and end-users have domain knowledge, but not necessarily data management expertise [5,10]. Traditionally, in OBDA, the DB is assumed to be relational, the ontology is expressed in the OWL 2 QL profile of the Web Ontology Language OWL 2 [15], the mapping DBs is specified in R2RML [7], and queries are formulated in SPARQL, the Semantic Web query language [11].

Our generalization extends the classical OBDA setting to arbitrary DBs. The approach enjoys all benefits already offered by OBDA, in particular hiding from the user low-level concerns such as data storage and access, and providing a high-level querying interface, closer to application needs. In the NoSQL case, an additional advantage is the possibility to formulate all queries in a familiar yet expressive language, namely SPARQL, which is both widespread and very similar to SQL dialects.

We then investigate the feasibility of the generalized OBDA framework when query answering is fully delegated to the DB engine, by focusing on MongoDB, a document-based DB, which is also one of the most popular NoSQL DBs as of today. OBDA appears as a solution of choice for MongoDB: MongoDB offers a very expressive query language, which however has a more procedural flavor than SQL or SPARQL, and can become very complex to manipulate for advanced information needs. Document-based DBs can leverage the *denormalized* structure of their data: a collection of documents can be seen as a materialized view over a (normalized) relational DB instance, essentially with joins being pre-computed. Therefore a natural question we try to answer in this paper is whether OBDA over MongoDB can take advantage of such structure in order to answer queries efficiently. We provide a first element towards a positive answer, by instantiating the generalized OBDA framework over MongoDB as an extension of the OBDA system *Ontop* [4], and comparing its performance with a triple store, which does not benefit from such denormalization.

The rest of the paper is structured as follows. Section 2 recalls the standard OBDA framework over relational data sources. Section 3 introduces our proposal for generalizing OBDA to access arbitrary DBs, and an architecture of a generalized OBDA system. Section 4 introduces MongoDB, and describes our extension of *Ontop* over MongoDB. Section 5 evaluates the performance of this system and compares it to the triple store Virtuoso, using as dataset an instance of the well-known Berlin SPARQL Benchmark (BSBM). Section 6 discusses related work, and Sect. 7 concludes the paper.

2   Ontology-Based Data Access

We recall the traditional OBDA paradigm for accessing relational DBs through an ontology [22]. An *OBDA specification* is a triple $\mathcal{P} = \langle \mathcal{T}, \mathcal{M}, \mathcal{S} \rangle$, where $\mathcal{T}$ is an ontology modeling the domain of interest in terms of classes and properties, S is a relational DB schema, and M is a mapping consisting of a finite set of mapping assertions. We note that T consists of axioms involving classes and properties, and does not mention individuals. In other words, T consists only of the intensional part of an ontology.

To define mapping assertions, we make use of (RDF) *term constructors*, each of which is a function $f(x_1, \ldots, x_n)$ mapping a tuple of DB values to an IRI or to an RDF literal. A *mapping assertion* [13] between S and T is an expression of the form

$$\varphi(\boldsymbol{x}) \rightsquigarrow (f(\boldsymbol{x}) \;\texttt{rdf:type}\; A) \qquad \text{or} \qquad \varphi'(\boldsymbol{x}, \boldsymbol{x}') \rightsquigarrow (f(\boldsymbol{x}) \; P \; f'(\boldsymbol{x}')),$$

where A is a class name in T, P is a property name in T, $\varphi(\boldsymbol{x})$ and $\varphi'(\boldsymbol{x}, \boldsymbol{x}')$ are arbitrary (SQL) queries expressed over S, and f and f' are term constructors. Mapping assertions allow one to define how classes and properties in T should be populated with objects constructed from values in a DB instance of S.

An *OBDA instance* is a pair $\langle P, D \rangle$, where $P = \langle T, M, S \rangle$ is an OBDA specification and D is a DB instance satisfying S. The semantics of $\langle P, D \rangle$ is given with respect to the RDF graph $M(D)$ *induced by M and D*, defined by

$$\{(f(\boldsymbol{o}) \;\texttt{rdf:type}\; A) \mid \boldsymbol{o} \in ans(\varphi, D) \text{ and } \varphi \rightsquigarrow (f(\boldsymbol{x}) \;\texttt{rdf:type}\; A) \text{ in } M\} \;\cup$$
$$\{(f(\boldsymbol{o}) \; P \; f'(\boldsymbol{o}')) \mid (\boldsymbol{o}, \boldsymbol{o}') \in ans(\varphi', D) \text{ and } \varphi' \rightsquigarrow (f(\boldsymbol{x}) \; P \; f'(\boldsymbol{x}')) \text{ in } M\},$$

where $ans(\varphi, D)$ denotes the result of the evaluation of φ over D. Then a *model* of $\langle P, D \rangle$ is simply a model of the ontology $T \cup M(D)$. We observe that in this ontology, $M(D)$ provides the set of extensional facts, but such facts are typically kept *virtual*, i.e., they are not actually materialized.

Queries are usually formulated in SPARQL, the Semantic Web query language that allows for formulating expressive high-level queries over an RDF graph [11, 17]. Such queries are answered over the ontology $T \cup M(D)$, according to the semantics of the chosen *entailment regime*. Typically, in OBDA, the ontology T is expressed in OWL 2 QL, and the corresponding entailment regime is that of OWL 2 QL [12].

3 Generalized OBDA Framework

In this section, we introduce a generalization of the OBDA framework to arbitrary DBs, and then propose an architecture for a generalized OBDA system.

3.1 OBDA over Arbitrary Databases

We assume to deal with a class $\mathbf{D}$ of DBs, e.g., relational DBs, XML DBs, or JSON stores, such as MongoDB. Moreover, we assume that $\mathbf{D}$ comes equipped with:

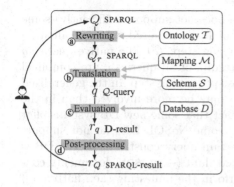

Fig. 1. Query answering in OBDA

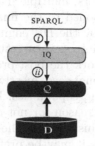

Fig. 2. SPARQL to native query translation

- Suitable forms of constraints, which might express both information about the structure of the stored data, e.g., the relational schema information in relational DBs, and "constraints" in the usual sense of relational DBs, e.g., primary and foreign keys. We call a collection of such constraints a **D**-*schema* (or simply, *schema*).
- A way to view **D**-instances as flat relational DB instances: for a **D**-instance D satisfying a **D**-schema $\mathcal{S}$, $[\![D]\!]$ is a flat relational DB over the relational schema $[\![\mathcal{S}]\!]$. The function $[\![\cdot]\!]$ is called *relational wrapper*.
- A *native* query language $\mathcal{Q}$, such that, for a query $q \in \mathcal{Q}$ and for a **D**-instance D, the answer $ans(q, D)$ of q over D is defined, and is itself a **D**-instance.

Now, given a **D**-schema $\mathcal{S}$, a *mapping* $\mathcal{M}$ is a set of classical mapping assertions $\varphi \rightsquigarrow h$, where φ is a SQL query over $[\![\mathcal{S}]\!]$. Then, as in the relational case, an *OBDA specification* is a triple $\langle \mathcal{T}, \mathcal{M}, \mathcal{S} \rangle$. An *OBDA instance* consists of an OBDA specification $\langle \mathcal{T}, \mathcal{M}, \mathcal{S} \rangle$ and a **D**-instance D satisfying $\mathcal{S}$. The semantics of such an instance is derived naturally from the relational wrapper $[\![\cdot]\!]$.

Note that our assumption that for the class **D** of DBs a relational wrapper is available is not in any way restrictive, since any form of data, independently of how it is structured, can be represented using relations. Observe also that the source query in a mapping assertion in our generalized setting is not a native $\mathcal{Q}$ query, but a SQL query. Our framework has the advantage of having a uniform and expressive mapping language that is independent of **D** and $\mathcal{Q}$. It does not mean, however, that the concrete user mapping language must strictly follow this specification. When it does not, the system should only be able to transform user mapping assertions into classical ones.

By default, when referring to OBDA, we mean the *virtual* approach, which avoids materializing the RDF graph, and instead delegates (part of) query answering to the DB. In this approach, the query answering process can be depicted as in Fig. 1, and done in 4 main steps: *(a)* An input SPARQL query Q is first rewritten with respect to the ontology $\mathcal{T}$ into Q_r (according to the semantics of the entailment regimes, this step only rewrites the basic graph pattern (BGPs) in Q [12]). *(b)* The rewritten SPARQL query Q_r is translated into one or several native queries $q \in \mathcal{Q}$. When the DB engine does not support (efficiently) some SPARQL operators, multiple native queries might be required, whose evaluation could be postponed to the final post-processing step. *(c)* The native queries q are evaluated by the DB engine. *(d)* The results of all queries q are combined and converted into SPARQL results in the post-processing step. In the generalized OBDA framework the post-processing step may be more involved than in the classical relational case, mostly due to the fact that some new DB systems offer limited querying capabilities. In particular, some NoSQL DBs do not support joins. Another reason for not delegating certain query constructs to the DB is efficiency. For instance, in the case of nested data (e.g., JSON documents containing arrays), it may be preferable to perform the unnesting (i.e., flattening) of nested objects into tuples as a post-processing step, so as to reduce network load between DB and client.

For the generalized OBDA framework, we propose to translate SPARQL queries to native queries in two steps (cf. Fig. 2): first translate the input SPARQL query to an *intermediate query*, subject to transformations, and then translate the (transformed) intermediate query to a native query. The *intermediate query language*, denoted IQ, is expected to be a more high-level language than $\mathcal{Q}$, and can vary depending on $\mathcal{Q}$, but also on the considered fragment of SPARQL. On the one hand, it should at least capture such fragment (e.g., for BGPs, joins are sufficient, while for a fragment with property paths, IQ should include some form of recursion). On the other hand, IQ may include other operators present/expressible in $\mathcal{Q}$ (e.g., an unnest operator for dealing with nested data). Note that Relational Algebra (RA) as IQ is sufficient for the first-order fragment of SPARQL and for relational DBs. Our framework relying on the use of IQ provides several advantages: *(i)* It better supports optimizations since IQ, unlike SPARQL, can take into account the structure of the data, without necessarily being as low-level as $\mathcal{Q}$. *(ii)* The optimization techniques devised for IQ are independent of $\mathcal{Q}$. *(iii)* The translation from SPARQL to IQ is standard and depends only on the mapping (since IQ strictly subsumes RA, such a translation has to extend the well-known translation from SPARQL to RA).

3.2   Architecture of an OBDA System over Heterogeneous Data Sources

We propose an architecture of an OBDA system able to answer SPARQL queries over heterogeneous data sources. This architecture, depicted in Fig. 3, assumes an offline and an online query answering stages.

The *offline* stage (steps ⓘ and ⓘⓘ) takes as input the ontology, the mapping, and the schema, and produces two elements, to be used during the online stage: the *classified* ontology, and the *saturated* mapping [18,20], which is constructed by saturating the input mapping with the classified ontology. Notably, the saturated mapping can be significantly simplified for the online stage, by using query containment-based optimization to remove redundant mapping assertions.

The *online* stage handles individual SPARQL queries, and can be split into 6 main steps: ① the input SPARQL query is rewritten according to the classified

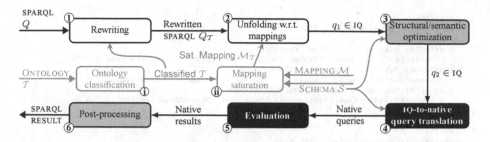

Fig. 3. Proposed architecture for an OBDA system

ontology; ② the rewritten query is unfolded w.r.t. the saturated-mapping by substituting each triple with its mapping definitions; ③ the resulting IQ is simplified by applying structural (e.g., replacing join of unions by union of joins) and semantic (e.g., redundant self-join elimination) optimization techniques; ④ the optimized IQ is translated into one or multiple native queries; ⑤ these are evaluated by the DB engine; ⑥ the native results are combined and transformed into SPARQL results.

Such an architecture allows for steps ⓘ, ⓘⓘ, ①, and ② to be independent of the actual class **D** of DBs (white boxes in Fig. 3). Steps ③ and ⑥ require an implementation specific to IQ (gray boxes), while ④ and ⑤ are specific to **D** (black boxes).

We emphasize that the structural and semantic optimization step is crucial for OBDA to work in practice. In general, SPARQL queries are not aware of the structure of the stored data, hence the unfolded query may contain significantly more joins than necessary. In the case of OBDA over a document-based DB, these techniques can be extended to take advantage of additional opportunities for optimization offered by the structure of the DB instance.

4   OBDA over MongoDB

We illustrate the generalized OBDA framework by focusing on a specific NoSQL DB, namely MongoDB,[2] a popular and representative instance of document DBs.

4.1   MongoDB

MongoDB stores and exposes data as collections of JSON-like documents.[3] A sample collection of two MongoDB documents consisting of (nested) key-value pairs and arrays, is given in Fig. 4, where each document contains information about a product: its id, name, and a list of offers, in the form of a JSON array. Each offer has itself an id, price, and vendor (in turn with id, name and homepage).

---

[2] https://docs.mongodb.org/manual/.
[3] JSON, or JavaScript Object Notation, is a tree-shaped format for structuring data.

```
{ _id: 23226,
  productName: "Olympus OM-D E-M10 Mark II",
  offers: [
    { offerId: 258, price: 747.14, vendor: {
        vendorId: 3785, name: "Yeppon Italia", homepage: "https://www.yeppon.it"} },
    { offerId: 895, price: 609.42, vendor: {
        vendorId: 481, name: "amazon.it", homepage: "https://www.amazon.it"} },
    { offerId: 922, price: 759.99, vendor: {
        vendorId: 481, name: "amazon.it", homepage: "https://www.amazon.it"} } ]
}

{ _id: 25887,
  productName: "Panasonic Lumix DMC-GX80",
  offers: [
    { offerId: 311, price: 500.32, vendor: {
        vendorId: 481, name: "amazon.it", homepage: "https://www.amazon.it"} } ]
}
```

Fig. 4. A collection of two MongoDB documents

product

nr	label
23226	Olympus OM-D E-M10 Mark II
25887	Panasonic Lumix DMC-GX80

vendor

nr	label	homepage
481	amazon.it	http://www.amazon.it
3785	Yeppon Italia	http://www.yeppon.it

offer

nr	price	product	vendor
258	747.14	23226	3785
311	500.32	25887	481
895	609.42	23226	481
922	759.99	23226	481

Fig. 5. Relational view of the collection in Fig. 4, following the BSBM schema

Note that in a normalized relational DB instance, this data would be spread across several tables. Indeed, our example is inspired by the e-commerce scenario of the BSBM benchmark [2], where the data is structured according to a relational schema consisting of multiple tables. Figure 5 provides the relational view corresponding to the above MongoDB collection, with distinct tables for products, offers, and vendors (the relational schema in the BSBM benchmark is actually more complex).

Note also that the JSON data in Fig. 4 is *denormalized*. In particular, it contains redundant information: the name and homepage of vendor 481 are present 3 times. Document-based DBMSs like MongoDB can take advantage of such redundancy. For instance, retrieving all vendors (with id, name, and homepage) of a given product over an instance of the relational schema of Fig. 5 requires 2 (potentially costly) join operations. But the same request over the denormalized data does not require any join: the relevant information is already grouped within a document. However, query execution can also be penalized by redundancy. For instance, given the value 481 for `offers.vendor.vendorId`, the value of `offers.vendor.name` associated to it can be retrieved from one document only. But in order to locate such data, MongoDB would check all documents with an occurrence of 481 for field `offers.vendor.vendorId`. Noticeably, this problem can be avoided by choosing a different document structure for the same data, with one document for each vendor rather than for each product, and consequently with redundant information about products. In general, the choice of a particular document structure is a trade-off, favoring some queries, and penalizing others. Thus, it should be done depending on the expected query workload, provided such information is available beforehand.

Like relational DBs, MongoDB allows for declaring indexes. By default, it creates a unique index over the (top-level) field `_id`, which serves as the primary key in a collection. Indexes can drastically speed up query execution. In particular, retrieving a (whole) document by a unique value of an indexed field (like the values of `offers.offerId` in Fig. 4) can be done very efficiently by looking up the value in the index, and then fetching from disk data that is likely to be contiguous. On the other hand, queries on values with non-unique occurrences (e.g., the values of `offers.offer.vendorId`) may be less efficient, because multiple (non-contiguous) documents might need to be fetched.

MongoDB provides an ad-hoc querying mechanism for formulating expressive queries by means of the *aggregation framework*[4]. A *MongoDB aggregate query (*MAQ*)* is a sequence of *stages*, each of which takes one or two collections of documents as input, and produces another collection as output. A fragment of this language has been shown in [3] to be equivalent in expressive power to Nested Relational Algebra (NRA).

Because the language is powerful, MAQs can be complex to read and to manipulate. As an illustration, the MAQ of Fig. 6 retrieves all products offered twice by the same vendor. In comparison, the SPARQL query of Fig. 7 satisfies the same information need, but in a more concise fashion. The MAQ language also has a more procedural (less declarative) flavor than SQL/SPARQL, in that the sequence of stages of an MAQ is closer to its actual execution, whereas relational DBs/triple stores hide from the user the complexity of query planning (e.g., the ordering of joins). Hence, from a user perspective, OBDA over MongoDB appears indeed as a promising alternative to manually devising MAQs.

4.2 Extension of *Ontop* for MongoDB

We built a proof-of-concept prototype for answering SPARQL queries over MongoDB, called *Ontop/MongoDB*, which extends the *Ontop* system [4] and implements the architecture described in Fig. 3. The current implementation supports the fragment of SPARQL including BGPs, FILTER, JOIN, OPTIONAL, and UNION over MongoDB 3.4. In this implementation of the virtual OBDA architecture, NRA serves as IQ, and MAQ as the native query language. The system is designed to fully delegate query execution to the MongoDB engine,[5] thus minimizing the amount of post-processing required in step ⑥ of Fig. 3. We now provide some details on the input accepted by *Ontop/MongoDB*, and on the implementation of steps ③ and ④.

---

[4] https://docs.mongodb.com/manual/reference/operator/aggregation-pipeline/.

[5] An exception is the step that builds the returned RDF strings (IRIs and literals) from the constants retrieved from the DB.

```
db.bios.aggregate([
  {$project: {
    "productName": true, "offer1": "$offers", "offer2": "$offers" }},
  {$unwind: "$offer1"},
  {$unwind: "$offer2"},
  {$project: {
    "productName": true, "offer1": true, "offer2": true,
    "sameVendor": { $and: [
        {$ne: ["$offer1.offerId", "$offer2.offerId"]},
        {$eq: ["$offer1.vendorId", "$offer2.vendorId"]} ]}}},
  {$match: {"sameVendor": true} },
  {$project: {
    "productName": true, "vendorName": "$offer1.vendor.label",
    "price1": "$offer1.price", "price2": "$offer2.price" }}
])
```

Fig. 6. A MongoDB aggregate query (MAQ)

```
SELECT ?productName ?vendorName ?price1 ?price2
WHERE {
  ?product rdfs:label ?productName .
  ?offer1 bsbm:product ?product . ?offer1 bsbm:price ?price1 .
  ?offer1 bsbm:vendor ?vendor . ?vendor rdfs:label ?vendorName .
  ?offer2 bsbm:product ?product . ?offer2 bsbm:price ?price2 .
  ?offer2 bsbm:vendor ?vendor .
  FILTER (?offer1 != ?offer2) }
```

Fig. 7. A SPARQL query corresponding to the MAQ in Fig. 6

Ontop/MongoDB takes as input an OWL 2 QL ontology, a mapping, and a set of constraints. In the current implementation, the source query φ of each mapping assertion is relatively inexpressive: it can either retrieve a whole collection, or apply a simple filter to it. From the paths mentioned in this mapping, the system extracts the structure of the JSON documents being queried.

The constraints are user-defined functional dependencies that hold over the JSON documents being queried. For instance, in the collection of Fig. 4, the value of path offers.vendor.vendorID uniquely defines the values of paths offers.vendor.name and offers.vendor.homepage. Note that, although MongoDB does not enforce such constraints, they can still hold over the data, and can be used for semantic optimization, e.g., to eliminate redundant joins. Note also that if the JSON collection is a denormalized version of an existing relational DB instance (as is the case for BSBM), then such dependencies can be directly inferred from keys declared in the relational schema.

In step ③, in addition to relational optimization techniques implemented by *Ontop*, *Ontop/MongoDB* also applies techniques specific to nested data, based on the equivalence with NRA mentioned above. In particular, it can take advantage of the constraints just mentioned. In step ④, *Ontop/MongoDB* uses an optimized version of the NRA-to-MAQ translation given in [3], which in theory makes full delegation of query answering to MongoDB feasible, but, if left unoptimized, may produce queries not executable in practice. An important consideration here is the internal limitations put by MongoDB on the size of in-memory intermediate results during query evaluation (16 MB for a single document, and 100 MB for a collection). Another purpose of this optimization is to take advantage of indexes available over the source JSON collection.

5   Evaluation

We have carried out an evaluation that aims at determining whether OBDA over MongoDB is a realistic solution performance-wise, and in particular whether it is able to leverage the document structure of MongoDB collections. We focus on answering queries over datasets that do not fit into memory. In such a setting, a key concern for performance is to limit disk access, i.e., the number of non-contiguous pages that need to be fetched into memory.

To this end, we compare *Ontop/MongoDB* to the triple store Virtuoso [9] representing a diametrically opposite approach to answering SPARQL queries, as far as the data and index structure are concerned. Indeed, Virtuoso stores data as quads (i.e., triples extended with the graph name), and for each element of the quads it maintains an extensive index structure, which is in particular highly optimized for retrieving (multiple) triples sharing a constant value[6]. Comparatively, retrieving all documents for a given value of an indexed field may be inefficient in MongoDB if the value is not unique in the index, as it requires fetching multiple (non-contiguous) documents from disk. On the other hand, when the value is unique, MongoDB can fetch the whole document containing this value very efficiently, whereas for Virtuoso fetching the same data may require multiple disk accesses.

We expect the evaluation to reflect these differences: *(i)* that *Ontop/MongoDB* outperforms Virtuoso on queries containing a unique constant in an indexed field and fetching a single document; *(ii)* that Virtuoso outperforms *Ontop/MongoDB* on queries containing only constants with multiple occurrences in the JSON collection.

An additional goal of the experiments is to determine whether the cost of query rewriting itself (i.e., generating the MAQ) introduces an excessive overhead.

5.1   Dataset and Evaluation Environment

As dataset we used an instance of the well-known BSBM benchmark [2], which emulates an e-commerce scenario, centered on offered products. The number of products in the instance is 4 million, giving 1.2 billion RDF triples, whose total size is 156 GB.

---

[6] http://docs.openlinksw.com/virtuoso/rdfperfrdfscheme/.

BSBM also provides a representation of this dataset as a relational DB instance, composed of 10 tables (product, offer, vendor, etc.). Based on the relational schema of this instance, we generated a 118 GB collection of JSON documents containing the same data. The structure of the documents in this collection extends the one of Fig. 4, grouping in each document all information pertaining to a single product.

The latest version of BSBM comes with 11 queries, numbered from 1 to 12 (there is no query 6 anymore). Among these, 3 were discarded, because they contain SPARQL features not (yet) supported by *Ontop/MongoDB* (DESCRIBE queries, *bound* operator, and variables over predicates). We instantiated 10 versions of each query, replacing constant placeholders with values randomly sampled from the data. One version of each query was set aside for a cold run, and the 8·9 remaining queries were shuffled as a query mix. Execution times reported below are averaged over these 9 versions.

The systems being compared are Virtuoso v7.2.4 (over the RDF triples), and *Ontop/MongoDB* with MongoDB v3.4.2 (over the JSON collection). Queries were run on a 24 cores Intel Xeon CPU at 3.47 GHz, with a 5.4 TB 15k RPM RAID-5 hard-drive cluster. 8 GB of RAM were dedicated to each system (MongoDB and Virtuoso) for caching and intermediate operations. The OS page cache was also flushed every 5 s, to ensure that each system could only exploit these 8 GB for caching. The query timeout was set to 500 s. For each constant appearing in a query, the corresponding field in the MongoDB collection was indexed.

An executable for *Ontop/MongoDB* is available online, together with the SPARQL queries, mapping, constraints, and both datasets (JSON and RDF), so that the experiment can be reproduced. The generated MAQs are also provided.[7]

5.2   Results and Analysis

As a first element of answer, we observed that all MAQs generated by *Ontop/-MongoDB* are optimal with respect to the document structure, in the sense that cross-document operations are only used for joins that cannot be performed within each document.

Table 1 reports the execution times for both systems. For *Ontop/MongoDB*, we distinguish query rewriting time ("rw"), i.e., the time spent generating the MAQ, from its actual evaluation ("eval") by MongoDB. Rewriting time does not depend on the size of the data, but only on the query, mapping, ontology, and constraints, which are less likely to grow out of proportion. Still, for some of the cheaper MAQs (<100 ms), this overhead represents the major part of the execution time. This can be partly explained by the wide range of optimizations performed by *Ontop/MongoDB*. But it is also an aspect to improve, for OBDA over MongoDB to be considered a viable alternative to MongoDB itself, at least in applications with high performance requirements.

---

[7] https://www.dropbox.com/sh/nz8dfas5ijpr76y/AACJzxHZUInrHi6Vq3Lk8f8ra?dl=0.

Table 1. Execution times (ms) for *Ontop/MongoDB* and Virtuoso, over the BSBM benchmark (4 million products). Values are averaged over 9 versions of each query

Query		1	2	4	5	7	8	10	12
Ontop/MongoDB	rw	26	179	102	NA	417	838	22	35
	eval	2672	43	3713	NA	53	66	34	40
Virtuoso	eval	258	308	403	1179	3995	1897	3966	327

We now focus on query evaluation times. For each of the 9 versions of Query 5, the evaluation either timed out, or exceeded MongoDB's memory limitations (see Sect. 4.2). This is explained by the fact that this query contains an anti-join, which requires a (close to) full collection scan from MongoDB. For the 7 remaining queries, we observe a sharp contrast in performance between the two systems, which matches the above expectations. Queries 1 and 4 present a very favorable setting for Virtuoso: the SPARQL BGPs are of limited size (≤ 5 triple patterns), and each of them contains 3 constants. On the other hand, because none of these constants is unique in the JSON collection, the evaluation by *Ontop/MongoDB* requires fetching multiple documents from disk. As expected, for these two queries, evaluating the SPARQL query with Virtuoso was one order of magnitude faster than evaluating the corresponding MAQ with *Ontop/MongoDB*. As for the 5 remaining queries, they all represent a setting where MongoDB can fully benefit from denormalization. First, all 5 queries require data contained in one document only. In addition, they all contain a constant in an indexed field, where the index is either declared as a unique (Queries 2, 7, 8 and 10), or contains only unique values (Query 12). For each of these queries, the evaluation was one to two orders of magnitude faster for MongoDB. This confirms that *Ontop/MongoDB* was able to generate MAQs that take full advantage of the document (and index) structure.

6 Related Work

The idea of using wrappers to access external data sources dates back to the 90s; see e.g., the Garlic data integration system [19]. In recent years, several practical systems were developed for querying MongoDB via SQL: Drill[8], Dremio[9], Studio 3T[10], and the MongoDB Connector for Spark[11]. With such systems, users can query MongoDB collections as nested tables. SQL queries are automatically translated to (basic) MongoDB queries, and post-processing is often required to compute advanced query constructs.

---

[8] https://drill.apache.org/.
[9] https://www.dremio.com/.
[10] https://studio3t.com/whats-new/how-to-query-mongodb-with-sql/.
[11] https://docs.mongodb.com/spark-connector/.

Another line of relevant research is the SQL++ extension of the SQL language for accessing, e.g., JSON data [16]. SQL++ has been supported by the DB engines Couchbase[12] and AsterixDB[13].

There already exist several mapping language proposals extending R2RML for converting non-relational data sources to RDF, e.g., RML [8], xR2RML [14], KR2RML [21], and D2RML [6]. These languages extend the relational model used in R2RML to more general cases (e.g., CSV, JSON, and Web Services). Their corresponding systems are mostly used for data conversion; the xR2RML implementation also supports SPARQL query answering by partially materializing the relevant RDF graph.

Finally, the approach of [1] is comparable in spirit to ours, in that it also aims at delegating query execution to a NoSQL source engine, and relies on an object-oriented (OO) intermediate representation, similar to our "relational view". A key difference though is that the mapping is from the ontology vocabulary to the OO layer, rather than from the source DB to the ontology vocabulary. The aim is to simplify the mapping specification, and make it independent of the underlying source DB. The expressivity of such a mapping is thus limited, essentially mapping OWL classes to (possibly nested) relations.

7 Conclusions

In this paper, we have presented a generalized OBDA framework for arbitrary (not only relational) DBs. It provides a convenient uniform querying interface, by means of a high-level vocabulary coupled with a familiar query language (SPARQL), as an alternative to the variety of ad-hoc query languages provided by native NoSQL DBs. We also propose a practical architecture for a generalized virtual OBDA approach, that allows one to answer SPARQL queries over arbitrary data sources.

We have instantiated this framework in the specific case of MongoDB, as an extension, called *Ontop/MongoDB*, of the OBDA system *Ontop*, and have compared its performance to that of a triple store. The evaluation we have carried out shows that *Ontop/MongoDB* was able to generate MAQs that take full advantage of the denormalized structure of the data.

As a continuation of this work, we plan to evaluate the impact of the different techniques implemented within *Ontop/MongoDB* to optimize the generated MAQ, using a wider range of queries, but also different document structures for the same dataset.

---

[12] http://couchbase.com/.
[13] https://asterixdb.apache.org/.

References

1. Araujo, T.H.D., Agena, B.T., Braghetto, K.R., Wassermann, R.: OntoMongo - ontology-based data access for NoSQL. In: Proceedings of the OntoBras. CEUR, ceur-ws.org, vol. 1908 (2017)
2. Bizer, C., Schultz, A.: The Berlin SPARQL benchmark. Int. J. Semant. Web Inf. Syst. 5(2), 1–24 (2009)
3. Botoeva, E., Calvanese, D., Cogrel, B., Xiao, G.: Expressivity and complexity of MongoDB queries. In: Proceedings of the ICDT. LIPIcs, vol. 98, pp. 9:1–9:22 (2018)
4. Calvanese, D., et al.: Ontop: answering SPARQL queries over relational databases. Semant. Web J. 8(3), 471–487 (2017)
5. Calvanese, D., Liuzzo, P., Mosca, A., Remesal, J., Rezk, M., Rull, G.: Ontology-based data integration in EPNet: production and distribution of food during the Roman Empire. Eng. Appl. Artif. Intell. 51, 212–229 (2016)
6. Chortaras, A., Stamou, G.: D2RML: Integrating heterogeneous data and web services into custom RDF graphs. In: Proceedings of the LDOW. CEUR, ceur-ws.org, vol. 2073 (2018)
7. Das, S., Sundara, S., Cyganiak, R.: R2RML: RDB to RDF mapping language. W3C Recommendation (2012). http://www.w3.org/TR/r2rml/
8. Dimou, A., Vander Sande, M., Colpaert, P., Verborgh, R., Mannens, E., Van de Walle, R.: RML: a generic language for integrated RDF mappings of heterogeneous data. In: Proceedings of the LDOW. CEUR, ceur-ws.org, vol. 1184 (2014)
9. Erling, O., Mikhailov, I.: RDF support in the Virtuoso DBMS. In: Pellegrini, T., Auer, S., Tochtermann, K., Schaffert, S. (eds.) Networked Knowledge - Networked Media. SCI, vol. 221. Springer, Berlin (2009). https://doi.org/10.1007/978-3-642-02184-8_2
10. Giese, M., et al.: Optique: zooming in on big data. IEEE Comput. 48(3), 60–67 (2015)
11. Harris, S., Seaborne, A.: SPARQL 1.1 query language. W3C Recommendation (2013). http://www.w3.org/TR/sparql11-query
12. Kontchakov, R., Rezk, M., Rodríguez-Muro, M., Xiao, G., Zakharyaschev, M.: Answering SPARQL queries over databases under OWL 2 QL entailment regime. In: Mika, P., et al. (eds.) ISWC 2014. LNCS, vol. 8796, pp. 552–567. Springer, Cham (2014). https://doi.org/10.1007/978-3-319-11964-9_35
13. Lenzerini, M.: Data integration: a theoretical perspective. In: Proceedings of the PODS (2002)
14. Michel, F., Djimenou, L., Faron-Zucker, C., Montagnat, J.: Translation of relational and non-relational databases into RDF with xR2RML. In: Proceedings of the WEBIST, pp. 443–454 (2015)
15. Motik, B., Fokoue, A., Horrocks, I., Wu, Z., Lutz, C., Cuenca Grau, B.: OWL web ontology language profiles. W3C Recommendation (2009). http://www.w3.org/TR/owl-profiles/
16. Ong, K.W., Papakonstantinou, Y., Vernoux, R.: The SQL++ query language: configurable, unifying and semi-structured. CoRR Technical Report abs/1405.3631, arXiv.org (2014)
17. Pérez, J., Arenas, M., Gutierrez, C.: Semantics and complexity of SPARQL. ACM TODS 34(3), 16:1–16:45 (2009)
18. Rodríguez-Muro, M., Kontchakov, R., Zakharyaschev, M.: Ontology-based data access: Ontop of databases. In: Alani, H., et al. (eds.) ISWC 2013. LNCS, vol. 8218, pp. 558–573. Springer, Heidelberg (2013). https://doi.org/10.1007/978-3-642-41335-3_35

19. Roth, M.T., Schwarz, P.M.: Don't scrap it, wrap it! A wrapper architecture for legacy data sources. In: Proceedings of the VLDB, pp. 266–275. Morgan Kaufmann (1997)
20. Sequeda, J.F., Arenas, M., Miranker, D.P.: OBDA: query rewriting or materialization? In practice, both!. In: Mika, P., et al. (eds.) ISWC 2014. LNCS, vol. 8796, pp. 535–551. Springer, Cham (2014). https://doi.org/10.1007/978-3-319-11964-9_34
21. Slepicka, J., Yin, C., Szekely, P.A., Knoblock, C.A.: KR2RML: an alternative interpretation of R2RML for heterogenous sources. In: Proceedings of the 6th International Workshop on Consuming Linked Data (COLD), co-located with ISWC. CEUR, ceur-ws.org, vol. 1426 (2015)
22. Xiao, G., et al.: Ontology-based data access: a survey. In: Proceedings of the IJCAI. AAAI Press (2018)

Knowledge Representation and Reasoning

Creative Concept Generation by Combining Description Logic of Typicality, Probabilities and Cognitive Heuristics

Antonio Lieto[1] and Gian Luca Pozzato[2(✉)]

[1] Dipartimento di Informatica, Università di Torino, and ICAR-CNR Palermo,
Turin, Palermo, Italy
antonio.lieto@unito.it
[2] Dipartimento di Informatica, Università di Torino, Turin, Italy
gianluca.pozzato@unito.it

Abstract. We propose a nonmonotonic Description Logic of typicality as a tool for the generation and the exploration of novel creative concepts, that could be useful in many applicative scenarios, ranging from video games to the creation of new movie characters. In particular, our logic is able to deal with the phenomenon of prototypical concept combination, which has been shown to be problematic to model for other formalisms like fuzzy logic. The proposed logic relies on the logic of typicality $\mathcal{ALC}+\mathbf{T_R}$, whose semantics is based on a notion of rational closure, as well as on the distributed semantics of probabilistic Description Logics, and takes into account the insights coming from the heuristics used by humans for concept composition. Besides providing framework able to account for typicality-based concept combination, we also outline that reasoning in the proposed Description Logic is ExpTime-complete as for the underlying $\mathcal{ALC}$.

1 Introduction

Inventing novel concepts by combining the typical knowledge of pre-existing ones is an important human creative ability. Dealing with this problem requires, from an AI perspective, the harmonization of two conflicting requirements that are hardly accommodated in symbolic systems: the need of a syntactic compositionality (typical of logical systems) and one concerning the exhibition of typicality effects [1]. According to a well-known argument [2], in fact, prototypical concepts are not compositional. The argument runs as follows: consider a concept like *pet fish*. It results from the composition of the concept *pet* and of the concept *fish*. However, the prototype of *pet fish* cannot result from the composition of the prototypes of a pet and a fish: e.g. a typical pet is furry and warm, a typical fish is grayish, but a typical pet fish is neither furry and warm nor grayish (typically, it is red).

In this work we provide a framework able to account for this type of human-like concept combination in the scenario of typical concept invention. We exploit

C. Ghidini et al. (Eds.): AI*IA 2018, LNAI 11298, pp. 183–196, 2018.
https://doi.org/10.1007/978-3-030-03840-3_14

a nonmonotonic Description Logic (from now on DL) of typicality called $\mathbf{T}^{CL}$ (typical compositional logic), that has been already shown able to capture well established examples in the literature of cognitive science concerning concept combination [3]. This logic combines two main ingredients. The first one relies on the DL of typicality $\mathcal{ALC}+\mathbf{T_R}$ introduced in [4]. In this logic, "typical" properties can be directly specified by means of a "typicality" operator $\mathbf{T}$ enriching the underlying DL, and a TBox can contain inclusions of the form $\mathbf{T}(C) \sqsubseteq D$ to represent that "typical Cs are also Ds". As a difference with standard DLs, in the logic $\mathcal{ALC} + \mathbf{T_R}$ one can consistently express exceptions and reason about defeasible inheritance as well. For instance, a knowledge base can consistently express that "normally, athletes are fit", whereas "sumo wrestlers usually are not fit" by $\mathbf{T}(Athlete) \sqsubseteq Fit$ and $\mathbf{T}(SumoWrestler) \sqsubseteq \neg Fit$, given that $SumoWreslter \sqsubseteq Athlete$. The semantics of the $\mathbf{T}$ operator is characterized by the properties of *rational logic* [5], recognized as the core properties of nonmonotonic reasoning. $\mathcal{ALC}+\mathbf{T_R}$ is characterized by a minimal model semantics corresponding to an extension to DLs of a notion of *rational closure* as defined in [5] for propositional logic: the idea is to adopt a preference relation among $\mathcal{ALC}+\mathbf{T_R}$ models, where intuitively a model is preferred to another one if it contains less exceptional elements, as well as a notion of *minimal entailment* restricted to models that are minimal with respect to such preference relation. As a consequence, $\mathbf{T}$ inherits well-established properties like *specificity* and *irrelevance*: in the example, the logic $\mathcal{ALC} + \mathbf{T_R}$ allows us to infer $\mathbf{T}(Athlete \sqcap Bald) \sqsubseteq Fit$ (being bald is irrelevant with respect to being fit) and, if one knows that Hiroyuki is a typical sumo wrestler, to infer that he is not fit, giving preference to the most specific information.

As a second ingredient, we consider a distributed semantics similar to the one of probabilistic DLs known as DISPONTE [6], allowing to label axioms with degrees representing probabilities, but restricted to typicality inclusions. The basic idea is to label inclusions $\mathbf{T}(C) \sqsubseteq D$ with a real number between 0.5 and 1, representing its probability[1]: such a number represents the probability of finding elements of C being also D, then we impose that it is at least 50% since we are only considering typicality properties. We assume that the axioms are independent from each other. The resulting knowledge base defines a probability distribution over *scenarios*: roughly speaking, a scenario is obtained by choosing, for each typicality inclusion, whether it is considered as true of false. In a slight extension of the above example, we could have the need of representing that both typicality inclusions about athletes and sumo wrestlers have a probability of 80%, whereas we also believe that athletes are usually young with a higher probability of 95%, with the following KB: (1) $SumoWrestler \sqsubseteq Athlete$; (2) $0.8 :: \mathbf{T}(Athlete) \sqsubseteq Fit$; (3) $0.8 :: \mathbf{T}(SumoWrestler) \sqsubseteq \neg Fit$; (4) $0.95 :: \mathbf{T}(Athlete) \sqsubseteq YoungPerson$. We consider eight different scenarios, representing all possible combinations of typicality inclusion: as an example, $\{((2),1),((3),0),((4),1)\}$ represents the scenario

---

[1] Here, we focus on the proposal of the formalism itself, therefore the machinery for obtaining probabilities from an application domain will not be discussed.

in which (2) and (4) hold, whereas (3) does not. We equip each scenario with a probability depending on those of the involved inclusions, then we restrict reasoning to scenarios whose probabilities belong to a given and fixed range.

As an additional element of the proposed formalization we employ a method inspired by cognitive semantics [7] for the identification of a dominance effect between the concepts to be combined: for every combination, we distinguish a HEAD, representing the stronger element of the combination, and a MODI-FIER. The basic idea is: given a KB and two concepts C_H (HEAD) and C_M (MODIFIER) occurring in it, we consider only *some* scenarios in order to define a revised knowledge base, enriched by typical properties of the combined concept $C \sqsubseteq C_H \sqcap C_M$ (the heuristics for the scenario selections are detailed in Sect. 2, Definition 7).

In this work, we show that the proposed logic $\mathbf{T}^{CL}$ is able to tackle the problem of composing prototypical concepts (by creating a novel, plausible, conceptual prototype) and we exploit the proposed formalism as a tool for the generation of novel creative concepts, that could be useful in many applicative scenarios. We also outline that the reasoning complexity of $\mathbf{T}^{CL}$ is ExpTime-complete, as in the standard $\mathcal{ALC}$ logic, witnessing that the proposed approach is essentially inexpensive.

2   A Logic for Concept Combination

The nonmonotonic Description Logic $\mathbf{T}^{CL}$ combines the semantics based on the rational closure of $\mathcal{ALC}+\mathbf{T_R}$ [4] with the probabilistic DISPONTE semantics [6]. By taking inspiration from [8], we consider two types of properties associated to a given concept: rigid and typical. Rigid properties are those that hold under any circumstance, e.g. $C \sqsubseteq D$ (all Cs are Ds). Typical properties are represented by inclusions equipped by a probability. Additionally, we employ a cognitive heuristic for the identification of a dominance effect between the concepts to be combined, distinguishing between HEAD and MODIFIER[2].

The language of $\mathbf{T}^{CL}$ extends the basic DL $\mathcal{ALC}$ by *typicality inclusions* of the form $\mathbf{T}(C) \sqsubseteq D$ equipped by a real number $p \in (0.5, 1)$ representing its probability, whose meaning is that "normally, Cs are also D with probability p".

Definition 1 (Language of $\mathbf{T}^{CL}$). *We consider an alphabet* C *of concept names,* R *of role names, and* O *of individual constants. Given $A \in$ C and $R \in$ R, we define:*
$$C, D := A \mid \top \mid \bot \mid \neg C \mid C \sqcap C \mid C \sqcup C \mid \forall R.C \mid \exists R.C$$

We define a knowledge base $\mathcal{K} = \langle \mathcal{R}, \mathcal{T}, \mathcal{A} \rangle$ where:

- $\mathcal{R}$ *is a finite set of rigid properties of the form $C \sqsubseteq D$;*
- $\mathcal{T}$ *is a finite set of typicality properties of the form $p :: \mathbf{T}(C) \sqsubseteq D$, where $p \in (0.5, 1) \subseteq \mathbb{R}$ is the probability of the inclusion;*

---

[2] Here we assume that some methods for the automatic assignment of the HEAD/MODIFER pairs are/may be available and focus on the discussion of the reasoning part.

- $\mathcal{A}$ is the *ABox*, i.e. *a finite set of formulas of the form either* $C(a)$ *or* $R(a, b)$, *where* $a, b \in \mathsf{O}$.

It is worth noticing that we avoid typicality inclusions with degree 1. Indeed, an inclusion $1 :: \mathbf{T}(C) \sqsubseteq D$ would mean that it is a certain property, that we represent with $C \sqsubseteq D \in \mathcal{R}$. Also, observe that we only allow typicality inclusions equipped with probabilities $p > 0.5$. Indeed, the very notion of typicality derives from the one of probability distribution, in particular typical properties attributed to entities are those characterizing the majority of instances involved. Moreover, in our effort of integrating two different semantics – DISPONTE and typicality logic – the choice of having probabilities higher than 0.5 for typicality inclusions seems to be the only compliant with both formalisms. In fact, despite the DISPONTE semantics allows to assign also low probabilities/degrees of belief to standard inclusions, in the logic $\mathbf{T}^{CL}$ it would be misleading to also allow low probabilities for typicality inclusions. Please, note that this is not a limitation of the expressivity of the logic $\mathbf{T}^{CL}$: we can in fact represent properties not holding for typical members of a category, for instance if one need to represent that typical students are not married, we can have that $0.8 :: \mathbf{T}(Student) \sqsubseteq \neg Married$.

Following from the DISPONTE semantics, each axiom is independent from each others. This allows us to deal with conflicting typical properties equipped with different probabilities.

A model $\mathcal{M}$ of $\mathbf{T}^{CL}$ extends standard $\mathcal{ALC}$ models by a preference relation among domain elements as in the logic of typicality [4]. In this respect, $x < y$ means that x is "more normal" than y, and that the typical members of a concept C are the minimal elements of C with respect to this relation. An element $x \in \Delta^{\mathcal{I}}$ is a *typical instance* of some concept C if $x \in C^{\mathcal{I}}$ and there is no element in $C^{\mathcal{I}}$ *more typical* than x.

Definition 2 (Model). *A model* $\mathcal{M}$ *is any structure* $\langle \Delta^{\mathcal{I}}, <, .^{\mathcal{I}} \rangle$ *where: (i)* $\Delta^{\mathcal{I}}$ *is a non empty set of items called the domain; (ii)* $<$ *is an irreflexive, transitive, well-founded and modular (for all* x, y, z *in* $\Delta^{\mathcal{I}}$, *if* $x < y$ *then either* $x < z$ *or* $z < y$) *relation over* $\Delta^{\mathcal{I}}$; *(iii)* $.^{\mathcal{I}}$ *is the extension function that maps each concept* C *to* $C^{\mathcal{I}} \subseteq \Delta^{\mathcal{I}}$, *and each role* R *to* $R^{\mathcal{I}} \subseteq \Delta^{\mathcal{I}} \times \Delta^{\mathcal{I}}$. *For concepts of* $\mathcal{ALC}$, $C^{\mathcal{I}}$ *is defined as usual. For the* $\mathbf{T}$ *operator, we have* $(\mathbf{T}(C))^{\mathcal{I}} = Min_<(C^{\mathcal{I}})$, *where* $Min_<(C^{\mathcal{I}}) = \{x \in C^{\mathcal{I}} \mid \nexists y \in C^{\mathcal{I}} \text{ s.t. } y < x\}$.

A model $\mathcal{M}$ can be equivalently defined by postulating the existence of a function $k_{\mathcal{M}} : \Delta^{\mathcal{I}} \longmapsto \mathbb{N}$, where $k_{\mathcal{M}}$ assigns a finite rank to each domain element [4]: the rank of x is the length of the longest chain $x_0 < \cdots < x$ from x to a minimal x_0, i.e. such that there is no x' such that $x' < x_0$. The rank function $k_{\mathcal{M}}$ and $<$ can be defined from each other by letting $x < y$ if and only if $k_{\mathcal{M}}(x) < k_{\mathcal{M}}(y)$.

Definition 3 (Model satisfying a KB). *Let* $\mathcal{K} = \langle \mathcal{R}, \mathcal{T}, \mathcal{A} \rangle$ *be a KB. Given a model* $\mathcal{M} = \langle \Delta^{\mathcal{I}}, <, .^{\mathcal{I}} \rangle$, *we assume that* $.^{\mathcal{I}}$ *is extended to assign a domain element* $a^{\mathcal{I}}$ *of* $\Delta^{\mathcal{I}}$ *to each individual constant* a *of* O. *We say that: (i)* $\mathcal{M}$ *satisfies* $\mathcal{R}$ *if, for all* $C \sqsubseteq D \in \mathcal{R}$, *we have* $C^{\mathcal{I}} \subseteq D^{\mathcal{I}}$; *(ii)* $\mathcal{M}$ *satisfies* $\mathcal{T}$ *if, for all* $q :: \mathbf{T}(C) \sqsubseteq D \in \mathcal{T}$, *we have that* $\mathbf{T}(C)^{\mathcal{I}} \subseteq D^{\mathcal{I}}$, *i.e.* $Min_<(C^{\mathcal{I}}) \subseteq D^{\mathcal{I}}$; *(iii)* $\mathcal{M}$

satisfies $\mathcal{A}$ *if, for each assertion* $F \in \mathcal{A}$*, if* $F = C(a)$ *then* $a^{\mathcal{I}} \in C^{\mathcal{I}}$*, otherwise if* $F = R(a, b)$ *then* $(a^{\mathcal{I}}, b^{\mathcal{I}}) \in R^{\mathcal{I}}$.

Even if the typicality operator $\mathbf{T}$ itself is nonmonotonic (i.e. $\mathbf{T}(C) \sqsubseteq E$ does not imply $\mathbf{T}(C \sqcap D) \sqsubseteq E$), what is inferred from a KB can still be inferred from any KB' with KB $\subseteq$ KB', i.e. the resulting logic is monotonic. In order to perform useful nonmonotonic inferences, in [4] the authors have strengthened the above semantics by restricting entailment to a class of minimal models. Intuitively, the idea is to restrict entailment to models that *minimize the untypical instances of a concept*. The resulting logic corresponds to a notion of *rational closure* on top of $\mathcal{ALC} + \mathbf{T_R}$. Such a notion is a natural extension of the rational closure construction provided in [5] for the propositional logic. This nonmonotonic semantics relies on minimal rational models that minimize the *rank of domain elements*. Informally, given two models of KB, one in which a given domain element x has rank 2 (because for instance $z < y < x$), and another in which it has rank 1 (because only $y < x$), we prefer the latter, as in this model the element x is assumed to be "more typical" than in the former. Query entailment is then restricted to minimal *canonical models*. The intuition is that a canonical model contains all the individuals that enjoy properties that are consistent with KB. This is needed when reasoning about the rank of the concepts: it is important to have them all represented. A query F is minimally entailed from a KB if it holds in all minimal canonical models of KB. In [4] it is shown that query entailment in the nonmonotonic $\mathcal{ALC} + \mathbf{T_R}$ is in ExpTime.

Definition 4 (Entailment). *Let* $\mathcal{K} = \langle \mathcal{R}, \mathcal{T}, \mathcal{A} \rangle$ *be a KB and let* F *be either* $C \sqsubseteq D$ *(C could be* $\mathbf{T}(C')$*) or* $C(a)$ *or* $R(a, b)$*. We say that* F *follows from* $\mathcal{K}$ *if, for all minimal* $\mathcal{M}$ *satisfying* $\mathcal{K}$*, then also* $\mathcal{M}$ *satisfies* F.

Let us now define the notion of *scenario* of the composition of concepts. Intuitively, a scenario is a knowledge base obtained by adding to all rigid properties in $\mathcal{R}$ and to all ABox facts in $\mathcal{A}$ only *some* typicality properties. More in detail, we define an *atomic choice* on each typicality inclusion, then we define a *selection* as a set of atomic choices in order to select which typicality inclusions have to be considered in a scenario.

Definition 5 (Atomic choice). *Given* $\mathcal{K} = \langle \mathcal{R}, \mathcal{T}, \mathcal{A} \rangle$*, where* $\mathcal{T} = \{E_1 = q_1 :: \mathbf{T}(C_1) \sqsubseteq D_1, \ldots, E_n = q_n :: \mathbf{T}(C_n) \sqsubseteq D_n\}$ *we define* (E_i, k_i) *an atomic choice for some* $i \in \{1, 2, \ldots, n\}$*, where* $k_i \in \{0, 1\}$.

Definition 6 (Selection). *Given* $\mathcal{K} = \langle \mathcal{R}, \mathcal{T}, \mathcal{A} \rangle$*, where* $\mathcal{T} = \{E_1 = q_1 :: \mathbf{T}(C_1) \sqsubseteq D_1, \ldots, E_n = q_n :: \mathbf{T}(C_n) \sqsubseteq D_n\}$ *and a set of atomic choices* ν*, we say that* ν *is a selection if, for each* E_i*, one decision is taken, i.e. either* $(E_i, 0) \in \nu$ *and* $(E_i, 1) \notin \nu$ *or* $(E_i, 1) \in \nu$ *and* $(E_i, 0) \notin \nu$ *for* $i = 1, 2, \ldots, n$*. The probability of* ν *is* $P(\nu) = \prod_{(E_i, 1) \in \nu} q_i \prod_{(E_i, 0) \in \nu} (1 - q_i)$.

Definition 7 (Scenario). *Given* $\mathcal{K} = \langle \mathcal{R}, \mathcal{T}, \mathcal{A} \rangle$*, where* $\mathcal{T} = \{E_1 = q_1 :: \mathbf{T}(C_1) \sqsubseteq D_1, \ldots, E_n = q_n :: \mathbf{T}(C_n) \sqsubseteq D_n\}$ *and given a selection* σ*, we define* a scenario $w_\sigma = \langle \mathcal{R}, \{E_i \mid (E_i, 1) \in \sigma\}, \mathcal{A} \rangle$. We also define the probability of a scenario w_σ as the probability of the corresponding selection, i.e. $P(w_\sigma) = P(\sigma)$. Last, we say that a scenario is consistent when it admits a model in the logic $\mathbf{T}^{CL}$.

We denote with $\mathcal{W}_{\mathcal{K}}$ the set of all scenarios. It immediately follows that the probability of a scenario $P(w_\sigma)$ is a probability distribution over scenarios, that is to say $\sum_{w \in \mathcal{W}_{\mathcal{K}}} P(w) = 1$.

Given a KB $\mathcal{K} = \langle \mathcal{R}, \mathcal{T}, \mathcal{A} \rangle$ and given two concepts C_H and C_M occurring in $\mathcal{K}$, our logic allows to define the compound concept C as the combination of the HEAD C_H and the MODIFIER C_M, where $C \sqsubseteq C_H \sqcap C_M$ and the typical properties of the form $\mathbf{T}(C) \sqsubseteq D$ to ascribe to the concept C are obtained in the set of scenarios that:

1. are consistent;
2. are not trivial, i.e. those with the highest probability, in the sense that the scenarios considering *all* properties that can be consistently ascribed to C are discarded;
3. are those giving preference to the typical properties of the HEAD C_H (with respect to those of the MODIFIER C_M) with the highest probability. Notice that, in case of conflicting properties like D and $\neg D$, given two scenarios w_1 and w_2, both belonging to the set of consistent scenarios with the highest probability and such that an inclusion $p_1 :: \mathbf{T}(C_H) \sqsubseteq D$ belongs to w_1 whereas $p_2 :: \mathbf{T}(C_M) \sqsubseteq \neg D$ belongs to w_2, the scenario w_2 is discarded in favor of w_1.

In order to select the wanted scenarios we apply points 1, 2, and 3 above to blocks of scenarios with the same probability, in decreasing order starting from the highest one. More in detail, we first discard all the inconsistent scenarios, then we consider the remaining (consistent) ones in decreasing order by their probabilities. We then consider the blocks of scenarios with the same probability, and we proceed as follows:

- we discard those considered as *trivial*, consistently inheriting all (or most of) the properties from the starting concepts to be combined;
- among the remaining ones, we discard those inheriting properties from the MODIFIER in conflict with properties inherited from the HEAD in another scenario of the same block (i.e., with the same probability);
- if the set of scenarios of the current block is empty, i.e. all the scenarios have been discarder either because trivial or because preferring the MODIFIER, we repeat the procedure by considering the block of scenarios, all having the immediately lower probability;
- the set of remaining scenarios are those selected by the logic $\mathbf{T}^{CL}$.

The knowledge base obtained as the result of combining concepts C_H and C_M into the compound concept C is called *C-revised* knowledge base:

$$\mathcal{K}_C = \langle \mathcal{R}, \mathcal{T} \cup \{p : \mathbf{T}(C) \sqsubseteq D\}, \mathcal{A} \rangle,$$

for all D such that $\mathbf{T}(C) \sqsubseteq D$ is entailed in w. The probability p is defined as follows: if D is a property inherited either from the HEAD (or from both the HEAD and the MODIFIER), then p corresponds to the probability of such inclusion of the HEAD in the initial knowledge base, i.e. $p :: \mathbf{T}(C_H) \sqsubseteq D \in \mathcal{T}$; otherwise, p corresponds to the probability of such inclusion of a MODIFIER in the initial knowledge base, i.e. $p :: \mathbf{T}(C_M) \sqsubseteq D \in \mathcal{T}$. Notice that, since the C-revised knowledge base is still in the language of the $\mathbf{T}^{CL}$ logic, we can iteratively repeat the same procedure in order to combine not only atomic concepts, but also compound concepts. We leave a detailed analysis of this topic for future works.

We conclude the section by showing that reasoning in $\mathbf{T}^{CL}$ remains in the same complexity class of standard $\mathcal{ALC}$. For the completeness, let n be the size of KB, then the number of typicality inclusions is $O(n)$. It is straightforward to observe that we have an exponential number of different scenarios, for each one we need to check whether the resulting KB is consistent in $\mathcal{ALC} + \mathbf{T_R}$ which is ExpTime-complete. Hardness immediately follows from the fact that $\mathbf{T}^{CL}$ extends $\mathcal{ALC} + \mathbf{T_R}$. In [3] we have shown that reasoning in $\mathbf{T}^{CL}$ in the revised knowledge is ExpTime-complete.

3 Artificial Prototypes Composition and Concept Invention

In this section we exploit the logic $\mathbf{T}^{CL}$ to show both (i) how it allows to automatically generate novel, plausible, prototypical concepts by composing two initial prototypes and (ii) how it can be used as a generative tool in the field of computational creativity (with applications in the so called creative industry). In detail, we first show how our logic can model the generation of a quite complex concept recently introduced in the field of narratology, i.e. that one of the ANTI-HERO (a role invented by narratologists to generate new story lines), by combining the typical properties of the concepts HERO and VILLAIN. Of course, the specific domain of the example is not relevant here; our goal is showing how $\mathbf{T}^{CL}$ can model this kind of prototypical concept composition (a crucial aspect of human concept invention) that, on the other hand, has been proven to be problematic for other kinds of logics (e.g fuzzy logic, [2,9]). We then show how the same machinery can be used as a creative support tool to generate a new type of villain for a video game or a movie.

3.1 The Anti Hero

We will take into account the concepts of HERO, ANTI-HERO and VILLAIN extracted by the common sense descriptions coming from the TvTropes repository (https://tvtropes.org). In such online repository, typical descriptions of character roles are provided. They can be useful for practitioners of the narrative field in order to design their own character according to the main assets presented in such schemas. In particular, Tropes can be seen as devices and conventions that a writer can reasonably rely on as being present in the audience members' minds and expectations. Regarding the HERO, TvTropes identifies the following relevant representative features: e.g. the fact that it is characterized by his/her fights against the VILLAIN of a story, the fact that his/her actions are necessarily guided by general goals to be achieved in the interest of the collectivity, the fact that he/she fights against the VILLAIN in a fair way and so on. Examples of such Trope are: Superman, Flash Gordon etc. The ANTI-HERO, on the other hand, is described as characterized by the fact of sharing most of its typical traits with the HERO (e.g. the fact that it is the protagonist of a plot fighting against the VILLAIN of the story); however, his/her moves are not guided by a general spirit of sacrifice for the collectivity but, rather, they are usually based on some personal motivations that, incidentally and/or indirectly, coincide with the needs of the collectivity. Furthermore the ANTI-HERO may also act in a not fair way in order to achieve the desired goal. A classical example of such Trope is Batman, whose moves are guided by his desire of revenge. Finally the VILLAIN is represented as a classic negative role in a plot and is characterized as the main opponent of the protagonist/HERO. In addition to this classical contraposition, TvTropes also reports some physical elements characterizing such role from a visual point of view. For example: the characters of this Trope are usually physically endowed with some demoniac cues (e.g. they have the "eyes of fire"). Finally, they are guided by negative moral values. Examples of such role can be easily taken from the classical literature to the modern comics. Some representative exemplars are Cruella de Vil in Disney's filmic saga or Voldemort in Harry Potter.

Let us now exploit our logic $\mathbf{T}^{\text{CL}}$ in order to define a prototype of ANTI-HERO. First of all, we define a knowledge base describing both rigid and typical properties of concepts HERO and VILLAIN, then we rely on the logic $\mathbf{T}^{\text{CL}}$ in order to formalize an *AntiHero*-revised knowledge base.

Let $\mathcal{K} = \langle \mathcal{R}, \mathcal{T}, \mathcal{A} \rangle$ be a KB, where the ABox $\mathcal{A}$ is empty. Concerning rigid properties, let $\mathcal{R}$ be as follows:

R1 *Hero* $\sqsubseteq \exists hasOpponent.Villain$
R2 *Villain* $\sqsubseteq \forall fightsFor.PersonalGoal$
R3 *Villain* $\sqsubseteq WithNegativeMoralValues$
R4 *CollectiveGoal* $\sqcap$ *PersonalGoal* $\sqsubseteq \bot$
R5 *WithPositiveMoralValues* $\sqcap$ *WithNegativeMoralValues* $\sqsubseteq \bot$
R6 *AngelicIconicity* $\sqcap$ *DemoniacIconicity* $\sqsubseteq \bot$.

Prototypical properties of villains and heroes are described in $\mathcal{T}$ as follows:

T1 $0.95 ::$ $\mathbf{T}(Hero) \sqsubseteq Protagonist$
T2 $0.85 ::$ $\mathbf{T}(Hero) \sqsubseteq \exists fightsFor.CollectiveGoal$
T3 $0.9 ::$ $\mathbf{T}(Hero) \sqsubseteq WithPositiveMoralValues$
T4 $0.6 ::$ $\mathbf{T}(Hero) \sqsubseteq AngelicIconicity$
T5 $0.75 ::$ $\mathbf{T}(Villain) \sqsubseteq DemoniacIconicity$

T6 0.8 :: $\mathbf{T}(Villain) \sqsubseteq Implulsive$
T7 0.75 :: $\mathbf{T}(Villain) \sqsubseteq Protagonist$.

We make use of the logic $\mathbf{T}^{CL}$ in order to build the compound concept *AntiHero* as the result of the combination of concepts *Hero* and *Villain*. Differently from what the natural language seems to suggest, we consider this compound concept by assuming that the HEAD is *Villain* (since the ANTI-HERO shares more typical traits with this concept than with the HERO concept).

First of all, we have that the compound concept inherits all the rigid properties of both its components (if not contradictory), therefore in the logic $\mathbf{T}^{CL}$ we have that:

(i) $AntiHero \sqsubseteq \exists hasOpponent.Villain$
(ii) $AntiHero \sqsubseteq \forall fightsFor.PersonalGoal$
(iii) $AntiHero \sqsubseteq WithNegativeMoralValues$.

For the typical properties, we consider all the $2^7 = 256$ different scenarios obtained from all possible selections about inclusion in $\mathcal{T}$. Some of them are inconsistent, namely those including either axiom T2 or axiom T3, since they would ascribe properties in contrast with inherited rigid properties of (ii) and (iii): rigid properties impose that an anti hero has negative moral values, and all his goals are personal, therefore he is an atypical hero in those respects (T2 states that typical heroes fights also for some collective goals, whereas T3 states that normally heroes have positive moral values). Also scenarios containing both axioms T4 and T5 are inconsistent, due to the fact that the concepts *AngelicIconicity* and *DemoniacIconicity* are disjoint (formalized by R6).

Let us consider the remaining, consistent scenarios: the one having the highest probability considers all the properties of both concepts by excluding only *AngelicIconicity*, that is to say the one with the lowest probability between the two properties in conflict. In $\mathbf{T}^{CL}$ this scenario is discarded since it is the most trivial one. When we consider scenarios less trivial, i.e., more surprising scenarios (we analyze scenarios in decreasing order of probability), we discard the scenario with probability 0.13%, which includes T4, associated to the MODIFIER, rather than T5, associated to the HEAD, allowing to conclude, in a counter intuitive way, that typical anti heroes have an angelic iconicity rather than a demoniac one.

Next scenarios, sharing the same probability (0.09%), are as follows:

T1 0.95 :: $\mathbf{T}(Hero) \sqsubseteq Protagonist$	T1 0.95 :: $\mathbf{T}(Hero) \sqsubseteq Protagonist$
T5 0.75 :: $\mathbf{T}(Villain) \sqsubseteq DemoniacIconicity$	T6 0.8 :: $\mathbf{T}(Villain) \sqsubseteq Implulsive$
T6 0.8 :: $\mathbf{T}(Villain) \sqsubseteq Implulsive$	T7 0.75 :: $\mathbf{T}(Villain) \sqsubseteq Protagonist$

According to the logic $\mathbf{T}^{CL}$, both are adequate and represent the outcome of the whole heuristic procedures adopted in $\mathbf{T}^{CL}$. Probably, in this case, it could be more useful to opt for the solution on the left allowing to inherit a further property (i.e. *DemoniacIconicity*) for the generated prototypical Anti-Hero. However, we remain agnostic about the selection of the final options provided by $\mathbf{T}^{CL}$. This choice can be plausibly left to human decision makers and based on their own goals.

A final element that is worth noticing in $\mathbf{T}^{CL}$ is the following: in our logic, adding a new inclusion, e.g. $\mathbf{T}(AntiHero) \sqsubseteq Brave$, would not be problematic. That is to say that our formalism is able to tackle the phenomenon of prototypical *attributes emergence* for the new compound concept, widely described in the Cognitive Science literature [7].

In the next subsection we show how $\mathbf{T}^{CL}$ can be used to invent novel concepts.

3.2 The Villain Chair

Let us assume to generate a novel concept obtained as the combination of concepts *Villain* (as HEAD) and *Chair* (as MODIFIER). Let $\mathcal{K} = \langle \mathcal{R}, \mathcal{T}, \emptyset \rangle$ be as follows:

R1 $Villain \sqsubseteq \exists fightsFor.PersonalGoal$
R2 $Villain \sqsubseteq Animate$
R3 $Villain \sqsubseteq WithNegativeMoralValues$
R4 $Chair \sqsubseteq \exists hasComponent.SupportingSeatComponent$
R5 $Chair \sqsubseteq \exists hasComponent.Seat$
R6 $CollectiveGoal \sqcap PersonalGoal \sqsubseteq \bot$

and $\mathcal{T}$ is as follows:

T1 0.9 :: $\mathbf{T}(Villain) \sqsubseteq DemoniacIconicity$
T2 0.75 :: $\mathbf{T}(Villain) \sqsubseteq \exists hasOpponent.Hero$
T3 0.75 :: $\mathbf{T}(Villain) \sqsubseteq Protagonist$
T4 0.8 :: $\mathbf{T}(Villain) \sqsubseteq Impulsive$
T5 0.95 :: $\mathbf{T}(Chair) \sqsubseteq \neg Animate$
T6 0.95 :: $\mathbf{T}(Chair) \sqsubseteq \exists hasComponent.Back$
T7 0.65 :: $\mathbf{T}(Chair) \sqsubseteq \exists madeOf.Wood$
T8 0.8 :: $\mathbf{T}(Chair) \sqsubseteq Comfortable$
T9 0.7 :: $\mathbf{T}(Chair) \sqsubseteq Inflammable.$

We consider the 512 scenarios, from which we discard the inconsistent ones, namely those including T5: indeed, since R2 imposes that villains are animate, in the underlying $\mathcal{ALC} + \mathbf{T_R}$ we conclude that $Villain \sqcap Chair \sqsubseteq Animate$, therefore all scenarios including T5, imposing that $Villain \sqcap Chair \sqsubseteq \neg Animate$ are inconsistent. We also discard the most obvious scenario including all the typicality inclusions of $\mathcal{R}$, having probability of 14%, and the ones containing all the inclusions related to the HEAD. The first suitable scenarios are those having probability 4.67% and contain all properties coming from the MODIFIER and three out of four properties coming from the HEAD. Such scenarios define two alternative revised knowledge bases: one containing T2 and not T3, the other one containing T3 and not T2. These scenarios are the preferred ones selected by the logic $\mathbf{T}^{CL}$.

However, in this application setting, we could imagine to use our framework as a creativity support tool and thus considering alternative - more surprising - scenarios by adding additional constraints. For example, we could impose that the compound concept should inherit exactly six properties. In this case, we would get that the scenario having the highest probability (3.2%) is the one including all the properties of the HEAD, namely T1, T2, T3 and T4, and two out of four properties of the MODIFIER, namely T6 and T8. Due to its triviality, this scenario is discarded, in favor of the following more creative scenarios, with probability 2.51%, obtained by excluding T7 of the MODIFIER and one out of four properties of the HEAD:

T1 0.9 :: $\mathbf{T}(Villain \sqcap Chair) \sqsubseteq DemoniacIconicity$
T2 0.75 :: $\mathbf{T}(Villain \sqcap Chair) \sqsubseteq \exists hasOpponent.Hero$
T4 0.8 :: $\mathbf{T}(Villain \sqcap Chair) \sqsubseteq Impulsive$
T6 0.95 :: $\mathbf{T}(Villain \sqcap Chair) \sqsubseteq \exists hasComponent.Back$
T8 0.8 :: $\mathbf{T}(Villain \sqcap Chair) \sqsubseteq Comfortable$
T9 0.7 :: $\mathbf{T}(Villain \sqcap Chair) \sqsubseteq Inflammable$

T1 0.9 :: $\mathbf{T}(Villain \sqcap Chair) \sqsubseteq DemoniacIconicity$
T3 0.75 :: $\mathbf{T}(Villain \sqcap Chair) \sqsubseteq Protagonist$
T4 0.8 :: $\mathbf{T}(Villain \sqcap Chair) \sqsubseteq Impulsive$
T6 0.95 :: $\mathbf{T}(Villain \sqcap Chair) \sqsubseteq \exists hasComponent.Back$
T8 0.8 :: $\mathbf{T}(Villain \sqcap Chair) \sqsubseteq Comfortable$
T9 0.7 :: $\mathbf{T}(Villain \sqcap Chair) \sqsubseteq Inflammable$

---

4 Related and Future Works

In this work we have considered a nonmonotonic Description Logic $\mathbf{T}^{CL}$, extending the DL of typicality $\mathcal{ALC} + \mathbf{T_R}$ with a DISPONTE semantics, in order to deal with the generation of novel creative concepts. This logic enjoys good computational properties, since entailment in it remains ExpTime as the underlying monotonic $\mathcal{ALC}$, and is able to take into account the concept combination of prototypical properties. To this aim, the logic $\mathbf{T}^{CL}$ allows to have inclusions of the form $p :: \mathbf{T}(C) \sqsubseteq D$, representing that, with a probability p, typical Cs are also Ds. Then, several different scenarios – having different probabilities – are described by including or not such inclusions, and prototypical properties of combinations of concepts are obtained by restricting reasoning services to scenarios having suitable probabilities, excluding "trivial" ones with the highest probabilities.

In AI, several approaches have been proposed to deal with the problem of prototypical concept composition in a human-like fashion. The authors of [10] present a detailed analysis of the limits of the set-theoretic approaches, the fuzzy logics (whose limitations was already shown in [11]), the vector-space models and quantum probability approaches proposed to model this phenomenon. In addition, they propose to use hierarchical conceptual spaces [12] to model the phenomenon in a way that accurately reflects how humans exploit their creativity in conjunctive concept combination. While we agree with the authors with the comments moved to the described approaches, we showed that our logic can equally model, in a cognitively compliant-way, the composition of prototypes by using a nonmonotonic formalism whose complexity remains in the same class of standard monotonic $\mathcal{ALC}$. Other attempts similar to the one proposed here concerns the conceptual blending: a task where the obtained concept is *entirely novel* and has no strong association with the two base concepts (while in concept combination the compound concept is always a subset of the base concepts, for details see [13]). In [14] the authors propose a mechanism for conceptual blending based on the DL $\mathcal{EL}^{++}$. They construct the generic space of two concepts by introducing an upward refinement operator that is used for finding common generalizations of $\mathcal{EL}^{++}$ concepts. However, differently from us, what they call prototypes are expressed in the standard monotonic DL, which does not allow to reason about typicality and defeasible inheritance. More recently, a different approach is proposed in [15], where the authors see the problem of concept blending as a nonmonotonic search problem and propose to use Answer Set Programming (ASP) to deal with this search problem in a nonmonotonic way. In a related work [16], the author extends the logic of typicality $\mathcal{ALC} + \mathbf{T_R}$ by means of probabilities equipping typicality inclusions of the form $\mathbf{T}(C) \sqsubseteq_p D$, whose intuitive meaning is that, "normally, Cs are Ds and we have a probability of $1 - p$ of having exceptional Cs not being Ds". Probabilities of exceptions are then used in order to reason about plausible scenarios, obtained by selecting only *some* typicality assumptions and whose probabilities belong to a given and fixed range. As a difference with the logic $\mathbf{T}^{CL}$, all typicality assumptions are systematically taken into account: as a consequence, one cannot exploit such a DL for capturing compositionality, since it is not possible to block inheritance of prototypical properties in concept combination. The logic $\mathbf{T}^{CL}$ extends the work of [16] in that it does not systematically take into account all typicality assumptions. As a consequence, $\mathbf{T}^{CL}$ allows to block inheritance of prototypical properties in concept combination. The same criticism applies also to the approach proposed in [17], where $\mathcal{ALC} + \mathbf{T_R}$ is extended by inclusions of the form $\mathbf{T}(C) \sqsubseteq_d D$, where d is a *degree of expectedness*, used to define a preference relation among extended ABoxes: entailment of queries is then restricted to ABoxes that are minimal with respect to such preference relations and that represent surprising scenarios. Also in this case, however, the resulting logic does not allow to define scenarios containing only some inclusions, since all of them are systematically considered. Similarly, probabilistic DLs [18] themselves cannot be employed as a framework for dealing with the combination of concepts, since these logics are not able to represent and reason about prototypical properties.

In future research we aim at extending our approach to more expressive DLs, such as those underlying the standard OWL language. Starting from the work of [19], applying the logic with the typicality operator and the rational closure to $\mathcal{SHIQ}$, we intend to study whether and how $\mathbf{T}^{CL}$ could provide an alternative solution to the problem of the "all or nothing" behavior of rational closure with respect to property inheritance. We also aim at implementing efficient reasoners for $\mathbf{T}^{CL}$, relying on the prover RAT-OWL [20] which allows to reason in the nonmonotonic logic $\mathcal{ALC} + \mathbf{T_R}$ underlying our approach.

The knowledge base obtained by adding typicality inclusions of a compound concept remains in the language of the logic $\mathbf{T}^{CL}$, allowing to iterate the process in order to define concepts as combinations of – not necessarily atomic – existing concepts. We plan to investigate this opportunity in future works.

Acknowledgements. This work has been partially supported by the project "ExceptionOWL: Nonmonotonic Extensions of Description Logics and OWL for defeasible inheritance with exceptions", Università di Torino and Compagnia di San Paolo, call 2014 "Excellent (young) PI". Gian Luca Pozzato has been also partially supported by the project "iNdAM GNCS" - Metodi di prova orientati al ragionamento automatico per logiche non-classiche.

References

1. Frixione, M., Lieto, A.: Representing concepts in formal ontologies: compositionality vs. typicality effects. Log. Log. Philos. **21**(4), 391–414 (2012)
2. Osherson, D.N., Smith, E.E.: On the adequacy of prototype theory as a theory of concepts. Cognition **9**(1), 35–58 (1981)
3. Lieto, A., Pozzato, G.L.: A description logic of typicality for conceptual combination. In: Ceci, M., Japkowicz, N., Liu, J., Papadopoulos, G.A., Raś, Z.W. (eds.) ISMIS 2018. LNCS (LNAI), vol. 11177, pp. 189–199. Springer, Cham (2018). https://doi.org/10.1007/978-3-030-01851-1_19
4. Giordano, L., Gliozzi, V., Olivetti, N., Pozzato, G.L.: Semantic characterization of rational closure: from propositional logic to description logics. Artif. Intell. **226**, 1–33 (2015)
5. Lehmann, D., Magidor, M.: What does a conditional knowledge base entail? Artif. Intell. **55**(1), 1–60 (1992)
6. Riguzzi, F., Bellodi, E., Lamma, E., Zese, R.: Reasoning with probabilistic ontologies. In: Yang, Q., Wooldridge, M., (eds.): Proceedings of the Twenty-Fourth International Joint Conference on Artificial Intelligence, IJCAI 2015, Buenos Aires, Argentina, 25–31 July 2015, pp. 4310–4316. AAAI Press (2015)
7. Hampton, J.A.: Inheritance of attributes in natural concept conjunctions. Mem. Cogn. **15**(1), 55–71 (1987)
8. Lieto, A., Minieri, A., Piana, A., Radicioni, D.P.: A knowledge-based system for prototypical reasoning. Connect. Sci. **27**, 137–152 (2015)
9. Hampton, J.A.: Conceptual combinations and fuzzy logic. Concepts Fuzzy Log. **209**, 209–232 (2011)
10. Lewis, M., Lawry, J.: Hierarchical conceptual spaces for concept combination. Artif. Intell. **237**, 204–227 (2016)
11. Smith, E.E., Osherson, D.N.: Conceptual combination with prototype concepts. Cogn. Sci. **8**(4), 337–361 (1984)
12. Gärdenfors, P.: The Geometry of Meaning: Semantics Based on Conceptual Spaces. MIT Press, Cambridge (2014)

13. Nagai, Y., Taura, T.: Formal description of concept-synthesizing process for creative design. In: Gero, J.S. (ed.) Design Computing and Cognition '06, pp. 443–460. Springer, Dordrecht (2006). https://doi.org/10.1007/978-1-4020-5131-9_23

14. Confalonieri, R., Schorlemmer, M., Kutz, O., Peñaloza, R., Plaza, E., Eppe, M.: Conceptual blending in EL++. In: Lenzerini, M., Peñaloza, R., (eds.): CEUR Workshop Proceedings of the 29th International Workshop on Description Logics, Cape Town, South Africa, 22–25 April 2016, vol. 1577. CEUR-WS.org (2016)

15. Eppe, M., et al.: A computational framework for conceptual blending. Artif. Intell. **256**, 105–129 (2018)

16. Pozzato, G.L.: Reasoning in description logics with typicalities and probabilities of exceptions. In: Antonucci, A., Cholvy, L., Papini, O. (eds.) ECSQARU 2017. LNCS (LNAI), vol. 10369, pp. 409–420. Springer, Cham (2017). https://doi.org/10.1007/978-3-319-61581-3_37

17. Pozzato, G.L.: Reasoning about plausible scenarios in description logics of typicality. Intell. Artif. **11**(1), 25–45 (2017)

18. Riguzzi, F., Bellodi, E., Lamma, E., Zese, R.: Probabilistic description logics under the distribution semantics. Semant. Web **6**(5), 477–501 (2015)

19. Giordano, L., Gliozzi, V., Olivetti, N., Pozzato, G.L.: Rational closure in $\mathcal{SHIQ}$. In: CEUR Workshop Proceedings DL 2014, 27th International Workshop on Description Logics, vol. 1193, pp. 543–555. CEUR-WS.org (2014)

20. Giordano, L., Gliozzi, V., Pozzato, G.L., Renzulli, R.: An efficient reasoner for description logics of typicality and rational closure. In: Artale, A., Glimm, B., Kontchakov, R., (eds.): CEUR Workshop Proceedings of the 30th International Workshop on Description Logics, Montpellier, France, 18–21 July 2017, vol. 1879. CEUR-WS.org (2017)

A Comparative Study of Defeasible Argumentation and Non-monotonic Fuzzy Reasoning for Elderly Survival Prediction Using Biomarkers

Lucas Rizzo[1](✉), Ljiljana Majnaric[2], and Luca Longo[1]

[1] School of Computing, Dublin Institute of Technology, Dublin, Ireland
lucas.rizzo@mydit.ie, luca.longo@dit.ie
[2] Department of Family Medicine, School of Medicine, University of Osijek, Osijek, Croatia

Abstract. Computational argumentation has been gaining momentum as a solid theoretical research discipline for inference under uncertainty with incomplete and contradicting knowledge. However, its practical counterpart is underdeveloped, with a lack of studies focused on the investigation of its impact in real-world settings and with real knowledge. In this study, computational argumentation is compared against non-monotonic fuzzy reasoning and evaluated in the domain of biological markers for the prediction of mortality in an elderly population. Different non-monotonic argument-based models and fuzzy reasoning models have been designed using an extensive knowledge base gathered from an expert in the field. An analysis of the true positive and false positive rate of the inferences of such models has been performed. Findings indicate a superior inferential capacity of the designed argument-based models.

Keywords: Argumentation Theory · Non-monotonic reasoning Defeasible reasoning · Fuzzy reasoning · Possibility Theory Biomarkers

1 Introduction

Inferences through knowledge driven approaches have been researched extensively in the field of Artificial Intelligence. Among such approaches computational argumentation has recently emerged as a solid theoretical research discipline for defeasible reasoning and inference under uncertainty. Unfortunately, there is a lack of studies which examine its impact in real-world settings by considering real knowledge surrounded by uncertainty, incompleteness and contradictions. In certain settings, like in health care, large amounts of data are not always available, due to the difficulties in gathering it and because of privacy issues. Nonetheless, inferences have to be made. Knowledge-driven approaches are likely better suited in such cases instead of data-driven approaches because

© Springer Nature Switzerland AG 2018
C. Ghidini et al. (Eds.): AI*IA 2018, LNAI 11298, pp. 197–209, 2018.
https://doi.org/10.1007/978-3-030-03840-3_15

they rely upon knowledge-bases derived by human experts and not automatically extracted from data. Various quantitative approaches of reasoning under uncertainty exist. One of these is Fuzzy reasoning which allows robust representation of linguistic information and provide designers with computational tools to describe incomplete, inconsistent or ambiguous knowledge.

In this research, the inferential capacity of computational argumentation is compared against the one of non-monotonic fuzzy reasoning. The domain that has been chosen for such a comparison is survival prediction using biological markers. Biomarkers can be defined as features of the state or condition of a human which can be objectively measured and assessed as indicators of normal or abnormal biological processes [10]. This domain has been chosen because of the availability of a small dataset built over a number of months by a doctor in medicine who also provided an extensive knowledge-base. The research question under investigation is: *to what extent can computational argumentation enhance the prediction of survival in elderly using biomarkers features when compared to non-monotonic fuzzy reasoning?*

The remainder of this paper is organised as follows: Sect. 2 introduces related work on computational argumentation, non-monotonic fuzzy reasoning and biomarkers. The design of a comparative experiment and the methods for the development of argument-based and fuzzy reasoning-based models are detailed in Sect. 3. Section 4 provides the results followed by a discussion while Sect. 5 concludes the study suggesting future avenues of research.

2   Related Work

Many approaches in the field of Artificial Intelligence (AI) have been studied for dealing with quantitative reasoning under uncertainty. Among them, Fuzzy Logic and Argumentation Theory (AT) have already been used for modeling non-monotonic (defeasible) reasoning, a type of reasoning characterised by incomplete, contradicting and uncertain knowledge.

Argumentation Theory (AT) provides computational models for the implementation of defeasible reasoning [14], or reasoning when a conclusion can be changed in the light of new evidence. It has become progressively central in the AI domain for implementing non-monotonic reasoning [2,5]. Furthermore, it is getting momentum thanks to its higher capacity and transparency to justify and retrace inferences [15,16]. In recent works [19,20] it is shown how different knowledge-bases can be translated into different argument-based models following a 5-layer schema upon which argumentation systems are generally built [13]. This schema includes the definition of the internal structure of arguments, the attacks and the resolution of conflicts as well as the computation of their dialectical status and the production of a final justifiable inference (schema adopted in this study and detailed in Sect. 3.3).

Fuzzy reasoning is well suited for modelling linguistic information and handling uncertain, imprecise knowledge providing a powerful framework for reasoning. However, not much work has been carried out on non-monotonic fuzzy reasoning. A few works have proposed some possible approaches for handling non-monotonicity. For example, in [4], the resolution of conflicting rules was tackled through aggregating their conclusions with an averaging function, or in [9], a rule base compression method is proposed for the reduction of the set of non-monotonic rules. A third approach can be found in [21]. It makes use of Possibility Theory [7] as a mechanism to solve conflicting information. Possibility Theory generalises the traditional fuzzy system in the sense that propositions have not one, but two truth values: *possibility* and *necessity*. Both are values within $[0, 1] \in \mathbb{R}$, but the first indicates the extent to which data fail to refute its truth while the second indicates the extent to which data supports its truth.

An example of a domain where inferences have to be made in condition of uncertainty, incomplete and contradicting knowledge is health care. Here, for example, mortality of elderly individuals has to be predicted and this is mainly caused by non-communicable diseases, such as cardiovascular disease [12]. Prognostic information is then of essential value for clinical decision making, that in turn is useful fort the development of advance care planning for higher risk patients [11]. Some works have tackled this problem and attempted to use new biomakers in the prediction of mortality. [6] compares a few biomarkers, such as homocysteine, against other classic risk scores for predicting cardiovascular mortality in older people. In another example [1] the use blood borne biomarkers is explored as potential predictors of mortality risk. Nonetheless, biomakers validation as prognostic factors is still an open issue [22] given the uncertainty of the knowledge applied. Also, when predicting mortality, available evidence might be partial and conflicting, adding burden to the decision making process.

3   Design and Methodology

In order to answer the research question a primary research study was designed. This includes a comparison between the inferences produced by AT and non-monotonic fuzzy reasoning within the biomarkers domain. A knowledge-base on mortality risk factors in elderly, produced by an expert in the field, was employed for the development of non-monotonic fuzzy reasoning and argument-based models. Both approaches require that firstly, the knowledge-base is translated into logical expressions that can be adapted as computational rules or arguments. Three main units compose the non-monotonic fuzzy reasoning models: (1) a fuzzification module, (2) an inference engine and (3) a defuzzification module (Fig. 1 left). The argument-based models are structured over 5 layers, as proposed in [13] (Fig. 1 right): (1) definition of the structure of arguments, (2) definition of their conflicts, (3) their evaluation (4) the computation of the dialectical status of each argument and (5) their final accrual. A comparison of the inferences produced by AT and fuzzy reasoning was done by assessing their true positive (TPR) and false positive (FPR) rates on a dataset of 93 elderly patients described by 51 biomarkers (feature set). This data was obtained in a primary health care European hospital and the survival status of the 93 patients was recorded 5 years after data collection. The design of the research is summarised in Fig. 1.

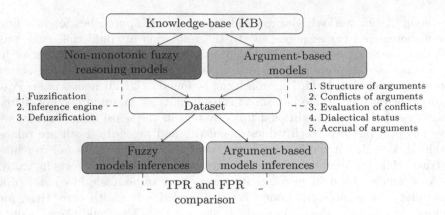

Fig. 1. Evaluation strategy schema.

3.1 Knowledge-Base

Fifty one biomarkers were described by a clinician and their association with mortality risk levels was defined. Each description was encapsulated in one or more sentences to facilitate their adaptation into formal rules and formal arguments. Six out of 51 biomarkers were discarded given the contradictory information in their descriptions. For instance, suppose the description given for serum iron (iron in the blood when red blood cells and clotting factors have been removed) and its respective encapsulation:

– Description 1: *'Testing serum iron is a part of complete blood count test. According to available knowledge, both, lower and upper extremes of the interval values, recorded in the sample, might be unbeneficial for survival.'*
– Encapsulation 1: *low* OR *high* `serum iron` *imply* `unbeneficial survival`.

Mortality risks were subsequently classified into five different categories: *no risk* (r_1), *low risk* (r_2), *medium risk* (r_3), *high risk* (r_4) and *extremely risk* (r_5). This classification was deducted from natural language descriptions such as: "may be non beneficial for survival", "major cause of mortality" and "unbeneficial for survival". Encapsulation 1 can then be extended to:

– Encapsulation 2: *low* OR *high* `serum iron` *imply* `low risk` (r_2).

Contradictions and preferences among biomarkers were also provided by the interviewed domain expert. Since the full knowledge-base is vast and due to space limitations in this paper, it can be found online.[1]

3.2 Non-monotonic Fuzzy Reasoning Models

Fuzzification Module. Rules in the form *"IF ... THEN ..."* were constructed given the encapsulated description. It is a straightforward process exemplified by the definition of rule R1 given Encapsulation 2:

---

[1] http://dx.doi.org/10.6084/m9.figshare.7028480.

– R1: **IF** *low* serum iron OR *high* serum iron **THEN** r_2.

Fuzzy membership functions (FMF) were defined for linguistic variables such as *low* serum iron and *high* serum iron. Not all biomakers had a fuzzy representation and they were incorporated into the fuzzy models as crisp variables (membership grade always 0 or 1). These include, for example, categorical biomarkers, such as hypertension, or numerical biomarkers with a strict threshold for their different levels, such as high-density lipoprotein cholesterol. Twenty one out of 45 biomakers could be modelled as fuzzy variables and had a FMF defined by the domain expert. Figure 2 depicts an example of FMF for *low* and *high* serum iron. The categories representing the five mortality risks also had an associated FMF (Fig. 3). Due to space limitation, the full list of FMFs can be found in the online knowledge-base (see footnote 1).

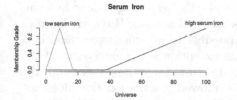

Fig. 2. Membership function for low serum iron (triangular) and high serum iron (linear).

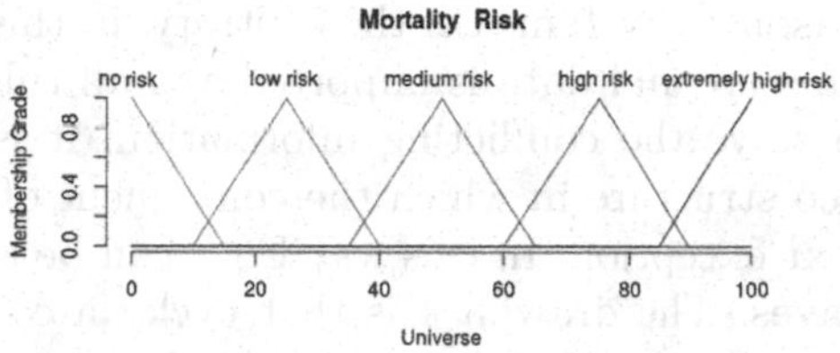

Fig. 3. Triangular membership functions for risks r_{2-4} and linear membership functions for risks r_1 and r_5.

Inference Engine. Once the knowledge-base has been fully operationalised in the fuzzification module, then the model could be extended to perform fuzzy inferences. Due to the presence of a high amount of contradicting information in the knowledge-base, a mechanism for resolving contradictions was required. An example of a contradiction for increased serum insulin (INS) and waist to hip ratio (w/h) exist:

– Contradiction 1: **IF** *low* INS **THEN** w/h is not high.

This information indicates that if INS is *low* then any rule whose antecedent contains "high w/h" is being refuted and its truth value should be re-evaluated. For example:

– R2: **IF** *high* w/h **THEN** low risk (r_2)
– Exception 1: *low* INS *refutes* R2.

A possible approach for dealing with these types of exceptions is through the use of Possibility Theory. The work [21] presents an implementation of fuzzy reasoning with rule-based systems. It expands the usual fuzzy system using not one but two truth values named *possibility* (Pos) and *necessity* (Nec). Possibility can be seen as the extent to which data fail to refute its truth, whereas the

Necessity of a proposition can be seen as the extent to which data supports its truth. Both possibility and necessity lies in the range $[0, 1] \in \mathbb{R}$. Possibility of a proposition can also be seen as the upper bound of the respective necessity (Pos $\geq$ Nec). Note that in a regular fuzzy system, necessity represents the membership grade of a proposition and possibility is always 1 for all propositions. The effect on the necessity of a proposition A by a set of propositions Q which refutes A is derivable in [21] and given by:

$$Nec(A) = min(Nec(A), \neg Nec(Q_1), \ldots, \neg Nec(Q_n)) \tag{1}$$

where $\neg Nec(Q) = 1 - Nec(Q)$. In this study, there is no consideration of supporting information but only attempts to refute information. Thus, Eq. (1) can deal with the contradictions in the knowledge-base when the membership grade of a proposition is interpreted as its necessity. It is important to highlight that the approach developed in [21] was inspired by a multi-step forward-chaining reasoning system. On the contrary, in this study, the reasoning is done in a single step, and data is imported and all rules are fired at once. However, in order to solve the conflicting information, it is possible to organise exceptions in a tree structure in which the consequent of an exception is the antecedent of the next exception. In this way Eq. 1 can be applied from the root or roots until the leaves. The drawback is that cycles are not allowed, a situation that does not occur in the knowledge-base considered in this study. Eventually, the effect of Exception 1 on the truth value of R2 is:

- Truth value R2 = Nec(*high* w/h) = min (Nec(*high* w/h), 1 - Nec(*low* INS)).

Nec(*high* w/h) is the membership grade of the linguistic variable high of biomarker w/h. If Nec(*low* INS) = 0 note that Exception 1 has no impact on R2 and if Nec(*low* INS) = 1 the new truth value of R2 is 0. Values between 1 and 0 indicates that R2 is partially refuted. The truth value of R2 represents the truth value of **low risk** in this respective rule.

Having a mechanism to solve conflicts, fuzzy logic operators can now be used to aggregate the antecedents of each rule and to aggregate the categories of mortality risks of consequents. Traditional fuzzy operators are selected for investigation: *Zadeh*, *Product* and *Lukasiewicz*. Table 1 lists the t-norms and t-conorms (fuzzy AND and fuzzy OR respectively) for each of them. Antecedents might employ OR or/and AND, while consequents (mortality risks) are aggregated by the OR operator. For instance, the truth value of **low risk** (r_2) in a context where only R1 and R2 infer r_2 is "Nec(R1) OR Nec(R2)".

Table 1. T-Norms and t-Conorms employed for two propositions a and b

Fuzzy operator	T-Norm	T-Conorm
Zadeh	$\min(a,b)$	$\max(a,b)$
Lukasiewicz	$\max(a + b - 1, 0)$	$\min(a + b, 1)$
Product	$a.b$	$a + b - a.b$

Defuzzification Module. The output of the inference engine is a graphic representation of the aggregation of the consequents (r_{1-5}) of rules as depicted in the example of Fig. 4. Several methods can be used for calculating a single defuzzified scalar. Two are selected here: *mean of max* and *centroid*. The former returns the average of all elements (in this case mortality risks) with maximal membership grade. The latter returns the coordinates (x, y) of the center of gravity of the geometric shape formed by the aggregation of the FMF of each mortality risk (example in Fig. 4) In summary, a set of models is constructed with different fuzzy logic operators and defuzzification techniques (Table 2). Each designed model produces a single scalar in the range $[0, 100] \in \Re$ as a final inference. However, beside this output, a final inference has to be produced for predicting mortality: death or survival. Several cutoffs of the scalar output are automatically applied to investigate how to separate the two possible outcomes.

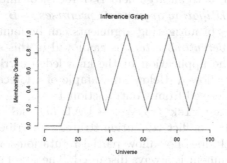

Fig. 4. Example of inference graph with truth values of $r_1 = 0$ and $r_{2-5} = 1$. The coordinates of the centroid are (58.52, 0.34) and the mean of max is 62.5.

Table 2. Set up of fuzzy models designed.

Model	Operators	Defuzzification method
$F1$	Zadeh	Centroid
$F2$	Zadeh	Mean of max
$F3$	Product	Centroid
$F4$	Product	Mean of max
$F5$	Lukasiewicz	Centroid
$F6$	Lukasiewicz	Mean of max

3.3   Argument-Based Models

The definition of argument based-models follows the 5-layer modelling approach proposed in [13] (and depicted in Fig. 1 right).

Layer 1 - Definition of the Structure of Arguments. The first step consists on the construction of *forecast arguments*. These can be represented like:

Forecast argument : *premises* → *conclusion*

This structure is composed by a set of premises related to some biomarkers from which a conclusion can be deducted by applying an inference rule →. These are defeasible argument and informally it means that if the set of premises holds, then the conclusion presumably holds. Here conclusions are represented by the 5 categories of mortality risks, r_{1-5} (Sect. 3.1). Arguments are constructed from the encapsulated descriptions of biomarkers provided by the domain expert. For example, the following argument is derived from Encapsulation 2:

A1: *low* OR *high* `serum iron` → `low risk` (r_2)

Layer 2 - Definition of the Conflicts of Arguments. The objective here is to model possible inconsistencies among arguments. *Mitigating arguments* [17] are constructed using the notion of attack. These are formed by a set of premises and an attack relation ⇒ to an argument B (forecast or mitigating):

Mitigating argument : *premises* ⇒ *B*

Different typologies of mitigating arguments can be found in [18]. However, only the notion of *undercutting attack* is employed in this study. It defines an exception by which the application of the knowledge carried in the attacked argument is no longer allowed. Below an example of a forecast argument and a mitigating argument derived from Contradiction 1:

- A2: *high* `w/h` → `low risk` (r_2) - UA1: *low* `INS` ⇒ A2

Differently than the conflict resolution strategy described in Sect. 3.2, here an undercutting attack does not allow partial refutation, rather full refutation whereby its target argument is always discarded. The set of arguments (forecast and mitigating) and the set of undercutting attacks, originated from mitigating arguments, form an *argumentation framework* (AF) (example in Fig. 5-Left).

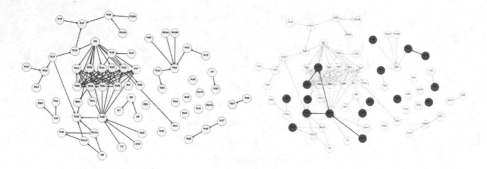

Fig. 5. Argumentation framework (Left): graphical representation of the knowledge-base employed in this primary research. Nodes are arguments, directed edges are attacks. Sub-Argumentation framework (Right): activated arguments (blue nodes) and surviving attacks for one record of the dataset. (Color figure online)

Layer 3 - Evaluation of the Conflicts of Arguments. The knowledge-base operationalised as an AF can now be elicited with real data. Arguments whose premises evaluate true are activated otherwise discarded. Attacks between activated arguments are considered valid. From activated arguments and valid attacks a *sub-argumentation framework* (sub-AF) emerges (Fig. 5-Right).

Layer 4 - Definition of the Dialectical Status of Arguments. Given a sub-AF, acceptability semantics are applied to compute the dialectical status of each argument (accepted or rejected). Each record of the dataset activates a different sub-AF and thus semantics have to be run for each of them. Among well-known semantics such as *grounded* and *preferred* [8], the grounded semantics is employed here. It returns only one *extension* (set) of arguments which is conflict free (it can be empty). It represents the least questionable set of arguments. Beside grounded semantics, also a ranking-based semantics is employed in this study. The goal is to rank-order arguments from the most to the least acceptable one. Note that, with a ranking-based semantics, arguments supporting different conclusions (here mortality risks) can be part of the same extension since they are simply ranked. Here, the *categorizer* semantic has been selected [3]. It ranks arguments based on the number of direct attacks in a way that attacks, from non attacked arguments, are stronger than attacks from arguments attacked multiple times. The detailed implementation of the categorizer semantics can be found in [3]. Figure 6 shows an example of a sub-AF evaluated by grounded and categorizer semantics. Note that arguments attacked only by rejected arguments can still be rejected under the categorizer semantics.

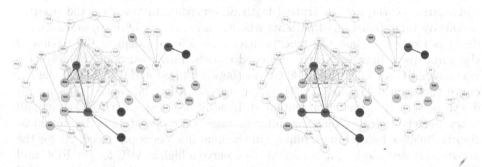

Fig. 6. Argumentation framework: acceptable arguments computed by the grounded semantics (left) and categorizer semantics (right). Blue nodes are activated but do not support a conclusion (mitigating arguments), so are not accepted neither rejected. Red and green nodes are forecast arguments rejected and accepted respectively. (Color figure online)

Layer 5 - Accrual of Acceptable Arguments. The last stage of the reasoning process is to produce a final inference (here a single scalar). This is defined by accrual of the accepted forecast arguments. Mitigating arguments do not support a conclusion and so have their role finalized by contributing to the resolution of conflicts. Each accepted forecast argument supports one mortality risk. In this case mortality risks have crisp values: $r_1 = 0, r_2 = 25, r_3 = 50, r_4 = 75, r_5 = 100$. It is important to highlight that there is no correct values for mortality risks, but for comparison purposes, argument-based models adopts the same values designed by the domain expert for the fuzzy membership functions (for the consequents of rules). In this research, the final scalar is proposed to be equal to the risk value supported by the highest number of accepted forecast arguments. In case of a tie, their average is returned. In the same way as in the defuzzification unit of the fuzzy reasoning approach, several cutoffs of the scalar inference are automatically used to separate the possible outcomes (death or survival).

4   Results

Data from 93 elderly patients and 51 different biomarkers was obtained from primary health care European hospital during the time span of two years.[2] This was used to instantiate argument-based models employing grounded and categorizer semantics and also fuzzy reasoning models as listed in Table 2 (Sect. 3.2). The percentage of death and survival records is 39% and 61% respectively, so not perfectly balanced. The evaluation metrics selected were true positive rate (TPR) and false positive rate (FPR), which can be visualised by a Receiver Operating Characteristic (ROC) curve and compared according to the Area Under the Curve (AUC). Different thresholds to separate the two type of inferences produced, (death and survival), are automatically generated, providing one TPR and one FPR for each model and each cutoff. The AUC of the Precision-Recall (PR) curve is also investigated. This has been chosen because of the imbalanced distribution of the grouth truth (death or survival). In this case the positive predictive value (fraction of patients who had an inference of death and actually died) is plotted against the true positive rate. Figure 7 depicts the results of the comparison between all the designed models. Fuzzy reasoning models have very low AUC for both the ROC curves (between 0.284 and 0.306), and the PR curve (between 0.232 and 0.264) which suggests a low inferential capacity for death regardless of the cutoff employed. In addition, the similar AUC among all fuzzy models indicates that the different fuzzy logic operators and defuzzification techniques had minimal impact in the final inferences produced. As for the argument-based models, it is possible to observe a higher AUC for the ROC and PR curves, 0.494 and 0.371 respectively for the model employing the grounded semantic and 0.502 and 0.377 for the model employing the categorizer semantic, which is significantly better than non-monotonic fuzzy reasoning.

4.1   Discussion

The AUC of the ROC curve for the fuzzy reasoning models shows a worse performance when compared to that of the argument-based models (approximately 67% lower on average). One factor that can likely explain the better performance of argumentation is its superior capacity in conflict resolution, thus actually better handling non-monotonicity as well as capturing and representing defeasible information. Another factor that might explain the lower

---

[2] https://doi.org/10.6084/m9.figshare.7028516.v1.

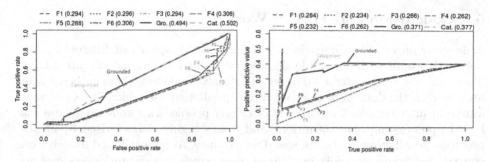

Fig. 7. True positive rate by false positive rate (left) and positive predictive value by true positive rate (right), for fuzzy and argument-based models for different cutoffs in the range $[0, 100] \in \Re$. The AUC is presented next to each model's name (top).

performance of fuzzy reasoning models is the higher number of crisp variables present in the knowledge-base. These variables can hide the vagueness associated to information, undermining the capacity of fuzzy reasoning models to capture non-monotonic reasoning. In relation to the PR curve, the peak of 0.5 positive predictive value (for models F1, F3, F4, F6) suggests that the models based upon fuzzy reasoning are able to achieve a higher fraction of correct death inferences, but only with a very low true positive rate. In other words, AT presents a more robust fraction of correct death inferences when the true positive rate is higher, which is a clear advantage in the prediction of mortality. Nonetheless, it is also important to highlight that the AUC of the ROC curve for all models is very similar to the area associated to a random binary classifier (0.5). Although someone can argue that this is very poor, the random classifier does not given any insight on the inferences produced. Therefore, such a comparison is not useful. However, findings here are in line to a previous work where it has been shown that not even some data-driven approach for classifying mortality, using the same dataset employed in this research, could significantly outperform a random classifier [20]. This indeed suggests that the knowledge available is actually incomplete, uncertain and fragmented. Further work can be done to extend the current knowledge-base with additional information and the argument-based approach, described in this study, can actually support such a task. For example, those cases that have been predicted incorrectly can be further analysed individually. Since the concept of argument is always used across the layers of the defeasible argumentative approach, this makes the retracement and explanation of its inferences easier. Thus for a non-expert it is easier to grasp whether something went wrong or some additional information is actually needed. If this additional information become available, it can then be added to the previous knowledge-base and the inferential process can be repeated again. This task is more intuitive for a non-expert when compared to the fuzzy reasoning approach which employs the fuzzification and defuzzification mechanisms that are not really intuitive.

5   Conclusion and Future Work

This study presented a comparison of the inferential capacity of different reasoning models built with defeasible argumentation and non-monotonic fuzzy logic. These models were constructed upon an extensive knowledge-base gathered from an expert in the domain of elderly survival prediction using biomakers and were aimed at inferring death or survival of elderly people. This knowledge-base was based upon assumptions, intuitions and it was highly characterised by incompleteness, conflicting information and uncertainty. Argument-based models were constructed based on a 5-layer schema upon which argumentation systems are generally built: from the definition of arguments and attacks to the resolution of their conflicts, the production of their dialectical status and their final accrual towards a final inference. The fuzzy reasoning models adopted Possibility Theory for modeling conflicts among designed rules. This allowed the expansion of an usual fuzzy system by using not only one but two truth values of a proposition namely *possibility* and *necessity*. The metrics selected for the investigation of the inferential capacity of designed models were the true positive rate, the false positive rate and the positive predictive value. Findings showed how the argument-based models outperformed the fuzzy reasoning models. Future work will be focused on the replication of this study by evaluating the impact of other argument-based acceptability semantics on the computation of the dialectical status of arguments and their final accrual. Other experts will be interviewed to build additional knowledge-bases for the same problem. This will help strengthening current findings and better demonstrate the impact of argumentation for defeasible inference across different knowledge-bases. Eventually, the explainability of defeasible argumentation and its capacity of presenting justifiable inferences will be investigated more precisely.

Acknowledgments. Lucas Middeldorf Rizzo would like to thank CNPq (Conselho Nacional de Desenvolvimento Científico e Tecnológico) for his Science Without Borders scholarship, proc n. 232822/2014-0.

References

1. Barron, E., Lara, J., White, M., Mathers, J.C.: Blood-borne biomarkers of mortality risk: systematic review of cohort studies. PloS One **10**(6), e0127550 (2015)
2. Bench-Capon, T.J., Dunne, P.E.: Argumentation in artificial intelligence. Artif. Intell. **171**(10–15), 619–641 (2007)
3. Besnard, P., Hunter, A.: A logic-based theory of deductive arguments. Artif. Intell. **128**(1–2), 203–235 (2001)
4. Castro, J.L., Trillas, E., Zurita, J.M.: Non-monotonic fuzzy reasoning. Fuzzy Sets Syst. **94**(2), 217–225 (1998)
5. Chesñevar, C.I., Maguitman, A.G., Loui, R.P.: Logical models of argument. ACM Comput. Surv. (CSUR) **32**(4), 337–383 (2000)
6. De Ruijter, W., et al.: Use of framingham risk score and new biomarkers to predict cardiovascular mortality in older people: population based observational cohort study. BMJ **338**, a3083 (2009)

7. Dubois, D., Prade, H.: Possibility theory: qualitative and quantitative aspects. In: Smets, P. (ed.) Quantified Representation of Uncertainty and Imprecision, pp. 169–226. Springer, Dordrecht (1998). https://doi.org/10.1007/978-94-017-1735-9_6

8. Dung, P.M.: On the acceptability of arguments and its fundamental role in non-monotonic reasoning, logic programming and N-person games. Artif. Intell. **77**(2), 321–358 (1995)

9. Gegov, A., Gobalakrishnan, N., Sanders, D.: Rule base compression in fuzzy systems by filtration of non-monotonic rules. J. Intell. Fuzzy Syst. **27**(4), 2029–2043 (2014)

10. Group, B.D.W., et al.: Biomarkers and surrogate endpoints: preferred definitions and conceptual framework. Clin. Pharmacol. Ther. **69**(3), 89–95 (2001)

11. Lee, S., Lindquist, K., Segal, M., Covinsky, K.: Development and validation of a prognostic index for 4-year mortality in older adults. Jama **295**(7), 801–808 (2006)

12. Lloyd-Jones, D., Adams, R., Carnethon, M., et al.: Heart disease and stroke statistics 2009 update: a report from the American heart association statistics committee and stroke statistics subcommittee. Circulation **119**(3), e21–e181 (2009)

13. Longo, L.: Argumentation for knowledge representation, conflict resolution, defeasible inference and its integration with machine learning. In: Holzinger, A. (ed.) Machine Learning for Health Informatics. LNCS (LNAI), vol. 9605, pp. 183–208. Springer, Cham (2016). https://doi.org/10.1007/978-3-319-50478-0_9

14. Longo, L., Dondio, P.: Defeasible reasoning and argument-based systems in medical fields: an informal overview. In: 2014 IEEE 27th International Symposium on Computer-Based Medical Systems, pp. 376–381, New York (2014)

15. Longo, L., Hederman, L.: Argumentation theory for decision support in healthcare: a comparison with machine learning. In: Imamura, K., Usui, S., Shirao, T., Kasamatsu, T., Schwabe, L., Zhong, N. (eds.) BHI 2013. LNCS (LNAI), vol. 8211, pp. 168–180. Springer, Cham (2013). https://doi.org/10.1007/978-3-319-02753-1_17

16. Longo, L., Kane, B., Hederman, L.: Argumentation theory in health care. In: Proceedings of CBMS 2012, The 25th IEEE International Symposium on Computer-Based Medical Systems, Rome, Italy, 20–22 June 2012, pp. 1–6 (2012)

17. Matt, P.A., Morgem, M., Toni, F.: Combining statistics and arguments to compute trust. In: 9th International Conference on Autonomous Agents and Multiagent Systems, Toronto, Canada, vol. 1, pp. 209–216. ACM, May 2010

18. Prakken, H.: An abstract framework for argumentation with structured arguments. Argum. Comput. **1**(2), 93–124 (2010)

19. Rizzo, L., Longo, L.: Representing and inferring mental workload via defeasible reasoning: a comparison with the NASA task load index and the workload profile. In: 1st Workshop on Advances in Argumentation in Artificial Intelligence, pp. 126–140 (2017)

20. Rizzo, L., Majnaric, L., Dondio, P., Longo, L.: An investigation of argumentation theory for the prediction of survival in elderly using biomarkers. In: Iliadis, L., Maglogiannis, I., Plagianakos, V. (eds.) AIAI 2018. IAICT, vol. 519, pp. 385–397. Springer, Cham (2018). https://doi.org/10.1007/978-3-319-92007-8_33

21. Siler, W., Buckley, J.J.: Fuzzy Expert Systems and Fuzzy Reasoning. Wiley, Hoboken (2005)

22. Strimbu, K., Tavel, J.A.: What are biomarkers? Curr. Opin. HIV AIDS **5**(6), 463 (2010)

Compact Preference Representation via Fuzzy Constraints in Stable Matching Problems: Theoretical and Experimental Studies

Maria Silvia Pini[1(✉)], Francesca Rossi[1,2], and Kristen Brent Venable[3]

[1] University of Padova, Padua, Italy
pini@dei.unipd.it
[2] IBM T.J. Watson Research Center, Yorktown Heights, NY, USA
frossi@math.unipd.it
[3] Tulane University and IHMC, New Orleans, USA
kvenabl@tulane.edu

Abstract. The stable matching problem has many practical applications in two-sided markets, like those that assign doctors to hospitals or students to schools. Usually it is assumed that all agents in each side explicitly express a preference ordering over those in the other side. This can be unfeasible and impractical when the set of agents is very big. However, usually this set has a combinatorial structure, since each agent is often described by some features. To tackle these scenarios, we define a framework for stable matching problems where agents are allowed to express their preferences over those of the other group in a compact way, via soft constraints over the features describing these agents. We focus on a special kind of soft constraints, namely fuzzy constraints. We provide a solving engine for this new kind of stable matching problems that does not increase the time complexity of the classical Gale-Shapley algorithm, while maintaining stability of the matching returned. We then evaluate the approach experimentally.

1 Introduction

The stable matching (SM) problem is a well-known problem with many practical applications. It considers two sets of agents, often called men and women, that should be matched in such a way that no man and woman, who are not married to each other, both prefer each other to their current partner [11,14]. This property is called stability. Problems of this kind arise in many real-life situations, such as assigning junior doctors to hospitals [21], children to schools [22], students to campus housing, and kidney transplant patients to donors.

F. Rossi—On leave from University of Padova.

C. Ghidini et al. (Eds.): AI*IA 2018, LNAI 11298, pp. 210–224, 2018.
https://doi.org/10.1007/978-3-030-03840-3_16

The most well-known and used algorithm to find a stable matching is the Gale-Shapley algorithm (GS) [9], that runs in polynomial time. It assumes that both men and women express a preference ordering over all members of the other gender. However, this can be unfeasible, since the number of men and women can be very large. For example, in China, over 10 million students apply for admission to higher education annually via a centralized process.

In addition, eliciting the preferences may be a costly and time-consuming process. However, the sets of men and women may have a combinatorial structure, which allows for expressing preferences in a compact way by referring to features rather than entire men or women. For instance, consider a large set of hospitals offering residencies to doctors. Doctors may not want to rank explicitly all the hospitals, but may rather wish to express preferences over some of their features. For example, they might say "I prefer a position close to my home town", or "If the hospital is far away from my home town, then I want a better salary". The same can be for hospitals over doctors, which may have preferences such as "We prefer doctors who excel in a certain skill".

In this paper we study how to adapt the GS algorithm to work with such preference statements over features, and the impact of this approach over the computational properties of the algorithm. The main operations performed by the GS algorithm are the following ones: men need to exploit their preferences over women to find their most preferred woman, and possibly also their next most preferred woman (several times), while women need to compare two men according to their preferences over men. Thus, we need to check what it means to perform such operations when preference statements are over features of men and women and they are modelled via soft constraints.

In the soft constraint formalism [15], preferences are modeled in a quantitative way, with several levels of acceptance to express the degrees of preference for the variable assignments. To use such formalism within the GS stable matching procedure, we need to model the GS operations mentioned above in a soft constraint setting. Soft constraints induce an order over men and women, possibly with ties. The GS algorithm requires a strict total order (that is, no ties) over men and women. We consider three linearizations, i.e., three ways to break ties, with particular attention to fuzzy constraints, where solutions which are less distant from optimal ones appear earlier in the linearized order.

We thus propose a setting where SM preference lists are modelled via soft constraints, and the GS algorithm is augmented by a soft constraint solver which performs the GS operations over the soft constraints representing preferences of men and women, when needed by the GS algorithm.

The use of soft constraints reduces the amount of time and space needed by each agent to specify its preference ordering. Moreover, there are benefits also for the stable matching procedure, which receives an input which is much smaller. Moreover, if we don't impose any restriction on the soft constraints of the women and if we require only that the *soft constraints of men* have a constraint graph with a bounded tree-width [7], the time complexity of the stable matching procedure does not suffer in terms of time, as shown both by our theoretical and experimental evaluation. Tree-shaped soft constraints (which have a constraint graph with tree-width = 1) are sufficiently expressive to model a wide range of preferences, such as those that are based on a hierarchical organization of the features. For example, in matching students to schools, it has been observed [1] that several schools give preferences over students as follows: priority 1 to students who have already attended that school or a feeder school, priority 2 to students who have a sibling at the school and live in the walk zone of the school and so on. This leads to a tree-shaped constraint graph.

A study similar to the one in this paper was done using CP-nets instead of soft constraints [16]. CP-nets [4] are a different compact model for preferences over combinatorial sets where preferences are qualitative, that is, expressed via orderings. In contrast to soft constraints, not all partial orders can be induced by a CP-net on the outcomes in the combinatorial set and outcomes can be incomparable but *not in a tie*. We note that, intuitively, in the SM setting it is more likely for two members of the same group to be regarded as in a tie vs incomparable. In both cases, the proposal-based nature of GS imposes a linearization. As different techniques are needed to reason with CP-nets and soft constraints in SMs, the linearization studied for CP-net in [16] is very different than those we define in this paper for soft constraints.

Constraints have been considered in the literature of stable matching only as a means to encode the problem and to solve it efficiently [2,10,13], rather than as a way to compactly model agents preferences and then to solve the problem by interleaving the GS algorithm and the constraint solver.

The paper is a revised and extended version of [17,18].

2   Background

2.1   Stable Matching Problems

A *stable matching problem* (SM) [11] of size n is the problem of finding a stable matching between n men and n women. Such men and women each have a strict preference ordering over the members of the other gender. A *matching* is a one-to-one correspondence between men and women. Given a matching M, a man m, and a woman w, the pair (m, w) is a *blocking pair* for M if m prefers w to his partner in M and w prefers m to her partner in M. A matching is said to be *stable* if it does not contain blocking pairs. Given a SM P, there may be many stable matchings for P and there is always at least one. Extended versions of SM allow for different numbers of men and women, ties and/or incomplete lists in the preference orderings [12,14].

The *Gale-Shapley algorithm* (GS) [9] is widely used to solve SMs. The algorithm takes $O(n^2)$ steps and constructs a stable matching. It consists of a number of rounds in which each un-engaged man proposes to his most preferred woman to whom he has not yet proposed. Each woman receiving a proposal becomes "engaged", provisionally accepting the proposal from her most preferred man. In subsequent rounds, an already engaged woman can "trade up", becoming engaged to a more preferred man and rejecting a previous proposal, or if she prefers him, she can stick with her current partner.

Given a matching M, we will denote with $M(w)$ (resp., $M(m)$) the man (resp., woman) associated to the woman w (resp., man m) in M. Also, $pref(x)$ denotes the preference list of a man or a woman x. The GS algorithm may be therefore rewritten as in Algorithm 1 below, which includes the following operations:

- $Opt(pref(m))$: Computes the optimal woman for m (i.e., m's first proposal).
- $Next(pref(m), w)$: computes the next best woman after w for man m (i.e., a new proposal for m).
- $Compare(pref(w), m, m')$: returns true if woman w prefers man m to m'. This is needed when woman w, currently matched with m', must decide whether to accept or decline a proposal from m.

Algorithm 1. GS

---

foreach *man m and woman w* **do**
$\quad$ | $M(m) \leftarrow null$;
$\quad$ | $M(w) \leftarrow null$;
while $\exists m$ *such that* $M(m) = null$ **do**
$\quad$ | $w \leftarrow Opt(pref(m))$;
$\quad$ | **while** $M(m) = null$ **do**
$\quad\quad$ | **if** $M(w) = null$ **then**
$\quad\quad\quad$ | $M(m) \leftarrow w$;
$\quad\quad\quad$ | $M(w) \leftarrow m$;
$\quad\quad$ **else**
$\quad\quad\quad$ | **if** $Compare(pref(w), m, M(w))$ **then**
$\quad\quad\quad\quad$ | $pref(M(w)) \leftarrow pref(M(w)) - w$;
$\quad\quad\quad\quad$ | $M(M(w)) \leftarrow null$;
$\quad\quad\quad\quad$ | $M(w) \leftarrow m$;
$\quad\quad\quad\quad$ | $M(m) \leftarrow w$;
$\quad\quad\quad$ **else**
$\quad\quad\quad\quad$ | $w \leftarrow Next(pref(m), w)$;

2.2 Soft Constraints

A *soft constraint* [15] involves a set of variables and it is defined by a preference function that associates a preference value from a (totally or partially ordered) set to each instantiation of its variables. This preference value is taken from a preference structure $\langle A, +, \times, 0, 1 \rangle$, where A is the set of preference values, $+$ induces an ordering over A (where $a \leq b$ iff $a + b = b$), $\times$ is used to combine preference values, and 0 and 1 are the worst and best preference value.

A *Soft Constraint Satisfaction Problem* (SCSP) is a tuple $\langle V, D, C, A \rangle$ where V is a set of variables, D is the domain of the variables, and C is a set of soft constraints (each one involving a subset of V) associating preference values from A.

An instance of the SCSP framework is obtained by choosing a specific preference structure. For instance, a *classical CSP* [8] is just an SCSP where the preference structure is $S_{CSP} = \langle \{false, true\}, \vee, \wedge, false, true \rangle$. Preference values are only true and false and they are combined via logical and.

Fuzzy CSPs [15] are instead modeled choosing $S_{FCSP} = \langle [0,1], max, min, 0, 1 \rangle$, i.e., preference values are in $[0,1]$ and we want to maximize the minimum preference value. Fuzzy CSPs are useful in safety-critical applications, since we focus on the worst preference value when we evaluate a complete variable assignment.

For weighted CSPs, the preference structure is $S_{WCSP} = \langle R^+, min, +, +\infty, 0 \rangle$: preferences are interpreted as costs from 0 to $+\infty$, and we want to minimize the sum of costs.

Figure 1 shows the constraint graph of a Fuzzy CSP with three variables x, y, and z with domain $D(x) = D(y) = D(z) = \{a, b\}$ and $C = \{c_x, c_y, c_z, c_{xy}, c_{yz}\}$. Each node models a variable and each arc models a binary constraint. There are also unary constraints. For example, c_y is a unary constraint that involves only variable y and it is specified by the preference function f_y that associates preference value 0.4 to $y = a$ and 0.7 to $y = b$, while c_{xy} is a binary constraint that involves variables x and y and it is specified by the preference function f_{xy} that associates a preference value to each possible combination of values of x and y in their domain. For example, c_{xy} associates preference value 0.9 to the tuple $(x = a, y = a)$. This Fuzzy CSP has a tree-shape constraint graph.

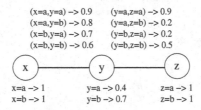

Fig. 1. A tree-shaped Fuzzy CSP, where we use notation "tuple -> preference value".

A *tuple* of a soft CSP P is a partial assignment of preference values to the variables. A *solution* of a soft CSP P is a complete assignment of preference values to all the variables. Given an assignment s to all the variables of a soft CSP P, its preference value, written $pref(P, s)$ (aka $pref(s)$), is the combination (which corresponds to the minimum in the fuzzy case and to the sum in the weighted case) of the preference values associated to the tuples of s in the constraints of P.

A solution of the Fuzzy CSP shown in Fig. 1 is $s = (x = a, y = a, z = b)$. The preference value of this solution, i.e., $pref(P, s)$, is $min(f_x(a), f_y(a), f_z(b), f_{xy}(a, a), f_{yz}(a, b)) = min(1, 0.4, 1, 0.9, 0.2) = 0.2$.

An *optimal solution* of a soft CSP P is a solution that has preference value that is the best possible. More formally, an optimal solution is a solution s such that there are no other solution s' with $pref(P, s) < pref(P, s')$, where $<$ is the preference ordering of the considered preference structure. We denote with opt its preference value.

In general, finding an optimal solution for a soft CSP is computationally hard, but is polynomial for some classes of soft constraints. This is the case for tree-shaped fuzzy CSPs, where a technique called directional arc-consistency, applied bottom-up on the tree shape of the problem, is enough to make the search for an optimal solution backtrack-free and thus polynomial.

A *tree-shaped fuzzy CSP* is a fuzzy CSP whose constraint graph (where nodes represent variables and arcs connect variables involved in the same constraint) is a tree.

Given a variable ordering o, a fuzzy CSP is *directional arc-consistent (DAC)* if, for any two variables x and y in a fuzzy binary constraint, such that x precedes y in the ordering o, we have that, for each a in the domain of x, $f_x(a) = max_{b \in D(y)}(min(f_x(a), f_{xy}(a, b), f_y(b)))$, where f_x, f_y, and f_{xy} are the preference functions of c_x, c_y and c_{xy}. If a fuzzy CSP is not DAC, it is possible to make it DAC in polynomial time. Once the fuzzy CSP is DAC, if its constraint graph is a tree (or has a bounded tree-width), we may find an optimal solution by instantiating each variable to its best value in the ordering o in linear time.

The tree-like restriction is not the only one to assure tractability. In fact, it is polynomial to find a solution even if, instead of a tree, we have a graph with cycles but with bounded tree-width. Many classes of graphs have bounded tree-width, such as cactus graphs (where every two cycles have at most one vertex in common), pseudo-forests and Apollonian networks [3].

Fuzzy CSPs can also be solved via a cut-based approach. Given a fuzzy CSP P, an α-cut of P, where α is between 0 and 1, is a classical CSP with the same variables, domains, and constraint topology as the given fuzzy CSP, and where each constraint allows only the tuples that have preference values above α in the fuzzy CSP. We will denote such a problem by $cut(P, \alpha)$. The set of solutions of P with preference value greater than or equal to α coincides with the set of solutions of $cut(P, \alpha)$. Thus, to find an optimal solution for a given fuzzy CSP, it is enough to find a solution of the CSP $cut(P, \alpha)$ with the highest α such that the problem has some solution.

Fuzzy and weighted CSPs generate a solution ordering which is a *total order with ties*, where the ties are given by all the solutions with the same preference value, and a solution dominates another one if its preference value is higher. Thus, linearizing the solution ordering just means giving an order over the elements in each tie. It has been shown in [5] that it is possible to define a linearization of the solution ordering of a tree-shaped fuzzy CSP where finding the next solution is computationally easy.

For weighted CSPs, instead, unfortunately there in no linearization with this property. However, in [7], it has been shown that, for weighted CSPs with bounded tree-width, it is polynomial to find the top k solutions when k is bounded. So, to find the next solution after we already have the top $k - 1$ ones, it is easy if k is bounded.

3   Soft Constraints in SM

We consider stable marriage problems with n men and n women, where each man and each woman specify their preferences over the members of the other gender via a set of soft constraints. We call this a Soft CSP based SM (SSM).

Each man and woman is described by a set of features, that are represented by the variables of the soft constraint problems. If each variable has d possible values, the number of variables, say f, of each soft constraint problem is $O(log_d n)$. Summarizing, we have $2f$ features, of which f describe men and f describe women.

We will now model the GS operations: Opt, $Compare$, and $Next$.

$Opt(pref(m))$ must return the optimal solution of a soft constraint problem defining the preferences of man m over the women. We recall that, in general, finding the optimal solution of a soft constraint problem is a computationally difficult problem. However, if the soft constraint problem has a tree-like shape, or bounded tree-width, it can be done in polynomial time [6]. Thus this operation takes polynomial time if the constraint graph is a tree (or has a bounded tree-width).

$Compare(pref(w), m_1, m_2)$ compares two complete assignments m_1 and m_2 and checks if m_1 is strictly more preferred to m_2 for w. In fuzzy constraint problems, this is computationally easy to do, if there is a polynomial number of constraints. In fact, m_1 is strictly preferred to m_2 when the preference value of m_1 for w is strictly greater than that of m_2 for w. Notice that women need only to perform Compare operations. Thus we do not need any restriction on the shape of the constraint graph for women's preferences to make Compare polynomial.

For the $Next(pref(m), w)$ operation, we need to understand how to linearize the solution ordering of a soft constraint problem. In fact, this operation is used to find the next most preferred woman in a man's preference ordering, so when two or more women are tied, we need to put an order over them to understand who to propose first.

Linearizations. In fuzzy constraint problems, the solution ordering is in general a total order with ties: some solutions are equally preferred and a solution dominates another one if its preference value is higher.

In this context, linearizing the solution ordering means giving an order over the elements in each tie.

We aim to define linearizations where finding the next best solution (that is, applying operation $Next$) is tractable and where solutions which are less distant from optimal ones appear earlier in the linearized order. In this respect we make a novel and significant technical contribution by allowing an ordered enumeration of solutions in decreasing order of preference values with minimal recomputation every time a new solution is generated. This plays a fundamental role in fully exploiting the benefits of the compact representation of preferences.

We will define three linearizations L_1, L_2, and L_3:

- L_1 breaks some ties by taking into account the distance of the preference value of a solution from the preference value of an optimal solution;
- L_2 does the same as L_1 and breaks additional ties by considering also the minimum number of preference values for parts of the solutions to be changed to make the solution optimal;
- L_3 does the same as L_2 and breaks additional ties by considering also the amount of change required to become optimal.

We recall that the preference value of an optimal solution is called *opt*.

Breaking ties in a smarter way allows for men to discriminate with a higher resolution when making proposals and to end up matched with more preferred partners. Fuzzy constraints do not distinguish among solutions that perform poorly on one or all the constraints as long as they have the same minimal preference. Linearization L_2 instead overcomes this by allowing to propose first to women with fewer low preferences in the constraints. L_3 extends this refinement further by considering also the other non-minimal preferences.

In all three linearizations we use a lexicographic order to break ties. This order which we denote as $\prec_{lex}$ assumes a linear ordering over variables and a linear ordering over the elements in their domain. Given two solutions, s_1 and s_2, $s_1 \prec_{lex} s_2$ if the first variable, according to the ordering over variables, on which s_1 and s_2 differ is assigned a value in s_1 which precedes the value assigned in s_2 according to the domain ordering. We also define $\prec_{oT}$, which orders partial assignments in decreasing order of preference and then breaks ties using $\prec_{lex}$.

Given a solution s, we define $tuple(s)$ as the first tuple of s according to $\prec_{lex}$ that has preference value equal to $pref(s)$. We can now define an ordering $\prec_t$ over solutions: $s_1 \prec_t s_2 \iff tuple(s_1) \prec_{oT} tuple(s_2)$.

We now define our linearizations:

- **L_1:** $s_1 \prec_{L_1} s_2$ iff
  - $(opt - pref(s_1)) < (opt - pref(s_2))$, or
  - $(opt - pref(s_1)) = (opt - pref(s_2))$ and $s_1 \prec_t s_2$, or
  - $(opt - pref(s_1)) = (opt - pref(s_2))$, $s_1 =_t s_2$ and $s_1 \prec_{lex} s_2$.
- **L_2:** $s_1 \prec_{L_2} s_2$ iff
  - $(opt - pref(s_1)) < (opt - pref(s_2))$, or
  - $(opt - pref(s_1)) = (opt - pref(s_2))$ and $t(s_1) < t(s_2)$, or
  - $(opt - pref(s_1)) = (opt - pref(s_2))$ and $t(s_1) = t(s_2)$ and $s_1 \prec_t s_2$, or
  - $(opt - pref(s_1)) = (opt - pref(s_2))$, $t(s_1) = t(s_2)$, $s_1 =_t s_2$, and $s_1 \prec_{lex} s_2$,
  where $t(s)$ is the minimum number of tuples of s that must be changed to make s optimal. For fuzzy constraints, this is the number of tuples of s with preference value less than *opt*.

- $\mathbf{L_3}$: $s_1 \prec_{L_3} s_2$ iff
    - $(opt - pref(s_1)) < (opt - pref(s_2))$, or
    - $(opt - pref(s_1)) = (opt - pref(s_2))$ and $ct(s_1) < ct(s_2)$, or
    - $(opt - pref(s_1)) = (opt - pref(s_2))$ and $ct(s_1) = ct(s_2)$ and $s_1 \prec_t s_2$, or
    - $(opt - pref(s_1)) = (opt - pref(s_2))$, $ct(s_1) = ct(s_2)$, $s_1 =_t s_2$, and $s_1 \prec_{lex}$ s_2,

  where $ct(s)$ is $sum_{t_i}(opt - pref(t_i))$, where t_i is any tuple of s with preference less than opt.

We will now see how to perform operations $Next$ on such three linearizations. We will call them $Next_i$, for $i = 1, 2, 3$.

Next$_1$. In Algorithm 2 we describe procedure $Next_1$ for fuzzy CSPs which is a modified version of the Next operation presented in [5]. In Algorithm 2:

- $next(p)$ is the preference value, among those appearing in P, following p in decreasing order;
- given a fuzzy CSP P and one of its tuples $t = (x_i = v, x_j = w)$, $fix(P, t)$ returns the fuzzy CSP obtained from P by removing from the domains of x_i and x_j all values except v and w;
- given a fuzzy CSP P and a preference p, $cut(P, p)$ returns the CSP obtained from P by zeroing all preferences less than p in all the constraints;
- given a tree-shaped CSP P, $cspSolve(P)$ returns the first solution in lexicographic order given the variable and domain orderings;
- given a tree-shaped CSP and one of its solutions s, $cspNext(P, s)$ returns the solution following s in lexicographic order if one exists.

In a fuzzy CSP, a solution has preference p only if it includes a tuple that has preference p. When a solution s is given in input, we look for t_s, the smallest tuple of s w.r.t. ordering o_T that has preference p in the corresponding constraint. This is the tuple that generates solution s. Thus, we fix tuple t_s via $fix(P, t_s)$ and cut the obtained fuzzy CSP at level p. By calling $cspNext$ we look for the solution lexicographically following s. If it doesn't exist, s must be the last solution generated by tuple t_s with preference p. The next solution may have preference p or lower. If it has preference p, such a preference must come from a tuple with preference p which follows t_s w.r.t. ordering o_T. To avoid finding solutions with preference p that come from tuples preceding t_s we zero out tuple t_s and all tuples with preference p preceding t_s w.r.t ordering o_T. If none of the tuples with preference p following t_s generates a valid solution with preference p, we move down one preference level, restoring all zeroed tuples back to their original values. This search continues until a solution is found or all tuples with preference greater than 0 have been considered.

Next$_2$ and Next$_3$. To perform $Next_2$ and $Next_3$ for tree-shaped fuzzy CSPs, when we already have the top $k-1$ solutions, we find the top k solution according to L_2 and L_3 by computing the top k solutions of a set of weighted CSPs. Our algorithm, which we call $KCheapest$, works for both L_2 and L_3. The input is a

---

Algorithm 2. Next1

Input : tree-shaped and DAC Fuzzy CSP P, orderings $o, o_1, \ldots, o_n, o_T$,
assignment s with preference p
Output : an assignment s', or "no more solutions"
compute tuple t_s
$t^* = t_s$; $p^* = p$; $P' = cut(fix(P, t^*), p^*)$
if $cspNext(P', s) \neq$ "no more solutions" **then**
$\qquad$ **return** $cspNext(P', s)$
$pref(t) = 0, \forall t \in T$ s.t. $pref(t) = p^*$ and $t \leq_{o_T} t^*$
$cpref = p*$
foreach tuple $t >_{o_T} t^*$ with $pref(t) > 0$ **do**
$\qquad$ **if** $pref(t) < cpref$ **then**
$\qquad\qquad$ L reset all preferences previuosly set to 0 to their original values
$\qquad$ **if** $pref(cspSolve(cut(fix(P, t), pref(t)))) = pref(t)$ **then**
$\qquad\qquad$ L **return** $cspSolve(cut(fix(P, t), pref(t)))$
$\qquad$ $cpref = pref(t)$
$\qquad$ L $pref(t) = 0$
return "no more solutions"

Algorithm 3. KCheapest

---

1. Find k optimal solutions of P, or all optimal solutions if they are less than k. If
the number of solutions found is k, we stop, otherwise let k' be the number of remaining
solutions to be found.
2. Look for the remaining top solutions within non-optimal solutions. More in
detail, until k' best solutions have been found or all solutions of P have been exhausted,
consider each preference pl associated to some tuple in P in decreasing order and, for each
tuple t of P with preference pl, perform the following:

1. Compute the new fuzzy CSP, $P_t = fix(P, t)$.
2. If $cspSolve(cut(P_t, pl))$ has no solution, restart the loop with next iteration from **2.**
3. Compute a new soft CSP, say P_t^w, associated to P_t as follows:
   (a) the constraint topology of P_t^w and P_t coincide;
   (b) each tuple with a preference greater than or equal to opt in P_t has weight 0 in P_t^w;
   (c) each tuple with a preference pt s. t. $pl \leq pt < opt$ in P_t has weight c in P_t^w defined
       as follows: $c = 1$ if $L = L_2$, $c = pt - opt$ if $L = L_3$;
   (d) each tuple with preference less than pl in P_t has weight $+\infty$ in P_t^w.
   Thus, P_t^w is a weighted CSP if $L = L_2$ or $L = L_3$;
4. Compute the k' best solutions or all the solutions if they are less than k' of P_t^w.
5. Take the k' top solutions (or all solutions if less than k') among the sets of best solutions
   computed for P_t^w, $\forall t$ with $pref(t) = pl$.

---

tree-shaped fuzzy CSP P, an integer k, and a linearization L (either L_2 or L_3).
The output is a set of top k solutions of P according to the given linearization.

The first step of *KCheapest* is to look for k optimal solutions of P. As
described in the background section, given a fuzzy CSP P with optimal preference opt, the set of optimal solutions of P coincides with the set of solutions
of the CSP $cut(P, opt)$, obtained by allowing only tuples mapped to preferences
equal or above opt. Thus, to look for k optimal solutions of P, it is sufficient to

compute *opt* and generate solutions of *cut*(P, opt). If there are at least k optimal solutions, *KCheapest* will return them and stop.

Otherwise, we need to consider other, non-optimal solutions, in decreasing order of preference. To do so, we exploit the fact that, in fuzzy CSPs, all solutions with a given preference level, say pl, must have at least a tuple with preference pl. Let us now consider the fuzzy CSP which we obtain from P by fixing a tuple, say t, with preference pl, in a constraint (that is, by forbidding all other tuples in that constraint), and by forbidding all tuples with preference smaller than pl. Such a problem will have either no solution (with a non-zero preference), or all its solutions will have preference pl. Let us consider the set of such problems which have at least one solution. It is easy to see that the set of all solutions with preference pl of P coincides with the union of the sets of optimal solutions of such new fuzzy problems. L_2 linearizes solutions with the same preference by counting the number of tuples that have preference lower than *opt*, and L_3 by weighting such a count with the distance from *opt*. To account for this we transform each of the fuzzy problems for preference pl, which have solutions, into a weighted problem. The main idea is to make solutions costs in the weighted problem coincide with the component of the L_2 and L_3 which depends on the changes to be performed to make a solution optimal. Thus, the weighted problems will have the same variables and the same constraint topology as the fuzzy CSPs. All tuples with preference below pl will be forbidden by setting their cost to be

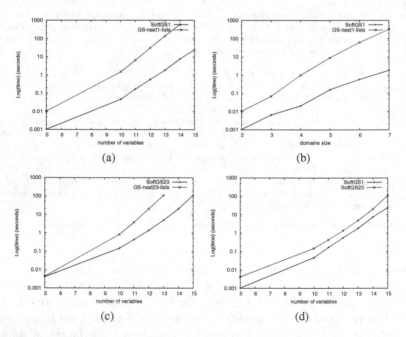

(a)   (b)

(c)   (d)

Fig. 2. Computation time varying the number of variables with $d = 2$, and varying d with 5 variables ($f = 5$).

$+\infty$, and all tuples with preference equal or above *opt* will have cost 0. All the remaining tuples, that is, tuples with a non-zero preference smaller than *opt*, are those that determine the distance to optimality of solutions, according to both L_2 and L_3. If we are linearizing according to L_2, they will be assigned cost 1, while, in the case of L_3, the cost will be the difference between *opt* and the preference of the tuple. Assuming we are still looking for $k' \leq k$ solutions we must compute the top k' solution for each weighted CSP and then compute the union of such sets. Once we have the union, we pick the top k' solutions of the union. Of course we may be able to obtain less than k' solutions, in which case we proceed as described above for each other preference level in decreasing order.

Theorem 1. *Given a fuzzy CSP P with a tree-shape, computing a set of top k outcomes according to L_2 and L_3 is in P when k is polynomial in f and d.*

From [16] we know that on average only 2% of all proposals are made, so the main idea is to call *KCheapest* with $k = 2\%$ of the maximum number of proposals and cache the returned set of solutions. Only when all cached solutions have already been returned, we need to call *KCheapest* again.

4   Complexity Issues and Stability

Let us now compare the worst case space and time complexity of using the GS algorithm with and without soft constraints. In the classical setting, with n men and n women, and preference lists given explicitly, an SM needs $O(n^2)$ space and $O(n^2)$ time [11]. When we use soft constraints, each man and woman needs $O(d^k m)$ space and time to state their preferences, where d is the size of domains, k is the number of features involved in the largest soft constraint, and m is the number of soft constraints. When we use soft constraints with bounded tree-width for the men, each proposal in the GS algorithm takes $O(poly(f))$ time, where f is the number of features and each Compare operation takes $O(poly(m))$. So, overall, the GS algorithm may need up to $O(n^2 \times poly(f) \times poly(m))$ time, although the number of proposals have been shown to be much lower in practice [16].

If we run the GS algorithm on any of the three linearizations we defined, by definition we obtain a matching which is stable w.r.t. this linearization. In SMs with ties [11], a matching is said to be *weakly stable* when there is no man and woman who *strictly prefer* each other to their partner in the matching. Since our linearizations order more pairs than the ordering of the soft CSPs, it is easy to see that any matching which is stable for the linearizations is also weakly stable for the initial orderings.

5   Experimental Setting and Results

The described linearizations can be used in two different ways within the GS algorithm. One way is to compute the whole preference lists for each man and then run GS. The other is to use the linearization only when GS requires a new proposal. We ran experiments to compare the running time of these two scenarios on a 2.4 Ghz Intel Core i5 machine with 8 GB of RAM, and averaged values over 100 executions, setting a time limit of 10 min. For each man, a tree-shaped fuzzy CSP over f features of domain size d is generated by randomizing the preference values. Each woman is represented by a randomly generated fuzzy CSP with a generic topology over the same number of f features and a constraint density of 50%. Thus, the whole generated SSM problem consists of $n = d^f$ individuals on each side.

In the first test we fixed d and measured the execution time needed to find a stable matching while increasing the number of features f. Results for $Next_1$ are shown in Fig. 2(a), where GS-next1-lists is GS run on precomputed lists obtained running $Next_1$ exactly n^2 times, whereas SoftGS1 is GS which calls $Next_1$ on demand. For $f = 15$ GS-next1-lists didn't complete within the time limit. Also, SoftGS1 substantially outperforms GS-next1-lists both in space and time. As expected from [16], GS makes on average only 2% of all possible proposals. This justifies the advantage of an on demand implementation.

We ran the same tests on $Next_{2-3}$, that is, the algorithm that calls $KCheapest$, only when needed, for either L_2 or L_3. The results are plotted in Fig. 2(c) where GS-next23-lists is again the implementation that runs over full precomputed lists while SoftGS23 only precomputes the first 2% of every preference list and then eventually asks for more. SoftGS23 is considerably better than its equivalent that runs on precomputed lists, with an average running time of $4.875\,s$ versus $107.202\,s$. In Fig. 2(d) we compared the performance of the different linearizations L_1 and L_{2-3}. As expected, solving the Weighted CSP cost minimization problem brings additional overhead to the Next operation, resulting in a worse performance compared to $Next_1$.

In the second test setting, we fixed f to 5, and measured execution time as a function of the domains cardinality d. As shown in Fig. 2(b), SoftGS1 behaves better than GS with precomputed lists, despite the fact that $n = d^f$. The performance of SoftGS1 is very promising as for a setting of $d = 2$ and $f = 12$ (which means 8192 individuals to be matched), the average computation time is $1.83\,s$ versus $137.43\,s$ of the version with precomputed lists. In a real world scenario of this size, ranking 8192 individuals of the opposite sex may be impractical, while the compact preference representation makes it feasible, as each individual only needs to express his/her preferences over 12 features.

6   Conclusions

We study and solve the problem of finding stable matchings when agents' preferences are expressed compactly via fuzzy constraints. Experiments suggest that this reduces the amount of time and space needed by each agent to specify its preference ordering, as well as the overall time complexity of the GS algorithm to find a stable matching. Our work may be extended by considering other matching problems (e.g. many-to-many), non-fuzzy compact preferences, and manipulation issues as done in [19, 20].

References

1. Abdulkadiroglu: Generalized matching for school choice. Working paper, Duke University (2011)
2. Bistarelli, S., Foley, S., O'Sullivan, B., Santini, F.: From marriages to coalitions: a soft CSP approach. In: Oddi, A., Fages, F., Rossi, F. (eds.) CSCLP 2008. LNCS (LNAI), vol. 5655, pp. 1–15. Springer, Heidelberg (2009). https://doi.org/10.1007/978-3-642-03251-6_1
3. Bodlaender, H.L.: A partial k-arboretum of graphs with bounded treewidth. Theor. Comput. Sci. **209**(1–2), 1–45 (1998)
4. Boutilier, C., Brafman, R.I., Domshlak, C., Hoos, H.H., Poole, D.: CP-nets: a tool for representing and reasoning with conditional ceteris paribus preference statements. JAIR **21**, 135–191 (2004)
5. Brafman, R.I., Rossi, F., Salvagnin, D., Venable, K.B., Walsh, T.: Finding the next solution in constraint- and preference-based knowledge representation formalisms. In: Proceedings of KR 2010 (2010)
6. Dechter, R.: Tractable structures for CSPs. In: Rossi, F., Van Beek, P., Walsh, T. (eds.) Handbook of Constraint Programming. Elsevier, Amsterdam (2005)
7. Dechter, R., Flerova, N., Marinescu, R.: Search algorithms for M best solutions for graphical models. In: Proceedings of AAAI 2012. AAAI Press (2012)
8. Dechter, R.: Constraint Processing. Morgan Kaufmann, Burlington (2003)
9. Gale, D., Shapley, L.S.: College admissions and the stability of marriage. Amer. Math. Monthly **69**, 9–14 (1962)
10. Gent, I.P., Irving, R.W., Manlove, D.F., Prosser, P., Smith, B.M.: A constraint programming approach to the stable marriage problem. In: Walsh, T. (ed.) CP 2001. LNCS, vol. 2239, pp. 225–239. Springer, Heidelberg (2001). https://doi.org/10.1007/3-540-45578-7_16
11. Gusfield, D., Irving, R.W.: The Stable Marriage Problem: Structure and Algorithms. MIT Press, Boston (1989)
12. Iwama, K., Miyazaki, S., Morita, Y., Manlove, D.: Stable marriage with incomplete lists and ties. In: Wiedermann, J., van Emde Boas, P., Nielsen, M. (eds.) ICALP 1999. LNCS, vol. 1644, pp. 443–452. Springer, Heidelberg (1999). https://doi.org/10.1007/3-540-48523-6_41
13. Manlove, D.F., O'Malley, G., Prosser, P., Unsworth, C.: A constraint programming approach to the hospitals/residents problem. In: Van Hentenryck, P., Wolsey, L. (eds.) CPAIOR 2007. LNCS, vol. 4510, pp. 155–170. Springer, Heidelberg (2007). https://doi.org/10.1007/978-3-540-72397-4_12
14. Manlove, D.F.: Algorithmics of Matching Under Preferences. World Scientific Publishing, Singapore (2013)
15. Meseguer, P., Rossi, F., Schiex, T.: Soft constraints. In: Rossi, F., Van Beek, P., Walsh, T. (eds.) Handbook of Constraint Programming. Elsevier, Amsterdam (2005)
16. Pilotto, E., Rossi, F., Venable, K.B., Walsh, T.: Compact preference representation in stable marriage problems. In: Rossi, F., Tsoukias, A. (eds.) ADT 2009. LNCS (LNAI), vol. 5783, pp. 390–401. Springer, Heidelberg (2009). https://doi.org/10.1007/978-3-642-04428-1_34
17. Pini, M.S., Rossi, F., Venable, K.B.: Stable matching problems with soft constraints. In: Proceedings of AAMAS 2014 - Extended Abstract, pp. 1511–1512 (2014)

18. Pini, M.S., Rossi, F., Venable, K.B.: Compact preference representation via fuzzy constraints in stable matching problems. In: Rothe, J. (ed.) ADT 2017. LNCS (LNAI), vol. 10576, pp. 333–338. Springer, Cham (2017). https://doi.org/10.1007/978-3-319-67504-6_23
19. Pini, M.S., Rossi, F., Venable, K.B., Walsh, T.: Manipulation complexity and gender neutrality in stable marriage procedures. Autonomous Agents and Multi-Agent Systems 22, 183–199 (2011)
20. Pini, M.S., Rossi, F., Venable, K.B., Walsh, T.: Stability, optimality and manipulation in matching problems with weighted preferences. Algorithms 6, 782–804 (2013)
21. Roth, A.E.: The evolution of the labor market for medical interns and residents: a case study in game theory. J. Polit. Econ. 92, 991–1016 (1984)
22. Teo, C.-P., Sethuraman, J., Tan, W.-P.: Gale-shapley stable marriage problem revisited: strategic issues and applications. Manag. Sci. 47(9), 1252–1267 (2001)

Answer Set Programming for Declarative Content Specification: A Scalable Partitioning-Based Approach

Francesco Calimeri[1,2], Stefano Germano[1,2], Giovambattista Ianni[1,2],
Francesco Pacenza[1,2], Armando Pezzimenti[1,2(✉)], and Andrea Tucci[1,2]

[1] Department of Mathematics and Computer Science, University of Calabria,
Rende, Italy
{calimeri,germano,ianni,pacenza}@mat.unical.it, armnd.6793@gmail.com
[2] Rocksteady Studios Ltd., London, UK
andrea.tucci.cs@gmail.com

Abstract. Procedural Content Generation is applied in the development process of many commercial games: automatically generated game contents are delivered to players in order to offer a constantly changing user experience and enrich the game itself. Usually, the generative process relies on search-based non-deterministic algorithms, which encode one or more techniques for guaranteeing "legal" yet diversified output. Declarative approaches to content generation, more properly defined as Declarative Content Specification techniques, like the ones based on Answer Set Programming, allow to focus on describing content requirements rather than programming ad-hoc generation engines, and to fast prototype generation techniques themselves. This work investigates to what extent ASP-based DCS is scalable enough for industrial contexts, by proposing a partitioning-based approach. A working prototype, available as an Unity Asset and as a GVGAI framework level generator is presented.

Keywords: Answer Set Programming
Procedural content generation · Game content generation
Artificial intelligence in games · Computational intelligence in games
Declarative Content Specification

1 Introduction

Procedural Content Generation (PCG) [20] is an important tool for modern video game development, and commonly used in both triple-A (i.e., high-budget games) and indie games. A good PCG framework allows the creation of new game content without the specific need to create it by hand: instead, a program is run and the produced output is used into the game itself in the form of landscapes, playable levels, open worlds, i.e., of what we will in general call *game artifacts*.

The game production workflow usually involves a number of professional profiles, whose jobs can partially overlap. In particular, the game *designer* is

© Springer Nature Switzerland AG 2018
C. Ghidini et al. (Eds.): AI*IA 2018, LNAI 11298, pp. 225–237, 2018.
https://doi.org/10.1007/978-3-030-03840-3_17

in charge of manually designing and combining game artifacts, while the *programmer* writes general purpose code, Artificial Intelligence (AI) code, and, in our context, content generation code. Designers and programmers have usually a strict collaboration, and interact in order to produce the right content generation code. There can be cases in which the designer has little inspiration and cannot converge to a concrete game world or to suitable new levels, nor explore novel ideas, etc. In this setting *PCG* might be very beneficial; however, finding a good content generation scheme might be a big burden on programmers' shoulders. In other development contexts, designers extensively collaborate with a programmer in order to modify the content creation algorithm, so that the generated game artifacts fit to the original ideas and description.

In both settings above, input ideas about the game world come from designers in terms of high-level rules and constraints, and such information is then used by programmers to encode algorithms which should generate the content specified; this, however, means that the programmer must devise not only what is supposed to be generated, but also the procedural algorithms in charge of the generation task.

It turns then out that a general technique, which is reusable and decoupled from the specific game domain and visual appearance, and results to be accessible to non-programmers and suitable for rapidly prototyping game content, can be significantly of help. In this respect, logic-based declarative tools, such as Answer Set Programming, can be a game changer, as they limit, if not eliminate, the need for imperative code, thus achieving the above benefits in several respects. On the one hand, a skilled game designer can declaratively express quantitative and qualitative desiderata in terms of ASP code; on the other hand, programmers themselves can define content generation strategies without the burden of programming detailed algorithms via imperative languages.

In other words, ASP can be used for evolving traditional PCG techniques to the notion of what might better be defined as Declarative Content Specification (DCS); in this respect, declarative specifications can be easily modified and incremented with new knowledge at will.

1.1   Our Contribution

In the vast literature concerning procedural content generation,[1] the first usage of ASP for content generation can be found in [15,21], with particular focus on the maze generation problem, where promising results are achieved. In particular, the work in [21] adopts a tile-by-tile generation model, and encouraging performance results are reported over 6×6 mazes.

Our contributions are detailed next:

- We investigate over the usage of a partition-based generation technique [19] in ASP. Approaches relying on partition-based generation are generally efficient

---

[1] The reader can refer to the last edition of [20] for a comprehensive survey of generation techniques and related research.

in terms of processing time and, if mixed with ASP, can benefit from the declarative properties of this latter;

– To the above end, we propose a multiple step-generation approach, set in the context of the 2-D caves generation domain, where each step is declaratively controlled by an ASP specification;

– With respect to existing literature [15,21], our approach promises to be better scalable to real contexts with higher size mazes; experiments aimed at confirming that are currently ongoing;

– We develop two plugins based on our generation technique, which were respectively deployed as an asset available in the Unity development[2] and in the GVGAI [18] frameworks;

– We report about some experiments and analyze possible improvements.

The remainder of the paper is structured as follows: we first give an overview of PCG techniques, and in particular of binary space partitioning in Sect. 2; an overview of ASP is given in Sect. 3. Our content generation strategy is reported in Sect. 4, and a prototype is illustrated in Sect. 5; we then report about performance and draw our conclusions in Sect. 6.

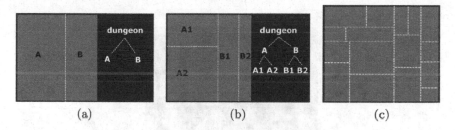

     (a)   (b)   (c)

Fig. 1. Steps of space partitioning. (a) First step: the level is divided by a vertical line and two sub zones are defined, A and B. (b) Further steps divide each zone into smaller areas. Here A has been divided by a horizontal line, while B has been split by a vertical line. (c) After n steps, a given criterion is met, and the level will be subdivided into sectors.

2 Procedural Content Generation: An Overview

Procedural Content Generation (PCG) can be defined as the algorithmic creation of game content with limited/indirect user input [22]: roughly, one can think of a software that automatically generates game contents, that might be possibly refined by a designer afterwards. There are several reasons for the use of PCG techniques in actual game development, such as fast content prototyping and improved design tasks: indeed, a software can be much faster than a

---

[2] https://unity3d.com/unity.

designer [20], and, in general, it might lead to comparatively better results in less time. Furthermore, the procedural generation of game content allows to tailor the gaming experience to several extents: different challenges can be proposed according to the game session, or even depending on the player profile that is currently playing the game. In general, PCG helps to obtain a game that can be played an arbitrary number of times with always new original content, while also improving the development phases.

Game content that can be automatically created ranges from game levels to music, textures, entire worlds. We focus here on the generation of 2-D levels and caves; in particular, we focus on a PCG technique called *space partitioning*, as we found it particularly suitable when combined with the ASP approach. Space partitioning is typically used in PCG to create dungeons, both 2-D and 3-D. It works by recursively dividing the level area into smaller zones, until all meet a certain criterion, such as a specific size. Once the partitioning is done, monsters and other game objects can be placed into each "room"; eventually, rooms can be connected. One of the most popular space partitioning algorithm is the Binary Space Partitioning (BSP), which recursively divides a given "space" into two subspaces. By splitting the space into two sub-zones, the algorithm creates a binary tree. Figure 1 illustrates the principle of this technique.

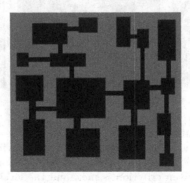

Fig. 2. Each obtained sector is filled with a room, which will be connected afterwards using the BSP tree.

As shown in Fig. 2, the binary space partitioning algorithm guarantees that no areas will be overlapping, and the result is very structured and uniform. Once the space has been partitioned, proper policies are adopted to create the areas and directly affect the structure of the dungeon; for instance, one can decide to randomly assign each final zone either the "room" or the "empty" property, thus creating a very symmetric dungeon. Room connections and additional level content can hence be created and placed either purely randomly, or using other techniques that don't rely on the space partitioning itself. A pseudo-code for an implementation of the binary space partitioning technique can be found in [20].

3   Answer Set Programming

Answer Set Programming (ASP) [4,6,9] is a declarative programming paradigm evolved from logic programming, deductive databases, knowledge representation, and non-monotonic reasoning. In ASP, a computational problem can be encoded by a logic program, that is, a collection of rules which describe a problem to be solved; the program, along with some input usually expressed using factual rules, possesses a collection of intended models (possibly also no model), called *answer sets*, which correspond one-to-one to the solutions of the modelled problem instance [14]. Formally, a rule is defined as follow:

$$b_1, b_2, ..., b_n, not\ c_1, not\ c_2, ..., not\ c_m, \leftarrow r_1 \lor r_2, ..., \lor r_k.$$

where each b_i and c_i are atoms (b_i) or negated atoms (c_i), while each r_i is an atom. Atoms in the rule body are in conjunction with each other: the comma here stands for the logical connective *AND*. The $\leftarrow$ symbol is a logical implication; what is to the left of the implication is called body, while the right part is the rule's head. The symbol not is the logical *NOT* operator; the symbol $\lor$ is the logical *OR* operator, also known as disjunction.

ASP is highly expressive, and allows to solve problems even beyond the complexity class NP. Rule are semantically interpreted according to common sense principles and to the classical *closed-world* assumption/semantics (CWA) of deductive databases; the field of ASP is growing, and several extensions of the basic language have been proposed and used in applications such as *ontology-based query answering* [2,17] according to the classical *open-world* semantics/assumption (OWA) of first-order logic [1].

Efficient systems for computing answer sets [3,8] are available. The typical computation combines two modules: grounder and solver [10]. The first module takes a program Π and instantiates it by producing a propositional program Π' semantically equivalent but containing no variables; the second module computes answer sets of Π' by adapting and significantly extending SAT solving techniques [13]. The availability of efficient and solid ASP systems have stimulated the development of a wide range of practical applications relying on ASP, both in academia and business, that include, and are not limited to, product configuration, decision support systems for space shuttle flight controllers, large-scale biological network repairs, data-integration and scheduling systems (cfr. [5,11]). In order to facilitate the use in real-world scenarios, a number of tools allowing to "embed" ASP into imperative code, are available. In particular, we took advantage of the EmbASP library [7], which allows to interoperate with an ASP solver in several development environments, such as the C# and Java toolchain.

4   Declarative Content Generation with Space Partitioning in ASP

We will use next some typical map generation terminology, as recalled here:

Map: a rectangular grid composed of square *tiles*;

Partition: the outcome of sectioning the map at hand obtained by dividing the map itself into non-overlapping parts;

Area: a component of a partition, usually a rectangle-shaped area made of tiles;

Structure: how areas composing partitions are connected to each other, for instance by means of a door object;

Type: the actual kind of an area, which can be either a room, a corridor or a filled zone, i.e., an area filled with walls;

Tile: a tile can be either a wall, i.e., a cell which is not accessible by a game character, a floor cell, i.e., a cell that can be walked on by a game character. A floor cell can be possibly occupied by a game object;

Object: a game object (such as keys, treasures, enemies, etc.); game objects fit in general in one or more tiles; we will assume to deal with single tile objects;

In this setting, given an empty map M of given size, the goal of a game content generation framework is to assign each tile of M an appropriate value and to properly put game objects in "floor" tiles. One could explore the search space of all the possible tile assignments: however, as soon as the required map size grows to common values for commercial video-games, such an exhaustive search approach is not viable anymore. This is the main reason for the choice of a space partitioning approach, as it should scale better on larger maps, in principle.

Our approach is conceived on a multiple step basis: each step is implemented using a different declarative specification, written in ASP; the output of each step is processed and glued to next stages using the EmbASP library. This tight, step-by-step, mix of imperative and declarative programming allows to overcome the limitations of both paradigms, and to cut the search space of each computation,

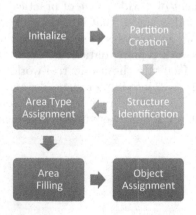

Fig. 3. Declarative Content Generation: work-flow of the proposed approach.

achieving better results in terms of performance and a higher scalability, as shown in Sect. 6.

Our content generation strategy is illustrated in Fig. 3. The behaviour of each step is summarized next:

Initialize: Initial step to create the basic structure of the map, i.e., a "base" Partition;

Partition Creation: Partitions are recursively created according to requirements, such as minimum size of areas, so that a raw structure is obtained similar to the one of Fig. 4. In this step we also place the doors connecting the areas according to specified desiderata, such as minimum allowed distance from corner walls, etc.;

Structure Identification: A graph model of the raw map is built, where nodes represent areas and arcs represent connections between areas; note that placed doors induce connections between areas;

Area type assignment: Each area is assigned a type according to specified qualitative requirements, i.e., the desired density of rooms with respect to corridors, etc.;

Area filling: According to the assigned area type, each tile of an area is assigned a floor type or a wall type. Three different specifications, each given by means of a logic program, are defined for rooms, corridors, and filled partitions, respectively; the three logic programs can be modified, thus allowing to tune rooms and corridor shapes according to design wishes. For instance, one can build square rooms instead of rounded caves by changing the corresponding specification;

Object Assignment: Eventually, game objects are assigned to selected rooms, and put in selected tiles. Note that this task is not trivial, in principle, given that some objects, such as keys, might be needed in order to enter some rooms and therefore they cannot be simply placed randomly.

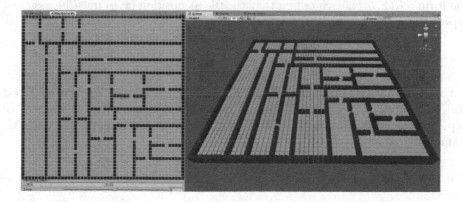

Fig. 4. A semi-finished map obtained after the **Partition Creation** step, shown in the Unity plugin.

We outline next some of the ASP logical specifications we used to develop the strategy described above. The **Partition Creation** step is repeatedly invoked; at each step, given a rectangular area, a partition is chosen consisting of two new rectangular areas, which share a wall having a door. The following rules, expressed in ASP, are used to achieve this result:

$$1 = \{new\_door(X, Y, D_{type}) \; : \; free\_cells(X, Y)\} = 1 \leftarrow door\_type(D_{type}).$$
$$cell(X, Y, D_{type}) \leftarrow new\_door(X, Y, \_), door\_type(D_{type}).$$

$$free\_cells(X, Y) \leftarrow row(X), col(Y), notunavailable\_cells(X, Y).$$

$$cell(X, Y_2, \text{``wall''}) \leftarrow new\_door(X, Y_1, \_), col(Y_2), Y_1 \neq Y_2,$$
$$orientation(horizontal),$$
$$Y_2 > Min, Y_2 < Max,$$
$$min\_col(Min), max\_col(Max).$$
$$cell(X_2, Y, \text{``wall''}) \leftarrow new\_door(X_1, Y, \_), row(X_2), X_1 \neq X_2,$$
$$orientation(vertical),$$
$$X_2 > Min, X_2 < Max,$$
$$min\_row(Min), max\_row(Max).$$

These rules specify how the input area at hand must be sectioned by expressing where it is possible to place a door with a surrounding wall. Intuitively, the first two rules express the requirement that a new door of type D_{type} must be positioned at some point (X, Y) in the range of *free_cells*; *free_cells* are the cells that are not considered as *unavailable_cells* (there is no wall, door or a general object in position X, Y); the following rules enforce that an horizontal or a vertical (depending on the *orientation* variable) line of "walls" should start from both sides of the newly placed door. Note that the value assigned to the *orientation* variable change from one execution to another depending on the parameter *same orientation percentage* previously set. When run along with proper input data, the above specification produces a set of logical assertions in the form $cell(x, y, t)$, each telling that the tile at position (x, y) must be assigned type t (for t either a *wall*, a *vertical_door*, etc.)

5   Prototype Overview

In this section we report about our prototype. It applies the techniques described above in order to generate dungeons by means of declarative languages. We deployed our application both in the Unity, as a Unity Asset, and in the GVGAI-framework, as an extension of the GVGAI-framework.

5.1   Unity Asset

Unity is a cross-platform game engine primarily used to develop video-games or simulations for more than 25 different platforms, such as mobile, computers and consoles. It supports 2-D and 3-D graphics, drag-and-drop functionalities

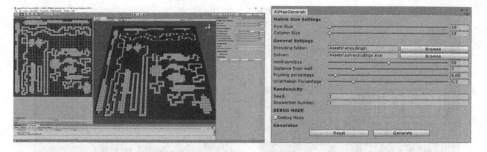

Fig. 5. The full Unity interface. A complete map where areas are transformed in rooms and corridors is shown. On the right, it is highlighted our Unity asset.

and scripting via the C# language. Rapid development speed, a very active and powerful community, cross-platform integration and the availability of 3-D models, ready-made scripts, shaders and other extensions that can be easily added to a game, make Unity a user-friendly game engine easy to learn and use also for beginners; indeed, Unity is currently the leader of the global game development engine market, holding the 45% market share (nearly three times the size of its nearest competitor). Among the wide range of assets offered by the Unity community, a lot of general level generator (both for 2-D and 3-D games) exist; nevertheless, none of them give the developers the possibility to generate the game content describing it in terms of rules and constraints.

It is worth observing that the common approach to content generation is usually built on a per-game, per-level basis, with little or no opportunity of reusing the same content generation module across different games. This is reflected by the Unity Asset Store, in which almost any level generator is very tailored to specific game domains, specific graphic game elements, etc. Our framework, instead, is capable of producing general purpose content, which has very few features depending from a specific game context. As shown in Fig. 5 our tool provides an easy-to-use graphical interface: the developer is free to set some specific parameters using the menu integrated into the Unity Editor. Among the parameters that can be set we have map size, number and minimum size of rooms, and also location of the ASP encodings; the developer can hence change the default style of the generated map. On the left side little 2-D preview of the generated map is presented, while in the middle of the Unity Editor the 3-D scene view is showed, ready to be integrated in the whole game code.

5.2   GVGAI Plug-in

GVGAI [18] is a Java framework that can be easily used to play any game described using the standard Video Game Description Language (VGDL) [16]. It is used for different purposes, such as an AI benchmark to test intelligent agents and as a framework for general level generation for any game. The framework is currently used for hosting the General Video Game Player (GVGP) competition. We deployed our application on top of the GVGAI-framework, in order to

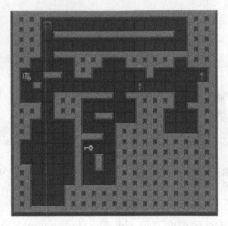

Fig. 6. GVGAI integration. On the left the main menu where it is possible to set some parameters for the map design, and choose a game between Zelda and Labyrinth. On the right, a game running on the generated map.

gain the possibility to reuse both games and controllers created by other participants of the GVGP competition [12]. Figure 6 shows Zelda game built using the GVGAI-framework and our level generator. When the application starts, the user is free to fill some fields (as in the Unity asset) and then specify the encoding folder he wants to use for the map generation. Eventually, the program generates a new example map and runs the previously selected game on the top of the generated level.

6   Performance Considerations and Conclusions

We performed a set of experiments with a two-fold aim: on the one hand, to have a first qualitative idea of the order of magnitude of execution times, in order to prove the practical viability of the approach; on the other hand, to assess scalability with respect to maze sizes. We report here about two different cases: in the first one (Setting 1) we required the generation of mazes featuring few rooms of big size, while in the second (Setting 2) we gave input specifications for having more rooms of smaller size. We considered sizes of 10×10, 20×20, 30×30, 40×40 and 50×50; for each size we performed 3 runs for both settings 1 and 2. This led to a total of 15 executions for each setting, that produced 30 random mazes.

Results are reported in Fig. 7, where times have been averaged over the maze size. The green line shows the execution time taken by the imperative code to connect the different declarative specification written in ASP. The blue one shows the execution time of the declarative specification while the red one shows the total execution time given by the sum of imperative time and declarative time. First of all, we notice that executions take a few seconds, even for significantly large mazes. Furthermore, performance in the two settings are almost

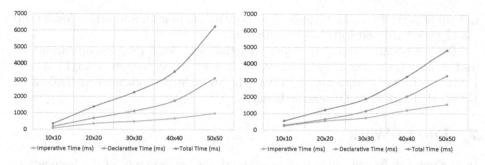

Fig. 7. Benchmark test on scalability over Setting 1 (left side) and Setting 2 (right side). Times are reported in milliseconds. (Color figure online)

the same, even though number and shape of generated rooms are significantly different; such difference and quality of the result can be appreciated in Fig. 8. Results confirm the effectiveness of the approach, and its capability of scaling when dealing with generation tasks of significant size. Compared to imperative based generators, the performance of our ASP based prototypical generator can be considered good; indeed, it is sufficient enough for runtime content generation during game, and it is especially well suited for generation and manual refinement at design time. It is worth noting that, in this latter case, ASP can be of great help in the design phase, by shortening the distance between designers and programmers, especially when fast prototyping is needed.

As for future work is concerned, we plan to define a number of predefined settings for typical desiderata in the context of maze generation (i.e., room shapes, size, etc.); furthermore, we want to take more advantage from the declarative

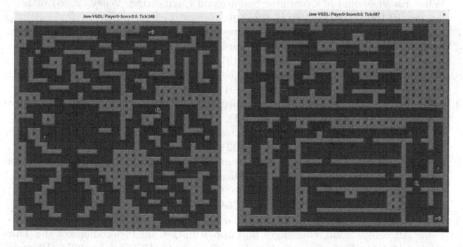

Fig. 8. Two sample maps obtained with Setting 1 (left-hand side) and with Setting 2 (right-hand side). (Color figure online)

nature of ASP, by making easier the specification of such and other desiderata, along with hard and soft design constraints.

Both versions of our prototypes, together with logic program specifications and source code are fully available online at https://github.com/DeMaCS-UNICAL/DCS-Maze_Generator-GVGAI and https://github.com/DeMaCS-UNICAL/DCS-Maze_Generator-Unity.

7   Future Work

In the ongoing future, we aim to benchmark the performance of the framework. After deploying the tool to the public, we will assess the usability of the framework by the end user and we will report in detail the obtained results.

References

1. Abiteboul, S., Hull, R., Vianu, V. (eds.): Foundations of Databases: The Logical Level. Addison-Wesley Longman Publishing Co., Inc., Boston (1995)
2. Calì, A., Gottlob, G., Lukasiewicz, T.: Tractable query answering over ontologies with datalog+/−. In: Description Logics, CEUR Workshop Proceedings, vol. 477. CEUR-WS.org (2009)
3. Calimeri, F., Gebser, M., Maratea, M., Ricca, F.: Design and results of the fifth answer set programming competition. Artif. Intell. **231**, 151–181 (2016). https://doi.org/10.1016/j.artint.2015.09.008
4. Eiter, T., Ianni, G., Krennwallner, T.: Answer set programming: a primer. In: Tessaris, S., et al. (eds.) Reasoning Web 2009. LNCS, vol. 5689, pp. 40–110. Springer, Heidelberg (2009). https://doi.org/10.1007/978-3-642-03754-2_2
5. Erdem, E., Gelfond, M., Leone, N.: Applications of answer set programming. AI Mag. **37**(3), 53–68 (2016)
6. Faber, W., Leone, N., Ricca, F.: Answer set programming. In: Wah, B.W. (ed.) Wiley Encyclopedia of Computer Science and Engineering. Wiley (2008) https://doi.org/10.1002/9780470050118.ecse226
7. Fuscà, D., Germano, S., Zangari, J., Anastasio, M., Calimeri, F., Perri, S.: A framework for easing the development of applications embedding answer set programming. In: PPDP, pp. 38–49. ACM (2016)
8. Gebser, M., Maratea, M., Ricca, F.: The sixth answer set programming competition. J. Artif. Intell. Res. **60**, 41–95 (2017). https://doi.org/10.1613/jair.5373
9. Gelfond, M., Lifschitz, V.: Classical negation in logic programs and disjunctive databases. New Gener. Comput. **9**(3/4), 365–386 (1991)
10. Kaufmann, B., Leone, N., Perri, S., Schaub, T.: Grounding and solving in answer set programming. AI Mag. **37**(3), 25–32 (2016)
11. Leone, N., Ricca, F.: Answer set programming: a tour from the basics to advanced development tools and industrial applications. In: Faber, W., Paschke, A. (eds.) Reasoning Web 2015. LNCS, vol. 9203, pp. 308–326. Springer, Cham (2015). https://doi.org/10.1007/978-3-319-21768-0_10
12. Liebana, D.P., Samothrakis, S., Togelius, J., Schaul, T., Lucas, S.M.: General video game AI: competition, challenges and opportunities. In: Proceedings of the Thirtieth AAAI Conference on Artificial Intelligence, 12–17 February 2016, Phoenix, Arizona, USA, pp. 4335–4337 (2016). http://www.aaai.org/ocs/index.php/AAAI/AAAI16/paper/view/11853

13. Lierler, Y., Maratea, M., Ricca, F.: Systems, engineering environments, and competitions. AI Mag. **37**(3), 45–52 (2016)
14. Lifschitz, V.: Answer set planning. In: ICLP, pp. 23–37. MIT Press (1999)
15. Nelson, M.J., Smith, A.M.: ASP with applications to mazes and levels. In: Shaker, N., Togelius, J., Nelson, M.J. (eds.) Procedural Content Generation in Games, pp. 143–157. Springer, Cham (2016). https://doi.org/10.1007/978-3-319-42716-4_8
16. Nielsen, T.S., Barros, G.A.B., Togelius, J., Nelson, M.J.: Towards generating arcade game rules with VGDL. In: 2015 IEEE Conference on Computational Intelligence and Games (CIG), pp. 185–192, August 2015. https://doi.org/10.1109/CIG.2015.7317941
17. Ortiz, M.: Ontology based query answering: the story so far. In: Proceedings of AMW (2013). http://ceur-ws.org/Vol-1087/keynote3.pdf
18. Pérez-Liébana, D., Liu, J., Khalifa, A., Gaina, R.D., Togelius, J., Lucas, S.M.: General video game AI: a multi-track framework for evaluating agents, games and content generation algorithms. CoRR abs/1802.10363 (2018). http://arxiv.org/abs/1802.10363
19. Shaker, N., Liapis, A., Togelius, J., Lopes, R., Bidarra, R.: Constructive generation methods for dungeons and levels. In: Shaker, N., Togelius, M., Nelson, M.J. (eds.) Procedural Content Generation in Games. CSCS, pp. 31–55. Springer, Cham (2016). https://doi.org/10.1007/978-3-319-42716-4_3
20. Shaker, N., Togelius, J., Nelson, M.J. (eds.): Procedural Content Generation in Games. CSACS. Springer, Cham (2016). https://doi.org/10.1007/978-3-319-42716-4
21. Smith, A.M., Mateas, M.: Answer set programming for procedural content generation: a design space approach. IEEE Trans. Comput. Intell. AI in Games **3**(3), 187–200 (2011). https://doi.org/10.1109/TCIAIG.2011.2158545
22. Togelius, J., Kastbjerg, E., Schedl, D., Yannakakis, G.N.: What is procedural content generation?: Mario on the borderline. In: Proceedings of the 2Nd International Workshop on Procedural Content Generation in Games, PCGames 2011, pp. 3:1–3:6. ACM, New York (2011). https://doi.org/10.1145/2000919.2000922

A Tableau Calculus for a Multi-modal Logic of Dishonesty

Sanja Pavlović and Hans Tompits[✉]

Institute of Logic and Computation, Knowledge-Based Systems Group E192-03,
Technische Universität Wien, Favoritenstraße 9-11, 1040 Vienna, Austria
{pavlovic,tompits}@kr.tuwien.ac.at

Abstract. In recent years, several approaches for formalising dishonest agents have been proposed in the artificial-intelligence literature. In particular, many of these approaches are based on a modal-logic setting. A prominent specimen of such a formalism is the multi-modal logic BIC, proposed by Sakama, Caminada, and Herzig, where the name "BIC" stands for *belief*, *intention*, and *communication*. In their work, Sakama et al. introduce a Kripke semantics for BIC and provide a corresponding Hilbert-style axiomatisation. In this paper, we complement this investigation by introducing a tableau calculus for BIC. Our approach is based on the *single-step tableau method*, an important proof method for automated deduction, originally proposed by Massacci for certain normal modal logics and subsequently elaborated by Goré. We provide soundness and completeness proofs, extending methods of Goré.

1 Introduction

Traditionally, research in artificial intelligence (AI) has focussed on the modelling of *ideal agents*, like, e.g., ideally rational agents. But understanding the properties of dishonest behaviour is also relevant in AI as dishonesty is an integral part of human life and thus AI systems which are able to not always tell the truth are one more step closer to human-level AI. Of course, one may argue why it would be desirable to have dishonest artificial agents. As argued by Castelfranchi [1], there are different reasons why there is a need for "deceitful agents". Much like humans, an agent in a heterogeneous multi-agent system might use a dishonest strategy in order to achieve its goals with a minimum amount of effort. Another example given by Castelfranchi includes personal assistants that "should probably deceive us in trying to influence us to do the right thing, to protect our interest against our short term preferences or biases" [1].

Indeed, there is a growing interest in the logic and AI literature on providing formalisations of dishonest behaviour [2,8,9,11–15,17,18]. In this paper, we consider the logic BIC, as introduced by Sakama, Caminada, and Herzig [14]. BIC is a propositional multi-modal logic that is able to express *beliefs*, *intentions*, and *communications* of agents, and as such is used to formulate a number of categories of dishonest behavior. In their work, Sakama et al. provide a Kripke

C. Ghidini et al. (Eds.): AI*IA 2018, LNAI 11298, pp. 238–251, 2018.
https://doi.org/10.1007/978-3-030-03840-3_18

semantics and a Hilbert-type axiomatisation of BIC. We complement this investigation by introducing a tableau calculus for BIC and showing soundness and completeness of our calculus.

Our tableau method is based on the *single-step approach*, first discussed by Massacci [6,7] and, independently, by Goré [5], which trace back in turn to *labelled tableaux* as discussed by Fitting [4] for a wide variety of different modal logics. In a labelled tableau, prefixes of formulae encode possible worlds and accessibility between them, and in single-step tableaux, the inference rules are such that the labels within a rule "are at most one step away from each other".

2 Preliminaries

We start with providing the basic elements of the logic BIC [14]. Syntactically, BIC is a multi-modal logic whose formulae are built over a set of atomic propositions using the usual sentential operators $\neg$, $\wedge$, $\vee$, and $\supset$, the logical constants $\top$ and $\bot$, and, for a fixed set A, whose elements are referred to as *agents*, the modal operators B_a, I_a, and C_{ab}, for every two agents $a, b \subset A$. The intended reading of $B_a\varphi$ is that agent a believes φ. Similarly, $I_a\varphi$ and $C_{ab}\varphi$ are understood as that agent a intends φ and that agent a communicates φ to agent b, respectively. Communication between two agents is assumed to include both verbal and non-verbal communication. Moreover, it is assumed to be *instantaneous*, i.e., a hearer recognises information at the same moment it is uttered by a speaker.

BIC allows to formulate diverse types of dishonest communication. For example, *sincere communication*, where agent a communicates to agent b a sentence φ he believes to be true, can be expressed in BIC as $SINC_{ab}(\varphi) := B_a\varphi \wedge C_{ab}\varphi$. Similarly, lying can be formalised by the formula $LIE_{ab}(\varphi) := C_{ab}\varphi \wedge B_a\neg\varphi \wedge I_a B_b\varphi$. This means that agent a lies to agent b on φ if he believes the opposite of φ (i.e., $\neg\varphi$) but communicates φ to agent b with the intention of making b believe φ. Also, *withholding information*, where a speaker does not communicate a believed-true sentence with the intention that the hearer does not believe that statement, can be expressed as $WI_{ab}(\varphi) := \neg C_{ab}\varphi \wedge B_a\varphi \wedge I_a\neg B_b\varphi$. Other forms of deceitful and insincere communication can be formalised likewise, cf. Sakama et al. [14] for details.

The semantics of BIC is given in terms of a Kripke-style semantics. To this end, we need the following notions: A binary relation $\mathcal{R}$ over a set X is (i) *serial*, if, for every $x \in X$, there is some $y \in X$ such that $x\mathcal{R}y$, (ii) *transitive*, if $x\mathcal{R}y$ and $y\mathcal{R}z$ implies $x\mathcal{R}z$, for every $x, y, z \in X$, and (iii) *Euclidean*, if $x\mathcal{R}y$ and $x\mathcal{R}z$ implies $y\mathcal{R}z$, for every $x, y, z \in X$. Furthermore, for binary relations $\mathcal{R}_1$ and $\mathcal{R}_2$ over X, $\mathcal{R}_1$ is said to be *Euclidean over* $\mathcal{R}_2$, if $x\mathcal{R}_2y$ and $x\mathcal{R}_1z$ imply $y\mathcal{R}_1z$, for every $x, y, z \in X$, and $\mathcal{R}_1$ is *transitive over* $\mathcal{R}_2$, if $x\mathcal{R}_2y$ and $y\mathcal{R}_1z$ imply $x\mathcal{R}_1z$, for every $x, y, z \in X$.

A BIC-*model*, $\mathcal{M}$, is a tuple $\langle W, (\mathcal{R}^{B_a})_{a \in A}, (\mathcal{R}^{I_a})_{a \in A}, (\mathcal{R}^{C_{ab}})_{a,b \in A}, \Vdash \rangle$, where, for each $a, b \in A$, $\mathcal{R}^{B_a}$ is serial, transitive, and Euclidean, $\mathcal{R}^{I_a}$ and $\mathcal{R}^{C_{ab}}$ are serial, $\mathcal{R}^{I_a}$ is transitive over $\mathcal{R}^{B_a}$ and Euclidean over $\mathcal{R}^{B_a}$, $\mathcal{R}^{C_{ab}}$ is transitive over $\mathcal{R}^{I_a}$ and $\mathcal{R}^{B_a}$ and Euclidean over $\mathcal{R}^{I_a}$ and $\mathcal{R}^{B_a}$, and $\Vdash$ is a binary relation between the set of possible worlds W and the set of formulae satisfying the following conditions, for any $w \in W$:

1. $\mathcal{M}, w \Vdash \top$ and $\mathcal{M}, w \not\Vdash \bot$;
2. $\mathcal{M}, w \Vdash \varphi \wedge \psi$ iff $\mathcal{M}, w \Vdash \varphi$ and $\mathcal{M}, w \Vdash \psi$;
3. $\mathcal{M}, w \Vdash \varphi \vee \psi$ iff $\mathcal{M}, w \Vdash \varphi$ or $M, w \Vdash \psi$;
4. $\mathcal{M}, w \Vdash \varphi \supset \psi$ iff $\mathcal{M}, w \not\Vdash \varphi$ or $M, w \Vdash \psi$;
5. $\mathcal{M}, w \Vdash \neg\varphi$ iff $\mathcal{M}, w \not\Vdash \varphi$; and
6. $\mathcal{M}, w \Vdash O\varphi$ iff $\mathcal{M}, u \Vdash \varphi$ for every $u \in W$ such that $w\mathcal{R}^{O}u$, where $O \in \{B_a, I_a, C_{ab} \mid a, b \in A\}$.

We say that a formula φ is *true* in a world w in a BIC-model $\mathcal{M}$ if $\mathcal{M}, w \Vdash \varphi$, and *false* otherwise. Furthermore, φ is true in a BIC-model $\mathcal{M}$ if it is true in every world in $\mathcal{M}$, and false otherwise. Finally, φ is *valid* if it is true in every BIC-model. In what follows, we also refer to BIC-models simply as *models*.

3   Single-Step Tableaux for BIC

We next introduce a single-step tableau calculus for BIC, based on a method proposed by Massacci [6] and show soundness and completeness extending methods from Goré [5].

Unifying Notation. We begin by extending the unified notation following Fitting [3] and Smullyan [16]. As customary in the unified notation, we work with *signed formulae*, built by prefixing (unsigned) formulae with either T or F. Intuitively, $T\varphi$ stands for "φ is true" and $F\varphi$ for "φ is false". Formally, given a model $\mathcal{M}$ and a world w in it, we define $\mathcal{M}, w \Vdash T\varphi$ iff $\mathcal{M}, w \Vdash \varphi$, and $\mathcal{M}, w \Vdash F\varphi$ iff $\mathcal{M}, w \not\Vdash \varphi$, i.e., $T\varphi$ is true in w iff φ is true in w and $F\varphi$ is true in w iff φ is false in w.

The unifying notation for BIC is defined according to the following tables, consisting of formulae of type α, β, π^O, and ν^O, along with their respective *components*, α_i and β_i ($i = 1, 2$) and π_0^O and ν_0^O, for $O \in \{B_a, I_a, C_{ab} \mid a, b \in A\}$ and $\bar{O}$ abbreviating $\neg O\neg$:

α	α_1	α_2		β	β_1	β_2		π^O	π_0^O		ν^O	ν_0^O
$T(\varphi \wedge \psi)$	$T\varphi$	$T\psi$		$F(\varphi \wedge \psi)$	$F\varphi$	$F\psi$		$FO\varphi$	$F\varphi$		$TO\varphi$	$T\varphi$
$F(\varphi \vee \psi)$	$F\varphi$	$F\psi$		$T(\varphi \vee \psi)$	$T\varphi$	$T\psi$		$T\bar{O}\varphi$	$T\varphi$		$F\bar{O}\varphi$	$F\varphi$
$F(\varphi \supset \psi)$	$T\varphi$	$F\psi$		$T(\varphi \supset \psi)$	$F\varphi$	$T\psi$						
$T\neg\varphi$	$F\varphi$	$F\varphi$										
$F\neg\varphi$	$T\varphi$	$T\varphi$										

From the semantic conditions of BIC, we immediately get corresponding properties for our unified notation:

Theorem 1. Let $\mathcal{M} = \langle W, (\mathcal{R}^{B_a})_{a \in A}, (\mathcal{R}^{I_a})_{a \in A}, (\mathcal{R}^{C_{ab}})_{a, b \in A}, \Vdash \rangle$ be a model. Then, for every α-, β-, π^O-, and ν^O-formula ($O \in \{B_a, I_a, C_{ab} \mid a, b \in A\}$), and every $w \in W$, the following conditions hold:

1. $\mathcal{M}, w \Vdash \mathsf{T}\top$ and $\mathcal{M}, w \Vdash \mathsf{F}\bot$;
2. $\mathcal{M}, w \Vdash \mathsf{T}\varphi$ iff $\mathcal{M}, w \nVdash \mathsf{F}\varphi$, for each unsigned formula φ;
3. $\mathcal{M}, w \Vdash \alpha$ iff $\mathcal{M}, w \Vdash \alpha_1$ and $\mathcal{M}, w \Vdash \alpha_2$;
4. $\mathcal{M}, w \Vdash \beta$ iff $\mathcal{M}, w \Vdash \beta_1$ or $\mathcal{M}, w \Vdash \beta_2$;
5. $\mathcal{M}, w \Vdash \pi^O$ iff there is a world v such that $w\mathcal{R}^O v$ and $\mathcal{M}, v \Vdash \pi_0^O$; and
6. $\mathcal{M}, w \Vdash \nu^O$ iff for every world $v \in W$, $w\mathcal{R}^O v$ implies $\mathcal{M}, v \Vdash \nu_0^O$.

Labels and Tableaux. Our tableau calculus for BIC uses *labelled signed formulae* [4–6]. Intuitively, labels represent symbolic names for worlds in a model. The core idea is that the structure of labels, along with accessibility relations among them, encodes reachability relations between worlds. We define, for the logic BIC, the structure of labels and the accessibility relations between them, and then use these to prove soundness and completeness of our calculus.

Definition 1. A *label* is given according to the following conditions: (i) 1 is a label; (ii) if σ is a label, then $\sigma; On$, for $O \in \{B_a, I_a, C_{ab} \mid a, b \in A\}$ and a number $n \geq 1$, is also a label. Furthermore, a *labelled signed formula*, or simply a *labelled formula*, is a signed formula prefixed by a label. The set of all labels appearing in a set Φ of labelled formulae is denoted by $lab(\Phi)$. $\qquad\square$

We use $|\sigma|$ to denote the length of a (part of a) label σ, which is defined as the number of semicolons it contains plus one. Further, for two labels σ and τ, $\sigma - \tau$ denotes the part of σ that σ and τ do not share. For example, $1; B_a 1; B_a 1; C_{ab} 1 - 1; B_a 1; B_a 1; I_a 1; C_{ab} 1 = C_{ab} 1; I_a 1$.

As previously stated, the structure of labels should encode the reachability relations between worlds. Suppose we have two labels, σ and $\tau = \sigma; B_a 1$, and two worlds, v and w, named by σ and τ, respectively. From the structure of σ and τ, we should be able to conclude that w is reachable from v via B_a, for some agent a. This idea will become more apparent when we discuss accessibility relations between labels. To this end, we introduce the notions of a simple extension and an extension of a label as follows:

Definition 2. Let σ and τ be two labels and let O be a modal operator. Then, τ is a *simple extension of σ with respect to O* if $\tau = \sigma; On$, for a number $n \geq 1$. Furthermore, τ is a *simple extension of σ* if τ is a simple extension of σ with respect to some modal operator O. Finally, τ is an *extension of σ* if $\tau = \sigma; O_1 n_1; O_2 n_2; \ldots; O_k n_k$, for $k, n_i \geq 1$ and $O_i \in \{B_a, I_a, C_{ab} \mid a, b \in A\}$, where $i = 1, \ldots, k$. $\qquad\square$

We are now ready to define our tableau calculus for BIC.

Definition 3. Given a finite set of signed formulae $\Phi = \{\varphi_1, \varphi_2, \ldots, \varphi_n\}$, a *labelled tableau for Φ*, or simply a *tableau for Φ*, is a (downwards oriented) tree with labelled formulae as nodes, obtained by putting elements from $\{1\varphi \mid \varphi \in \Phi\}$ as initial branch, and then possibly extending it with the following rules:

$$(\alpha) \ \frac{\sigma\alpha}{\begin{array}{c}\sigma\alpha_1\\\sigma\alpha_2\end{array}} \qquad (\beta) \ \frac{\sigma\beta}{\sigma\beta_1 \mid \sigma\beta_2} \qquad (\pi^O) \ \frac{\sigma\pi^O}{\sigma; On\pi_0^O} \qquad (\nu^O) \ \frac{\sigma\nu^O}{\sigma; On\nu_0^O}$$

$$(D^O) \ \frac{\sigma\nu^O}{\sigma\pi^O} \ , \ \text{providing} \ \pi_0^O = \nu_0^O \qquad (4^{Ba}) \ \frac{\sigma\nu^{Ba}}{\sigma; B_a n\nu^{Ba}} \qquad (4r^{Ba}) \ \frac{\sigma; B_a n\nu^{Ba}}{\sigma\nu^{Ba}}$$

$$(4^{I_a Ba}) \ \frac{\sigma\nu^{I_a}}{\sigma; B_a n\nu^{I_a}} \qquad (4^{C_{ab} Ba}) \ \frac{\sigma\nu^{C_{ab}}}{\sigma; B_a n\nu^{C_{ab}}} \qquad (4^{C_{ab} I_a}) \ \frac{\sigma\nu^{C_{ab}}}{\sigma; I_a n\nu^{C_{ab}}}$$

$$(4r^{I_a Ba}) \ \frac{\sigma; B_a n\nu^{I_a}}{\sigma\nu^{I_a}} \qquad (4r^{C_{ab} Ba}) \ \frac{\sigma; B_a n\nu^{C_{ab}}}{\sigma\nu^{C_{ab}}} \qquad (4r^{C_{ab} Ba}) \ \frac{\sigma; I_a n\nu^{C_{ab}}}{\sigma\nu^{C_{ab}}}$$

A branch of a tableau, i.e., a path from the root of the tree to some leaf, is *closed* if $\sigma T\bot$, σFT, or both $\sigma T\varphi$ and $\sigma F\varphi$, for some label σ and formula φ, appear on the branch. A tableau is closed if each of its branches is closed. A (*labelled*) *tableau proof* of an unsigned formula φ is a closed tableau for $F\varphi$.   □

Note that the labels within a given rule are at most one step away from each other, hence these tableaux are also referred to as "single-step tableaux", following Massacci [6] and Goré [5]. Note also that the (π^O)-rule comes with the constraint that $\sigma; On$ must not already appear on the current branch. All other rules require that labels appearing in them must already be present on the current branch.

The intuition behind the tableau rules is rather simple. The (α) and (β) rules are the standard tableau rules for classical propositional logic. As for the modal rules, consider, e.g., the (π^O)-rule, and assume we have a π^O-formula that holds in a world with the symbolic name σ. From the semantics of π^O-formulae, it follows that there must be a world reachable from σ by $\mathcal{R}^O$ where π_0^O holds. Therefore, the (π^O)-rule allows us to create a new label, as a symbolic name for this world, and assert that π_0^O holds in it. Analogous considerations apply for the (ν^O)-rule as well, taking the semantics of ν^O-formulae into account.

The remaining rules carry the name of the frame conditions they implicitly represent. Following the standard modal-logic nomenclature, "4" stands for transitivity, and "D" for seriality. Rules containing the symbols "$4r$" represent *reverse transitivity*, which we get as a side effect of transitivity and Euclideanity.

The (D^O)-rule is obtained from the seriality of BIC operators. If a formula ν^O holds in some world named by σ, then there must be at least one world reachable by $\mathcal{R}^O$ in which ν_0^O holds. The (D^O)-rule creates a corresponding π^O formula, thus granting us the use of the (π^O)-rule that in turn creates a new label naming this world.

Rules (4^{Ba}) and $(4r^{Ba})$ tell us what we can conclude from a ν^{Ba}-formula based on transitivity and Euclideanity of $\mathcal{R}^{Ba}$. Let us consider the rule $(4r^{Ba})$ and assume that ν^{Ba} holds in some world w named by $\sigma; B_a n$. Let us furthermore consider a world v named by σ. Obviously, w is reachable from v, since w is named by a simple extension of σ. From the Euclideanity of $\mathcal{R}^{Ba}$, we know that any other world u reachable from v by $\mathcal{R}^{Ba}$ is also reachable from w using the same relation. Since ν^{Ba} holds in w, ν_0^{Ba} must hold in all $\mathcal{R}^{Ba}$-successors of w, and therefore also in all $\mathcal{R}^{Ba}$-successors of v. This in turn means that ν^{Ba} holds in v, which is exactly what the rule asserts. The intuition behind the remaining rules can be given in a similar manner.

Example 1. Consider the formula $\psi = (C_{ab}\varphi \wedge B_a\varphi) \supset B_a(C_{ab}\varphi \wedge B_a\varphi)$, formalising that if agent a believes φ and communicates it to agent b, then it also believes that it believes φ and that the communication took place. The following tree is a tableau proof of ψ (with justifications for each node in square brackets):

1. $1\mathrm{F}(C_{ab}\varphi \wedge B_a\varphi) \supset B_a(C_{ab}\varphi \wedge B_a\varphi)$ [assumption]
2. $1\mathrm{T}C_{ab}\varphi \wedge B_a\varphi$ $[1, (\alpha)]$
3. $1\mathrm{F}B_a(C_{ab}\varphi \wedge B_a\varphi)$ $[1, (\alpha)]$
4. $1\mathrm{T}C_{ab}\varphi$ $[2, (\alpha)]$
5. $1\mathrm{T}B_a\varphi$ $[2, (\alpha)]$
6. $1; B_a 1 \mathrm{F}C_{ab}\varphi \wedge B_a\varphi$ $[3, (\pi^{B_a})]$

7. $1; B_a 1 \mathrm{F}C_{ab}\varphi$ $[6, (\beta)]$		8. $1; B_a 1 \mathrm{F}B_a\varphi$ $[6, (\beta)]$
9. $1; B_a 1; C_{ab} 1 \mathrm{F}\varphi$ $[7, (\pi^{C_{ab}})]$		10. $1; B_a 1; B_a 1 \mathrm{F}\varphi$ $[8, (\pi^{B_a})]$
11. $1; B_a 1 \mathrm{T}C_{ab}\varphi$ $[4, (4^{C_{ab}B_a})]$		12. $1; B_a 1 \mathrm{T}B_a\varphi$ $[5, (4^{B_a})]$
13. $1; B_a 1; C_{ab} 1 \mathrm{T}\varphi$ $[1, (\nu^{C_{ab}})]$		14. $1; B_a 1; B_a 1 \mathrm{T}\varphi$ $[12, (\nu^{B_a})]$
$\times$ [closure, 9,13]		$\times$ [closure, 10,14]

4 Adequacy of the Tableau Calculus

4.1 Soundness

We first show soundness, i.e., that every formula provable in the tableau calculus is valid in BIC. We start with defining what it means for a tableau to be satisfiable. To this end, we introduce some notation: By $frm(\theta)$ we denote the set of all labelled formulae appearing on some tableau branch θ. Further, we abbreviate the set $lab(frm(\theta))$, i.e., the set of all labels appearing on the formulae of θ, by $lab(\theta)$.

Definition 4. Let Φ be a set of labelled formulae and let $\mathcal{M}$ be a model. A *label interpretation* of Φ in $\mathcal{M}$ is a mapping $\mathcal{N}$ from $lab(\Phi)$ to the set of possible worlds in $\mathcal{M}$ such that, for every $\sigma \in lab(\Phi)$, every number n, and every $O \in \{B_a, I_a, C_{ab} \mid a, b \in A\}$, $\sigma; On \in lab(\Phi)$ implies $\mathcal{N}(\sigma)\mathcal{R}^O\mathcal{N}(\sigma; On)$.   □

Definition 5. A BIC-*interpretation* (or, simply, *interpretation*) of a set Φ of labelled formulae is a pair $\langle \mathcal{M}, \mathcal{N} \rangle$, where $\mathcal{M}$ is a model and $\mathcal{N}$ is a label interpretation of Φ in $\mathcal{M}$.   □

An interpretation *satisfies* a set Φ of labelled formulae if for every formula $\sigma\varphi \in \Phi$, $\mathcal{M}, \mathcal{N}(\sigma) \Vdash \varphi$ holds. We say that Φ is *satisfiable* if there exists a satisfying interpretation. Further, a branch θ of a tableau is satisfiable if $frm(\theta)$ is satisfiable, and a tableau is satisfiable if it has a satisfiable branch.

We call a set L of labels *rooted* if it is non-empty and $\sigma; On \in L$ implies $\sigma \in L$, for all $n \geq 1$ and all $O \in \{B_a, I_a, C_{ab} \mid a, b \in A\}$. Note that, if L is rooted, then it contains in particular the label 1 which is called the *root* of L.

Lemma 1. For every branch θ in a tableau, the set of all labels on θ is rooted.

Proof. Since the initial branch of every tableau contains the label 1, and θ is obtained from the initial branch by applying tableau rules, we have that $1 \in lab(\theta)$, and hence $lab(\theta)$ is non-empty. Consider now an arbitrary label $\sigma; On \in lab(\theta)$, for $O \in \{B_a, I_a, C_{ab} \mid a, b \in A\}$. This label must have been introduced by an application of the (π^O)-rule to some formula $\sigma\pi^O$ that already appears on θ, as π-rules are the only rules allowed to introduce new labels. Hence, $\sigma \in lab(\theta)$, and so $lab(\theta)$ is rooted. □

Lemma 2. If a tableau is satisfiable, then every tableau obtained from it by one application of a tableau rule is also satisfiable.

Proof. Suppose $\mathcal{T}$ is a satisfiable tableau. Then, $\mathcal{T}$ contains a satisfiable branch, say θ. Consider $\mathcal{T}'$ obtained from $\mathcal{T}$ by applying some tableau rule to $\mathcal{T}$. If the rule was applied to some branch other than θ, then θ remains unchanged and therefore $\mathcal{T}'$ has a satisfiable branch. Otherwise, we make a case distinction depending on what rule was applied. We only show the result for one type of rule; the others are similar.

Suppose the $(4^{O_1 O_2})$-rule has been applied to some ν^{O_1}-formula $\sigma\nu^{O_1} \in frm(\theta)$, where $(O_1, O_2) \in \{(B_a, B_a), (I_a, B_a), (C_{ab}, B_a), (C_{ab}, I_a)\}$.[1] Then, we obtain an extended branch θ' by adding $\sigma; O_2 n\nu^{O_1}$ to θ, for some $\sigma; O_2 n \in lab(\theta)$. As θ is satisfiable, there is an interpretation $\langle \mathcal{M}, \mathcal{N} \rangle$ that satisfies $frm(\theta)$. In particular, $\mathcal{M}, \mathcal{N}(\sigma) \Vdash \nu^{O_1}$ holds. By the semantics of ν^{O_1}-formulae, for every world w in $\mathcal{M}$, $\mathcal{N}(\sigma)\mathcal{R}^{O_1} w$ implies $\mathcal{M}, w \Vdash \nu_0^{O_1}$. Further, as $\sigma; O_2 n \in lab(\theta)$, there must be a world in $\mathcal{M}$ that $\sigma; O_2 n$ is mapped to such that $\mathcal{N}(\sigma)\mathcal{R}^{O_2}\mathcal{N}(\sigma; O_2 n)$ holds. Moreover, as $\mathcal{M}$ requires $\mathcal{R}^{O_1}$ to be transitive over $\mathcal{R}^{O_2}$, it follows that for every world v in $\mathcal{M}$, $\mathcal{N}(\sigma; O_2 n)\mathcal{R}^{O_1}$ implies $\mathcal{N}(\sigma)\mathcal{R}^{O_1} v$. Combining this with the previous observation, we get that $\mathcal{N}(\sigma; O_2 n)\mathcal{R}^{O_1} v$ implies $\mathcal{M}, v \Vdash \nu_0^{O_1}$. It follows from the semantics of ν^{O_1}-formulae that $\mathcal{M}, \mathcal{N}(\sigma; O_2 n) \Vdash \nu^{O_1}$. Next, observe that $lab(\theta') = lab(\theta)$ and therefore $\langle \mathcal{M}, \mathcal{N} \rangle$ is also an interpretation of $frm(\theta')$. As $frm(\theta') = frm(\theta) \cup \{\sigma; O_2 n\nu^{O_1}\}$, $\langle \mathcal{M}, \mathcal{N} \rangle$ satisfies $frm(\theta)$ by assumption, showing that $\langle \mathcal{M}, \mathcal{N} \rangle$ satisfies $\sigma; O_2 n\nu^{O_1}$. We conclude that $\langle \mathcal{M}, \mathcal{N} \rangle$ satisfies $frm(\theta')$, and therefore $\mathcal{T}'$ is satisfiable. □

Theorem 2 (Soundness). If a formula has a tableau proof, then it is valid.

Proof. Let φ be a formula having a tableau proof, $\mathcal{T}$, and assume that φ is not valid, i.e., there is some model $\mathcal{M}$ and some world w in $\mathcal{M}$ such that $\mathcal{M}, w \not\Vdash \varphi$. Let θ_0 be the initial branch of $\mathcal{T}$. Then, by definition, $frm(\theta_0) = \{1F\varphi\}$. By defining a label interpretation $\mathcal{N}$ of $frm(\theta_0)$ in $\mathcal{M}$ by setting $\mathcal{N}(1) = w$, we get that the tableau consisting of just the initial branch θ_0 of $\mathcal{T}$ is satisfiable since $\mathcal{M}, \mathcal{N}(1) \not\Vdash \varphi$, i.e., $\mathcal{M}, \mathcal{N}(1) \Vdash F\varphi$. Hence, in view of Lemma 2, it follows that $\mathcal{T}$ is satisfiable too. As a satisfiable tableau cannot be closed, this violates our assumption that φ has a tableau proof. Thus, φ must be valid. □

---

[1] Here, $(4^{B_a B_a})$ refers to the rule (4^{B_a}).

4.2 Completeness

A Systematic Tableau Procedure. We show completeness by using a *systematic tableau procedure* which, given a finite set Φ of signed formulae, systematically constructs a tableau proof of Φ if there is one, by applying all possible applicable rules, or provides sufficient information to construct a countermodel. This is a well-known approach for showing completeness of a tableau calculus and our construction follows the one given by Goré [5] for certain modal and temporal logics.

Our systematic tableau construction for a given finite set Φ of signed formulae is depicted in Fig. 1. Note that the way we process π-formulae guarantees that every ν-formula is considered again when a new label, that could allow additional applications of a tableau rule, is added to the branch. We call a tableau produced by the systematic tableau procedure a *systematic tableau*.

STAGE 1: Construct the initial branch by putting the labelled formulae $1\varphi_1, 1\varphi_2, \ldots, 1\varphi_n$ in a vertical linear sequence of nodes, one beneath another and mark them all as awake. While the tableau is open and some formula is awake do:

Begin STAGE $n + 1$: Choose the topmost labelled formula $\sigma\varphi$ that is awake in the tree. If there are several candidates, choose the one on the leftmost branch. If $\sigma\varphi$ is atomic, mark it as finished and stop stage $n + 1$. Otherwise, for every *open* branch θ that passes through $\sigma\varphi$ do:

(α) If φ is of form α update θ with $\sigma\alpha_1$ and then update the obtained branch with $\sigma\alpha_2$.

(β) If φ is of form β split the end of θ and update the left fork with $\sigma\beta_1$ and the right fork with $\sigma\beta_2$. If any of these formulae is already present on the branch, delete the corresponding fork (possibly having θ unaltered or with no fork).

(π^O) If φ is of form π^O, $O \in \{B_a, I_a, C_{ab} \mid a, b \in A\}$, then let k be the smallest integer such that the label $\sigma; Ok$ does not appear in $lab(\theta)$. Update θ with $\sigma; Ok\pi_0^O$. If some formula of type $\sigma\nu^{O'}$, $O' \in \{B_a, I_a, C_{ab} \mid a, b \in A\}$ appears on θ, update θ with the conclusions of the rules applicable to it.

(ν^O) If φ is of form ν^O, $O \in \{B_a, I_a, C_{ab} \mid a, b \in A\}$, then for every rule in the calculus that is applicable to $\sigma\nu^O$ update θ with the corresponding conclusion.

Here, "updating a branch with a formula" means adding that formula to the end of the branch and marking it as awake if it does not already appear on that branch (regardless of its marking).

End STAGE $n + 1$: Once all the branches passing through $\sigma\varphi$ have been updated, mark $\sigma\varphi$ as finished and terminate the stage n+1.

Fig. 1. Systematic tableau construction for $\Phi = \{\varphi_1, \varphi_2, \ldots, \varphi_n\}$.

A systematic tableau is a finitely generated tree, as each node of it has at most two successors. It may happen that the systematic construction of a tableau continues ad infinitum, i.e., we would obtain an infinite tableau. Then, from König's Lemma (cf., e.g., Fitting [4]), it follows that such a tableau must have an infinite branch. Now, in principle, the following cases can be distinguished:

(I_1) There is an infinite branch that contains a sequence of infinitely many distinct labelled formulae, all with the same label σ.

(I_2) There is an infinite branch that contains a sequence of infinitely many labelled formulae, where all the labels are simple extensions of a common label σ.

(I_3) There is an infinite branch that contains a sequence of infinitely many labelled formulae, where all labels are different.

(I_4) There is an infinite branch obtained by considering a set of ν-formulae over and over again, infinitely many times.

The first item on the list is impossible as there are only finitely many different formulae in a systematic tableau, up to label differences. This follows from the fact that, apart from the D^O-rule, for $O \in \{B_a, I_a, C_{ab} \mid a, b \in A\}$, all other tableau rules satisfy the subformula property, i.e., only subformulae of the formulae on the initial branch are introduced. But there are also only finitely many formulae introduced by the (D^O)-rule, as they must result from a ν^O-formula, of which there are only finitely many.

Also, (I_2) is not possible, as it can be shown that for every branch in a systematic tableau for a finite set Φ of signed formulae, the number of distinct labels of a given length is finite. Likewise, it holds that (I_4) is impossible in a systematic tableau.

Hence, the only possible way to have an infinite tableau is to have at least one branch with an infinite sequence of formulae where all the labels are different. Since, as stated above, we have at most finitely many formulae of any given length n, our labels must get longer and longer. Moreover, in order for a label σ', $|\sigma'| > 1$, to be introduced to a branch, there must exist a label σ with $|\sigma| = |\sigma'| - 1$ already present on the branch. Therefore, our infinite sequence of labels must have the following form: $\sigma, \sigma; O_1 n_1, \sigma; O_1 n_1; O_2 n_2, \sigma; O_1 n_1; O_2 n_2; O_3 n_3, \ldots$, where each $O_i \in \{B_a, I_a, C_{ab} \mid a, b \in A\}$.

As the only label of length 1 is the label 1, we define a *chain* of labels as a sequence $1, \sigma_1, \sigma_2, \ldots$ of labels if each label in a sequence is a simple extension of its predecessor. Moreover, a chain $1, \sigma_1, \sigma_2, \ldots$ of labels in some (infinite) set Φ of labelled formulae is *periodic* if there exist distinct labels σ_i and σ_j such that σ_i precedes σ_j on the chain and, for any given (unlabelled) formula φ, $\sigma_i \varphi$ is in Φ iff $\sigma_j \varphi$ is in Φ. Furthermore, a branch θ is periodic if every infinite chain of labels in $frm(\theta)$ is periodic.

We obtain the following result, whose proof is similar to an analogous result given by Fitting [4].

Lemma 3. In a systematic tableau for a finite set Φ of signed formulae, every infinite branch must be periodic.

The proof of the lemma follows from the fact that on every infinite branch θ there are only finitely many different formulae up to label differences. Each label σ appearing on θ is associated with a set of unlabelled formulae (formulae that appear on θ with the label σ). Notice that there are only finitely many such sets. Now, an arbitrary infinite chain on θ has infinitely many different labels. Hence, there must be two labels that are associated with the same set of unlabelled formulae and thus the chain is periodic, and so is the branch.

Label Accessibility and Completeness. We continue with showing how to extract a countermodel for a formula φ from an open branch θ of the systematic tableau for $F\varphi$. As labels represent symbolic names for possible worlds in a model, the intuitive approach would be to take the set of labels that appear on θ as the set of possible worlds. Further, we mentioned that the structure of labels should encode the reachability relations between worlds. We next formalise this by introducing the notion of accessibility relations between labels in a rooted set and showing that these relations satisfy all the conditions imposed on the reachability relations between possible worlds.

Definition 6. The accessibility relations $\rhd^*_{B_a}, \rhd^*_{I_a}, \rhd^*_{C_{ab}}$ between two labels σ_1 and σ_2 are defined as follows:

(i) $\sigma_1 \rhd^*_{B_a} \sigma_2$ iff there exists a label σ such that $\sigma_1 = \sigma;\tau$ and $\sigma_2 = \sigma;\rho;B_aL$, where $\tau = B_aN_1;\ldots;B_aN_n$, $\rho = B_aM_1;\ldots;B_aM_m$, $|\sigma| \geq 1, |\tau|, |\rho| \geq 0, L \geq 1$, and $N_i, M_j \geq 1$, for $i = 1,\ldots,n, j = 1,\ldots,m$;

(ii) $\sigma_1 \rhd^*_{I_a} \sigma_2$ iff there exists a label σ such that $\sigma_1 = \sigma;\tau$ and $\sigma_2 = \sigma;\rho;I_aL$, where $\tau = B_aN_1;\ldots;B_aN_n$, $\rho = B_aM_1;\ldots;B_aM_m$, $|\sigma| \geq 1, |\tau|, |\rho| \geq 0, L \geq 1$, and $N_i, M_j \geq 1$, for $i = 1,\ldots,n, j = 1,\ldots,m$;

(iii) $\sigma_1 \rhd^*_{C_{ab}} \sigma_2$ iff there exists a label σ such that $\sigma_1 = \sigma;\tau$ and $\sigma_2 = \sigma;\rho;C_{ab}L$, where $\tau = O_1n_1;\ldots;O_nN_n$, $\rho = O'_1M_1;\ldots;O'_mM_m$, $|\sigma| \geq 1, |\tau|, |\rho| \geq 0, L \geq 1, N_i, M_j \geq 1$, and $O_i, O'_j \in \{B_a, I_a\}$, for $i = 1,\ldots,n, j = 1,\ldots,m$. $\square$

Concerning the intuitions behind these relations, let us consider $\rhd^*_{C_{ab}}$ for illustration (the other relations can be explained similarly). For a possible world named by a label σ, any simple extension $\sigma;C_{ab}N$ of σ with respect to C_{ab} names a world that is reachable from σ via $\mathcal{R}^{C_{ab}}$ and so it is natural to have $\sigma \rhd^*_{C_{ab}} \sigma;C_{ab}N$. Consider now the label $\sigma;O_1N_1;\ldots;O_nN_n;C_{ab}L$, where $L \geq 1, n \geq 0$, and $O_i \subset \{B_a, I_a\}$, for $i = 1,\ldots,n$. Assume the case where $n \geq 1$. Then, we have that the world named by $\sigma;O_1N_1;\ldots;O_nN_n;C_{ab}L$ is reachable via $\mathcal{R}^{C_{ab}}$ from the world named by $\sigma;O_1N_1;\ldots;O_nN_n$, as we are dealing with a simple extension of $\sigma;O_1N_1;\ldots;O_nN_n$ with respect to C_{ab}. Similarly, the world named by $\sigma;O_1N_1;\ldots;O_nN_n$ is reachable from the world named by $\sigma;O_1N_1;\ldots;O_{n-1}N_{n-1}$ via $\mathcal{R}^{O_{n-1}}$. Since $O_{n-1} \in \{B_a, I_a\}$, and $\mathcal{R}^{C_{ab}}$ is transitive over both $\mathcal{R}^{B_a}$ and $\mathcal{R}^{I_a}$, we have that the world named by $\sigma;O_1N_1;\ldots;O_nN_n;C_{ab}L$ can be reached, the world named by $\sigma;O_1N_1;\ldots;O_{n-1}N_{n-1}$ via $\mathcal{R}^{C_{ab}}$. Following this approach, we can go backwards step by step and eventually obtain that the world named by $\sigma;O_1N_1;\ldots;O_nN_n;C_{ab}L$ can be reached from σ via $\mathcal{R}^{C_{ab}}$. Hence, it is desirable to have $\sigma \rhd^*_{C_{ab}} \sigma;O_1N_1;\ldots;O_nN_n;C_{ab}L$.

Consider now the label $\sigma;O'_1M_1;\ldots;O'_mM_m$, where $m \geq 0$ and $O'_j \in \{B_a, I_a\}$, for $j = 1,\ldots,m$. If $m = 0$, then we have the same situation as above. If $m \geq 1$, as $\sigma;O'_1M_1$ is a simple extension of σ with respect to O'_1, we have that the world named by $\sigma;O'_1M_1$ is reachable from the world named by σ via $\mathcal{R}^{O'_1}$. Since we have shown that the world named by $\sigma;O_1N_1;\ldots;O_nN_n;C_{ab}L$ is reachable from σ via $\mathcal{R}^{C_{ab}}$, we conclude, from the fact that $O'_1 \in \{B_a, I_a\}$ and $\mathcal{R}^{C_{ab}}$ is Euclidean over both B_a and I_a, that the world with the symbolic name $\sigma; O_1 N_1; \ldots; O_n N_n; C_{ab} L$ is reachable from the world named by $\sigma; O_1' M_1$ via $\mathcal{R}^{C_{ab}}$. Once again, we proceed step by step (this time going forward), and apply the same argument until we eventually get that the world named by $\sigma; O_1 N_1; \ldots; O_n N_n; C_{ab} L$ is reachable from the world named by $\sigma; O_1' M_1; \ldots; O_m' M_m$ via $\mathcal{R}^{C_{ab}}$. Note that chains $O_1 N_1; \ldots; O_n N_n$ and $O_1' M_1; \ldots; O_m' M_m$ can be arbitrarily short or long. This yields the definition above.

Theorem 3. (i) $\rhd_{B_a}^*$ is transitive and Euclidean; (ii) $\rhd_{I_a}^*$ is transitive and Euclidean over $\rhd_{B_a}^*$; and (iii) $\rhd_{C_{ab}}^*$ is transitive and Euclidean over $\rhd_{B_a}^*$ and $\rhd_{I_a}^*$.

The proof of this result is quite extensive with several case distinctions with repetitive arguments, and therefore omitted due to space reasons. It can be found in the thesis of the first author [10].

As each accessibility relation in a model must be serial, for each label accessibility relation $\rhd_O^*$, $O \in \{B_a, I_a, C_{ab} \mid a, b \in A\}$, we define the *serial closure*, $\rhd_O^D$, of $\rhd_O^*$ by demanding that all those labels from which no other label is accessible be reflexive. Note that it suffices to define the serial closure as above, as every infinite chain of labels, on an open branch of a systematic tableau, eventually becomes periodical. Hence, it is possible to compute the serial closure in a finite amount of time.

Although $\rhd_{I_a}^*$ is transitive and Euclidean over $\rhd_{B_a}^*$ and $\rhd_{C_{ab}}^*$ is transitive and Euclidean over both $\rhd_{B_a}^*$ and $\rhd_{I_a}^*$, unfortunately this is not the case for their respective serial closures. Hence, we need one more step to obtain label accessibility relations which fully capture the reachability relations between worlds.

Definition 7. The extended accessibility relations $\rhd_{B_a}^\circ$, $\rhd_{I_a}^\circ$, and $\rhd_{C_{ab}}^\circ$ are given as follows, where σ_1 and σ_2 are labels:

(i) $\sigma_1 \rhd_{B_a}^\circ \sigma_2$ iff $\sigma_1 \rhd_{B_a}^D \sigma_2$.

(ii) $\sigma_1 \rhd_{I_a}^\circ \sigma_2$ iff (a) $\sigma_1 \rhd_{I_a}^D \sigma_2$ or (b) $\sigma_2 \rhd_{I_a}^D \sigma_2$ and there exists a label σ, $|\sigma| \geq 1$, and some $\sigma' = B_a N_1; \ldots; B_a N_n, \sigma'' = B_a M_1; \ldots; B_a M_m$, such that $\sigma_1 = \sigma; \sigma'$ and $\sigma_2 = \sigma; \sigma''$, where $N_i, M_j \geq 1$, for $i = 1, \ldots, n$, $j = 1, \ldots, m$.

(iii) $\sigma_1 \rhd_{C_{ab}}^\circ \sigma_2$ iff (a) $\sigma_1 \rhd_{C_{ab}}^D \sigma_2$ or (b) $\sigma_2 \rhd_{C_{ab}}^D \sigma_2$ and there exists a label $\sigma, |\sigma| \geq 1$, and some $\sigma' = O_1 N_1; \ldots; O_n N_n, \sigma'' = O_1' M_1; \ldots; O_m' M_m$ such that $\sigma_1 = \sigma; \sigma'$, $\sigma_2 = \sigma; \sigma''$, where $N_i, M_j \geq 1$, $O_i, O_j' \in \{B_a, I_a \mid a \in A\}$, for $i = 1, \ldots, n$, $j = 1, \ldots, m$. □

Theorem 4. The relations $\rhd_{B_a}^\circ$, $\rhd_{I_a}^\circ$, and $\rhd_{C_{ab}}^\circ$ are serial. Moreover, (i) $\rhd_{B_a}^\circ$ is transitive and Euclidean, (ii) $\rhd_{I_a}^\circ$ is transitive and Euclidean over $\rhd_{B_a}^\circ$, (iii) $\rhd_{C_{ab}}^\circ$ is transitive and Euclidean over $\rhd_{B_a}^\circ$, and (iv) $\rhd_{C_{ab}}^\circ$ is transitive and Euclidean over $\rhd_{I_a}^\circ$.

As before, the proof can be found in the thesis of the first author [10].

Definition 8. Let Φ be a rooted set of labelled formulae. Then, Φ is BIC -*downward saturated* if it satisfies the following conditions (for $O \in \{B_a, I_a, C_{ab} \mid a, b \in A\}$):

(S_0) $\{\sigma T\varphi, \sigma F\varphi\} \not\subseteq \Phi$, $\{\sigma T\bot, \sigma F\top\} \cap \Phi = \emptyset$, for any unsigned formula φ and label σ;

(S_1) if $\sigma\alpha \in \Phi$, then $\sigma\alpha_1 \in \Phi$ and $\sigma\alpha_2 \in \Phi$;

(S_2) if $\sigma\beta \in \Phi$, then $\sigma\beta_1 \in \Phi$ or $\sigma\beta_2 \in \Phi$;

(S_3) $\sigma\pi^O \in \Phi$ implies $\tau\pi_0^O \in \Phi$, for at least one $\tau \in lab(\Phi)$ with $\sigma \rhd_O^\circ \tau$; and

(S_4) $\sigma\nu^O \in \Phi$ implies $\tau\nu_0^O \in \Phi$, for every $\tau \in lab(\Phi)$ such that $\sigma \rhd_O^\circ \tau$. □

Lemma 4. *If Φ is a rooted set of labelled formulae that is BIC-downward saturated, then Φ is satisfiable in a model whose possible worlds are labels that appear in Φ.*

Proof. Let Φ be a rooted set of labelled formulae that is BIC-downward saturated. Let $\mathcal{M} = \langle lab(\Phi), (\mathcal{R}^{B_a})_{a\in A}, (\mathcal{R}^{I_a})_{a\in A}, (\mathcal{R}^{C_{ab}})_{a,b\in A}, \Vdash \rangle$ be a model such that $\sigma\mathcal{R}^O\tau$ iff $\sigma \rhd_O^\circ \tau$, $O \in \{B_a, I_a, C_{ab} \mid a, b \in A\}$, and $\mathcal{M}, \sigma \Vdash P$ iff $\sigma TP \in \Phi$, for every atom P. Further, we define a label interpretation $\mathcal{N}$ of Φ in $\mathcal{M}$ as the identity mapping $\mathcal{N}(\sigma) = \sigma$. Using Theorem 4, it can be shown, by induction on the logical complexity of φ, that $\mathcal{M}, \sigma \Vdash \varphi$, for every formula $\sigma\varphi \in \Phi$. Hence, $\langle \mathcal{M}, \mathcal{N} \rangle$ satisfies Φ. □

We proceed with showing that every open branch of a systematic tableau is BIC-downward saturated. To this end, we say that a branch is *processed with respect to a tableau rule* if whenever the rule is applicable, then it has already been applied. Further, we call an open tableau *completed* if it is infinite or no formula on it is awake (cf. Fig. 1 for the notion of awakeness).

In what follows, we refer to the sequence in which the systematic tableau procedure expands the nodes (formulae) in a tableau under construction, as a *visit sequence* of the tableau. Note that if a labelled formula occurrence $\sigma\varphi$ on the visit sequence is awake at the end of stage n, the systematic procedure is guaranteed to either visit it at some later stage or close the tableau. Indeed, since no formula occurrence on the visit sequence can be awakened once it is marked as finished, each subsequent stage will visit the next formula occurrence on the sequence. Therefore, if at stage n, there are l formula occurrences which are awake on the visit sequence that precede $\sigma\phi$, this label will be visited at stage $n + l + 1$.

Lemma 5. *If θ is an open branch of a completed systematic tableau, then θ is processed with respect to every tableau rule in the calculus.*

Proof. First, observe that α-, β-, and π^O-rules, for $O \in \{B_a, I_a, C_{ab} \mid a, b \in A\}$, are applied whenever some formula of the corresponding type is visited. As each formula on θ is visited at least once, θ must be processed with respect to α-, β- and π^O-rules.

Now, suppose some ν^O-rule is applicable to a formula $\sigma\nu^O$ because some label τ was used on the branch. Then, if τ was present on the branch when $\sigma\nu^O$ was first visited, the rule must have been applied then. Otherwise, the label τ must be of form $\sigma; On$ and it must have been created at some later stage by some awake formula $\sigma\pi^O$. But in that case, at the end of the stage when τ was created, the formula $\sigma\nu^O$ is visited again and once again all applicable rules are applied to it, in particular also the ν^O-rule. Therefore, θ must be processed with respect to the rest of the tableau rules.

Lemma 6. If θ is an open branch of a completed systematic tableau, then θ is BIC-downward saturated.

Proof. We show that conditions (S_0)–(S_4) in Definition 8 are satisfied. Condition (S_0) holds as θ is an open branch. By Lemma 5, θ is processed with respect to all rules in the calculus. Thus, Conditions (S_1) and (S_2) hold as well. In particular, as θ is processed with respect to the π^O-rule, for $O \in \{B_a, I_a, C_{ab} \mid a, b \in A\}$, whenever we have a formula of the form $\sigma\pi^O$ on θ, then the (π^O)-rule must have been applied and hence there is a label $\sigma; On$ on θ such that $\sigma; On\pi_0^O \in frm(\theta)$. Thus, Condition (S_3) holds. The proof of Condition (S_4) depends on the type of the ν-formula and is omitted due to space reasons. $\qquad\square$

Theorem 5. If the systematic tableau for a set of signed formulae Φ does not close, then Φ is satisfiable.

Proof. Let $\mathcal{T}$ be the systematic tableau for Φ and suppose that $\mathcal{T}$ does not close. As $\mathcal{T}$ was created by the systematic procedure, it must be completed and, by definition, it must contain an open branch θ. By Lemma 6, θ is BIC-downward saturated. As $frm(\theta)$ is a rooted set, we have, by Lemma 4, that $frm(\theta)$ is satisfiable under the identity interpretation $\mathcal{N}$ (i.e., where $\mathcal{N}(\sigma) = \sigma$ holds for each σ) in a model $\mathcal{M} = \langle lab(\theta), (\rhd_{B_a}^\circ), (\rhd_{I_a}^\circ), (\rhd_{C_{ab}}^\circ), \Vdash \rangle$. Furthermore, if $\sigma\phi \in frm(\theta)$, then $\mathcal{M}, \sigma \Vdash \phi$. Since the tableau starts with $1\phi_i$, for each $\phi_i \in \Phi$, $1\phi_i \in frm(\theta)$ holds. Therefore, we obtain that $\mathcal{M}, 1 \Vdash \Phi$. $\qquad\square$

Theorem 6 (Completeness). If an unsigned formula is valid, then it is provable.

Proof. If ϕ is valid, then by the semantics of signed formulae, $T\phi$ is also valid, which means that $F\phi$ is unsatisfiable. Hence, by Theorem 5, the systematic tableau for $\{F\phi\}$ provides a tableau proof for ϕ. $\qquad\square$

In concluding, we note that our calculus can be extended in the usual manner by employing *local* and *global assumption rules* for accommodating logical consequence, where, following Fitting [4], a set V of formulae is a *logical consequence* of a set of *local assumptions* U and a set of *global assumptions* S, denoted by $S \vDash_{\mathsf{BIC}} (U \longrightarrow V)$, iff in every BIC-model $\mathcal{M}$ in which all formulae of S are true (forced by every world in $\mathcal{M}$), whenever all elements of U are true in some world w, then at least one element of V must be true in w. For details, we again refer to the thesis of the first author [10].

References

1. Castelfranchi, C.: Artificial liars: Why computers will (necessarily) deceive us and each other. Ethics Inf. Technol. **2**(2), 113–119 (2000)
2. Firozabadi, B.S., Tan, Y.H., Lee, R.M.: Formal definitions of fraud. In: Norms, Logics and Information Systems, pp. 275–288 (1998)
3. Fitting, M.: Tableau methods of proof for modal logics. Notre Dame J. Form. Log. **13**(2), 237–247 (1972)

4. Fitting, M.: Proof Methods for Modal and Intuitionistic Logics, vol. 169. Springer, Dordrecht (1983). https://doi.org/10.1007/978-94-017-2794-5
5. Goré, R.: Tableau methods for modal and temporal logics. In: D'Agostino, M., Gabbay, D.M., Hähnle, R., Posegga, J. (eds.) Handbook of Tableau Methods, pp. 297–396. Springer, Dordrecht (1999). https://doi.org/10.1007/978-94-017-1754-0_6
6. Massacci, F.: Strongly analytic tableaux for normal modal logics. In: Bundy, A. (ed.) CADE 1994. LNCS, vol. 814, pp. 723–737. Springer, Heidelberg (1994). https://doi.org/10.1007/3-540-58156-1_52
7. Massacci, F.: Single step tableaux for modal logics. J. Autom. Reason. **24**(3), 319–364 (2000)
8. O'Neill, B.: A formal system for understanding lies and deceit. In: Jerusalem Conference on Biblical Economics (2003)
9. Pan, Y., Cao, C., Sui, Y.: A formal system for lies based on speech acts in multi-agent systems. In: Proceedings of the First IEEE Symposium on Foundations of Computational Intelligence, FOCI 2007, pp. 228–234. IEEE (2007)
10. Pavlović, S.: A tableau calculus for a multi-modal logic of dishonesty. Bachelor's thesis, Technische Universität Wien, Institute for Logic and Computation (2018)
11. Sakama, C.: Dishonest reasoning by abduction. In: Proceedings of the 22nd International Joint Conference on Artificial Intelligence, IJCAI 2011, pp. 1063–1064. IJCAI/AAAI (2011)
12. Sakama, C.: Dishonest arguments in debate games. In: Proceedings of the Fourth International Conference on Computational Models of Argument, COMMA 2012. Frontiers in Artificial Intelligence and Applications, vol. 245, pp. 177–184. IOS Press (2012)
13. Sakama, C.: Learning dishonesty. In: Riguzzi, F., Železný, F. (eds.) ILP 2012. LNCS, vol. 7842, pp. 225–240. Springer, Heidelberg (2013). https://doi.org/10.1007/978-3-642-38812-5_16
14. Sakama, C., Caminada, M., Herzig, A.: A formal account of dishonesty. Log. J. IGPL **23**(2), 259–294 (2015)
15. Sakama, C., Inoue, K.: Abduction, conversational implicature and misleading in human dialogues. Log. J. IGPL **24**(4), 526–541 (2016)
16. Smullyan, R.M.: A unifying principle in quantification theory. Proc. Natl. Acad. Sci. **49**(6), 828–832 (1963)
17. Tzouvaras, A.: Logic of knowledge and utterance and the liar. J. Philos. Log. **27**(1), 85–108 (1998)
18. van Ditmarsch, H., van Eijck, J., Sietsma, F., Wang, Y.: On the logic of lying. In: van Eijck, J., Verbrugge, R. (eds.) Games, Actions and Social Software. LNCS, vol. 7010, pp. 41–72. Springer, Heidelberg (2012). https://doi.org/10.1007/978-3-642-29326-9_4

Goal Distribution in Business Process Models

Matteo Baldoni$^{(\boxtimes)}$ (iD), Cristina Baroglio(iD), and Roberto Micalizio(iD)

Dipartimento di Informatica, Università degli Studi di Torino, c.so Svizzera 185, 10149 Turin, Italy
{matteo.baldoni,cristina.baroglio,roberto.micalizio}@unito.it

Abstract. Business processes are widely used to capture how a service is realized or a product is delivered by a set of combined tasks. It is a recommended practice to implement a business goal through a single business process; in many cases, however, this is impossible or it is not efficient. The choice is, then, to split the process into a number of interacting processes. In order to realize this kind of solution, the business goal is broken up and distributed through many "actors", who will depend on one another in carrying out their tasks. We explain, in this work, some weaknesses that emerge in this picture, and also how they would be overcome by introducing an explicit representation of responsibilities and accountabilities. We rely, as a running example, on the Hiring Process as described by Silver in [13].

Keywords: Accountability · Responsibility · BPM · Goals

1 Introduction

Most of the methodologies for the design and development of complex distributed systems turn around the notion of *goal* as a way to specify the functional behavior of the system under development. In the agent-oriented programming, for instance, the Gaia methodology [20] is specifically concerned with how a society of agents cooperate to realize the *system-level goals*.

The notion of goal is also relevant in the specification of business processes. Specifically, a business process can be defined as "a set of activities that are performed in coordination in an organizational and technical environment. These activities jointly realize a business goal." [19] As a general practice, it is desirable to design an end-to-end process [13]: a single process is triggered by a specific request and ends up with a proper answer for that request (e.g., a service or a product). In other words, since the Business Process Modeling and Notation (BPMN) is one of the most widely used languages for modeling business processes, the description of how satisfying a business request should be encompassed within a single BPMN process, whenever possible, so that any instance of such a process would be a specific *case*.

© Springer Nature Switzerland AG 2018
C. Ghidini et al. (Eds.): AI*IA 2018, LNAI 11298, pp. 252–265, 2018.
https://doi.org/10.1007/978-3-030-03840-3_19

Sometimes, however, such a practice cannot be implemented, for instance because the activity instances are not aligned across the whole end-to-end process. To cope with this problem, the engineer cannot but resort to model the end-to-end process as multiple BPMN processes, realizing in this way the one-to-many coordination pattern [10,13]. In the one-to-many pattern, the designer must model a number of independent BPMN processes that interact with each other either by exchanging messages, or by means of a synchronized access to a shared data storage. Since these processes are independent, each of them has its own start and end events, however, none of them alone can bring about the business goal. Such a goal, in fact, is only achieved when all the processes are considered as a whole. This represents a first pitfall of the one-to-many pattern because the business goal is no longer explicitly represented by a single BPMN process. Moreover, interactions among the processes may be only indirectly represented – as synchronized accesses to data storages. As a consequence, the BPMN models lose part of their descriptive power because relevant coordination aspects are actually missing. Thus, an engineer has to deal with several processes at design time, but she has not adequate abstractions to model, and check, how these processes will actually interact.

We deem that providing an engineer with explicit abstractions for capturing interactions at the level of goals is essential for the realization of complex distributed systems, and in particular, systems where multiple, concurrent business processes interact with each other to achieve a business goal. To support the achievement of goals in a distributed way, we resort to notions that underlie human coordination, namely, *accountability* and *responsibility*. The two terms are strictly related, and often used interchangeably in the literature, but in our perspective they assume distinct meaning and purpose. For instance, in [11] responsibilities are seen as charges assigned to some actor. Being responsible for a task, however, does not necessarily mean to directly carry out the very same task. A task, in fact, can be decomposed into subtasks, each of which is then under the responsibility of a different actor. Here comes into play the notion of accountability that is broadly defined as: the obligation to give account to someone else under the threat of sanction(s) [5,8,14]. In other works, e.g. [6], accountability is a directed relationship between two principals, which reflects the legitimate *expectations* the second principal has of the first about the achievement of a condition. Moreover, thanks to the inherent expectations created by an accountability relationship, accountability is seen as a major driving force of individuals when it comes to decide about their own behavior [1]. In our perspective, see the information model described in [3], accountability is characterized by two fundamental facets. First, as already noted, the legitimate expectation that an actor has on the behavior of another actor. Second, the *control* over the condition for which one is held accountable. The intuitive meaning, here, is that an actor declares (or accepts) to be accountable for a given condition when it has the capabilities for bringing about the condition on its own, or when it can rely on the accountability relationships provided by other actors. In both cases the actor has control over the condition –direct in the former case, indirect in

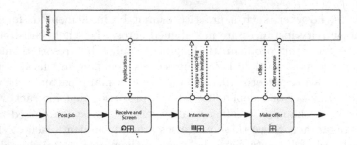

Fig. 1. The hiring process example: ineffective solution.

the latter. In fact, an actor that can hold another to account exerts a form of authority having the right of asking the second actor an account of its actions about a condition of interest. Accountability, thus, plays a twofold role. On the one side, it is the instrument through which responsibilities are discharged [11]. On the other side, it is the trigger that makes interactions progress as agents tend to discharge their duties lest being sanctioned.

In this paper, we first point out some modeling issues related to the one-to-many pattern for coordinating independent business processes (Sect. 2). We then describe our proposal (Sect. 3), and argue how responsibility and account-ability can be accommodated in the context of business processes to keep an explicit trace of (1) how a business goal is distributed over concurrent processes, each responsible for a specific portion of the goal, and (2) how the coordination among these processes is represented via accountability relationships. Having an explicit model of goal distribution has several beneficial consequences. First of all, it becomes clear what is the (sub)goal carried out by each business process and how this is functional for the achievement of the overall goal. Moreover, having a formal model, the engineer can verify whether the processes she has designed actually achieve the overall goal, and hence detect in advance flaws. In particular, we will show (Sect. 4) that thanks to the recursive feature of control associated with accountability, an engineer can establish whether each process is properly supported by the others, and what is potentially missing. Finally, we show how, driven by the goal distribution model, the interaction among the processes can be implemented as commitment-based protocols, provided that some specific conditions on the creation and shape of commitments are respected (Sect. 5). Finally, we conclude with a comparison between our proposal and novel approaches to modeling business process choreographies (Sect. 6).

2   Challenges in Business Goal Distribution

To understand the issues hidden in the one-to-many pattern, we shortly recall how Silver [13] illustrates this problem by means of the Hiring Process example. Suppose a case consisting of one open job position; the goal is to hire a new

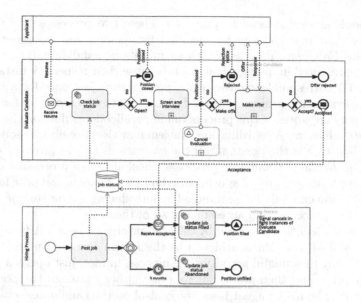

Fig. 2. The hiring process example: correct solution.

employee for that job. Many candidates will likely apply. As long as the position remains open, each interested candidate walks through an evaluation process, that may take some time to be completed. When a candidate is deemed apt for the position, the job is assigned and the position is closed.

Silver explains how such a procedure cannot be modeled as a single BPMN process since, inherently, the activities managing the candidates (e.g., accepting and processing their applications), have a different multiplicity than the activity managing the position, which is only one. A first intuitive solution is showed in Fig. 1 where the multiplicity of the candidates is dealt with by means of an iterative task (i.e., `Receive and Screen`) and a parallel task (i.e., `Interview`). Although this solution is formally correct, it does not meet the goal. Indeed, the goal of the hirer is to assign the position as soon as an adequate candidate is found. The process in Fig. 1, instead, awaits to collect a certain number of applications, and then starts the interviews (in parallel). A first weakness of the process is that the hirer has to set the number of applications she is willing to wait before starting the interviews. Once this number is reached, it is not possible to accept other applications. Thus, it may be the case that the position remains unfilled because none of the interviews were satisfactory and no new application is admissible. Moreover, the hirer moves to step `Make Offer` only after having interviewed all the candidates. This process, thus, does not represent the intended goal since an offer is not made as soon as a good candidate is found.

In order to deal with many candidates for a single job, so as to meet the goal, Silver suggests the adoption of two distinct BPMN processes, that, although potentially performed by the same people, are formally represented in two separate pools since *independent processes*. These two processes are: the *Hiring Process*, that manages the job position by opening and assigning it, and the *Evaluate Candidate* process, which examines one candidate. The two processes are represented in independent pools because their respective instances do not have a 1:1 correspondence: the hiring process runs just once for a position, whereas the evaluation process runs for each candidate who shows up for the job. Possibly, many instances of this process run in parallel depending on the number of available evaluators. A coordination problem now rises because, as soon as one of the candidates fills the position, all the evaluations still in progress must be stopped. The *Evaluate Candidate* processes, thus, although processing different candidate applications, are all synchronized on the status of the position. Such a synchronization can only be guaranteed by introducing a *data storage* (Fig. 2), external to the processes and accessible to all of them.

We see in the solution proposed by Silver some critical issues. A first problem is that the goal *fill position* is achieved by the *Hiring Process*, but this process is cleared off any meaningful activity. The process, in fact, just opens a position in the beginning, and then awaits for an event either to assign the position or to abandon it. The hiring agent loses the control on the candidates' evaluation. When a candidate is accepted by an evaluator, the hiring agent does not know how the evaluation process has been carried out. On the other hand, in case the three-month timeout expires, the hiring agent cannot know whether all the candidates were rejected, or no candidate at all showed up. Looking at the *Evaluate Candidate* process, instead, one knows how an evaluator manages a candidate, but cannot contextualize the process: the evaluator does not know how many positions are open, nor she knows there is a time limit. The (sub)goal *evaluate candidate* is functional to the achievement of the original business goal *fill position*, but the relationship between these two goals (and processes) is hidden in the synchronized access to the data store. Data are used as a sort of synchronization signals, but then the semantics associated with data falls outside the model. Arguably, the engineer adds an annotation to the model through which she explains data semantics, but then the correct development of the processes relies on the skills of the careful developer.

Our goal, on the contrary, is to maintain the dependencies between the *Hiring* and the *Evaluate Candidate* processes in an explicit, formal way that allows one to develop them so as to be compliant with the coordination designed by the engineer. We believe that the notions of responsibility and accountability serve this purpose in an intuitive, yet effective way, and in the rest of the paper we discuss how to achieve this result.

3   Distributing Goals via Accountability and Responsibility

In order to support the achievement of distributed goals, we resort to the notions of *accountability* and *responsibility*. Specifically, we take as a starting point the ReMMo conceptual model proposed by Feltus [11], which is, to the best of our knowledge, the first proposal that relates responsibility and accountability in a computational model. ReMMo, in fact, defines responsibility as "a charge assigned to a unique actor to signify its accountabilities concerning a unique business task." Responsibility is therefore seen as a charge assigned to an agent, which is always linked at least to one accountability.

Accountability, on the other hand, has distinctive traits which do not allow making it a special kind of responsibility. It involves two agents, the one who gives the account (a-giver) and the one who takes the account (a-taker). The a-taker can only be someone who has some kind of authority on the account giver [7]. The origin of such an authority may be various; for instance, it may be due to a principal-agent relationship, or to a delegation. Moreover, accountability is defined into a context (or condition), and concerns either to-do or to-achieve a specific goal (or task). Accountability may also involve a sanction, as a social consequence of the account giver's achievement or non-achievement of what expected, and of its providing or not providing an account. So, for instance, both a doctor and a nurse will be responsible – in different ways – for a treatment task to be given to a patient. The different ways in which they are responsible depend on the many accountabilities they will have concerning this task (e.g., towards the head physician, towards the administration, towards the patient, the nurse towards the doctor, . . .). The nurse will be accountable to do (herself) certain procedures, the doctor to achieve (relying on others) certain results.

The ReMMo model is surely a valuable contribution, but it fails in providing a proper characterization of accountability. The notion of expectation, for instance, is just informally assumed but it is not explicitly captured within the model. Moreover, we deem that an agent can be held accountable for a given goal only when it has the control over the goal. Control can be defined as the ability, possibly distributed among agents, of bringing about events [12]. In fact, without control, the agent does not have an impact on the situation. It will be ineffectual. Again, the notion of control is not part of the ReMMo model. Discussing how the ReMMo model could be enhanced with a more precise characterization of accountability is out the scope of this paper, a first attempt is discussed in [3]. In the rest of the paper, we assume that each accountability relationship brings over the two features of legitimate expectation and control.

We now illustrate in abstract terms how a business model can be complemented with accountabilities. Let us suppose that a modeler has devised a set of independent business processes that, working in a choreography, achieve a given business goal. As discussed above, the goal is clearly in the mind of the modeler, but since it has been distributed over a number of processes, in the resulting BPMN model, BP, the business goal remains substantially implicit. To make the goal explicit, first, we consider each process assigned to a role x in BP as an objective ob, whose achievement contributes to the achievement of the business goal, and, second, we say that role x is responsible for that specific objective, denoted by $R(x, ob)$. In other terms, we can think of an objective as a high-level task that abstracts from execution details. The set of responsibilities make explicit what high-level tasks are needed to achieve a business goal, and which role is in charge for each task. However, the responsibilities do not model how an objective is related to another objective, that is, how it is functional to, and coordinated with, other objectives.

To this end, we follow the same idea of grounding responsibilities on accountabilities, followed also in [11], and characterize each $R(x, ob)$ with a set of accountability relationships of form $A(x, y, p, q)$: role y, the a-taker, is entitled to ask role x, the account-giver, for a proof about the (non-)realization of condition q, when condition p is realized. In his case, x must provide the account, that is, x will produce a sequence of events that prove the satisfaction of the expectations y has on x. Events in the proof amount to the execution of a (sub)process meeting condition q. Generally speaking, the two conditions p and q need not to be causally nor temporally related, i.e. q can be brought about even if p does not hold yet. Condition p just circumscribes the context under which x is held to account for q. When modeling the coordination of distributed business processes, however, the intuition is that q should be actually achieved after p.

More precisely, x and y are roles in BP, whereas p and q can be thought of as events representing portions of the BP process relevant for expressing the accountability relation. Intuitively, events in p and q corresponds to the sending/reception of messages, the throwing/catching of signals, and the execution of activities as indicated in BP. (At the time being, the language for expressing the antecedent and consequent conditions is not relevant in this abstract presentation, a specific formalism is introduced for a concrete scenario in the next section, where we show how the coordination between antecedent and consequent conditions can be obtained.) However, not all the events in q may be under the direct control of x. On the other hand, we demand that the consequent condition be under the control of the a-giver. This requires an indirect form of control that is achieved only when all the accountability relationships associated with every role in BP are *closed*.

Definition 1. *Let BP be a business process achieving a given business goal, and let A be the set of all the accountability relationships $A(x, y, p, q)$ for each pair of roles x and y in BP. We say that A is* closed *if for each accountability relationship $A(x, y, p, q) \in A$, every event e occurring in q is such that either x can bring about e directly, or there exists in A another accountability relationship $A(z, x, p', q')$ such that e holds when q' holds (i.e., $q' \models e$), and x has direct control over p'.*

Control over condition q is therefore exerted by agent x in two ways. For *direct control* we mean that x can bring about every event in q directly via its own behaviors. For *indirect control* we mean that x can bring about some of the events in q by relying on the collaboration of other agents, that are subjected to x via accountability relationships through which x can pressure them, having the control of the antecedent condition, to pull their weight on achieving the condition q.

4 Responsibility and Accountability in the One-to-Many Pattern

In this section we exemplify in the hiring process scenario how our accountability framework is used to model the one-to-many pattern. In the hiring process scenario, it is quite natural to individuate three roles: the hirer, the evaluator, and the candidate. For each available position, then, there will be just one actor hi playing the hirer role, whereas many evaluators and candidates will be admissible. To simplify the exposition, we will assume that a candidate i will be evaluated by a specific evaluator ev_i; this does not exclude, however, that the same agent be an evaluator for different candidates. Namely, ev_i and i are role instances of roles evaluator and candidate, respectively. To each role we ascribe part of the responsibility of achieving the business goal, namely with $R(hi, fill\ position)$ we denote that the hirer is in charge of fulfilling the objective *fill position*, whereas $R(ev_i, evaluate\ candidate)$ denotes that evaluator ev_i is in charge of the evaluation of a single candidate, finally, with $R(i, follow\text{-}through\ application)$ we specify that every candidate has the objective to complete its application process.

Each responsibility is, then, characterized by a set of accountabilities describing how a role player can meet that responsibility. The set of accountabilities for the hiring process is showed in Fig. 3, where antecedent and consequent conditions are expressed in precedence logic.[1] It is interesting to study first the accountabilities that each evaluator ev_i assumes having part of the responsibilities over the goal. These accountabilities derive directly from the *Evaluate Candidate* process in Fig. 2, which describes the procedure an evaluator is expected to follow. Roughly speaking, the hirer expects that the evaluator be compliant with the evaluation process (e.g., always perform *Screen and Interview* before a *Make Offer*). Moreover, the evaluator should interrupt the evaluation as soon as the position is assigned. On the other hand, a candidate submitting an application expects from an evaluator to be answered, either with a notification of rejection, or with a message of position filled, or possibly with an offer. All these considerations bring us to characterize $R(ev_i, evaluate\ candidate)$ with the accountability relationships a_1 and a_2. Each event occurring in the expressions is adorned, as subscript, with the role that brings it about. Intuitively, accountability a_1 means that evaluator ev_i is accountable towards hirer hi for evaluating a candidate i, but only in the context where hirer has posted a position (post-job$_{hi}$) and candidate i has applied for the position (apply$_i$), to guarantee this strict ordering,

---

[1] Precedence logic is an event-based linear temporal logic introduced in [16] and in [17, Chap. 14] for Web service composition. The interpretation of such a logic deals with occurrences of events along runs (i.e., sequence of instanced events). Under this respect, event occurrences are assumed as nonrepeating and persistent: once an event has occurred, it has occurred forever. The precedence logic has three primary operators: '∨' (choice), '∧' (concurrency), and '·' (before). The *before* operator allows one to constrain the order with which two events must occur, e.g., $a \cdot b$ means that a must occur before b, but the two events do not need to occur immediately after one another.

the sequence post-job$_{hi}$ · apply$_i$ appears both as the antecedent condition and as a prefix of the consequent condition, preceding the candidate evaluation. The same pattern is used throughout the subsequent relationships. The evaluation is encoded as the sequence of events that may occur during an evaluation according to the *Evaluate Candidate* process in Fig. 2.

a_1 : A(ev_i, hi, post-job$_{hi}$ · apply$_i$, post-job$_{hi}$ · apply$_i$ · evaluate-candidate$_{ev_i}$)

    evaluate-candidate$_{ev_i}$ ≡ position-filled$_{hi}$ · msg-position-closed$_{ev_i}$ ∨

                    check-position$_{ev_i}$ · msg-position-closed$_{ev_i}$ ∨

                    (check-position$_{ev_i}$ · screen-interview$_{ev_i}$ ·

                    (msg-rejection-notice$_{ev_i}$ ∨ make-offer$_{ev_i}$ ·

                    (response-yes$_i$ · accepted$_{ev_i}$ ∨ response-no$_i$ · offer-rejected$_{ev_i}$)))

a_2 : A(ev_i, i, post-job$_{hi}$ · apply$_i$, post-job$_{hi}$ · apply$_i$ · inform-outcome$_{ev_i}$)

    inform-outcome$_{ev_i}$ ≡ msg-position-closed$_{ev_i}$ ∨ msg-rejection-notice$_{ev_i}$ ∨ make-offer$_{ev_i}$.

a_3 : A(hi, ev_i, accept$_{ev_j}$, accept$_{ev_j}$ · position-filled$_{hi}$), where $ev_i \neq ev_j$.

a_4 : A(i, ev_i, make-offer$_{ev_i}$, make-offer$_{ev_i}$ · (response-yes$_i$ ∨ response-no$_i$))

a_5 : A(hi, $boss$, open-position$_{boss}$, open-position$_{boss}$ · post-job$_{hi}$)

a_6 : A(hi, $boss$, post-job$_{hi}$ · (accepted$_{ev_i}$ ∨ timeout_3months$_{hi}$), hiring$_{hi}$)

    hiring$_{hi}$ ≡ post-job$_{hi}$ · (accepted$_{ev_i}$ · position-filled$_{hi}$

              ∨ timeout_3months$_{hi}$ · position-abandoned$_{hi}$)

Fig. 3. The set of accountabilities relationships for the *Hiring Process* scenario.

Accountability a_2 represents the expectation candidate i has on ev_i: in the context in which a job is posted and candidate i has applied for it, ev_i is expected to inform i with the outcome of the evaluation process, this can either be, a message with content "position closed", a rejection notification, or an offer for the job.

It is important to observe that, to be properly grounded, the accountability relationships must be such to guarantee the *a-giver* has the control (possibly indirect) over the consequent condition. Under this respect, a_1 is not properly founded since there are events in expression evaluate-candidate$_{ev_i}$ that are not generated by ev_i. First of all, event position-filled$_{hi}$ occurs when the hirer has assigned the position, in this case the evaluation process carried on by ev_i has to terminate by informing the candidate that the position is no longer available (msg-position-closed$_{ev_i}$). To grant ev_i control over this event, thus, R(hi, *fill position*) must be characterized by accountability a_3, which states that hi is accountable towards every evaluator ev_i still processing a candidate that, as soon as the position gets filled due to the acceptance event coming from an evaluator

ev_j, hi will notify this change (position-filled$_{hi}$). In other words, notifying that the position has been assigned is part of the responsibilities of the hirer role. Note that, even if ev_i and ev_j are distinct, they are role instances of the same role evaluator, and hence a_3 satisfies the definition of indirect control in Definition 1.

More critically, also the events response-yes$_i$ and response-no$_i$ are not under the control of ev_i. In case of an offer made to candidate i, ev_i awaits an answer, either response-yes$_i$ or response-no$_i$, from i. However, the candidate could never answer, and if this happened, the error would be ascribed to the evaluator for not having completed its process, rather than to the candidate for not having answered. Noticeably, this is exactly the scenario modeled in the BPMN processes in Fig. 2. In fact, the BPMN model does not specify the internal process of the candidate, thus there is no guarantee that the candidate will ever answer to the evaluator's offer. The lack of proper abstractions for explicitly modeling interactions at the goal level, rather than just at the data level via message exchanges, makes the overall system fragile to unexpected conditions. We properly handle this issue thanks to the notions of *expectation* and *control* characterizing the accountability relationships. Since every accountability must be properly grounded over control, the engineer makes a_1 closed by associating accountability a_4 to R(i, *follow-through application*). a_4 means that candidate i is accountable towards ev_i for answering either response-yes$_i$ or response-no$_i$ in case it receives an offer from ev_i. This correctly captures the expectation of ev_i to receive an answer, and enables ev_i to control (even indirectly) all the events in the consequent condition of a_1.

Since a business goal, put in a context, is usually functional to other goals, it is reasonable to characterize the responsibility of the hirer with the accountability it has towards its boss. Accountability a_5 means that hi is accountable towards *boss* for posting a job vacancy when *boss* open a position for that job, this triggers the whole hiring process. Accountability a_6 models the fact that hi is accountable for managing the hiring process until either the assignment of the position to a candidate or to the abandoned. In particular, timeout_3months$_{hi}$ means position-filled$_{hi}$, that is, the complementary event of position-filled$_{hi}$ representing the fact that, after a three-month period, the position is no longer assignable. Thus, when a candidate is accepted (accepted$_{ev_i}$), hi is expected to assign the position to that candidate position-filled$_{hi}$. Otherwise, in case the three-month period expires without the occurrence of an acceptance (timeout_3months$_{hi}$), hi is expected to abandon the position (position-abandoned$_{hi}$). Here *boss* can be thought of as an abstraction of the rest of the organization to which hirer and evaluator belong. This allows us to express the relations the hiring process has with other processes within the same organization. In fact, the hirer is not necessarily the same agent who opens a position, since the opening of a position might depend on decisions taken at the top level of an organization. The hirer, instead, is the agent who has the responsibility of managing the hiring process. The result achieved by this process will reasonably become the input for a downstream process.

Accountabilities Framework in Action. It is worth noting that our proposal is not only useful at the modeling stage (e.g., to recognize flaws in the interaction among business processes), but it also provides runtime support for handling exceptions. In fact, via the accountability relationships it is possible to isolate the actors responsible for unexpected executions. Let us assume, for instance, that after a reasonable amount of time, candidate i complains that it has not received a response about its application, yet the position results assigned to a different candidate. The isolation of the actor(s) that misbehaved would in general require the examination of the processes' logs to reconstruct the actual sequence of events that has led to the missing notification. Our accountability framework, instead, does this in a more direct and effective way. If i has not received an answer, then ev_i has not satisfied a_2, that is, ev_i has not sent none of the three possible messages. Thus ev_i is surely to blame for its misbehavior. Our framework allows for a more in-depth analysis, if we detect that also a_3 has not been satisfied, then hi, too, is responsible for the unexpected behavior since event position-filled$_{hi}$ is necessary for ev_i in order to send msg-position-closed$_{ev_i}$ (see a_1). In a different scenario where hi fails in satisfying a_3 and ev_i behaves correctly, ev_i will carry out the evaluation and will issue to i either an offer or a rejection notice. This anomalous behavior is detectable and explainable by simply observing rejection notices or offers instead of "position closed" messages after that the position has been assigned.

5   Implementing Accountabilities

So far we have discussed how the notions of accountability and responsibility can be used at design time to model a one-to-many pattern of interaction among independent processes. In particular, we have shown how, taking into account the expectation and control facets of accountability, the engineer can verify, at design time, whether the interaction among the processes is well founded. To be an effective instrument in the hands of the engineer, however, responsibility and accountability should also be means for implementing process coordination in a way which is compliant with the model. Interestingly, accountabilities (as we proposed them) can be mapped, under certain conditions, into commitment-based protocols, and hence any platform supporting them (see for instance JaCaMo+ [2]), is a good candidate for implementing the coordination among the business processes.

Roughly speaking, a commitment-based protocol $\mathcal{P}$ is a set of social commitments [15] that agents can manipulate via a predefined set of operations. Formally, a commitment is denoted as $C(x, y, p, q)$, meaning that agent x, the debtor, is committed towards y, the creditor, to bring about the consequent condition q in case the antecedent condition p is satisfied. A commitment thus formalizes a promise, or a contract, between the two agents. It creates a *legitimate expectation* in y that q will be brought about whenever p holds. This aspect is therefore very similar to what an accountability relationship $A(x, y, p, q)$ creates. Intuitively, thus, for each accountability relationship an analogous commitment can be defined. However, the mapping is not always so trivial. As noticed in [6], commitments are just a way to express accountability relations, others are, for instance, authorizations and prohibitions. Therefore, in general, not every accountability relationship can be mapped into a commitment. In this paper, however, we have characterized accountability in terms of expectation and control, meaning that the *a-giver* is expected *to do*, or *to achieve*, a given condition. This specific characterization of accountability is indeed mappable into commitments since a commitment, implicitly, suggests that the debtor will behave so as to achieve the consequent condition. In order to use properly commitments for representing accountability relationships, we have, however, to pay special care on how these commitments are created and defined.

First of all, a commitment can only be created by its debtor. This in general enables flexible executions w.r.t. obligations since agents can decide what commitments create depending on contextual conditions. However, this flexibility may create some problems because responsibilities and accountabilities are not necessarily taken on voluntarily by an agent, but may be part of a role definition in an organization. In our hiring scenario, for instance, an agent playing the evaluator role is expected to satisfy its accountabilities related to the objective *evaluate candidate*, it is not a matter of the evaluator's initiative. To cope with this problem, we impose that an agent willing to play a given role r in $\mathcal{P}$ accepts, explicitly, all the commitments C_r in $\mathcal{P}$ that mention r as debtor. In [4] we present the ADOPT protocol as a means for an agent and an organization to create an accountable agreement upon the powers and commitments that the agent will take as a player of a specific role in the organization. A second feature of commitments is that, similarly to accountability relationships, there is no causal nor temporal dependency between the antecedent condition p and the consequent one q: q can be satisfied even before condition p.

Finally, and more importantly, in a commitment the antecedent and consequent conditions are not necessarily under the control of the creditor and debtor agents, respectively. In other words, agent x can create the commitment $C(x, y, p, q)$ even though it has no control over q. This feature is again justified by the sake of flexibility, but this freedom endangers the realization of sound accountabilities. As argued above, in fact, our accountability relationships demand that the *a-giver* has control, possibly indirect, over the consequent condition. This means that also the corresponding commitments must retain the same property. Noticeably, it can be proved that when a set commitments implement a set of *closed* accountability relationships, all the commitments are safe as defined in [12]: "a commitment is safe for its debtor if either the debtor controls the negation of the antecedent or whenever the antecedent holds, the debtor controls the residuation of the consequent." In other words, the safeness of the commitments is obtained as a side effect of the closeness of the accountability relationships.

6   Discussion and Conclusions

Goals are the final purposes that justify every activity in business processes. Surprisingly enough, however, goals are not modeled explicitly in the standard modeling languages for business applications (e.g., BPMN). Especially in cross-organizational settings, the lack of an explicit representation of the business goal raises many problems, including documentation, design checking, and compliance of the implementation. Cross organizational business processes are often modeled via *choreographies* which define "the sequence and conditions under which multiple cooperating, independent agents exchange messages in order to perform a task to achieve a goal" [18]. Choreographies are therefore a means for reaching goals in a distributed way, but the goal is in the mind of the modeler, whereas the model itself boils down to an exchange of messages that may be not sufficiently informative. As discussed in [9], the *interconnection model* style of BPMN hampers the modularity and reuse of the processes, and creates situations where the interaction is easily ill-modeled. Decker et al. propose a novel modeling style for choreographies: the *interaction model*, and introduce iBPMN as an extension to BPMN. In iBPMN a choreography becomes a first-class component as it lays outside the business processes. Specific language elements allow the modeler to express how the interaction progresses through a workflow, where elementary activities include the (atomic) send-receive of messages, and decision and split gates. iBPMN allows the modeler to define ordering constraints between the interaction activities, and it is certainly a more powerful tool for expressing choreographies than standard BPMN, however, the goal of the interaction is still in the mind of the modeler and it is not made explicit.

In this paper we have shown how the notions of responsibility and accountability provide the engineer with explicit modeling tools, through which it becomes possible to distribute a business goal among different processes, yet maintaining precise dependencies among them via accountability relationships. For the sake of exposition, we have presented our approach through an example of the one-to-many coordination pattern. However, our proposal is applicable for cross-organization integration in the broad sense. An explicit representation of accountability relationships has several advantages. First of all, it makes the assessment of the correctness of an interaction model possible. As shown in the simple hiring scenario, for instance, we have singled out a flaw in the BPMN model proposed by Silver, thanks to the formal characterization of control associated with an accountability relationships. Moreover, our proposal paves the way to *compatibility* and *conformance* checks. Intuitively, compatibility centers around whether a set of process models can interact successfully. Conformance, on the other hand, focuses on whether a process model is a valid refinement or implementation of a given specification [9]. We have also pointed out that our accountability relationships are not just an abstract modeling tool, but find a proper implementation in commitment-based protocols. The obvious advantage, thus, is to translate the interaction model into a compliant implementation.

References

1. Anderson, P.A.: Justifications and precedents as constraints in foreign policy decision-making. Am. J. Polit. Sci. **25**(4), 738–761 (1981)
2. Baldoni, M., Baroglio, C., Capuzzimati, F., Micalizio, R.: Commitment-based agent interaction in JaCaMo+. Fundam. Inform. **159**(1–2), 1–33 (2018)
3. Baldoni, M., Baroglio, C., May, K.M., Micalizio, R., Tedeschi, S.: An information model for computing accountabilities. In: Ghidini, C., et al. (eds.) AI*IA 2018. LNCS, vol. 11298, pp. 30–44. Springer, Cham (2018)
4. Baldoni, M., Baroglio, C., May, K.M., Micalizio, R., Tedeschi, S.: Computational accountability in MAS organizations with ADOPT. Appl. Sci. **8**(4), 489 (2018)
5. Bovens, M.: Two concepts of accountability: accountability as a virtue and as a mechanism. West Eur. Polit. **33**(5), 946–967 (2010). https://doi.org/10.1080/01402382.2010.486119
6. Chopra, A.K., Singh, M.P.: From social machines to social protocols: software engineering foundations for sociotechnical systems. In: Proceedings of the 25th International Conference on WWW (2016)
7. Darwall, S.: Civil recourse as mutual accountability. In: Morality, Authority, and Law: Essays in Second-Personal Ethics I. Oxford University Press (2013)
8. Day, P., Klein, R.: Accountabilities: Five Public Services. Social Science Paperbacks. Tavistock, London (1987)
9. Decker, G., Weske, M.: Interaction-centric modeling of process choreographies. Inf. Syst. **36**(2), 292–312 (2011)
10. Dumas, M.: On the convergence of data and process engineering. In: Eder, J., Bielikova, M., Tjoa, A.M. (eds.) ADBIS 2011. LNCS, vol. 6909, pp. 19–26. Springer, Heidelberg (2011). https://doi.org/10.1007/978-3-642-23737-9_2
11. Feltus, C.: Aligning access rights to governance needs with the responsibility metamodel (ReMMo) in the frame of enterprise architecture. Ph.D. thesis. University of Namur, Belgium (2014)
12. Marengo, E., Baldoni, M., Baroglio, C., Chopra, A., Patti, V., Singh, M.: Commitments with regulations: reasoning about safety and control in REGULA. In: Proceedings of the 10th International Conference on Autonomous Agents and Multiagent Systems, AAMAS, vol. 2, pp. 467–474 (2011)
13. Silver, B.: BPMN Method and Style, with BPMN Implementer's Guide, 2nd edn. Cody-Cassidy Press, Aptos (2012)
14. Sinclair, A.: The chameleon of accountability: forms and discourses. Account. Org. Soc. **20**(2–3), 219–237 (1995)
15. Singh, M.P.: An ontology for commitments in multiagent systems. Artif. Intell. Law **7**(1), 97–113 (1999)
16. Singh, M.P.: Distributed enactment of multiagent workflows: temporal logic for web service composition. In: Proceedings of the Second International Joint Conference on Autonomous Agents & Multiagent Systems, AAMAS 2003, Melbourne, Victoria, Australia, 14–18 July 2003, pp. 907–914. ACM (2003)
17. Singh, M.P., Huhns, M.N.: Service-Oriented Computing - Semantics, Processes, Agents. Wiley, Hoboken (2005)
18. W3C: W3C Glossary and Dictionary (2003). http://www.w3.org/2003/glossary/
19. Weske, M.: Business Process Management: Concepts, Languages, Architectures. Springer, Heidelberg (2007). https://doi.org/10.1007/978-3-540-73522-9
20. Wooldridge, M., Jennings, N.R., Kinny, D.: The GAIA methodology for agent-oriented analysis and design. Auton. Agents Multi-Agent Syst. **3**(3), 285–312 (2000)

A Tool for the Verification of Data-Aware Business Processes

Luca Sabiucciu, Marco Montali(ID), and Sergio Tessaris(✉)(ID)

Free University of Bozen–Bolzano, Bolzano, Italy
lsabiucciu@unibz.it, {montali,tessaris}@inf.unibz.it

Abstract. Verification of data-aware Business Processes is a highly complex and time consuming activity. As Business Processes tend to increase in terms of both size and complexity, the process of verifying such, becomes difficult even for experts. Data values may cause, for example, a deadlock in the control-flow of a Business Process, due to unsatisfied constraints on the data values, preventing the procedure of the process. Although commercial and non-commercial suites handling both control-flow and data-flow are available on the market, they struggle to produce an impact, due to the fact that the data-flow is on a separated layer from the control-flow.

In this paper we present the experimental results of the first prototype of the RAW-SYS framework, a framework for the verification of data-aware Business Processes, using small sized Business Process models, but arbitrarily complex, with updates on the data values and relying on data-constraints in order, for the process, to proceed. Despite the restricted size of the models, results are good and suggest that planning techniques are a valid way of verifying data-aware Business Processes.

Keywords: Business processes · Automated planning
Data-aware workflow verification

1 Introduction

In recent years, organisations have increasingly adopted *business process management* (BPM) to understand, structure, monitor, and govern their internal work, and better achieve their strategic goals [10]. At the same time, processes have grown both in size and complexity, dealing with concurrent activities, data stored in different information systems, and many types of resources (employees, managers, consultants, etc.).

Business Process Management professionals reserve a first-class citizenship to processes, downplaying the importance of data [3]. As a result, it is often hidden inside the logic of activities how the data is modified, e.g. within Java code. Therefore, it is not possible to verify data related aspects since how the data is modified is not formally captured. Several theoretical frameworks have been developed in order to verify formal properties considering the interplay

C. Ghidini et al. (Eds.): AI*IA 2018, LNAI 11298, pp. 266–276, 2018.
https://doi.org/10.1007/978-3-030-03840-3_20

between both aspects. However, such frameworks are often too far from the modelling languages adopted in practice, or do not properly represent data in real world scenarios. To overcame these limitations the formal framework *RAW-SYS* has been recently introduced combining process and data modelling which captures a wide range of features provided by commercial BPM systems [4]. RAW-SYS is based on *Petri Nets* (a formal representation of BPs capturing the control-flow) to model the control-flow, and relational databases (the most widely used and well-known persistent data model) to represent persistent data; moreover it enables the formal verification of BP models leveraging state of the art automated planning systems.

In this paper we present the results obtained from the development of a first prototype for the RAW-SYS framework. Results are promising as the framework efficiently verifies moderately complex BP models enriched with data.

2   Background

In this section we introduce some basic concepts that are used further in the paper.

2.1   Business Processes

A Business Process (BP), is a set of activities, belonging to a Business, organized such that, when performed, a particular goal/objective is reached. BPs represent flows of activities that are performed sequentially, in parallel or exclusively in order to achieved a certain goal. The Business Process Management Notation, described in [8] makes use of simple symbols and is thus easy to understand even from non-experts of the field (e.g. managers).

2.2   Petri Nets

A Petri Net (PN) is a bipartite graph, whose nodes are of two types, namely transitions and places [1]. It is the most widely used formal language for representing the control-flow of BPs. Rectangles, named transitions, represent activities, while circles represent momentary phases, from one transition to the following. Arcs denote the flow relation, that is, the sequence flow of activities. Two objects of the same type cannot be connected via an arc.

Moreover we rely on the *Petri Net Markup Language* [9] for storing the PN on a file. Such representation allows for portability and a standardized way of persistently storing PNs. A simple example of PN is shown in Fig. 1.

2.3   Action Language

Action languages are formal models of parts of the natural language that are used for talking about the effects of actions [5]. Action languages are part of the reasoning branch of Artificial Intelligence, which make use of planning techniques.

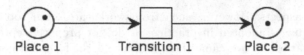

Fig. 1. Simple PN example

In particular, we make use of the *PDDL Action Language*, a language derived from *STRIPS* and used for planning competitions. The language is described by means of *actions*, having a set of *preconditions*, representing the necessary condition(s) in order to execute the action, and a set of *postconditions*, a set of conditions that will be true (or false, depending on the specification) after executing the action.

2.4 RAW-SYS Model

The RAW-SYS framework, described in [4], is a framework for verifying data-aware Business Processes. On the one hand, it graphically represents BPs by means of Petri Nets. On the other hand, it stores data on the well-known relational model of databases, called *data store* in RAW-SYS.

In RAW-SYS, the class of Petri Nets is restricted to Workflow-nets (WF-nets), Petri Nets with a single starting place and one sinking place. Additionally, the Petri Nets used are limited to 1-safeness. That is, only one token may be assigned to each place. WF-nets are equipped with a data store. This new type of nets is called Relational-AWare workflow nets, namely RAW-nets. The particularity of RAW-nets, is that transitions are equipped with guards. Guards are queries over the data store which represent either a condition on the data store that has to be satisfied, or an effect of the firing (i.e. execution) of a transition that is executed when performing the activity. An unsatisfied guard prevents the transition from being fired.

3 Petri Net Conversion

In order to convert the BP, from the PN notation, to a planning domain and problem, in PDDL, we created a *Java* program that performs such conversion. The underlying idea of the conversion is described in this section.

3.1 Domain Definition

As simple as it sounds, in action languages, including PDDL, actions represent, literally, an action. Thus PN's transitions are be mapped to PDDL's actions, since they have the same meaning. A PDDL action has preconditions and effects for regulating the execution of it. On the other side, the firing of a Petri Net's transition, is regulated by tokens, marking the places in the preset of the transition and the postset of it. Therefore in the action language representation, PN's places have to be present along with tokens, and will be managed by predicates, moving tokens from one place to another, after the execution of an action. Since we focus on 1-safe networks, then we just need to represent the fact that in a place there is at least a token; therefore we don't need to store the actual number of tokens. The state of the marking is encoded using a binary predicate where the first argument is the process id (to deal with multi process cases) and the second the place id.

Since RAW-SYS guards are FO (First Order) queries, which verify with the local database whether the transition can be fired, in PDDL the constraint can be seen as part of an action's *precondition*, which has to be satisfied in order to execute the action. Therefore a guard's constraint is part of a PDDL action. On the other side, RAW-SYS actions are updates of the data values and are therefore associated with the firing of a transition. In PDDL, the only way to modify the values of predicates is via the *effect* of an action, since the precondition only verifies that a constraint is satisfied. Therefore the RAW-SYS action is translated into PDDL predicates and inserted into the *effect* of the action.

3.2   Problem Definition

Problems in PDDL are separated from domains, as a domain may be posed several problems. In order to verify the PN represented in the domain, the problem first declares the set of objects that may be involved for finding a solution, then describes the initial state of the PN, from the marking to the data. Lastly, it defines a goal that has to be satisfied in order for the sequence of actions to be a solution. In our case the goal is to reach the sinking place, that is, the final state that ends the process.

4   Evaluation Methodology

In this section we first provide a description of how the experiment has been conducted. Next, we provide a description of the BP models used for testing, followed by a description of the testing environment.

4.1   Experimental Approach

To investigate the behavior of the planner, we explore the relation between BP model's characteristics and time needed to verify the model. In particular we focus on two types of models: *(i)* single process instance and *(ii)* multiple process instance. On the one hand, *(i)* represents independent processes that do not need any other process instance to access nor to modify data values in order to prosecute. On the other hand, *(ii)*, represents process instances that rely on each other in order to either create, remove or update data values in order, for the process flow, to proceed. The two process types are of particular importance because of their expressibility, in terms of models, capturing most of the BP models that may be needed.

The planner used for the experiments is a generic planner, *Fast-Downward* [6], developed for planning competitions and accepting the *PDDL* action language, as described in Sect. 2.3. The language supported by the planner is not the complete PDDL language specification, but a subset, rich enough for our purpose. Other planners can be adopted, depending on the considered model and on the process related activities. We chose to use such planner because of it's generality and performances.

The goal the planner has to satisfy is to find an execution path, from the start to the end, of the given BP such that guards (i.e. the constraints on transitions) are not violated. Guards are added on transitions as FO queries in the PDDL language, referencing the data objects declared in the domain and problem. RAW-SYS actions are written in the PDDL language as well, but not all of them affect the process flow (they are added for the sake of representing a more realistic scenario).

For the single process instance models, we varied the number of objects, while the number of concurrent process instances was free. Instead, the multiple process instance models had a fixed amount of objects, but we varied number of concurrent process instances that were running.

On the one hand, the single process model was tested with the same values 10 times and the resulting times were averaged, for each step of increasing the number of data object. The number of data objects was initially set to 5, and incremented by 5 units until 25 data objects (latter included). On the other hand, the multiple process models were tested with a fixed number of data objects (5), and a varying number of process instances, starting from 2 to 10, incrementing at each step by 2 process instances. As before, the same configuration is run 10 times and timing is averaged.

For all tests the same search strategy for the planner is used, a greedy search with no memory nor time bounds. This search strategy makes use of the *FF* heuristic [6].

4.2   Business Process Models

For our experiments we considered three different BPs, each of different size and complexity. The first example that we considered is taken from [2] and represents the process for claims to a car insurance company. As Fig. 2 shows, the process starts with two activities that can be performed in parallel: *check_insurance* and *contact_garage*. In this two activities a data value is updated and such value is used, afterwards, when the process flow is converged, where depending on the data constraint, either the *pay_damage* activity is performed or the *send_letter* activity is performed. The process flow ends after one of the two activities is performed.

FO queries have been added on *check_insurance* and *contact_garage* transitions, updating a data object such that a particular activity is selected when choosing between *pay_damage* and *send_letter*. The value to be used for updating the data object has been defined a priori, since the value depended on an external factors (the garage and the insurance).

For simplicity, we will refer at it as *insurance model*.

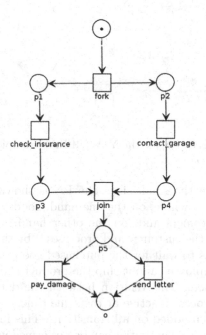

Fig. 2. PN for the insurance model example

The second considered BP is taken from the YAWL foundation and is described in [7]. It represents the workflow for a film production. Since the example was available only in the form of workflow-net, we converted it into a *RAW-SYS* model. As Fig. 3 shows, the size is quite big, and we will thus, only describe the underlying idea. The number of shooting days is decided a priori and inserted, along with other data values, into the system via a first phase. Once such phase terminates, the process starts cycling over a series of activities, representing a shooting day. The number of cycles is defined by the number of shooting days. After the shooting days have ended, the process flow ends too in a final state. Several data updates are performed during the cycles on the same data objects, which are inserted during the first phase.

FO queries have been added on almost all transitions. Most of the queries simply update some data objects, with no influence on the process-flow. On the other hand, some queries influence the process-flow, in particular the counter keeping track of the number of shooting days. If the number of shooting days reaches a threshold defined a priori, no new shooting day is started, instead, the process ends.

We will refer at this model as *YAWL4FILM*.

The last example used, is a synthetic one, specially designed to stress the updates on the data from concurrent process, which have to collaborate in order

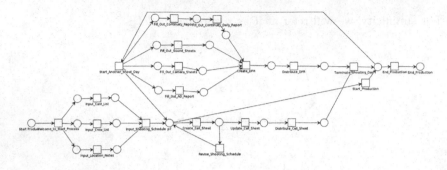

Fig. 3. PN for the YAWL4FILM example

to terminate. Therefore the small size. The PN is shown in Fig. 4 and represents a shipping domain, where, on the one hand, goods are chosen, purchased and received from customers and, on the other hand, a warehouse employee receives the order from the customer and processes it by shipping it to the client. Note that the client has to wait for the purchased goods to be shipped from an employee, while the employee cannot ship the products before the customer has purchased those products. This relation between the data, leads to having at least two concurrent processes active at the same time.

FO queries have been added on all transitions. This model has two types of users, based on which certain activities can be performed while other not. Therefore the planner has to decide whether the user is a customer or an employee at the start of the process. When a customer buys the selected products, a RAW-SYS action is triggered, setting all purchased products as ordered, but not delivered. At least one good has to be ordered, for a warehouse employee to ship those products and label them as delivered (in this case we assume that the shipping does not require any time). The warehouse employee's process will then end. Only after shipping, the customer will receive the products, ending the process.

We will refer at this model as *Goods Shipping*.

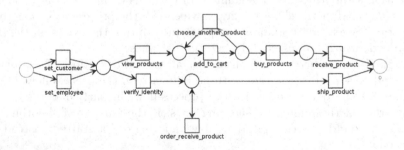

Fig. 4. PN for the *Goods Shipping* example

4.3   Testing Environment

The timings are taken with the *time* command of the *Linux System*, considering the total time taken, from the conversion of the PN to PDDL, to the solution (there is always one), by the process, including waiting times for *I/O* operations. All the tests are conducted on a *64-bit Ubuntu 17.04* machine, mounting an *Intel Core i7-4710HQ* processor (2.5 GHz, 4 cores, 8 threads), 8 GBs of RAM and 3, 4 GBs of swap space on a mechanical hard-disk.

5   Results

In this section we present the results obtained from testing the prototype within the environment described in Sect. 4. We start describing the results of single process instance models, followed by the results of multiple process instance models.

5.1   Single Process Instance Models

We first tested the running time of the single process instance models, as they were expected to take less time than the multiple process instance model. The obtained results of both single process instance models are shown in Fig. 5, providing a visual comparison of the running time. Expectable is that the size and the complexity of the business model influence the running time of the planner.

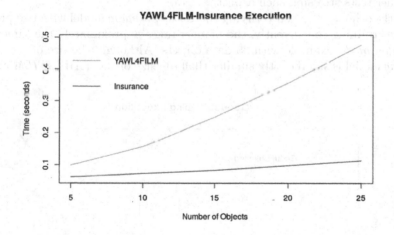

Fig. 5. Running time for single process instance

As the graph in Fig. 5 shows, time grows along with the number of objects the planner has to handle. Notable is also the growing gap between the two models. The bigger and more complex the model, the more time is needed to verify such. Overall, the planner provides an answer rather quickly: in the worst case, slightly less than 0.5 s for the *YAWL4FILM* model with 25 data objects, while slightly less than 0.1 s for the *insurance model*.

5.2   Multiple Process Instance Model

As expected, the multiple process instance model takes more than the single process instances. This is due to the fact that the number of possible choices of the planner increase exponentially, as the number of concurrent processes increases. The increase in time required by the planner is much drastic with respect to the other models.

6   Discussion

The obtained results reveal that verification of data-aware Business Processes via planning techniques is feasible, for small models at least. The three major influences on the running time, that we could notice, are size, complexity (the number of data objects as well as the constraints and loops) and number of concurrent processes in the model.

For single process instance models, the growth of time needed to verify the model, increases as expected, with the number of data objects. Noticeable is the increase of the gap between the two models with increasing number of objects. This gap suggests that the growth of time needed to discover a solution, along with the increase of data objects to handle, depends on both size and complexity of the model. In particular, we believe that loops play a significant role in such increase for single process instance models. This hypothesis shall be confirmed by further tests stressing such aspect.

On the other side, when verifying the *Goods Shipping* model with two process instances running concurrently, the planner takes approximately the same time of the *film model* example with 25 data objects. Although, the size of the *Goods Shipping* model is significantly smaller than the size of the *YAWL4FILM* model,

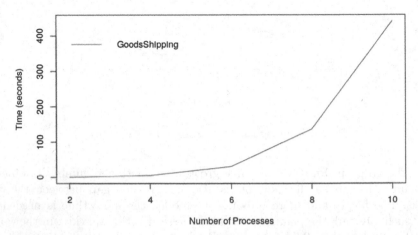

Fig. 6. Running time for multiple process instances

with a different number of data objects, multi process instance models require more time in order to discover a solution, with respect to single process instance models. From this fact, we can deduce that the running time is heavily influenced by the number of concurrent processes and the dependency among them.

Other planners may perform differently, as we used an off-the-shelf planner, Fast-Downward. Planning techniques, such as search algorithms and search space representation, may vary from planner to planner and thus, may affect the running time. Also the search strategy of the planner may influence the running time of the planner. Finally, the number of threads of the machine may influence the running time as well and the support, of the planner, of multi-thread (Fig. 6).

7   Future Work and Conclusions

Formal verification of BP models is an important aspect of BP modeling, that has been studied only theoretically. In this paper we have shown the results of a prototype for the RAW-SYS framework, for modeling and verifying data-aware processes, based on the well-established PNs for representing BP models and the planning language PDDL for solving the verification problem. Results look promising and support the usage of planners for verification of data-aware business processes. Although very big and complex BP models may not perform as well as smaller ones, we recall the fact that the planner used for the tests is an off-the-shelf planner, which is likely to be outperformed by other, more task-specific, ones. In this regard, the system will be further developed for accommodating other planners. Performances of other planners will be tested with respect to other BP models.

Additional, complex, object types are part of the next implementation steps for our tool. Moreover, support for other planning languages that provide different features than the ones provided by classical planning (o.g. temporal planning), are part of the next implementation steps as well.

References

1. van der Aalst, W.: Verification of workflow nets. Appl. Theory Petri Nets **1997**, 407–426 (1997)
2. van der Aalst, W., Stahl, C.: Modeling Business Processes: A Petri Net-Oriented Approach. MIT Press, Cambridge (2011)
3. Calvanese, D., Giacomo, G.D., Montali, M.: Foundations of data-aware process analysis: a database theory perspective. In: Hull, R., Fan, W. (eds.) Proceedings of the 32nd ACM SIGACT SIGMOD SIGART Symposium on Principles of Database Systems (PODS), pp. 1–12. ACM Press (2013). https://doi.org/10.1145/2463664.2467796
4. De Masellis, R., Francescomarino, C.D., Ghidini, C., Montali, M., Tessaris, S.: Add data into business process verification: bridging the gap between theory and practice. In: Proceedings of the Thirty-First AAAI Conference on Artificial Intelligence, pp. 1091–1099 (2017). http://aaai.org/ocs/index.php/AAAI/AAAI17/paper/view/14627

5. Fox, M., Long, D.: PDDL2. 1: an extension to PDDL for expressing temporal planning domains. J. Artif. Intell. Res. **20**, 61–124 (2003)
6. Helmert, M.: The fast downward planning system. J. Artif. Intell. Res. **26**, 191–246 (2006)
7. ter Hofstede, A., van der Aalst, W., Adams, M., Russell, N.: Modern Business Process Automation: YAWL and its Support Environment. Springer, Heidelberg (2009). https://doi.org/10.1007/978-3-642-03121-2
8. Business Process Model: Notation (BPMN) version 2.0. OMG Specification. Object Management Group, pp. 22–31 (2011)
9. Treves, N., Hillah, L.M., Kordon, F., Petrucci, L.: A primer on the Petri Net markup language and ISO/IEC 15909–2. In: 10th International workshop on Practical Use of Colored Petri Nets and the CPN Tools (CPN 2009), Aarhus, Denmark, p. 19, October 2009. https://hal.archives-ouvertes.fr/hal-01126017
10. Weske, M.: Business Process Management - Concepts, Languages, Architectures, 2nd edn. Springer, Heidelberg (2012). https://doi.org/10.1007/978-3-642-28616-2

Machine Learning

Exploring Abstract Argumentation-Based Approaches to Tackle Inconsistent Observations in Inductive Logic Programming

Andrea Pazienza[✉] and Stefano Ferilli

Dipartimento di Informatica, Università di Bari, Bari, Italy
{andrea.pazienza,stefano.ferilli}@uniba.it

Abstract. Noisy (uncertain, missing, or inconsistent) information, typical of many real-world domains, may dramatically affect the performance of logic-based Machine Learning. Multistrategy Learning approaches have been tried to solve this problem by coupling Inductive Logic Programming with other kinds of inference. While uncertainty has been tackled using probabilistic approaches, and abduction has been used to deal with missing data, inconsistency is still an open problem. In the Multistrategy Learning perspective, this paper proposes to attack this latter kind of noise using (abstract) Argumentation, an inferential strategy aimed at handling conflicting information. More specifically, it defines a pre-processing operator based on abstract argumentation that can detect and remove noisy atoms from the observations before running the learning system on the polished data. Quantitative and qualitative experiments point out some strengths and weaknesses of the proposed approach, and suggest lines for future research on this topic.

Keywords: Inductive Logic Programming · Conflicting information
Abstract argumentation · Multistrategy Learning

1 Introduction and Related Work

Machine Learning approaches based on First-Order Logic (FOL) representations, such as Inductive Logic Programming (ILP), are particularly suited for tasks in which the relationships among objects play a relevant role in the definition of the concepts of interest. Unfortunately, logic-based approaches are very sensitive to noise in the data, in the form of missing, uncertain or inconsistent information.

Multistrategy Learning (MSL) is an approach to Machine Learning based on the cooperation between purely inductive operators and other kinds of inference strategies. Some MSL solutions have been attempted to tackle the problem of noisy data. Abductive Logic Programming (ALP) coupled pure induction with abduction in order to handle missing information by hypothesizing likely but unknown facts, provided that they are consistent with a set of integrity

C. Ghidini et al. (Eds.): AI*IA 2018, LNAI 11298, pp. 279–292, 2018.
https://doi.org/10.1007/978-3-030-03840-3_21

constraints. Statistical Relational Learning (SRL) coupled purely logical and probabilistic approaches in order to handle uncertainty by associating a degree of likelihood to information items. In this landscape, an attempt to deal with inconsistency in the data is still missing and any contribution would be extremely important.

Since argumentation is the kind of logical inference specifically devoted to settling conflicts, in this paper we propose a novel MSL approach that couples ILP with abstract argumentation in order to tackle the problem inconsistent data. More specifically, we define a pre-processing operator that is able to detect conflicting information in the available data, to select a subset of consistent data, and to remove the inconsistent portion of the data before running the inductive operators. The proposed approach uses background knowledge, provided in the form of integrity constraints based on various kinds of logical operators (AND, OR, NAND, NOR, XOR, IF, IFF), to build the argument graphs to be input to the argumentative reasoner.

This paper is organized as follows. After quickly discussing related work in the next section, Sect. 3 defines the problem and Sect. 4 describes the proposed solution. Section 5 evaluates the performance of our approach. Finally, Sect. 6 concludes the paper.

2   Related Work

In the following, after describing some ILP systems that were reported to be capable of handling some kind of noise, we will introduce the Abstract Argumentation notions on which the proposed approach relies.

2.1   Noise Handling in ILP

The problem of noise handling, and the need to tackle it, was clearly perceived in the ILP research field since its very beginning [5]. However, the concepts of 'noise' were initially very primitive, and the approaches to tackle them often unsuitable to really attack the problem, as the following list shows.

- FOIL [16] may stop extending a clause, or expanding a set of clauses, based on the idea that approximate concepts can be more valuable than overspecified rules that "fit the noise".
- mFOIL [7] is claimed to be "more robust against noise" because its concept descriptions compete to classify test examples based on the likelihood ratios that are assigned to clauses that make up the descriptions.
- GOLEM [15] allows hypotheses to cover a certain number of negative examples based on information theoretic thresholds.
- LINUS [12] uses pre-pruning and post-pruning in the construction of decision trees.
- HYDRA [1] presents a method to increase predictive accuracy on noisy domains using likelihood multipliers that reduces the small disjuncts problem.

It is clear that these systems consider as noise the presence of wrong examples, or of superfluous wrong features in example descriptions. This allows them to cast the problem as overfitting or polymorphism, and thus to handle it simply using generalizations, disjunctive concepts or partial example coverage.

Further developments in this landscape are tackled in the LIME system [14] with the help of Bayesian heuristics for inducing a hypothesis with the maximum posterior probability; or in the CN2 system [11] by adapting compression measures, based on the Minimum Description Length principle, for grading candidate hypotheses. Recently, in [9], an ILP system has been hybridized by connecting it with neural networks over ambiguous data in order to be applied to domains which ILP cannot address, while providing data efficiency and generalization beyond what neural networks on their own can achieve.

2.2 Abstract Argumentation

Argumentation is an inferential strategy that aims at selecting acceptable (i.e., justified) items in a set of conflicting claims (the *arguments*). It has been a very active topic in Artificial Intelligence since more than two decades now (see [2] for a comprehensive and up-to-date view of the state of the art and current trends). The Abstract Argumentation Frameworks introduced by Dung [6] are not interested in the internal structure and actual content of the claims; they just consider the interactions among arguments. Such interactions are expressed by a directed graph in which nodes represent arguments, and arcs represent attacks between pairs of arguments. Several non-monotonic reasoning approaches have been defined to determine 'consistent' subsets of arguments in the graph, based on the fact that they defend each other from attacks of arguments not included in the subset. These acceptable subsets of arguments, called *extensions*, correspond to various positions one may take based on the available arguments. The precise conditions for arguments acceptance are defined by different semantics, that produce different acceptable subsets. It should be noted that most extension-based semantics in the literature are not single-status, that is, they may produce several alternative solutions (extensions).

Dung's original framework has been extended along many lines (see [17] for an overview). The extension that is relevant for the purpose of this paper is the Bipolar Argumentation Framework (*BAF*) [3] in which a support relation between pairs of arguments can be considered, in addition to the attack relation. So, a BAF can be represented by a directed graph in which two kinds of arcs are used, in order to differentiate between the two relations (see Fig. 1 for an example in which normal arrows depict attack relations, and dashed arrows depict support relations). More formally, we have the following definition:

Definition 1. *A **BAF** is a triplet $B = \langle \mathcal{A}, \mathcal{R}_{att}, \mathcal{R}_{sup} \rangle$, where $\mathcal{A}$ is a set of arguments, $\mathcal{R}_{att}$ is a binary relation on $\mathcal{A}$ called attack relation and $\mathcal{R}_{sup}$ is another binary relation on $\mathcal{A}$ called support relation. For two arguments a and b, $a\mathcal{R}_{att}b$ (resp., $a\mathcal{R}_{sup}b$) means that a attacks b (resp., a supports b).*

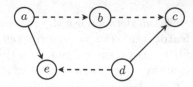

Fig. 1. BAF example

In BAFs, new kinds of attack emerge from the interaction between the direct attacks and the supports: there is a *supported attack* for an argument b by an argument a iff there is a sequence of supports followed by one attack, while, there is an *indirect attack* for an argument b by an argument a iff there is an attack followed by a sequence of supports. Taking into account sequences of supports and attacks leads to the following definition applying to sets of arguments [3].

Definition 2. *Let $B = \langle \mathcal{A}, \mathcal{R}_{att}, \mathcal{R}_{sup} \rangle$ be a BAF. A set $S \subseteq \mathcal{A}$ set-attacks an argument $b \in \mathcal{A}$, iff there exists a supported attack or an indirect attack for b from an element of S. A set $S \subseteq \mathcal{A}$ set-supports an argument $b \in \mathcal{A}$, iff there exists a sequence $a_1 \mathcal{R}_{sup} \ldots \mathcal{R}_{sup} a_n$, $n \geq 2$, such that $a_n = b$ and $a_1 \in S$. A set $S \subseteq \mathcal{A}$ defends an argument $a \in \mathcal{A}$, iff for each argument $b \in \mathcal{A}$, if $\{b\}$ set-attacks a, then b is set-attacked by S.*

The semantics for acceptability in BAFs are as follows.

Definition 3. *Let $B = \langle \mathcal{A}, \mathcal{R}_{att}, \mathcal{R}_{sup} \rangle$ be a BAF and $S \subseteq \mathcal{A}$. Then, S is:*

- *conflict-free (cf for short), iff $\nexists a, b \in S$ s.t. $\{a\}$ set-attacks b;*
- *S is a stable extension, iff S is cf and $\forall a \notin S$, S set-attacks a;*
- *a admissible set, iff S is conflict-free and $\forall a \in S$, a is defended by S;*
- *a preferred extension is a $\subseteq$-maximal d-admissible subset of $\mathcal{A}$.*

3   Problem Definition and Setting

Given a background knowledge $\mathcal{B}$, a theory $\mathcal{T}$, and a set of observations $\mathcal{O}$, the fundamental equation of reasoning is $\mathcal{B} \cup \mathcal{T} \models \mathcal{O}$ (i.e., the theory, along with the background knowledge, must explain the observations), where $\mathcal{B}$, $\mathcal{T}$ and $\mathcal{O}$ are sets of logical formulas. In inductive learning, $\mathcal{B}$ and $\mathcal{O}$ are given, and the objective is finding a $\mathcal{T}$ which is consistent with $\mathcal{B}$ and $\mathcal{O}$ and satisfies the fundamental equation. Clearly, if $\mathcal{O}$ is inconsistent in itself, no $\mathcal{T}$ whatsoever can be found for which $\mathcal{T} \cup \mathcal{O}$ is consistent, and thus the inductive learning problem cannot be solved. This paper aims at solving this fundamental problem.

The Inductive Logic Programming (ILP) approach, specifically, works in the Logic Programming setting [13], where formulas are *Horn clauses*. Clauses are disjunctions of literals, where a literal is an atom or a negated atom[1]. They correspond to implications: given $\{p_i\}_{i=1,\ldots,n}$ and $\{q_i\}_{i=1,\ldots,m}$ sets of atoms,

---

[1] An atom is an n-ary predicate applied to n terms as arguments, where a term is a constant, a variable, or an n-ary function applied to n terms as arguments.

$p_1 \vee \cdots \vee p_n \vee \neg q_1 \vee \cdots \vee \neg q_m \equiv q_1 \wedge \cdots \wedge q_m \Rightarrow p_1 \vee \cdots \vee p_n$. The conclusion is called the *head* of the clause, while the premises are called the *body*. Horn clauses contain at most one literal in their head. A Horn clause having non-empty head and body is a *rule*; one having only the head is called a *fact*. Rules are typically found in $\mathcal{T}$, while facts are typically found in $\mathcal{O}$. In an informal interpretation, $\mathcal{O}$ is the set of claims (atom) that describe what we know about the given domain. Many learning framework adopt the *Datalog* [4] sublanguage of Prolog, where terms can only be variables or constants (functions are not permitted). It has the same expressive power as Prolog [20].

In this setting, having an inconsistent set of observations $\mathcal{O}$ means that there must be pairs of claims in $\mathcal{O}$ that are inconsistent to each other. Since this prevents the application of inductive learning on these data, we need to remove either of the claims in each pair in order to obtain a subset $\mathcal{C} \subset \mathcal{O}$ of the original observations in which consistency is restored. Of course, one cannot work at the level of single pairs of inconsistent atoms, and the removal approach must adopt a global strategy. Our proposal is to represent all pairwise inconsistencies in the observations as an argumentation graph, and to apply an abstract argumentation operator to obtain $\mathcal{C}$, so that the inductive learning approach can be applied to the modified fundamental equation $\mathcal{B} \cup \mathcal{T} \models \mathcal{C}$.

More in general, given a pair of claims in $\mathcal{O}$, various cases may apply: either of the two attacks the other, or they are mutually inconsistent, or either of the two supports the other, or they support each other, or they are unrelated. If we have knowledge about all these cases, we should adopt a bipolar approach to argumentation, in order to leverage not only knowledge about attacks but also knowledge about supports, when determining the consistent subset of claims.

4   Argumentative Integrity Constraints

The main issue in the proposed approach is how to determine automatically the arcs in the argumentation graph (nodes are the atoms in $\mathcal{O}$). Indeed, manually building such a graph for each given dataset would be infeasible, and a general technique is needed so that the learning system may autonomously obtain the graph starting from general knowledge about the domain at hand. We propose to place such knowledge in the background knowledge component $\mathcal{B}$ of the fundamental equation, and to express it in the form of constraints. In a nutshell, constraints are applied in all possible ways to the available observations in $\mathcal{O}$, and each instance of such applications may generate a set of arcs in the graph.

As to the constraints, we adopted the typed integrity constraints as proposed in [10] (a preliminary version of which can be found in [19]) for abduction. This has several advantages: first, it implements a real MultiStrategy approach, in which different inference strategies are really integrated because they exploit the same background knowledge items; second, we may leverage existing techniques for checking these constraints; third, this saves costly expert time to define the constraints, since constraints may be defined once and used for both abduction and argumentation. Given two claims A and B, the following types of constraints can be expressed on A and B, and generate the pieces of BAF shown in Fig. 2 (also involving the negations of A and B, $\neg A$ and $\neg B$).

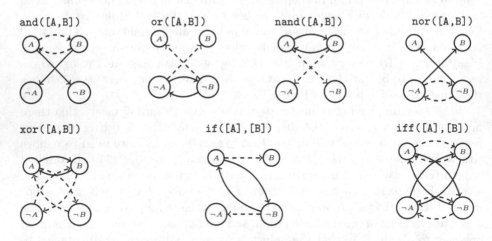

Fig. 2. Pieces of BAF generated by the constraints

AND($[A, B]$): A and B must both survive in $\mathcal{C}$. In abstract argumentation terms, A supports B and attacks $\neg B$, and B supports A and attacks $\neg A$.

OR($[A, B]$): at least one between A and B must survive in $\mathcal{C}$. In abstract argumentation terms, $\neg A$ and $\neg B$ attack each other, $\neg B$ being true supports A, and $\neg A$ being true supports B.

NAND($[A, B]$): A and B cannot both survive in $\mathcal{C}$. In abstract argumentation terms, it has the opposite behavior of the AND constraint: A and B attack each other, A being true supports $\neg B$, B being true supports $\neg A$.

NOR($[A, B]$): neither A nor B must survive in $\mathcal{C}$. In abstract argumentation terms, it has the opposite behavior of the OR constraint: $\neg A$ and $\neg B$ support each other, $\neg A$ being true attacks B, and $\neg B$ being true attacks A.

XOR($[A, B]$): either A or B, but not both, must survive in $\mathcal{C}$. This means that A and B attack each other, and $\neg A$ and B, as well as A and $\neg B$, support each other.

IF($[A], [B]$): if A survives in $\mathcal{C}$, then also B must survive (*modus ponens*); if B does not survive in $\mathcal{C}$, then also A must not survive (*modus tollens*). In abstract argumentation terms, A supports B and $\neg B$ supports $\neg A$, while A and $\neg B$ attack each other.

IFF($[A], [B]$): either both A and B survive in $\mathcal{C}$, or none of them survives. In the graph translation A and B, as well as $\neg A$ and $\neg B$, support each other, while A and $\neg B$, as well as B and $\neg A$, attack each other.

For any claim A, the obvious denial $nand([A, \neg A])$ is implicitly considered and automatically applied.

5   Experiments

To run experiments aimed at evaluating the behavior of our operator we selected the domain of family relationships, both because it allows an immediate understanding by the reader, and because benchmark datasets are available for it. According to the proposed approach, we expressed constraints concerning family relationships in the background knowledge, applied them on an inconsistent set of observations in order to build an argumentation graph, applied a semantics to obtain a consistent subset of the observations, and finally ran a learning system on such a subset in order to obtain a theory defining family relationships. Since the dataset reports complete and consistent information, we purposely corrupted it before applying our approach. This allowed us to check the behavior of our operator under qualitatively and quantitatively different conditions of inconsistency. We will report about all the above steps in the following.

5.1   Experimental Setting

We considered the family dataset from [18]. It involves 86 people across 5 generations, reporting 744 examples of family relationships among them, plus 1488 randomly generated negative examples for those relationships that we ignore in our experiments. The observations are described in terms of predicates *male/1*, *female/1*, *parent/2* (where the former argument is the parent and the latter is the child) and *married/2* (where the former argument is the husband and the latter is the wife), plus predicates *husband/2*, *wife/2*, *mother/2*, *father/2*, *daughter/2*, *son/2*, *sister/2*, *brother/2*, *aunt/2*, *uncle/2*, *niece/2*, and *nephew/2* which are the concepts to be learned.

For corrupting the observations, in order to obtain the inconsistencies to be detected and cleaned by our approach, we proceeded as follows. A corruption ratio $p \in |0,1|$ means that each atom in the observations built on a descriptive predicate had probability p of being corrupted. Depending on the specific predicate, different kinds of corruptions were possible, as shown in Table 1. Atoms selected for corruption were replaced by one of the associated possible corruption chosen at random (where variable Z, is present, was replaced by the name of another individual from the dataset). Basically, sex predicates were switched, or the roles of the arguments were swapped, or an impossible relation was introduced.

Table 1. Possible corruptions for atoms based on descriptive predicates

Atom	Possible corruptions
male(A)	female(A)
female(A)	male(A)
married(A,B)	married(B,A), married(A,Z), married(Z,B), parent(A,B), parent(B,A)
parent(A,B)	parent(B,A), parent(A,Z), parent(Z,B), married(A,B), married(B,A)

Table 2 reports the set of integrity constraints we placed in the background knowledge for the descriptive predicates in the family domain. The argumentation graph was built by starting from the empty graph, then applying the constraints in all possible ways on the observation atoms and adding the to the graph the nodes and arcs associated to each such application. In these preliminary experiments, we decided to use only limited subsets of one or two constraint types in each run, in order to investigate their specific behavior. On the resulting BAF we applied the ASPARTIX argumentation system [8] to compute an extension-based semantics that would select a subset of conflict-free atoms, to be used as reliable (consistent, noise-free) observations for the learning step. Specifically, we focused on the preferred and stable semantics, in order to have different levels of skepticism in the justification and acceptability of extensions.

Table 2. Family integrity constraints

AND	married(A,B) $\wedge$ female(A)	XOR	married(A,B) $\oplus$ parent(A,B)
	married(A,B) $\wedge$ male(B)		married(A,B) $\oplus$ parent(B,A)
OR	parent(A,B) $\vee$ parent(C,A)		married(A,C) $\oplus$ male(A)
NAND	married(A,B) $\uparrow$ male(A)		married(C,B) $\oplus$ female(B)
	married(A,B) $\uparrow$ female(B)		parent(A,B) $\oplus$ parent(B,A)
	married(A,B) $\uparrow$ married(B,A)		male(A) $\oplus$ female(A)
	parent(A,B) $\uparrow$ married(A,B)	IF	married(A,B) $\rightarrow$ female(A)
	parent(A,B) $\uparrow$ married(B,A)		married(A,B) $\rightarrow$ male(B)
	parent(A,B) $\uparrow$ parent(B,A)		parent(A,C) $\rightarrow$ married(A,B)
	male(A) $\uparrow$ female(A)		parent(A,C) $\rightarrow$ married(B,A)
NOR	parent(A,B) $\downarrow$ parent(A,C)	IFF	parent(A,B) $\leftrightarrow$ parent(C,B)
			parent(A,B) $\leftrightarrow$ married(A,C)
			parent(A,B) $\leftrightarrow$ married(C,A)

For each experimental configuration (set of constraint types, corruption ratio), all the target concepts were learned (based on the positive examples in the dataset) using InTheLEx, an ILP system that is able to learn *hierarchical* (i.e., non-recursive) theories from positive and negative examples. It is *fully incremental*: it is able not only to refine existing theories, but also to start learning from an empty theory and from the first available example. It works on Datalog representations interpreted under the Object Identity (OI) assumption ("within a clause, terms denoted by different symbols must be distinct"). The resulting language, $Datalog^{OI}$, has the same expressive power as Datalog [21]. It takes examples in the form of Horn clauses where the head is the atom labeling a target class instance, and the body is the set of (non-negated) atoms in the observation that are provided to the system as relevant to that instance. InTheLEx adopts the Closed World Assumption, by which what is not reported in the example description is assumed to be false. In our case, each example reported in the body the full set of observations. The theories learned by InTheLEx are made up of general rules (whose head expresses the target concept and whose body reports a conjunctive definition for it) and, possibly, of specific exceptions (examples for which the inductive operators available in InTheLEx could not find a correct refinement of the existing theory).

5.2   Evaluation of the Argumentation Step

A first (qualitative) evaluation of the proposed approach was aimed at understanding how the number of integrity constraints and the degree of dataset corruption affected the following features of the argumentation step:

- Number of arguments in the graph
- Number of supports in the graph
- Number of attacks in the graph
- Number of solutions obtained for preferred semantics
- Average length of the solutions obtained for the preferred extensions
- Number of solutions obtained for stable semantics
- Average length of the solutions obtained for stable extensions.

We focused in turn on graphs built on a single type of constraints, and tried different levels of corruption, ranging from 10% to 50% with 10% steps. Since for some graphs ASPARTIX returned hundreds of solutions, for practical reasons we decided to stop the argumentation system after finding the first 50 solutions. This may be considered enough for the objectives of our study. Also, we stopped extension computations which did not terminate within a 10 minutes time limit.

The results, reported in Table 3, suggest a number of considerations:

- When the number of solutions increases, the average length of the solutions also increases, and few solutions correspond to a small graph and small extensions.
- Exclusive constraints (NAND and XOR) build smaller graphs and therefore lead to shorter extensions. Inclusive constraints (such as OR) behave the opposite way, generating larger graphs and leading to more, longer solutions.
- Using exclusive constraints, the increase in the length of the solutions is directly proportional to the increase in corruption. Intuitively, this was expected: e.g., XOR generates two alternative solutions and mutually exclusive solutions, because the two atoms cannot coexist in the same solution but each of them might in principle be reliable individually.
- The IFF constraint tends to yield less, shorter extensions as the corruption ratio increases. We may call it a 'strict' operator compared to exclusive ones, because when the latter generate two alternative solutions it does not generate any solution. The results also show that IFF might be considered a 'strong' operator, since in all combinations with other operators it retains the characteristic of reducing the number and size of the solutions as the corruption ratio in the data increases.

Table 3. Quantitative evaluation of the argumentation step

OP	Corr	Arg	Att	Supp	# pref	Avg pref size	# stable	Avg stable size
AND	.1	22	36	14	16	11	16	11
	.2	20	32	12	16	10	16	10
	.3	20	32	12	16	10	16	10
	.4	32	52	20	50	16	50	16
	.5	38	64	26	50	19	50	19
AND,OR	.1	60	122	63	50	30	50	30
	.2	54	106	52	50	27	50	27
	.3	58	116	58	50	29	50	29
	.4	68	131	63	50	34	50	34
	.5	70	124	54	50	35	50	35
OR	.1	86	230	144	50	43	50	43
	.4	68	185	117	50	34	50	34
	.5	68	168	100	50	34	50	34
NAND	.1	10	16	6	15	5	15	5
	.2	14	22	8	45	7	45	7
	.3	20	34	14	50	10	50	10
	.4	32	53	21	50	16	50	16
	.5	34	54	20	50	17	50	17
NOR	.1	32	54	22	32	16	32	16
	.2	32	54	22	32	16	32	16
	.3	34	58	24	32	17	32	17
	.4	26	46	20	16	13	16	13
	.5	34	54	20	50	17	50	17
XOR	.1	10	16	12	15	5	15	5
	.2	14	22	16	45	7	45	7
	.3	20	34	28	50	10	50	10
	.4	32	53	42	50	16	50	16
	.5	34	54	40	50	17	50	17
IF	.1	66	122	56	50	33	50	30
	.2	58	110	52	50	29	50	27
	.3	64	118	54	50	32	50	30
	.4	64	122	58	50	32	50	30
	.5	76	164	88	50	38	50	36
IF,IFF	.2	58	158	100	50	28	50	28
	.3	64	158	94	50	31	50	31
IFF	.1	50	170	120	50	24	50	24
	.2	32	104	72	50	15	50	15
	.3	26	86	60	32	12	32	12
	.4	16	52	36	8	7	8	7
	.5	6	18	12	2	3	2	3

5.3   Evaluation of the Learning Step

Another (qualitative) evaluation concerned the correctness of theories learned by InTheLEx for the target concepts. Since the extensions computed in the argumentation step may contain both positive and negative atoms, only the set of positive atoms was provided to InTheLEx for use as observations. Also, when many alternative extensions were generated by a given setting, since from a logical viewpoint there is no reason to prefer one over another, we decided to use one at random as the set of observations for learning. An overview of the results for selected subsets of constraint types is reported in Table 4, reporting for each combination (concept, constraint types) a 4-tuple of values: number of corrected definitions/number of under-specified definitions/number of over-specified definitions/number of wrong definitions. The results show that, albeit the correct definition is almost never learned, most of the errors are in the under-specified or over-specified cases. Most wrong definitions are associated to XOR/OR-type constraints, and a detailed analysis reveals that they are due to corrupted atoms that were not detected as inconsistencies by the argumentation step due to the lack of attacks on them. This should be solved by using all the types of constraints together. As regards over-specified definitions, this is the easiest case, because it may be expected that having further examples available may lead to theory refinements that finally converge to the correct definition. Finally, the presence of under-specified definitions can be explained by the fact that InTheLEx worked without the help of negative examples to limit the extent of generalizations. Coupled with the argumentation step removing wrong atoms, but not replacing them with correct ones, this explains why relevant parts of the definitions were removed. In a Multistrategy Learning perspective, abductive operators might fill this missing information (InTheLEx provides an abductive

Table 4. Quantitative evaluation of the learning step

Concept	OR	XOR	AND-OR	IF	IFF	IF-IFF
wife/2	0/2/3/2	0/9/0/7	0/5/5/1	1/1/3/1	0/0/10/0	0/2/8/2
husband/2	0/3/3/1	0/9/0/7	0/5/5/1	1/2/3/0	0/0/10/0	0/3/8/1
mother/2	0/4/3/1	0/14/0/6	0/7/3/1	0/5/2/0	0/2/11/0	0/3/10/0
father/2	0/5/1/1	0/11/0/7	0/7/5/0	0/7/2/0	0/2/9/0	0/4/6/0
daughter/2	0/1/3/2	0/12/0/0	0/5/5/1	0/3/3/0	0/0/9/0	0/0/12/0
son/2	0/5/2/0	0/17/0/4	0/7/3/1	0/7/1/0	0/0/9/0	0/4/9/1
sister/2	0/2/2/1	0/5/0/0	0/6/3/2	0/4/3/0	0/0/7/0	0/1/6/0
brother/2	0/6/0/0	0/8/0/4	0/7/3/0	0/3/1/0	0/0/9/0	0/1/7/0
aunt/2	0/6/2/2	0/7/0/4	0/9/3/0	0/6/0/0	0/6/3/0	0/4/6/0
uncle/2	0/3/2/1	0/8/0/3	0/5/2/0	0/4/0/0	0/7/1/0	0/4/4/0
niece/2	0/4/2/1	0/12/0/1	0/7/4/1	0/8/0/0	0/6/2/0	0/1/8/0
nephew/2	0/3/3/1	0/8/0/2	0/3/2/0	0/6/0/0	0/7/2/0	0/3/8/0

operator that works on exactly the same constraints as those used here for the proposed argumentation-based approach). So, overall, while the figures are not good, they still provide room for solutions.

Let us provide some insight into the learned theories:

IF. Theories learned using the IF constraint are very simple and never wrong, typically made up of a single rule. An example is `wife(A,B) :- female(A), male(B).`, which is clearly incomplete (the *married(B,A)* atom is missing).

IFF. This operator was considered a strong operator because, combined with the others, it maintained its peculiarities, overriding those of the other operators. With 0.1 corruption ratio, we got a mixture of quite general theories (e.g., for concept `mother/2`) with much longer theories (as for concept `sister/2`). With higher corruption ratios, theories are not wrong but incomplete (missing information about sex), and typically short (2–5 literals per rule), except for the `aunt/2` concept, which turned out to be one of the most difficult to learn.

IF-IFF. Since for this combination of constraints the argumentation step did not terminate within 10 min for corruption ratios 0.1, 0.4, and 0.5, only ratios 0.2 and 0.3 were used for the learning step, both with the *preferred* and the *stable* semantics. Theories learned based on the preferred semantics are not wrong; their rules are very long but often incomplete (they seldom include information about sex). With the stable semantics, the length of the rules still increases slightly and sex information is more present.

OR. This operator (not used for 0.20 and 0.30 corruption ratios, where the argumentation step did not terminate within 10 min) returned interesting results: generally, the theories were short (1–4 literals per rule) and sound, detecting also correct atoms about sex, but sometimes both incomplete and redundant. It behaved worse on the concepts of indirect kinship (`aunt/2`, `uncle/2`).

XOR. Rules learned based on the XOR constraint are typically very short (at most 2 atoms in the body) and not wrong (e.g., `wife(A,B) :- married(A,B).`), but they sometimes include positive exceptions.

AND-OR. With 0.1 corruption ratio, the AND-OR combination neatly tends to generate longer rules, full of useless information, but always capturing sex information correctly. With 0.4 corruption ratio, the rule size drops below 10 atoms. With 0.5 corruption ratio, the behavior is hybrid: some learned rules are extremely short and general, others long and include superfluous information.

In general, as expected, concepts having easier definitions (those in the upper part of Table 4, expressing more direct kinship) were learned 'better' than those having a more complex definition (those in the lower part of Table 4). Indeed, the need for longer definitions (and hence more data) to learn the latter increases the chance of involving missing or incorrect information in the data, leading to more wrong definitions. On the other hand, the former suffered from incomplete definitions due to missing information. Often, the concepts that differ only in the sex of one of the involved persons are learned in a similar way, with rules that differ only, in fact, for sex. In general, sex information was learned with difficulty when using constraints AND, OR, and XOR, and their combinations.

6 Conclusion

The research carried out so far aimed at making logic-based learning approaches, and specifically Inductive Logic Programming, able to deal with noisy data, focused on uncertain and missing information. Carrying on this stream of interest, this work represents a first step towards solving the relevant problem of inconsistent data. The proposed solution relies on constraint-based computational argumentation techniques to remove inconsistency from the data, so that a subsequent learning step may work on consistent information only. In a Multistrategy Learning perspective, our approach is smoothly integrated with other inference strategies, and specifically abduction.

Experiments ran on a dataset about family relationships, purposely aimed at studying the behavior of the proposed approach, highlighted some strengths and weaknesses. They allowed us to understand the features and behavior of single types of constraints, and to identify directions for overcoming the problems. Using the full set of constraints will probably allow to remove further inconsistencies, thanks to their complementary features. Coupling argumentation with abstraction should allow the latter to restore the missing information dropped by the former. These are the issues that we plan to explore in our future work.

References

1. Ali, K.M., Pazzani, M.J.: HYDRA: a noise-tolerant relational concept learning algorithm. In: IJCAI, pp. 1064–1071 (1993)
2. Baroni, P., Gabbay, D., Giacomin, M., van der Torre, L.: Handbook of Formal Argumentation, vol. 1. College Publications, Joplin (2018)
3. Cayrol, C., Lagasquie-Schiex, M.C.: On the acceptability of arguments in bipolar argumentation frameworks. In: Godo, L. (ed.) ECSQARU 2005. LNCS (LNAI), vol. 3571, pp. 378–389. Springer, Heidelberg (2005). https://doi.org/10.1007/11518655_33
4. Ceri, S., Gottlöb, G., Tanca, L.: Logic Programming and Databases. Springer, Heidelberg (1990). https://doi.org/10.1007/978-3-642-83952-8
5. De Raedt, L., Lavrač, N.: Multiple predicate learning in two inductive logic programming settings. Log. J. IGPL 4(2), 227–254 (1996)
6. Dung, P.M.: On the acceptability of arguments and its fundamental role in non-monotonic reasoning, logic programming and n-person games. Artif. intell. 77(2), 321–357 (1995)
7. Džeroski, S.: Handling imperfect data in inductive logic programming. In: Proceedings of the Fourth Scandinavian Conference on Artificial Intelligence–93, SCAI93, pp. 111–125 (1993)
8. Egly, U., Gaggl, S.A., Woltran, S.: ASPARTIX: implementing argumentation frameworks using answer-set programming. In: Garcia de la Banda, M., Pontelli, E. (eds.) ICLP 2008. LNCS, vol. 5366, pp. 734–738. Springer, Heidelberg (2008). https://doi.org/10.1007/978-3-540-89982-2_67

9. Evans, R., Grefenstette, E.: Learning explanatory rules from noisy data. J. Artif. Intell. Res. **61**, 1–64 (2018)
10. Ferilli, S.: Extending expressivity and flexibility of abductive logic programming. J. Intell. Inf. Syst. (2018). https://doi.org/10.1007/s10844-018-0531-6, ISSN: 1573-7675
11. Gamberger, D., Lavrač, N., Džeroski, S.: Noise elimination in inductive concept learning: a case study in medical diagnosis. In: Arikawa, S., Sharma, A.K. (eds.) ALT 1996. LNCS, vol. 1160, pp. 199–212. Springer, Heidelberg (1996). https://doi.org/10.1007/3-540-61863-5_47
12. Lavrač, N., Džeroski, S., Grobelnik, M.: Learning nonrecursive definitions of relations with linus. In: Kodratoff, Y. (ed.) EWSL 1991. LNCS, vol. 482, pp. 265–281. Springer, Heidelberg (1991). https://doi.org/10.1007/BFb0017020
13. Lloyd, J.W.: Foundations of Logic Programming, 2nd edn. Springer, Berlin (1987). https://doi.org/10.1007/978-3-642-83189-8
14. McCreath, E., Sharma, A.: ILP with noise and fixed example size: a Bayesian approach. In: IJCAI, vol. 97, pp. 1310–1315 (1997)
15. Muggleton, S., Feng, C.: Efficient induction of logic programs. In: New Generation Computing. Academic Press (1990)
16. Quinlan, J.R.: Learning logical definitions from relations. Mach.learn. **5**(3), 239–266 (1990)
17. Rahwan, I., Simari, G.R., van Benthem, J.: Argumentation in Artificial Intelligence, vol. 47. Springer, Heidelberg (2009). https://doi.org/10.1007/978-0-387-98197-0
18. Richards, B.L., Mooney, R.J.: Automated refinement of first-order horn-clause domain theories. Mach. Learn. **19**(2), 95–131 (1995)
19. Rotella, F., Ferilli, S.: Probabilistic abductive logic programming using possible worlds. In: Proceedings of the 28th Italian Convention on Computational Logic (CILC-2013), Central Europe (CEUR) Workshop Proceedings, vol. 1068, pp. 131–145 (2013)
20. Rouveirol, C.: Extensions of inversion of resolution applied to theory completion. In: Inductive Logic Programming, pp. 64–90. Academic Press (1992)
21. Semeraro, G., Esposito, F., Malerba, D., Fanizzi, N., Ferilli, S.: A logic framework for the incremental inductive synthesis of datalog theories. In: Fuchs, N.E. (ed.) LOPSTR 1997. LNCS, vol. 1463, pp. 300–321. Springer, Heidelberg (1998). https://doi.org/10.1007/3-540-49674-2_16

Expectation Maximization in Deep Probabilistic Logic Programming

Arnaud Nguembang Fadja[1]([⊠]), Fabrizio Riguzzi[2]([⊠]), and Evelina Lamma[1]([⊠])

[1] Dipartimento di Ingegneria, University of Ferrara,
Via Saragat 1, 44122 Ferrara, Italy
{arnaud.nguembafadja,fabrizio.riguzzi,evelina.lamma}@unife.it
[2] Dipartimento di Matematica e Informatica, University of Ferrara,
Via Saragat 1, 44122 Ferrara, Italy

Abstract. Probabilistic Logic Programming (PLP) combines logic and probability for representing and reasoning over domains with uncertainty. Hierarchical probability Logic Programming (HPLP) is a recent language of PLP whose clauses are hierarchically organized forming a deep neural network or arithmetic circuit. Inference in HPLP is done by circuit evaluation and learning is therefore cheaper than any generic PLP language. We present in this paper an Expectation Maximization algorithm, called Expectation Maximization Parameter learning for HIerarchical Probabilistic Logic programs (EMPHIL), for learning HPLP parameters. The algorithm converts an arithmetic circuit into a Bayesian network and performs the belief propagation algorithm over the corresponding factor graph.

Keywords: Hierarchical probabilistic logic programming
Arithmetic circuits · Expectation Maximization · Factor graph
Belief propagation

1 Introduction

Due to it expressiveness and intuitiveness, Probabilistic Logic Programming (PLP) has been recently used in many fields such as natural language processing [12,17], link prediction [8] and bioinformatics [3,9]. Hierarchical PLP (HPLP) [11] is a type of PLP where clauses and predicates are hierarchically organized forming deep neural networks or arithmetic circuits (AC). In this paper we present an algorithm, called "Expectation Maximization Parameter learning for HIerarchical Probabilistic Logic programs" (EMPHIL), that performs parameter learning of HPLP using Expectation Maximization. The algorithm computes the required expectations by performing two passes over ACs.

The paper is organized as follows: Sect. 2 describes PLP and hierarchical PLP. Section 3 presents EMPHIL. Related work is discussed in Sects. 4 and 5 concludes the paper.

© Springer Nature Switzerland AG 2018
C. Ghidini et al. (Eds.): AI*IA 2018, LNAI 11298, pp. 293–306, 2018.
https://doi.org/10.1007/978-3-030-03840-3_22

2   Probabilistic Logic Programming and Hierarchical PLP

PLP languages under the distribution semantics [18] have been shown expressive enough to represent a wide variety of domains [1,2,16]. A program in PLP under the distribution semantics defines a probability distribution over normal logic programs called *instances*. We consider in this paper a PLP language with a general syntax called *Logic Programs with Annotated Disjunctions* (LPADs) [19] in which each clause head is a disjunction of atoms annotated with probabilities. Consider a program T with p clauses: $P = \{C_1, \ldots, C_p\}$. Each clause C_i takes the form:

$$h_{i1} : \pi_{i1}; \ldots; h_{in_i} : \pi_{in_i} :- b_{i1}, \ldots, b_{im_i}$$

where $h_{i1}, \ldots, h_{in_i}$ are logical atoms, $b_{i1}, \ldots, b_{im_i}$ are logical literals and $\pi_{i1}, \ldots, \pi_{in_i}$ are real numbers in the interval $[0, 1]$ that sum up to 1. $b_{i1}, \ldots, b_{im_i}$ is indicated with $body(C_i)$. Note that if $n_i = 1$ the clause corresponds to a non-disjunctive clause. We denote by $ground(T)$ the grounding of an LPAD T. Each grounding $C_i\theta_j$ of a clause C_i corresponds to a random variable X_{ij} with values $\{1, \ldots, n_i\}$. The random variables X_{ij} are independent of each other. An *atomic choice* [15] is a triple (C_i, θ_j, k) where $C_i \in T$, θ_j is a substitution that grounds C_i and $k \in \{1, \ldots, n_i\}$ identifies one of the head atoms. In practice (C_i, θ_j, k) corresponds to an assignment $X_{ij} = k$.

A *selection* σ is a set of atomic choices that, for each clause $C_i\theta_j$ in $ground(T)$, contains an atomic choice (C_i, θ_j, k). A selection σ identifies a normal logic program l_σ defined as $l_\sigma = \{(h_{ik} :- body(C_i))\theta_j | (C_i, \theta_j, k) \in \sigma\}$. l_σ is called an *instance* of T. Since the random variables associated to ground clauses are independent, we can assign a probability to instances: $P(l_\sigma) = \prod_{(C_i, \theta_j, k) \in \sigma} \Pi_{ik}$.

We write $l_\sigma \models q$ to mean that the query q is true in the well-founded model of the program l_σ. We denote the set of all instances by L_T. Let $P(L_T)$ be the distribution over instances. The probability of a query q given an instance l is $P(q|l) = 1$ if $l \models q$ and 0 otherwise. The probability of a query q is given by

$$P(q) = \sum_{l \in L_T} P(q, l) = \sum_{l \in L_T} P(q|l)P(l) = \sum_{l \in L_T : l \models q} P(l) \tag{1}$$

In the hierarchical PLP language [11], clauses are restricted to the following form:

$$C = p(\boldsymbol{X}) : \pi :- \phi(\boldsymbol{X}, \boldsymbol{Y}), b_1(\boldsymbol{X}, \boldsymbol{Y}), \ldots, b_k(\boldsymbol{X}, \boldsymbol{Y})$$

where $p(\boldsymbol{X})$ is the single atom in the head annotated with the probability π, $\phi(\boldsymbol{X}, \boldsymbol{Y})$ is a conjunction of input literals (that is their definitions are given in input and are non-probabilistic) and $b_i(\boldsymbol{X}, \boldsymbol{Y})$ for $i = 1, \ldots, k$ literals for are *hidden predicate*. This means that clauses and predicates are hierarchically organized forming a tree that can be translated into a neural networks or Arithmetic Circuit (AC). Inference can be performed with HPLP programs by generating their groundings that, similarly to clauses, form a tree. Such a tree can be used for inference by translating it into an Arithmetic Circuit (AC). The AC has a × node for each clause computing the product of the values of its children, and a

$\oplus$ node for each clause head, computing the function $\bigoplus_i p_i = 1 - \prod_i(1 - p_i)$. Moreover, $\neg$ nodes are associated with negative literals in bodies, computing the function $1 - p$ where p is the value of their only child, Each leaf is associated to the Boolean random variable X_i of a clause and takes value π. The AC can be evaluated bottom-up from the leaves to the root. Because of the constraints that HPLP programs must respect, literals in bodies are mutually independent and bodies of different clauses are mutually independent as well, so the value that is computed at the root is the probability that the atom associated with the root is true according to the distribution semantics. Let us call v(N) the value of node N in the arithmetic circuit. Circuits generation and inference are described in [11].

Example 1. Consider the UW-CSE domain [6] where the objective is to predict the "advised by" relation between students and professors. An example of an HPLP program for *advisedby*/2 may be

$$C_1 \quad = advisedby(A, B) : 0.3 : -$$
$$student(A), professor(B), project(C, A), project(C, B),$$
$$r_{11}(A, B, C).$$
$$C_2 \quad = advisedby(A, B) : 0.6 : -$$
$$student(A), professor(B), ta(C, A), taughtby(C, B).$$
$$C_{111} = r_{11}(A, B, C) : 0.2 : -$$
$$publication(D, A, C), publication(D, B, C).$$

where $project(C, A)$ means that C is a project with participant A, $ta(C, A)$ means that A is a teaching assistant (TA) for course C and $taughtby(C, B)$ means that course C is taught by B. $publication(A, B, C)$ means that A is a publication with author B produced in project C. $student/1$, $professor/1$, $project/2$, $ta/2$, $taughtby/2$ and $publication/3$ are input predicates and $r_{11}/3$ is a hidden predicate.

The probability of $q = advisedby(harry, ben)$ depends on the number of joint courses and projects and on the number of joint publications from projects. The clause for $r_{11}(A, B, C)$ computes an aggregation over publications of a projects and the clause level above aggregates over projects. Supposing harry and ben have two joint courses c1 and c2, two joint projects pr1 and pr2, two joint publications p1 and p2 from project pr1 and two joint publications p3 and p4 from project pr2, the AC of such ground program is shown in Fig. 1.

3   EMPHIL

EMPHIL performs parameter learning of HPLP using Expectation Maximization (EM). The parameter learning problem is: given an HPLP P and a training set of positive and negative examples, $E = \{e_1, \dots, e_M, \textbf{not } e_{M+1}, \dots, \textbf{not } e_N\}$, find the parameters Π of P that maximize the log-likelihood (LL):

$$\arg\max_{\Pi} \sum_{i=1}^{M} \log P(e_i) + \sum_{i=M+1}^{N} \log(\textbf{not } P(e_i)) \qquad (2)$$

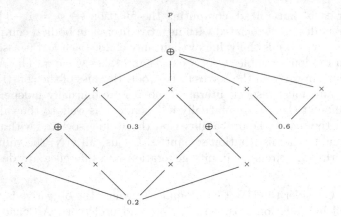

Fig. 1. Arithmetic circuit.

where $P(e_i)$ is the probability assigned to e_i by P. EMPHIL alternates between Expectation (E) and Maximization (M) steps. For a single example e, the Expectation step computes $\mathbf{E}[c_{i0}|e]$ and $\mathbf{E}[c_{i1}|e]$ for all rules C_i where c_{ix} is the number of times a variable X_{ij} takes value x for $x \in \{0,1\}$ and for all $j \in g(i)$ i.e.

$$\mathbf{E}[c_{ix}|e] = \sum_{j \in g(i)} P(X_{ij} = x|e)$$

where $g(i) = \{j|\theta_j$ is a substitution grounding $C_i\}$. These values are aggregated over all examples obtaining $E[c_{i0}] = \sum_{e \in E} \sum_{j \in g(i)} P(X_{ij} = 0|e)$ and $E[c_{i1}] = \sum_{e \in E} \sum_{j \in g(i)} P(X_{ij} = 1|e)$.

Then the Maximization computes

$$\pi_i = \frac{\mathbf{E}[c_{i1}]}{\mathbf{E}[c_{i0}] + \mathbf{E}[c_{i1}]}$$

For a single substitution θ_j of clause C_i we have that $P(X_{ij} = 0|e) + P(X_{ij} = 1|e) = 1$. So $E[c_{i0}] + E[c_{i1}] = \sum_{e \in E} |g(i)|$

Therefore to perform EMPHIL, we have to compute $P(X_{ij} = 1|e)$ for each example e. We do it using two passes over the AC, one bottom-up and one top-down. In order to illustrate the passes, we construct a graphical model associated with the AC and then apply the *belief propagation* (BP) algorithm [14].

A Bayesian Network (BN) can be obtained from the AC by replacing each node with a random variable. The variables associated with an $\oplus$ node have a conditional probabilistic table (CPT) that encodes an OR deterministic function, while variables associated with an $\times$ node have a CPT encoding an AND. Variables associated with a $\neg$ node have a CPT encoding the NOT function. Leaf nodes associated with the same parameter are split into as many nodes X_{ij} as the groundings of the rule C_i, each associated with a CPT such that

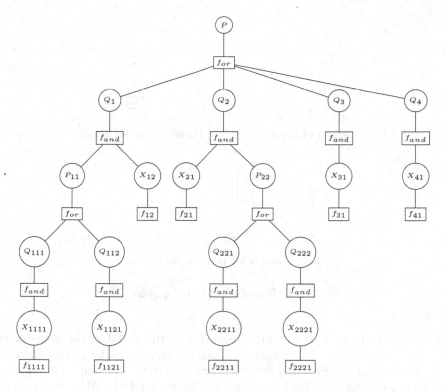

Fig. 2. Factor graph.

$P(X_{ij} = 1) = \pi_i$. We convert the BN into a Factor Graph (FG) using the standard translation because BN can be expressed in a simpler way for FGs. The FG corresponding to the AC of Fig. 1 is shown in Fig. 2.

After constructing the FG, $P(X_{ij} = 0|e)$ and $P(X_{ij} = 1|e)$ are computed by exchanging messages among nodes and factors until convergence. In the case of FG obtained from an AC, the graph is a tree and it is sufficient to propagate the message first bottom-up and then top-down. The message from a variable N to a factor f is [14]

$$\mu_{N \to f}(n) = \prod_{h \in nb(N) \setminus f} \mu_{h \to N}(n) \qquad (3)$$

where $nb(X)$ is the set of neighbor of X (the set of factors X appears in). The message from a factor f to a variable N is.

$$\mu_{f \to N}(n) = \sum_{\neg N} (f(n, \mathbf{s}) \prod_{Y \in nb(f) \setminus N} \mu_{Y \to f}(y)) \qquad (4)$$

where $nb(f)$ is the set of arguments of f. After convergence, the belief of each variable N is defined as follows:

$$b(n) = \prod_{f \in nb(N)} \mu_{f \to N}(n) \qquad (5)$$

(a) Factor graph of not node.   (b) Factor graph for a leaf node.

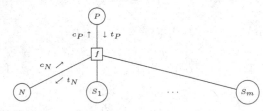

(c) Factor graph for inner or root node.

Fig. 3. Examples of factor graph

that is the product of all incoming messages to the variable. By normalizing $b(n)$ we obtain $P(N = n|e)$. Evidence is taken into account by setting the cells of the factor that are incompatible with evidence to 0. We want to develop an algorithm for computing $b(n)$ over the AC. So we want the AC nodes to send messages. We call c_N the normalized message, $\mu_{f \to N}(N = 1)$, in the bottom-up pass and t_N the normalized message, $\mu_{f \to N}(N = 1)$, in the top-down pass. Let us now compute the messages in the forward pass. Different cases can occur: the leaf, the inner and the root node. For a leaf node X, we have the factor graph in Fig. 3b From Table 1d, the message from f_x to X is given by:

$$\mu_{f_x \to X} = [\pi(x), 1 - \pi(x)] = [v(x), 1 - v(x)] \tag{6}$$

Note that the message is equal to the value of the node. Moreover, because of the construction of HPLP, for any variable node N

$$\mu_{f \to P}(p) = \mu_{P \to f}(p) \tag{7}$$

where P is the parent of N.

Let us consider a node P with children $N, S_1 \ldots S_m$ as shown in Fig. 3c. We define $\mathbf{S} = S_1 \ldots S_m$ and $\mathbf{s} = s_1 \ldots s_m$. We prove by induction that $c_P = v(P)$. For leaf nodes it was proved above. Suppose that $c_C = v(C)$ for all children $N, S_1, \ldots S_m$:

Table 1. Cpts of factors

(a) P is an *or* node

p	n = 1	n = 0, **S** = **0**	n = 1, ¬ (**S** = **0**)
0	0	1	0
1	1	0	1

(b) P is an *and* node

p	n = 0	n = 1, **S** = **1**	n = 1, ¬ (**S** = **1**)
0	1	0	1
1	0	1	0

(c) P is a not node

p	n = 0	n = 1
0	0	1
1	1	0

(d) Leaf node $f_x = \pi(x)$

x	f_x
0	1-$\pi(x)$
1	$\pi(x)$

If P is an $\times$ node, the cpt of P given its children is described in Table 1b and $\mu_{C \to f}(c) = v(c)$ for all children C. According to Eq. 4 we have:

$$\mu_{f \to P}(1) = \sum_{\neg P} f(p, n, \mathbf{s}) \prod_{Y \in nb(f) \backslash P} \mu_{Y \to f}(y)$$

$$= \sum_{n, \mathbf{s}} (f(p, n, \mathbf{s}) \prod_{Y \in \{N, \mathbf{S}\}} \mu_{Y \to f}(y) \qquad (8)$$

$$= \mu_{N \to f}(1) \cdot \prod_{S_k} \mu_{S_k \to f}(1)$$

$$= v(N) \cdot \prod_{s_k} v(S_k) = v(P)$$

In the same way, from Eq. 8 we have:

$$\mu_{f \to P}(0) = 1 - \mu_{N \to f}(1) \cdot \prod_{S_k} \mu_{S_k \to f}(1)$$

$$= 1 - v(N) \cdot \prod_{s_k} v(S_k) = 1 - v(P)$$

So $c_P = v(P)$

If P is an $\oplus$ node, the cpt of P given its children is described in Table 1a. From Eq. 8 we have:

$$\mu_{f \to P}(1) = \sum_{n,s} f(p,n,\mathbf{s}) \prod_{Y \in \{N,S\}} \mu_{Y \to f}(y)$$

$$= 1 - \mu_{N \to .}(0) \cdot \prod_{S_k} \mu_{S_k \to f}(0) = 1 - v(N) \cdot \prod_{S_k} v(S_k)$$

$$= 1 - (1 - v(N)) \cdot \prod_{S_k}(1 - v(S_k)) = v(P)$$

In the same way we have:

$$\mu_{f \to P}(0) = \mu_{N \to f}(0) \cdot \prod_{S_k} \mu_{S_k \to f}(0) = v(N = 0) \cdot \prod_{S_k} v(N = 0)$$

$$= 1 - [1 - (1 - v(N) \cdot \prod_{S_k} v(S_k)] = 1 - v(P)$$

If P is a $\neg$ node with the single child N, its cpt us shown in Table 1c and we have:

$$\mu_{f \to P}(1) = \sum_{n} f(p,n) \prod_{Y \in \{N\}} \mu_{Y \to f}(y)$$

$$= \mu_{N \to f}(0) = 1 - v(N)$$

and

$$\mu_{f \to P}(0) = \mu_{N \to f}(1) = v(N)$$

Overall, exchanging message in the forward pass means evaluating the value of each node in the AC. This leads to Algorithm 1.

Now let us compute the messages in the backward pass. Considering the factor graph in Fig. 3c, we consider the message $t_P = \mu_{P \to f}(1)$ as known and we want to compute the message $t_N = \mu_{f \to N}(1)$.

If P is an *inner* $\oplus$ node (with children $N, S_1, ...S_m$), its cpt is shown in Table 1a. Let us compute the messages $\mu_{f \to N}(1)$ and $\mu_{f \to N}(0)$:

$$\mu_{f \to N}(1) = \sum_{\neg N}(f(p,n,\mathbf{s}) \prod_{Y \in nb(f) \backslash N} \mu_{Y \to f}(y))$$

$$= [\sum_{p,s}(f(p,n,\mathbf{s}) \prod_{S} v(s)] \cdot [\mu_{P \to f}(1)]$$

$$= \mu_{P \to f}(1) = t_P \tag{9}$$

In the same way

$$\mu_{f \to N}(0) = \sum_{p,s} f(p,n,\mathbf{s}) \prod_{S} v(s)[\mu_{P \to f}(p)] \tag{10}$$

$$= [1 - \prod_{S}(1 - v(S))] \cdot [\mu_{P \to f}(1)] + \prod_{S}(1 - v(S))[\mu_{P \to f}(0)]$$

$$= v(P) \ominus v(N) \cdot t_P + (1 - v(P) \ominus v(N)) \cdot (1 - t_P)$$

Algorithm 1. FUNCTION FORWARD

```
 1: function FORWARD(node)                                          ▷ node is an AC
 2:     if node = not(n) then
 3:         v(node) ← 1 − FORWARD(n)
 4:         return v(node)
 5:     else
 6:         ▷ Compute the output example by recursively call Forward on its sub AC
 7:         if node = ⊕(n₁,...nₘ)  then                              ▷ ⊕ node
 8:             for all nⱼ do
 9:                 v(nⱼ) ← FORWARD(nⱼ)
10:             end for
11:             v(node) ← v(n₁) ⊕ ... ⊕ v(nₘ)
12:             return v(node)
13:         else                                                    ▷ and Node
14:             if node = ×(πᵢ, n₁,...nₘ) then
15:                 for all nⱼ do
16:                     v(nⱼ) ← FORWARD(nⱼ)
17:                 end for
18:                 v(node) ← πᵢ · v(n₁) · ... · v(nₘ)
19:                 return v(node)
20:             end if
21:         end if
22:     end if
23: end function
```

where the operator $\ominus$ is defined as follows:

$$v(p) \ominus v(n) = 1 - \prod_s (1 - v(s)) = 1 - \frac{1 - v(p)}{1 - v(n)} \tag{11}$$

So we have

$$t_N = \frac{t_P}{t_P + v(P) \ominus v(N) \cdot t_P + (1 - v(P) \ominus v(n)) \cdot (1 - t_P)} \tag{12}$$

If P is a $\times$ node, its cpt is shown in Table 1b and we have:

$$\mu_{f \to N}(1) = \sum_{\neg N} (f(p, n, \mathbf{s}) \prod_{Y \in nb(f) \backslash N} \mu_{Y \to f}(y))$$

$$= \mu_{P \to f}(P = 1) \cdot \prod_S \mu_{S \to f}(1) + \mu_{P \to f}(0) \cdot (1 - \prod_S \mu_{S \to f}(1))$$

$$= t_P \cdot \prod_S v(S) + (1 - t_P) \cdot (1 - \prod_S v(S))$$

$$= t_P \cdot \frac{v(P)}{v(N)} + (1 - t_P) \cdot (1 - \frac{v(P)}{v(N)})$$

In the same way,

$$\mu_{f \to N}(0) = \mu_{P \to f}(0) \cdot \sum_{\mathbf{s}}(f(p, n, \mathbf{s}) \prod_{\mathbf{s}} \mu_{S \to f}(s)) = 1 - t_P$$

So we have

$$t_N = \frac{t_P \cdot \frac{v(P)}{v(N)} + (1 - t_P) \cdot (1 - \frac{v(P)}{v(N)})}{t_P \cdot \frac{v(P)}{v(N)} + (1 - t_P).(1 - \frac{v(P)}{v(N)}) + (1 - t_P)} \tag{13}$$

If P is a $\neg$ node, its cpt is shown in Table 1c and we have:

$$\mu_{f \to N}(1) = \sum_p f(p, n) \prod_{Y \in \{P\}} \mu_{Y \to f}(y) = \mu_{P \to f}(0) = 1 - t_P$$

Equivalently

$$\mu_{f \to N}(0) = \sum_p f(p, n) \prod_{Y \in \{P\}} \mu_{Y \to f}(y) = \mu_{P \to f}(1) = t_P$$

And then

$$t_N = \frac{1 - t_P}{1 - t_P + t_P} = 1 - t_P \tag{14}$$

To take into account evidence, we consider $\mu_{P \to f} = [1, 0]$ as the initial messages in the backward pass (where P is the root) and use Eq. 12 for $\oplus$ node. Overall, in the backward pass we have:

$$t_N = \begin{cases} \frac{t_P}{t_P + v(P) \ominus v(N) \cdot t_P + (1 - v(P) \ominus v(N)) \cdot (1 - t_p)} & \text{if } P \text{ is a } \oplus \text{ node} \\ \frac{t_P \cdot \frac{v(P)}{v(P)} + (1 - t_P) \cdot (1 - \frac{v(P)}{v(N)})}{t_P \cdot \frac{v(P)}{v(N)} + (1 - t_P) \cdot (1 - \frac{v(P)}{v(N)}) + (1 - t_P)} & \text{if } P \text{ is a } \times \text{ node} \\ 1 - t_P & \text{if } P \text{ is a } \neg \text{ node} \end{cases} \tag{15}$$

Since the belief propagation algorithm (for AC) converges after two passes, we can compute the unnormalized belief of each parameter during the backward pass by multiplying t_N by $v(N)$ (that is all incoming messages). Algorithm 2 perform the backward pass of belief propagation algorithm and computes the normalized belief of each parameter. It also counts the number of clause groundings using the parameter, lines 17–18.

We present EMPHIL in Algorithm 3. After building the ACs (sharing parameters) for positive and negative examples and initializing the parameters, the expectations and the counters, lines 2–5, EMPHIL proceeds by alternating between expectation step 8–13 and maximization step 13–17. The algorithm stops when the difference between the current value of the LL and the previous one is below a given threshold or when such a difference relative to the absolute value of the current one is below a given threshold. The theory is then updated and returned (lines 19–20).

Algorithm 2. PROCEDURE BACKWARD

1: **procedure** BACKWARD(t_p, $node$, B, $Count$)
2:     **if** $node = not(n)$ **then**
3:         BACKWARD($1 - t_p$, n, B, $Count$)
4:     **else**
5:         **if** $node = \bigoplus(n_1, \ldots n_m)$ **then**   ▷ $\bigoplus$ node
6:             **for all** child n_i **do**
7:                 $t_{n_i} \leftarrow \frac{t_p}{t_p + v(node) \ominus v(n_i) \cdot t_p + (1 - v(node) \ominus v(n_i)) \cdot (1 - t_p)}$
8:                 BACKWARD(t_{n_i}, n_i, B, $Count$)
9:             **end for**
10:         **else**
11:             **if** $node = \times(n_1, \ldots n_m)$ **then**   ▷ $\times$ node
12:                 **for all** child n_i **do**
13:                     $t_{n_i} \leftarrow \frac{t_p \cdot \frac{v(node)}{v(n_i)} + (1 - t_p) \cdot (1 - \frac{v(node)}{v(n_i)})}{t_p \cdot \frac{v(node)}{v(n_i)} + (1 - t_p) \cdot (1 - \frac{v(node)}{v(n_i)}) + (1 - t_p)}$
14:                     BACKWARD(t_{n_i}, n_i, B, $Count$)
15:                 **end for**
16:             **else**   ▷ leaf node π_i
17:                 $B[i] \leftarrow B[i] + \frac{\pi_i t_p}{(\pi_i t_p + (1 - \pi_i)(1 - t_p)}$
18:                 $Count[i] \leftarrow Count[i] + 1$
19:             **end if**
20:         **end if**
21:     **end if**
22: **end procedure**

---

4   Related Work

EMPHIL is related to Deep Parameter learning for Hierarchical probabilistic Logic programs (DPHIL) [13] that learns hierarchical PLP parameters using gradient descent and back-propagation. Similarly to EMPHIL, DPHIL performs two passes over the ACs: the Forward pass evaluates the AC, as EMPHIL, and the backward pass computes the gradient of the cross entropy error with respect to each parameter. A method for stochastic optimization, Adam [5], is used to update the parameters (shared over the ACs). Since EMPHIL is strongly related to EMPHIL we plan in our future work to implement EMPHIL and compare the performance of both algorithms.

Hierarchical PLP is also related to [4,7,10] where the probability of a query is computed by combining the contribution of different rules and grounding of rules with noisy-Or or Mean combining rules. In First-Order Probabilistic Logic (FOPL), [7] and Bayesian Logic Programs (BLP), [4], each ground atoms is considered as a random variables and rules have a single atom in the head and only positive literals in the body. Each rule is associated with a CPT defining the dependence of the head variable given the body ones. Similarly to HPLP, FOPL and BLP allow multiple layers of rules. Differently from FOPL and HPLP, BLP allows different combining rules. Like FOLP, BLP and hierarchical PLP, First-Order Conditional Influence Language (FOCIL) [10], uses probabilistic rules

Algorithm 3. Function EMPHIL.

1: **function** EMPHIL($Theory, \epsilon, \delta, Max$)
2:     $Examples \leftarrow$ BUILDACs($Theory$)   ▷ Build the set of ACs
3:     **for** $i \leftarrow 1 \rightarrow |Theory|$ **do**
4:         $\Pi[i] \leftarrow random; B[i], Count[i] \leftarrow 0$ ▷ Initialize the parameters
5:     **end for**
6:     $LL \leftarrow -inf; Iter \leftarrow 0$
7:     **repeat**
8:         $LL_0 \leftarrow LL, LL \leftarrow 0$ ▷ Expectation step
9:         **for all** $node \in Examples$ **do**
10:             $P \leftarrow$ FORWARD($node$)
11:             BACKWARD($1, node, B, Count$)
12:             $LL \leftarrow LL + \log P$
13:         **end for**   ▷ Maximization step
14:         **for** $i \leftarrow 1 \rightarrow |Theory|$ **do**
15:             $\Pi[i] \leftarrow \frac{B[i]}{Count[i]}$
16:             $B[i], Count[i] \leftarrow 0$
17:         **end for**
18:     **until** $LL - LL_0 < \epsilon \vee LL - LL_0 < -LL.\delta \vee Iter > Max$
19:     $FinalTheory \leftarrow$ UPDATETHEORY($Theory, \Pi$)
20:     **return** $FinalTheory$
21: **end function**

---

for compactly encoding probabilistic dependencies. The probability of a query is computed using two combining rules: the contributions of different groundings of the same rule with the same random variable in the head are combined by taking the *Mean* and the contributions of different rules are combined either with a weighted mean or with a *noisy-OR* combining rule. HPLP instead uses the noisy-OR combining rule for both cases. FOPL, BLP and FOCIL implement parameter learning using gradient descent, or Expectation Maximization, as EMPHIL. In this paper we specialized the results of [4,7,10] for the HPLP language obtaining formulas that can be easily implemented into an algorithm.

5   Conclusion

We present in this paper the algorithm EMPHIL for learning the parameters of hierarchical PLP using Expectation Maximization. The formula for expectations are obtained by converting an arithmetic circuit into a Bayesian network and performing belief propagation algorithm over the corresponding factor graph. We plan in our future work to implement and compare EMPHIL with DPHIL, an algorithm that performs parameter learning of HPLP using gradient descent. We also plan to design an algorithm for learning the structure of hierarchical PLP in order to search in the space of HPLP the program that best described the data using EMPHIL or DPHIL as sub-procedures.

References

1. Alberti, M., Bellodi, E., Cota, G., Riguzzi, F., Zese, R.: cplint on SWISH: probabilistic logical inference with a web browser. Intell. Artif. 11(1), 47–64 (2017)
2. Alberti, M., Cota, G., Riguzzi, F., Zese, R.: Probabilistic logical inference on the web. In: Adorni, G., Cagnoni, S., Gori, M., Maratea, M. (eds.) AI*IA 2016. LNCS (LNAI), vol. 10037, pp. 351–363. Springer, Cham (2016). https://doi.org/10.1007/978-3-319-49130-1_26
3. De Raedt, L., Kimmig, A., Toivonen, H.: ProbLog: a probabilistic Prolog and its application in link discovery. In: Veloso, M.M. (ed.) IJCAI 2007, vol. 7, pp. 2462–2467. AAAI Press/IJCAI (2007)
4. Kersting, K., De Raedt, L.: Basic principles of learning Bayesian logic programs. Institute for Computer Science, University of Freiburg. Citeseer (2002)
5. Kingma, D., Ba, J.: Adam: a method for stochastic optimization. arXiv preprint arXiv:1412.6980 (2014)
6. Kok, S., Domingos, P.: Learning the structure of Markov logic networks. In: ICML 2005, pp. 441–448. ACM (2005)
7. Koller, D., Pfeffer, A.: Learning probabilities for noisy first-order rules. In: IJCAI, pp. 1316–1323 (1997)
8. Meert, W., Struyf, J., Blockeel, H.: CP-logic theory inference with contextual variable elimination and comparison to BDD based inference methods. In: De Raedt, L. (ed.) ILP 2009. LNCS (LNAI), vol. 5989, pp. 96–109. Springer, Heidelberg (2010). https://doi.org/10.1007/978-3-642-13840-9_10
9. Mørk, S., Holmes, I.: Evaluating bacterial gene-finding HMM structures as probabilistic logic programs. Bioinformatics 28(5), 636–642 (2012)
10. Natarajan, S., Tadepalli, P., Kunapuli, G., Shavlik, J.: Learning parameters for relational probabilistic models with noisy-or combining rule. In: 2009 International Conference on Machine Learning and Applications, ICMLA 2009, pp. 141–146. IEEE (2009)
11. Nguembang Fadja, A., Lamma, E., Riguzzi, F.: Deep probabilistic logic programming. In: Theil Have, C., Zese, R. (eds.) Proceedings of the 4th International Workshop on Probabilistic Logic Programming (PLP 2017), CEUR Workshop Proceedings, vol. 1916, pp. 3–14. Sun SITE Central Europe, Aachen (2017)
12. Holzinger, A., Goebel, R., Palade, V., Ferri, M.: Towards integrative machine learning and knowledge extraction. In: Holzinger, A., Goebel, R., Ferri, M., Palade, V. (eds.) Towards Integrative Machine Learning and Knowledge Extraction. LNCS (LNAI), vol. 10344, pp. 1–12. Springer, Cham (2017). https://doi.org/10.1007/978-3-319-69775-8_1
13. Nguembang Fadja, A., Riguzzi, F., Lamma, E.: Deep parameter learning for probabilistic logic programming (2018, submitted)
14. Pearl, J.: Probabilistic Reasoning in Intelligent Systems: Networks of Plausible Inference. Morgan Kaufmann, Burlington (1988)
15. Poole, D.: The independent choice logic for modelling multiple agents under uncertainty. Artif. Intell. 94, 7–56 (1997)
16. Riguzzi, F., Bellodi, E., Lamma, E., Zese, R., Cota, G.: Probabilistic logic programming on the web. Softw.-Pract. Exper. 46(10), 1381–1396 (2016)
17. Riguzzi, F., Lamma, E., Alberti, M., Bellodi, E., Zese, R., Cota, G.: Probabilistic logic programming for natural language processing. In: Chesani, F., Mello, P., Milano, M. (eds.) Workshop on Deep Understanding and Reasoning, URANIA 2016. CEUR Workshop Proceedings, vol. 1802, pp. 30–37. Sun SITE Central Europe, Aachen, Germany (2017)

18. Sato, T.: A statistical learning method for logic programs with distribution semantics. In: Sterling, L. (ed.) ICLP 1995, pp. 715–729. MIT Press (1995)
19. Vennekens, J., Verbaeten, S., Bruynooghe, M.: Logic programs with annotated disjunctions. In: Demoen, B., Lifschitz, V. (eds.) ICLP 2004. LNCS, vol. 3132, pp. 431–445. Springer, Heidelberg (2004). https://doi.org/10.1007/978-3-540-27775-0_30

Neural Random Access Machines Optimized by Differential Evolution

Marco Baioletti, Valerio Belli, Gabriele Di Bari, and Valentina Poggioni[✉]

Dip. Matematica e Informatica, Università di Perugia, Perugia, Italy
{marco.baioletti,valentina.poggioni}@unipg.it, belli.valerio@gmail.com,
dbgabri@gmail.com

Abstract. Recently a research trend of learning algorithms by means of deep learning techniques has started. Most of these are different implementations of the controller-interface abstraction: they use a neural controller as a "processor" and provide different interfaces for input, output and memory management. In this trend, we consider of particular interest the Neural Random-Access Machines, called NRAM, because this model is also able to solve problems which require indirect memory references. In this paper we propose a version of the Neural Random-Access Machines, where the core neural controller is trained with Differential Evolution meta-heuristic instead of the usual backpropagation algorithm. Some experimental results showing that this approach is effective and competitive are also presented.

Keywords: NRAM · Differential Evolution · Neural networks

1 Introduction

A new learning algorithms' research trend, by means of deep learning techniques, has been recently started by various works [5,7–9,11,12]. The basic idea is to learn regularities in sequences of symbols, each sequence generated by simple algorithms. The learning of the regularities can be performed only by models having the ability to count and memorize. Most of the implementations are based on the controller-interface abstraction as they use a neural controller as a "processor" and provide different interfaces for input, output and memory. The most influential model is the Differentiable Neural Computer (DNC) [6]. In order to make these models trainable with gradient descent, sometimes the authors made them "artificiously" fully differentiable modifying the discrete nature of their interfaces [5,9].

In this trend, we consider of particular interest the Neural Random-Access Machines (NRAM) [9] as the proposed model is able to solve problems using pointers. The algorithm can learn to solve problems that require explicit manipulation and dereferencing of pointers as well as it can learn to solve a number of algorithmic problems. Moreover, the authors show that the solutions can generalize well to inputs longer than ones used during the training and for some

C. Ghidini et al. (Eds.): AI*IA 2018, LNAI 11298, pp. 307–319, 2018.
https://doi.org/10.1007/978-3-030-03840-3_23

problems they generalize to inputs of arbitrary length. However, as reported by the authors, the optimization problem resulting from the backpropagation through the execution trace of the program is very challenging for standard optimization techniques.

Moreover, the continuity condition of the optimization function and the "fuzzyfication" process add further complexity to the optimization problem. For example, since the gates are connected in a fuzzy way to each other and to the registers, computing the circuit results is an expensive operation. From further analysis, since the additional cost of computing circuit results is due to the use of gradient descent, different optimization methods not requiring differentiability can help to reduce the complexity of the operation.

This work is part of a wider project aiming to rewrite a NRAM model which does not require the differentiability condition for the neural controller. The main idea is to train the controller with an evolutionary optimization algorithm, in line with the approach used in previous work [7] where an evolutionary algorithm is used to learn the controller of a Neural Turing Machine [5].

In this paper we present a new version of the Neural Random-Access Machines using the same model proposed in the original paper [9], where the core neural controller is trained with Differential Evolution meta-heuristic instead of backpropagation algorithm. In particular, we employ the Differential Evolution for Neural Networks (DENN) method [1,4], to evolve neural networks by means of Differential Evolution. With respect to the optimization methods based on gradient descent, DENN is less influenced by the choice of starting points, it has lower chances to be trapped in local minima and it has a more exploratory attitude.

Experiments are conducted to evaluate the system from two different points of view: the ability of DENN technique to optimize the network and compete with backpropagation, and the generalization capability of our solution. Moreover, some DE variants have been tested in order to find the best for this kind of problems. In the experiments, some algorithmic problems whose solutions require pointer manipulation and chasing are chosen.

DENN approach has been applied in its simplest form, by flattening the network depth. The results are encouraging and prove that further analysis and investigation should be undertaken in a more advanced manner.

2 Neural Random Access Machines

In this section we briefly recall the NRAM model presented in [9]. This model can be included in the recent research trend of learning algorithms [5,7,8,11, 12]. Like others, NRAM model is an implementation of the controller-interface abstraction: it uses a neural controller as a "processor" and provides different interfaces for input, output and memory.

In particular the NRAM model can learn to solve problems that require explicit manipulation and dereferencing of pointers. The controller, the core part of the NRAM model, can be a feedforward neural network or an LSTM, and it is the only trainable part of the model.

The idea of NRAM is that the controller, at each time-step, produces a small set of elementary operations, described with a circuit, which are executed. The execution terminates after a given number of time-steps or when the controller signals the willingness of termination.

The NRAM model can be divided in four main pieces: the controller, which can be a feed-forward or a Long-Short Term Memory (LSTM) neural network, a set of R registers $r_1, \ldots, r_R$, the gates (also called modules), and a variable-sized memory tape.

Registers and memory cells contain integers from the set $N = \{0, 1, \ldots, I-1\}$, where I is an integer constant. Moreover, the memory has I cells numbered from 0 to $I - 1$, hence any integer of N can also be seen as a valid address.

In order to have a fully differentiable model the NRAM does not work directly with integers but with probability distributions $p \in \mathbb{R}^I$. Hence, each register or memory cell plays the role of random variable. The content memory can be represented by a square matrix $\mathcal{M}$ of size I, whose rows are the probability distributions of the content of their cells. In this way, the model is fully differentiable.

There are $Q = 14$ gates, representing the elementary operations, divided in constant, unary and binary. Each gate is represented as a function m_i with 0, 1, or 2 arguments from the set N and a result is in N. There are

- 3 constant gates: Zero() = 0, One() = 1, Two() = 2
- 3 unary gates: $\mathrm{Inc}(a) = (a + 1) \mod I$, $\mathrm{Dec}(a) = (a - 1) \mod I$, Read($p$)
- 8 binary gates: $\mathrm{Add}(a, b) = (a + b) \mod I$, $\mathrm{Sub}(a, b) = (a - b) \mod I$, Less-Than$(a, b) = [a < b]$, Less-Or-Equal-Than$(a, b) = [a \leq b]$, Equal-Than$(a, b) = [a = b]$, $\mathrm{Min}(a, b) = \min(a, b)$, $\mathrm{Max}(a, b) = \max(a, b)$, Write($p, a$)

The controller at each time step is given as input the vector $(p_{r_1}(0), \ldots, p_{r_R}(0))$, i.e. the probability that each register contains 0. This choice gives the controller only a partial information about the content of the registers, in this way the controller can generalize to different memory sizes.

The controller produces the description of a "fuzzy" circuit which contains all the Q gates, exactly once and taken in the same order (Read, Zero, One, Two, Inc, Add, Sub, Dec, Less-Than, Less-Or-Equal-Than, Equal-Than, Min, Max, Write). The circuit is described by three sequence of vectors $a_1, \ldots, a_Q$, $b_1, \ldots, b_Q$, and $c_1, \ldots, c_R$. For the i-th gate, the vectors a_i and b_i have size $R + i - 1$, while all the vectors c_j have size $R + Q$.

We denote by o_i the output produced by the i-th gate, which is computed as follows. Denoting by $v_i = (r_1, \ldots, r_R, o_1, \ldots, o_{i-1})$ the vector composed by the values of all the R registers and the output of the previous $i - 1$ gates, if the gate is unary, then

$$o_i = m_i(v_i^T \cdot softmax(a_i)),$$

while if it is binary, then

$$o_i = m_i(v_i^T \cdot softmax(a_i), v_i^T \cdot softmax(b_i)).$$

Clearly, if the gate is constant, $o_i = m_i()$.

The vector c_i, for $i = 1, \ldots, R$, determines how the register r_i is updated for the next iteration, by the formula

$$r_i \leftarrow v_{Q+1}^T \cdot softmax(c_i)$$

where the vector v_{Q+1} is composed by the current values of the register r_i and the outputs of all the gates $m_1, \cdots, m_Q$.

Note that, as for the registers, the gates have to work over probability distributions: since the inputs are probability distributions also the output is a probability distribution. For instance if the module m_i is binary, A and B are its input, the probability of having the value $\gamma \in N$ as result is given by

$$P(m_i(A, B) = \gamma) = \sum_{\alpha, \beta \in N} P(A = \alpha) P(B = \beta) [m_i(\alpha, \beta) = \gamma] \qquad (1)$$

The result of the gate $Read(p)$ is defined by the probability distribution $\mathcal{M}^T p$, while the effect of $Write(p, a)$, where p is the address and a is the data to be written (both are probability distributions), is to change the content of the memory using the following equation

$$\mathcal{M} \leftarrow (J - p) \cdot J^T \star \mathcal{M} + p \cdot a^T$$

where J is a column vector composed by I ones and $\star$ denotes a coordinate-wise multiplication.

For each time step t the controller also outputs a value $\xi_t \in \mathbb{R}$. The value $f_t = sigmoid(\xi_t) \in [0, 1]$ represents the willingness of finishing the execution at the time step t. Hence, the probability that the output is produced in t can be computed as $p_t = f_t \cdot \prod_{i=1}^{t-1} (1 - f_i)$. Anyway, the execution continues at most for a given maximum number of time-steps T or when f_t is above given a threshold θ.

The global procedure to execute the NRAM program is the following:

- Initialize the registers and the memory
- For each time-step $t = 1, \ldots, T$
  1. the controller gets the input from the registers and computes its output, i.e. the data describing the circuit
  2. if the controller is a LSTM, it also updates its internal state
  3. the circuit is executed
  4. the values of the registers and the memory is updated
  5. if $f_t > \theta$ the execution is stopped

During the learning process we feed the network with examples, each of them described by a couple $(x, y) \in N^I \times N^I$ which contains the starting input sequence and the expected output sequence.

The cost function to be minimized can be computed using the memory matrix $\mathcal{M}^{(t)}$ at the end of the execution of the time-step t as the expected negative log-likelihood of producing the correct output, i.e.

$$C(x, y) = -\sum_{t=1}^{T} \left(p_t \cdot \sum_{i=0}^{I-1} \log \left(\mathcal{M}_{i, y_i}^{(t)} \right) \right) \qquad (2)$$

where y_i is the expected integer value at memory cell number i.

3   DENN: Differential Evolution for Neural Networks

In this section we briefly describe the algorithm DENN, an enhancement of a previous algorithm already presented in [1], which optimizes artificial neural networks using Differential Evolution (DE). In particular we use DENN to train the neural controller of the NRAM model using a dataset of examples D.

We decided to use this approach because it is the only method we know that has been tested with relatively large neural networks.

DE is applied according the conventional neuroevolution approach, i.e. to evolve the network weights instead of backpropagation or other optimization methods based on backpropagation. A batch system, similar to that one used in stochastic gradient descent, is adopted to reduce the computation time.

DENN evolves a population $\mathcal{P}$ of N feed-forward neural networks $\{\xi_1, \ldots, \xi_N\}$ with a given fixed topology and fixed activation functions.

The representation of neural networks as population elements is defined as follows.

Each neural network has L levels, numbered from 1 to L and each network level l is defined by a real valued matrix $\mathbf{W}^{(l)}$, representing the connection weights, and by the bias vector $\mathbf{b}^{(l)}$.

Then, each population element ξ_i is described by a sequence

$$\langle (\mathbf{w}^{(i,1)}, \mathbf{b}^{(i,1)}), \ldots, (\mathbf{w}^{(i,L)}, \mathbf{b}^{(i,L)}) \rangle,$$

where $\mathbf{w}^{(i,l)}$ is the vector obtained by linearizing the matrix $\mathbf{W}^{(i,l)}$, for $l = 1, \ldots, L$.

For a given population element ξ_i, we denote by $\xi_i^{(h)}$ its h–th component, for $h = 1, \ldots, 2L$, i.e. $\xi_i^{(h)} = \mathbf{w}^{(l,(h+1)/2)}$, it h is odd, while $\xi_i^{(h)} = \mathbf{b}^{(l,h/2)}$ it h is even. Note that each component $\xi_i^{(h)}$ of a solution x_i is a vector whose size $d^{(h)}$ depends on the number of neurons in the level h.

The population elements are evolved by applying mutation and crossover operators in a component-wise way. For instance, the mutation $rand/1$ for the element ξ_i is applied in the following way: three indexes $r1, r2, r3$ are randomly chosen in the set $\{1, \ldots, N\} \setminus \{i\}$ without repetition; then, for $h = 1, \ldots, 2L$, the h th component $v_i^{(h)}$ of the donor element v_i is obtained as the linear combination

$$v_i^{(h)} = \xi_{r1}^{(h)} + F(\xi_{r2}^{(h)} - \xi_{r3}^{(h)}).$$

We have implemented three mutation operators, namely $rand/1$, DEGL and Current-to-pbest (see for instance [2,3]).

Each trial ζ_i, for $i = 1, \ldots, N$, is produced by applying the usual crossover operator bin to ξ_i and v_i.

The evaluation of each population element ξ_i should be performed by computing the sum of the cost function $C(x_j, y_j)$ for each example (x_j, y_j) in the dataset D.

Anyway, the computation of this quantity is the most time consuming operation in the overall algorithm and it will lead to unacceptable computation time. For this motivation we have decided to follow a batching method similar to the one proposed in [10].

The dataset D is split in three different sets: a training set TS used for the training phase, a validation set VS used for a uniform evaluation of the individuals selected at the end of each training phase, and a test set ES used to evaluate the performance of the best neural network.

Then, the training set TS is randomly partitioned in k batches $B_0, \ldots, B_{k-1}$ of size $b = |TS|/k$. Moreover, the fitness function f is computed using the records present in a "window" U of size b, which is composed by examples both from the current batch B_i and from the next one B_{i+1}.

The window is changed after s generations, by replacing b/r examples of U from B_i with b/r examples taken from B_{i+1} and not already present in U. s is called *sub-epoch* dimension and the window completely passes from a batch to the next one in r sub-epoch, i.e. in rs generations (we call *epoch* this period). In this way the evolution has enough time to learn from the batch because the window is updated after s generations.

Since the fitness function depends also on the batch and we need a fixed way to compare the elements, at the end of every epoch the best neural network ξ_e^* of the epoch e is selected as the neural network in $\mathcal{P}$ reaching the lowest cost in the validation set VS. The global best network ξ^{**} found so far is then eventually updated.

At the beginning of each epoch, the fitness of every element in $\mathcal{P}$ is re-evaluated by computing the fitness on the new batch and the window U becomes exactly the current batch.

To avoid a premature convergence of the algorithm, a restart method is applied: all the elements in the current population, except the best element, are discarded and the search continues with a new randomly generated population. The restart mechanism is performed at the end of each epoch, if the fitness evaluation of ξ^{**} has remained unchanged for a given number M of epochs.

The complete DENN algorithm is depicted in Algorithm 1.

In DENN algorithm, the function *generate_offspring* computes the mutation and the crossover operators that produce the *trial element*, while the function *best_score* returns the best network ξ^*, and its score f^*, among all the elements in the population.

4   Experiments

The experiments has been performed by using DENN, as described in Sect. 3, to train the controller of the system described in Sect. 2. Since DE has never been applied before to this kind of problems, we decided to test different DE variants and mutation strategies. Moreover, as suggested in NRAM paper [9], a curriculum learning method has been applied.

Algorithm 1. The algorithm DENN

1: Initialize the population
2: $k \leftarrow |TS|/b$
3: Extract the k batches $B_0, \ldots, B_{k-1}$
4: $h \leftarrow 0$
5: **for** $e \leftarrow 0$ **to** $G/(rs) - 1$ **do**
6:     Set the current batch as $B_{e \bmod k}$
7:     Re-evaluate all the elements $(\xi_1, \ldots, \xi_N)$
8:     **for** $z \leftarrow 1$ **to** r **do**
9:         **for** $j \leftarrow 1$ **to** s **do**
10:            **for** $i \leftarrow 1$ **to** N **do**
11:                $\zeta_i \leftarrow$ generate_offspring(ξ_i)
12:            **end for**
13:            **for** $i \leftarrow 1$ **to** N **do**
14:                **if** $f(\zeta_i) < f(\xi_i)$ **then**
15:                    $\xi_i \leftarrow \zeta_i$
16:                **end if**
17:            **end for**
18:         **end for**
19:         Update the window U
20:     **end for**
21:     $\xi_e^*, f_e^* \leftarrow$ best_score$(\xi_1, \ldots, \xi_N)$
22:     Update ξ^{**}, f^{**}
23:     **if** ξ^{**} is not changed **then**
24:         **if** $h > M$ **then**
25:             Restart the population
26:             $h \leftarrow 0$
27:         **else**
28:             $h \leftarrow h + 1$
29:         **end if**
30:     **end if**
31: **end for**
32: **return** ξ^{**}

4.1 Curriculum Learning

For each task, we defined a set of problems of increasing difficulty, where the difficulty d is defined as a tuple containing the length of the working sequence and the number of timesteps of running. During the training, a tuple is selected according to the current difficulty D as follows:

- with probability 10%: pick d randomly from the set of all difficulties according to a uniform distribution
- with probability 25%: pick d randomly from the set $[1, D + e]$ according to a uniform distribution, with e generated from a geometric distribution with a success probability of 0.5
- with probability 65%: set $d = D + e$, where e is sampled as above.

The difficulty is increased when $1 - \frac{c}{m} < \lambda$, where c represents the correct modified cells, m the cells that should be modified and λ is a threshold chosen by the user. Furthermore, we ensure that the difficulty is increased at least after a given number of generations.

We test the impact of curriculum learning approach because the authors of the original paper [9] claimed it is of crucial importance. They explicitly claim that without curriculum learning the training of some controllers is impossible.

4.2 Settings

The DE variants used for testing are *JADE*, *SHADE* and *L-SHADE*. Each of them has been combined with the mutation methods *DEGL* and *Current-to-pbest*. The crossover method is *bin*. In each test we set population to 100 individuals, for DEGL the neighborhood is in the interval $[4, 8]$, and we set $p = 0.1$ for Current-to-pbest.

All the tests are executed with a feedforward neural network with two hidden levels, each containing 260 neurons. The training set is composed of batches of 1000 examples generated at runtime. The generalization tests are executed with input sequences up to 1000 values. The Curriculum Learning was set up with an interval of batches in $[25, 250]$ and a threshold $\lambda = 0.1$.

4.3 Tasks

The tasks used in these experiments are a subset of the ones proposed in [9]. In the following descriptions, capital and small letters represent respectively arrays and pointers, *NULL* denotes the value 0 and it is used both as an ending character and a placeholder for missing next element in the lists.

- **Access** Given a value k and an array $\mathbf{A}$, return $\mathbf{A}[k]$. Input is given as $k, A[0], \ldots, \mathbf{A}[n-1]$, *NULL* and the network should replace the first memory cell with $\mathbf{A}[k]$.
- **Copy** Given an array and a pointer to the destination, copy all elements from the array to the given location. Input is given as $p, \mathbf{A}[0], \ldots, \mathbf{A}[n-1]$ where p points to one element after $\mathbf{A}[n-1]$. The expected output is $\mathbf{A}[0], \ldots, \mathbf{A}[n-1]$ at positions $p, \ldots, p+n-1$ respectively.
- **Reverse** Given an array and a pointer to the destination, copy all elements from the array in reversed order. Input is given as $p, \mathbf{A}[0], \ldots, \mathbf{A}[n-1]$ where p points one element after $\mathbf{A}[n-1]$. The expected output is $\mathbf{A}[n-1], \ldots, \mathbf{A}[0]$ at positions $p, \ldots, p+n-1$ respectively.
- **Increment** Given an array $\mathbf{A}$, increment all its elements by 1. Input is given as $\mathbf{A}[0], \ldots, \mathbf{A}[n-1]$, *NULL* and the expected output is $\mathbf{A}[0] + 1, \ldots, A[n-1] + 1$.

5 Results

We have conducted the experiments following the structure proposed in NRAM paper [9]. The main objective was to have comparable results with the ones in the original paper, with and without Curriculum Learning, focusing especially on the generalization ability of the discovered solutions. In this paper the most significant results are shown. Complete results can be retrieved on GitHUB[1]. Training values for parameter I, number of timesteps T, and number of registers R are similar to those used by Kurach et al. [9].

Table 1. Results of the tests comparing the optimization and generalization ability of the system with and without curriculum learning.

Task	Train complexity		Cost=0		Train error		Generalization	
	No CL	CL	No CL	CL	No CL	CL	No CL	CL
DENN *JADE/Current-to-pbest/1/bin*								
Access	$len(A) = 8, t = 3$	$len(A) \leq 10$	✓	✓	0	0	Perfect	Perfect
Increment	$len(A) = 9, t = 9$	$len(A) \leq 11$	✓	✓	0	0	Perfect	Perfect
Copy	$len(A) = 5, t = 12$	$len(A) \leq 9$	✓	×	0	—	Semi-perfect	—
Reverse	$len(A) = 4, t = 9$	$len(A) \leq 8$	✓	✓	0	0	Perfect	Perfect
ADAM [9]								
Access	$len(A) = 8, t = 3$	$len(A) \leq 10$	×	✓		0	—	Perfect
Increment	$len(A) = 9, t = 9$	$len(A) \leq 11$	×	✓	—	0	—	Perfect
Copy	$len(A) = 5, t = 12$	$len(A) \leq 9$	×	✓	—	0	—	Perfect
Reverse	$len(A) = 4, t = 9$	$len(A) \leq 8$	×	✓	—	0	—	Perfect

In Table 1 we present the results that compare optimization and generalization ability of our system with and without curriculum learning. In particular, these results are obtained by means of the JADE version of DENN with the mutation *Currenttopbest* and crossover *bin*. The column *Train complexity* represents the length of the sequences and the timesteps used in the training without Curriculum Learning (No CL), while it represents the maximum length of the sequences used in the training with Curriculum Learning (CL). The column *Reached cost 0* is checked when the cost function C reached the value 0 during the training phase. The column *Train Error* represents the lowest error rate $1 - c/m$ reached by the trained controller. The *Generalization* column represents the behaviour of the trained controller with memory sequences longer and more available timesteps for running with respect to those used in training. The keyword *Perfect* is used when the controller produces circuits able to generalize independently from the test length and the number of timesteps; the keyword *Semi-Perfect* means that the solution generalizes well only with input sequences and number of timesteps similar to those used in the training.

The first result we can note is the different contribution of curriculum learning application in our system with respect to the original one in NRAM paper [9]. While Kurach et al. claim that their system cannot be trained without CL, we have obtained good results also without it. As in [9], all these problems have been solved with zero errors and producing circuits with perfect or semi-perfect generalization ability.

---

[1] https://github.com/Gabriele91/DENN-NRAM-RESULTS-2018.

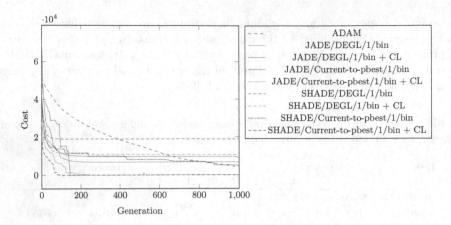

Fig. 1. Costs reached by DE variants with task **Increment**.

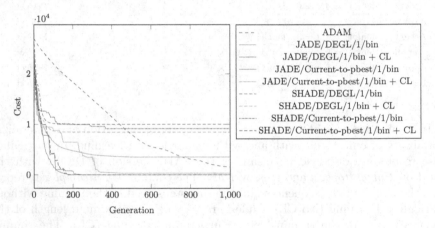

Fig. 2. Costs trend by DE variants with task **Reverse**.

5.1   DENN Variants Results

In this section the charts obtained plotting the values of the cost function are shown. For each generation and for each combination of DE variant, mutation and crossover, the convergence ability can be analyzed. For sake of space, just the plots for the problems *Increment* and *Reverse* are respectively shown in Fig. 1 and in Fig. 2. The legends report all the combinations tested except the ones for L-SHADE that cannot compete with the others, hence are not shown here. In this way we can compare the costs reached by the DENN variants with the cost of the reimplementation of the original system (trained with the ADAM optimization algorithm) (Fig. 3).

Even if these experiments are preliminary and more tests have yet to be run, we can see that, while some DENN variants cannot reach the convergence to

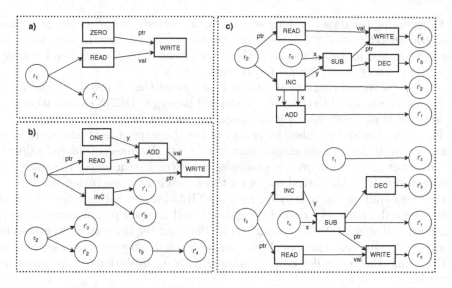

Fig. 3. The circuits generated respectively for **(a)** the tasks *Access* when $t \geq 2$, **(b)** *Increment* when $t \in [2, \text{len}(A)]$ and **(c)** *Reverse* when, in the first, $t \in [2, \text{len}(A)]$ and, in the second, when t is even and $t > \text{len}(A)$.

zero, some other variants reach the convergence better than the original system with ADAM, like for example the JADE variant with *current_to_pbest* mutation.

5.2 Circuits

In the following we present the circuits generated by the controller trained by the JADE/current_to_pbest/1/bin variant. For the sake of readability, only the necessary gates and registers are shown in the circuits.

Overall it is important to note that the circuits generated differ from those shown in [9]. Even if a criterion to evaluate the circuit quality has not provided, it is evident that the circuits generated by the controller trained by DENN are more intuitive and easy to understand than the ones shown in [9]. Moreover, we observed also that, in the case of DENN, the circuits generated depend to the DE variant used in the training.

6   Conclusions and Future Works

In this work a version of NRAM with Differential Evolution as optimization engine has been presented. In particular the DENN framework [4] has been used instead of ADAM optimization algorithm.

As shown in the experiments, we can conclude that Differential Evolution and DENN behave well with this kind of problems and with large neural networks. For the *Access*, *Increment* and *Reverse* tasks, solutions that generalize perfectly are reached, also without the use of Curriculum Learning.

Considering the data obtained so far we can conclude that, excluding the case of *JADE/DEGL/1/bin + CL*, the best performing variants are the ones with the *Current-to-pbest* mutation method. The contribution of the Curriculum Learning is crucial in some cases, like for the Increment task.

We also observed that the solutions found using DENN produce more intuitive circuits compared to those in the original paper [9]. DENN exploitation and exploration is more effective with respect to Gradient Descent.

For future work, we plan to complete all the experiments including new tasks. In particular, we are considering to evaluate the ones considered *difficult* by Kurach et al. [9]. Moreover, we consider the current structure of the gates too stringent, requiring the forced use of all them, making the execution excessively static. One of our objective is to upgrade the NRAM model with a more advanced system for a dynamic selection of the gates. Finally, we are planning to rewrite a enhanced and simpler NRAM model which does not require the differentiability condition. In this case the model can not be trained using the gradient descent method, but the controller can be trained with an evolutionary optimization algorithm.

References

1. Baioletti, M., Di Bari, G., Poggioni, V., Tracolli, M.: Can differential evolution be an efficient engine to optimize neural networks? In: Nicosia, G., Pardalos, P., Giuffrida, G., Umeton, R. (eds.) MOD 2017. LNCS, vol. 10710, pp. 401–413. Springer, Cham (2018). https://doi.org/10.1007/978-3-319-72926-8_33
2. Das, S., Mullick, S.S., Suganthan, P.N.: Recent advances in differential evolution an updated survey. Swarm Evol. Comput. **27**, 1–30 (2016)
3. Swagatam Das and Ponnuthurai Nagaratnam Suganthan: Differential evolution: a survey of the state-of-the-art. IEEE Trans. Evol. Comput. **15**(1), 4–31 (2011)
4. Di Bari, G., Poggioni, V., Baioletti, M., Tracolli, M.: Differential evolution for learning large neural networks. Technical report (2018). https://github.com/Gabriele91/DENN-RESULTS-2018
5. Graves, A., Wayne, G., Danihelka, I.: Neural turing machines. CoRR abs/1410.5401 (2014)
6. Graves, A., et al.: Hybrid computing using a neural network with dynamic external memory. Nature **538**(7626), 471–476 (2016)
7. Greve, R.B., Jacobsen, E.J., Risi, S.: Evolving neural turing machines for reward-based learning. In: Proceedings of the Genetic and Evolutionary Computation Conference 2016, GECCO 2016, pp. 117–124. ACM, New York (2016)
8. Joulin, A., Mikolov, T.: Inferring algorithmic patterns with stack-augmented recurrent nets. In: Proceedings of the GECCO 2016, pp. 190–198 (2015)
9. Kurach, K., Andrychowicz, M., Sutskever, I.: Neural random-access machines. CoRR abs/1511.06392 (2015)
10. Morse, G., Stanley, K.O.: Simple evolutionary optimization can rival stochastic gradient descent in neural networks. In: Proceedings of the GECCO 2016, pp. 477–484 (2016)

11. Zaremba, W., Mikolov, T., Joulin, A., Fergus, R.: Learning simple algorithms from examples. In: Proceedings of the 33rd International Conference on International Conference on Machine Learning, ICML 2016, vol. 48, pp. 421–429. JMLR.org (2016)
12. Zaremba, W., Sutskever, I.: Reinforcement learning neural turing machines. CoRR abs/1505.00521 (2015)

The Role of Coherence in Facial Expression Recognition

Lisa Graziani[1]([envelope]), Stefano Melacci[2], and Marco Gori[2]

[1] DINFO, University of Florence, Florence, Italy
lisa.graziani@unifi.it
[2] DIISM, University of Siena, Siena, Italy
{mela,marco}@diism.unisi.it

Abstract. Recognizing facial expressions from static images or video sequences is a widely studied but still challenging problem. The recent progresses obtained by deep neural architectures, or by ensembles of heterogeneous models, have shown that integrating multiple input representations leads to state-of-the-art results. In particular, the appearance and the shape of the input face, or the representations of some face parts, are commonly used to boost the quality of the recognizer. This paper investigates the application of Convolutional Neural Networks (CNNs) with the aim of building a versatile recognizer of expressions in static images that can be further applied to video sequences. We first study the importance of different face parts in the recognition task, focussing on appearance and shape-related features. Then we cast the learning problem in the Semi-Supervised setting, exploiting video data, where only a few frames are supervised. The unsupervised portion of the training data is used to enforce two types of coherence, namely temporal coherence and coherence among the predictions on the face parts. Our experimental analysis shows that coherence constraints can improve the quality of the expression recognizer, thus offering a suitable basis to profitably exploit unsupervised video sequences.

Keywords: Facial expression recognition
Convolutional Neural Networks · Learning from constraints
Coherence constraints

1 Introduction

Facial expression recognition is the problem of detecting emotions in facial images or videos. The research activity on this problem involves the scientific community that is about psychology but also the one that is about computer science and artificial intelligence. Although this task is widely studied and much progress has been made, it still remains a challenging problem, due to the variability and complexity of facial expressions. As a matter of fact, facial expressions can be categorized with respect to multiple classes of emotions. The most

C. Ghidini et al. (Eds.): AI*IA 2018, LNAI 11298, pp. 320–333, 2018.
https://doi.org/10.1007/978-3-030-03840-3_24

widely followed approach consists in considering six basic emotions plus the neutral case, and it is due to the studies of Paul Ekman [2], while other scientists provided more fine grained descriptions [14]. Facial features of expressions are mostly located around mouth, nose, and eyes, and their locations are essential in explaining and categorizing expressions [1]. Despite the large number of advanced psychological experiments about the human perception and recognition of emotions, we can trivially figure out that different face parts have a different impact in the way humans recognize emotions: the role of eyebrows when we are angry or the way we treat our mouth when we are happy or surprised, for example.

We can find several approaches that exploit Machine Learning with the aim of learning to categorize emotions from examples. Most of them are about using still images [10,13], while several more recent works also consider video sequences where actors start with a neutral expression and generate a non-neutral one [9,16]. The learning framework is usually fully supervised, and supervision is either about each training image or about each video sequence. Works that exploit video data focus on the importance of the temporal evolution of the input face. The system proposed by Fan and Tjahjadi [3] processes four sub-regions of the face: forehead, eyes/eyebrows, nose and mouth. They used an extension of the spatial pyramid histogram of gradients and dense optical flow to extract spatial and dynamic features from video sequences, and adopted a multi-class SVM-based classifier with one-to-one strategy to recognise facial expressions. Jung et al. [7] propose a neural-network-based method where two different networks are exploited: the first one extracts appearance features from image sequences, learning temporal correlations, while the other network extracts shape features from a set of facial landmarks. The two nets are combined to yield the final decision on the emotion class. Happy and Routray [5] identify salient areas with generalized discriminative features for expression classification. They only use appearance-based features, and they do not consider the time domain. The framework from Jain et al. [6] recognizes facial expressions from video sequences by modeling temporal variations within shapes. They show that shape provides important information that is sometimes hard to grasp from appearance only. Zhang and Huang [16] propose a mixed model which include a "temporal" and a "spatial" network. The former captures dynamic features from consecutive frames, while the latter is about extracting static features from still frames. More generally, we can roughly characterize the popular trends in the existing literature by the usage of (i) appearance-related (i.e., visual) features, (ii) shape-related features, (iii) features from face parts, (iv) the temporal domain (i.e., video data).

This paper investigates the application of a pool of Convolutional Neural Networks (CNNs) with the aim of building recognizers of expressions in static images, that can be further applied to video sequences. We consider both (i) appearance and (ii) shape features, but, differently from most of the existing works, we do not hand-engineer shape features, and we let the CNNs learn the right representations from special shape-only images. We propose a model that considers (iii) sub-parts of the face in addition to the entire face, motivated by the need of gaining deeper insights in the role of each component. Then, we move to the Semi-Supervised setting, exploiting (*iv*) video data. The unsupervised portion of the training data is used to enforce "temporal coherence" among consecutive frames, and "part coherence" in each frame, i.e., a coherent prediction among the CNNs that operate on the different face parts. Our experimental analysis shows that coherence constraints can improve the quality of the expression recognizer, thus offering a suitable basis to profitably exploit unsupervised video sequences.

This paper is organized as follows. The next Section formalizes the problem of facial expression recognition. Section 3 introduces our model. The role of coherence is described in Sect. 4, while experiments and conclusions (and future work) are collected in Sects. 5 and 6, respectively.

2 Facial Expression Recognition

The task of facial expression recognition that we consider in this paper consists in building a classifier that predicts one of the six universal emotions [2], that are *anger, disgust, fear, happiness, sadness, surprise*, plus the *neutral* case, and that we collect into the set Y, codified with indices from 1 to 7. The most popular inputs of the recognizer are images of faces, represented in foreground, usually with frontal orientation. When video data is considered, the recognition problem focusses on short video clips where a transition from the *neutral* state toward one the six emotions is recorded. Processing videos instead of still images can improve the recognition performance because facial expressions involve variations of the facial muscles along the temporal dimension. However, classifiers that are specifically trained to build a latent representation from a video clip $\mathcal{V}$ before taking a decision [7], cannot be immediately applied to classify images. Differently, image-based classifiers can process single frames $\{\mathcal{I}_t\}$ of a video (being t the time index) to produce a final decision over a time window, so they are more versatile from the point of view of easiness of deployment in different real-world applications. The facial expression recognition problem is usually faced in the "Fully-Supervised" setting, and, in the case of videos, the available datasets are composed of labeled video clips where we do not have access to the labelings of the single frames[1]. Nonetheless, obtaining supervised data is costly, while nowadays is pretty easy to have access to collections of unsupervised frontal view faces (web, social networks, smartphones, ...) or unsupervised video recordings (video conference/call applications). This suggests that studying the "Semi-Supervised" setting, where a portion of the training data is labeled and a larger portion is unsupervised, can be a promising way to approach the recognition task.

Motivated by the need of building a versatile emotion recognition system, we focus on a predictor that operates on still images and that we can use to make predictions on video data. The system can be trained exploiting both video and image data in a Semi-Supervised setting, taking advantage of the temporal evolution described by the video format. In detail, we consider a classifier $f(\cdot)$

---

[1] See CK+ http://www.consortium.ri.cmu.edu/ckagree/, Oulu-CASIA http://www.cse.oulu.fi/CMV/Downloads/Oulu-CASIA, MMI https://mmifacedb.eu/.

that produces a decision $y \in Y$ for each input image $\mathcal{I}$, or for a set of consecutive frames belonging to a time window W (that covers a video clip, for example),

$$y = f(\mathcal{I}) \tag{1}$$

$$y = \mathtt{majority}_{t \in W} \{f(\mathcal{I}_t)\}, \tag{2}$$

where $\mathtt{majority}$ is the majority-voting function, that returns the most frequent prediction in the time window W. Differently from the existing approaches, our system can be trained using labeled and unlabeled image databases, collected in $\mathcal{D}_{\mathcal{I}}$, or labeled and unlabeled frames extracted from the previously described labeled video sequences, collected in $\mathcal{D}_\mathcal{V}$. Due to the aforementioned properties of the existing video datasets (containing transitions from *neutral* to a certain emotion), we can artificially generate $\mathcal{D}_\mathcal{V}$ by labeling as *neutral* the very first frames of each video clip, and by assigning the provided video label to the last frames of the sequence. The frames in the internal portion of the sequence are not labeled. Formally, we have

$$\mathcal{D}_{\mathcal{I}} = \{(\mathcal{I}_i, y_i), \; i = 1, \ldots, l\} \cup \{(\mathcal{I}_i, \mathtt{none}), \; i = l+1, \ldots, l+u\},$$

where $y_i \in Y$ is the image label, and the rightmost set is fully unlabeled. Then,

$$\mathcal{D}_\mathcal{V} = \{\mathcal{D}_{\mathcal{V}_z}, \; z = 1, \ldots, v\},$$

where v is the number of available video clips and $\mathcal{D}_{\mathcal{V}_z}$ is a sequence extracted from the z-th clip,

$$\mathcal{D}_{\mathcal{V}_z} = ((\mathcal{I}_{z,t}, \mathtt{neutral}), \; t = 1, \ldots, \alpha|\mathcal{V}_z|) \oplus$$
$$((\mathcal{I}_{z,t}, \mathtt{none}), \; t = \alpha|\mathcal{V}_z| + 1, \ldots, \beta|\mathcal{V}_z|) \oplus$$
$$((\mathcal{I}_{z,t}, y_z), \; t = \beta|\mathcal{V}_z| + 1, \ldots, |\mathcal{V}_z|),$$

being $\oplus$ the sequence concatenation operator, $\mathcal{I}_{z,t} \in \mathcal{V}_z$ the t-th frame of the z-th video, and $0 < \alpha < \beta < 1$, arbitrarily chosen. In this case $y_z \in Y \setminus \{\mathtt{neutral}\}$ is the label provided with the video clip $\mathcal{V}_z$ ($\mathtt{neutral}$ is the identifier of the *neutral* class). We notice that $\mathcal{D}_\mathcal{V}$ is more informed than $\mathcal{D}_{\mathcal{I}}$, since it also stores the image/frame order and the frame grouping with respect to the videos. For this reason, we can consider $\mathcal{D}_{\mathcal{I}}$ to be an instance of the more general representation $\mathcal{D}_\mathcal{V}$, and in the rest of the paper we will focus on data represented as in $\mathcal{D}_\mathcal{V}$ without reducing the generality of what we described so far, and we will compactly indicate it with $\mathcal{D}$.

3   Model

Our model is based on CNNs that process two categories of representations of the input image/frame $\mathcal{I}$. Such categories consist in *appearance*-based (i.e., visual) representations and a *shape*-based representations.

In both the cases, we do not consider the whole $\mathcal{I}$, but only the rectangular area that is covered by the target face. We localize the face first, and then we crop the image accordingly. This choice is crucial when processing inputs with multiple faces or when the face is not well positioned at the center of the image (or more generally, at a position incoherent with the training data). The *appearance*-based representation of the face is simply a grayscale instance of the cropped face. In the case of the *shape*-based representation, we still focus on the same cropped region, but we extract a set of shape features that essentially describe the contours of the face parts, and that, in this work, consist of a set of facial landmark points. However, instead of stacking their 2D coordinates into a vector (that is only possible if the set of points is consistent among different faces), we consider a more generic approach in which the shape is simply represented by an artificial image with uniform background and in which the landmarks points are depicted at their coordinates. This allows us to treat the shape in a way that is similar to what we do with the appearance, and it opens the possibility of providing different shape "sketches" that are not only based on landmark points (but also on contour lines, for example).

In order to study the effects of the different face parts in the recognition process, we computed the appearance and shape representations for the face (as just described) and for all the face parts: mouth, nose, eyes, eyebrows. We localized the face area and a set of 68 landmark points using the localizer of Viola and Jones [15] and a landmark detector [8][2]. The detector uses the classic Histogram of Oriented Gradients (HOG) features combined with a linear classifier, an image pyramid, and a sliding window detection scheme. Cropping around each set of part-related landmarks (adding a small padding), we obtained 7 instances of appearance-based representations of the input $\mathcal{I}$ and 8 shape-based ones, since in the case of shape we also included the landmarks associated to the jaw contour. Figure 1 shows the overall 15 representations that we generate. We resized these representations to the following sizes: face area 200×200, mouth area 80×50, eye area 60×30, eyebrow area 100×30, nose area 60×100 pixels, jaw area 200×170.

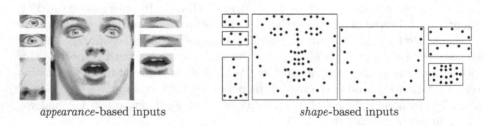

appearance-based inputs   *shape*-based inputs

Fig. 1. Representations extracted from an input image. On the left there are the 7 appearance-based representations. On the right there are the 8 shape-based representations, that we implement by sketching landmark points in artificial images.

We implemented a pool of 15 CNNs, each of them processing one of the aforementioned representations (Fig. 2). The generic CNN_h associated to the

---

[2] We used OpenCV https://opencv.org/ and the "dlib" library http://dlib.net/.

h-th representation has two convolutional layers followed by max pooling, and some fully connected layers terminated with a softmax activation that outputs a probability distribution over the emotions in Y. We indicate with $p_h(\cdot)$ the function computed by such CNN_h. All the hidden neural units have ReLu activation functions. The face-related CNNs have 32 and 64 filters on the two convolutional layers, respectively, and two fully connected layers (64 and $|Y| = 7$ neurons). The other CNNs, that are based on inputs with smaller sizes, exploit 16 and 32 filters, and a single fully connected layer ($|Y| = 7$ neurons).

The output of each of the 15 CNNs, when followed by an arg max operation (assuming 1-based indexing), is a possible instance of the function f in Eqs. (1) and (2). Formally, for a given h,

$$x_h = \texttt{representation}_h(\mathcal{I})$$
$$p_h(x_h) = \texttt{CNN}_h(x_h)$$
$$f(\mathcal{I}) = \arg\max p_h(x_h),$$

where x_h is the h-representation of the input, and $p_h(x_h)$ outputs a vector of size $|Y|$ that sums to 1. Even if our final goal is to focus on the case in which h is the index of the full-face-based classifier, in Sect. 5 we will evaluate the quality of multiple instances of f, considering the predictors on the face parts too. In the next Section we will introduce a link between the full-face and face parts.

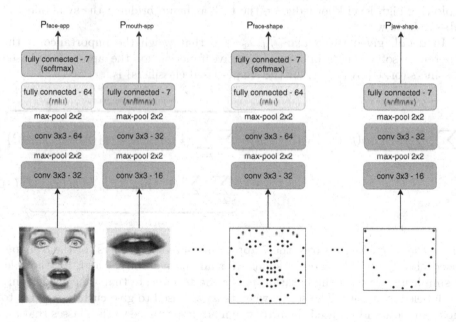

Fig. 2. Structure of CNNs employed.

4   Learning by Enforcing Coherence

We trained the pool of CNNs by minimizing an objective function involving the cross-entropy $L(p_h(x_h), y)$ between the outputs of the networks and the available labels (one-hot encoding), considering the training data $\mathcal{T} \subset \mathcal{D}$. The cross-entropy only exploits the labeled pairs in $\mathcal{T}$. However, our objective function is also composed by the penalties associated to the fulfilment of "coherence constraints" that we enforce on all the samples of $\mathcal{T}$, being them labeled or not. We have considered two types of coherence, namely "temporal coherence" and "coherence among the predictions on the face parts". The former enforces the CNNs to be coherent over time for each video sequence, i.e., it enforces the predictions to smoothly change along the time axis. This constraint introduces a regularizing effect, since it prevents the system from developing unstable models that abruptly change their decisions among consecutive frames[3]. The part-based coherence enforces each full-face-representation-based classifiers to take decisions that are coherent with the ones taken (*on average*) by the other part-based classifiers (and vice-versa). The idea behind this constraint is that the committee of the local (i.e. part-based) predictors could provide important fine-grained information that the global (face-based) predictor might not have been able to capture. We already experimented some related constraints in the case of multi-view object recognition [12], and these ideas are borrowed by the generic framework of "Learning from Constraints" [4], where a predictor is constrained exploiting high-level knowledge on the task at hand, bridging the symbolic and sub-symbolic worlds.

In detail, given two scalars $\lambda_t, \lambda_c \geq 0$ that weigh the importance of the coherence (soft) constraints, our objective function for the appearance-based classifiers (or, equivalently, for the shape-based classifiers) is

$$\sum_{h} \sum_{\substack{i=1 \\ y_i \neq \text{none}}} w_i \cdot L(p_h(x_{h,i}), y_i) + \lambda_t \overbrace{\sum_{h} \sum_{z=1}^{v} \sum_{t=2}^{|\mathcal{V}_z|} \left(1 - p_h(x_{h,(z,t-1)})' \cdot p_h(x_{h,(z,t)})\right)}^{\text{temporal coherence}}$$

$$+ \lambda_c \underbrace{\sum_{h \neq \text{face}} \sum_{i} \left(1 - p_{\text{face}}(x_{h,i})' \cdot p_h(x_{h,i})\right)}_{\text{part coherence}} \quad (3)$$

where the index h spans over the 7 appearance-based classifiers (or the 8 shape-based classifiers). The index i spans over all the pairs in $\mathcal{T}$, and, for the sake of simplicity, we used the notation $y_i \neq \text{none}$ to indicate that we consider only the labeled examples. The scalar weights w_i are used to give custom weights to the examples, and we used them to give more importance to the classes that are less represented in $\mathcal{T}$. The notation (z, t) is the index of the t-th frame in the

---

[3] We remark that the enforcement of both the coherence constraints only happens at training time.

z-th video sequence belonging to $\mathcal{T}$. Finally, `face` is used to indicate the index associated with the full-face input, and $'$ is the transpose operator.

We notice that since $p.(\cdot)$ is a probability distribution, the dot products involving two instances of $p.(\cdot)$ are 1 when such instances are equivalent (and the coherence constraints are fulfilled). The temporal constraint involves dot products between the predictions on pairs of consecutive frames in the same video clip. We kept the same structure to build the part-based constraint, where the averaging operation on the part-based classifiers is evident when $\sum_{h \neq \text{face}}$ is moved right before the second term of the dot product $p_{\text{face}}(x_{h,i})' \cdot p_h(x_{h,i})$.

5   Experimental Results

In order to validate our model, we used the popular Extended Cohn-Kanade dataset (CK+) [11]. It consists of 593 frames belonging to a set of short video sequences, where 120 subjects (different age and gender) generate expressions belonging to the following list: anger, contempt, disgust, fear, happiness, sadness and surprise. We excluded the sequences associated to "contempt", which is not included into the six universal emotions. The video sequences are composed of 10–60 frames, they start with a neutral expression and they end with the peak of one of the previously listed expressions. Each sequence is associated with an emotion label.

In order to build the Semi-Supervised set $\mathcal{D}$ described in Sect. 2, we selected $\alpha = 0.1$ and $\beta = 0.7$. We generated 5 randomizations of the whole dataset, and divided each of them into training (70%), validation (15%), and test sets (15%), keeping the original distribution of the classes in each set. The validation data was used to validate the model parameters and excluded from training. The test partition was used to measure the quality of the model, and the results presented in this Section are averaged over the 5 test partitions (when available, we also report the standard deviation in brackets). Each collection of training data consists of about $\approx 4,000$ frames, out of which $\approx 1,500$ are labeled, and they are organized into ≈ 200 sequences, while the validation data is composed of ≈ 600 frames, out of which ≈ 200 are labeled, and organized into ≈ 30 sequences. Since examples from the "neutral" class are much more represented with respect to other examples, we set $w_i = 0.1$ in Eq. (3) if i is an example from the neutral class, $w_i = 1$ otherwise. We selected the optimal λ_c, λ_t by a grid-search in $\{10^{-10}, 10^{-8}, 10^{-7}, 10^{-6}, 10^{-4}, 10^{-2}\}$, measuring frame-level accuracy (i.e., only the labeled validation frames are considered). We implemented our model using TensorFlow, and we minimized Eq. (3) by the Adam-based optimizer (starting learning rate 0.001), mini-batches of size 96, and we have trained the model for multiple epochs, stopping the procedure when the validation error started increasing.

We performed experiments comparing a system with no-coherence-constraints ($\lambda_c = \lambda_t = 0$) with other models that include either temporal or part-based coherence. We compared the cases of single-frame-level predictions (where only the labeled portion of the test set is considered) and the case of video-sequence-level predictions, following the decision rules of Eqs. (1) and (2), respectively (where W covers the full video sequence). Since examples of the different classes are not balanced in the given dataset, and in order to provide a more informative set of results, we measured two types of accuracies, namely Micro and Macro accuracies. The former is simply the percentage of correctly labeled frames/sequences, while the latter is the average of the percentages of correctly labeled frames/sequences in each emotion class.

Table 1 shows the results we obtain when testing the classifiers that operate on the full-face inputs, considering both appearance and shape representations. We also report results of an additional classifier obtained by averaging the outputs of the full set of 15 classifiers (thus mixing appearance and shape data).

Table 1. Micro and macro accuracies (std dev. in brackets) at image and video (sequence) level of the full-face-based classifiers (appearance and shape representations) and of an ensemble of the 15 classifiers (average of 15 outputs, both shape and appearance). Results without coherence constraints (NONE), with PART-based coherence and TEMP-oral coherence (results where coherence improves the accuracy are in bold).

	IMAGES					
	% Micro Acc			% Macro Acc		
	NONE	PART	TEMP	NONE	PART	TEMP
Face$_{app.}$	78.9 (3.6)	78.0 (2.0)	**81.1** (3.0)	71.2 (2.8)	**72.8** (2.2)	**72.2** (7.4)
Face$_{shape}$	71.8 (3.0)	**71.9** (3.1)	**72.5** (2.9)	61.1 (2.9)	**61.3** (3.0)	**62.1** (2.7)
Avg$_{all}$	73.7 (4.1)	71.4 (3.1)	72.1 (4.8)	71.9 (3.9)	70.2 (3.3)	69.7 (3.7)
	VIDEOS					
	% Micro Acc			% Macro Acc		
	NONE	PART	TEMP	NONE	PART	TEMP
Face$_{app.}$	75.3 (5.1)	**77.0** (3.4)	**80.0** (2.9)	64.0 (3.2)	**66.8** (3.1)	**64.4** (10.3)
Face$_{shape}$	68.5 (3.0)	68.1 (3.1)	**69.4** (2.9)	54.0 (2.9)	53.5 (3.0)	**55.5** (2.7)
Avg$_{all}$	78.3 (4.9)	77.9 (2.5)	**80.4** (5.5)	65.6 (6.5)	**65.9** (3.9)	64.8 (7.4)

Temporal coherence always improves the quality of the face-based classifiers, up to 5% in the case of sequences (micro). In the case of macro-accuracy we observe larger standard deviations, that are due to the effects of the predictions on the classes with a smaller number of examples. Such classes are less-frequently predicted, and asking for a strong temporal regularization sometimes further reduces such frequency. Coherence among parts helps in a less evident manner, especially when using shapes. Shape is less informative than appearance, resulting in a performance drop of $\approx 10\%$. The average-based classifier is only in some cases better that the face-based ones. Constraints are less effective in this case (even if we get a strong micro accuracy in videos + temporal coherence). This suggests that mixing the 15 classifiers together is not a promising

Table 2. Micro and macro accuracies (std dev. in brackets) at image and video level of all the part-based classifiers (appearance and shape representation). Results without coherence constraints (NONE), with PART-based coherence and TEMP-oral coherence (results where coherence improves the accuracy are in bold).

	IMAGES					
	% Micro Acc			*% Macro Acc*		
	NONE	PART	TEMP	NONE	PART	TEMP
Mouth$_{app.}$	70.5 (3.5)	68.6 (3.0)	**72.8** (2.6)	71.5 (6.7)	70.8 (5.8)	**73.3** (4.4)
Left-eye$_{app.}$	42.3 (6.0)	41.4 (6.0)	40.0 (4.2)	41.3 (6.5)	39.1 (4.9)	38.5 (3.9)
Right-eye$_{app.}$	42.0 (5.6)	42.0 (7.3)	40.6 (5.2)	40.8 (5.7)	40.5 (5.7)	38.8 (5.6)
Left-eyebrow$_{app.}$	40.5 (6.8)	37.7 (7.3)	38.4 (9.1)	40.1 (6.1)	37.4 (7.5)	37.6 (8.4)
Right-eyebrow$_{app.}$	40.1 (2.5)	39.7 (2.4)	**40.4** (2.9)	40.1 (3.5)	39.5 (2.8)	**40.3** (3.1)
Nose$_{app.}$	43.6 (2.9)	**44.1** (5.5)	43.4 (4.0)	41.6 (3.4)	**42.4** (4.8)	42.0 (3.7)
Mouth$_{shape}$	64.3 (2.3)	63.8 (3.5)	63.4 (3.2)	64.4 (4.7)	63.4 (4.8)	**66.2** (4.9)
Left-eye$_{shape}$	35.8 (3.4)	34.5 (3.7)	35.2 (2.6)	33.2 (3.9)	33.0 (3.4)	32.5 (2.3)
Right-eye$_{shape}$	40.7 (3.2)	40.6 (2.7)	**41.5** (3.0)	36.9 (2.4)	**37.2** (2.1)	**37.9** (2.0)
Left-eyebrow$_{shape}$	31.2 (4.4)	31.0 (3.8)	30.1 (3.5)	31.8 (1.8)	**31.9** (2.0)	31.7 (3.7)
Right-eyebrow$_{shape}$	34.3 (4.2)	33.9 (3.7)	34.1 (3.5)	34.3 (5.2)	33.4 (4.5)	33.6 (4.9)
Nose$_{shape}$	30.8 (3.7)	30.4 (3.2)	**30.9** (4.2)	30.6 (5.6)	**31.0** (5.0)	**31.6** (5.2)
Jaw$_{shape}$	37.4 (3.7)	37.2 (3.7)	37.0 (3.5)	34.1 (4.6)	**34.9** (4.3)	33.8 (4.0)
	VIDEOS					
	% Micro Acc			*% Macro Acc*		
	NONE	PART	TEMP	NONE	PART	TEMP
Mouth$_{app.}$	77.5 (7.7)	72.3 (9.0)	75.7 (6.4)	73.0 (9.5)	66.4 (8.4)	69.9 (8.7)
Left-eye$_{app.}$	49.4 (8.4)	**50.6** (4.1)	47.2 (5.9)	42.7 (5.8)	41.3 (2.7)	40.2 (6.3)
Right-eye$_{app.}$	46.8 (2.3)	**47.2** (4.9)	**47.7** (2.9)	39.8 (1.7)	39.2 (3.0)	38.9 (3.7)
Left-eyebrow$_{app.}$	43.0 (0.7)	41.7 (9.2)	42.1 (11.1)	35.2 (7.7)	34.3 (9.1)	34.3 (9.6)
Right-eyebrow$_{app.}$	43.4 (4.6)	42.5 (5.5)	**43.8** (3.2)	36.5 (6.6)	35.6 (6.8)	35.9 (4.0)
Nose$_{app.}$	44.3 (4.9)	**47.7** (5.1)	**47.2** (2.8)	35.4 (4.3)	**38.8** (4.3)	**38.9** (3.1)
Mouth$_{shape}$	71.9 (2.5)	**74.0** (3.7)	70.6 (2.8)	64.3 (4.2)	**66.1** (6.0)	**67.3** (5.0)
Left-eye$_{shape}$	45.1 (5.8)	44.7 (8.5)	45.1 (4.5)	36.6 (7.1)	**37.2** (6.1)	**38.3** (4.1)
Right-eye$_{shape}$	51.9 (2.2)	**52.8** (3.7)	**56.2** (3.7)	39.4 (3.1)	**41.5** (3.3)	**44.9** (3.9)
Left-eyebrow$_{shape}$	36.2 (6.7)	34.5 (3.4)	34.9 (3.5)	28.7 (5.1)	28.7 (3.0)	**29.3** (4.1)
Right-eyebrow$_{shape}$	40.4 (5.0)	40.0 (5.9)	**41.3** (6.7)	33.9 (5.6)	33.1 (5.0)	33.8 (7.0)
Nose$_{shape}$	37.5 (5.0)	35.7 (3.7)	34.0 (1.4)	31.4 (5.4)	28.5 (5.6)	**31.8**(4.4)
Jaw$_{shape}$	40.9 (2.5)	40.9 (2.1)	40.0 (3.7)	30.5 (2.5)	**31.3** (2.7)	29.8 (2.7)

direction, mostly because some of them have low performances that can degrade the average quality of the system.

To gain better insights about the last comment, Table 2 reports the accuracies for all the part-based classifiers. The mouth area is a very effective input for facial expression recognition, that can sometimes compete with the full-face. This is more evident in the case of videos, when comparing shape-based representations of face and mouth. As expected, the other parts are worse than the full-face, since they are just local views. The addition of both coherences sparsely helps in improving the local classifiers, with a preference toward temporal coherence. The worst results are obtained by eyebrows and nose in shape-based classification. Interestingly, the eye-based predictors score the most effective results after face and mouth in video sequences. While their appearance representation is altered when eyes get closed, their shape representation is more stable. This analysis suggests that an accurate choice of a sub-portion of the face parts could significantly help the part-based coherence constraint (since some of the parts are not very informative).

We deepened the analysis on the temporal-constrained classifiers in the case of making predictions in video sequences. Since the number of sequences is small, we selected the optimal λ_t using image-level predictions on the validation data (as already stated), leading to $\lambda_t = 10^{-8}$ and $\lambda_t = 10^{-2}$ in the case of micro and macro accuracy, respectively. Figure 3 reports the performances on videos with different values of λ_t (appearance only). We can see that the distributions of the performances are multimodal, and if we focus on the macro accuracy we observe that we could have obtained much better results with different values of λ_t. This suggests that the validation procedure has room for being improved in the case of video data.

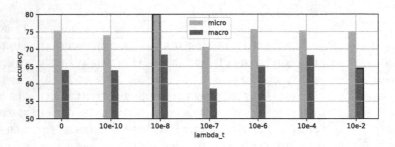

Fig. 3. Micro and macro accuracies in the case of video data, full-face-based classifier (appearance), for different values of λ_t. The black-bordered bars are the results we reported in Table 1.

In Table 3 we show the results on single emotion classes for face and mouth appearance-based classification, focussing on the case where no-coherence is introduced and the ones with a selection of the best $\lambda_c > 0$ and $\lambda_t > 0$ from the previously described experiments. "Fear" and "sadness" classes are difficult to classify because they do not involve strong facial movements, while "happiness" and "surprise" are easy to recognize. The mouth-based model has difficulties in the "neutral" class, since some emotions do not evidently alter the mouth area (the face model does not show this issue). In the "sadness" class, where the face-based model scores low accuracies, the mouth-based classifier is much more performant. This suggests that the face-related network has difficulties in developing a generalizable representation for the whole face to identify "sadness". Larger training data could help in this case.

Table 3. Accuracies (std dev. in brackets) on each class of full-face and mouth classifiers (appearance). Results without coherence constraints, with PART-based coherence and TEMPORAL coherence (results where coherence improves the accuracy are in bold).

	IMAGES						
	Anger	*Disgust*	*Fear*	*Happiness*	*Sadness*	*Surprise*	*Neutral*
face$_{app.}$ NONE	73.7 (8.8)	69.2 (12.4)	56.1 (28.9)	92.5 (9.8)	29.5 (27.7)	96.1 (1.3)	81.1 (14.9)
face$_{app.}$ PART	68.0 (28.0)	**78.2** (10.0)	**75.2** (11.8)	**98.2** (2.9)	24.3 (21.0)	**97.4** (0.7)	68.6 (9.3)
face$_{app.}$ TEMP	**77.1** (18.6)	**81.8** (14.2)	50.0 (27.7)	**97.5** (4.9)	26.2 (21.5)	95.5 (2.7)	**81.8** (15.1)
mouth$_{app.}$ NONE	66.4 (18.5)	69.6 (19.1)	59.4 (9.5)	92.7 (7.0)	75.6 (16.0)	96.6 (2.5)	40.2 (11.8)
mouth$_{app.}$ PART	66.4 (31.8)	**81.8** (14.5)	**65.1** (13.3)	**95.0** (3.8)	59.6 (27.5)	95.5 (3.1)	32.2 (12.2)
mouth$_{app.}$ TEMP	**67.8** (19.8)	**80.4** (12.3)	58.8 (9.7)	**94.8** (5.9)	72.0 (20.8)	95.2 (3.4)	**44.1** (6.8)
	VIDEOS						
	Anger	*Disgust*	*Fear*	*Happiness*	*Sadness*	*Surprise*	*Neutral*
face$_{app.}$ NONE	77.1 (7.0)	62.2 (13.3)	33.3 (21.1)	90.9 (14.1)	25.0 (27.4)	95.4 (6.2)	–
face$_{app.}$ PART	68.6 (31.8)	**71.1** (16.6)	**53.3** (16.3)	90.9 (11.5)	20.0 (18.7)	**96.9** (3.8)	–
face$_{app.}$ TEMP	77.1 (26.5)	**73.3** (11.3)	**40.0** (13.3)	**98.2** (3.6)	25.0 (15.8)	**96.9** (3.8)	–
mouth$_{app.}$ NONE	77.1 (17.1)	73.3 (16.6)	46.7 (26.7)	78.2 (14.8)	75.0 (27.4)	87.7 (11.5)	–
mouth$_{app.}$ PART	62.9 (34.5)	**77.8** (14.1)	46.7 (16.3)	74.6 (15.6)	55.0 (36.7)	81.5 (9.2)	–
mouth$_{app.}$ TEMP	74.3 (21.0)	**77.8** (14.1)	40.0 (24.9)	74.6 (14.6)	65.0 (33.9)	87.7 (10.4)	–

Temporal coherence shows better performance in "neutral", "anger" (image-level only), and "disgust" emotions. It is also helpful in the "happiness" class, where the face model performs a close-to-flawless classification. Introducing coherence among parts improves the recognition of "disgust", "fear" (face only), "happiness" (image-level only), and it slightly improves the accuracy of "surprise" for the face-based predictor.

In addiction to these results, we report that eye-based recognition reaches very good results for the "surprise" class; the accuracy of right-eye classifier with temporal coherence is 88.2%. This is due to the fact that the eyes in surprise expressions are wide open, so easily recognizable. Differently, the "neutral" class is not recognizable at all from the eyebrows. Nose-based classification (appearance) reaches an accuracy of 79.4% with temporal coherence in the "disgust" class, where the nose is wrinkled. As a final comment, we have also tried to perform some preliminary experiments involving both temporal and part-based coherences activated, and while we obtained good results on average (showing improvements with respect to the unconstrained case), they were not better than the "best" ones we obtained by activating only one of the two coherences. However, we will further investigate this point with a more detailed cross-validation and larger data collections.

6   Conclusions and Future Work

We presented a Convolutional Neural Network (CNN)-based approach to Facial Expression Recognition. Our model is based on a pool of CNNs that process distinct face parts, represented using visual (appearance) or shape-only features. In the latter case, we treated shape as a generic input of the learnable model, without manually engineering its representation. We studied the importance of the different representations on the task at hand, showing an analysis that involved all the considered face parts, and reporting results of experiments on a popular dataset composed of six basic emotions, plus the neutral case. We proposed the introduction of coherence constraints among the face-part predictors and between predictions on consecutive time instants, casting the learning problem in the Semi-Supervised setting and using video data. Our results have shown that using unsupervised training data paired with coherence constraints improves the quality of the recognizer, especially in the case of temporal coherence. Our future work will include a more detailed study on the face-part coherence, selecting only on the most promising face parts, according to the results of this study. We will also consider introducing coherence between shape and appearance-based predictors, and the use of larger collections of data, to grasp the importance of large-scale unsupervised data obtained from video conferences.

References

1. Duchenne, G.B., de Boulogne, G.B.D.: The Mechanism of Human Facial Expression. Cambridge University Press, Cambridge (1990)
2. Ekman, P., Friesen, W.V.: Constants across cultures in the face and emotion. J. Pers. Soc. Psychol. **17**(2), 124 (1971)
3. Fan, X., Tjahjadi, T.: A spatial-temporal framework based on histogram of gradients and optical flow for facial expression recognition in video sequences. Pattern Recogn. **48**(11), 3407–3416 (2015)
4. Gnecco, G., Gori, M., Melacci, S., Sanguineti, M.: Foundations of support constraint machines. Neural Comput. **27**(2), 388–480 (2015)
5. Happy, S., Routray, A.: Automatic facial expression recognition using features of salient facial patches. IEEE Trans. Affect. Comput. **6**(1), 1–12 (2015)
6. Jain, S., Hu, C., Aggarwal, J.K.: Facial expression recognition with temporal modeling of shapes. In: 2011 IEEE International Conference on Computer Vision Workshops (ICCV Workshops), pp. 1642–1649. IEEE (2011)
7. Jung, H., Lee, S., Yim, J., Park, S., Kim, J.: Joint fine-tuning in deep neural networks for facial expression recognition. In: 2015 IEEE International Conference on Computer Vision (ICCV), pp. 2983–2991. IEEE (2015)
8. Kazemi, V., Sullivan, J.: One millisecond face alignment with an ensemble of regression trees. In: Proceedings of the IEEE Conference on Computer Vision and Pattern Recognition, pp. 1867–1874 (2014)
9. Long, F., Bartlett, M.S.: Video-based facial expression recognition using learned spatiotemporal pyramid sparse coding features. Neurocomputing **173**, 2049–2054 (2016)

10. Lopes, A.T., de Aguiar, E., De Souza, A.F., Oliveira-Santos, T.: Facial expression recognition with convolutional neural networks: coping with few data and the training sample order. Pattern Recogn. **61**, 610–628 (2017)
11. Lucey, P., Cohn, J.F., Kanade, T., Saragih, J., Ambadar, Z., Matthews, I.: The Extended Cohn-Kanade dataset (CK+): a complete dataset for action unit and emotion-specified expression. In: 2010 IEEE Computer Society Conference on Computer Vision and Pattern Recognition Workshops (CVPRW), pp. 94–101. IEEE (2010)
12. Melacci, S., Maggini, M., Gori, M.: Semi–supervised learning with constraints for multi–view object recognition. In: Alippi, C., Polycarpou, M., Panayiotou, C., Ellinas, G. (eds.) ICANN 2009. LNCS, vol. 5769, pp. 653–662. Springer, Heidelberg (2009). https://doi.org/10.1007/978-3-642-04277-5_66
13. Mollahosseini, A., Chan, D., Mahoor, M.H.: Going deeper in facial expression recognition using deep neural networks. In: 2016 IEEE Winter Conference on Applications of Computer Vision (WACV), pp. 1–10. IEEE (2016)
14. Plutchik, R.: The nature of emotions: human emotions have deep evolutionary roots, a fact that may explain their complexity and provide tools for clinical practice. Am. Sci. **89**(4), 344–350 (2001)
15. Viola, P., Jones, M.: Rapid object detection using a boosted cascade of simple features. In: Proceedings of the 2001 IEEE Computer Society Conference on Computer Vision and Pattern Recognition, CVPR 2001, vol. 1, p. I. IEEE (2001)
16. Zhang, K., Huang, Y., Du, Y., Wang, L.: Facial expression recognition based on deep evolutional spatial-temporal networks. IEEE Trans. Image Process. **26**(9), 4193–4203 (2017)

Extremely Randomized CNets for Multi-label Classification

Teresa M. A. Basile[2,3](✉), Nicola Di Mauro[1], and Floriana Esposito[1]

[1] Department of Computer Science, University of Bari "Aldo Moro", Bari, Italy
[2] Department of Physics, University of Bari "Aldo Moro", Bari, Italy
teresamaria.basile@uniba.it
[3] National Institute for Nuclear Physics (INFN), Bari Division, Bari, Italy

Abstract. Multi-label classification (MLC) is a challenging task in machine learning consisting in the prediction of multiple labels associated with a single instance. Promising approaches for MLC are those able to capture label dependencies by learning a single probabilistic model—differently from other competitive approaches requiring to learn many models. The model is then exploited to compute the most probable label configuration given the observed attributes. Cutset Networks (CNets) are density estimators leveraging context-specific independencies providing exact inference in polynomial time. The recently introduced Extremely Randomized CNets (XCNets) reduce the structure learning complexity making able to learn ensembles of XCNets outperforming state-of-the-art density estimators. In this paper we employ XCNets for MLC by exploiting efficient Most Probable Explanations (MPE). An experimental evaluation on real-world datasets shows how the proposed approach is competitive w.r.t. other sophisticated methods for MLC.

Keywords: Multi-label classification · Cutset networks
Tractable probabilistic models

1 Introduction

Many real world classification problems, such as image and video annotation, functional genomics in bioinformatics, text categorization, and others [16], involve multiple label classes. Multi-Label Classification (MLC) aims at learning a mapping from an instance to a set of relevant labels. A quite common approach to MLC is to adopt a problem transformation technique—the multi-label problem is transformed into one or more single-label problems. *Binary relevance* (BR) [2,25] is a popular problem transformation method that decomposes the MLC problem into a set of single label classification problems, learning the classifiers independently, thus possibly losing the dependencies among the label variables. On the contrary, as reported in [8], it is well known that exploiting the label dependencies can significantly improve the classification performance. For instance, the *classifier chain* approach (CC) [22] exploits potential label correlations by transforming a MLC problem into a chain of binary classification

© Springer Nature Switzerland AG 2018
C. Ghidini et al. (Eds.): AI*IA 2018, LNAI 11298, pp. 334–347, 2018.
https://doi.org/10.1007/978-3-030-03840-3_25

problems—subsequent binary classifiers in the chain are built upon the predictions of preceding ones.

Density estimators like Probabilistic Graphical Models (PGMs) [13], such as Bayesian Networks (BNs), represent a powerful formalism to model and reason about MLC problems, since they are able to capture the conditional independence assumptions among random variables (RVs) into a graph-based representation. Inference routines in PGMs, such as conditional probability inference and Most Probable Explanation (MPE) inference can be exploited to solve MLC [1,6]. In a MLC scenario, we assume to have a set of N training instances $\mathcal{D} = \{(\mathbf{x}^i, \mathbf{y}^i)\}_{i=1}^N$, where each instance has a component $\mathbf{x}^i$ as a vector of M feature values $x_k^i \in \mathbb{R}$. The set $\mathcal{L} = \{y_1, \ldots, y_L\}$ denotes the output domain of possible labels. Each vector $\mathbf{x}^i$ is associated to a subset $\mathcal{Y}_i \subseteq \mathcal{L}$ of these labels, represented by an vector of L binary values $\mathbf{y}^i = [y_1^i, \ldots, y_L^i]$. The instances are assumed to to be i.i.d. according to a probability distribution $P(\mathbf{X}, \mathbf{Y})$. A common way for probabilistic classifiers to tackle the MLC problem is to learn a model h able to compute a prediction $\hat{\mathbf{y}} = [\hat{y}_1, \ldots, \hat{y}_L] = h(\hat{\mathbf{x}})$ for a given attribute instance $\hat{\mathbf{x}}$, usually solved by computing the MPE assignment for the $\mathbf{Y}$—solving $\hat{\mathbf{y}} = \mathrm{argmax}_{\mathbf{y} \in \{0,1\}^L} P(\mathbf{y}|\mathbf{x}) = \mathrm{argmax}_{\mathbf{y} \in \{0,1\}^L} P(\mathbf{y}, \mathbf{x})$, where the $\mathbf{X}$ is assumed to be observed as evidence.

However, learning and inference with PGMs can be challenging—computing exact inference is an NP-Hard problem and some approximate inference routines can be intractable in practice [23]. The need for exact and efficient inference procedures has lead to the introduction of *Tractable Probabilistic Models* (TPMs). An example of TPMs are tractable PGMs, such as mixture of tree distributions [17], trading off expressiveness in exchange of tractable inference. Recent TPMs include, among the others, Sum-Product Networks (SPNs) [19]: deep architectures encoding probability distributions by layering hidden variables as mixtures of independent components. Similarly, *Cutset Networks* (CNets), a particular kind of SPNs, have been recently proposed as easy-to-learn TPMs [21]. CNets are weighted probabilistic model trees in the form of OR-trees having tree-structured probabilistic models as leaves, and positive weights on inner edges. Inner nodes—conditioning OR nodes—are associated to random variables and outgoing branches represent conditioning on the values for those variables. Structure learning algorithmic variants for CNets have been proven to be both accurate and scalable [9,11].

Recently, both SPNs [14] and *Restricted CNets* (RCNets) [12] have been successfully applied to solve MLC problems obtaining state-of-the-art results learning a single model and exploiting its (exact) tractable inference routines to obtain the correct label predictions. In order to increase the predictive accuracy one can leverage the very well know statistical tool for robust parameter estimation: *bagging*. However, learning an optimal single CNet is a costly operation. *Extremely Randomized CNets* (XCNets) have been recently introduced in [10], as CNets that can be learned in a simple, fast and yet effective approach by performing random conditioning to grow the OR tree. While the likelihood of a single XCNet is not greater than an optimally learned CNet, ensembles of XCNets outperformed state-of-the-art density estimators.

In this work we show *Extremely Randomized Restricted CNets* (XRCNets) combining RCNets and XCNets for solving MLC problems. In particular we focus on learning *ensembles of random RCNets* (XRCNets), and then we prove them to be very competitive against more sophisticated approaches like RAkEL [24], CC [22] and SPNs based. In a thorough empirical comparison on many real-world benchmark datasets, we show our model effectiveness under commonly used metrics for MLC, like accuracy, Hamming and exact match scores.

2   Cutset Networks

Let RVs be denoted by upper-case letters, e.g. X, and their values as the corresponding lower-case letters, e.g. x. Let set of RVs be denoted by $\mathbf{X}$ and their values as $\mathbf{x}$. Given a set of RVs $\mathbf{X}$, $\mathbf{X}_{\setminus i}$ will denote $\mathbf{X} \setminus \{X_i\}$, while $\mathbf{X}_{|\mathbf{Y}}$ the restriction of $\mathbf{X}$ to $\mathbf{Y} \subseteq \mathbf{X}$. Before describing the multi-label scenario, here we assume $\mathcal{D}$ to be a set of N n-dimensional i.i.d. samples drawn from an unknown joint probability distribution $p(\mathbf{X})$. The primary goal is to learn a model $\mathcal{M}$ from $\mathcal{D}$ estimating a density $p_{\mathcal{M}}(\mathbf{X})$ as close as possible to $p(\mathbf{X})$.

2.1   Tree-Structured Models

A *directed tree-structured model* [17] over a set of RVs $\mathbf{X}$ is a BN in which each node $X_i \in \mathbf{X}$ has at most one parent. It is a tractable probabilistic model—less expressive than general BNs but performing exact complete and marginal inference in $O(n)$ [17]—encoding a distribution that factorizes as:

$$p(\mathbf{x}) = \prod_{i=1}^{n} \mathsf{p}(x_i | \mathrm{Pa}_{x_i}),\tag{1}$$

where Pa_{x_i} denotes the projection of the assignment $\mathbf{x}$ on the parent of X_i.

To learn a tree-structured model $\mathcal{M}$, one has to estimate both a tree structure $\mathcal{T}$ and the corresponding conditional probabilities $\theta_{i|\mathrm{Pa}_{X_i}} = \mathsf{p}_{\mathcal{M}}(X_i | \mathrm{Pa}_{X_i})$. An optimal model, according to the KL-divergence, can be obtained by employing the classical result from Chow and Liu [4]. We will refer to tree-structured models as Chow-Liu trees, or CLtrees, assuming the Chow-Liu algorithm has been employed to learn them. CLTrees have been employed as the core components of many tractable probabilistic models ranging from mixtures of them [17], SPNs [26] and CNets [9,11,21].

2.2   Cutset Networks

CNets, introduced in [21], are TPMs represented as a hybrid of OR trees and CLTrees as the tree leaves. Their definition has been generalized to comprise generic TPMs as leaf distributions in [10]. In particular, a CNet $\mathcal{C}$ over a set of

RVs $\mathbf{X}$, is a probabilistic weighted model tree defined via a rooted OR tree $\mathcal{G}$ and a set of TPMs $\{\mathcal{M}_i\}_{i=1}^{L}$ as leaves encoding distributions $\mathsf{p}_{\mathcal{M}_i}$ over a subset of $\mathbf{X}$, called *scope* and denoted as $\mathsf{sc}(\mathcal{M}_i)$. The scope of a CNet $\mathcal{C}$, $\mathsf{sc}(\mathcal{C})$, is the set of RVs appearing in it. Figure 1 shows a CNet over binary RVs where each circled node is an OR tree node labeled by a variable X_i. Outgoing edges are weighted by the probability w_i^0, resp. w_i^1, of conditioning X_i to the value 0 (left), resp. 1 (right). In order to encode a probability distribution it must hold $w_i^0 + w_i^1 = 1$.

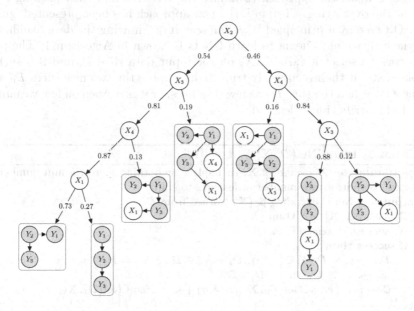

Fig. 1. Example of a CNet over the binary RVs $X_1, \dots, X_4, Y_1, \dots, Y_3$. Inner nodes, with weighted outgoing edges, on variables X_i are OR nodes, while leaf nodes—RVs grouped in a plate—represent CLtrees.

Definition 1 (Cutset network [10]). *Given binary RVs* $\mathbf{X}$, *a CNet is: 1) a TPM* $\mathcal{M}$, *with* $\mathsf{sc}(\mathcal{M}) = \mathbf{X}$; *or 2) a weighted disjunction of two CNets* $\mathcal{C}_0$ *and* $\mathcal{C}_1$ *graphically represented as an OR node conditioned on RV* $X_i \in \mathbf{X}$, *with associated weights* w_i^0 *and* w_i^1 *s.t.* $w_i^0 + w_i^1 = 1$, *where* $\mathsf{sc}(\mathcal{C}_0) = \mathsf{sc}(\mathcal{C}_1) = \mathbf{X}_{\backslash i}$.

A CNet $\mathcal{C}$ encodes a distribution factorizing as follows:

$$\mathsf{p}(\mathbf{x}) = \mathsf{p}_l(\mathbf{x}_{|\mathsf{sc}(\mathcal{C})\backslash\mathsf{sc}(\mathcal{M}_l)})\mathsf{p}_{\mathcal{M}_l}(\mathbf{x}_{|\mathsf{sc}(\mathcal{M}_l)}), \tag{2}$$

where $\mathsf{p}_l(\mathbf{x}_{|\mathsf{sc}(\mathcal{C})\backslash\mathsf{sc}(\mathcal{M}_l)}) = \prod_i (w_i^0)^{1-x_i}(w_i^1)^{x_i}$ is a factor obtained by multiplying all the weights attached to the edges of the path in the OR tree starting from the root of $\mathcal{C}$ and reaching a unique leaf node l; while, $\mathsf{p}_{\mathcal{M}_l}(\mathbf{x}_{|\mathsf{sc}(\mathcal{M}_l)})$ is the distribution encoded by the reached leaf l.

Learning CNets. Learning the structure and parameters of a CNet from data equals to perform searching in the space of probabilistic weighted model trees, requiring an exponential time w.r.t. its height k. The learning problem is tackled in a two-stage greedy fashion by: first performing a top-down search in the space of weighted OR trees, and then learning TPMs as leaf distributions according to a conditioned subset of the data.

In [21] has been introduced the first structure learning algorithm for CNets, leveraging a heuristic approach to induce the OR tree and then pruning it to overcome the overfitting. Then in [11] a new approach has been presented, growing the OR tree by a principled Bayesian search maximizing the data likelihood. The general learning schema to learn CNets is shown in Algorithm 1. The procedure tries to select a variable X_i on the input data slice $\mathcal{D}$, and if a such a variable exists, it then recursively tries to decompose the two new slices $\mathcal{D}_0$ and $\mathcal{D}_1$ over $\mathbf{X}_{\backslash i}$. When the slice $\mathcal{D}$ has few instances, or it is defined on few variables, then a leaf distribution is learned.

Algorithm 1. LearnCNet($\mathcal{D}$, $\mathbf{X}$, α, δ, σ) [10]

1: **Input:** a dataset $\mathcal{D}$ over RVs $\mathbf{X}$; α: Laplace smoothing factor; δ min number of samples to split; σ min number of features to split
2: **Output:** a CNet $\mathcal{C}$ encoding $p_\mathcal{C}(\mathbf{X})$ learned from $\mathcal{D}$
3: **if** $|\mathcal{D}| > \delta$ **and** $|\mathbf{X}| > \sigma$ **then**
4:     X_i, success $\leftarrow$ select($\mathcal{D}, \mathbf{X}, \alpha$)
5:     **if** success **then**
6:         $\mathcal{D}_0 \leftarrow \{\xi \in \mathcal{D} : \xi[X_i] = 0\}$, $\mathcal{D}_1 \leftarrow \{\xi \in \mathcal{D} : \xi[X_i] = 1\}$
7:         $w_0 \leftarrow |\mathcal{D}_0|/|\mathcal{D}|$, $w_1 \leftarrow |\mathcal{D}_1|/|\mathcal{D}|$
8:         $\mathcal{C} \leftarrow w_0 \cdot$ LearnCNet($\mathcal{D}_0, \mathbf{X}_{\backslash i}, \alpha, \delta, \sigma$) $+ w_1 \cdot$ LearnCNet($\mathcal{D}_1, \mathbf{X}_{\backslash i}, \alpha, \delta, \sigma$)
9: **else**
10:    $\mathcal{C} \leftarrow$ learnDistribution($\mathcal{D}, \mathbf{X}, \alpha$)
11: **return** $\mathcal{C}$

The algorithm proposed in [21], performs a greedy top-down search in the OR-trees space. It implements the select function as a procedure to determine the RV X_i that maximizes a reformulation of the information gain from decision tree theory. To cope with the systematic overfitting, then a post-pruning method on a validation set is introduced. As shown in [10], growing a full binary OR tree using this approach when learning a CNet on $\mathcal{D}$ over RVs $\mathbf{X}$ has time complexity $O(kmn^2)$, where $m = |\mathcal{D}|$, $n = |\mathbf{X}|$, and k is the height of the OR tree.

The approach proposed in [11] to learn CNets exploits a different approach from that in [21], by avoiding decision tree heuristics while choosing the best variable directly maximizing the data log-likelihood. As already reported in [11], the log-likelihood function of a CNet may be recursively decomposed. By exploiting the recursive nature of CNets, a CNet is grown top-down, allowing further expansion—the substitution of a CLtree with an OR node—only if it improves the structure log-likelihood. In particular, one starts with a single CLtree, learned from $\mathcal{D}$ over $\mathbf{X}$, and then checks whether there is a decomposition—an OR node on the best variable X_i applied on two CLtrees—providing a better log-likelihood than that scored by the initial tree. If such a decomposition exists, than the decomposition process is recursively applied to the sub-slices $\mathcal{D}_0$ and $\mathcal{D}_1$ over $\mathbf{X}_{\backslash i}$, testing each leaf for a possible substitution. Growing a full binary OR tree on $\mathcal{D}$ over RVs $\mathbf{X}$ with this new proposed approach has time complexity $O(kmn^3)$.

Extremely Randomized CNets. *Extremely Randomized CNets* (XCNets), proposed in [10], are CNets that are built following the procedure sketched in the Algorithm 1, where the OR split node procedure—the select function—is simplified in the most straightforward way: selecting a RV uniformly at random. As a consequence, the cost of the new select function does not directly depend anymore on the number of features and can be considered to be constant. For XCNets, growing a full binary OR tree on $\mathcal{D}$ over $\mathbf{X}$ has time complexity $O(km)$.

Ensembles of CNets. To improve the accuracy of a single model, in [21] CNets have been employed as components of a mixture of the form: $p(\mathbf{X}) = \sum_{i=1}^{c} \lambda_i \mathcal{C}_i(\mathbf{X})$, being $\lambda_i \geq 0 : \sum_{i=1}^{c} \lambda_i = 1$ the mixture coefficients. Learning such a mixture can be obtained employing EM to alternatively learn both the weights and the mixture components. A more efficient method to learn Mixtures of CNets, presented in [11], adopts bagging. For bagged CNets, mixture coefficients are set equally probable and the mixture components can be learned independently on different bootstrapped data samples. An approach adding random subspace projection to bagged CNets has been introduced in [9]. While its worst case complexity is the same as for bagging, the cost of growing the OR tree reduced by random sub-spacing is effective in practice. Finally, mixtures of CNets have been learned by exploiting some boosting approaches proposed in [20], having time complexity equals to that for bagging or even worst.

3   Sum-Product Networks for MLC

Recently, in [14] has been investigated the use of SPNs for multi-label classification, showing that SPN-based multi-label classifiers are competitive against state-of-the-art classifiers.

Sum-Product Networks [19] are deep probabilistic-models that have obtained impressive results in many tasks. An SPN represents a probability distribution over a set of random variables by a rooted directed-acyclic graph with tractable distributions as leaves, sums and products as inner nodes and weighted edges. In order to deal with MLC different approaches have been proposed in [14]. The two most effective ones that we are reporting here are one based on MPE inference and the other on pool of sequential classification.

In particular, since learning an SPN is a costly operation—differently from learning an XCNet—the general approach is to learn a single SPN $\mathcal{S}$ from the whole training set $\mathcal{D}$, using a structure learner algorithm such as those reported in [15, 26], and then perform the classification on an instance $\hat{\mathbf{x}}$ by solving:

$$\hat{\mathbf{y}} = \mathrm{argmax}_{\mathbf{y}} P_S(\mathbf{y}|\mathbf{x}).$$

The first approach (SPN$_{\mathsf{mpe}}$) solves the problem, as done in [12] for CNets, by computing the MPE inference as proposed in [19]. However, differently from CNets computing exact MPE in SPNs is NP-hard in general [5, 18]. Being the adopted MPE inference approximate, in order to improve the quality of the predictions another approach (SPN$_{\mathsf{psc}}$) inspired by the classifier chain [22] one has been proposed. Let θ be an ordering of the labels, then the θ_j-th label could be predicted by solving:

$$y_{\theta_j} = \mathrm{argmax}_{y_{\theta_j}} P_S(Y_k = 1|\mathbf{x}, y_{\theta_1}, \ldots, y_{\theta_{j-1}}).$$

Instead of fixing a single ordering, SPN$_{\mathsf{psc}}$ uses an ensemble approach, by considering a set of label orderings $\{\theta^1, \ldots, \theta^k\}$, and then computing the set $\mathcal{CC} = \{(y_1^i, \ldots, y_L^i)\}_{i=1}^k$ of classifications obtained for each order. Finally, a method to aggregate the results for producing the single prediction is adopted such as majority voting: $y_j = 1$ iff $1/k \sum_{i=1}^k y_j^i \geq 0.5$.

4   Cutset Networks for MLC

We start to explain how to exploit CNets for MLC as reported in [12], where Restricted CNets have been introduced. As already stated in the introduction, in MLC we assume to have a set of N training instances $\mathcal{D} = \{(\mathbf{x}^i, \mathbf{y}^i)\}_{i=1}^N$, where each instance has a component $\mathbf{x}^i$ as a vector of M feature values $x_k^i \in \mathbb{R}$. We assume the instances to be i.i.d. according to a probability distribution $P(\mathbf{X}, \mathbf{Y})$. We want to learn a model h able to compute a prediction $\hat{\mathbf{y}}$ for a given attribute instance $\hat{\mathbf{x}}$: $\hat{\mathbf{y}} = [\hat{y}_1, \ldots, \hat{y}_L] = h(\hat{\mathbf{x}}) = \mathrm{argmax}_{\mathbf{y} \in \{0,1\}^L} P(\hat{\mathbf{x}}, \mathbf{y})$.

CNets tackle the MLC problem computing the MPE assignment for the $\mathbf{Y}$—solving $\hat{\mathbf{y}} = \mathrm{argmax}_{\mathbf{y} \in \{0,1\}^L} P(\mathbf{y}|\mathbf{x})$. As showed in [12], differently from SPNs, even MPE queries can be answered in time linear to the size of the network. After having computed the MPE assignment for each leaf node, one can continue visiting all the OR nodes up to the root, obtaining a complete assignment. The leaf node MPE assignment associated to their scope can be computed by employing the max-out variant of the Variable Elimination Algorithm—guaranteed to be linear in the size of the trees [13].

4.1   Restricted CNets

Probabilistic multi-label classifiers can be learned by optimizing one particular loss function, trying to elicit the marginal (resp. conditional) label dependencies if they focus on modeling $p(\mathbf{Y})$ (resp. $p(\mathbf{Y}|\mathbf{X})$) [8]. The approach proposed in [12] consists in learning a CNet while optimizing the joint likelihood, but guiding the structure learning algorithm to focus on the label dependence relationships. This has been obtained by i) limiting the OR split tests to be taken on the $\mathbf{X}$ variables only while growing a CNet, and by ii) constraining both label variables and feature variables in the BNs in the leaves to have as a parent a label variable. This leads to particular networks called *Restricted CNets* (RCNets). The former constraint forces the $\mathbf{Y}$ to be strictly dependent from the $\mathbf{X}$ appearing in the internal nodes, helping the Chow-Liu algorithm to better focus on the $\mathbf{Y}$ variable interactions. The CNet in Fig. 1 is an RCNet as well, since label variables are represented only in the leaves. The latter constraint implies that features variables shall be independent given the label variables. In this way the algorithm is forced to model the dependencies among the class variables, and giving the feature to independently contribute in the MPE inference evaluation.

4.2   Extremely Randomized Restricted CNets

Here, in order to improve the classification results for a multi-label classification problem we combine the Extremely Randomized CNets (XCNet) and the Restricted CNets leading to *Extremely Randomized Restricted CNets* (XRCNets). Since the score of a single XCNet is lesser than that obtained with a regular CNet, due to its random process, we learned a mixture of XCNets adopting bagging. However, while for a single CNet the MPE inference is exact, for ensemble of CNets this in not longer true, like for SPNs—being the mixture modeled as a sum node over k models, where k is the number of the components. Hence, we have to use a kind of approximate MPE inference.

In particular, let k be the number of XRCNets used to build the mixture model. Given a test instance $\hat{\mathbf{x}}$, each XRCNet in the mixture can be queried to compute an exact MPE assignment $\hat{\mathbf{y}}_i = [\hat{y}_{i1}, \ldots, \hat{y}_{iL}], i = 1, \ldots, k$. Then, the final prediction $\hat{\mathbf{y}}$ for the instance $\hat{\mathbf{x}}$ can be computed using a simple aggregation function as follows:

$$\hat{\mathbf{y}} = \left[\mathbb{1}\left(\sum_{i=1}^{k} \hat{y}_{i1} > L/2 \right), \ldots, \mathbb{1}\left(\sum_{i=1}^{k} \hat{y}_{iL} > L/2 \right) \right].$$

Other more sophisticated approaches to better approximate the exact MPE assignment for mixtures of CNets deserves a further study.

5   Experimental Results

Here we detail the performance evaluation metrics, the datasets, the algorithms and their experimental settings. The source code of our algorithm and all the scripts to reproduce the experiments reported in this paper are made publicly available[1].

---

[1] https://github.com/nicoladimauro/mlxcnet.

5.1   Evaluation Metrics and Datasets

Given a multi-label dataset consisting of N multi-label instances $(\mathbf{x}_i, \mathbf{y}_i)_{i=1}^N$, where each $\mathbf{y}_i$ is a vector of L binary values $\mathbf{y}_i \in \{0, 1\}^L$. Let h a multi-label classifier and $\hat{\mathbf{y}}^i = h(\mathbf{x}_i) \in \{0, 1\}^L$ be the set of label memberships predicted by h for the instance $\mathbf{x}_i$. In order to assess the classifier performance, different metrics focus on different dependency relationships among the labels, and are better optimized by taking into account those dependencies [8]. We employ three different metrics to assess the performance of the considered models, namely: accuracy score $= \frac{1}{N} \sum_{i=1}^N \frac{|\mathbf{y}^i \wedge \hat{\mathbf{y}}^i|}{|\mathbf{y}^i \vee \hat{\mathbf{y}}^i|}$, Hamming score $= \frac{1}{NL} \sum_{i=1}^N \sum_{j=1}^L \mathbb{1}(y_j^i = \hat{y}_j^i)$, and exact match score $= \frac{1}{N} \sum_{i=1}^N \mathbb{1}(\mathbf{y}^i = \hat{\mathbf{y}}^i)$, where $\mathbb{1}(C)$ is the indicator function, while $\wedge$ and $\vee$ are the bitwise logical AND and OR operations, respectively [16], applied vector-wise. The accuracy score is a label set-based measure defined by the Jaccard similarity coefficients between the predicted and true set of labels. The Hamming score rewards methods for predicting individual labels well, while the exact match score computes the percentage of instances whose predicted set of labels $\hat{\mathbf{y}}$ matches the true set of labels $\mathbf{y}$ *exactly*.

We considered 10 numerical traditional multi-label datasets—accessible from the MULAN[2], MEKA[3], and LABIC[4] websites—belonging to a wide variety of application domains with their labels ranging from 6 to 174, the number of attributes ranging from 19 to 500, and the number of examples ranging from 194 to 11214. Table 1 reports the information about the adopted datasets, where M, N and L represent the number of attributes, instances, and possible labels respectively. Furthermore, for each dataset $\mathcal{D}$ the following statistics are also reported: *Label Cardinality*: $LCard(\mathcal{D}) = \frac{1}{N} \sum_{i=1}^N \sum_{j=1}^L y_j^i$, *Label Density*: $LDens(\mathcal{D}) = \frac{LCard(S)}{L}$ and *Distinct Labels*: $LDist(\mathcal{D}) = |\{\mathbf{y} | \exists (\mathbf{x}, \mathbf{y}) \in \mathcal{D}\}|$.

As reported in [12], we discretized all the numeric features for each dataset implementing the Label-Attribute Interdependence Maximization (LAIM) [3] discretization method for multi-label data. All the algorithms have been ran on the datasets preprocessed by LAIM.

5.2   Algorithms

For the experimental evaluation, we compared both RCNets (RCN) and an ensemble of 10 XRCNets (XRCN)[5], to different algorithms. First, we include in the comparison the RAndom k-labELsets (RAkEL) algorithm [24], an ensemble method for multi-label classification that constructs each member of the ensemble by considering a small random subset of labels and learning a single-label classifier for the prediction of each element in the powerset of this subset. Another competitive algorithm included is Classifier Chains (CC) [22], a chaining method that can model label correlations while maintaining acceptable computational

---

[2] http://mulan.sourceforge.net/.
[3] http://meka.sourceforge.net/.
[4] http://computer.njnu.edu.cn/Lab/LABIC/LABIC_Software.html.
[5] Both have be run with `-d 0.1`, leaving all the other parameters set to default value.

Table 1. Datasets: number of attributes (M), instances (N), and labels (L).

	Domain	M	N	L	LCard	LDens	LDist
Arts-Yahoo	Text	500	7484	26	1.653	0.063	599
Business-Yahoo	Text	500	11214	30	1.598	0.053	233
CAL500	Music	68	502	174	26.043	0.149	502
Emotions	Music	72	593	6	1.868	0.311	27
Flags	Images	19	194	7	3.391	0.484	54
Health-Yahoo	Text	500	9205	32	1.644	0.051	335
Human	Biology	440	3106	14	1.185	0.084	85
Plant	Biology	440	978	12	1.078	0.089	32
Scene	Images	294	2407	6	1.073	0.178	15
Yeast	Biology	103	2417	14	4.237	0.302	198

complexity. Both RAkEL and CC have been run using their openly available implementations in MEKA (See footnote 3) (release 1.9.2), with parameters set as default values[6].

Finally, we included the two algorithms based on SPNs [14], SPN_{mpe} and SPN_{psc}[7]. After having learned an SPN on the training dataset $(\mathbf{x}_i, \mathbf{y}_i)$, SPN_{mpe} performs classification on an instance $\mathbf{x}$ by computing the approximate MPE $argmax_\mathbf{y} P(\mathbf{y}|\mathbf{x})$, while SPN_{psc} combines by majority voting the predictions of an ensemble of sequential classifications.

All experiments have been run on a 8-core Intel Xeon E5-1620 @3.5 GHz with 16 Gb of RAM and Linux kernel 4.4.0-59.

5.3   Results and Discussion

The results over a 10-fold cross validation for each evaluation metric and for each classification algorithm on all the datasets are reported in Table 2 for the accuracy score, Table 3 for the Hamming score, and Table 4 for the exact match score. In order to assess whether the differences of the scores reported in Tables 2, 3 and 4 are statistically significant, a t-test has been adopted comparing the means with a significance level $p = 0.05$. In each column of the tables, a ↑ (resp. ↓) denotes that XRCN (resp. the competitor) outperforms the competitor (resp. XRCN) with a difference statistically significant.

---

[6] RAkEL, resp. CC, has been executed with Support Vector Machines with polynomial kernel, resp. with C4.5 decision trees, as base classifier.

[7] We executed the code avalible at https://github.com/giulianavll/MLC-SPN to reproduce the results reported in this paper. The algorithm used for learning the structure of SPNs corresponds to that reported in [26].

Table 2. Accuracy scores of CNets and the competitors on the ten datasets.

Dataset	CNets		Competitors			
	XRCN	RCN	SPN$_{psc}$	SPN$_{mpe}$	RAkEL	CC
Arts	0.429	0.425	0.334↑	0.379↑	0.293↑	0.402↑
Business	0.720	0.728	0.732↓	0.720	0.729	0.729
Cal	0.172	0.184	0.220↓	0.217↓	0.001↑	0.199↓
Emotions	0.584	0.524	0.586	0.555↑	0.532↑	0.493↑
Flags	0.548	0.544	0.537	0.541	0.576	0.554
Health	0.586	0.609	0.627↓	0.619↓	0.560↑	0.616↓
Human	0.330	0.335	0.180↑	0.209↑	0.276↑	0.318
Plants	0.337	0.322	0.146↑	0.218↑	0.301↑	0.298↑
Scene	0.705	0.680	0.682↑	0.634↑	0.687	0.606↑
Yeast	0.471	0.441	0.472	0.459	0.508↓	0.444↑
↑/↓			4/3	5/2	6/1	5/2
Avrg score	0.488	0.479	0.452	0.455	0.446	0.466

First of all, as we can see, the ensemble of XRCNets obtains on average scores better that those obtained with a single RCNet, proving the validity of the ensemble approach—even if each components of the ensemble are learned completely at random, their aggregation provides more precise predictions when compared to a single RCNet. Furthermore, for each metric the average score over all the datasets is always greater than that obtained by other competitors.

Table 3. Hamming scores of CNets and the competitors on the ten datasets.

Dataset	CNets		Competitors			
	XRCN	RCN	SPN$_{psc}$	SPN$_{mpe}$	RAkEL	CC
Arts	0.939	0.937	0.945↓	0.942↓	0.947↓	0.936↑
Business	0.972	0.974	0.976↓	0.975↓	0.976↓	0.975↓
Cal	0.860	0.854	0.856↑	0.833↑	0.850↑	0.845↑
Emotions	0.811	0.770	0.799	0.783↑	0.773↑	0.748↑
Flags	0.707	0.701	0.689	0.697	0.714	0.705
Health	0.963	0.966	0.969↓	0.968↓	0.965↓	0.967↓
Human	0.914	0.890	0.917↓	0.912↑	0.886↑	0.890↑
Plants	0.913	0.881	0.910	0.899	0.870↑	0.884↑
Scene	0.902	0.882	0.903	0.892	0.895	0.863↑
Yeast	0.790	0.753	0.770↑	0.757↑	0.779↑	0.752↑
↑/↓			2/4	4/3	5/3	7/2
Avrg score	0.877	0.861	0.873	0.866	0.865	0.857

Table 4. Exact match scores of CNets and the competitors on the ten datasets.

Dataset	CNets		Competitors			
	XRCN	RCN	SPN$_{psc}$	SPN$_{mpe}$	RAkEL	CC
Arts	0.304	0.327	0.278↑	0.309	0.222↑	0.319
Business	0.558	0.571	0.584↓	0.570↓	0.570	0.575
Cal	0.000	0.000	0.000	0.000	0.000	0.000
Emotions	0.336	0.246	0.352	0.325	0.260↑	0.265↑
Flags	0.155	0.140	0.139	0.144	0.170	0.170
Health	0.436	0.473	0.514↓	0.504↓	0.387↑	0.496↓
Human	0.275	0.251	0.161↑	0.186↑	0.176↑	0.254
Plants	0.316	0.292	0.139↑	0.207↑	0.183↑	0.267↑
Scene	0.612	0.569	0.644↓	0.599	0.589	0.561↑
Yeast	0.147	0.138	0.160	0.158	0.141	0.156
↑/↓			3/3	2/2	5/0	3/1
Avrg score	0.314	0.301	0.297	0.300	0.270	0.306

As regards the accuracy score, XRCN obtains better results when compared to all the competitors, while for the Hamming and exact match scores the values seems to be comparable to that of SPN$_{psc}$. Indeed, XRCN outperforms the competitors in 6 (RAkEL), 5 (SPN$_{mpe}$ and CC), and 4 (SPN$_{psc}$) in terms of the accuracy score. In terms of the Hamming score, XRCN is superior to the others in 7 (CC), 5 (RAkEL), 4 (SPN$_{mpe}$), and 2 (SPN$_{pcs}$) cases. Regarding the exact match score, XRCN is superior to the competitors in 5 (RAkEL), 3 (SPN$_{psc}$ and CC), and 2 (SPN$_{mpe}$) cases.

It is important to note that, even if we used a fixed inference procedure, i.e. MPE, it is robust for each score. Indeed, as reported in [7], MPE inference is maximizer of the exact match score, while marginal inference for each label is a maximizer for the Hamming score.

Overall, while XRCN outperforms problem transformation schemes such a RAkEL and CC, it is competitive with respect to the approaches based on SPNs for the Hamming and exact match scores and outperforming them for the accuracy score. Adopting sophisticated schemes to infer the correct label predictions such those used in SPN$_{psc}$ represent an interesting future work.

6   Conclusion

In this paper, we employed the recently introduced tractable probabilistic model XCNets to tackle the MLC problem. XCNets reduce the structure learning complexity making able to learn ensembles of XCNets outperforming state-of-the-art density estimators. The experimental evaluation on real-world datasets showed how our approach can effectively improve the accuracy, exact match and Hamming scores, proving itself to be highly competitive against complex approaches.

References

1. Antonucci, A., Corani, G., Mauá, D.D., Gabaglio, S.: An ensemble of Bayesian networks for multilabel classification. In: IJCAI, pp. 1220–1225 (2013)
2. Boutell, M.R., Luo, J., Shen, X., Brown, C.M.: Learning multi-label scene classification. Pattern Recogn. **37**(9), 1757–1771 (2004)
3. Cano, A., Luna, J.M., Gibaja, E.L., Ventura, S.: LAIM discretization for multilabel data. Inf. Sci. **330**, 370–384 (2016)
4. Chow, C., Liu, C.: Approximating discrete probability distributions with dependence trees. IEEE Trans. Inf. Theory **14**(3), 462–467 (1968)
5. Conaty, D., de Campos, C.P., Mauá, D.D.: Approximation complexity of maximum a posteriori inference in sum-product networks. In: UAI (2017)
6. Corani, G., Antonucci, A., Mauá, D.D., Gabaglio, S.: Trading off speed and accuracy in multilabel classification. In: van der Gaag, L.C., Feelders, A.J. (eds.) PGM 2014. LNCS (LNAI), vol. 8754, pp. 145–159. Springer, Cham (2014). https://doi.org/10.1007/978-3-319-11433-0_10
7. Dembczyński, K., Cheng, W., Hüllermeier, E.: Bayes optimal multilabel classification via probabilistic classifier chains. In: ICML, pp. 279–286 (2010)
8. Dembczyński, K., Waegeman, W., Cheng, W., Hüllermeier, E.: On label dependence and loss minimization in multi-label classification. Mach. Learn. **88**(1), 5–45 (2012)
9. Di Mauro, N., Vergari, A., Basile, T.M.A.: Learning Bayesian random cutset forests. In: Esposito, F., Pivert, O., Hacid, M.-S., Raś, Z.W., Ferilli, S. (eds.) ISMIS 2015. LNCS (LNAI), vol. 9384, pp. 122–132. Springer, Cham (2015). https://doi.org/10.1007/978-3-319-25252-0_13
10. Di Mauro, N., Vergari, A., Basile, T.M.A., Esposito, F.: Fast and accurate density estimation with extremely randomized cutset networks. In: Ceci, M., Hollmén, J., Todorovski, L., Vens, C., Džeroski, S. (eds.) ECML PKDD 2017. LNCS (LNAI), vol. 10534, pp. 203–219. Springer, Cham (2017). https://doi.org/10.1007/978-3-319-71249-9_13
11. Di Mauro, N., Vergari, A., Esposito, F.: Learning accurate cutset networks by exploiting decomposability. In: Gavanelli, M., Lamma, E., Riguzzi, F. (eds.) AI*IA 2015. LNCS (LNAI), vol. 9336, pp. 221–232. Springer, Cham (2015). https://doi.org/10.1007/978-3-319-24309-2_17
12. Di Mauro, N., Vergari, A., Esposito, F.: Multi-label classification with cutset networks. In: PGM, vol. 52, pp. 147–158 (2016)
13. Koller, D., Friedman, N.: Probabilistic Graphical Models: Principles and Techniques. MIT Press, Cambridge (2009)
14. Llerena, J.V., Mauá, D.D.: On using sum-product networks for multi-label classification. In: BRACIS, pp. 25–30 (2017)
15. Lowd, D., Rooshenas, A.: The libra toolkit for probabilistic models. JMLR **16**, 2459–2463 (2015)
16. Madjarov, G., Kocev, D., Gjorgjevikj, D., Deroski, S.: An extensive experimental comparison of methods for multi-label learning. Pattern Recogn. **45**(9), 3084–3104 (2012)
17. Meila, M., Jordan, M.I.: Learning with mixtures of trees. JMLR **1**, 1–48 (2000)
18. Peharz, R., Gens, R., Pernkopf, F., Domingos, P.: On the latent variable interpretation in sum-product networks. IEEE Trans. Pattern Anal. Mach. Intell. **39**(10), 2030–2044 (2017)

19. Poon, H., Domingos, P.: Sum-product network: a new deep architecture. In: NIPS 2010 Workshop on Deep Learning and Unsupervised Feature Learning (2011)
20. Rahman, T., Gogate, V.: Learning ensembles of cutset networks. In: AAAI (2016)
21. Rahman, T., Kothalkar, P., Gogate, V.: Cutset networks: a simple, tractable, and scalable approach for improving the accuracy of Chow-Liu trees. In: Calders, T., Esposito, F., Hüllermeier, E., Meo, R. (eds.) ECML PKDD 2014. LNCS (LNAI), vol. 8725, pp. 630–645. Springer, Heidelberg (2014). https://doi.org/10.1007/978-3-662-44851-9_40
22. Read, J., Pfahringer, B., Holmes, G., Frank, E.: Classifier chains for multi-label classification. In: Buntine, W., Grobelnik, M., Mladenić, D., Shawe-Taylor, J. (eds.) ECML PKDD 2009. LNCS (LNAI), vol. 5782, pp. 254–269. Springer, Heidelberg (2009). https://doi.org/10.1007/978-3-642-04174-7_17
23. Roth, D.: On the hardness of approximate reasoning. Artif. Intell. **82**(1–2), 273–302 (1996)
24. Tsoumakas, G., Katakis, I., Vlahavas, I.: Random k-labelsets for multilabel classification. IEEE Trans. Knowl. Data Eng. **23**(7), 1079–1089 (2011)
25. Tsoumakas, G., Katakis, I., Vlahavas, I.: Mining multi-label data. In: Maimon, O., Rokach, L. (eds.) Data Mining and Knowledge Discovery Handbook, 2nd edn, pp. 667 685. Springer, Boston (2009). https://doi.org/10.1007/978 0 387 09823 4_34
26. Vergari, A., Di Mauro, N., Esposito, F.: Simplifying, regularizing and strengthening sum-product network structure learning. In: Appice, A., Rodrigues, P.P., Santos Costa, V., Gama, J., Jorge, A., Soares, C. (eds.) ECML PKDD 2015. LNCS (LNAI), vol. 9285, pp. 343–358. Springer, Cham (2015). https://doi.org/10.1007/978-3-319-23525-7_21

Bayesian Markov Logic Networks
Bayesian Inference for Statistical Relational Learning

Radim Nedbal[(⊠)] and Luciano Serafini[(⊠)]

Fondazione Bruno Kessler, Via Sommarive 18, 38123 Trento, Italy
{nedbal,serafini}@fbk.eu

Abstract. One of the most important foundational challenge of Statistical relational learning is the development of a uniform framework in which learning and logical reasoning are seamlessly integrated. State of the art approaches propose to modify well known machine learning methods based on parameter optimization (e.g., neural networks and graphical models) in order to take into account structural knowledge expressed by logical constraints. In this paper, we follow an alternative direction, considering the Bayesian approach to machine learning. In particular, given a partial knowledge in hybrid domains (i.e., domains that contains relational structure and continuous features) as a set T of axioms and a stochastic (in)dependence hypothesis $\mathscr{F}$ encoded in a first order language $\mathcal{L}$, we propose to model it by a probability distribution function (PDF) $p(\mathbf{x} \mid T, \mathscr{F})$ over the $\mathcal{L}$-interpretations $\mathbf{x}$. The stochastic (in)dependence $\mathscr{F}$ is represented as a Bayesian Markov Logic Network w.r.t. a parametric undirected graph, interpreted as the PDF. We propose to approximate $P(\mathbf{x} \mid T, \mathscr{F})$ by variational inference and show that such approximation is possible if and only if $\mathscr{F}$ satisfies a property called *orthogonality*. This property can be achieved also by extending $\mathcal{L}$, and adjusting T and $\mathscr{F}$.

1 Introduction and Related Work

The last decade has seen the emergence of a powerful new framework for building sophisticated real-world applications based on *statistical relational learning* (SRL). A corner stone of this framework is the use of graphical models to represent complex *probability density functions* (PDFs) of continuous and discrete random variables. Another, more recent corner stone, is *Markov logic* [5] that builds on the theory of *Markov random fields* (MRFs) [7]. In Markov logic, a *first-order logic* (FOL) theory is represented as a template for constructing undirected graphs. This is the main step towards lifting up MRFs to FOL. In particular, *hybrid Markov logic networks* (HMLNs) [5,15] are very expressive: they can represent PDFs over interpretations of a FOL fragment that contains numeric functions. In theory, also an infinite number of constants is allowed [13]. However, to the best of our knowledge, none of the implementations of Markov logic allows for infinite domains. *Alchemy* [8] is arguably the best known and most developed one. It calculates a *maximum a posteriori* (MAP) or *maximum-likelihood*

© Springer Nature Switzerland AG 2018
C. Ghidini et al. (Eds.): AI*IA 2018, LNAI 11298, pp. 348–361, 2018.
https://doi.org/10.1007/978-3-030-03840-3_26

[11, Chapter 20] approximation of the posterior PDF using the *stochastic approximation schema* presented by *sampling methods* [1, Chapter 11].

The learning and inference in graphical models have been based on maximum likelihood or MAP approaches, and sampling techniques for a long time. Unfortunately, sampling techniques tend to be computationally costly and do not scale well to real-world applications involving large data sets [2]. Nevertheless, it has been recognized in machine learning community that adoption of Bayesian viewpoint and variational approach [1, Chapter 10] provides a principled way to the development of fast, deterministic, approximate inference algorithms. There are some attempts in this direction aimed at probabilistic programming [16], Bayesian networks [3,17], arbitrary graphical probability models [6,14] or even arbitrary probability models [9] that have the potential to scale well to real-world applications involving large data sets. However, an attempt that aims at integrating (graphical) probability models with FOL is still missing. This paper takes up this challenge and elaborates on adoption of Bayesian viewpoint and variational approach in a framework for SRL. We call it *Bayesian Markov logic network* (BMLN) to highlight the fact that it builds on the Markov logic, and in fact, it can be seen as a variational analogue of HMLNs.

In BMLN as well as in HMLN, the domain is specified in FOL. The underlying model of both HMLN and BMLN is a Gibbs random field (GRF). The first main difference between HMLN and BMLN is constituted by the shape of the potential functions. In HMLN, the potential function reflects the number of grounding of the formula that are satisfied by a variable assignment and any positive function for the continuous terms; the potential function in BMLN (defined in (4)), is a weighted PDF. Though this might look as a technical internal difference, this is indeed one of the key contribution of this work. Thanks to the shape of the weight function, we were able to develop a Bayesian inference algorithm for SRL. The deeper difference between the two approaches, which can be seen also as one of the main contribution of the paper is the fact that BMLN does not need parameter learning, as it applies a Bayesian inference, marginalizing out all the parameters of the model. In HMLN, instead, inference is performed by first, learning the parameters that better fit the data, via optimize the pseudo-likelihood, and then the inference is performed with the network instantiated with the found parameters.

2   The Model and Its Random Vector Representation

In general, SRL is concerned with *domain models* that exhibit both uncertainty and complex *relational structure*. Intuitively, a domain model is a probability distribution over the set of interpretations of a first order language. In what follows, we describe the language and how a model can be specified and queried in such a language.

2.1   The Intended Model

We suppose a FOL language $\mathcal{L}$. Let $S_\mathcal{O}$ and $S_\mathbb{R}$ be logical constants interpreted as a set $\mathcal{O}$ of non-numerical *objects* and $\mathbb{R}$, respectively. Each n-ary predicate symbol is of sort $S_\mathcal{O}^n$ or $S_\mathbb{R}^n$ (i.e., no mixed sort predicates are admitted), while n-functions (including constants as 0-ary functions) are of sort $S_\mathcal{O}^n \to S_\mathcal{O}$ or $S_\mathcal{O}^n \to S_\mathbb{R}$. Functions of sort $S_\mathcal{O}^n \to S_\mathbb{R}$ are also called *numeric functions*, and they describe numeric attributes of the domain objects. $\mathcal{L}$ also includes real functions (i.e., functions of sort $S_\mathbb{R}^n \to S_\mathbb{R}$).

- Function symbols of sort $S_\mathcal{O}^n \to S_\mathcal{O}$, $S_\mathcal{O}^n \to S_\mathbb{R}$ are respective mappings $\mathcal{O}^n \to \mathcal{O}$, $\mathcal{O}^n \to \mathbb{R}$;
- n-ary predicate symbols are mappings from $\mathcal{O}^n$ to the truth values $\{true, false\}$.
- symbols of sort $S_\mathbb{R}$ are interpreted as the usual real functions (e.g., $+$ as the summation, $<$ as the less then, 1.5 as itself).

Example 1. We introduce a variation of the well known "Smoking, Friendship, Cancer" example introduced in [5]. For the sake of simplicity, we consider three non-numerical constants: *Ann*, *Bob*, and *Cole*. Besides, we consider three predicate symbols: *Sm* is short for *Smokes*, *Ca* for *Cancer*, and *Fr* for *Friends*; and one function symbol *cig*, which is short for *cigarettes*. Note that *Sm* and *Ca* are of the type $S_\mathcal{O}$, *Fr* is of the type $S_\mathcal{O}^2$, and *cig* is of the type $S_\mathcal{O} \to S_\mathbb{R}$. An example of a function symbol of the type $S_\mathcal{O} \to S_\mathcal{O}$ would be *fatOf*, where *fatOf* is short for *fatherOf*. An example of a function symbol of the type $S_\mathbb{R}^2 \to S_\mathbb{R}$ would be *sum*, where *sum* is a logical constant for summation. Some well formed formulae of this language are: $cig(Bob) = 50$, $\neg\exists x\, cig(x) < 0$, $\forall x, y \colon \neg Sm(x) \wedge cig(y) > 50 \to \neg Fr(x, y)$.   ◁

Following the approach of *Markov logic networks* (MLNs) [5,10] and HMLNs [5,15], we propose that the domain model be specified by a pair $\langle \mathcal{T}, \mathcal{F} \rangle$ where $\mathcal{T}$ is a set of axioms in $\mathcal{L}$, e.g., $\forall x \colon Sm(x) \leftrightarrow cig(x) > 0$, $\forall x \colon 0 \le cig(x) \le 100$, and $cig(Cole) = 9$ and $\mathcal{F}$ is a set of so called *dependence terms* (DT).

Definition 1 (Dependence term). *A DT is a pair $\langle \varphi, \tau \rangle$ of an $\mathcal{L}$-formula φ that contains no numeric term and a (possibly empty) set τ of tuples of* numeric terms[1].   ◇

A DT specifies stochastic dependence among ground atoms and ground terms that appear together in at least one grounding of the DT. The numeric terms from τ play the role of numeric properties of φ.

Example 2 (Smoking, friendship, cancer) **Axioms** include

- $\neg Sm(Ann)$
- $cig(Ann) = 0, cig(Bob) = 50, cig(Cole) = 9$
- $\neg Fr(Ann, Cole)$

---

[1] A numeric term is a term that evaluates to a (real) number.

– $\forall x, y \colon Fr(x, y) \to Fr(y, x)$;
– $\forall x \colon Sm(x) \leftrightarrow cig(x) > 0$.

Stochastic (in)dependence encoded as **DTs** are

(F_1) $\varphi_1 \overset{\triangle}{=} \forall x, y, z \colon Fr(x, y) \wedge Fr(y, z) \to Fr(x, z)$, $\tau_1 = \{\}$. Friends of friends are friends (notice that this is not given as an axiom but as a dependence term with $\tau_1 = \{\}$ since it is not always true; it does not depend on numeric features);

(F_2) $\varphi_2 \overset{\triangle}{=} \forall x \colon Sm(x) \wedge Ca(x)$, $\tau_2 \overset{\triangle}{=} \{\langle cig(x) \rangle\}$, smoking, cancer and a number of cigarettes smoked are stochastically dependent;

(F_3) $\varphi_3 \overset{\triangle}{=} \forall x, y \colon Fr(x, y) \to (Sm(x) \leftrightarrow Sm(y))$,
$\tau_3 \overset{\triangle}{=} \{\langle |age(x) - age(y)|, |cig(x) - cig(y)| \rangle\}$, if two people are friends, either both smoke or neither does, but it depends also on the age difference and the difference of numbers of smoked cigarettes. ◁

The intended domain model is a probability space[2] in which we can measure probability $P(\mathcal{T})$ of every theory $\mathcal{T}$ specified in $\mathcal{L}$. In general, a query is formulated as a conditional probability $P(\mathcal{T}_2 \mid \mathcal{T}_1, \mathscr{F})$ of a $\mathcal{L}$-theory $\mathcal{T}_2$ given a domain model specification $\mathcal{T}_1, \mathscr{F}$.

Example 3. Examples of queries are: What is

(Q1) the posterior probability that *Ann* smokes: $P(Sm(Ann) \mid \mathcal{T}, \mathscr{F})$;
(Q2) the posterior probability that smoking causes cancer: $P(\forall x \colon Sm(x) \leftrightarrow Ca(x) \mid \mathcal{T}, \mathscr{F})$;
(Q3) the posterior probability that a smoker has cancer: $P(Ca(x) \mid Sm(x), \mathcal{T}, \mathscr{F})$;
(Q4) the PDF of the posterior probability $P(n > cig(x) \mid \mathcal{T}, \mathscr{F})$ of smoked cigarettes;
(Q5) the PDF of the posterior probability $P(n > cig(x) \mid Ca(x), \mathcal{T}, \mathscr{F})$ of cigarettes that are smoked by people who develop cancer;
(Q6) the posterior probability of developing cancer if one smokes a specific number n of cigarettes daily: $P(Ca(x) \mid cig(x) = n, \mathcal{T}, \mathscr{F})$. ◁

2.2 Random Vector Representation of the Intended Model

Prominent approaches to SRL are characterized by the representation that they use to capture the input information about the domain model in a framework suitable for efficient query-answering algorithms. Specifically, a theory can by represented as a set of Herbrand interpretations, which, under *Known functions assumption* (KFA), can be encoded as a numeric vector. This leads naturally to the representation by a random vector.

Consider $(\mathbb{R}^k, \mathcal{B}^k)$, the *Borel σ-field* on $\mathbb{R}^k$. The Borel function, whose domain coincides with the set of all $\mathcal{L}$-interpretations is a random vector and will be denoted by $\mathbf{X} \colon \mathcal{I} \mapsto \mathbf{x}$, where $\mathbf{x} \in \mathbb{R}^k$, defined as follows.

---

[2] Familiarity with probability theory as presented in e.g., [12, Sects. 1.1 and 1.2] is assumed.

Definition 2 (Random vector X). *The random vector* $\mathbf{X}$ *contains*

- *random variables* $X_{R(c_1,\ldots,c_n)}$ *for grounded atomic formulas* $R(c_1,\ldots,c_n)$, *where* R *is a relation symbol and* $c_1,\ldots,c_n$ *constants of sort* $S_{\mathcal{O}}$. *We define* $X_{R(c_1,\ldots,c_n)}(\mathcal{I}) \stackrel{\triangle}{=} 1$ *if* $\mathcal{I} \models R(c_1,\ldots,c_n)$ *and* 0 *otherwise;*
- *one real random variable* $X_{g(c_1,\ldots,c_n)}$ *for each grounded term* $g(c_1,\ldots,c_n)$, *with* g *of type* $S_{\mathcal{O}}^n \to S_{\mathbb{R}}$. *We define* $X_{g(c_1,\ldots,c_n)}(\mathcal{I}) \stackrel{\triangle}{=} \mathcal{I}(g(c_1,\ldots,c_n))$.

Example 4 (Continued from Example 2). The random vector $\mathbf{X}$ is a vector of random variables. Every ground atom $Sm(Ann)$, $Sm(Bob)$, $Sm(Cole)$, $Ca(Ann)$, $Ca(Bob)$, $Ca(Cole)$, and another 9 ground atoms for Fr has its respective binary random variable X_i. For instance $X_{Sm(Ann)}(\mathcal{I}) = 1$ iff $\mathcal{I} \models Sm(Ann)$. Besides, every ground numeric term $cig(Ann)$, $cig(Bob)$, $cig(Cole)$ has its respective real random variable. For instance, $X_{cig(Ann)}(\mathcal{I}) = \mathcal{I}(cig(Ann))$. So we can write $\mathbf{x} \in \mathbb{R}^{18}$.   ◁

Note that $\mathbf{X}$ never contains random variables for ground non-numeric terms (e.g., *fatOf*) since, by KFA, their interpretation is always known. Similarly, $\mathbf{X}$ never contains random variables for ground atoms or ground numeric terms of logical constants (e.g., $=$, $<$, summation), whose interpretation is fixed. In particular, observe that every ground numeric term is either of type $S_{\mathcal{O}}^n \to S_{\mathbb{R}}$ for some $n \geq 0$, and it is denoted as X_j for some j, $1 \leq j \leq k$. Or we get it by grounding a term of type $S_{\mathbb{R}}^n \to S_{\mathbb{R}}$ for some $n \geq 1$. In this latter case, the term denotes an interpreted function, whose arguments are interpreted functions or/and functions of types $S_{\mathcal{O}}^n \to S_{\mathbb{R}}$, $n \geq 0$. By finite induction, we get a finite number of, say m, ground numeric terms $X_{i_1}, \ldots, X_{i_m}$ of types $S_{\mathcal{O}}^n \to S_{\mathbb{R}}$, $n \geq 0$, that occur in the ground term of type $S_{\mathbb{R}}^n \to S_{\mathbb{R}}$.

The representation based on $\mathbf{X}$ restricts us to the domain model $(\mathbf{Dom\,X}, \sigma(\mathbf{X}), P)$, where $\mathbf{Dom\,X}$ is the set of Herbrand interpretations of $\mathcal{L}$, and P is a probability measure on a sigma algebra $\sigma(\mathbf{X})$ of $\mathbf{Dom\,X}$. The domain model is represented as $(\mathbb{R}^k, \mathcal{B}^k, P_{\mathbf{X}})$.

Since $\mathbf{Ran\,X} = \{0,1\}^\ell \times \mathbb{R}^{k-\ell}$, we define ν as the *product measure*

$$\nu = \nu_c^\ell \times m^{k-\ell} \tag{1}$$

on $(\mathbb{R}^k, \mathcal{B}^k)$, where

- ℓ is the number of components of $\mathbf{X}$ that represent respective ground atoms;
- ν_c is a *counting measure* on $(\mathbb{R}, \mathcal{B})$ defined for every $B \in \mathcal{B}$ as $B \mapsto |B \cap \{0,1\}|$;
- m denotes the *Lebesgue measure* on $(\mathbb{R}, \mathcal{B})$.

Clearly, ν is σ-finite, and it can be verified that ν fulfils $\mathbf{X}^{-1}(B) = \emptyset \implies \nu(B) = 0$ for $B \in \mathcal{B}^k$. To this end, observe that for an arbitrary B, $\mathbf{X}^{-1}(B) = \emptyset$ iff B is disjoint with $\mathbf{Ran\,X}$, and $\nu_c(B) = 0$ for every B that includes neither 0 nor 1. Consequently, we can formulate the following Theorem.

Theorem 1 (Interpretation). *There is a one-to-one correspondence between probability measures P on $\sigma(\mathbf{X})$ that fulfil*

$$\nu(B) = 0 \implies P\left(\mathbf{X}^{-1}(B)\right) = 0, \qquad B \in \mathcal{B}^k, \tag{2}$$

and classes of a.e. ν identical PDFs on $\mathbb{R}^k$. This bijection is given by

$$P\left(\mathbf{X}^{-1}(B)\right) = \int_B p_{\mathbf{X}} \, d\nu, \qquad B \in \mathcal{B}^k. \tag{3}$$

The interpretation based on PDFs w.r.t. ν imposes another restriction on P given by (2) and the Definition (1) of the measure ν on $\mathcal{B}^k$. Note that (2) in conjunction with using the Lebesgue measure in the Definition (1) of ν imply that $P(\mathcal{T}) = 0$ for every $\mathcal{T}$, $\mathcal{T} = \{\mathcal{I} \mid \mathcal{I}(g)(\mathbf{b}) = x_k\}$, where $g(\mathbf{b})$ denotes a ground numeric term and x_k is a real. Indeed, let X_k be w.l.o.g. the random variable of $\mathbf{X}$ that represents $g(\mathbf{b})$. It follows from (1) and $m(\{x_k\}) = 0$ that $\nu\left(\{0,1\}^\ell \times \mathbb{R}^{k-1-\ell} \times \{x_k\}\right) = 0$. Then (2) implies $P(\mathcal{T}) = 0$. Intuitively speaking, we do not allow the probability to be concentrated "too much" in a single point on the real axis.   ◇

Example 5 (Smoking, friendship, cancer – notation). Observe that

$$P(Sm(Ann)) = \int_{\mathbf{x} \models Sm(Ann)} p_{\mathbf{X}} \, d\nu = \int_{\{1\}} p_{Sm(Ann)} \, d\nu_c = p_{Sm(Ann)}(1)$$

where $p_{Sm(Ann)}$ is the marginal *discrete* PDF. Taking the perspective on $Sm(Ann)$ as a binary random variable, we get that $P(Sm(Ann)) = p(Sm(Ann))$. Also, observe that in accordance with (3),

$$P(0 < cig(Ann) < 10) = \int_{\mathbf{X}(A)} p(\mathbf{x}) \, d\nu = \int_{(0,10)} p_{cig(Ann)}(x) \, dm,$$

where $A = \{\mathcal{I} \mid \mathcal{I} \models 0 < cig(Ann) < 10\}$ and $p_{cig(Ann)}(x)$ is the marginal *Lebesgue* PDF.   ◁

3   Bayesian MLN

A set $\mathscr{F}$ defines an undirected graph with nodes $X_1, \ldots, X_k$ that compose $\mathbf{X}$; there is an edge between X_i, X_j iff X_i, X_j appear together in at least one grounding of a DT.

Example 6 (Smoking causes cancer). A grounding $\langle Sm(a) \wedge Ca(a), \{\langle cig(a)\rangle\}\rangle$ of the dependence terms F_2 from Example 2 is represented as shown in Fig. 1a. It includes binary random variables for $Sm(a)$, $Ca(a)$, and a real-valued random variable for $cig(a)$.   ◁

A set $\mathscr{F}$ can be viewed as a template for constructing undirected graphs. Given different sets of constants, it will produce different networks. These may be of greatly varying size, but all will have certain regularities in structure.

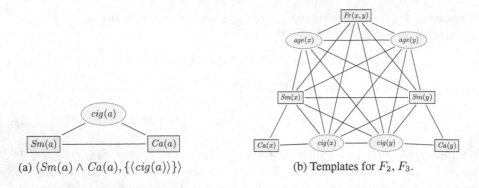

(a) $\langle Sm(a) \wedge Ca(a), \{\langle cig(a) \rangle\}\rangle$

(b) Templates for F_2, F_3.

Fig. 1. Ground DTs are represented by a *clique* in an *undirected graph*. Non ground DTs can be seen as templates for cliques. Binary random variables are indicated by rectangles, real-valued random variables by ovals.

Example 7 (Smoking, friendship, cancer – representation). The representation of dependence terms F_2, F_3 from Example 2 is depicted in Fig. 1b.   ◁

We require that $\mathbf{X}$ be a MRF w.r.t. the undirected graph defined by $\mathscr{F}$. That is, intuitively speaking, an absence of an edge in the graph represents stochastic independence between the nodes. This implies that each node represents a different object, which is guaranteed if we use the *unique names assumption* (UNA), which requires that different constants refer to different objects in a domain of an $\mathcal{L}$-interpretation. Note that KFA and UNA restrict the domain of $\mathbf{X}$. Accordingly, in the following text, $\mathbf{Dom\,X}$ will denote the set of all interpretations that satisfy KFA and UNA.

The MRF is interpreted in accordance with Hammersley-Clifford theorem [4] as a GRF – a PDF given by a product of *potential functions* normalized by a *partition function*. The choice of the shape of the potential function has an impact on the feasibility of the development of query answering algorithms. In particular, the potential functions introduced in [10] and [5] for MLN and HMLN are suitable neither for Bayesian approach nor for variational inference. We, therefore, focus on identification of the properties that define what exactly the Bayesian and variational friendly potential function is. We call the resulting graphical model *Bayesian Markov logic network (BMLN)*. Before defining BMLN, we introduce some more notation.

Given a DT $\langle \varphi_i, \tau_i \rangle$, we denote its j-grounding by $\langle \varphi_{ij}, \tau_{ij} \rangle$. The expression $\varphi_{ij}(\mathbf{x})$ denotes the truth value (0 or 1) of φ_{ij} under the assignment $\mathbf{x}$. We write $\tau_{ij}(\mathbf{x})$ for $\sum_{\tau \in \tau_{ij}} |\tau|$-vector that is the concatenation of all $|\tau|$-tuples (from τ_{ij}) of evaluations of ground numeric terms in τ (cf. Definition 2).

Example 8 (Smoking causes cancer). Consider the DT $\langle \varphi_2, \tau_2 \rangle$. A possible grounding $\langle \varphi_{2j}, \tau_{2j} \rangle$, where $\varphi_{2j} = Sm(a) \wedge Ca(a)$ and $\tau_{2j} = \langle cig(a) \rangle$, is represented as the clique depicted in Fig. 1a.

$$\varphi_{2j}(\mathbf{x}) = \varphi_{2j}\left(x_{Sm(a)}, x_{Ca(a)}\right), \qquad \tau_{2j}(\mathbf{x}) = x_{cig(a)},$$

where, in accordance with the standard inductive definition of truth,

$$\varphi_{2j}(\mathbf{x}) = x_{Sm(a)} \vee x_{Ca(a)} \text{ and } x_{cig(a)} \text{ is a real.} \qquad \triangleleft$$

Definition 3 (BMLN). *A Bayesian MLN is a set of pairs $((\langle \varphi_i, \tau_i \rangle, \omega_i)$, where $\langle \varphi_i, \tau_i \rangle$ is a DT and ω_i is a parameter vector of the following weight functions*[3]

$$w_{ij}(\mathbf{x}, \omega_i) = h_{ij}\left(\varphi_{ij}(\mathbf{x}), \tau_{ij}(\mathbf{x})\right) \cdot p_{dt}\left(\varphi_{ij}(\mathbf{x}), \tau_{ij}(\mathbf{x}) \mid \omega_i\right), \tag{4}$$

where both $h_{ij}, p_{dt} \colon \{0,1\} \times \mathbb{R}^{\sum_{\tau \in \tau_{ij}} |\tau|} \to \mathbb{R}$ are Borel functions, strictly positive on **Ran** $\mathscr{F}$. *In addition, p_{dt} is a joint PDF of $\varphi_{ij}(\mathbf{x})$ and $\tau_{ij}(\mathbf{x})$, parameterized by ω_i.* ◇

A BMLN specified by a set $\mathscr{F}$ of DTs has regularities because each DT $\langle \varphi_i, \tau_i \rangle$ can be viewed as a template for constructing J cliques of ground atoms and terms that appear in $\langle \varphi_{ij}, \tau_{ij} \rangle$, for $j = 1, \ldots J$, and all these cliques are associated with weight functions that share a common ω_i.

Note that, by choosing the form of weight function (4), we are not imposing any restriction on the MRF specified by the BMLN, since every real strictly positive function g_{ij} of $\varphi_{ij}(\mathbf{x})$ and $\tau_{ij}(\mathbf{x})$ can be expressed as the above product of a real strictly positive function h_{ij} and a strictly positive PDF. Furthermore, if τ_i is empty (e.g., in (F_1) of Example 2) then $w_{ij}(\mathbf{x}, \omega_i) = h_{ij}\left(\varphi_{ij}(\mathbf{x})\right) \cdot p_{dt}\left(\varphi_{ij}(\mathbf{x}) \mid \omega_i\right)$.

Therefore, the probability distribution defined by a BMLN is:

$$p(\mathbf{x} \mid \omega) = \frac{1}{Z(\omega)} \prod_{ij} w_{ij}(\mathbf{x}, \omega_i), \tag{5}$$

where, if ω denotes the vector $\langle \omega_1, \ldots, \omega_I \rangle$,

$$Z(\omega) = \int \prod_{ij} w_{ij}(\mathbf{x}, \omega_i) \, d\nu. \tag{6}$$

4 Query Answering via Bayesian Inference on BMLN

The general form of a query on the intended model is $P(\mathcal{T}_2 \mid \mathcal{T}_1, \mathscr{F})$. To answer this query using the representation $\mathbf{X}$ w.r.t. ν, we have to calculate

$$\int_{\mathbf{Ran\,X}} \mathcal{T}_2(\mathbf{x}) \cdot p(\mathbf{x} \mid \mathcal{T}_1, \mathscr{F}) \, d\nu.$$

---

[3] The term weight function is used to highlight the analogy with (H)MLNs, in which $w_{ij}(\mathbf{x}, \omega_i)$ is $e^{w_i s_i(\varphi_{ij}(\mathbf{x}), \tau_{ij}(\mathbf{x}))}$, where w_i is a constant, called weight, and s_i is a real function.

Each BMLN is parameterized by a vector ω that determines a specific configuration of the BMLN filter, which allows through exactly one PDF $p(\mathbf{x} \mid \omega)$. It is clear upon reflection that

$$p(\mathbf{x} \mid \omega, \mathcal{T}) = \frac{\mathcal{T}(\mathbf{x}) \cdot p(\mathbf{x} \mid \omega)}{\int_{\mathbf{Ran\,X}} \mathcal{T}(\mathbf{x}) \cdot p(\mathbf{x} \mid \omega) \, d\nu} = \frac{\mathcal{T}(\mathbf{x}) \cdot \prod_{ij} w_{ij}(\mathbf{x}, \omega_i)}{\int_{\mathbf{Ran\,X}} \mathcal{T}(\mathbf{x}) \cdot \prod_{ij} w_{ij}(\mathbf{x}, \omega_i) \, d\nu} \quad (7)$$

where we have made use of the substitution of (5).

Applying the Bayesian viewpoint, each parameter in ω is seen as a hypothesis, and predictions are made by using all the hypotheses, weighted by their prior probability $p(\omega \mid \mathscr{F})$. The product $p(\mathbf{x} \mid \omega, \mathcal{T})p(\omega \mid \mathscr{F})$ yields the joint PDF $p(\mathbf{x}, \omega \mid \mathcal{T}, \mathscr{F})$.

To answer queries of the form $P(\mathcal{T}_2 \mid \mathcal{T}_1, \mathscr{F})$, we need to calculate the posterior PDFs $p(\mathbf{x} \mid \mathcal{T}_1, \mathscr{F})$, $p(\omega \mid \mathcal{T}_1, \mathscr{F})$. However, it is unfeasible to marginalize out ω, or $\mathbf{x}$ from $p(\mathbf{x}, \omega \mid \mathcal{T}_1, \mathscr{F})$ for many models of practical interest. This may be because the dimensionality of the domain of ω or $\mathbf{x}$ is too high to work with directly or because $p(\mathbf{x}, \omega \mid \mathcal{T}_1, \mathscr{F})$ has a highly complex form. In the case of continuous variables, the required integrations may not have *closed-form* or *analytic* solutions, while the dimensionality of the space and the complexity may prohibit numeric integration. For discrete variables, the marginalizations involve summing over all possible configurations, and though this is always possible in principle, we often find an exact calculation prohibitively expensive in practice. In the above situations, we need to resort to approximation schemes, and these fall broadly into two classes, according whether they rely on stochastic or deterministic approximations [1, Chap. 10].

- Sampling methods can be computationally demanding, often limiting their use to small-scale problems. Also, it may be difficult to know whether a sampling scheme is generating independent samples from the required distributions.
- Deterministic approximation schemes are based on analytical approximations to the posterior distribution. Approximations like *variational inference* may scale well to large applications.

We apply variational techniques. In general, each analytic expression for a PDF represented as a GRF includes a *partition function* [1, Chapter 8], which leads to prohibitive numeric integration in variational inference. However, the particular form of potential functions of BMLNs in conjunction with the Bayesian viewpoint make it possible to find a general solution based on symbolic (instead of numeric calculations of) iterations of variational inference [1, Chap. 10]. This is crucial for the efficiency.

The variational solution yields analytic expressions $p^\star(\omega \mid \mathcal{T}_1, \mathscr{F})$, $p^\star(\mathbf{x} \mid \mathcal{T}_1, \mathscr{F})$ for the best approximations of the posterior PDFs $p(\omega \mid \mathcal{T}_1, \mathscr{F})$, $p(\mathbf{x} \mid \mathcal{T}_1, \mathscr{F})$, respectively. Then $p(\mathcal{T}_2 \mid \mathcal{T}_1, \mathscr{F})$ can be expressed in terms of $p^\star(\mathbf{x} \mid \mathcal{T}_1, \mathscr{F})$.

Example 9 (Continued from Example 4).

(Q1) $P(Sm(Ann) \mid \mathcal{T}, \mathscr{F}) \triangleq p^\star(X_{Sm(Ann)} = 1 \mid \mathcal{T}, \mathscr{F})$;

(Q2) $P(\forall x \colon Sm(x) \leftrightarrow Ca(x) \mid \mathcal{T}, \mathscr{F}) \triangleq p^\star(\forall x \colon Sm(x) \leftrightarrow Ca(x) \mid \mathcal{T}, \mathscr{F})$,

(Q3) $P(Ca(x) \mid Sm(x), \mathcal{T}, \mathscr{F})$

$$\triangleq \tfrac{1}{3} \sum_{x \in \{Ann, Bob, Cole\}} p^\star(X_{Ca(x)} = 1 \mid X_{Sm(x)} = 1, \mathcal{T}, \mathscr{F});$$

Alternatively, we can suppose w.l.o.g. a constant, say a, that occurs neither in $\mathcal{T}$ nor in $\mathscr{F}$. (If there is no such a constant, we introduce it to the language $\mathcal{L}$.)

(Q3) $P(Ca(a) \mid Sm(a), \mathcal{T}, \mathscr{F}) \triangleq p^\star(X_{Ca(a)} = 1 \mid X_{Sm(a)} = 1, \mathcal{T}, \mathscr{F})$;

(Q4) $p(X_{cig(a)} \mid \mathcal{T}, \mathscr{F}) \triangleq p^\star(X_{cig(a)} \mid \mathcal{T}, \mathscr{F})$;

(Q5) $p(X_{cig(a)} \mid X_{Ca(a)}, \mathcal{T}, \mathscr{F}) \triangleq p^\star(X_{cig(a)} \mid X_{Ca(a)} = 1, \mathcal{T}, \mathscr{F})$;

(Q6) $P(Ca(a) \mid cig(a) = n, \mathcal{T}, \mathscr{F}) \triangleq p^\star(X_{Ca(a)} = 1 \mid X_{cig(a)} = n, \mathcal{T}, \mathscr{F})$.   ◁

5 Variational Inference

This section reviews very briefly the variational technique applied on BMLNs. Our goal is to arrive at an approximation of the conditional PDF $p(\mathbf{x}, \boldsymbol{\omega} \mid \mathcal{T}, \mathscr{F})$ that renders the problem of marginalizing out $\boldsymbol{\omega}$ simple. To this end, consider an approximation

$$p(\mathbf{x}, \boldsymbol{\omega} \mid \mathcal{T}, \mathscr{F}) \approx q(\mathbf{x}, \boldsymbol{\omega}), \tag{8}$$

where q is a product of PDFs:

$$q(\mathbf{x}, \boldsymbol{\omega}) = \prod_i q_i(\mathbf{Z}_i), \tag{9}$$

where $\{\mathbf{Z}_i\}$ is a partition of the arguments $\mathbf{x}, \boldsymbol{\omega}$ of q.

To calculate (9), we use a functional

$$\mathcal{L}(q) = \int q(\mathbf{x}, \boldsymbol{\omega}) \cdot \ln \frac{p(\mathbf{x}, \boldsymbol{\omega}, \mathcal{T} \mid \mathscr{F})}{q(\mathbf{x}, \boldsymbol{\omega})} \, \nu(d\mathbf{x}, d\boldsymbol{\omega}),$$

where ν is a product of Lebesgue and counting measures for continuous and discrete components of $\mathbf{X}$ and the parameter vector, respectively. It can be shown [1, Chap. 10] that $\mathcal{L}(q)$ reaches its maximum $\ln p(\mathcal{T} \mid \mathscr{F})$ when $q(\mathbf{x}, \boldsymbol{\omega}) \equiv p(\mathbf{x}, \boldsymbol{\omega} \mid \mathcal{T}, \mathscr{F})$. The difference $\ln p(\mathcal{T} \mid \mathscr{F}) - \mathcal{L}(q)$ is called *Kullback–Leibler divergence* (or KL divergence) between the PDFs $q(\mathbf{x}, \boldsymbol{\omega})$ and $p(\mathbf{x}, \boldsymbol{\omega} \mid \mathcal{T}, \mathscr{F})$, denoted $\mathrm{KL}(q(\mathbf{x}, \boldsymbol{\omega}) \parallel p(\mathbf{Z} \mid \mathcal{T}, \mathscr{F}))$.

The required factorization (9) restricts the set of functions over which the maximization of $\mathcal{L}(q)$ is performed. The maximum, which minimizes the KL divergence, defines the best approximation of $p(\mathbf{x}, \boldsymbol{\omega} \mid \mathcal{T}, \mathscr{F})$ over this set. It can be shown [1, Chapter 10] that $\mathcal{L}(q)$ reaches its maximum iff

$$\ln q_j^\star(\mathbf{Z}_j) = \mathbb{E}_{i \neq j}[\ln p(\mathbf{x}, \boldsymbol{\omega}, \mathcal{T} \mid \mathscr{F})] + \text{const}, \tag{10}$$

where $\mathbb{E}_{i \neq j}[\ln p(\mathbf{x}, \boldsymbol{\omega}, \mathcal{T} \mid \mathscr{F})] = \int \ln p(\mathbf{x}, \boldsymbol{\omega}, \mathcal{T} \mid \mathscr{F}) \prod_{i \colon i \neq j} q_i(\mathbf{Z}_i) \, \nu(d\mathbf{Z}_i)$.

Note that (10) presents a system of coupled update equations that are solved by iterating until reaching a fixpoint. The complexity of the calculations depends on the form of the joint PDF $p(\mathbf{x}, \omega, \mathcal{T} \mid \mathcal{F})$ and also on (9). It is easily seen[4] that

$$p(\mathbf{x}, \omega, \mathcal{T} \mid \mathcal{F}) = \mathcal{T}(\mathbf{x}) \cdot p(\mathbf{x} \mid \omega) \cdot p(\omega \mid \mathcal{F}). \tag{11}$$

The presence of the partition function $Z(\omega)$ is one of the major limitations of GRFs w.r.t. variational inference. The evaluation of $Z(\omega)$ for an undirected graph with M binary nodes involves summing over 2^M states and so is exponential in the size of the graph. Moreover, $Z(\omega)$ depends on all the parameters that govern the weight functions (4). This leads to problems in the variational treatment because of integrals like $\int \ln Z(\omega) \cdot q_i^\star \, \nu(d\omega_i)$, which are even more difficult than $\int_\Omega p(\mathbf{x}, \omega \mid \mathcal{T}, \mathcal{F}) \, d\omega$, marginalizing out ω as mentioned at the beginning of Sect. 4.

We make the following assumption: $Z(\omega)$ is approximately constant, i.e., there is a strictly positive and finite real z s.t. $Z(\omega) \approx z$ for all ω. This amounts to an approximation of the joint PDF,

$$p(\mathbf{x}, \omega, \mathcal{T} \mid \mathcal{F}) \approx p^\star(\mathbf{x}, \omega, \mathcal{T} \mid \mathcal{F}) = \frac{Z(\omega)}{z} \cdot p(\mathbf{x}, \omega, \mathcal{T} \mid \mathcal{F}), \tag{12}$$

and in accordance with (11) and (5),

$$p^\star(\mathbf{x}, \omega, \mathcal{T} \mid \mathcal{F}) \propto p(\mathcal{T} \mid \mathbf{x}) \cdot \prod_{ij} w_{ij}(\mathbf{x}, \omega_i) \cdot p(\omega \mid \mathcal{F}).$$

That is, the approximated joint PDF can be factorized in a way that is suitable for variational treatment.

To sum up, the iteration until reaching fixpoint of the system of coupled update Eq. (10) yields a good approximation (8) if $p(\mathbf{x}, \omega, \mathcal{T} \mid \mathcal{F})$ is represented as a BMLN for which the partition function is constant or quasi constant. Most importantly, the iterations can be computed efficiently if the integrals in (10) can be calculated symbolically. To this end, we need not only "variational–friendly" weight functions (4) but also a "suitable" prior PDF $p(\omega \mid \mathcal{F})$.

6   Restriction to a Constant Partition Function

In this section, we analyze the approximation (12). First, we analyze the partition function Z (6) and show that Z is constant under some specific assumptions that define the concept of *orthogonality* of DTs.

It follows readily from Definition 1 that the first ℓ entries of $\mathbf{x}$ determine $\varphi_{ij}(\mathbf{x})$'s and the remaining $k - \ell$ entries determine $\tau_{ij}(\mathbf{x})$'s. We will denote them by $\mathbf{x}_\varphi$ and $\mathbf{x}_\tau$, respectively. Furthermore, we will denote the entries of $\mathbf{x}$ that determine $\tau_{ij}(\mathbf{x})$ by $\mathbf{x}_{\tau_{ij}}$. For example, $\tau_{2j} = \{\langle cig(a)\rangle\}$ and $\mathbf{x}_{\tau_{2j}} = cig(a)$ in Example 8. Let φ denote a map $\mathbf{x}_\varphi \mapsto \mathbf{s}, \mathbf{s} \in \{0,1\}^{|\{\langle i,j\rangle\}|}$ where $s_{ij} \triangleq \varphi_{ij}(\mathbf{x}_\varphi)$.

---

[4] Note that we get this equality also by multiplying (7) by $p(\mathcal{T} \mid \omega) \cdot p(\omega \mid \mathcal{F})$.

Let $\tau(\cdot)$ denote a map $\mathbf{x}_\tau \mapsto \mathbf{t}$ where $t_{ij} \stackrel{\Delta}{=} \tau_{ij}(\mathbf{x}_\tau)$, where t_{ij} is a $\sum_{\tau \in \tau_{ij}} |\tau|$-vector.

We use the following notational shorthand, where $\mathbf{s} \in \{0,1\}^{|\{\langle i,j \rangle\}|}$, $\mathbf{t} \in \mathbb{R}^{\sum_{ij}|t_{ij}|}$:

$$p_{dt}(\mathbf{s}, \mathbf{t} \mid \boldsymbol{\omega}) \stackrel{\Delta}{=} \prod_{ij} p_{dt}(s_{ij}, t_{ij} \mid \boldsymbol{\omega}_i), \qquad h(\mathbf{s}, \mathbf{t}) \stackrel{\Delta}{=} \prod_{ij} h_{ij}(s_{ij}, t_{ij}).$$

6.1   Partition Function

The partition function Z (6) depends on $\boldsymbol{\omega}$, which is the parameter vector of $p_{dt}(\cdot \mid \boldsymbol{\omega})$. Accordingly, we can study this relationship between Z and $\boldsymbol{\omega}$ through the relationship between Z and p_{dt}. To this end, we apply the change of variables [12, Theorem 1.2], from $\mathbf{x}$ to $(\mathbf{s}, \mathbf{t})$.

In accordance with (1), the definition of the counting measure ν_c, and the definition of φ, it is easily verified that

$$\frac{d\left(\nu_c^\ell \circ \varphi^{-1}\right)}{d\nu_c^{|\mathbf{s}|}}(\mathbf{s}) = \nu_c^\ell \circ \varphi^{-1}(\{\mathbf{s}\}) = \left|\varphi^{-1}(\{\mathbf{s}\})\right| \qquad \text{æ } \nu_c^{|\mathbf{s}|}.$$

◇

Theorem 2 (Partition function). *Suppose that $m^{|\mathbf{x}_\tau|} \circ \tau^{-1}$ is absolutely continuous w.r.t. $m^{|\mathbf{t}|}$ on $(\mathbf{Ran}\,\tau, \mathcal{B}_{\mathbf{Ran}\,\tau})$. Then the partition function, defined by (6),*

$$Z(\boldsymbol{\omega}) = \mathbb{E}_{p_{dt}(\cdot|\boldsymbol{\omega})}[q(\mathbf{s}, \mathbf{t})],$$

where

$$q(\mathbf{s}, \mathbf{t}) = h(\mathbf{s}, \mathbf{t}) \cdot \left|\varphi^{-1}(\{\mathbf{s}\})\right| \frac{d\left(m^{|\mathbf{x}_\tau|} \circ \tau^{-1}\right)}{dm^{|\mathbf{t}|}}(\mathbf{t}) \qquad \text{æ } \nu_c^{|\mathbf{s}|} \times m^{|\mathbf{t}|}.$$

The approximation (12) is precise iff the partition function $Z(\boldsymbol{\omega})$ doesn't depend on $\boldsymbol{\omega}$, i.e., $Z(\boldsymbol{\omega})$ is a *constant function*. Otherwise, (12) defines the approximation in which $p^\star(\mathbf{x}, \boldsymbol{\omega}, \mathcal{T} \mid \mathcal{F})$ differs from $p(\mathbf{x}, \boldsymbol{\omega}, \mathcal{T} \mid \mathcal{F})$ by the factor $\frac{Z(\boldsymbol{\omega})}{z}$, which can be understood as another probability prior for $\boldsymbol{\omega}$.

It follows from Theorem 2 that, speaking in broad terms, Z increases with $\boldsymbol{\omega}$'s that define higher probability for bigger values of $q(\mathbf{s}, \mathbf{t})$. Assuming $\arg\max q(\mathbf{s}, \mathbf{t})$, $\arg\min q(\mathbf{s}, \mathbf{t})$ in the *interior* of $\mathbf{Dom}\,q$, and q continuous, Z reaches its maximum in $\boldsymbol{\omega}_{\max}$ s.t. the support of $p_{dt}(\cdot \mid \boldsymbol{\omega}_{\max})$ coincides with an infinitesimally small neighborhood of $\arg\max q(\mathbf{s}, \mathbf{t})$ w.r.t. $\nu_c^{|\mathbf{s}|} \times m^{|\mathbf{t}|}$. Analogically, Z reaches its minimum in $\boldsymbol{\omega}_{\min}$ s.t. $\mathrm{supp}\,p_{dt}(\cdot \mid \boldsymbol{\omega}_{\min})$ coincides with an infinitesimally small neighborhood of $\arg\min q(\mathbf{s}, \mathbf{t})$ w.r.t. $\nu_c^{|\mathbf{s}|} \times m^{|\mathbf{t}|}$. It is clear that $Z(\boldsymbol{\omega}_{\max}) - Z(\boldsymbol{\omega}_{\min})$ increases with $\max q(\mathbf{s}, \mathbf{t}) - \min q(\mathbf{s}, \mathbf{t})$. On the other hand, $\frac{Z(\boldsymbol{\omega})}{z}$ presents a uniform prior iff Z is a constant function, which is the case iff q is a constant function and the support of $p_{dt}(\cdot \mid \boldsymbol{\omega})$ is a subset of $\mathbf{Dom}\,q$ for every $\boldsymbol{\omega}$ from $\mathbf{Dom}\,Z$.

For example, consider a continuous q and $U, V \subset \mathbf{Dom}\, q$ s.t. $\max_U q < \min_V q$. Then it can be observed that $Z(\omega_1) \leq Z(\omega_2)$ if $p_{dt}(\,\cdot\mid\omega_1), p_{dt}(\,\cdot\mid\omega_2)$ differ only on $U \cup V$ s.t. $p_{dt}(\,\cdot\mid\omega_1) \leq p_{dt}(\,\cdot\mid\omega_2)$ on V and $p_{dt}(\,\cdot\mid\omega_1) \geq p_{dt}(\,\cdot\mid\omega_2)$ on U. To sum up, $Z(\omega)$ increases with

(a) decreasing entropy of $p_{dt}(\,\cdot\mid\omega)$;
(b) ϵ s.t. q reaches the biggest values on $\{\langle \mathbf{s}, \mathbf{t}\rangle \mid p_{dt}(\mathbf{s}, \mathbf{t}\mid\omega) > \epsilon\}$.

6.2   Orthogonality of a Set of Dependence Terms

Theorem 2 motivates the following definition of the concept that captures important properties of DTs (refer to Definition 1) $\mathscr{F}$.

Definition 4 (Orthogonality). *We say that a set $\mathscr{F}$ of DTs is orthogonal on $C \subseteq \mathbf{Ran}\,\mathscr{F}$ iff the following equation,*

$$\prod_{ij} h_{ij}(s_{ij}, t_{ij}) = \frac{d\nu_c^{|\mathbf{s}|}}{d\left(\nu_c^{|x_\varphi|} \circ \varphi^{-1}\right)}(\mathbf{s}) \frac{dm^{|\mathbf{t}|}}{d\left(m^{|x_\tau|} \circ \tau^{-1}\right)}(\mathbf{t}), \quad \langle \mathbf{s}, \mathbf{t}\rangle \in C, \quad (13)$$

has a solution. ◇

Corollary 1 (Orthogonality). *$Z(\omega)$ (see (6)) is a constant function if (13) holds and $\mathrm{supp}\, p_{dt}(\,\cdot\mid\omega) \subseteq \mathbf{Ran}\,\mathscr{F}$ for every ω.*

The following theorem states that we can define variational friendly GRF iff $\mathscr{F}$ is orthogonal and the support of p_{dt} coincides with $\mathbf{Ran}\,\mathscr{F}$ for every ω.

Theorem 3 (Joint PDF). *The BMLN specified by $\mathscr{F}$ defines the PDF:*

$$p(\mathbf{x}, \omega, \mathcal{T}\mid\mathscr{F}) = p(\mathcal{T}\mid\mathbf{x}) \cdot \prod_{ij} w_{ij}(\mathbf{x}, \omega_i) \cdot p(\omega\mid\mathscr{F})$$

iff h_{ij} in Definition 3 are given by (13), and $\mathrm{supp}\, p_{dt}(\,\cdot\mid\omega) = \mathbf{Ran}\,\mathscr{F}$ for every ω.

7   Conclusions

Orthogonality (Definition 4) of $\mathscr{F}$ enables to define the BMLN s.t. the partition function is eliminated in the joint PDF, which plays role of the so-called variational distribution in variational inference. This leads to purely symbolic calculations in variational inference which is crucial for efficiency. In cases when $\mathscr{F}$ is not orthogonal, we can always extend the language $\mathcal{L}$ and the set of axioms to achieve the orthogonality with an logically equivalent set of DTs. To this end, we replace every formula or numeric term in $\mathscr{F}$ with a new symbol that we add to the $\mathcal{L}$-signature. The logical relationship between the new symbol and a formula or a numeric term is encoded as a new axiom. This procedure always yields an orthogonal set of DTs and trades off the background knowledge for efficiency of calculations.

References

1. Bishop, C.M.: Pattern Recognition and Machine Learning (Information Science and Statistics). Springer, New York (2006)
2. Bishop, C.M.: A new framework for machine learning. In: Zurada, J.M., Yen, G.G., Wang, J. (eds.) WCCI 2008. LNCS, vol. 5050, pp. 1–24. Springer, Heidelberg (2008). https://doi.org/10.1007/978-3-540-68860-0_1
3. Bishop, C.M., Spiegelhalter, D., Winn, J.: VIBES: a variational inference engine for Bayesian networks. In: Becker, S., Thrun, S., Obermayer, K., (eds.) Advances in Neural Information Processing Systems 15, pp. 777–784. MIT Press (2002). [Neural Information Processing Systems, NIPS 2002, 9–14 December 2002, Vancouver, British Columbia, Canada]
4. Clifford, P.: Markov random fields in statistics. In: Grimmett, G., Welsh, D. (eds.) Disorder in Physical Systems: A Volume in Honour of John M. Hammersley, pp. 19–32. Oxford University Press, Oxford (1990)
5. Domingos, P., Lowd, D.: Markov Logic: An Interface Layer for Artificial Intelligence. Morgan and Claypool Publishers, San Rafael/California (2009)
6. Jordan, M.I., Ghahramani, Z., Jaakkola, T.S., Saul, L.K.: An introduction to variational methods for graphical models. Mach. Learn. **37**(2), 183–233 (1999)
7. Kindermann, R., Laurie Snell, J.: Markov Random Fields and Their Applications. AMS, Providence (1980)
8. Kok, S., et al.: The alchemy system for statistical relational AI. Technical report, Department of Computer Science and Engineering, University of Washington (2007)
9. Ranganath, R., Gerrish, S., Blei, D.M.: Black box variational inference. In: Proceedings of the Seventeenth International Conference on Artificial Intelligence and Statistics, AISTATS 2014, Reykjavik, Iceland, 22–25 April 2014, Volume 33 of JMLR Proceedings, pp. 814–822. JMLR.org (2014)
10. Richardson, M., Domingos, P.M.: Markov logic networks. Mach. Learn. **62**(1–2), 107–136 (2006)
11. Russell, S.J., Norvig, P.: Artificial Intelligence - A Modern Approach. Pearson Education, London (2010). (3. internat. ed.)
12. Shao, J.: Mathematical Statistics. Springer, New York (1999). https://doi.org/10.1007/b97553. Springer texts in statistics
13. Singla, P., Domingos, P.M.: Markov logic in infinite domains. CoRR, abs/1206.5292 (2012)
14. Wainwright, M.J., Jordan, M.I.: Graphical models, exponential families, and variational inference. Found. Trends Mach. Learn. **1**(1–2), 1–305 (2008)
15. Wang, J., Domingos, P.M.: Hybrid Markov logic networks. In: Fox, D., Gomes, C.P. (eds.) Proceedings of the Twenty-Third AAAI Conference on Artificial Intelligence, AAAI 2008, Chicago, Illinois, USA, 13–17 July 2008, pp. 1106–1111. AAAI Press (2008)
16. Wingate, D., Weber, T.: Automated variational inference in probabilistic programming. CoRR, abs/1301.1299 (2013)
17. Winn, J.M., Bishop, C.M.: Variational message passing. J. Mach. Learn. Res. **6**, 661–694 (2005)

An Integration-Based Approach
to Pattern Clustering and Classification

Laura Sani[1], Gianluca D'Addese[2], Riccardo Pecori[1,3(✉)], Monica Mordonini[1],
Marco Villani[2], and Stefano Cagnoni[1]

[1] Department of Engineering and Architecture, University of Parma, Parma, Italy
[2] FIM Department, University of Modena and Reggio Emilia, Modena, Italy
[3] SMARTEST Research Centre, eCAMPUS University, Novedrate, CO, Italy
`riccardo.pecori@uniecampus.it`

Abstract. Methods based on information theory, such as the Relevance Index (RI), have been employed to study complex systems for their ability to detect significant groups of variables, well integrated among one another and well separated from the others, which provide a functional block description of the system under analysis. The integration (or zI in its standardized form) is a metric that can express the significance of a group of variables for the system under consideration: the higher the zI, the more significant the group. In this paper, we use this metric for an unusual application to a pattern clustering and classification problem. The results show that the centroids of the clusters of patterns identified by the method are effective for distance-based classification algorithms. We compare such a method with other conventional classification approaches to highlight its main features and to address future research towards the refinement of its accuracy and computational efficiency.

Keywords: Classification · Clustering · Complex systems · RI metrics

1 Introduction and Related Work

Methods that detect relevant groups of variables in a complex system have been described and applied to several fields, such as molecular biology, chemistry, physiology, etc. [12,16]. They rely on the analysis of a set of observations, represented as a matrix where each row represents the status of the system at a certain time, while columns represent the status variables of the system. Abstractly, one can say that such methods are able to find clusters of columns that exhibit some correlated properties or behaviors.

So, what would happen if one just transposed the matrix, to cluster events (status) instead of variables? And what would happen if one represented the status of the corresponding pixels in a set of patterns along the rows, and the patterns themselves along the columns?

© Springer Nature Switzerland AG 2018
C. Ghidini et al. (Eds.): AI*IA 2018, LNAI 11298, pp. 362–374, 2018.
https://doi.org/10.1007/978-3-030-03840-3_27

In this paper, we show that if we "turn the world upside down" (or, better, we rotate it by 90°), the same method that could be employed to find groups of correlated variables can be used for clustering similar patterns. This work aims to provide a proof of concept for such a theory and, with no pretense to reach state-of-the-art performances, to show that the hypothesis is reasonable and already competitive with existing classical clustering and classification approaches.

The reference method from which this application derives is the so-called Relevance Index (RI) method [15], an information-theoretic approach aimed at assigning a relevance score to each group of variables. This method measures the degree of integration (I, which is to be maximized) of a group, versus its independence from the rest of the system, which can be assessed by computing, and minimizing, the corresponding mutual information (MI). I, MI and RI, and their normalized counterparts, which solve some issues with their dependency on group size, constitute a family of information-theoretical metrics that we denote as *RI metrics*, for simplicity. Among these, in this paper we consider, in particular, the zI index, a normalized integration measure that accounts for the standardized distance of a group of variables from a reference condition of statistical independence.

As described above, using such indices to perform clustering can be somehow assimilated to some other information theoretic approaches to clustering. In most such methods, cluster labels (represented by random variable Y) are assigned to data points (represented by random variable X), such that the mutual information between data and labels is maximized [5,8,18]. However, Ver Steeg *et al.* [13] demonstrated that this approach is fundamentally flawed, so that clustering performance deteriorates as the amount of data increases. The authors propose an alternative approach based on the optimization of the *Total Cluster Uncertainty*, which is a particular estimator of the conditional entropy $H(Y|X)$. Optimizing such a metric over all possible partitions is a difficult problem. The authors consider a heuristic approach that involves solving a tractable semidefinite problem. A radically different approach, which is probably the closest to the one we propose, was introduced by Aldana-Bobadilla *et al.* [1]. There, the best dataset partition $\Pi = \{C_1, C_2, .., C_k\}$ is obtained by maximizing the entropy $H(\Pi) = \sum_{C_i} H(X|C = C_i)$ and minimizing $\sum_i \sigma(C_i)$, at the same time. The partition space is explored by means of an evolutionary approach.

This paper presents our approach to clustering, firstly introducing the zI index and how to compute it for analyzing complex systems. We then describe the application of the method to clustering and classification problems, reporting results obtained both on controlled synthetic data and on a real-world set of images of low-resolution digits extracted from license plates.

2   Theoretical Basis of the Approach

In this section, we describe the entropy-based zI metric, the strategies we have implemented to compute it, and the "iterative sieving" procedure we use to cluster data based on the zI values.

Considering a system U described by n random variables $X_1, X_2, ..., X_n$, we suppose that S_k is a subset composed of k elements, with $k < n$. Our purpose is to identify subsets of variables that behave in a somehow coordinated way, i.e., the variables belonging to the subset are integrated with one another much more than with the other variables of the system. As these subsets can be used to describe the whole system organization, they are named *Relevant Subsets (RSs)*.

In order to find these structures, we rely on an index initially conceived by Edelman and Tononi (the *Functional Cluster Index*, or *CI*) [11], aimed at detecting functional clusters in brain regions. In our previous works [15], we relaxed the stationary constraint and extended the CI to dynamical systems, to apply it to a wider range of system classes. Following [11], we initially computed it by combining integration and mutual information, introducing also the Relevance (RI) Index metric.

The integration, denoted as I, measures the mutual dependence among the k elements composing a subset S_k. It is the difference between the sum of entropies of the single variables in S_k and the total entropy of subset S_k itself:

$$I(S_k) = \sum_{s \in S_k} H(s) - H(S_k) \tag{1}$$

Conversely, the mutual information MI measures the mutual dependence between subset S_k and the remaining part of the system $U \backslash S_k$. Finally, the Relevance Index RI is defined as the ratio between the integration I of S_k and the mutual information MI between S_k and the rest of the system. Normalizing the RI to remove its dependency on the group size requires the computation of the statistics of a reference "homogeneous" system U_h, whose variables are mutually independent, that needs to be as large as the one under consideration [15]. This obviously imposes a very heavy computational burden on the method.

However, in many cases, the integration I itself provides relevant information. In [4], it was shown that the product $2mI$ (m being the number of observations) has a Chi Square distribution whose degrees of freedom depend on the size of the analyzed subset and on the cardinality of its alphabet. As a consequence, in this paper we only rely on the integration, defining a metric, termed zI, more effective and faster to be computed than the RI, whose name is related to its being a sort of z-score. The zI metric is defined in Eq. 2, where S_k is a subset of k out of n variables of system U, and S_k^h is a subset of dimension k, extracted from a homogeneous system U_h described by n uncorrelated variables. The terms $\langle 2mI(S_k^h) \rangle$ and $\sigma(2mI(S_k^h))$ are the average and the standard deviation of the Chi Square distribution of all subsets of dimension k of the homogeneous system U_h.

$$zI(S_k) = \frac{2mI(S_k) - \langle 2mI(S_k^h) \rangle}{\sigma(2mI(S_k^h))} \tag{2}$$

2.1 zI Computation

The zI metric expresses the significance of a group of variables for the system under consideration: the larger the zI value, the more significant the group. A list of relevant sets can be obtained, in principle, by enumerating all possible subsets of the system variables and ranking them according to the zI values. The exhaustive search soon reaches unrealistic requirements for computational resources, because the number of subsets increases exponentially with the number of variables. When large systems are analyzed, it is impossible to compute the zI for every possible subset, even using parallel hardware such as GPUs.

To quickly find the most relevant subsets, we used a metaheuristic (HyReSS) [9,10], which hybridizes a genetic algorithm with local search strategies, driven by statistics, computed at runtime, on the results that the algorithm is obtaining.

HyReSS searches the N_s highest-zI sets, as the evolutionary search is enhanced by a niching technique that maintains population diversity, exploring many peaks in parallel. The zI computation, which is the most computation-intensive module within the algorithm, is parallelized for large blocks of sets through a CUDA[1] kernel which fits the computational needs of this problem particularly well [14].

2.2   Iterative Sieving Procedure

As a further and final step, a sieving algorithm [6,17], performed iteratively, is used to reduce the list of N_s sets found by HyReSS to the most representative ones. The sieving algorithm is based on the following criterion: if set $S1$ is a proper subset, or superset, of set $S2$ and ranks higher than $S2$ according to the zI, then $S1$ is considered more relevant than $S2$. Therefore, the algorithm keeps only those sets that are not included in, or do not include, any other higher-zI set. This sieving action stops when no more eliminations are possible: the remaining subsets can not be decomposed any further, and thus represent the building blocks of the dynamical organization of the system.

The sieving procedure allows one to analyze the organization of the system in terms of its lowest-level, possibly overlapping, subsets of variables. Nevertheless, to analyze also the aggregated hierarchical relations among the identified sets, we devised an iterative version of the sieving method that groups one or more sets into a single entity to derive a hierarchy. The simplest, yet effective, way to do so consists of iteratively running the sieving algorithm on the same data, each time using a new representation of the variables, where the top-ranked set, in terms of zI value, of the previous iteration is considered atomic and is substituted by a single variable (group variable) [17].

2.3 zI Clustering and Classification

When the zI is used for clustering, the iterative sieving operates by subsequently merging the highest-zI set of patterns into a new cluster in each step. By iterating the procedure, considering each time the merged variables as a new atomic entity, the final cluster set is composed by all the clusters, generated by such

---

[1] https://developer.nvidia.com

mergers, that have been detected at the time of the final iteration, i.e., the one in which the zI falls below a conventional value of 3.0 (i.e., 3 standard deviations from the reference condition of variable independence).

The experiments described in the following section, in which we have analyzed a synthetic and a more complex real-world dataset, have been aimed at proving that, if the zI metric is applied to a matrix where columns represent patterns and rows represent values of corresponding features, it can detect clusters of patterns based on their similarity, which can be effective for the classification.

We considered two approaches to classification, one based on a distance criterion, and another based on the computation of the zI index. As concerns the first approach, considering that the resulting values of centroid pixels are an estimation of the *a priori* probability that the pixel is on when a pattern belongs to the cluster, we defined the distance $d(x, c_i)$, between the pattern x to be classified and each centroid c_i, as the pixel-wise sum of the absolute values of the differences between x and c_i. In the fully zI-based approach, instead, the classification relies on the computation of the same index zI used for computing the clusters. Substantially, the pattern x to be classified is subsequently included as an extra pattern into each cluster c_i, generating a new cluster $\tilde{c}_i$. Finally, we assign to x the label of the cluster c_i, from which the cluster $\tilde{c}_i$ having the highest zI has been generated.

3   Validation of the Method

The main aim of the experiments we carried out has been, firstly, to validate the assumption that our method can detect groups of patterns that meet the requirements for being properly termed "clusters". Secondly, to demonstrate that such clusters can be effectively used as a basis for a minimum distance (1-Nearest Neighbor) classifier. Thus, in evaluating the classification performance of the cluster set we detected, and in comparing it with that of other commonly-used classifiers, we did not make any effort to optimize the number of clusters using, for instance, the classical cluster removal/splitting/merging strategies.

In the first part of this section we describe the results obtained in experiments made on a synthetic dataset. After that, we compare the classification, made using the clusters detected based on their zI values, with the performances: (i) of a baseline 1-Nearest Neighbor classifier based on a random selection of the training patterns, (ii) of other more "standard" distance-based classifiers of similar complexity, and (iii) of other commonly-used classifiers based on different principles.

When the zI is used to detect the subsets of a complex system, the analysis can only use the values of the variables which describe the system status. When the goal is clustering, as in this case, and each instance of the training set is a pattern that we want to classify, most often a labeled dataset is available. The question, then, is whether one should approach the problem in an unsupervised or a supervised way.

The former option would imply extracting clusters (groups of patterns) from the whole dataset at the same time, regardless of the class to which they belong, and would represent the most natural and direct application of the method. Conversely, in the latter case, the clustering procedure would be repeated for each subset of patterns belonging to a certain class. In any case, the method is intrinsically unsupervised: the subdivision of the training set into distinct subsets corresponds to exploiting the knowledge about the problem, which allows one to move up one abstraction level and use the method to detect different nuances of the same class of patterns, instead of identifying generic clusters that would then need to be subsequently matched to class labels.

The unsupervised approach would have the obvious advantage of being applicable even in the absence of knowledge about the data. However, such an approach might have the drawback of highlighting correlations among feature sets which may, in turn, be totally uncorrelated with the actual classes to which the patterns belong. The supervised approach has the intrinsic advantage of avoiding *a priori* all possible hybridizations caused by the inclusion of patterns of different classes into the cluster.

The results described in the following have been obtained using the supervised approach, based on these considerations and on the nature of the datasets to which we have applied it.

3.1   Experiments on a Synthetic Dataset

In order to test our approach and permit an easier observation of its behavior, we created a synthetic set of patterns representing the ten digits from 0 to 9. To do so, we designed a "perfect" pattern for each of the ten digits (of size 13×8 pixels each), of which we then generated corrupted versions by adding noise at different levels, from 5% to 30%. In a first set of patterns, noise was more likely to be added to the foreground (the actual pixels composing the digit) than to the background. At the same time, we created other pattern sets by adding noise uniformly distributed all over the image, whose level was tuned to obtain the same average noise level as in the first set[2]. During the experiments, in each iteration of the sieving algorithm we considered all possible clusters having size lower than 5, merged the variables belonging to the highest-ranked group into a single cluster, and launched a new iteration where the new cluster was treated as a single entity, until the zI of the highest-ranked group was lower than 3.0.

Cluster Detection. In a first experiment, in which we considered only the ten "perfect" patterns, the method identified two clusters, including digits $0, 9, 6, 8, 3, 5$ and $2, 7, 1, 4$, respectively. This shows that a completely unsupervised strategy is unsuitable when too few training patterns are available.

The analysis of a moderately larger dataset, including six noisy patterns for each digit, provided some evidence in favor of the use of a totally unsupervised strategy. In fact, we could observe that: (i) the first mergers always include

---

[2] Patterns obtained by both strategies are represented with the tags 005, 010, 015, 020 and 030, even if these numbers represent the actual percent noise levels only for the first set.

patterns representing the instances of the same digit, regardless the merged patterns are single patterns or larger clusters, and that (ii) the sequence of zI values associated to the new cluster obtained in subsequent mergers is characterized by a large drop, corresponding to the appearance of the first cluster including patterns representing different digits. In other words, as long as the dataset is "clean" enough, and possibly large enough but not too large, one can reach an ideal situation, in which each merger creates a new high-zI homogeneous cluster for a digit that has not been represented yet, until clusters representing all digits have been detected (Figs. 1 and 2).

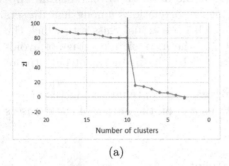
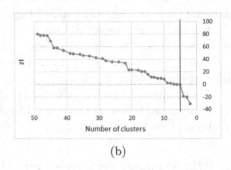

(a)   (b)

Fig. 1. zI analysis of (a) a system composed of 20 patterns (two for each of the ten digits) and (b) a system composed of 50 patterns (ten for each digit from 0 to 4) with noise level equal to 10%. Notice that the zI suddenly drops after detecting a number of clusters equal to the number of digits.

In fact, one can notice that, with the set we have taken into consideration, such a drop occurs typically when a number of homogeneous clusters equal to the number of classes has been reached. This coincidence shows that, in such a dataset, pattern homogeneity is preserved in spite of the addition of relevant noise levels.

Classification. The analysis of the intra-cluster and inter-cluster distances confirmed this observation; moreover, it showed that the centroids also satisfied the requirement, critical for a classifier, that the distances among cluster centroids should be larger than the distances between each centroid and the patterns belonging to the corresponding cluster.

We tested this approach on a set of 200 patterns, generated by the same random process, obtaining a perfect classification also using the zI-based classification.

3.2   Experiments on a Real-World Dataset

The real-world dataset used in our experiments[3] was collected by Società Autostrade SpA at highway toll booths. It includes 11034 patterns representing

---

[3] Downloadable at ftp://ftp.ce.unipr.it/pub/cagnoni/license_plate.

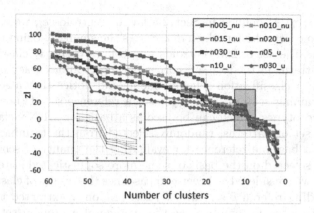

Fig. 2. zI analysis of eight sets composed of 60 noisy patterns (six patterns for each digit). Five sets are affected by noise which is more likely to be added to foreground pixels (xxxx_nu on the figure legend), whereas the digits of the other three sets are affected by uniform noise (xxxx_u on the figure legend); nxxx tags indicate the level of noise that was added. The inset shows an enlargement of the iterations around the one in which heterogeneous clusters start appearing. All clusters detected before the drop correspond to homogeneous groups with the only exception of one very distorted pattern of set n030_u.

the ten digits from 0 to 9, roughly uniformly distributed among the ten classes under consideration. The patterns have a size of 13 × 8 pixels, and have been trivially binarized pixel-wise using a threshold of 0.5 (considering pixel values normalized between 0 and 1). This resulted in strings of 104 binary features. We used part of the full dataset to compute the relevant groups, building a training set with 2000 patterns, 200 per digit, to compute the clusters, and a test set with 3000 patterns, 300 per digit, to assess the accuracy of the classifiers.

In the following, we describe and analyze in detail the results we have obtained using the supervised approach.

Cluster Detection and Distance-Based Classification. By applying HyReSS to our dataset, we detected 296 clusters, well distributed among the ten classes, with an isolated minimum of 22 clusters for digit "7" and between 27 and 34 clusters for all others. Each cluster includes from 3 to 18 training patterns. The patterns comprised in the same cluster appear to be visually homogeneous and morphologically similar, which is particularly true for the "cleanest" patterns. We evaluated the quality of such clusters by applying to them a supervised classifier, and analyzing the performances both of classical distance-based classifiers and of the classification strategy based on the zI.

The most direct assessment of the quality of the centroids of a set of clusters is provided by the accuracy of the 1-Nearest Neighbor (minimum-distance or 1-NN) classifier, whose reference set includes the centroids of all clusters that have been detected by the zI method. Therefore, to classify a pattern x, after computing $d(x, c_i)$ as defined in Sect. 2.3 for all centroids c_i, we assigned x to the class of the centroid $\hat{c}$ for which $d(x, \hat{c})$ was the smallest. Using the distance-based classifier, the set of 296 centroids was able to correctly classify 2948 out of the 3000 patterns in the test set, corresponding to an accuracy of 98.27%.

Adopting such a classification scheme, one should notice that a set of labeled data as the training set can itself represent a reference set of (possibly widely redundant) prototypes, which can be used as a basis for a 1-NN classifier. This means that a set of patterns, randomly selected from the training set, can be considered as a baseline reference for evaluating the quality of schemes, where protoypes are selected on the basis of some more sophisticated criteria.

Therefore, we considered as lower-end baselines the results of classifiers where the corresponding reference sets are: (i) 296 randomly extracted training patterns; (ii) 296 centroids computed as the average of a random set of patterns belonging to the same class.

Considering the stochasticity of the selection procedure, we repeated it 10 times, always obtaining accuracy values well below those yielded using the clusters detected by the zI clustering method for both the random pattern selector (average 96.70%, median 96.73%, worst 95.87%, best 97.43%) and the random centroid selector (average 96.17%, median 96.09%, worst 95.07%, best 97.10%).

Since we used a niching genetic algorithm to compute the zI-based clusters in a reasonable time, we also analyzed the repeatability of the results of cluster detection. We computed for five times the clusters pertaining to class "0" and class "1" and compared the results we globally obtained on the whole test set for all the 25 different centroid sets which include all their possible combinations.

As can be observed in Fig. 3(a), using the five different cluster sets for class "0" does not affect accuracy at all, while some slight changes can be observed between the best and worst result for class "1", amounting to a difference in the number of correctly classified patterns of 5 or 0.17%. Considering the worst-case scenario, based on these data, we can estimate in about 0.4% the range of variability of the results we could expect if we generated five clusters for all the ten classes as well.

Finally, we compared the results of the 296 centroids detected by the zI method with the results obtained by Kohonen's Learning Vector Quantization (LVQ) [7] algorithm, which is a very commonly used centroid-based minimum-distance supervised classifier. Using LVQ, the user has to specify the number of centroids, so it is easy to set up experiments to compare classifiers of a certain size with similarly-sized LVQ classifiers.

We first compared the set of all 296 zI-based centroids with a 296-centroid LVQ classifier, running LVQ ten times. This "full" classifier exhibited an average accuracy of 98.37% (median 98.38%, worst 98.27%, best 98.50%). Then, we applied OSLVQ [3], an LVQ variant which optimizes the number of centroids during the training phase based on the results obtained on a validation set. This algorithm gave us an idea of a reasonable optimal size and, possibly, performance, for such a classifier. Running OSLVQ ten times resulted in classifiers of size ranging from 71 to 81 centroids, with an average accuracy of 98.37%

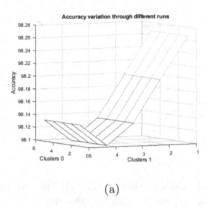

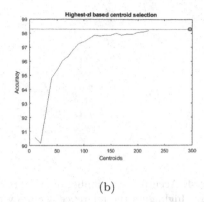

(a)   (b)

Fig. 3. (a) Variation of accuracy over different runs of the zI-based clustering algorithm. (b) Accuracy vs. size of the zI-based classifiers. The red line above highlights the reference accuracy obtained by the full 296-cluster classifier (circle on the top right-hand of the graph). (Color figure online)

(median 98.40%, worst 98.13%, best 98.57%). Based on these results, we finally trained an 80-centroid LVQ classifier for 10 times, obtaining an average accuracy of 97.65% (median 97.77%, worst 97.13%, best 97.90%).

To obtain a classifier of arbitrary size, we needed a centroid selection strategy. Once again, we wanted an immediate implementation, not based on any *a posteriori* consideration on the distribution of the centroids. Therefore, we used directly the zI value associated to each cluster, building a $10 \times n$-cluster classifier by naïvely selecting the n highest-zI centroids for each class.

Doing so, one can observe (Fig. 3(b)) that the performance of the classifiers increases smoothly with the classifier size, which proves that the centroids are well distributed over the pattern space, even if not as efficiently as possible. A less smooth accuracy increase, noticeable for the largest-size classifiers, is probably due both to some redundancy introduced in the centroid set, which may cause some partial overfitting effect, and to the way we selected the centroids. In fact, we kept adding one centroid per class in each step, while, certainly, the most efficient centroid distribution would correspond to a different number of centroids for each class.

This justifies with high probability the fact that a larger set of zI-based centroids seems to be needed to match the accuracy of a LVQ classifier. For instance, Fig. 3(b) shows that we could approximately match the performance of the 80-centroid LVQ classifier (97.65%) building a 110-centroid classifier.

Fully zI-Based Classification. Operating as described in Sect. 2.3, we applied to our test set the zI-based classifier including all 296 clusters, obtaining an accuracy level of 97.77%. As for the distance-based classifiers, we checked the performance of the zI-based clusters against random choices, choosing 296 random patterns and using them as reference clusters. This experiment was repeated ten times, with an average accuracy of 96.49% (median 96.70%, worst 94.30%, best

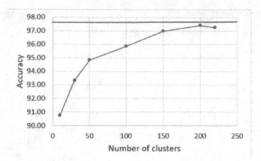

Fig. 4. Accuracy vs. number of clusters (ordered by decreasing zI values). The red line above highlights the reference accuracy obtained by the 296-cluster classifier.

97.23%). Finally, as for the distance-based classification, we created 296 clusters of random training patterns, obtaining an average accuracy of 92.08% (median 93.22%, worst 84.70%, best 94.93%).

Finally, we ranked the clusters in descending zI-value order, and tested the classification power of the subsets of these clusters, including the best-ranked ones (the best 1, 3, 5, 10, 15, 20, 22 clusters for each digit). A priori, the zI index simply evaluates the internal correlation level of each cluster and not its classification power. Nevertheless, also in this case (Fig. 4) we can make similar remarks as for the results of the 1-NN classifier reported in Fig. 3(b).

Other Classifiers. A final comparison was made with classifiers based on other principles, as provided by Weka [2]. Again, since our main goal was to confirm that the zI method is able to detect a set of clusters which can effectively be used for classification and not to reach the best possible performance, we just considered the default configurations of the classifiers we took into consideration. In particular, we classified the patterns in the test set using the following classifiers: Naïve Bayes Multinomial, J48, J48 Consolidated, SVM, Random Forest.

Table 1 summarizes all the results we have obtained on the real-world dataset, repeating the classification of the test set for ten times for the classifiers with a stochastic component, or repeating ten times a 10-fold cross-validation on the training set for the deterministic ones. The zI-based classifier reached a worse (average, if applicable) accuracy than SVM and Random Forest classifiers (98.77% and 99.02%, respectively), but better than J48, J48 Consolidated, and Naïve Bayes Multinomial (95.77%, 95.72% and 97.17%), respectively.

Even if we did not make any effort to tune the classifiers and optimize their performances, these results give an idea of the performance range that can be spanned by different classifiers on the dataset, and of the reasonably average rank of the classifiers obtained by the zI-method (98.27% and 97.77% accuracy for the 296-centroid distance-based and the fully zI-based classifiers, respectively).

Table 1. Summary of the classification accuracy of the classifiers we used as references, assessed on ten runs on the test set. Above: distance-based classifiers (see Sect. 3.2); below: classifiers based on other principles. Results of classifiers marked with a star refer to ten executions of a ten-fold cross-validation.

Classifier	Mean	Median	Worst	Best
296-centroid LVQ	98.37%	98.38%	98.27%	98.50%
80-centroid LVQ	97.65%	97.77%	97.13%	97.90%
OSLVQ (71-81 centroids)	98.37%	98.40%	98.13%	98.57%
J48*	94.12%	94.15%	93.75%	94.35%
J48 Consolidated	95.72%	95.67%	95.00%	96.63%
Naïve Bayes Multinomial*	96.05%	96.07%	95.95%	96.15%
SVM*	98.54%	98.53%	98.40%	98.70%
Random Forest	99.02%	99.03%	98.93%	99.13%

4   Conclusion

The experiments reported in this paper have proven that approaches derived from the RI metrics can be used effectively both to analyze the dynamical behavior of a complex system, and as cluster detectors for pattern classification.

In particular, the results of the experiments show that, without any further strategy aimed at selecting optimal cluster subsets and enhancing the classification performance, the accuracy of classifiers relying on clusters detected using the zI metric is competitive with other commonly-used classifiers.

Based on these basic results we expect to further develop this research along different directions, such as (1) analyzing more in depth the relationships between the relevance of a cluster for classification and its corresponding zI value; (ii) applying cluster pruning/splitting/merging strategies to the zI-based clusters; (iii) using the unsupervised approach, which apparently requires training sets that are possibly too large to be dealt with even using metaheuristics; (iv) optimizing the efficiency of the code used to compute the zI, to limit the computational overhead of that phase.

Acknowledgments. The authors would like to thank Chiara Lasagni for the many tests and for helping us reach full awareness of some of the finer details of the method.

References

1. Aldana-Bobadilla, E., Kuri-Morales, A.: A clustering method based on the maximum entropy principle. Entropy **17**(1), 151–180 (2015)
2. Bouckaert, R.R., et al.: WEKA manual for version 3-7-8. University of Waikato, NZ (2013)
3. Cagnoni, S., Valli, G.: OSLVQ: a training strategy for optimum-size learning vector quantization classifiers. In: IEEE International Conference on Neural Networks, IEEE WCCI 1994, vol. 2, pp. 762–765 (1994)

4. D'Addese, G.: Individuazione di Sottoinsiemi Rilevanti in Sistemi Dinamici. Bachelor thesis, University of Modena and Reggio Emilia, Italy (2017)
5. Faivishevsky, L., Goldberger, J.: A nonparametric information theoretic clustering algorithm. In: Proceedings of the 27th International Conference on Machine Learning ICML 2010, pp. 351–358 (2010)
6. Filisetti, A., Villani, M., Roli, A., Fiorucci, M., Serra, R.: Exploring the organisation of complex systems through the dynamical interactions among their relevant subsets. In: Andrews, P., et al. (eds.) ECAL 2015, pp. 286–293. The MIT Press, Cambridge (2015)
7. Kohonen, T.: Learning vector quantization. In: Arbib, M.A. (ed.) The Handbook of Brain Theory and Neural Networks, pp. 537–540. MIT Press, Cambridge (1998)
8. Müller, A.C., Nowozin, S., Lampert, C.H.: Information theoretic clustering using minimum spanning trees. In: Pinz, A., Pock, T., Bischof, H., Leberl, F. (eds.) DAGM/OAGM 2012. LNCS, vol. 7476, pp. 205–215. Springer, Heidelberg (2012). https://doi.org/10.1007/978-3-642-32717-9_21
9. Sani, L., et al.: Efficient search of relevant structures in complex systems. In: Adorni, G., Cagnoni, S., Gori, M., Maratea, M. (eds.) AI*IA 2016. LNCS (LNAI), vol. 10037, pp. 35–48. Springer, Cham (2016). https://doi.org/10.1007/978-3-319-49130-1_4
10. Silvestri, G., et al.: Searching relevant variable subsets in complex systems using k-means PSO. In: Pelillo, M., Poli, I., Roli, A., Serra, R., Slanzi, D., Villani, M. (eds.) WIVACE 2017. CCIS, vol. 830, pp. 308–321. Springer, Cham (2018). https://doi.org/10.1007/978-3-319-78658-2_23
11. Tononi, G., McIntosh, A., Russel, D., Edelman, G.: Functional clustering: Identifying strongly interactive brain regions in neuroimaging data. Neuroimage 7, 133–149 (1998)
12. Tononi, G., Sporns, O., Edelman, G.M.: A measure for brain complexity: relating functional segregation and integration in the nervous system. Proc. Nat. Acad. Sci. 91(11), 5033–5037 (1994)
13. Ver Steeg, G., Galstyan, A., Sha, F., DeDeo, S.: Demystifying information-theoretic clustering. In: Proceedings of the 31st International Conference on International Conference on Machine Learning ICML 2014, pp. I-19–I-27 (2014)
14. Vicari, E., et al.: GPU-based parallel search of relevant variable sets in complex systems. In: Rossi, F., Piotto, S., Concilio, S. (eds.) WIVACE 2016. CCIS, vol. 708, pp. 14–25. Springer, Cham (2017). https://doi.org/10.1007/978-3-319-57711-1_2
15. Villani, M., Roli, A., Filisetti, A., Fiorucci, M., Poli, I., Serra, R.: The search for candidate relevant subsets of variables in complex systems. Artif. Life 21(4), 412–431 (2015)
16. Villani, M., et al.: A relevance index method to infer global properties of biological networks. In: Pelillo, M., Poli, I., Roli, A., Serra, R., Slanzi, D., Villani, M. (eds.) WIVACE 2017. CCIS, vol. 830, pp. 129–141. Springer, Cham (2018). https://doi.org/10.1007/978-3-319-78658-2_10
17. Villani, M., et al.: An iterative information-theoretic approach to the detection of structures in complex systems. Complexity (2018, in press)
18. Wang, M., Sha, F.: Information theoretical clustering via semidefinite programming. In: Proceedings of the Fourteenth International Conference on Artificial Intelligence and Statistics, pp. 761–769 (2011)

Top-Down Attention Recurrent VLAD Encoding for Action Recognition in Videos

Swathikiran Sudhakaran[1,2]([⊠]) and Oswald Lanz[1]

[1] Fondazione Bruno Kessler, Trento, Italy
[2] University of Trento, Trento, Italy
{sudhakaran,lanz}@fbk.eu

Abstract. Most recent approaches for action recognition from video leverage deep architectures to encode the video clip into a fixed length representation vector that is then used for classification. For this to be successful, the network must be capable of suppressing irrelevant scene background and extract the representation from the most discriminative part of the video. Our contribution builds on the observation that spatio-temporal patterns characterizing actions in videos are highly correlated with objects and their location in the video. We propose Top-down Attention Action VLAD (TA-VLAD), a deep recurrent architecture with built-in spatial attention that performs temporally aggregated VLAD encoding for action recognition from videos. We adopt a top-down approach of attention, by using class specific activation maps obtained from a deep CNN pre-trained for image classification, to weight appearance features before encoding them into a fixed-length video descriptor using Gated Recurrent Units. Our method achieves state of the art recognition accuracy on HMDB51 and UCF101 benchmarks.

Keywords: Recurrent neural networks · Attention
Action recognition · Computer vision · Deep learning

1 Introduction

Despite the recent advancements in deep learning which resulted in huge performance improvements in computer vision tasks such as image recognition [1], object detection [2], semantic segmentation [3], etc., video action recognition still remains a challenging task. This can be attributed mainly to two major reasons, one being the lack of large scale video datasets to enable deep networks with millions of parameters to be tuned effectively to the given task, which can be partly solved by making use of large image datasets such as imagenet for pre-training the network. The second and the most important challenge is present in the nature of the data itself, i.e., the varying duration of action instances and the huge variability of action-specific spatio-temporal patterns in videos. The former can be addressed by sampling operations such as max pooling or average

© Springer Nature Switzerland AG 2018
C. Ghidini et al. (Eds.): AI*IA 2018, LNAI 11298, pp. 375–386, 2018.
https://doi.org/10.1007/978-3-030-03840-3_28

pooling while the latter requires a careful design of network structure capable of encoding the spatial information present in each frame in relation to how it evolves in subsequent frames with each action instance.

Several techniques have been proposed for encoding spatio-temporal information present in videos. Simonyan and Zisserman [4] propose to use stacked optical flow along with video frames for encoding both appearance and motion information present in the video. A huge performance improvement was observed after incorporating the optical flow stream to the image based convolutional neural network (CNN) which confirms the fact that a simple CNN has limited capability in capturing spatio-temporal information. Wang et al. [5] propose to combine improved dense trajectory method with the two stream network of [4] to perform an effective pooling of the convolutional feature maps. The original two stream network [4] is further improved by adding residual connections from the motion stream to the appearance stream in [6]. Wang et al. [7] propose to use several segments of the video on a two stream network and predict the action class of each segment followed by a segment consensus function for predicting the action class of the video. This enables the network to model long term temporal changes. A 3D convolutional network is proposed by Tran et al. [8] to encode spatio-temporal information from RGB images. Carreira and Zisserman [9] propose to combine this model with the two stream model to further improve the spatio-temporal information captured by the network. Several techniques that use recurrent neural networks such as LSTM [10,11], ConvLSTM [12,13], have also been proposed for encoding long term temporal changes. Girdhar et al. [14] propose an end-to-end trainable CNN with a learnable spatio-temporal aggregation technique.

The majority of the methods mentioned above use optical flow images along with RGB frames for improving the recognition performance. The major drawback associated with this is the huge amount of computations required for optical flow image generation. An interesting observation that we noticed is that the performance improvement brought about by the addition of the optical flow stream to these methods were almost the same ($\approx 17\%$ in the state of the art techniques that use a flow stream in addition to the RGB stream) [4–6,9,14]. This emphasizes the importance in improving the appearance stream, which uses RGB frames instead of optical flow, in order to further improve the performance of action recognition methods.

In this paper, we propose to use spatial attention during the feature encoding process to address this problem. Spatial attention have been proved to be useful in several applications such as image captioning [15], object localization [16], saliency prediction [17], action recognition [11]. Majority of these works use bottom-up attention whereas we propose to use top-down attention. Both these attention mechanisms are used by the human brain for processing visual information [18]. Bottom-up attention is based on the salient features of regions in the scene such as how one region differs from another, while top-down attention uses internally guided information based on prior knowledge such as the presence of objects and how they are spatially arranged. Since majority of the actions are correlated with the objects being handled, we propose to make use of the prior information embedded in a CNN trained for image classification task for identifying the location of the objects present in the scene. The location information is decoded from the raw video frames in the form of attention maps for weighting the spatial regions that provide discriminant information in differentiating one class from another. We leverage on class activation mapping [19] which was originally proposed for fine-grained image recognition for generating the attention map. Once the pertinent objects in the frames are identified and located, we aggregate the features from the regions into a fixed-length descriptor of the video. This is illustrated in Fig. 1 in which the object that is representative of the action class, the bow, is changing its position in subsequent frames. We use recurrent memory cells with parameters to learn such spatio-temporal aggregation for video classification. In summary,

- We propose Top-down Attention Action VLAD (TA-VLAD), a novel architecture that integrates top-down spatial attention with temporally aggregated VLAD encoding for action recognition from videos;
- We use class specific activation maps obtained from a deep CNN trained for image classification as the spatial attention mechanism and Gated Recurrent Units for flexible temporal encoding;
- We perform experimental validation of the proposed method on two most popular datasets and compare the results with state of the art.

The paper is organized as follows. TA-VLAD is presented in Sect. 2, followed by our analysis of experimental results in Sect. 3. In Sect. 4 we present our conclusions.

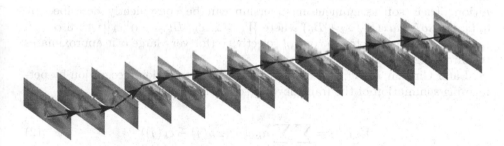

Fig. 1. The figure shows the video frames taken from the action class 'shoot bow'. The object that is representative of the action class, the bow, is changing its position in subsequent frames and determines the frame regions for feature extraction. In addition, the temporal order with which the image objects evolve into the action is relevant for aggregating frame features into a video descriptor.

2   Proposed Method

This section details our proposed method called Top-down Attention Action VLAD (TA-VLAD). We build our method on the recently proposed Action-

VLAD [14] for action recognition. In this, the authors develop an end-to-end trainable architecture that can perform VLAD aggregation of convolutional features extracted from a CNN. In order for the paper to be self-contained, we briefly explain VLAD encoding for action recognition and then present the details of our model.

2.1   VLAD Encoding

Vector of locally aggregated descriptors (VLAD) has been originally proposed for image retrieval application [20]. The method first generates a codebook of visual words c_k from local feature vectors extracted from a set of training images using k-means clustering. Given a new image with local feature vectors x_i of length P (i indexes location), the residual vectors $(x_i - c_k)$ are aggregated to form an image level descriptor V using membership values $a_k(x_i)$

$$V(j,k) = \sum_{i=1}^{N} a_k(x_i)(x_i(j) - c_k(j)) \qquad (1)$$

where $j \in P$. The matrix V is then intra-normalized, reshaped into a vector and L2-normalized to obtain the final image descriptor. A key element here is the definition of membership value $a_k(x_i)$.

In the original paper [20] the feature vectors were hand-crafted and aggregated with hard assignment, that is, $a_k(x_i)$ will be 1 if x_i is closest to c_k and 0 otherwise. The hard assignment was later replaced with a soft-assignment in [21] to form an end-to-end trainable CNN-VLAD network for place recognition. Their soft-assignment membership can be conveniently described by $a_k(x_i) = softmax(W_k^T x_i + B_k)$ where $W_k = 2\alpha c_k$, $B_k = -\alpha||c_k||^2$ with $\alpha \gg 0$ being a hyper-parameter to control selectivity (for very large α it approximates to hard assignment).

Later Girdhar et al. [14] extended this method to action recognition by performing summation of the frame level descriptors, that is

$$V(j,k) = \sum_{t=1}^{T} \sum_{i=1}^{N} a_k(x_{it})(x_{it}(j) - c_k(j)) \qquad (2)$$

where T represents the total number of frames under consideration.

Kim and Kim [22] propose an extension to the original VLAD approach by weighting the descriptors depending on their importance. For determining the spatial image locations which contain discriminant information, a saliency map of the image is used. Their method resulted in performance improvements in image retrieval application. We build upon this idea of weighted aggregation of VLAD descriptors for encoding visual features for action recognition. Instead of using a saliency detection algorithm, we develop a deep neural network with built-in weighting mechanism whose parameters are trained and which adds only minimal

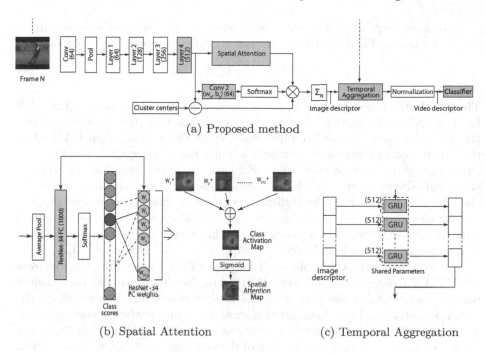

(a) Proposed method

(b) Spatial Attention   (c) Temporal Aggregation

Fig. 2. Block diagram of the proposed action recognition schema is given in figure (a). We use ResNet-34 for frame-based feature extraction and attention map generation, and temporally aggregated VLAD encoding to predict the action class from a frame sequence. Colored blocks indicate trained network layers, we use a two-stage strategy: stage 1 green, stage 2 green + orange. The proposed spatial attention and temporal aggregation methods are shown in figures (b) and (c) respectively. (Color figure online)

computation overhead to training and inference stages of the whole pipeline. Our image descriptor is computed using Eq. (1) with membership values

$$a_k(x_{it}) = m_{it} \cdot softmax(W_k^T x_{it} + B_k) \tag{3}$$

where m_{it} is used to weight the residual $(x_{it} - c_k)$ at each spatial location i. This will be detailed in Sects. 2.2 and 2.3.

2.2   Class Activation Maps for Top-Down Attention

Saliency detection involves identifying the regions of interest present in an image. In action recognition, this constitutes the image regions where humans and the objects that they are interacting with are present. We propose to utilize the class activation map (CAM) generation technique proposed in [19] for generating class specific saliency map of the video frames under consideration. The idea of CAMs is to project back the weights of the output layer to the convolutional feature map in the preceding layer. Let $f_l(i)$ be the activation of a unit l in the final convolutional layer at spatial location i and w_l^c be the weight corresponding to class c for unit l. Then the CAM for class c, $M_c(i)$, can be represented as

$$M_c(i) = \sum_l w_l^c f_l(i) \tag{4}$$

The CAM, M_c, gives the regions of the image that have been used by the CNN for identifying the particular class c. In other words, if the classes on which the CNN has been trained is representative of the actions, then CAM gives the saliency of an image if we compute it using the winning class, i.e., the class category with the highest probability. For instance, in the case of actions such as shoot ball, draw sword, brush hair, ride bike, etc., the objects being handled by the person for performing the action gives valuable information and we propose to take advantage of this. One disadvantage of CAM is that it can be computed only on CNNs that contain a global average layer preceding the fully connected classification layer, such as ResNet [1], SqueezeNet [23], DenseNet [24].

Figure 3 shows the CAM obtained for some of the frames from the videos of HMDB51 [25] dataset (second row). We used ResNet-34 pre-trained on imagenet dataset and the class category with the highest probability is selected for the CAM computation. In the figure, the regions in the image where the objects that are part of the action are getting activated such as the ball in Figs. 3a and b. Thus, it can be seen that irrespective of the fact that the CNN was pre-trained on a different dataset for a different application, the CAM generated is able to identify the salient regions present in the frames, i.e., regions that provide discriminative information in identifying the action taking place in the frame.

2.3 Top-Down Attention VLAD Encoding

In this section, we will detail how CAM can be used for weighting the image regions in order to improve the action recognition performance. A block diagram of the proposed approach is shown in Fig. 2. In this, a ResNet-34 CNN pre-trained on imagenet dataset is used for feature extraction (x_{it}) and top-down attention (m_{it}) computation. Feature extraction from frames and top-down attention computation can be carried out in a single forward pass across this network. The purpose of the top-down attention is to assign a higher weight to the regions present in the image that are useful for discriminating one action class from another while assigning a lower weight value to those regions that possess less discriminant information. Top-down attention is obtained using the following equation

$$m_{it} = sigmoid(\sum_l w_l^c f_l(i)) \tag{5}$$

where c is the winning class, w_l^c is the weight in the final layer corresponding to class c, f_l is the activation at the final convolutional layer. The *sigmoid* function is used to map the values of $M_c(i)$ in Eq. 4 to the range $[0, 1]$. The sigmoid function can be represented as

$$sigmoid(x) = \frac{1}{1 + e^{-x}} \tag{6}$$

The weights and bias of convolutional layer 'Conv 2' is initialized with W_k and B_k, respectively, as given in Sect. 2.1. Once the attention weighted VLAD descriptor is obtained as in Eq. 3, we perform summation operation across the spatial dimension to obtain a $K \times 512$ descriptor. Girdhar et al. performed summation across the temporal dimension (summation of image descriptors obtained from all frames) for generating the video descriptor. This simple summation operation is not capable of encoding the temporal evolution of the frame level features as it does not take it account the temporal ordering of frames. Following previous works [10–12], we choose to apply an RNN for this purpose. Chung et al. [26] have found that both LSTM [27] and GRU [28] perform comparably when evaluated on the tasks of polyphonic music modeling and speech signal modeling. With GRU having the added advantage of less parameters, we decided to use GRU in order to effectively encode how the frame level features evolve as an action progresses. Our temporal aggregation method using GRU is illustrated in Fig. 2c. We use K GRU modules with shared parameters (K is the number of clusters) in order to encode how the features associated with each of the clusters change with time. Once all the video frames are processed, we concatenate the final memory state of all the GRU modules to generate the temporally encoded descriptor. Then intra-normalization is applied as proposed in [29] followed by reshaping operation to obtain the vector and L2-normalization to get the final feature descriptor of the input video. This is followed by a single fully-connected layer for classification.

3 Experimental Results

The proposed method is tested on two popular action recognition datasets, namely, HMDB51 [25] and UCF101 [30] and compared against state of the art deep learning techniques. HMDB51 dataset consists of videos divided into 51 action classes collected from movies and Youtube. The dataset is composed of 6849 video clips. UCF101 dataset consists of 13320 videos collected from Youtube and has 101 action categories. For both the datasets, three train/test splits are provided by the dataset developers. Following standard practice, the recognition performance on the datasets is reported as the average of the recognition accuracy obtained on the three splits.

3.1 Implementation Details

As mentioned in Sect. 2, we use ResNet-34 for feature extraction and CAM computation. We use the feature map obtained from the final convolutional layer of ResNet-34 as the input features. The proposed method is implemented using Pytorch framework. The method consists of the following steps: (1) Extract convolutional features from random frames from the videos present in the training set to obtain the cluster centers. (2) Stage 1 training in which only the fully connected classifier layer and GRU network are trained while all the other parameters remain fixed. (3) Stage 2 training in which all the convolutional layers in the final block and fully-connected layer of ResNet-34, VLAD layers, GRU network and the classifier are trained. Stage 1 training acts as an initialization of the classifier and the GRU network while stage 2 training optimizes the features extracted from the frames, the clusters, and the attention to specialize to the given action recognition task. For the clustering step, we extracted features from random frames that are then clustered into 64 clusters using k-means algorithm. We chose the number of clusters based on the analysis carried out in [14]. The network is trained for 50 epochs in stage 1 with a learning rate of 10^{-2} and 30 epochs in stage 2 with a learning rate of 10^{-4}. In both stages, the learning rate is decayed by a factor of 0.5 after every 5 epochs. The network is trained using ADAM optimization algorithm with a batch size of 32. We also apply dropout at the final fully-connected layer at a rate of 0.5. The value of α, explained in Sect. 2.1, is chosen as 1000 following [14].

We used 25 frames from each video that are uniformly sampled across time during training and evaluation. The corner cropping and scale jittering techniques proposed in [7] is used as data augmentation during training. The center crop of frames are used for determining the action class during evaluation.

Table 1. Recognition accuracy (in %) obtained on the first split of HMDB51 for various network configurations

Configuration	Accuracy
ActionVLAD-Resnet34	53.1
VLAD+GRU(512)	54.4
VLAD+GRU(256)	54.7
VLAD+GRU(128)	54.1
TA-VLAD	56.1

3.2 Results and Discussion

We first evaluated the performance of the proposed approach on the first split of HMDB51 dataset with various settings. The results obtained are summarized in Table 1. We first adapted the ActionVLAD implementation from the authors of [14] using Resnet-34 for fair comparison and to establish a baseline since we are proposing to use Resnet-34 for frame level feature extraction. Then we added the proposed temporal aggregation method consisting of GRU networks. We evaluated the performance of the approach using different GRU memory size and found that a GRU network with 256 memory size gives the optimum performance. Thus we chose to use a GRU network of size 256 for temporal aggregation. By replacing the temporal summation with the proposed temporal aggregation method consisting of GRU network, we improved the performance by 1.6% over ActionVLAD. This shows the importance of keeping temporal ordering during feature descriptor generation of a video. In the next step, we evaluated the performance of the proposed approach, TA-VLAD by adding the proposed top-down attention mechanism during the image level feature encoding stage and an improvement of 3% is obtained over ActionVLAD.

(a) Dribble   (b) Kick ball   (c) Ride horse   (d) Golf

(e) Hug   (f) Shake hands   (g) Walk   (h) Wave

Fig. 3. Class activation maps (CAM) for some frames in HMDB51 dataset with action classes containing objects (top) and without objects (bottom). Top row: original frames, second row: CAM obtained using ResNet-34 trained on imagenet, bottom row: CAM obtained using the network trained for action recognition (after stage 2 training)

For validating that training the layers of the network used for CAM computation is useful, we decoupled the ResNet-34 used for generating CAM from the rest of the trainable layers. With the CAM branch not fine-tuned, a recognition accuracy of 55.3% is obtained on the split 1 of HMDB51 dataset, as opposed to 56.1% with the fully trained TA-VLAD. This shows that joint training, as explained in Sect. 3.1, enables the network to improve the prior knowledge encoded within it, i.e., the relevance of objects and their locations in relation to the action performed. This can be interpreted from the example images shown in Fig. 3. From the figure, we can see that the network learns to attend to regions that contain discernible information about the action class. In addition, the network has adapted its attention for both actions containing objects (3c and d) as well as actions that are performed in the absence of objects (3e and g).

Table 2. Comparison of proposed approach against state of the art methods on HMDB51 and UCF101 datasets (recognition accuracy in %).

Method	Backbone	HMDB51	UCF101
Two-stream VGG [4]	VGG-M	40.5	73.0
Two-stream ResNet [6]	ResNet-50	43.4	82.3
TDD [5]	VGG-M	50	82.8
I3D [9]	Inception V1	49.8	84.5
TSN [7]	Inception V2	51	85.1
LSTM soft attention [11]	GoogleNet	41.3	84.9
ActionVLAD [14]	VGG-16	49.8	80.3
TA-VLAD	ResNet-34	**54.1**	**85.7**

Table 2 compares the proposed approach, TA-VLAD, with state of the art techniques. The results are the average of the recognition accuracy in % obtained over all three splits. For fair comparison, we report the performance of the compared methods using RGB frames only and consider those methods that are based on deep learning and use imagenet for pre-training. For each of the three splits in HMDB51, we obtained recognition accuracies of 56.1%, 52.4% and 53.7% and on UCF101 dataset, 85.9%, 85.7% and 85.4%. From the table, it can be seen that the proposed approach performs better than the state of the art deep learning methods for action recognition.

4   Conclusions

We presented a novel end-to-end trainable deep neural network architecture for video action recognition which makes use of top-down attention mechanism for weighting spatial regions that possess discriminant information regarding the action class. For this, we used class activation maps generated from a network pre-trained on imagenet. Experiments show that prior information about the objects present in the scene, which is applied as top-down attention, improves recognition performance of the network. We also developed a temporal aggregation scheme that encodes frame level features into a fixed length video descriptor using a GRU network that inherits the cluster structure of the feature space. The boost in the performance obtained shows the importance in considering the temporal ordering of video frames during the feature encoding process. The proposed method is tested on two most popular action recognition datasets and achieves state of the art performance in terms of recognition accuracy. In addition, it was also found that the network is able to improve the prior knowledge about the scene when the top-down attention generation network is trained jointly with the video descriptor generation network. In order to improve the performance, existing approaches use optical flow as a second modality to explicitly encode motion changes and as a future work, we will explore the possibility of adding attention mechanism to the flow modality to further improve the performance of our method.

References

1. He, K., Zhang, X., Ren, S., Sun, J.: Deep residual learning for image recognition. In: IEEE Conference on Computer Vision and Pattern Recognition (CVPR) (2016)
2. Ren, S., He, K., Girshick, R., Sun, J.: Faster R-CNN: towards real-time object detection with region proposal networks. IEEE Trans. Pattern Anal. Mach. Intell. **39**(6), 1137–1149 (2017)
3. Peng, C., Zhang, X., Yu, G., Luo, G., Sun, J.: Large kernel matters - improve semantic segmentation by global convolutional network. In: Proceedings of CVPR (2017)
4. Simonyan, K., Zisserman, A.: Two-stream convolutional networks for action recognition in videos. In: Conference on Neural Information Processing Systems (NIPS) (2014)
5. Wang, L., Qiao, Y., Tang, X.: Action recognition with trajectory-pooled deep-convolutional descriptors. In: IEEE Conference on Computer Vision and Pattern Recognition (CVPR) (2015)
6. Feichtenhofer, C., Pinz, A., Wildes, R.: Spatiotemporal residual networks for video action recognition. In: Conference on Neural Information Processing Systems (NIPS) (2016)
7. Wang, L., et al.: Temporal segment networks: towards good practices for deep action recognition. In: Leibe, B., Matas, J., Sebe, N., Welling, M. (eds.) ECCV 2016. LNCS, vol. 9912, pp. 20–36. Springer, Cham (2016). https://doi.org/10.1007/978-3-319-46484-8_2
8. Tran, D., Bourdev, L., Fergus, R., Torresani, L., Paluri, M.: Learning spatiotemporal features with 3D convolutional networks. In: IEEE International Conference on Computer Vision (ICCV) (2015)
9. Carreira, J., Zisserman, A.: Quo vadis, action recognition? A new model and the kinetics dataset. In: IEEE Conference on Computer Vision and Pattern Recognition (CVPR) (2017)
10. Donahue, J., et al.: Long-term recurrent convolutional networks for visual recognition and description. In: IEEE Conference on Computer Vision and Pattern Recognition (CVPR) (2015)
11. Sharma, S., Kiros, R., Salakhutdinov, R.: Action recognition using visual attention. In: NIPS Workshop on Time Series (2015)
12. Sudhakaran, S., Lanz, O.: Convolutional long short-term memory networks for recognizing first person interactions. In: IEEE International Conference on Computer Vision Workshops (ICCVW) (2017)
13. Sudhakaran, S., Lanz, O.: Learning to detect violent videos using convolutional long short-term memory. In: IEEE International Conference on Advanced Video and Signal Based Surveillance (AVSS), pp. 1–6 (2017)
14. Girdhar, R., Ramanan, D., Gupta, A., Sivic, J., Russell, B.: ActionVLAD: learning spatio-temporal aggregation for action classification. In: IEEE Conference on Computer Vision and Pattern Recognition (CVPR) (2017)
15. Xu, K., et al.: Show, attend and tell: neural image caption generation with visual attention. In: International Conference on Machine Learning (ICML) (2015)

16. Teh, E.W., Rochan, M., Wang, Y.: Attention networks for weakly supervised object localization. In: British Machine Vision Conference (BMVC) (2016)
17. Wang, W., Shen, J.: Deep visual attention prediction. arXiv preprint arXiv:1705.02544 (2017)
18. Kastner, S., Ungerleider, L.G.: Mechanisms of visual attention in the human cortex. Ann. Rev. Neurosci. **23**(1), 315–341 (2000)
19. Zhou, B., Khosla, A., Lapedriza, A., Oliva, A., Torralba, A.: Learning deep features for discriminative localization. In: IEEE Conference on Computer Vision and Pattern Recognition (CVPR) (2016)
20. Jégou, H., Douze, M., Schmid, C., Pérez, P.: Aggregating local descriptors into a compact image representation. In: IEEE Conference on Computer Vision and Pattern Recognition (CVPR) (2010)
21. Arandjelovic, R., Gronat, P., Torii, A., Pajdla, T., Sivic, J.: NetVLAD: CNN architecture for weakly supervised place recognition. In: IEEE Conference on Computer Vision and Pattern Recognition (CVPR) (2016)
22. Kim, T., Kim, M.H.: Improving the search accuracy of the VLAD through weighted aggregation of local descriptors. J. Vis. Commun. Image Represent. **31**, 237–252 (2015)
23. Iandola, F.N., Han, S., Moskewicz, M.W., Ashraf, K., Dally, W.J., Keutzer, K.: SqueezeNet: AlexNet-level accuracy with 50x fewer parameters and ¡0.5 MB model size. arXiv preprint arXiv:1602.07360 (2016)
24. Huang, G., Liu, Z., Weinberger, K.Q., van der Maaten, L.: Densely connected convolutional networks. In: IEEE Conference on Computer Vision and Pattern Recognition (CVPR) (2017)
25. Kuehne, H., Jhuang, H., Stiefelhagen, R., Serre, T.: HMDB51: a large video database for human motion recognition. In: Nagel, W., Kröner, D., Resch, M. (eds.) High Performance Computing in Science and Engineering 2012, pp. 571–582. Springer, Berlin (2013). https://doi.org/10.1007/978-3-642-33374-3_41
26. Chung, J., Gulcehre, C., Cho, K.H., Bengio, Y.: Empirical evaluation of gated recurrent neural networks on sequence modeling. In: Proceedings of the NIPS Workshop on Deep Learning (2014)
27. Hochreiter, S., Schmidhuber, J.: Long short-term memory. Neural Comput. **9**(8), 1735–1780 (1997)
28. Cho, K., et al.: Learning phrase representations using RNN encoder-decoder for statistical machine translation. In: Conference on Empirical Methods in Natural Language Processing (EMNLP), pp. 1724–1734 (2014)
29. Arandjelovic, R., Zisserman, A.: All about VLAD. In: IEEE Conference on Computer Vision and Pattern Recognition (CVPR) (2013)
30. Soomro, K., Zamir, A.R., Shah, M.: UCF101: a dataset of 101 human actions classes from videos in the wild. arXiv preprint arXiv:1212.0402 (2012)

Natural Language Processing

Neural Learning for Question Answering
in Italian

Danilo Croce[✉], Alexandra Zelenanska, and Roberto Basili

Department of Enterprise Engineering, University of Roma Tor Vergata, Rome, Italy
{croce,basili}@info.uniroma2.it

Abstract. The recent breakthroughs in the field of deep learning have
lead to state-of-the-art results in several NLP tasks such as Question Answering (QA). Nevertheless, the training requirements in cross-
linguistic settings are not satisfied: the datasets suitable for training of
question answering systems for non English languages are often not available, which represents a significant barrier for most neural methods. This
paper explores the possibility of acquiring a large scale although lower
quality dataset for an open-domain factoid questions answering system
in Italian. It consists of more than 60 thousands question-answer pairs
and was used to train a system able to answer factoid questions against
the Italian Wikipedia. The paper describes the dataset and the experiments, inspired by an equivalent counterpart for English. These show
that results achievable for Italian are worse, even though they are already
applicable to concrete QA tasks.

1 Introduction

Question Answering (QA) [8] tackles the problem of returning one or more
answers to a question posed by a user in natural language, using as source a
large knowledge base or, even more often, a large scale text collection: in this
setting, the answers correspond to sentences (or their fragments) stored in the
text collection. A typical QA process consists of three main steps: the question
processing that aims at extracting requirements and objectives of the user query,
the retrieval phase where documents and sentences that include the answers are
retrieved from the text collection and the answer extraction phase that locates
the answer within the candidate sentences [7,11]. According to the above complexity, various QA architectures have been proposed so far. Some of these rely
on structured resources, such as Freebase, while others use unstructured information of sources such as Wikipedia (an example of such a system is the Microsoft's
AskMSR [3]), or the Web, e.g. the QuASE system [16]. Hybrid models exist as
well, that make use of both the structured and the unstructured information.
These include IBM's DeepQA [6] and YodaQA [1].

In order to initialize such systems, a manually constructed and annotated
dataset is crucial, from which the mapping between questions and answers can
be learned. Datasets designed for structured-knowledge based systems, such as

© Springer Nature Switzerland AG 2018
C. Ghidini et al. (Eds.): AI*IA 2018, LNAI 11298, pp. 389–402, 2018.
https://doi.org/10.1007/978-3-030-03840-3_29

WebQuestions [2], usually contain the questions, their logical forms and the answers. On the other side, datasets over unstructured information are usually composed of question-answer pairs: WikiMovies [13] is an example of this class of systems and it is made of a collection of texts of the movie domain. Finally, some datasets contain the entire triplets made of the questions, the paragraphs and the answers, that are expressed as specific spans of the paragraph and thus located in the paragraph. This is the case of the recently proposed SQuAD dataset [15].

The systems proposed in literature are often strongly language specific that adds a further level of complexity. Even if the proposed approaches might be portable across different languages, the low availability of training data for languages different from English still remains an important problem. Even though multilingual data collections, such as Wikipedia, do exist for many languages, the portability of the corresponding annotated resources for supervised learning algorithms remains low: large-scale annotated data mostly exist only for the English language. Small datasets for QA in Italian exists, such as the dataset consisting of about one thousand examples presented in [4], but their size is still quite limited. The manual acquisition of large datasets for a new language requires a significant effort and, as of now, human-annotated datasets only exist for few languages, including English. As a consequence, training a supervised model in a different language (such as Italian) is a challenging problem.

In this paper, we propose a weakly supervised method for the training of a QA system in the Italian language, where the annotated resource is obtained by *automatically translating* an existing QA dataset for English. While being less expensive, the method is harder due to the lower quality of the resulting training material. Specifically, the SQuAD dataset (one of the largest QA datasets in English consisting of more than 100,000 question/answer pairs) was automatically translated into Italian and the first large scale QA resource for this language was produced[1]. The basic research question follows: how can we leverage an accurate QA system from annotated data of a quality far below the human annotation standards? How can we make our QA system resilient to the inevitable noise introduced by the machine translation process applied to the English annotations? For this study, we adopted a recent state-of-the-art neural-based QA architecture, presented in [5] that allowed us to release the first neural-based QA system over Italian texts. The experimental outcomes are encouraging when compared to the English QA system. Finally, since the adoption of a noisy dataset may affect the precision of the system, an extension of the investigated model was created that introduces the possibility of training a system able not to respond if the answer is probably incorrect. The paper will discuss the process, the neural architecture and the dataset to finally outline interesting extensions for future investigation.

In the paper, the adopted neural QA approach is discussed in Sect. 2. Section 3 describes the SQuAD dataset. The acquired novel Italian dataset, named SQuAD-IT, is presented in Sect. 4. The experimental evaluation of the

---

[1] The dataset can be downloaded at http://sag.art.uniroma2.it/squadit.html.

model w.r.t. SQuAD-IT dataset is presented in Sect. 5, while Sect. 6 draws the conclusions.

2 Neural Networks for Question Answering

Among the existing approaches to question answering, we investigated the model presented in [5], namely DrQA. The approach was chosen mostly due to its reduced dependence on the language of the input dataset and for its significant performance, that makes it a crucial reference paradigm in the current research on QA. The DrQA question answering system was designed in order to use Wikipedia as the only source of information. Wikipedia is here adopted just as a plain collection of articles, without making use of its graph structure: this makes the approach highly reusable in any other context. Given a question and a (possibly huge) set of texts that contain the answer to the question, the system first finds a few among the relevant documents (as in a *classic* IR task) and then identifies the answer span within these. An example is reported in Fig. 2. The DrQA component responsible for finding the most relevant documents to the query is referred to as the *Retriever* while the *Reader Component* is a component that retrieves the correct answer span from the documents, [5]. In order to better understand the processes triggered by a new input query, the overall information flow is displayed in Fig. 1.

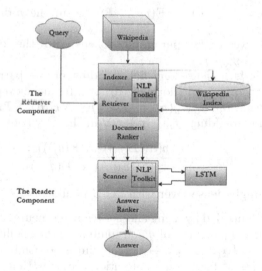

Fig. 1. The architecture of the DrQA system.

When a user makes a query, the *Retriever Component* exploits its *Indexer*. This takes in input all available Wikipedia articles in English and creates the corresponding *Wikipedia Index*. The stored data consist of tf-idf vectors and relevant metadata necessary for the retrieval process triggered by an input query.

The *Retriever* uses unigram and bigram counts of the documents in order to compile the tf-idf vectors. It makes use of a hashing function to support efficient vector retrieval. When a query is issued, the documents are retrieved from the *Index*: their tf-idf representation is compared with the query through the cosine similarity between the query-document vector pairs. Given the similarity ranking, the *Document Ranker* returns the top documents to the *Reader Component*.

The *Reader Component* triggers first the *Scanner* that seeks possible answer spans. The *Ranker* is then applied to compile the ranking of the candidate answers. The ranking is performed by making use of a LSTM neural network [9]. Such a network is trained to detect particular passages of the documents retrieved in the previous step. The answers obtained from each paragraph are then aggregated in order to make the final prediction and the best one is returned to the user. Consistently with [5], the training of the network is based on the features created from both the paragraph and the query. First, the sequence of tokens $\{p_1, \ldots, p_m\}$ in a target paragraph P_t is represented as feature vectors $\mathbf{p}_i \in \mathbb{R}^d$. The paragraph encoding is obtained by applying a Recurrent Neural Network (RNN) to a sequence of input embeddings $\{\tilde{\mathbf{p}}_1, \ldots, \tilde{\mathbf{p}}_m\}$ representing each input token: $\mathbf{p}_1, \ldots, \mathbf{p}_m = RNN(\tilde{\mathbf{p}}_1, \ldots, \tilde{\mathbf{p}}_m)$.

Specifically, a multi-layer bidirectional long short-term memory (LSTM) network is applied and the resulting $\mathbf{p}_i$ is the concatenation of the hidden units of the three layers in the end. Each input token for the specific token p_i consists of the concatenation $\tilde{\mathbf{p}}_i$ of different feature vectors summarized as follows:

- word embeddings: $f_{emb}(p_i) = \mathbf{E}(p_i) \in \mathbb{R}^n$ i.e. in the n-dimensional word embedding space
- exact match between the paragraph tokens and the question tokens: $f_{\text{exact\_match}}(p_i) = \mathbb{I}(p_i \in q)^2$
- token features, it is a dense one hot encoding of the part-of-speech tags, named entity categories and (normalized) term frequency represented as the following concatenation: $f_{\text{token}}(p_i) = (POS(p_i), NER(p_i), TF(p_i))$
- aligned question embedding: $f_{\text{align}}(p_i) = \Sigma_j a_{i,j} \mathbf{E}(q_j)$ where

$$a_{i,j} = \frac{exp(\alpha((\mathbf{E}(p_i)) \cdot \alpha(\mathbf{E}(q_j))))}{\Sigma_{j'} exp(\alpha((\mathbf{E}(p_i)) \cdot \alpha(\mathbf{E}(q_{j'}))))}$$

where $\alpha(\cdot)$ is a single dense layer with ReLU nonlinearity.

The question q is encoded by using another recurrent neural network on top of the word embeddings $\{q_1, \ldots, q_l\}$ of q and combining the resulting hidden units into one single vector $\{\mathbf{q}_1, \ldots, \mathbf{q}_l\} \rightarrow \mathbf{q}$. The aim is to combine the individual words through weights b_j based on an attention vector $\mathbf{w}$ that is trained during the learning stage, such that $\mathbf{q} = \Sigma_j b_j \cdot \mathbf{q}_j$ where $b_j = \frac{exp(\mathbf{w} \cdot \mathbf{q}_j)}{\Sigma_j' exp(\mathbf{w} \cdot \mathbf{q}_j')}$.

The overall model is thus a 3-layer bidirectional LSTM neural network. In [5], both the paragraph and the question encodings use $d = 128$ hidden units.

---

[2] A 3-dimensional binary vector represents the match with respect to the original, lowercase or lemma form of the given input token.

The best performing system reported in [5] uses GloVe embeddings [14] trained on Common Crawl of dimension $n = 300$ with more than 2 millions of tokens. The data was processed in mini-batches of length of 32. Adamax was used for the optimization as well as a dropout of 0.3 in the RNN encoding.

On top of the question and paragraph encoder, two classifiers are used to predict the start and the end of the answer span in the input paragraph. The probabilities of a token being a *start* or an *end* token are than modeled as

$$P_{start}(i) \propto exp(\mathbf{p}_i \mathbf{W}_s \mathbf{q}) \quad P_{end}(i) \propto exp(\mathbf{p}_i \mathbf{W}_e \mathbf{q}) \tag{1}$$

The best span is chosen such that its length is not superior to 15 tokens, and $P_{start} \times P_{end}$ is maximized over all the spans chosen in the given paragraph. The exponential in Eq. 1 is not normalized in order to obtain results compatible among various paragraphs. The creation of all the features needed by the system requires a significant preprocessing of the text. The original DrQA system uses the Stanford CoreNLP tool-kit [12]. It is worth noticing that almost all the features used to represent the input questions and the texts can be adapted to any other language without an excessive effort: the word embeddings can be acquired in an unsupervised fashion over any document collection. The linguistic features (e.g. the recognition of the Named Entities) can be made available through a language-specific processing chain.

3   Resources for the Question Answering System

The resources for the training and the functioning of the original DrQA system include a document collection necessary for questioning the system and a dataset used for the training of the answer ranking LSTM component. The information source used in DrQA is derived from an English Wikipedia dump. The data was filtered in order to get rid of link pages, disambiguation pages and similar, and $5,075,182$ pages were obtained in total.

QUESTION: *What was Marie Curie the first female recipient of?*

WIKIPEDIA PARAGRAPH: One of the most famous people born in Warsaw was Maria Skłodowska-Curie, who achieved international recognition for her research on radioactivity and was the first female recipient of the Nobel Prize.[198] Famous musicians include Władysław Szpilman and Frederic Chopin. Though Chopin was born in the village of Zelazowa Wola, about 60 km (37 mi) from Warsaw, he moved to the city with his family when he was seven months old.[199] Casimir Pulaski, a Polish general and hero of the American Revolutionary War, was born here in 1745.[200]

GROUND TRUTH ANSWER: *Nobel Prize*

Fig. 2. An example of the SQuAD dataset [15].

In order to create the data for the training of the question answering system, articles from a wide range of topics from Wikipedia were selected. This lead to the creation of the SQuAD dataset [15] made of more than 100,000 question-answer pairs about passages from the articles. The question-answer pairs were created by crowd-workers. These answered up to 5 questions about the content of a chosen paragraph, where each question's answer was a span from the corresponding paragraph. Other crowd-workers were also asked to provide answers to the questions created previously, in order to obtain human performance and mark the questions that might be unanswerable. This increased the quality of the data, since the unanswerable questions were deleted from the dataset. An example from the SQuAD dataset, showing the Wikipedia answer to the question *"What was Marie Curie the first female recipient of?"* is reported in Fig. 2. The dataset presents a few challenges. First of all, since the crowd-workers were asked to write the questions in their own words, it might be difficult to understand the question as the users may not use the Wikipedia prose. The system should deal with complex phenomena such as syntactic variability (due to the difference in the prose style and the lexical choice) and the synonymy between Wikipedia texts and the queries. Another challenge is the lexical variation, where external knowledge is needed in order to be able to understand some generalizations that are not included in the passage. This includes differences in the vocabulary used by different users when referring a target concept in the text. Sometimes the syntactic variability in the question and answer pair is high, as the structure of their syntactic parse trees differs significantly: this makes it more difficult to locate the correct answer. Lastly, correct answers might span through multiple sentences, which introduces additional complexity. The number of questions, paragraphs and answers in the dataset are displayed in Table 1. Notice that only the training and development sets are made available.

Table 1. The quantities of the SQuAD dataset elements.

Element	Training set	Development set
Paragraphs	18,896	2,067
Questions	87,599	10,570
Answers	87,599	34,726

4   Acquiring the Resources for Italian

In order to create an equivalent DrQA system for Italian, new training data are needed: a collection of examples, i.e. (question, paragraph, answer span) triples, is needed to suitably induce the correct answer selection function. For this purpose, a database was created from a dump of the Italian Wikipedia and the documents were processed by the tf-idf creator. The quantity of the stored documents is lower than the original, also due to the smaller size of the Italian Wikipedia counterpart. In order to store only meaningful articles, these were filtered and only those that contain more than one phrase in the document text were chosen, with a resulting dataset of 772,342 documents.

In order to create the DrQA equivalent dataset for Italian, automatic translation was applied to the Italian texts. Although being of a lower quality with respect to the original one due to the precision in the currently available automatic translation systems, such collection would definitely represent a reasonably large scale resource. Each of the answer paragraphs was translated automatically[3] together with all its corresponding questions and respective answers. Notice that the translation was obtained over a unique pseudo document collecting all the above information in order to favor the consistency of contextual information and increase the disambiguation capability of the translation system. Some parts of the original dataset were not translated by the system due to unknown characters or particular words in the text. The size of the translated data of the training and the development set is displayed in Table 2. One of the most important features of the data is that the answer for each question about the paragraph must be contained in the paragraph; it means that it can be expressed numerically as [start token:end token]. In fact, the dataset contains the answer start feature for each answer.

Table 2. The quantities of the documents in the English and the Italian Wikipedia dump, with the percentage of material w.r.t. the original dataset.

Element	Training set			Test set		
	English	Italian	Percent	English	Italian	Percent
Paragraphs	18,896	18,506	97.9%	2,067	2,010	97.2%
Questions	87,599	81,965	93.6%	10,570	9,578	90.6%
Answers	87,599	81,965	93.6%	34,726	30,979	89.2%

It was observed that often the translated answer was not part of the translated paragraph any more (mostly because of morphological differences, errors in the translation, etc.). These answers were not suitable for the training of the model: to obtain the highest possible percentage of the original data, a similar answer was looked for in the paragraph in this case. The morphologically different but equivalent answers that were searched for are the following ones:

- The lower-cased answer was looked up in the lower-cased paragraph.
- Answer with diverse punctuation was searched for in the original paragraph.
- The original English answer was looked up in the Italian paragraph.
- Lemmatized answer was looked for in the lemmatized paragraph.
- In case of a two word answer, a phrase with exchanged word order was searched in the paragraph.

---

[3] One of the currently best performing systems, deepl.com system, was used.

In case no such string was found in the paragraph, the question-answer pair was discarded from the translated dataset. It was observed that most of the discarded answers were phrases that were incorrect in the Italian language, some others were synonyms not compatible with the meaning of the paragraph and other errors were found as well. Having revised the dataset, the quantity of training and development data displayed in Table 3 was obtained.

Table 3. The quantities of the elements of the final dataset obtained by translating the SQuAD dataset, with the percentage of material w.r.t. the original dataset.

Element	Training set			Test set		
	English	Italian	Percent	English	Italian	Percent
Paragraphs	18,896	18,506	97.9%	2,067	2,010	97.2%
Questions	87,599	54,159	61.8%	10,570	7,609	72.0%
Answers	87,599	54,159	61.8%	34,726	21,489	61.9%

This dataset preserves almost all the paragraphs from Wikipedia, while discarding almost 40% of question/answer pairs. However, at the best of our knowledge, the size of the obtained dataset is far greater than any existing QA dataset in Italian. We will refer to such a dataset as **SQuAD-IT**.

5   Experimental Evaluation

The aim of the experiments was to measure the quality of the QA process for Italian given the indirect supervision obtained from the translated SQuAD dataset. The direct evaluation of the acquired translations would be too vague and costly. We measured instead its impact through the indirect evaluation corresponding to the application of the DrQA architecture to the new Italian corpus. In this way, we verify the differences in the performance with respect to the original counterpart, trained over the well-formed English dataset[4].

First, the adaptation of the original DrQA architecture with the aim of analyzing the Italian version of the SQuAD dataset will be described. Then, the results of the application of the *Reader Component*, i.e. the core answer matching algorithms, in English and Italian will be presented and some evidences about their performances will be provided. Although the DrQA system is a pipeline of the *Retriever* and the *Reader* components, we concentrate our analysis onto the evaluation of the neural network used by the answer matching stage, consistently with [5].

Experimental Set Up. In our work, most of the original DrQA architecture was preserved, although minor changes were made. First, the data storage needed

---

[4] Obviously, this measure is indicative, since the dataset will be different and the quality of the subset used as test set was not manually validated.

for further elaboration was changed. It is to be noticed that the distribution of the lengths of individual documents was not uniform: the system often produced errors just when dealing with the selection of the target documents. The ranking scores of the chosen documents (produced by the *Retriever*) were slightly biased (i.e. higher) towards longer documents against the shorter ones. Some documents have an excessive length, only 12 documents contain more than 300 paragraphs.

In order to improve the document ranking, we implemented a new ranking model for the retrieved documents as follows:

$$rank_{\text{doc new}} = \frac{rank_{\text{doc old}}}{log(\text{length of the document}) + 1}. \tag{2}$$

This makes longer documents stay lower in the final ranking, which is what we want. The SpaCy NLP tool-kit, [10], was used, for both the English and the Italian setting, since the original CoreNLP tool-kit is not available in Italian. The differences between the two languages are reflected also in the variety of the features created by the tool-kit. Whilst the English SpaCy offers 74 features, most of which are various POS-tags and named entity classes, the Italian SpaCy identified 267 features. Most of these include POS-tags and NEs as well, but it also differentiates various subclasses of these, such as Number, Person, Gender, Type (for pronouns), Tenses (for verbs), etc. Notice that 267 features correspond to a much larger and a more sparse feature space.

Experimental Results. A first evaluation was carried out as a consistency check aiming at reproducing the experiments reported in [15] by repeating those measures in our setting (e.g., by adopting a different language processor). The comparative results w.r.t. the official evaluation are reported in Table 4. The parameters of the neural network were set equal to those of the original work, including the word embeddings resource. Two evaluation metrics are used: exact string match (EM) and the F1 score, which measures the weighted average of precision and recall at the token level. EM is a stricter measure evaluated as the percentage of answers perfectly retrieved by the systems, i.e. the text extracted by the span produced by the system is exactly the same as the gold-standard. The adopted token-based F1 score smooths this constraint by measuring the overlap (the number of shared tokens) between the provided answers and the gold standard. Although the DrQA architecture is the same, the results of our setting are slightly lower due to differences in the NLP tool-kit used.

In a second experiment the DrQA was evaluated after being trained over the Italian SQuAD-IT proposed in this work. Given the high cost of the fine-tuning of the network parameters, these were kept equal to those of the original model. An embedding set of more than 300,000 words with dimension 250 was used, applying the GloVe architecture to a dump of the Italian Wikipedia.

Results in Table 5 were obtained though the official evaluation script for the SQuAD dataset[5]. Both EM and F1 scores of the Italian Architecture (DrQA-IT) are lower when compared with the English ones (DrQA-EN full), however

---

[5] The script is available at https://rajpurkar.github.io/SQuAD-explorer/. We applied some updates to translate stop words from the English to the Italian ones.

Table 4. The performance of the English system. The cells filled with (*) are not known, since the test set is not available. DrQA system is the original English system as discussed in [5]. The human performance refers to [15].

System	Test		Test	
	EM	F1	EM	F1
DrQA (Chen et al. [5])	69.5%	78.8%	70.0%	79.0%
DrQA (Our setting)	69.4%	78.5%	*	*
Human	*	*	82.3%	91.2%

they are encouraging given the complexity of the task and the simplicity of our methodology. We also investigated if the gap is due to the differences in terms of the training set size: the Italian training set covers only 60% of the questions of the English one. We thus sampled 60% of the examples from the English training material and then used them to train the DrQA English version: this setting corresponds to the row "DrQA-EN reduced". As expected, the results lowered (e.g., 64.0 of EM) although they are still higher with respect to the Italian performance (i.e. 56.1 of EM). We speculate that the difference of such performances is due to the lower quality of the Italian data set and the problems introduced during its translation. Moreover, different lexicons are used: the embedding files include 300,000 words in Italian with respect to the English lexicon made of more than 2 million tokens.

Table 5. The performance evaluation of the Italian system.

System	EM	F1
DrQA-EN (full)	69.4%	78.5%
DrQA-EN (reduced)	64.0%	75.9%
DrQA-IT	56.1%	65.9%

Notice that, in a real scenario, a QA system may provide more than one answer (with the corresponding snippets containing them) and the user may get the possibility of assessing their correctness. Considering that the DrQA architecture returns a list of answers ranked according to Eq. 1, we thus evaluated the quality of the DrQA-IT by considering the top five answers, i.e. the ones receiving the highest scores. In this setting, among the top five provided answers, we selected only the one that maximizes the overlap with the gold-standard answer and this one was used for evaluating EM and F1. As expected, the performances increases and EM of 75.0% and F1 score of 82.2% are achieved: even if the correct answers are not characterized by the highest scores, this measure shows that the system is able to target the correct answers. More work is thus required to improve the ranking necessary to reward the correct answers.

Extending the DrQA System. The original system does not include the case in which no answer is available for a given question. On the contrary, it always produces a selected, i.e. most likely, span. However, in a real scenario, it is often the case that the Retriever is unable to locate the correct paragraph. In this case, one can expect that the probability of the answer being correct is very low. In a new setting, we trained a system able to provide a NULL outcome as well, i.e. to deal with cases in which the system decide not to provide any answer to the user query.

The extended system, namely the Open World DrQA-IT, is correspondingly created such that, in case the answer is probably incorrect, it returns a "no answer" reply to the user. The SQuAD-IT dataset was extended with labeled cases for the NULL span category, in turn used to train a new model.

The extended part of the dataset should inform the system about cases where no answer is the correct outcome. Remember that, after the translation, many of the question-answer pairs were removed from the training data set as the answer was no longer contained in the translated paragraph. On the contrary, these cases are of interest for training the system against the NULL answer situation. We adopted here a distant supervision algorithm in order to retrieve interesting training paragraphs. In particular, selected paragraphs contain the answer but they show a low similarity with the question. In this way we simulate cases close enough to correct answers, useful to locate the answer-start feature in all the paragraphs of the dataset, but still unsupportive of the correct answer. This was true for several paragraphs removed from the previous tests, that were analyzed and added as new positive training examples of the NULL class for the Open World DrQA. Once this distantly supervised dataset was created, all the NULL answers in this part of the dataset were substituted by a special pseudo-token made of randomly chosen characters. The same token was used for all the answers. The token was added to all the paragraphs in the dataset, both the original and the distantly supervised ones. The quantity of the data obtained in such a way is displayed in Table 6.

Table 6. The dataset created for the training of the Open World Italian system. The first row consists of the whole SQuAD Italian dataset, whilst the second line refers to the data generated by distant supervision.

Data	Training set		Test set	
	Questions	Answers	Questions	Answers
SQuAD Italian	54,159	54,159	7,609	21,489
Questions w/o answers	19,776	19,776	2,644	2,644
Total	73,935	73,935	10,253	24,133

The performance was measured on the original DrQA data with the added random token. The evaluation is performed on Exact Match and Precision and

Recall at token level. The results are displayed in Table 7, where the new setting is referred to as DrQA-IT with no answer. The most significant increase of nearly 1% point is observed in the Exact Match measurement. Moreover a slight improvement in terms of Precision is observed, which was the main motivation of such a simple extension of the DrQA model.

The above model gives rise to a working application dealing with the Italian version of Wikipedia. Some examples are reported below. The question *"Qual è la capitale della Slovacchia?"* receives the correct answer *Bratislava* matched in the retrieved page concerning the Danube river, from the Italian Wikipedia[6].

The question *"Dove si trovano le isole Marshall?"* triggers the retrieval of three answers. The first answer is *Pacifico* from the Italian Wikipedia entry about the Marshall Islands[7], specifically at the paragraph: *"Facente parte della Micronesia, le Isole Marshall sono un gruppo di atolli e Isole situate nel [Pacifico], poco a nord dell'Equatore. La capitale, la cittá di Majuro ...".*

The second ranked answer is *Likiep* and it is much less precise. However, the matching in the paragraph *"...L'isola piú grande della Repubblica delle Isole Marshall é Kwajalein, un atollo con la laguna piú grande del mondo. Il punto piú alto del paese, che raggiunge soli i 10 metri di altitudine, si trova nell'atollo di [Likiep]. ..."* suggests a surprisingly good ability of the system to deal with information spread across multiple sentences.

Finally, the third answer *"Stati Federati di Micronesia a ovest e Kiribati a est"* is extracted from the paragraph *"La nazione (una repubblica presidenziale) é composta dagli arcipelaghi Ratak e Ralik situati fra gli [Stati Federati di Micronesia a ovest e Kiribati a est]."* and again it is a very good response, adding further details.

Table 7. The performance evaluation of the Open World Italian system.

System	EM	Precision	Recall
DrQA-IT	56.09%	67.38%	68.45%
DrQA-IT (no answ.)	57.00%	67.82%	68.12%

6   Conclusions

This paper introduced a new dataset for the task of Question Answering for the Italian language. The data were created by making use of the automatic translation and a large-scale dataset for the Italian question answering task on factoid questions was created, that might be reused and extended in the future.

We argue that the results obtained by the Italian DrQA system are satisfying, even though there is certainly space for future improvement of both the network

---

[6] https://it.wikipedia.org/wiki/Danubio.

[7] https://it.wikipedia.org/wiki/Isole_Marshall.

architecture and the dataset. Nevertheless, the overall training method and the resource obtained by a simple methodology lead to the creation of, possibly, the first neural network based QA system for the Italian language.

Lastly, an extension of the Italian QA system was set up, which includes the possibility of the system not to answer, which increased slightly the precision with respect to the original system and represents an interesting extension of the capabilities of the original model. As a future improvement, the quality of the document retrieval and the indexes creation in the Italian language can be improved by a major computational capacity. This might also enable the evaluation of the whole system pipeline. Further steps might include the structural or parameter optimization of the neural network for the Italian system and an improvement of the quality of the text processing for the Italian language.

References

1. Baudiš, P., Šedivý, J.: Modeling of the question answering task in the YodaQA system. In: Mothe, J., et al. (eds.) CLEF 2015. LNCS, vol. 9283, pp. 222–228. Springer, Cham (2015). https://doi.org/10.1007/978-3-319-24027-5_20
2. Berant, J., Chou, A., Frostig, R., Liang, P.: Semantic parsing on freebase from question-answer pairs. In: EMNLP, pp. 1533–1544. ACL (2013)
3. Brill, E., Dumais, S., Banko, M., Brill, E., Banko, M., Dumais, S.: An analysis of the AskMSR question-answering system. In: Proceedings of EMNLP 2002, January 2002
4. Caputo, A., de Gemmis, M., Lops, P., Lovecchio, F., Manzari, V.: Overview of the EVALITA 2016 question answering for frequently asked questions (QA4FAQ) task. In: CLiC-it/EVALITA. CEUR Workshop Proceedings, vol. 1749. CEUR-WS.org (2016)
5. Chen, D., Fisch, A., Weston, J., Bordes, A.: Reading Wikipedia to answer open-domain questions. In: Proceedings of the 55th Annual Meeting of the Association for Computational Linguistics, Long Papers, vol. 1, pp. 1870–1879 (2017)
6. Ferrucci, D.A., et al.: Building Watson: an overview of the DeepQA project. AI Mag. **31**(3), 59–79 (2010)
7. Harabagiu, S.M., et al.: FALCON: boosting knowledge for answer engines. In: Proceedings of The Ninth Text REtrieval Conference, TREC 2000, Gaithersburg, Maryland, USA, 13–16 November 2000 (2000)
8. Hirschman, L., Gaizauskas, R.: Natural language question answering: the view from here. Nat. Lang. Eng. **7**(4), 275–300 (2001)
9. Hochreiter, S., Schmidhuber, J.: Long short-term memory. Neural Comput. **9**(8), 1735–1780 (1997). https://doi.org/10.1162/neco.1997.9.8.1735
10. Honnibal, M., Montani, I.: spaCy 2: natural language understanding with bloom embeddings, convolutional neural networks and incremental parsing (2017, to appear)
11. Kwok, C.C.T., Etzioni, O., Weld, D.S.: Scaling question answering to the web. In: WWW, pp. 150–161 (2001)
12. Manning, C.D., Surdeanu, M., Bauer, J., Finkel, J., Bethard, S.J., McClosky, D.: The Stanford CoreNLP natural language processing toolkit. In: Association for Computational Linguistics (ACL) System Demonstrations, pp. 55–60 (2014)

13. Miller, A.H., Fisch, A., Dodge, J., Karimi, A.H., Bordes, A., Weston, J.: Key-value memory networks for directly reading documents. In: EMNLP (2016)
14. Pennington, J., Socher, R., Manning, C.D.: GloVe: global vectors for word representation. In: EMNLP, vol. 14, pp. 1532–1543 (2014)
15. Rajpurkar, P., Zhang, J., Lopyrev, K., Liang, P.: SQuAD: 100.000+ questions for machine comprehension of text. CoRR abs/1606.05250 (2016)
16. Sun, H., Ma, H., Yih, W.T., Tsai, C.T., Liu, J., Chang, M.W.: Open domain question answering via semantic enrichment. In: WWW (2015)

Detecting Inappropriate Comments to News

Patrizio Bellan[1] and Carlo Strapparava[2(✉)]

[1] University of Trento, CIMeC, Trento, Italy
patrizio.bellan@gmail.com
[2] FBK-irst, Trento, Italy
strappa@fbk.eu

Abstract. *Inappropriate* comments, defined as deliberately offensive, off-topic, troll-like, or direct attacks based on religious, sexual, racial, gender, or ethnic posts, are becoming increasingly problematic in user-generated content on the internet, because they can either derail the conversation or spread out harassment. Furthermore, the computational analysis of this kind of content, posted in response to professional news-papers, is not well investigated yet. To such an extent, the most predictive linguistic and cognitive features were seldom been addressed, and *inappropriateness* was not investigated deeply. After collecting a new dataset of inappropriate comments, three classic machine learning models were tested over two possible representations for the data to fed in: normal and distorted. *Text distortion* technique, thanks to its ability to mask thematic information, enhanced classification performance resulting in the valuable ground in which extract features from. Lexicon based features showed to be the most valuable characteristics to consider. Logistic regression turned out to be the most efficient algorithm.

Keywords: Journal news comments · Inappropriateness · Off-topic
Text distortion

1 Introduction

The new ways of communication are quickly transforming the everyday language into new forms. Abbreviation, emoticons, emojis, digital slang, globalization, anonymity, invisibility, and instant communication are only a bunch of factors that continuously change the language usage. Nowadays, journalists can experiment the resonance of their articles throughout the comments posted by the readers. However, we can often find uncivil comments that derail the conversation from the main discourse, consequently degrading the effectiveness of the user experiences. Margins *et al.* [12] depicted that "the anonymity of the Internet can provide opportunities for freer speech because people can say what they think without fear". Christians *et al.* [5] highlighted the importance of online users

C. Ghidini et al. (Eds.): AI*IA 2018, LNAI 11298, pp. 403–414, 2018.
https://doi.org/10.1007/978-3-030-03840-3_30

participation as an opportunity for readers to debate current events. In such context, instant responses are encouraged, with the possible escalation of the cyberhate [1]. This emphasizes two problematic aspects of online content: *mutability* and *adaptability*. Indeed, virtual harassment can become highly domain specific and avoided detection with hidden but human-understandable languages. Moreover, the huge number of user generated content published daily prevents a manual filtering [14]. Moreira *et al.* [14], and Warner and Hirschberg [18] highlighted that in long text toxic words tend to appear more frequently then in short ones. Furthermore, obfuscation of words and phrases to evade manual or automatic checking makes detection difficult. Basic methods make use of black-lists and regular expressions, however these measures fail in different situations [7,14,15]. Indeed, lists continuously change due to language evolution. Thus, it seems that it is impossible for simple keyword spotting metrics to be successful. Benefits from character *n-grams* in harmful-detection have been drawn down by Waseem [20]. The analysis of subjective language has proven to be a key feature for classification of opinions and emotions in text [3,4,10]. Although novel deep learning-based approaches for automatically identifying inappropriate language were a success [21], they require a huge collection of labeled examples, and thus they often prove to be unfeasible in many real settings.

In this paper, we introduce the task of detecting *inappropriate* comments to news. The task is different with respect to hate speech detection or offensive language detection because inappropriate post does not necessarily contain noxious speech.

After collecting a dataset, we looked for a solution based on a mixture of words lists and text statistics to enhance some classical machine learning algorithms. This paper is organized as follows. Section 2 describes the data collection process, the features extracted from dataset and the algorithms used in experiments. Section 3 reports the experimental results, while Sect. 4 discusses them. Finally, Sect. 5 presents our conclusions.

2   Data Collection and Features

We opted for *The Guardian* [22] to collect news and comments for investigating the phenomenon. The dataset was extracted from the collection of comments crawled on the newspaper website in a period of time starting from the beginning of November 2017 until the end of January 2018. We collected articles and comments posted among public available sections of the journal, checking for new comments daily. Because moderators delete inappropriate messages, a continuous check of its presence allowed us to label it in two distinct categories: *appropriate comment* and *inappropriate comment*. So, there was no need of any further operations in labeling the data, as well avoiding the annotator agreement issue highlighted by Wassem [19].

The dataset was extracted from the collection of comments grabbed, and then balanced by keeping all the posts removed by the moderators, while the appropriate comments were randomly selected. Thus, we ended up with 1386 samples in total, 693 inappropriate and 693 appropriate comments. Some examples are reported in Table 1. As an additional experiment, we also tested the best models in a different context to check if our classifiers were able to generalize across domains. Because the context plays a major role in the scope of posting and in language's style of the message, we opted for the Twitter setting. We built up the cross-domain dataset by concatenating samples from the work of Davidson et al. [6] to those from Golbeck et al. [11] because both represent some forms of inappropriateness. In the Davidson's dataset the 5% of samples were representative of *hate speech*, while in the Golbeck's dataset the 15% of texts were examples of *on-line harassment*.

The same policy applied for extraction of the first dataset, were performed here; so we ended with a balanced dataset for cross-domain experiments.

Table 1. Reports examples of comments posted in response to news article.

News headline	Inappropriate comment	Appropriate comment
Little lord Jesus, fruitcake-style: the worst nativity scenes of 2017	Are you black?	It is an interfaith nativity...
Keith Pitt Nationals defection rumour fuels Queensland LNP split debate	Roll on the Renaissance!	Oh, and remind the taxpayers, who picked up the bill for their incompetence?
Senate approves most drastic changes to US tax code in 30 years	Poor baby...	Ilaha! That is a good joke. Oh wait you were serious. There is no help for you now
	I wish there was the option available to report you for stupidity	You believe that they paid 91% tax or just gave it away to employees
Our selective blindness is lethal to the living world	"My strong advice is not to have children" Yeah I said that to your parents, but obviously they didn't listen to me	I blame the mainstream media

2.1 Sets of Features

Stamatatos *et al.* [17] demonstrated the efficacy of applying *text distortion*, method in which the input text is distorted by masking thematic information, and in the meanwhile it is still possible to generalize over topics. Features were extracted from both *normal* and *distorted* version of the text. We report the list of features, grouping them together under macro-categories. This list comprehends the most promising features reported in the literature. We run final step of dimensionality reduction by PCA, over each set of features, obtaining vectors in a more feed-able representation for the machine learning procedures.

- **Grammar**, to report statistics about *Sentences*, *Words*, and *Noun phrases*, were included for capturing the general spectrum of the text. Although, these features are in general not quite predictive, their use in conjunction with other statistics can enhance classifiers' performance. We tracked the use of grammatical categories by unigrams, bigrams, and trigrams of *Part-Of-Speech* (POS).
- **Space** and **Punctuation** statistics. The former intercepted space characters spectrum, the latter recorded punctuation symbols use by mean of k-grams schema.
- **Characters** (letters) were captured in forms of bigrams and trigrams of successive characters. Inspired by the work of Martinc [13], we added *Characters Flooding* to capture word-exaggeration that can be voluntary typed to hide harmful message.
- **Educational level** of the author was assessed by *Readability* [23] statistics and *SpellCheck* [24] errors.
- **Relations** among persons, organizations, and locations were extracted by mean of *Name Entity Recognition* (NER) [8] and *Dependency Parser* [16].
- **Semantic embeddings** has been computed by Doc2Vec.
- **Emotional features** were extracted by *VADER* and *SenticNet*. [25] The former was chosen because Gilbert *et al.* [9] proved its ability to outperform individual human raters in predicting sentiments expressed in social media. The latter would extend sentimental information.
- **Lexicon-based** counters were added to track down the presence of specific words.
  Lemma statistics kept the use of the most common words. *Concrete-Abstract* set was formed by considering the work of Brysbaert *et al.* [2]. *Imageability* depicted use of imaginable words and the level of strength associated for imaging them [27]. *Lexicon* represented a miscellaneous collection of terms. It was designed to grab psychological factors that can be informative of harassment. The list was formed by the refined version of a "hate lexicon" proposed by Davidson *et al.* [6], a list of common interjections, a list of common slangs and slurs associated with religious, genders, stereotypes, misogynies, misandry, sexual orientations, and ethnic extracted from Wikipedia. Because we aimed at capturing the *us versus them* thinking, common anti-words (such as anti-American) were also added.

2.2 Experiments

We run the classification experiments using three machine learning algorithms: Logistic regression, Naïve Bayes, and Decision Tree, assessing the evaluation with F1 metrics. Artificial neural network models were not tested because of dataset size. Hyper-parameters optimization was performed by mean of Grid search CV, with a factor of 10 for k-folds. This stage was necessary to identify the kernel and the C parameter in Logistic regression models, criterion and splitter in Decision Tree models.

The kernel research space was formed by newton-cg, lbfgs, and liblinear. The range of possible values for the inverse of regularization strength was (0.1, 1.0, 10, 100). In decision tree algorithm two measures the quality of a split were searched during Grid search: Gini and Entropy; while the split strategy was searched between best and random. For all algorithms we exploited the Scikit-Learn machine learning environment [26].

Following the text distortion approach, each word in the list of the top-k was replaced by a star character ('*'), producing a new version of the text. The list of words to mask was identified by words statistics computed on all the comments collected. So, we decided to feed ours models with two different representations for each group of features, one computed on the normal view of the text and another one using the distorted version, testing three different values for the factor k: 1000, 3500, and 5000.

Then, we applied to each algorithm an ablation stage with Recursive feature elimination (RFE) schema. The longest a group of features is kept the more it is informative, otherwise it was excluded previously during this stage.

Finally, the best performing models were tested on the Twitter dataset. The baseline has been set to the chance level.

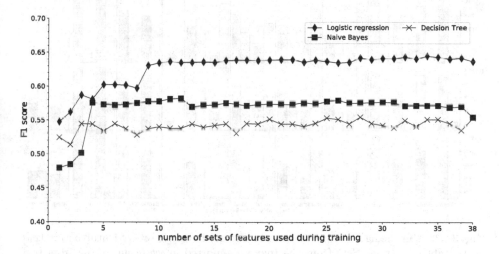

Fig. 1. The figure displays performances of models trained and tested on comments. The x-axis reports the number of sets of features during model training (models at the different points on the x-axis were trained on respective different sets of features).

3   Results

The section reports the results for each class of machine learning algorithms. Scores reported refer to models with the highest scores in *F1* metric. Classifiers

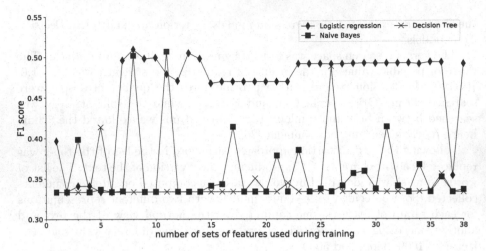

Fig. 2. The figure displays the performance of models trained on comments and tested on tweets. The x-axis reports the number of sets of features during model training (models at the different points on the x-axis were trained on respective different sets of features).

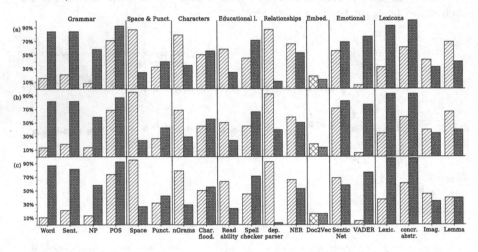

Fig. 3. Plots in the figure represent (in percentage) how long sets of features were kept by the ablation stage. Sets from the text are reported in *white* and those from text distortion in *gray*. Embeddings are colored in *white* those extracted on article, in *gray* those from comments. *(a)* Logistic regression; *(b)* Decision Tree; *(c)* Naïve Bayes.

are ordered by the number of sets of features used during training. So, the 1st classifier was trained with one set of features, the 2nd with two, and so on. Thus, the ordinal number corresponds to its position into Figs. 1 and 2.

Table 2. The table reports some scores on comments and tweets. The highest score for each algorithm in both context is underlined; in bold the best ones. It is also reported classifier's algorithm, number of features sets used during training (**sets**), and the distortion factor (k).

Algorithm	Sets	(k)	F1 comments	F1 tweets
Logistic regression	1	1000	.547	.397
	2	3500	.562	.333
	3	5000	.587	.341
	8	3500	.597	**.509**
	10	1000	.635	.499
	34	3500	**.645**	.491
Decision tree	1	3500	.524	.333
	2	3500	.514	.333
	3	5000	.545	.333
	26	5000	.551	.489
	29	3500	.555	.333
Naïve bayes	1	3500	.479	.333
	2	5000	.485	.333
	3	5000	.501	.398
	4	3500	.578	.333
	8	3500	.576	.502
	11	3500	.582	.507
	12	3500	.582	.333

Logistic Regression. performed always above chance level, with good performance on the comments dataset. Figure 1 displays a marked positive uptrend pretty close to 0.645 overall. Also, the plot reveals a large increase in the first five models followed by two plateaus. The first one includes four models that scored 0.61, whereas the second one is pretty stable at 0.63 (+0.02). As reported in Table 2, the 34th model reached the absolute highest score at 0.645 with a distortion factor k of 3500. The model was trained only on 10 groups of features, but with text distortion set to 1000, peaked 0.635, with a very small gap from the best model (−0.01). The list of sets used during training for these two models is reported in Table 3. Concrete-Abstract, Lexicon, Part-of-speech and Word summaries extracted from text distortion always enhanced performance. In addition to those, the most predictive features extracted from the raw version of the text were: Space, Dependency parser, and n-grams statistics. Embeddings were discharged early during ablation stage.

Figure 2 reports the results of the cross-domain test. In general, this algorithm scored beneath chance level. The plot shows the larger negative drop in performance for the 2nd model. After that, an inconstant behavior is displayed

Table 3. The table below reports sets of features used during training for the 34th model ($k = 3500$), the 10th ($k = 1000$), and the 8th ($k = 3500$) in Logistic regression.

Normal	34th	10th	8th	Distorted	34th	10th	8th	Embeddings	34th	10th	8th
nGrams	x	x		nGrams	x			Article	x		
Character flood	x			Character flood	x			Comment	x		
Concrete-Abstract	x			Concrete-Abstract	x	x	x				
Dependency parser	x	x	x	Dependency parser	x						
Imageability	x			Imageability	x						
Lemma	x			Lemma	x						
Lexicon				Lexicon	x	x	x				
NER	x			NER	x						
Noun phrases				Noun phrases	x						
Part-of-speech	x			Part-of-speech	x	x	x				
Punctuation	x			Punctuation	x						
Readability	x			Readability	x						
SenticNet	x		x	SenticNet	x	x					
Sentences	x			Sentences	x	x	x				
Space	x	x	x	Space	x						
Spell checker	x			Spell checker	x						
Words				Words	x	x					
VADER				VADER	x						

on the subsequent models, broken by the highest peak at the 8th model, that scored 0.509; sets used to train this model are list in Table 3. This was the best performance in the Twitter domain, overall. The input representation for this classifier has been formed by the concatenation of Concrete-Abstract, Lexicon, Part-of-speech, Word, and Sentence summaries from text distortion with Space, Dependency parser, and SenticNet statistics. Two plateaus marked the rest of the trend, but none of them scored above baseline.

In general, these models took benefits from data represented by text distortion, specifically with a factor k of 3500. Grid search CV identified the value of *1.0* for the inverse of regularization strength and *liblinear* as kernel method.

Decision Tree. performed worst but above baseline on the comments dataset. The trend shows a waved behavior around 0.54. The 3rd classifier showed the major step up, scoring 0.545, but the 29th model scored the highest peak for the algorithm at 0.555.

Twitter test results are presented in Fig. 2. The situation depicted shows that only three models behaved off the main trend of 0.333, but only one peaked remarkably. As reported in Table 2, the highest peak is found at the 26th classifier, that scored 0.489 by representing the input with a factor k of 5000.

The most useful distortion parameter was 3500. The best criterion found out by Grid search CV was *Gini*, while the best node splitter strategy was *best*.

Naïve Bayes. scored above baseline in comment domain in most of the cases. As shown in Fig. 1, it increased sharply, till peaking almost the top with 4 sets only. The 1st model performed 0.479 using Space summary only computed on the normal representation of the data. The 2nd and the 3rd models adopted sets entirely extracted from the distorted view with a factor-gain of 5000. The former, that reached 0.485, has been trained with the concatenation of Concrete-Abstract with Lexicon; the latter, that also included Part-of-speech to the input representation, obtained a score of 0.501. The 4th model peaked almost the best for this class at 0.578, with a factor k equal to 3500. The input representation was obtained by the concatenation of Space, Concrete-Abstract, Lexicon, and Dependency parser features.

After this point, the trend results almost stable around this value. Upper bound performance was marked to 0.582 by both the 11th and the 12th model with text distortion parameter of 3500.

Twitter tests reported in Fig. 2 show a very irregular trend, but in most of the cases the accuracy metric is pretty close to 0.333. Only two scores are above 0.50.

3.1   Sets of Features

Figure 3 reveals informativeness of each group of features. The information conveyed to the classifiers is directly linked to times of retention during the ablation phase. So, the more a set is retained, the more information it conveys.

Overall, there is a clearly preference for sets of features extracted by mean of text distortion, but with few exceptions, among algorithms.

Grammar category turned out to be the most predictive group of features. Specifically, Words and Sentences from text distortion and Part-of-speech from both the versions of the text were good predictors.

In the **Syntax** group there is a marked preference for Space features only, extracted from the normal text.

Characters ngrams, extracted from the normal text were chosen more than the others members of this group. Instead, Character flooding shows a slightly preference for the distorted version of the text.

The **Educational level** was captured most likely by Spell-checker errors extracted form text distortion, and Readability summary computed over the two versions, but with a little preference for the distorted one.

Relations among places, people, objects were successfully captured on both normal and distorted texts by the NER. Instead, Dependency parser conveyed information to classifiers mainly from the unaltered text.

Semantic embeddings were the worst group of features; in fact they were excluded very early during ablation stage.

Emotional features present a strong preference for text distortion in the VADER setting only. Although this selection is not so marked in SenticNet, this set of features turned out to be a great predictor of the phenomenon.

Lexicon-based group comprehend the most predictive features, overall. Specifically, Lexicon and Concrete-Abstract features, extracted from text distortion were the most predictive features.

4   Discussion

Logistic regression turned out to be the best algorithm to deploy, while the others were not able to provide interesting results. The 34th Logistic regression classifier hit the highest score of 0.645, with a factor of distortion of 3500. Naïve Bayes classifiers could have failed due to violations on the base assumption that could have misled classifiers. In fact, features are not independent to each others. Instead, Decision Tree models were not able to split data optimally.

The paper argued for a conjunction of features from both normal and masked texts as efficient input representation for machine learning classifiers. Tracking use specific words can predict inappropriateness. As Fig. 3 reveals, the concatenation of *Lexicon-based*, *Grammar*, and *Syntax* are the most valuable features to consider in this task. The most predictive features are found in the two versions of the text, but not distributed equally. Indeed, there is a strong preference for sets of features extracted by mean of text distortion. Specifically, Concrete-Abstract, Part-of-speech, Lexicon, Sentences, and Words from text distortion were kept most of the times during ablation step. From the other side, Space, Dependency parser, and nGrams of character were extracted from the unaltered text. Worthy to note, the lack of semantic embeddings, that were not able to offer any valuable information to classifiers.

Furthermore, the study agree with Gilbert *et al.* that "A comprehensive, high quality lexicon is often essential" [9], because the two most predictive sets of features are of this type: Lexicon and Concrete-Abstract. Results hold for the conclusion that *text distortion* technique enhanced classifier quality. Moreover, we agree with Stamatatos *et al.* [17] on 3500 as the best choice for the distortion parameter k, providing solid evidence in favor of its deployment.

Twitter tests revealed high dependency of the task with the environment under investigation. Probably, the incompatibility of linguistic factors such as language styles, idiom, the scope of posting, broader *vs.* narrow public, caused the bad performance recorded in this setting, evidencing also a possible scalability issue.

5   Conclusion

We propose a novel approach for inappropriate comments detection posted in response to professional articles in on-line newspapers. This kind of investigation has rarely been addressed. The lack of availability of a representative dataset imposed us the need to collect one of this kind. The study focused on which are the most predictive features of inappropriateness, and it tested the efficacy of text distortion technique in text-classification tasks. Benefit from using a text distortion representation has been well demonstrated. In fact, the situations depicted suggests of representing input data as concatenation of features extracted from both distorted and unaltered texts. Specifically, a gain factor k of 3500 provided the most powerful text representation in which extract features from. Moreover, the most predictive groups of characteristics turned out to be *Lexicon-based*, *Grammar*, and *Syntax*.

Results of Twitter tests suggested a higher context specificity of the investigated phenomenon.

We would like to apply the depicted workflow to other similar problems such as *hate speech*, *toxicity*, and *harmful* detection. Furthermore, the use of ensemble methods should show better results. Such design can also benefit from a more focused investigation on the k value of text distortion, because a specific domain and the choice of k could be tied together. Along this way, other social media environments should also be investigated.

References

1. Brown, A.: What is so special about online (as compared to offline) hate speech? Ethnicities **18**(3), 297–326 (2018)
2. Brysbaert, M., Warriner, B., Kuperman, V.: Concreteness ratings for 40 thousand generally known English word lemmas. Behav. Res. Methods **46**(3), 904–911 (2014)
3. Burnap, P., Williams, M.L.: Us and them: identifying cyber hate on Twitter across multiple protected characteristics. EPJ Data Sci. **5**(11), 11 (2016)
4. Burnap, P., Williams, M.: Hate speech, machine classification and statistical modelling of information flows on Twitter: interpretation and communication for policy decision making. Internet Policy Polit. 1–18. (2014). https://doi.org/10.1002/poi3.85
5. Christians, C.G., Richardson, K.B., Fackler, M., Kreshel, P., Woods, R.H.: Media Ethics: Cases and Moral Reasoning, CourseSmart eTextbook, 9th edn. Routledge, Abingdon (2015)
6. Davidson, T., Warmsley, D., Macy, M., Weber, I.: Automated hate speech detection and the problem of offensive language. In: Proceedings of the 11th International AAAI Conference on Web and Social Media, pp. 512–515. AAAI Press, Montréal (2017)
7. Djuric, N., Zhou, J., Morris, R., Grbovic, M., Radosavljevic, V., Bhamidipati, N.: Hate speech detection with comment embeddings. In: Proceedings of the 24th International Conference on World Wide Web Companion, pp. 29–30. ACM, Florence (2015)
8. Finkel, J.R., Grenager, T., Manning, C.: Incorporating non-local information into information extraction systems by Gibbs sampling. In: 43rd Annual Meeting of the Association for Computational Linguistics, pp. 363–370. ACL, University of Michigan, USA (2005)
9. Gilbert, E., Hutto, C.J.: Vader: a parsimonious rule-based model for sentiment analysis of social media text. In: Proceedings of the Eighth International Conference on Weblogs and Social Media. AAAI Press, Ann Arbor (2014)

10. Gitari, N.D., Zuping, Z., Damien, H., Long, J.: A lexicon-based approach for hate speech detection. Int. J. Multimedia Ubiquit. Eng. **10**(4), 215–230 (2015)
11. Golbeck, J., Ashktorab, Z., Banjo, R., et al.: A large labeled corpus for online harassment research. In: Proceedings of the 2017 ACM on Web Science Conference, pp. 229–233. ACM, New York (2017)
12. Kirby, A.: The communicative features of online hate in temporary social networks in Twitter and YouTube. Multilingual Margins: J. Multiling. Peripher. **2**(2), 74 (2017)
13. Martinc, M., Skrjanec, I., Zupan, K., Pollak, S.: PAN 2017: author profiling - gender and language variety prediction. In: Working Notes of CLEF - Conference and Labs of the Evaluation Forum. CEUR-WS.org, Dublin (2017)
14. Pelle, R.D., Moreira, V.P.: Offensive comments in the Brazilian web: a dataset and baseline results. In: Proceedings of the 6th Brazillian Workshop on Social Network Analysis and Mining, Sao Paulo, SP, Brazil, pp. 510–519 (2017)
15. Mubarak, H., Darwish, K., Magdy, W.: Abusive language detection on Arabic social media. In: Proceedings of the First Workshop on Abusive Language Online, Vancouver, BC, Canada, pp. 52–56. ACL (2017)
16. Schuster, S., Manning, C.D.: Enhanced English universal dependencies: an improved representation for natural language understanding tasks. In: Proceedings of the Tenth International Conference on Language Resources and Evaluation. European Language Resources Association, Portorož (2016)
17. Stamatatos, E.: Authorship attribution using text distortion. In: Proceedings of the 15th Conference of the European Chapter of the Association for Computational Linguistics, Valencia, Spain, vol. 1, pp. 1138–1149. ACL (2017)
18. Warner, W., Hirschberg, J.: Detecting hate speech on the world wide web. In: Proceedings of the Second Workshop on Language in Social Media, Montreal, Canada, pp. 19–26. ACL (2012)
19. Waseem, Z.: Are you a racist or am I seeing things? Annotator influence on hate speech detection on Twitter. In: Proceedings of the First Workshop on NLP and Computational Social Science, Austin, TX, USA, pp. 138–142. ACL (2016)
20. Waseem, Z., Hovy, D.: Hateful symbols or hateful people? Predictive features for hate speech detection on Twitter. In: Proceedings of the Student Research Workshop, SRW@HLT-NAACL 2016, The 2016 Conference of the North American Chapter of the Association for Computational Linguistics: Human Language Technologies, San Diego, California, USA, pp. 88–93. ACL (2016)
21. Yenala, H., Jhanwar, A., Chinnakotla, M.K., et al.: Deep learning for detecting inappropriate content in text. Int. J. Data Sci. Anal. 1–14 (2017)
22. The Guardian. http://www.theguardian.com. Accessed 31 Jan 2018
23. TextSTAT. https://github.com/shivam5992/textstat. Accessed 30 Nov 2017
24. Pattern.en. https://www.clips.uantwerpen.be/pages/pattern-en. Accessed 30 Nov 2017
25. SenticNet. http://sentic.net/. Accessed 31 Jan 2018
26. Scikit-Learn. http://scikit-learn.org/. Accessed 31 Jan 2018
27. Tsvetkov, Y., Boytsov, L., Gershman, A., Nyberg, E., Dyer, C.: Metaphor detection with cross-lingual model transfer. In: Proceedings of the 52nd Annual Meeting of the Association for Computational Linguistics, ACL 2014, Baltimore, Maryland, USA (2014)

Annotating Concept Abstractness
by Common-Sense Knowledge

Enrico Mensa, Aureliano Porporato, and Daniele P. Radicioni[✉]

Dipartimento di Informatica, Università degli Studi di Torino, Turin, Italy
{enrico.mensa,daniele.radicioni}@unito.it,
aureliano.porporato@edu.unito.it

Abstract. Dealing with semantic representations of concepts involves collecting information on many aspects that collectively contribute to (lexical, semantic and ultimately) linguistic competence. In the last few years mounting experimental evidences have been gathered in the fields of Neuroscience and Cognitive Science on conceptual access and retrieval dynamics that posit novel issues, such as the imageability associated to terms and concepts, or abstractness features as a correlate of figurative uses of language. However, this body of research has not yet penetrated Computational Linguistics: specifically, as regards as Lexical Semantics, in the last few years the field has been dominated by distributional models and vectorial representations. We recently proposed COVER, that relies on a partly different approach. Conceptual descriptions herein are aimed at putting together the lexicographic precision of BabelNet and the common-sense available in ConceptNet. We now propose ABS-COVER, that extends the existing lexical resource by associating an abstractness score to the concepts contained therein. We introduce the detailed algorithms and report about an extensive evaluation on the renewed resource, where we obtained correlations with human judgements in line or higher compared to state of the art approaches.

Keywords: Concept abstractness · Concept representation
Lexical Resources · Knowledge representation · Figurative language
NL semantics

1 Introduction

Ordinary experience shows that semantic representation and lexical access and processing of concepts can be affected by concepts' concrete/abstract status: concrete meanings, more ingrained in the perceptual experience, are acknowledged to be more quickly and easily delivered in human communication than abstract meanings [1]. Such kind of information grasps a complex combination of experiential (e.g., sensory, motor) and strictly linguistic features, such as verbal associations arising through co-occurrence patterns and syntactic information [20]. These features make conceptual abstractness matter of broad interest

© Springer Nature Switzerland AG 2018
C. Ghidini et al. (Eds.): AI*IA 2018, LNAI 11298, pp. 415–428, 2018.
https://doi.org/10.1007/978-3-030-03840-3_31

for computational linguistics, and the investigation on conceptual abstractness a challenging though only superficially explored field. Information on conceptual abstractness impacts on many diverse NLP tasks, such as the word sense disambiguation task [10], the semantic processing of figurative language [3,14,18], the automatic translation and simplification [22], the characterisation of web queries with difficulty scores [21], the processing of social tagging information [2], and many others, as well.

One very first issue is, of course, that it is not straightforward to define abstractness [9]. Provided that more fine grained distinctions on abstract and concrete word meanings can be drawn, the term 'abstract' has two main interpretations: *(i)* what is far from perception (as opposed to perceptible directly through the senses), and *(ii)* what is more general (as opposed to low-level, specific). To implement the second view, the concreteness or *specificity*—the opposite of abstractness—can be defined as a function of the distance intervening between a concept and a parent of that concept in the top-level of a taxonomy or ontology [5]. In this setting, the second definition can be used to automatically compute abstractness given an ontology-like resource (like WordNet or BabelNet [17]) without any additional information from human beings. On the other side, the first definition seems to better correlate with what is perceived as "abstract" in human judgement [19].

In this work we basically refer to the first aspect – perceptually salient abstractness, and enrich it with common-sense information; additionally, different from most existing literature (e.g., [4]), we consider abstractness as a feature of word meanings (concepts) rather than a feature of word forms (terms): our work thus consists of annotating with abstractness information the concepts in COVER [15], a lexical resource developed in the frame of a long-standing research aimed at combining ontological and common-sense reasoning [8,11,13]. As a result, we propose an extended lexical resource, ABS-COVER,[1] where each and every concept is automatically annotated with an abstractness score ranging in the $[0,1]$ interval, where the left bound 0.0 features fully concrete concepts, and the right bound 1.0 stands for maximally abstract concept.

The paper is organised as follows. We first propose a review of the related work on this and close issues (Sect. 2); in Sect. 3 we then illustrate how the abstractness score featuring COVER concepts is computed. Later on we extensively evaluate the proposed annotation and discuss the obtained results (Sect. 4). We conclude by pointing out future work, to refine our approach and improve the quality of the abstractness annotation.

2   Related Work

An automatic approach has been devised using abstractness information to analyse web image queries, and to characterise them in terms of difficulty [21]. In particular, the authors compute the abstractness associated to nouns by checking the presence of the *physical entity* synset among the hypernyms of senses in the

---

[1] ABS-COVER is available for download at https://ls.di.unito.it.

WordNet taxonomy. This approach also involves a disambiguation step, which is performed through a model trained on the SemCor *corpus* [16]. The technique carried out in [5] also relies on WordNet information, but the abstractness of a concept (also called *specificity*) is here defined as the distance between the corresponding node in WordNet, and the root of the ontology. The more specific (lower in the hierarchy) is a concept, the more concrete, according to the second definition of abstractness reported in the previous Section. Given that in WordNet we have at most 17 levels of depth, conceptual concreteness varies over the interval $[0, 16]$. A closely related strategy [9], based on similar assumptions, proposes the notions of *precision by depth* (P-depth), together with other two abstractness measures: *precision by inclusiveness* (P-inclusiveness), based on the fraction of descendants of a node with respect to the overall number of nodes in WordNet; and *concreteness*, based on the sensory definition of abstractness.

The authors of the work [19] compare the first two methods, one based on the definition of abstractness that checks for the presence of *physical entity* among the hypernyms of a concept, and one based on the second—specificity-based—notion of abstractness. Interestingly enough, the authors report a 0.17 Spearman correlation between scores obtained with the method in [5] and those obtained in [21], in line with the findings about the correlation of values based on the two different definitions [9]. This measure can be considered as an estimation of the overlap of the two notions of abstractness: the poor correlation seems to confirm that they are rather distinct. Furthermore, the two sets of scores have been compared with those in the MRC data set, reporting a 0.60 Spearman correlation between the abstractness scores proposed by [21] and the human judgements, and a 0.29 correlation between the scores by [5] and human ratings. Such experimental evidence suggested us to adopt the first definition of abstractness.

The role of abstractness has also been explored in the context of the Word Sense Disambiguation [10], leading to the finding that words with very high or very low score of abstractness are easier to disambiguate. Along this line, the association of word senses with senses of different words have been examined, finding that concrete concepts tend to be related to concrete concepts and abstract concepts tend to be related to abstract ones. In particular, concrete concepts would be more related to concrete concepts than are abstract concepts to abstract concepts. Similar conclusions have been recently reached in [7].

3   COVER Annotation

In this Section we describe how the common-sense knowledge already present in COVER has been used to enrich it with abstractness information. Before providing the annotation algorithm, for the sake of self containedness, we briefly introduce COVER.

3.1   Introduction to COVER

COVER is a lexical resource aimed at hosting general conceptual representations. Full details on COVER and on the algorithm designed to build it by

---

Algorithm 1. The COVER Annotation Algorithm.

Data: a set of COVER elements C, a set of COVER dimensions D
Result: a set of pairs (e, a), with $e \in C$ and a updated abstractness score for e
First Step $T \longleftarrow \bigcup_{c \in C}(c, \text{IsAbstract}(c.\text{wnsi}, c.\text{bsi}))$
Second Step **return** $\bigcup_{c \in C}(c, \text{RefineAbstracness}(c, D, T))$

---

integrating BabelNet and ConceptNet can be found in [15]. Each concept c in COVER is identified through a BabelNet synset ID and described as a vector representation $\vec{c}$, composed by a set of semantic dimensions $\mathcal{D} = \{d_1, d_2, \ldots d_n\}$. Each such dimension encodes a relationship like, e.g., IsA, UsedFor, *etc.* and reports the concepts connected to c along the dimension d_i. The vector space dimensions are based on ConceptNet relationships.[2] The dimensions are filled with BabelNet synset IDs, so that finally each concept c in COVER can be defined as

$$\vec{c} = \bigcup_{d \in \mathcal{D}} \{\langle ID_d, \{c_1, \cdots, c_k\}\rangle\} \tag{1}$$

where ID_d is the identifier of the d-th dimension, and $\{c_1, \cdots, c_k\}$ is the set of values (concepts themselves) filling d.

3.2   COVER Annotation Algorithm

In order to enrich COVER with abstractness information, we took inspiration from the concreteness criterion exposed in [21], and we follow this idea: a concept is concrete if it descends from *physical entity* in WordNet, abstract otherwise. Algorithm 1 shows the main procedure for the abstractness annotation, that consists of two steps:

1. **First Step** (Algorithm 2): this function is designed to compute a base abstractness score for each element e in COVER, where an *element* is a concept (i.e., a BabelNet synset ID) that either has a vector representation or is a value inside a vector. In order to compute this score, we perform the following steps:

   (a) we attempt to retrieve the list of WordNet synset IDs associated to e in BabelNet, and from those we collect the WordNet hypernyms set (Algorithm 2, (1)); if in this set we find the synset of *physical entity*,[3] the abstractness score of e is set to 0.0; otherwise it is set to 1.0 (3);

   (b) if (a) fails (i.e., no WordNet synset ID can be found for e), we collect the direct BabelNet hypernyms of e and the search described in (a) is performed for each such hypernym (4). If at least one of e hypernyms has *physical entity* among its hypernyms, the base abstractness score of e is set to 0.0, and to 1.0 otherwise (6);

---

[2] The most relevant relationships include: RELATEDTO, IsA, ATLOCATION, USEDFOR, CAPABLEOF, PARTOF, HASPROPERTY, MADEOF, HASA, INSTANCEOF.

[3] The synset for *physical entity* has ID WN:00001930N in WordNet 3.0.

(c) if (b) fails (that is, e has no hypernyms in BabelNet or none of them has an associated WordNet synset ID), we retrieve the BabelNet main gloss for e (7), disambiguate it,[4] thus obtaining a set of concepts N. In order to compute the abstractness score for each noun in the gloss, steps (a) and (b) are performed on each $n \in N$. Finally, the valid scores associated to the nouns are averaged and the result is assigned as the abstractness score of e (9–11).

If the function fails in all of these steps, the abstractness score is set to -1, indicating that no suitable score could be computed (12).

2. **Second Step** (Algorithm 3): the first step enriches every concept in COVER with a base score of abstractness. The goal of the second step is to smooth such scores by following human perception accounts; to do so, we employ the common-sense knowledge available in COVER. Given a vector $\vec{c}$ in the resource, we explore a subset of its dimensions:[5] all the base abstractness scores of the concepts that are values for these dimensions are retrieved, and the average score $s_{\text{values-avg}}$ is computed. Concepts having an invalid score are discarded (1, 2). The score $s_{\text{values-avg}}$ is then in turn averaged with $s_{\text{vec-base}}$, that is the base score of $\vec{c}$ (3), thus obtaining the final score for the COVER vector. If either $s_{\text{vec-base}}$ or $s_{\text{values-avg}}$ are invalid scores, the final score of c is set to the only valid score available.

It is important to note that the scores computed in the first step are frozen, and they are not dynamically updated during the execution of the second step. This is important to ensure that the order in which the vectors are considered does not impact on the final result of the annotation. Moreover, we did not iterate the second step, since it would potentially drift the scores from the precise information given by WordNet. In the end, any element defined as a *physical entity* in WordNet retains an abstractness score lesser than or equal to 0.5.

4   Evaluation

In order to assess the abstractness scores of ABS-COVER we make use the Medical Research Council Psycholinguistic Dataset (MRC hereafter) [6] and the Brysbaert Dataset (BRYS hereafter) [4]. The MRC *corpus* has been built by merging three handcrafted corpora containing words abstractness information. The MRC also provides additional information: each word has up to 25 associated features, such as imageability (i.e., how easily a word can evoke mental images) or meaningfulness (i.e., the confidence that a subject has about his understanding of the actual meaning of a word or expression), or its common part of speech. From this data set, containing in total 8, 228 terms with an abstractness value, we extracted 3, 977 nouns. On the other hand, the BRYS

---

[4] At the present stage the disambiguation is performed by using Babelfy APIs (http://babelfy.org/).

[5] We presently consider the following dimensions: RELATEDTO, FORMOF, ISA, SYNONYM, DERIVEDFROM, SIMILARTO and ATLOCATION.

Algorithm 2. Auxiliary `IsAbstract` function.

Input: a BabelNet synset b
Output: the base abstractness score of the COVER element corresponding to b
Function IsAbstract(b):

```
1     S ←— WordNetHypernyms(b)
2     if S ≠ ∅ then
3         if physical entity ∈ S then
          |   return 0
          else
          └ return 1
      else
          H ←— BabelNetHypernyms(b)
4         W ←— ∪_{h∈H} WordNetHypernyms(h)
5         if W ≠ ∅ then
6             if physical entity ∈ W then
              |   return 0
              else
              └ return 1
          else
7             g ←— GetMainBabelNetGloss(b)
8             N ←— Babelfy(g)
              G ←— []
              for each n noun concept ∈ N do
9                 q ←— GetGlossConceptAbstractness(n)
10                if q ≥ 0 then
                  └ append q to G
11            if G is not empty then
              |   return average of scores in G
              else
12            └ return −1
```

---

data set consists of a large of set of words annotated with abstractness scores through crowdsourcing, for a total of $39,945$ terms. We only use a portion of these terms (that is, the nouns contained in ABS-COVER).

We preliminarily observe that vectors associated to abstract concepts are well separated from those associated to concrete ones, as illustrated in Fig. 1, showing how abstractness scores are distributed. In particular, the average score of concrete vectors (that is, the score of concepts featured by abstractness score lower than or equal to 0.5) is 0.153 and the average score of abstract vectors (whose abstractness score is greater than 0.5) is 0.837. Concrete vectors are slightly more frequent than abstract vectors: out of the $31,837$ vectors in COVER, we count overall $17,295$ and $14,542$ vectors, respectively.

A first evaluation of the annotation is based on *internal coherence*. We recorded the average abstractness of the values along all dimensions: also based on literature (see, e.g., [7,10]) we expect that concrete vectors are, on average, more connected to other concrete concepts (e.g., through the SYNONYM relation). In Table 1 we report, over 15 of the most relevant (populated) relationships in

---

Algorithm 3. Auxiliary `RefineAbstracness` function.

Input: a COVER element *elem*, a set of COVER dimensions D, a set A of
       pairs (c, a), with c COVER element and a base abstractness score of c
Output: the refined abstractness score for *elem*
Function `RefineAbstracness`$(elem, D, A)$:

    $s_{\text{vec-base}} \longleftarrow A(elem)$ `// find the score of v in A`
    if *elem is a* COVER *vector* **then**
        $L \longleftarrow [\,]$
        for *each dimension* $dim \in D$ **do**
            for *each value* $v \in elem.dim$ **do**
                $abstr_v \longleftarrow A(v)$
1   **if** $abstr_v \geq 0$ **then**
                    append $abstr_v$ to L
2   **if** L *is not empty* **then**
        $s_{\text{values-avg}} \longleftarrow$ average of scores in L
      else
        $s_{\text{values-avg}} \longleftarrow -1$
3   **case** $s_{\text{vec-base}} \geq 0$ AND $s_{\text{values-avg}} \geq 0$ **return** $\frac{s_{\text{vec-base}} + s_{\text{values-avg}}}{2}$
4   **case** $s_{\text{values-avg}} \geq 0$ **return** $s_{\text{values-avg}}$
5   **otherwise return** $s_{\text{vec-base}}$
    else
6   **return** $s_{\text{vec-base}}$

COVER, the average scores that have been obtained by collecting all values along a given dimension. For example, we observe that the average abstractness score for the values in the IsA relation is 0.215 when the vector involved is concrete, and 0.787 when the vector is abstract. The relations marked with '*' are those actually employed by the auxiliary function `RefineAbstractness`, (Algorithm 3). The only notable exception to this basic homogeneity principle is represented by vectors connected through the HASCONTEXT relation, where also concrete concepts are related to abstract concepts.

Although such figures are in accord with cited literature and seem to be reasonable on purely introspective accounts (thus qualitatively corroborating the proposed approach), an extensive experimentation has been devised to fully assess the annotated abstractness scores.

4.1 Correlation with Human Judgement

The second evaluation has been carried out by comparing the computed abstractness scores against human judgements. In particular, we considered the MRC and the BRYS data sets, whose scores were scaled into the range $[0, 1]$.

Before analysing the result, however, it should be noted that these data sets and ours are not directly comparable: while our scores are based on *concept* abstractness, such data sets are based on *word* abstractness. To overcome this problem, we exploited the information available in the label of each COVER vector, a set of words associated to the concept represented by the vector itself.

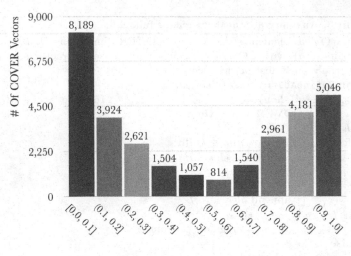

Fig. 1. Distribution of COVER vectors by abstractness score.

For example, given the word "mother", 5 conceptual descriptions can be found in COVER:

- *mother*, `bn:00029439n`, "The earth conceived of as the female principle of fertility";
- *mother/psi*, `bn:14001852n`, "Role-playing video game series by Shigesato Itoi";
- *mother*, `bn:03824293n`, "Energy drink from Coca-Cola";
- *mother/mommy/mom/motherhood*, `bn:00034027n`, "A woman who has given birth to a child (also used as a term of address to your mother)";
- *mother*, `bn:03322691n`, "A Broadway musical".

Clearly, in order to select one given sense, some sort of disambiguation is needed. Before evaluating the ABS-COVER scores in a pipeline that also includes this disambiguation step, we performed a preliminary exploration of the abstractness scores on a randomly chosen set of 150 terms present in both the MRC data set and in the BRYS data set. We computed the correlation between the abstractness values contained in each data sets, and those in ABS-COVER. Not to mix disambiguation errors with the evaluation of the abstractness scores, we manually performed the word sense disambiguation by selecting the sense of the word that seemed more relevant (taken in isolation, with no disambiguation context). Table 2 reports Pearson's r and Spearman's ρ correlations between the abstractness scores in these data sets and those in ABS-COVER. As it can be seen, the correlation between the two human-annotated sets is very high (although it shows that even human ratings are far from full agreement), and the correlation with ABS-COVER scores is high. We consider this sample test as an upper bound to the correlation that can be reached by undertaking some algorithmic

Table 1. Average abstractness score in COVER vectors' dimensions. Starred dimensions indicate the relations actually used in the Second Step. Concrete concepts are featured by abstractness score ($abs \leq 0.5$), while abstract concepts are those with $abs > 0.5$.

Dimension	Average abstractness	
	Concrete concepts	Abstract concepts
RELATEDTO*	0.293	0.694
ISA*	0.215	0.787
SYNONYM*	0.254	0.772
HASCONTEXT	0.632	0.805
FORMOF*	0.127	0.777
DERIVEDFROM*	0.227	0.736
ANTONYM	0.312	0.750
ATLOCATION*	0.261	0.537
HASA	0.150	0.682
PARTOF	0.181	0.681
SIMILARTO*	0.241	0.751
USEDFOR	0.464	0.719
HASPROPERTY	0.385	0.727
CAUSE	0.450	0.811
CAPABLEOF	0.473	0.687
HASPREREQUISITE	0.339	0.723

Table 2. Pearson's r and Spearman's ρ correlation scores between the computed abstractness and human judgements, on a set of 150 manually disambiguated terms.

	MRC [6]	BRY [4]	ABS-COVER
MRC	$r = 1$	$r = 0.941$	$r = 0.795$
	$\rho = 1$	$\rho = 0.871$	$\rho = 0.663$
BRYS		$r = 1$	$r = 0.766$
		$\rho = 1$	$\rho = 0.649$
ABS-COVER			$r = 1$
			$\rho = 1$

approach to select a given sense in ABS-COVER. In the following, we consider the full problem of calculating the abstractness score for a word by using one or more vectors (concepts) from ABS-COVER.

Baseline. As the simplest strategy to retrieve ABS-COVER scores for comparison with the terms in the MRC and BRYS *corpora*, we took the average of the abstractness scores featuring all senses available in ABS-COVER for a given

Table 3. Pearson (r) and Spearman (ρ) correlation scores obtained by computing the abstractness scores from ABS-COVER senses according to several strategies.

	MRC	BRYS
Baseline – simple average r	0.614	0.588
Baseline – simple average ρ	0.612	0.590
No common-sense KW r	0.547	0.524
No common-sense KW ρ	0.544	0.518
Weighted average r	0.655	0.608
Weighted average ρ	0.648	0.612
Most salient sense r	0.627	0.594
Most salient sense ρ	0.646	0.615
SemCor-frequency r	0.732	0.653
SemCor-frequency ρ	0.704	0.639

input term. Table 3 reports Pearson and Spearman's correlation values obtained through simple average. From the MRC, we were able to retrieve overall 3,977 nouns, 431 of which do not appear in the label (i.e., the set of lexicalizations) of any ABS-COVER vector. About the remaining 3,546 nouns, 1,158 are associated to 1 concept, and on average a word occurs in the label of 2.56 conceptual descriptions. The BRYS data set lacks of the part of speech annotation, so out of the total 39,954 words (or compound expressions), 15,779 occur in some vector's label (8,722 only once, 1.88 times on average).

No Common-Sense KW. In order to investigate how relevant is common-sense information, we devised a subtractive experiment. We created a version of ABS-COVER annotated without executing the second step of the annotation algorithm (Algorithms 1 and 3). We obtained a version of COVER with 14 unlabelled vectors (while no vector remains without abstractness annotation after executing the whole algorithm), 15,649 zero-valued vectors (+547.99%) and 12,832 one-valued vectors (+799.86%). As expected, the first step of the algorithm alone produced less smoothed scores, which were compared with human ratings. The correlation figures are reported in Table 3.

Weighted Average. Some senses underlying any term (e.g., the term "mother") are by far more common than other ones: in order to individuate one chief sense – which is ideally that considered by human annotators, we examined the cardinality (that is, the sum of all concepts) of all dimensions featuring each ABS-COVER vector. The assumption is that the more broadly a sense is used in language and available to annotators, the larger the set of its connections to other senses. More on the possible criteria to perform selection, clustering and/or filtering of the sense inventory can be found in [12]. For example, the sense bn:03824293n associated to the term *mother* (an energy drink) has, over all dimensions, 6 values in COVER, while for the sense bn:00034027n (a woman who has given birth to a child) we find 119 values. In this experiment, the abstractness scores have been averaged over senses based on the overall amount of information available for each sense. The correlation values are reported in Table 3.

Most Salient Sense. Based on the same rationale, we designed another experimental condition. Instead of using all the senses extracted from ABS-COVER, weighted by the number of the concepts related with them, in this case we used only the most salient concept. As anticipated, the most salient sense is chosen as the vector featured by the highest number of concepts filling its dimensions. The results obtained by individuating abstractness scores through this strategy are reported in Table 3.

SemCor-Based Frequency. Another strategy to define suitable weights for word senses is to take into account their frequency in some *corpus*, assuming it reflects the distribution of senses in the considered language. So we collected sense frequency information based on the SemCor corpus [16], where words are annotated with information on part-of-speech and WordNet synset ID. Exploiting such information, we collected a set of word senses that are present in ABS-COVER and in the considered *corpora*. Namely, we took $2,417$ words that are present both in SemCor and in the MRC data set that have at least one associated WordNet Synset ID in ABS-COVER (including $1,433$ terms with only one sense, 1.76 senses per word on average); and $6,383$ words both in SemCor and in the BRYS data set (including $4,785$ terms with only one sense, 1.43 senses per word on average). Note that we not only considered only words present in both SemCor and the selected data set, but we restricted to the WordNet senses for the terms present in both the SemCor and COVER, thus finally reducing the number of both words and concepts: for example, in this setting the word "mother" is linked to a single sense (with ID wn:10332385n), "A woman who has given birth to a child". Table 3 reports the correlation obtained with the abstractness scores in ABS-COVER weighted according to the sense frequencies in the SemCor *corpus*.

4.2 Discussion

The reported figures are either in line or directly improve on state of the art approaches, such as [19,21]. We first computed the correlation between the human ratings contained in the MRC and BRYS data sets ($r = 0.94$, and $\rho = 0.87$, as shown in Table 2). This makes these figures a solid experimental base for comparison with the scores computed to annotate COVER. This datum is not new; in essence, it replicates previous experiments made by the authors of the BRYS data set [4]. Nevertheless, it was relevant to preliminarily verify the agreement between the two. As regards as the evaluation of our abstractness scores, as expected, we obtained the highest correlation in the first experimental condition where a small sample of terms was disambiguated by hand (Table 2). This datum shows that WSD is still an open issue (though of secondary relevance, in the present setting), as the task of choosing one best sense for a given term.

The results obtained in the *baseline* experimental condition by computing a simple average among all senses' abstractness show a significant drop in the Pearson correlation with respect to results in Table 2: around 15% and 10% on the MRC on the BRYS data sets, respectively, as reported in Table 3. Similar drop is observed on the Spearman coefficients, with a more limited reduction, in the order of 4% in both data sets. The results obtained in the *No common-sense KW* condition seem to confirm the central role of common-sense knowledge in determining how abstract/concrete concepts are: in fact, these figures are the worst ones, with a reduction in the correlation with human judgement in the order of 20% for the r metrics, and 10% for the ρ metrics on both data sets. The *weighted average* condition obtained correlation above the baseline on both data sets and correlation metrics. It may be interpreted as a cue that the coverage of our resource is sufficient to provide information on the relevance of senses associated to a given term. Also, additional evidence should be collected to investigate on the aptitude of human annotators: when assessing the abstractness of a word, did they consider only one (most salient) concept taken in isolation, or a pool of concepts, where the most salient is the most prominent one surrounded by a set of satellite senses? Systems for Natural Interaction would benefit from this sort of information. The last experimental condition, based on the *SemCor frequency*, is that maximally approaching the first condition results (Table 2). Here we observe good correlation with human ratings (in the specific case of MRC data set and ρ metrics resulting in an improved correlation with scores obtained); also, it confirms the quality of the contribution provided by the SemCor *corpus* to the tasks ingrained in senses disambiguation.

5   Conclusions

In this paper we have proposed Abs-COVER, the novel version of COVER annotated with abstractness scores. At first, we have introduced the research question underlying the present work, and shown that this sort of information may be relevant to different NLP tasks. We have then introduced related work, and illustrated existing research efforts and approaches. Then the algorithms devised to compute abstractness have been introduced and illustrated in full detail. We have finally reported about an experimentation where we obtained valuable agreement with human ratings on concepts abstractness.

Finally, we realised that although the BRYS data set provides a great deal of information, some further elements would be beneficial for NLP experiments. Terms should be sense-annotated, hopefully by adopting the *de-facto* standard naming convention of BabelNet; additionally, some measure of inter-annotator agreement should be reported, so to distinguish cases that are straightforward (at least for human rating) from those more complicated, to further refine systems' accuracy on the latter ones.

References

1. Bambini, V., Resta, D., Grimaldi, M.: A dataset of metaphors from the Italian literature: exploring psycholinguistic variables and the role of context. PloS One **9**(9), 1–13 (2014)
2. Benz, D., Körner, C., Hotho, A., Stumme, G., Strohmaier, M.: One tag to bind them all: measuring term abstractness in social metadata. In: Antoniou, G., et al. (eds.) ESWC 2011. LNCS, vol. 6644, pp. 360–374. Springer, Heidelberg (2011). https://doi.org/10.1007/978-3-642-21064-8_25
3. Birke, J., Sarkar, A.: A clustering approach for nearly unsupervised recognition of nonliteral language. In: Proceedings of the 11th Conference of EACL (2006)
4. Brysbaert, M., Warriner, A.B., Kuperman, V.: Concreteness ratings for 40,000 generally known english word lemmas. Behav. Res. Methods **46**(3), 904–911 (2014)
5. Changizi, M.A.: Economically organized hierarchies in wordnet and the Oxford English dictionary. Cogn. Syst. Res. **9**, 214–228 (2008)
6. Coltheart, M.: The MRC psycholinguistic database. Q. J. Exp. Psychol. Sect. A **33**(4), 497–505 (1981)
7. Frassinelli, D., Naumann, D., Utt, J., Walde, I., Schulte, S.: Contextual characteristics of concrete and abstract words. In: IWCS 2017 (2017)
8. Ghignone, L., Lieto, A., Radicioni, D.P.: Typicality-based inference by plugging conceptual spaces into ontologies. In: Proceedings of AIC. CEUR (2013)
9. Iliev, R., Axelrod, R.: The paradox of abstraction: precision versus concreteness. J. Psycholinguist. Res. **46**(3), 715–729 (2017)
10. Kwong, O.Y.: Sense abstractness, semantic activation, and word sense disambiguation. Int. J. Speech Technol. **11**(3–4), 135 (2008)
11. Lieto, A., Mensa, E., Radicioni, D.P.: A resource-driven approach for anchoring linguistic resources to conceptual spaces. In: Adorni, G., Cagnoni, S., Gori, M., Maratea, M. (eds.) AI*IA 2016. LNCS (LNAI), vol. 10037, pp. 435–449. Springer, Cham (2016). https://doi.org/10.1007/978-3-319-49130-1_32
12. Lieto, A., Mensa, E., Radicioni, D.P.: Taming sense sparsity: a common-sense approach. In: Proceedings of CLiC-it 2016 (2016)
13. Lieto, A., Minieri, A., Piana, A., Radicioni, D.P.: A knowledge-based system for prototypical reasoning. Connect. Sci. **27**(2), 137–152 (2015)
14. Mensa, E., Porporato, A., Radicioni, D.P.: Grasping metaphors: lexical semantics in metaphor analysis. In: Gangemi, A., et al. (eds.) ESWC 2018. LNCS, vol. 11155, pp. 192–195. Springer, Cham (2018). https://doi.org/10.1007/978-3-319-98192-5_36
15. Mensa, E., Radicioni, D.P., Lieto, A.: COVER: a linguistic resource combining common sense and lexicographic information. Lang. Resour. Eval. **52**(4), 921–948 (2018)
16. Miller, G.A., Leacock, C., Tengi, R., Bunker, R.T.: A semantic concordance. In: Proceedings of the Workshop on Human Language Technology, pp. 303–308. ACL (1993)
17. Navigli, R., Ponzetto, S.P.: BabelNet: building a very large multilingual semantic network. In: Proceedings of the 48th ACL, pp. 216–225. ACL (2010)
18. Neuman, Y., et al.: Metaphor identification in large texts corpora. PloS One **8**(4), e62343 (2013)
19. Theijssen, D., van Halteren, H., Boves, L., Oostdijk, N.: On the difficulty of making concreteness concrete. CLIN J. **1**, 61–77 (2011)

20. Vigliocco, G., Meteyard, L., Andrews, M., Kousta, S.: Toward a theory of semantic representation. Lang. Cogn. **1**(2), 219–247 (2009)
21. Xing, X., Zhang, Y., Han, M.: Query difficulty prediction for contextual image retrieval. In: Gurrin, C., et al. (eds.) ECIR 2010. LNCS, vol. 5993, pp. 581–585. Springer, Heidelberg (2010). https://doi.org/10.1007/978-3-642-12275-0_52
22. Zhu, Z., Bernhard, D., Gurevych, I.: A monolingual tree-based translation model for sentence simplification. In: Proceedings of the 23rd International Conference on Computational Linguistics, pp. 1353–1361. ACL (2010)

Planning and Scheduling

Iterative Width Search for Multi Agent Privacy-Preserving Planning

Gabriele Bazzotti[1], Alfonso Emilio Gerevini[1], Nir Lipovetzky[2],
Francesco Percassi[1], Alessandro Saetti[1(✉)], and Ivan Serina[1]

[1] Dipartimento di Ingegneria dell'Informazione, Università degli Studi di Brescia,
Via Branze 38, 25123 Brescia, Italy
alessandro.saetti@unibs.it
[2] School of Computing and Information Systems, The University of Melbourne,
Melbourne, Victoria, Australia

Abstract. In multi-agent planning, preserving the agents' privacy has become an increasingly popular research topic. In multi-agent privacy-preserving planning, agents jointly compute a plan that achieves mutual goals by keeping certain information private to the individual agents. Unfortunately, preserving the privacy of such information can severely restrict the accuracy of the heuristic functions used while searching for solutions. Recently, it has been shown that centralized planning based on Width-based search is a very effective approach over several benchmark domains, even when the search is driven by uninformed heuristics. In this paper, we investigate the usage of Width-based search in the context of (decentralised) multi-agent privacy-preserving planning, addressing the challenges related to the agents' privacy and performance. An experimental study analyses the effectiveness of our techniques and compares them with the state-of-the-art.

1 Introduction

Over the last years, several frameworks for multi-agent (MA) planning have been proposed (e.g., [1–3]). Most of them consider, in different ways, the agents' privacy: some or all agents have private knowledge that cannot be communicated to other agents during the planning process and plan execution. This prevents the straightforward usage of most of the modern techniques developed for centralized (classical) planning, which are based on heuristic functions computed by using the knowledge of all the involved agents.

Recently, it has been shown that many instances of popular planning benchmarks can be solved by a polynomial algorithm, called Iterative Width (IW), provided that the instances feature a single goal atom [4]. Such an algorithm is based on the notion of "novelty". The novelty of a state s is defined as the size of the smallest tuple of facts that holds in s for the first time in the search, i.e. among all previously generated states. Essentially, IW search consists of a sequence of breadth-first searches (BFS) with an increasing integer value k for

© Springer Nature Switzerland AG 2018
C. Ghidini et al. (Eds.): AI*IA 2018, LNAI 11298, pp. 431–444, 2018.
https://doi.org/10.1007/978-3-030-03840-3_32

which all states with novelty greater than k are pruned. The success of this simple pruning technique derives from the fact that usually actions in optimal plans achieve a tuple of at least k facts that was not true in any preceding state on the solution path [4].

For planning problems with multiple goal atoms, IW search is less effective, but there are some variants of this search algorithm that perform well for many planning benchmarks [4]. One of these variants, called Serialized Iterative Width (SIW), restarts the Iterative Width search from each reached state s that achieves at least one more goal since the last restart. Notably, since SIW does not heuristically evaluate the expanded states, it is a good candidate to solve MA-planning problems without affecting the agents' privacy.

The usage of IW search for solving MA-planning problems raises some synchronization issues, since each search conducted by the IW procedure is a breadth-first search (BFS) and, at a given time, the search tree depth reached by an agent's BFS can be quite different from the depth reached by the BFS of other agents. This happens because in MA-planning each agent is capable of executing a different set of actions, and hence the searches conducted by two different agents can have a different branching factor. Even the usage of SIW raises some issues about the synchronization of the IW search: when an agent α_i reaches a state achieving a new problem goal, all the agents should restart a new IW search from that state, but accidentally a state s generated by α_i after the restart may arrive to another agent α_j before that agent restarts its own IW search. In such a case, when α_j restarts its IW search to synchronize herself with α_i, state s will be discarded and won't be visited by α_j's restarted search.

The contribution of the paper is investigating the usage of SIW for decentralized multi-agent privacy-preserving planning, proposing solutions addressing the agent search synchronization needed for using SIW in the MA-planning setting. An experimental study compares the investigated approach with a state-of-the-art planner (addressing privacy in a form weaker than our approach), showing that SIW is also a competitive planner for MA-planning.

The paper is organized as follows. Section 2 gives the necessary background; Sect. 3 presents a new version of the SIW procedure that can solve multi-agent privacy-preserving planning problems; Sect. 4 shows the results of our experimental analysis; finally, Sect. 5 gives the conclusions and mentions future work.

2   Background

In this section, first we introduce the MA-STRIPS planning problem, then we describe the IW search and the SIW procedure developed for classical planning.

2.1   The MA-STRIPS Planning Problem

Our work relies on *MA-STRIPS*, a "minimalistic" extension of the STRIPS language for multi-agent planning [1], that is the basis of the most popular definition of multi-agent planning problem (see, e.g., [2,5–9]).

Definition 1. *A* MA-STRIPS *planning problem for a set of agents* $\Sigma = \{\alpha_i\}_{i=1}^n$ *is a 4-tuple* $\langle \{A_i\}_{i=1}^n, P, I, G \rangle$ *where:*

- A_i *is the set of actions agent* α_i *is capable of executing, and such that for every pair of agents* α_i *and* α_j $A_i \cap A_j = \emptyset$;
- *P is a finite set of propositions;*
- *I* $\subseteq$ *P is the initial state;*
- *G* $\subseteq$ *P is the set of goals.*

Each action consists in a name, a set of additive effects representing facts that the action makes true, a set of positive facts representing its additive effects, and a set of deleting effects representing facts that the action makes false. A fact is *private* for an agent if other agents can neither achieve, destroy or require the fact [1]. A fact is *public* otherwise. An action is private if all its preconditions and effects are private; the action is public, otherwise.

To maintain agents' privacy, the private knowledge shared among agents can be encrypted. We distinguish two modes for sharing the encrypted description of private facts. An agent can share with the other agents a description of its search state in which each private fact that is true in a state is substituted with a string obtained by encrypting the fact name [10].[1] In the rest of the paper, E0 denotes this encryption of search states. Another way to share search states containing private knowledge during the search is substituting all the private facts that are true in a state with a string obtained by encrypting all the private fact names together [11]. This encryption of the search state is called E1.

While both methods do not reveal the names of the private facts of each agent α_i to other agents, with E0 agent α_i can realize the existence of a private fact of another agent and monitor its truth value during the search process. This allows the other agents to infer the existence of some private actions of α_i, as well as try to infer their causal effects. With E1, the other agents can only infer the existence of a group of private facts, as the encrypted string contained in the exchanged states substitutes a group of an arbitrary number of private facts.

2.2 Width-Based Search

Pure width-based search algorithms are exploration algorithms that do not look at the goal at all. The simplest such algorithm is $IW(1)$, which is a plain breadth-first search where newly generated states that do not make an atom $X = x$ true for the first time in the search are pruned. The algorithm $IW(2)$ is similar except that a state s is pruned when there are no atoms $X = x$ and $Y = y$ such that the pair of atoms $X = x, Y = y$ is true in s and false in all the states generated before s.

$IW(k)$ is a normal breadth-first except that newly generated states s are pruned when their "novelty" is greater than k, where the novelty of s is i iff there is a tuple t of i atoms such that s is the first state in the search that makes

---

[1] Private facts that are false in the search state are omitted from the shared description of the state.

all the atoms in t true, with no tuple of smaller size having this property [4]. While simple, it has been shown that $IW(k)$ manages to solve arbitrary instances of many of the standard single agent benchmark domains in low polynomial time provided that the goal is a single atom. Such domains can be shown to have a small and bounded width w that does not depend on the instance size, which implies that they can be solved (optimally) by running $IW(w)$. Moreover, $IW(k)$ runs in time and space that are exponential in k and not in the number of problem variables.

The procedure IW, that calls the procedures $IW(1)$ and $IW(2)$, sequentially, has been used to solve instances featuring multiple (conjunctive) atomic goals, in the context of Serialized IW (SIW) [4], an algorithm that calls IW for achieving one atomic goal at a time. In other words, the j-th subcall of SIW stops when IW generates a state s_j that consistently achieves j goals from G. The search state s_j *consistently achieves* $G_j \subseteq G$ if s_j achieves G_j, and G_j does not need to be undone in order to achieve G. This last condition is checked by testing whether $h_{max}(s_j) = \infty$ is true once the actions that delete atoms from G_j are excluded. (Heuristic h_{max} is described in [12].)

While SIW is an incomplete blind search procedure (it can get trapped into dead-ends), it turns out to perform much better than a greedy best-first search guided by the standard delete relaxation heuristics [4].

3   Serialized Online IW for MA Planning

Classical planning problems solved by SIW can be understood as casting the offline problem into an online planning problem. Each subproblem induced by the serialization is an online j episode solved by IW, returning a path to a state where one more goal has been achieved with respect to the last episode $j - 1$.

Algorithm 1 shows the multi-agent version of SIW search for an agent α_i of the MA-planning problem. Each agent considers a separate search space, since each agent maintains its own list of open states, *open*, and, when an agent expands an open state, it generates a set of states using only its own actions. Moreover, each agent also maintains its own list of received messages to process, *open_msgs*. Algorithm 1 assumes the presence of a separated thread listening for incoming messages sent from other agents; each time a message is received, it is added to the end of the *open_msgs* list.

During the search, each agent α_i sends two types of messages to other agents, *restart messages* and *state messages*. A restart message contains the encrypted description of a state s to start a new episode, an identifier of the episode, and the number of episodes required to achieve s from the problem initial state. Similarly, a state message contains the encrypted description of a search state s for the current episode, the depth of s in the episode search tree of α_i, and the identifier of the current episode. Given a message m, $State(m)$ and $Episode(m)$, respectively, denote the search state and the episode identifier in m. $Depth(m)$ denotes the depth of s in the episode search tree of α_i.

The episode of each agent α_i can terminate if it achieves a state with a new goal, or if it receives a restart message from another agent. The exchange of

```
1  Procedure MA-SIW(s_I, G, A_i, k, E, e)
       Input: An initial episode search state s_I, a set G of goals, a set A_i of actions agent α_i
              is capable of executing, a novelty bound k, a (initially empty) set E of episode
              identifiers, an (initially null) episode identifier e;
       Output: A solution single-agent plan π_i for agent α_i, or failure.
2      open ← s_I
3      while open is not empty or open_msg is not empty do
4          received_msgs ← Dequeue(open_msgs)                    /* Receive messages */
5          foreach m ∈ received_msgs do
6              if m is a restart message then                    /* Process restart msg */
7                  E ← E ∪ Episode(m)
8                  if isEpisodeBetter(State(m), s_I) then
9                      return MA-SIW(State(m), G, A_i, k, E, Episode(m))
10                 end
11             end
12             else                                              /* Process state msg */
13                 if Episode(m) = e then
14                     Enqueue(State(m), open)
15                 end
16                 else
17                     if Episode(m) ∉ E then
18                         Enqueue(m, open_msgs)                  /* Process later */
19                     end
20                 end
21             end
22         end
23         s ← Dequeue(open)
24         if G ∈ s then                                         /* Plan found */
25             return ReconstructPlan(s)
26         end
27         if isStateBetter(s, s_I) then                         /* Restart */
28             e ← GenerateNewEpisodeIdentifier()
29             SendRestartMessage(⟨s, e⟩)
30             return MA-SIW(s, G, A_i, k, E ∪ {e}, e)
31         end
32         if s is public then                                   /* Send state */
33             SendStateMessage(⟨s, Depth(s), e⟩)
34         end
35         foreach a ∈ A_i s.t. Prec(a) ⊆ s do                   /* Expand */
36             s' ← s \ Del(a) ∪ Add(a)
37             d ← Depth(s')
38             if Novelty_{1...d}(s') ≤ k then
39                 Enqueue(s', open)
40             end
41         end
42     end
43     return failure
```

Algorithm 1. SIW search run by agent α_i.

messages raise a crucial issue about the synchronization of the IW episodes of each agent. Accidentally a state message from another agent containing a state generated after a restart may arrive before the actual restart message. Even when a restart message is received, α_i has to assess weather the new restart state is better than the starting state of the current episode. These kind of synchronization issues can often occur if the agents reside on interconnected machines through a networked infrastructure.

Agent α_i iteratively processes the messages received in the *open_msgs* list (steps 4–22) and expands the states in the *open* list (step 23–42). Loop 4–43 is repeated until the lists *open* and *open_msgs* are not empty. Each time a restart message m is received, function $isEpisodeBetter(State(m), s_I)$ evaluates whether the current episode really ends (steps 6–11). This happens if the restart state $State(m)$ contains more goals than the initial state s_I of the current episode. If both achieve the same number goals, we break ties choosing $State(m)$ if it was achieved with less episodes than s_I, and finally break ties if needed by choosing the state whose IP is alphanumerically smaller.

If a state message m is received, agent α_i checks if $State(m)$ belongs to the current episode (steps 13–15). If it does, α_i includes $State(m)$ in its IW search, by adding the state to its *open* list using the $Depth(m)$, ensuring a BFS expansion order. Otherwise, if $State(m)$ belongs to another episode, α_i checks if the episode it belongs to has already been marked as worst, and simply ignores the message. If the episode identifier has not been evaluated yet, i.e., $Episode(m) \notin E$, then α_i re-inserts the new state into the *open_msgs* list in order to process it later, once the restart message with the same episode identifier arrives (steps 16–20).

Another issue raising in MA-planning is that at a given time the depth reached by agent α_i in its own episode search tree can be quite different from the depth reached by other agents, since the searches conducted by two different agents have different branching factor, as each agent has its own set of actions. If α_i extracted the first state in the *open* list, it could happen that a state is expanded before another state achieved with fewer actions. To overcome this issue, Algorithm 1 manages the list of open states, *open*, as a priority list in which the priority of a state is the depth of the state in the episode search tree of the agent who expanded the state. If the state is expanded by an agent different from α_i the depth of the state comes from the same message with which the state is communicated to α_i. Thereby, agent α_i iteratively extracts a state s from the *open* priority list, selecting the first state in *open* with lowest depth.

Each time a state s is extracted from *open*, first α_i checks if the state satisfies the goal of the planning problem. If it does, agent α_i, together with the other agents, reconstructs the plan achieving s and returns the solution plan (steps 24–26). Otherwise, function $isStateBetter(s, s_I)$ evaluates whether s is a final search state of the current episode (steps 27–31). This is the case when s contains more goals than the initial state s_I of the current episode, and the number of goals reachable from s by using actions A_i is the same as those reachable from s using set A_i minus the set of actions deleting the goals in s that are not in s_I. The set of goals reachable from a given state is estimated by constructing a relaxed planning graph from the state using the set A_i of actions. A relaxed planning graph is a planning graph [13] constructed by ignoring deleting effects of actions. Intuitively, the second part of the condition checked by *isStateBetter* estimates if the remaining unachieved goals are reachable without destroying the new goals achieved by s. The condition is different from the condition used in the version of SIW for classical planning, because in MA-planning the h_{max} value that an agent computes for a state s using its own actions gives no valuable information about the solvability of the planning problem from s, since in MA-planning each agent is capable of executing only a subset of the problem actions. Essentially, $h_{max}(s)$ can be infinite each time reaching the problem goals from s requires the (joint) work of more than one agent.

Then, agent α_i checks if the state s is the result of the application of a public action, and in this case it sends a state message containing state s, its depth, and the identifier of the current episode e to other agents (steps 32–34). Finally, α_i expands state s by applying the executable actions and, for each successor state s' of s, α_i decides whether to include s' in its IW search according to the novelty of the state. In classical planning, a state s produces a new tuple of atoms t iff s is the first state generated in the episode search that makes t true. In the setting of MA-planning, the computation of the novelty is more difficult because, at a given time, the depth in episode search trees constructed by each agent can be quite different. In MA-planning, state s' with search depth d produces a new tuple of atoms t for agent α_i iff s' is the first state with depth lower than or equal to d in the episode search tree of α_i that makes t true. Notation $Novelty_{1...d}(s')$ denotes the novelty value of state s' computed with respect to states in the episode search tree with depth lower than or equal to its depth d. So, if $Novelty_{1...d}(s')$ is lower than the novelty bound k, α_i adds s' to its *open* list (steps 35–41). A similar idea is exploited in the recently introduced rollout-IW [14] and alternative formulations of novelty for heuristic search [15].

Algorithm 1 works with both encryption E0 and E1. The encryption affects the definition of novelty. E.g., consider states $s_1 = \{p, q\}$, $s_2 = \{p\}$, $s_3 = \{q\}$, where p and q are private facts of some agents different from α_i. Let $[x]$ denote the encrypted string representing one or more private facts x of other agents. With E0, the descriptions of states s_1, s_2, and s_3 that agent α_i handles are $\{[p], [q]\}, \{[p]\}, \{[q]\}$, respectively. With E1, these descriptions are $\{[p, q]\}, \{[p]\}, \{[q]\}$. Assume that the order with which these states are processed is s_1, s_2, s_3. Then, with E0, $novelty(s_2) = novelty(s_3) = \infty$, while with E1 we have $novelty(s_2) = novelty(s_3) = 1$. Thus, with E0, Algorithm 1 prunes s_2 and s_3, while with E1 it expands these states.

4   Experimental Results

In this section, we present an experimental study aimed at testing the effectiveness of our procedure MA-SIW. We also evaluate the usefulness of two simple extensions to MA-SIW. The first one regards the usage of an additional secondary queue. Each time MA-SIW achieves a successor state which has a novelty greater than the novelty bound k, MA-SIW adds the state to a secondary queue; if *open* and *open_msgs* become empty, then the states in this secondary queue are moved into *open*. Essentially, with this secondary queue the novelty is not used to prune the search, but it is used as a heuristic that prefers to expand search states with novelty lower than or equal to the novelty bound (states with higher novelty, instead of being discharged, are postponed). In the following, SQ denotes the usage of this secondary queue. This change renders novelty as a preference rather than a pruning mechanism, akin to the Best First Width Search algorithm [16].

The second extension to MA-SIW that we evaluate in this section regards reducing the agent communication burden by identifying situations in which an agent can autonomously reach all problem goals by herself. Given a search state, if an agent can reach all problem goals from this state, then the planning problem can be solved by the agent without further interactions with the other agents. In the proposed extension, the problem goals are *estimated* to be reachable by an agent from a given search state if the relaxed planning graph constructed from this state, using the set of actions of the agent, reaches all problem goals. If so, the agent does not send and receive messages anymore, until a goal state is reached or its *open* list becomes empty.

Note that the attempt of the agent to solve the planning problem by herself alone can fail, because the fact that all problem goals are reachable from a certain search state is only estimated to be true. For this reason, during the search that the agent conducts without communicating with the other agents, the messages that the agent does not send or receive are not discarded, but they are maintained in two queues. If the *open* list becomes empty, the received messages that were (temporarily) ignored are added to the *open_msg* list, while the messages that were (temporarily) not sent to the other agents are now sent, and the communication with the other agents is re-activated to its normal modality. In the following, DA denotes the usage of this search strategy.

Our code is written in C++, and exploits the Nanomsg open-source library to share messages [17].[2] In particular, this code is written on top of the code developed by Bonisoli et al. [10]. However, their approach is different from ours, Bonisoli et al. propose a distributed version of best first search for MA-STRIPS planning, while here we study the use of a blind search along with pruning by novelty.

Each agent uses three threads, two of which send and receive messages, while the other one conducts the search, so that the search is asynchronous w.r.t. the communication routines. The behavior of MA-SIW depends on the order with which the messages are received by an agent. Each time a run of MA-SIW is repeated, the agents' threads can be scheduled by the operative system differently, so that the behavior of MA-SIW can also be different. Thereby, for each problem of our benchmark, we run MA-SIW five times and consider the performance of the algorithm as the median over the five experimental runs.

---

[2] Our code and experimental data will be available on request.

When MA-SIW exceeded the CPU-time limit for more than two of the five runs, we consider the problem unsolved.

The considered benchmarks are the problems and domains of the distributed track of the first international competition on distributed and multi-agent planning [18,19]. In classical planning, SIW performs best using novelty bound $k = 2$. Since we have empirically observed a similar behavior also for our benchmark, all the results in the paper are derived using $k = 2$.

All tests are run on an Intel Xeon E5-2620 CPUs (24 nodes with 2.20 GHz) and 128 GB of RAM. Given a MA-planning problem, for each agent in the problem we limited the usage of resources to 3 CPU cores and 8 GB of RAM. Moreover, the time limit was 5 min, after which the termination of all threads was forced.

Table 1. Number of problems solved by SIW, SIW-DA and SIW-DA-SQ with encryptions E0 and E1 for the benchmark domains of the Distributed Track of the first competition on MA-planning.

Domain	With encryption E0			With encryption E1		
	SIW	*SIW-DA*	*SIW-DA-SQ*	*SIW*	*SIW-DA*	*SIW-DA-SQ*
Blocksworld	19	20	20	18	18	20
Depot	10	10	9	8	7	8
Driverlog	20	19	20	18	20	20
Elevators'08	16	17	20	16	16	20
Logistics'00	20	20	20	20	20	18
Rovers	20	20	20	20	20	20
Satellites	20	20	20	20	20	20
Sokoban	1	2	6	3	1	1
Taxi	19	20	20	13	20	20
Wireless	0	0	0	0	0	0
Woodworking'08	0	1	2	0	0	1
Zenotravel	20	20	20	20	20	20
Total (240)	168	169	177	156	165	171

Table 1 shows the number of solved instances of SIW, SIW using DA, and SIW using both DA and SQ, with encryptions E0 and E1 for the exchanged private facts. Table 2 shows their performance in terms of average CPU-time (in seconds), average plan length, time score, quality score, number of exchanged messages, and number of expanded states. The CPU time of the unsolved problem is considered to be equal to the time limit. The average CPU time is computed over all the problems, while the average plan length is computed over the solved problems. The time score and quality score are popular measures, originally proposed for the seventh international planning competition [20]; they are

Table 2. Average CPU-time (in seconds), average plan length, time score, quality score, number of thousands of exchanged messages, and number of thousands of expanded states of SIW, SIW-DA and SIW-DA-SQ with encryptions E0 and E1.

Domain	With encryption E0			With encryption E1		
	SIW	*SIW-DA*	*SIW-DA-SQ*	*SIW*	*SIW-DA*	*SIW-DA-SQ*
Average time	92.47	90.5	85.42	109.04	96.32	94.17
Time score	153.41	157.65	150.43	137.21	147.24	141.08
Average plan length	74.71	76.44	82.52	80.32	77.51	85.35
Quality score	154.81	156.06	161.65	141.07	148.99	152.51
kMessages	32.04	26.63	325.98	25.93	25.37	267.7
kStates	27.55	23.24	187.46	25.69	24.0	141.93

defined as follows. If a planner P solves a problem π using t CPU time, it gets a *time score* equal to $\frac{1}{1+\log_{10}(t/t^*)}$, where t^* is the best time over the times required by the planners under comparison for solving π. Similarly, for plan quality if P generates a plan with l actions solving π, it gets a *quality score* equal to $\frac{l^*}{l}$, where l^* is the number of actions in the shortest plan over those computed by the compared planners for π. If P does not solve π, then it gets zero score (both for speed and quality). The time (quality) score of planner P is the sum of the time (quality) scores assigned to P over all the considered test problems.

The results in Tables 1 and 2 show that, using encryption E0, SIW with DA solves one more problem and, on average, is slightly faster than SIW without DA. Notably, with DA the number of expanded states and exchanged messages is significantly reduced. This is important because, if fewer messages are exchanged, less (private) knowledge is shared and hence the agents' privacy is better preserved. Moreover, SIW with both DA and SQ is on average slightly faster, and solves several more problems than SIW with DA.

The relative performance of the compared algorithms using encryption E1 is similar: SIW with both DA and SQ is the fastest, and has the best number of solved instances. As expected, the performance obtained using E1 are worse than using E0. Indeed, it can be shown that the novelty of a state computed by E1 is always smaller than the novelty computed by E0, and hence the pruning obtained by E1 is less effective than E0. On the other hand, as discussed before, the knowledge than could be inferred by using E0 includes the existence of private facts and the effects of private actions, while using E1 the private knowledge that could be inferred in much more limited. Interestingly, the results in Tables 1 and 2 show that SIW-DA-SQ using E1 solves few less problems than using E0, and that in terms of speed using E0 or E1 gives similar performance.

We also have run SIW-SQ with the competition benchmark domains used in our experiments. Overall, SIW-SQ solves fewer problems than SIW-DA-SQ: SIW-SQ using E0 solves 175 problems, while using E1 solves 167 problems.

Finally, we compare SIW-DA-SQ with the state-of-the-art multi-agent planner MAPlan [11,21], which showed the best performance at the first international

Table 3. Number of solved problems of SIW-DA-SQ using encryptions E0 and E1 w.r.t. MAPlan.

Domain	SIW-DA-SQ with encryption E0	SIW-DA-SQ with encryption E1	MAPlan FF + DTG
Blocksworld	20	20	20
Depot	9	8	9
Driverlog	20	20	16
Elevators08	20	20	8
Logistics00	20	18	17
Rovers	20	20	20
Satellites	20	20	20
Sokoban	6	4	13
Taxi	20	20	20
Wireless	0	0	3
Woodworking'08	2	1	16
Zenotravel	20	20	20
Total (240)	177	171	182

competition on distributed and multi-agent planning [18]. MAPlan conducts two consecutive best-first searches: the first search is guided by the LM-cut heuristic [22]; the second one is guided by the FF heuristic adapted for the multi-agent context [23]. The version of MAPlan that took part at the competition also terminates after 5 min.

Differently from MAPlan, the agents in SIW-DA-SQ do not exchange heuristic information during the search. From the heuristic information exchanged by MAPlan an agent could derive private knowledge of other agents, such as the existence of a certain number of other agents private actions, which is a disadvantage w.r.t. using SIW. On the other hand, as expected, without guiding the search by heuristics SIW-DA-SQ performs worse than MAPlan, although according to the results in Tables 3 and 4 the performance gap is quite small. MAPlan has the best number of solved instances, but SIW-DA-SQ with encryption E0 solves only few less problems. Moreover, the speed of SIW-DA-SQ with both encryptions E0 and E1 is similar to MAPlan. In terms of plan length the compared approaches perform similarly, although the average plan length for MAPlan is almost double of the one for SIW-DA-SQ. This is due to the Woodworking domain, whose problems are mostly unsolved by SIW-DA-SQ, while MAPlan solves them with quite long plans (containing more than one thousands actions). If we rule out Woodworking from the experimental analysis, the performance of MAPlan is comparable with that of SIW-DA-SQ in terms of both average plan length and quality score. We think that the reason of the poor performance of our approach in Woodworking is the presence of some bugs in the code that instantiates the problem, since we have noticed that there are actions necessary for solving the problem that are not grounded.

Table 4. Average CPU-time (in seconds), average plan length, time score, and quality score of SIW-DA-SQ using encryptions E0 and E1 w.r.t. MAPlan.

Domain	SIW-DA-SQ with encryption E0	SIW-DA-SQ with encryption E1	MAPlan FF+DTG
Average time	85.42	94.17	93.63
Time score	143.82	134.04	159.3
Average plan length	82.52	85.35	145.77
Quality score	159.66	150.33	149.6

5   Conclusion

In multi-agent privacy-preserving planning, the goal of the agents is to compute a joint plan that achieves mutual goals by keeping certain information private to the individual agents. However, typically, during the search each agent exchanges information with others, and the exchanged information could be used to infer private knowledge [5]. In this paper, we investigate the usage of SIW for multi-agent planning. Differently from the approaches proposed for multi-agent planning in the current literature, SIW conducts a "blind" search, and hence it does not require that agents exchange heuristic values. As a consequence, we claim that the agents' privacy can be better preserved by SIW than by the existing approaches to MA-planning.

The usage of IW search for solving MA-planning problems raises some synchronization issues that we have observed in this paper. We have proposed a new SIW procedure solving these issues, and have developed some improvements to the basic procedure that either speedup the search or reduce the number of exchanged messages, improving the agents' privacy. An experimental analysis shows that our approach is competitive with the state-of-the-art planner MAPlan, which by exchanging heuristic information among agents is weaker than our approach in terms of privacy preservation.

An interesting direction for future work is to investigate the usage and adaptation of recent heuristics based on the notion of novelty, that have been developed for centralized planning, in the setting of MA-planning [16]. Moreover, in order to preserve the agents' privacy even further, we plan to study the techniques that we have proposed also in the context of the definition of MA-planning problem presented in [10,24], which allows to constrain the information that can be shared among agents.

References

1. Brafman, R.I., Domshlak, C.: From one to many: planning for loosely coupled multi-agent systems. In: Proceedings of the Eighteenth International Conference on Automated Planning and Scheduling, ICAPS, pp. 28–35 (2008)
2. Nissim, R., Brafman, R.I.: Distributed heuristic forward search for multi-agent planning. J. Artif. Intell. Res. **51**(1), 293–332 (2014)
3. Torreño, A., Onaindia, E., Sapena, Ó.: An approach to multi-agent planning with incomplete information. In: Proceedings of the 20th European Conference on Artificial Intelligence, ECAI, pp. 762–767 (2012)
4. Lipovetzky, N., Geffner, H.: Width and serialization of classical planning problems. In: 20th European Conference on Artificial Intelligence, ECAI 2012, pp. 540–545 (2012)
5. Brafman, R.I.: A privacy preserving algorithm for multi-agent planning and search. In: International Joint Conference on Artificial Intelligence, IJCAI, pp. 1530–1536 (2015)
6. Maliah, S., Shani, G., Stern, R.: Privacy preserving landmark detection. In: Proceedings of European Conference on Artificial Intelligence, ECAI, vol. 14 (2014)
7. Maliah, S., Stern, R., Shani, G.: Privacy preserving LAMA. In: Proceedings of the Fourth Workshop on Distributed and Multi-agent Planning, ICAPS, pp. 100–108 (2016)
8. Nissim, R., Apsel, U., Brafman, R.I.: Tunneling and decomposition-based state reduction for optimal planning. In: 20th European Conference on Artificial Intelligence, ECAI, pp. 624–629 (2012)
9. Nissim, R., Brafman, R.I.: Multi-agent A* for parallel and distributed systems. In: Proceedings of the Workshop on Heuristics and Search for Domain-Independent Planning, ICAPS, pp. 42–51 (2012)
10. Bonisoli, A., Gerevini, A.E., Saetti, A., Serina, I.: A privacy-preserving model for multi-agent propositional planning. J. Exp. Theor. Artif. Intell. (2018, in press)
11. Fišer, D., Štolba, M., Komenda, A.: MAPlan. In: Proceedings of the Competition of Distributed and Multi-agent Planners, ICAPS, pp. 8–10 (2015)
12. Bonet, B., Geffner, H.: Planning as heuristic search. Artif. Intell. **129**(1–2), 5–33 (2001)
13. Blum, A.L., Furst, M.L.: Fast planning through planning graph analysis. Artif. Intell. **90**(1–2), 281–300 (1997)
14. Bandres, W., Bonet, B., Geffner, H.: Planning with pixels in (almost) real time. In: AAAI (2018)
15. Katz, M., Lipovetzky, N., Moshkovich, D., Tuisov, A.: Adapting novelty to classical planning as heuristic search. In: ICAPS, pp. 172–180 (2017)
16. Lipovetzky, N., Geffner, H.: Best-first width search: exploration and exploitation in classical planning. In: Singh, S.P., Markovitch, S. (eds.) Proceedings of the Thirty-First AAAI Conference on Artificial Intelligence, 4–9 February 2017, San Francisco, California, USA, pp. 3590–3596. AAAI Press (2017)
17. Sustrik, M.: nanomsg (2016). http://nanomsg.org/
18. Štolba, M., Komenda, A., Kovacs, D.L.: Competition of distributed and multiagent planners (2015). http://agents.fel.cvut.cz/codmap/
19. Štolba, M., Komenda, A., Kovacs, D.L.: Competition of distributed and multiagent planners (codmap). In: The International Planning Competition (WIPC-15), vol. 24 (2015)

20. Olaya, A., G., López C., L., Jiménez, S., C.: Deterministic part of the 7th International Planning Competition IPC7. In: ICAPS (2011). http://www.plg.inf.uc3m.es/ipc2011-deterministic
21. Štolba, M., Fišer, D., Komenda, A.: Admissible landmark heuristic for multi-agent planning. In: Proceedings of the Twenty-Fifth International Conference on Automated Planning and Scheduling, ICAPS (2015)
22. Bonet, B., Helmert, M.: Strengthening landmark heuristics via hitting sets. In: ECAI 2010–19th European Conference on Artificial Intelligence, pp. 329–334 (2010)
23. Štolba, M., Komenda, A.: Relaxation heuristics for multiagent planning. In: Proceedings of the Twenty-Fourth International Conference on Automated Planning and Scheduling, ICAPS, pp. 298–306 (2014)
24. Bonisoli, A., Gerevini, A.E., Saetti, A., Serina, I.: A privacy-preserving model for the multi-agent propositional planning problem. In: Proceedings of the Twenty-First European Conference on Artificial Intelligence, ECAI, pp. 973–974 (2014)

Operating Room Scheduling via Answer Set Programming

Carmine Dodaro[1], Giuseppe Galatà[2], Marco Maratea[1(✉)], and Ivan Porro[2]

[1] DIBRIS, University of Genova, Genova, Italy
{dodaro,marco}@dibris.unige.it
[2] SurgiQ srl, Genova, Italy
{giuseppe.galata,ivan.porro}@surgiq.com

Abstract. The Operating Room Scheduling (ORS) problem is the task of assigning patients to operating rooms, taking in account different specialties, the surgery and operating room shift durations and different priorities. Given that Answer Set Programming (ASP) has been recently employed for solving real-life scheduling and planning problems, in this paper we first present an off-line solution based on ASP for solving the ORS problem. Then, we present techniques for re-scheduling on-line in case the off-line schedule can not be fully applied. Results of an experimental analysis conducted on benchmarks with realistic sizes and parameters show that ASP is a suitable solving methodology also for the ORS problem.

1 Introduction

The Operating Room Scheduling (ORS) [1,5,18,20] problem is the task of assigning patients to operating rooms, taking in account different specialties, surgery durations, and operating room shift durations. Given that patients may have priorities, the solution has to find an accommodation for the patients with highest priorities, and then to the other with lower priorities if space is still available. A proper solution to the ORS problem is crucial for improving the whole quality of the health-care and the satisfaction of patients. Indeed, modern hospitals are often characterized by long surgical waiting lists, which is caused by inefficiencies in operating room planning, leading to an obvious dissatisfaction of patients.

Complex combinatorial problems, possibly involving optimizations, such as the ORS problem, are usually the target applications of knowledge representation and reasoning formalisms such as Answer Set Programming (ASP). Indeed, its simple but rich syntax [9], which includes optimization statements as well as powerful database-inspired constructs such as aggregates, and its intuitive semantics, combined with the readability of specifications (always appreciated by users) and availability of efficient solvers (see, e.g., [3,17,19]), make ASP an ideal candidate for addressing such problems. Indeed, ASP has been already successfully used for solving hard combinatorial and application problems in several research areas, including Artificial Intelligence [6,12], Bioinformatics [14], Hydroinformatics [16], and also employed in industrial applications (see, e.g., [2,11]).

C. Ghidini et al. (Eds.): AI*IA 2018, LNAI 11298, pp. 445–459, 2018.
https://doi.org/10.1007/978-3-030-03840-3_33

In this paper we first present an off-line solution schedule based on ASP for solving the ORS problem, where problem's specifications are modularly expressed as ASP rules, and ASP solvers are used to solve the resulting ASP program. Then, we also present techniques for re-scheduling on-line in case the off-line solution can not be fully applied given, e.g., some patients could not be operated in their assigned slot and have to be reallocated; in this case, the aim is of minimizing the changes needed to accommodate the new situation. Again, the re-scheduling is specified by modularly adding ASP rules to (part of) the original ASP program. We have finally run a wide experimental analysis on ORS benchmarks with realistic sizes and parameters inspired from data of a hospital in the north-east of Italy. Additionally, we have also performed a scalability analysis on the performance of the employed ASP solver and encoding for the scheduling problem w.r.t. schedule length. Overall, results show that ASP is a suitable solving methodology also for ORS, given that a high efficiency, defined in terms of room's occupation, can be achieved in short timings in line with the need of the application.

2   Background on ASP

Answer Set Programming (ASP) [7] is a programming paradigm developed in the field of nonmonotonic reasoning and logic programming. In this section we overview the language of ASP. More detailed descriptions and a more formal account of ASP, including the features of the language employed in this paper, can be found in [7,9]. Hereafter, we assume the reader is familiar with logic programming conventions.

Syntax. The syntax of ASP is similar to the one of Prolog. Variables are strings starting with uppercase letter and constants are non-negative integers or strings starting with lowercase letters. A *term* is either a variable or a constant. A *standard atom* is an expression $p(t_1, \ldots, t_n)$, where p is a *predicate* of arity n and $t_1, \ldots, t_n$ are terms. An atom $p(t_1, \ldots, t_n)$ is ground if $t_1, \ldots, t_n$ are constants. A *ground set* is a set of pairs of the form $\langle consts : conj \rangle$, where *consts* is a list of constants and *conj* is a conjunction of ground standard atoms. A *symbolic set* is a set specified syntactically as $\{Terms_1 : Conj_1; \cdots ; Terms_t : Conj_t\}$, where $t > 0$, and for all $i \in [1, t]$, each $Terms_i$ is a list of terms such that $|Terms_i| = k > 0$, and each $Conj_i$ is a conjunction of standard atoms. A *set term* is either a symbolic set or a ground set. Intuitively, a set term $\{X : a(X, c), p(X); Y : b(Y, m)\}$ stands for the union of two sets: the first one contains the X-values making the conjunction $a(X, c), p(X)$ true, and the second one contains the Y-values making the conjunction $b(Y, m)$ true. An *aggregate function* is of the form $f(S)$, where S is a set term, and f is an *aggregate function symbol*. Basically, aggregate functions map multisets of constants to a constant. The most common functions implemented in ASP systems are the following:

- #*count*, number of terms;
- #*sum*, sum of integers.

An *aggregate atom* is of the form $f(S) \prec T$, where $f(S)$ is an aggregate function, $\prec \in \{<, \leq, >, \geq\}$ is a comparison operator, and T is a term called guard. An aggregate atom $f(S) \prec T$ is ground if T is a constant and S is a ground set. An *atom* is either a standard atom or an aggregate atom. A *rule r* has the following form:

$$a_1 \vee \ldots \vee a_n :\!- b_1, \ldots, b_k, not\ b_{k+1}, \ldots, not\ b_m.$$

where $a_1, \ldots, a_n$ are standard atoms, $b_1, \ldots, b_k$ are atoms, $b_{k+1}, \ldots, b_m$ are standard atoms, and $n, k, m \geq 0$. A literal is either a standard atom a or its negation *not a*. The disjunction $a_1 \vee \ldots \vee a_n$ is the *head* of r, while the conjunction $b_1, \ldots, b_k, not\ b_{k+1}, \ldots, not\ b_m$ is its *body*. Rules with empty body are called *facts*. Rules with empty head are called *constraints*. A variable that appears uniquely in set terms of a rule r is said to be *local* in r, otherwise it is a *global* variable of r. An ASP program is a set of *safe* rules. A rule r is *safe* if both the following conditions hold: *(i)* for each global variable X of r there is a positive standard atom ℓ in the body of r such that X appears in ℓ; *(ii)* each local variable of r appearing in a symbolic set $\{Terms : Conj\}$ also appears in $Conj$.

A *weak constraint* [8] ω is of the form:

$$:\!\sim b_1, \ldots, b_k, not\ b_{k+1}, \ldots, not\ b_m. \ [w@l]$$

where w and l are the weight and level of ω. (Intuitively, $[w@l]$ is read "as weight w at level l", where weight is the "cost" of violating the condition in the body of w, whereas levels can be specified for defining a priority among preference criteria). An ASP program with weak constraints is $\Pi = \langle P, W \rangle$, where P is a program and W is a set of weak constraints.

A standard atom, a literal, a rule, a program or a weak constraint is *ground* if no variables appear in it.

Semantics. Let P be an ASP program. The *Herbrand universe* U_P and the *Herbrand base* B_P of P are defined as usual. The ground instantiation G_P of P is the set of all the ground instances of rules of P that can be obtained by substituting variables with constants from U_P.

An *interpretation* I for P is a subset I of B_P. A ground literal ℓ (resp., *not* ℓ) is true w.r.t. I if $\ell \in I$ (resp., $\ell \notin I$), and false (resp., true) otherwise. An aggregate atom is true w.r.t. I if the evaluation of its aggregate function (i.e., the result of the application of f on the multiset S) with respect to I satisfies the guard; otherwise, it is false.

A ground rule r is *satisfied* by I if at least one atom in the head is true w.r.t. I whenever all conjuncts of the body of r are true w.r.t. I.

A model is an interpretation that satisfies all the rules of a program. Given a ground program G_P and an interpretation I, the *reduct* [15] of G_P w.r.t. I is the subset G_P^I of G_P obtained by deleting from G_P the rules in which a body literal is false w.r.t. I. An interpretation I for P is an *answer set* (or stable model) for P if I is a minimal model (under subset inclusion) of G_P^I (i.e., I is a minimal model for G_P^I) [15].

Given a program with weak constraints $\Pi = \langle P, W \rangle$, the semantics of Π extends from the basic case defined above. Thus, let $G_\Pi = \langle G_P, G_W \rangle$ be the instantiation of Π; a constraint $\omega \in G_W$ is violated by an interpretation I if all the literals in ω are true w.r.t. I. An *optimum answer set* O for Π is an answer set of G_P that minimizes the sum of the weights of the violated weak constraints in G_W in a prioritized way.

3   Problem Description

Most modern hospitals are characterized by a very long surgical waiting list, often worsened, if not altogether caused, by inefficiencies in operating room planning. In this paper, the elements of the waiting list are called *registrations*. Each registration links a particular surgical procedure, with a predicted duration, to a patient.

The overall goal of the ORS problem is to assign the maximum number of registrations to the operating rooms (ORs). As first requirement, the assignments must guarantee that the sum of the predicted duration of surgeries assigned to a particular OR shift does not exceed the length of the shift itself, this is referred in the following as *surgery requirement*. Moreover, registrations are not all equal: they can be related to different pathologies and they can be in the waiting list for different periods of time. These two factors can be unified in a singular concept: *priority*. Registrations are classified according to three different priority categories, namely P_1, P_2 and P_3. The first one gathers either very urgent registrations or the ones that have been in the waiting list for a long period of time; we require that these registrations are all assigned to an OR. Then, the registrations of the other two categories are assigned to the top of the ORs capacity, prioritizing the P_2 over the P_3 ones (*minimization*).

However, in hospital units it is frequent that one planned assignment of ORs cannot be fulfilled due to complications or conflicts that may occur either during the surgery or before. In particular, surgeries may last longer than expected or some patients may delete the registration. Therefore, in such cases it is required to compute a new schedule which reallocates the ORs and, at the same time, minimizes the differences with a previous computed schedule. This problem is usually referred to as *rescheduling*. It is important to emphasize here that such situations are usually independent from the quality of the original schedule, indeed they are often due to unpredictable events.

The ORS problem can be split into two subproblems: (i) computation of an initial schedule for a given planning period (usually one week in hospitals, which is thus our target), and (ii) the rescheduling, i.e., the generation of an altered schedule based on complications or conflicts that require changes in the initial schedule.

The implementation described in Sect. 4 supports both the generation of an optimized initial schedule of the surgeries and its alteration and rearrangement in case of needed rescheduling, where the case of canceled registrations is considered.

4   ASP Encoding

In this section the scheduling and rescheduling problems are described in the Answer Set Programming language, in particular following the ASP-CORE-2 input language specification [9], in two separate sub-sections.

4.1   OR Scheduling

Data Model. The input data is specified by means of the predicates described in this paragraph. The predicates representing the facts of our encoding are the following:

- Instances of *registration(R, P, SU, SP)* represent the registrations, characterized by an id (R), a priority score (P), a surgery duration (SU) and the id of the specialty (SP) it belongs to.
- Instances of *mss(O, S, SP,D)* link each operating room (O) to a shift (S) for each specialty and planning day (D) as established by the hospital Master Surgical Schedule (MSS), i.e., a cyclic timetable constructed to define the specific assignment of OR shifts to specialties. Note that every value of the variable S represents an unique period of time, called shift, and that each day contains two shifts in our choice of MSS. Thus, $S = 1$ denotes the Monday $(D = 1)$ AM shift, $S = 2$ the Monday $(D = 1)$ PM one, $S - 3$ the Tuesday $(D = 2)$ AM one and so on.
- The OR shifts are represented by the instances of the predicate *duration(N, O, S)*, where N is the shift duration.
- Assignments are stored in the instances of *x(R, P, O, S, D)*, representing that the registration R with priority P is assigned to the operating room O during the shift S and the day D.

Encoding. Here we describe the ASP rules used for solving the ORS problem. The encoding is based on the well-known *Guess&Check* programming methodology. In particular, the following rule guesses an assignment for the registrations to an operating room in a given day and shift among the ones permitted by the MSS for the particular specialty the registration belongs to.

$$x(R, P, O, S, D) \lor nx(R, P, O, S, D) :- \ registration(R, P, \_, SP), \\ mss(O, S, SP, D). \tag{1}$$

Note that $nx(R, P, O, S, D)$ is a fresh atom representing that a registration is not assigned to an operating room in a specific day. The same registration should not be assigned more than once, in different operating rooms or shifts. This is assured by the constraints:

$$. :- x(R, P, O, S1, \_), \ x(R, P, O, S2, \_), \ S1 \ ! = \ S2.$$
$$:- x(R, P, O1, S, \_), \ x(R, P, O2, S, \_), \ O1 \ ! = \ O2. \tag{2}$$
$$:- x(R, P, O1, S1, \_), \ x(R, P, O2, S2, \_), \ O1 \ ! = \ O2, \ S1 \ ! = \ S2.$$

Note that in our setting there is no requirement that every registration must actually be assigned.

Surgery Requirement. With this constraint, we impose that the total length of surgery durations assigned to a shift is less than or equal to the shift duration.

$$surgery(R, SU, O, S) :\!- x(R, \_, O, S, \_), registration(R, \_, SU, \_, \_, \_).$$

$$:\!- x(\_, \_, O, S, \_), \#sum\{SU, R : surgery(R, SU, O, S)\} > N, duration(N, O, S). \tag{3}$$

Minimization. Registrations are characterized by the three priority levels P_1, P_2 and P_3. We want to be sure that every registration having priority 1 is assigned, then we assign as much as possible of the others, giving precedence to registrations having priority 2 over those having priority 3. This procedure is accomplished through constraint (4) for the priority 1 and the weak constraints (5) and (6) for priority 2 and 3, respectively.

$$:\!- N = totRegsP1 - \#count\{R : x(R, 1, \_, \_, \_)\}, \; N > 0. \tag{4}$$

$$:\!\sim N = totRegsP2 - \#count\{R : x(R, 2, \_, \_, \_)\}. \; [N@3] \tag{5}$$

$$:\!\sim N = totRegsP3 - \#count\{R : x(R, 3, \_, \_, \_)\}. \; [N@2] \tag{6}$$

totRegsP1, *totRegsP2* and *totRegsP3* are constants representing the total number of registrations having priority 1, 2 and 3, respectively.

Minimizing the number of unassigned registrations could cause an implicit preference towards the assignments of the registrations with shorter surgery durations. To avoid this effect, one can consider to minimize the idle time, however this is in general slower from a computational point of view and unnecessary, since the shorter surgeries preference is already mitigated by our three-tiered priority system.

4.2   Rescheduling

In the rescheduling problem, we start from an already-defined schedule that for some reasons could not be followed to the end and must be partially scheduled again. In particular, we took into account the case where some patients could not be operated in their assigned slot and must be reallocated in one of the slots in the remaining part of the original planning period.

Data Model. The predicates representing the facts of our encoding are the following:

- The old planning is encoded through facts represented by instances of the predicate *x(R, P, O, S, D)*.
- MSS, registrations and shifts are described by the same predicates as in the previous section.
- The new assignments are described using a novel predicate *y*.

Encoding. The new encoding includes only rules (1), (2) and (3) from the previous encoding, where atoms over the predicate x and nx are replaced with y and ny, respectively. Additionally, a constraint must be added to ensure that for every single registration in the old schedule (x predicate) there is an assignment in the new one (y predicate):

$$:- not\ y(R, P, \_, \_, \_),\ x(R, P, \_, \_, \_). \tag{7}$$

The main objective of the scheduling was to assign the largest possible number of registrations to the OR shifts. On the contrary, in the rescheduling problem the objective is to reassign all the previously allocated registrations and the reallocated ones with the least possible disruption to the old schedule. In order to do so, we compute and minimize the difference in days between the new and old assignments for each registration. This means that the rules (4), (5) and (6) are replaced by:

$$difference(DF, R):-\ y(R, \_, \_, \_, D),\ x(R, \_, \_, \_, OldD),\ DF = |D - OldD|.$$
$$:\sim\ T = \#sum\{DF, R:\ difference(DF, R)\}.\ [T@1] \tag{8}$$

5   Experimental Results

In this section we report about the results of an empirical analysis of the scheduling and rescheduling problems. For the initial scheduling problem, data have been randomly generated but having parameters and sizes inspired by real data, then a part of the results of the planning has been used as input for the rescheduling (as we will detail later). Both experiments were run on a Intel® Core™ i7-7500U CPU @ 2.70 GHz with 7.6 GB of physical RAM. The ASP system used was CLINGO [17], version 5.5.2.

5.1   ORS

The test case we have assembled for the initial planning is based on the requirements of a typical middle sized hospital, with five surgical specialties to be managed. To test scalability, other than the 5-days planning period, which is the one that is widely used in Italian hospital units, seven benchmarks of different dimension were created. Each benchmark was tested 10 times with different randomly generated input. The characteristics of the tests are the following:

- 7 different benchmarks, comprising a planning period of respectively 15, 10, 7, 5, 3, 2 and 1 work days;
- 10 operating rooms unevenly distributed among the specialties;
- 5 h long morning and afternoon shifts for each operating room, summing up to a total of respectively 1500, 1000, 700, 500, 300, 200 and 100 hours of OR available time for the 7 benchmarks;

Table 1. Parameters for the random generation of the scheduler input.

Specialty	Registrations							ORs	Avg. surgery duration (min)	Coefficient of variation
	15-day	10-day	7-day	5-day	3-day	2-day	1-day			
1	240	160	112	80	48	32	16	3	124	48%
2	210	140	98	70	42	28	14	2	99	18%
3	210	140	98	70	42	28	14	2	134	19%
4	180	120	84	60	36	24	12	1	95	21%
5	210	140	98	70	42	28	14	2	105	29%
Total	1050	700	490	350	210	140	70	10		

- for each benchmark, we generated 1050, 700, 490, 350, 210, 140 and 70 registrations, respectively, from which the scheduler will draw the assignments. Registrations are characterized by a surgery duration, a specialty and a priority. In this way, we simulate the common situation where a hospital manager takes the beginning of an ordered, w.r.t. priorities, waiting list and tries to assign as many elements as possible to each OR.

The surgery durations have been generated assuming a normal distribution, while the priorities have been generated from a quasi-uniform distribution of three possible values (with weights respectively of 0.30, 0.33 and 0.37 for registrations having priority 1, 2 and 3, respectively). The parameters of the test have been summed up in Table 1. In particular, for each specialty (1 to 5), we reported the number of registrations generated for each benchmark (15-, 10-, 7-, 5-, 3-, 2- and 1-day), the number of ORs assigned to the specialty, the average duration of surgeries, and the coefficient of variation (defined as the standard deviation over the mean), respectively.

Results of the experiment are reported in Table 2, as the average of 10 runs for each benchmark. Table 2 reports, for each benchmark, the average number of assigned registrations (shown as assigned/generated ratio). The efficiency column shows the percentage of the total OR time occupied by the assigned registrations. A time limit of 20 s was given in view of a practical use of the program: on the target 5-days planning length, an efficiency of the 95% was reached. As a general observation, we report that with all the considered benchmarks, except with the one having planning length of 15-day, we obtained an efficiency greater than or equal to 90%. The 1-day test managed to converge after 10 s.

A detailed analysis of the performance is reported in Table 3 for the target 5-day planning period. In particular, for each of the 10 runs executed, Table 3 reports the number of the assigned registrations out of the generated ones for each priority, and a measure of the total time occupied by the assigned registrations as a percentage of the total OR time available. In this case, it is possible to observe that the efficiency is always greater or equal than 95%, but for an instance having efficiency of 92%.

Table 2. Averages of the results for the 15, 10, 7, 5, 3, 2 and 1-day benchmarks.

Benchmark	Priority 1	Priority 2	Priority 3	Total	Efficiency
15 days	319/319	169/342	42/389	530/1050	66%
10 days	210/210	201/229	81/261	492/700	90%
7 days	147/147	152/166	55/177	353/490	92%
5 days	106/106	102/113	50/130	258/350	95%
3 days	62/62	62/67	35/81	159/210	94%
2 days	42/42	40/46	22/52	104/140	95%
1 day	21/21	20/23	12/26	53/70	96%

Table 3. Scheduling results for the 5-day benchmark.

Assigned registrations				OR time efficiency
Priority 1	Priority 2	Priority 3	Total	
103 out of 103	104 out of 121	61 out of 126	268 out of 350	96%
114 out of 114	90 out of 94	54 out of 142	258 out of 350	95%
102 out of 102	116 out of 116	43 out of 123	261 out of 350	95%
112 out of 112	90 out of 102	50 out of 136	252 out of 350	95%
103 out of 103	95 out of 107	35 out of 140	233 out of 350	92%
99 out of 99	99 out of 122	66 out of 129	264 out of 350	95%
101 out of 101	108 out of 110	44 out of 139	253 out of 350	95%
114 out of 114	115 out of 124	41 out of 112	270 out of 350	96%
114 out of 114	114 out of 129	34 out of 107	262 out of 350	96%
98 out of 98	91 out of 108	73 out of 144	262 out of 350	95%

Finally, in 5 plots of Fig. 1 we (partially) present the results achieved on one instance (i.e., the first instance of Table 3) with 350 registrations for 5 days. Each colored block in the respective plots corresponds to a registration assigned to one of the 10 operating rooms. The remaining space up to the 300 min limit represent the idle time of the OR. Only the data about the morning assignments are showed; the ones for the afternoon are similar (qualitatively). The bottom-right plot shows, instead, the evolution of the solution quality when 600 s are granted to the same instance.

5.2   Rescheduling

The rescheduling is applied to a previously planned schedule in the case this could not be carried on to the end. Once planned, a specialty schedule does not normally influence the other specialties, thus it makes sense to re-schedule one specialty at a time.

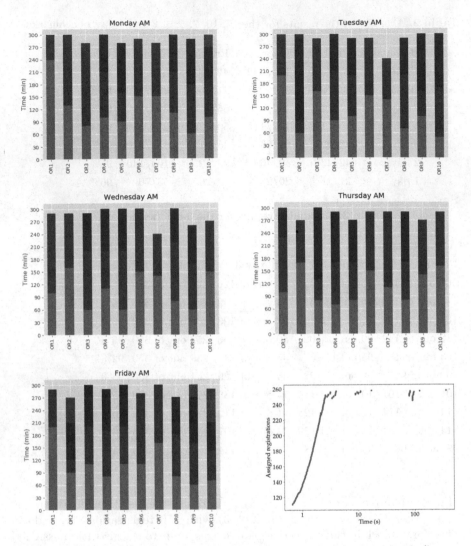

Fig. 1. Example of scheduling with 350 registrations for 5 days, and time scale (bottom-right).

To test the rescheduler we have defined three different scenarios. Considering the target planning schedule of 5-day, we assumed that in the second day a number of surgeries in specialty 1 had to be postponed to the next day. This number was set to 1 (scenario A), 3 (scenario B) or 6 (scenario C), respectively. Thus, we have to re-schedule the three remaining days of the planning.

In order to be able to insert the postponed registrations, we have to make sure that the starting schedule leaves enough available OR time by removing the necessary registrations from the old schedule, beginning from the last day of the period and from the registrations in the priority 3 category. The three tests performed had the following characteristics: *(i)* in all scenarios the postponed registrations have been generated with an average surgery duration of 100 min, *(ii)* the number of registrations present in the old schedule is 43, *(iii)* 0, 1 and 4 priority 3 old schedule registrations had to be removed from the last planning day in scenarios A, B and C, respectively.

The results are summarized in Table 4, where we report the scenario, the number of registrations that were inserted in each scenario (Postponed Registrations), the number of registrations coming from the old schedule (Old Registrations), and the total displacement, calculated as described in (8), showing the sum of all day displacements the old registrations were subject to in the resulting new schedule.

Table 4. Results for the three rescheduling scenarios.

Scenario	Postponed registrations	Old registrations	Total displacements (days)
A	1	43	3
B	3	42	4
C	6	39	6

6 Application of Our ASP Solution

Our ASP solution presented in this paper is part of a more general real-life application that we are developing. The application can be accessed through a web-interface where the parameters of the problem can be specified. Moreover, the interface allows the user to interact with the ASP encoding by offering web forms for adding the so called "customizable constraints", that express user requirements and preferences. We have identified five different constraints that combined together cover most user needs, and are detailed in the following paragraph. Finally, note that such customizable constraints can be used for both scheduling and rescheduling.

Customizable Constraints. The customizable constraints are not strictly required for the working of the program but allow the user to tweak as they prefer the final results. Each of these constraints can be activated at runtime for multiple registrations and can involve different selection of days, ORs, and shifts.

Given a set of n registrations, defined by the user through the app interface and characterized by the ids $r_i i = 1, ..., n$, the first imposes that the set can be assigned only in a chosen period, defined as all the operating room shifts between the initial (i) and the final (f) days, where i and f are parameters provided by the user. For each registration we impose:

$$:- \ x(r_i, \_, \_, S, \_), \ S < i.$$
$$:- \ x(r_i, \_, \_, S, \_), \ S > f. \tag{9}$$

The second constraint can be used to forbid a specific shift s to the chosen registrations:

$$:- x(r_i, \_, \_, s, \_). \tag{10}$$

The third and fourth customizable constraints regard forbidding or enforcing the use of a specific OR o for a set of registrations, respectively:

$$:- x(r_i, \_, o, \_, \_), registration(r_i, \_, \_, \_), mss(o, \_, \_, \_).$$
$$:- not\ x(r_i, \_, o, \_, \_), registration(r_i, \_, \_, \_), mss(o, \_, \_, \_). \tag{11}$$

The last constraint can be used if the user wants to assign a set of registrations as temporally close as possible to a specific OR shift, without actually enforcing it. This can be accomplished by defining a predicate ($distance(N, R)$) that computes the $distance$ (N) between the assigned (S) and suggested (represented by the parameter $prefS$) shifts and tries to minimize it:

$$distance(N, r_i) :- x(r_i, \_, \_, S, \_),\ N = |S - prefS|.$$
$$:\sim T = \#sum\{N, R :\ distance(N, R)\}.\ [T@4] \tag{12}$$

All these constraints can be applied to different sets of registrations at the same time, using different user provided parameters.

7   Related Work

We are not aware of any previous attempt to solve the ORS problem using ASP algorithms, however an extensive literature approaching this problem with different techniques has been developed.

Aringhieri et al. [5] addressed the joint OR planning (MSS) and scheduling problem, described as the allocation of OR time blocks to specialties together with the subsets of patients to be scheduled within each time block over a one week planning horizon. They developed a 0–1 linear programming formulation of the problem and used a two level meta-heuristic to solve it. Its effectiveness was demonstrated through extensive numerical experiments carried out on a large set of instances based on real data. In [18], the same authors introduced a hybrid two-phase optimization algorithm which exploits the potentiality of neighborhood search techniques combined with Monte Carlo simulation, in order to solve the joint advance and allocation scheduling problem taking into account the inherent uncertainty of surgery durations. Abedini et al. [1] developed a bin packing model with a multi-step approach and a priority-type-duration (PTD) rule. The model maximizes utilization and minimizes the idle time, which consequently affects the cost at the planning phase and was programmed using MATLAB. Molina-Pariente et al. [20] tackled the problem of assigning an intervention date and an operating room to a set of surgeries on the waiting list, minimizing access time for patients with diverse clinical priority values. The algorithms used to allocate surgeries were various bin packing (BP) operators. They adapted existing heuristics to the problem and compared them to their own heuristics using a test bed based on the literature. The tests were performed with the software Gurobi.

The rescheduling problem was addressed by Shu et al. [22], using an extension of the Longest Processing Time (LPT) algorithm, which was used to solve the atomic job shop scheduling problem. Zhang et al. [23] addressed the problem of OR planning with different demands from both elective patients and non-elective ones, with priorities in accordance with urgency levels and waiting times. This problem is formulated as a penalty stochastic shortest-path Markov Decision Process (MDP) with dead ends (fSSPDE), and solved using MATLAB by the method of asynchronous value iteration.

Finally, in the introduction we have already reported that ASP has been already successfully used for solving hard combinatorial and application problems in several research areas. ASP encodings were proposed for scheduling problems other than ORS, as examples *Incremental Scheduling Problem* [10], where the goal is to assign jobs to devices such that their executions do not overlap one another; *Team Building Problem* [21], where the goal is to allocate the available personnel of a seaport for serving the incoming ships; and *Nurse Scheduling Problem* [4,13], where the goal is to create a scheduling for nurses working in hospital units.

8 Conclusions

In this paper we presented an ASP encoding to provide a solution to the ORS problem, where specifications of the problem are modularly expressed as ASP rules. Then, we also presented techniques for re-scheduling on-line in case the off-line solution can not be fully applied given, e.g., canceled registrations. In this case, the goal is to minimize the changes needed to accommodate the new situation. Again, the re-scheduling is specified by modularly adding ASP rules to (part of) the original ASP program. Finally, we presented the results of an experimental analysis on ORS benchmarks with realistic sizes and parameters showing that our scheduling solution obtains around 95% of efficiency after few seconds of computation on planning length of 5 days usually used in Italian hospitals. Our solution also enjoys good scalability property, having an efficiency over or equal to 90% for planning periods up to 10 days, i.e., double w.r.t. the target period. Also our rescheduling solution reached positive results.

All benchmarks and encodings employed in this work can be found at: http://www.star.dist.unige.it/~marco/AIIA2018/material.zip.

References

1. Abedini, A., Ye, H., Li, W.: Operating room planning under surgery type and priority constraints. Proc. Manuf. **5**, 15–25 (2016)
2. Abseher, M., Gebser, M., Musliu, N., Schaub, T., Woltran, S.: Shift design with answer set programming. Fundam. Inf. **147**(1), 1–25 (2016)
3. Alviano, M., Dodaro, C.: Anytime answer set optimization via unsatisfiable core shrinking. TPLP **16**(5–6), 533–551 (2016)
4. Alviano, M., Dodaro, C., Maratea, M.: An advanced answer set programming encoding for nurse scheduling. In: Esposito, F., Basili, R., Ferilli, S., Lisi, F. (eds.) AI*IA 2017. LNCS, vol. 10640, pp. 468–482. Springer, Cham (2017). https://doi.org/10.1007/978-3-319-70169-1_35
5. Aringhieri, R., Landa, P., Soriano, P., Tànfani, E., Testi, A.: A two level meta-heuristic for the operating room scheduling and assignment problem. Comput. Oper. Res. **54**, 21–34 (2015)
6. Balduccini, M., Gelfond, M., Watson, R., Nogueira, M.: The USA-advisor: a case study in answer set planning. In: Eiter, T., Faber, W., Truszczyński, M. (eds.) LPNMR 2001. LNCS (LNAI), vol. 2173, pp. 439–442. Springer, Heidelberg (2001). https://doi.org/10.1007/3-540-45402-0_39
7. Brewka, G., Eiter, T., Truszczynski, M.: Answer set programming at a glance. Commun. ACM **54**(12), 92–103 (2011)
8. Buccafurri, F., Leone, N., Rullo, P.: Enhancing disjunctive datalog by constraints. IEEE Trans. Knowl. Data Eng. **12**(5), 845–860 (2000)
9. Calimeri, F., et al.: ASP-Core-2 Input Language Format (2013). https://www.mat.unical.it/aspcomp2013/files/ASP-CORE-2.01c.pdf
10. Calimeri, F., Gebser, M., Maratea, M., Ricca, F.: Design and results of the fifth answer set programming competition. Artif. Intell. **231**, 151–181 (2016)
11. Dodaro, C., Gasteiger, P., Leone, N., Musitsch, B., Ricca, F., Schekotihin, K.: Combining answer set programming and domain heuristics for solving hard industrial problems (application paper). TPLP **16**(5–6), 653–669 (2016)
12. Dodaro, C., Leone, N., Nardi, B., Ricca, F.: Allotment problem in travel industry: a solution based on ASP. In: ten Cate, B., Mileo, A. (eds.) RR 2015. LNCS, vol. 9209, pp. 77–92. Springer, Cham (2015). https://doi.org/10.1007/978-3-319-22002-4_7
13. Dodaro, C., Maratea, M.: Nurse scheduling via answer set programming. In: Balduccini, M., Janhunen, T. (eds.) LPNMR 2017. LNCS (LNAI), vol. 10377, pp. 301–307. Springer, Cham (2017). https://doi.org/10.1007/978-3-319-61660-5_27
14. Erdem, E., Öztok, U.: Generating explanations for biomedical queries. TPLP **15**(1), 35–78 (2015)
15. Faber, W., Pfeifer, G., Leone, N.: Semantics and complexity of recursive aggregates in answer set programming. Artif. Intell. **175**(1), 278–298 (2011)
16. Gavanelli, M., Nonato, M., Peano, A.: An ASP approach for the valves positioning optimization in a water distribution system. J. Log. Comput. **25**(6), 1351–1369 (2015)
17. Gebser, M., Kaminski, R., Kaufmann, B., Ostrowski, M., Schaub, T., Wanko, P.: Theory solving made easy with clingo 5. In: ICLP (Technical Communications). OASICS, vol. 52, pp. 2:1–2:15. Schloss Dagstuhl - Leibniz-Zentrum fuer Informatik (2016)
18. Landa, P., Aringhieri, R., Soriano, P., Tànfani, E., Testi, A.: A hybrid optimization algorithm for surgeries scheduling. Oper. Res. Health Care **8**, 103–114 (2016)

19. Maratea, M., Pulina, L., Ricca, F.: A multi-engine approach to answer-set programming. TPLP **14**(6), 841–868 (2014)
20. Molina-Pariente, J.M., Hans, E.W., Framinan, J.M., Gomez-Cia, T.: New heuristics for planning operating rooms. Comput. Indus. Eng. **90**, 429–443 (2015)
21. Ricca, F., Grasso, G., Alviano, M., Manna, M., Lio, V., Iiritano, S., Leone, N.: Team-building with answer set programming in the gioia-tauro seaport. TPLP **12**(3), 361–381 (2012)
22. Shu, A.C., Subbaraj, I., Phan, L.: Operating Room Rescheduler (2015)
23. Zhang, J., Dridi, M., El Moudni, A.: A stochastic shortest-path MDP model with dead ends for operating rooms planning, pp. 1–6, September 2017

A Goal Triggering Mechanism for Continuous Human-Robot Interaction

Alessandro Umbrico[✉], Amedeo Cesta, Gabriella Cortellessa,
and Andrea Orlandini

CNR – Italian National Research Council, ISTC – Institute of Cognitive Sciences and
Technologies, Via S. Martino della Battaglia, 44, 00185 Rome, Italy
{Alessandro.Umbrico,Amedeo.Cesta,Gabriella.Cortellessa,
Andrea.Orlandini}@istc.cnr.it

Abstract. The deployment of autonomous robots capable to both socially interact and proactively offer support to human users in a common life scenario remains challenging despite the recent technical advancements. For instance, research for endowing autonomous robots with the capability of acting in "non-ideal" and partially observable environments as well as socially interacting with humans is still an area in which improvements are specifically needed. To this aim, this paper elaborates on the need for integrating different Artificial Intelligence (AI) techniques to foster the development of personal robotic assistants continuously supporting older adults. Recently, the authors have been working on proposing an AI-based cognitive architecture that integrates knowledge representation and automated planning techniques in order to endow assistive robots with proactive and context situated abilities. This paper particularly describes a goal triggering mechanism to allow a robot to reason over the status of the user and the living environment with the aim of dynamically generating high-level goals to be planned accordingly.

Keywords: Goal reasoning · Knowledge reasoning
Planning and acting · Timeline-based planning
Sensor networks · Intelligent capabilities integration

1 Introduction

The deployment of autonomous robots in common life situations raises many research challenges that are still open despite the current technical advancements. In order to be fully reliable, autonomous robots must be capable of safely acting in "non-ideal" environments as well as socially interacting with humans when needed. The integration of different techniques coming from different fields like e.g., robotics, artificial intelligence (AI) or psychology, is key to realize *hybrid* cognitive capabilities that allow robots to effectively interact with humans in socially common situations [2,14,17]. In such contexts, autonomous robots should be able to represent and reason over a wide and heterogeneous set

© Springer Nature Switzerland AG 2018
C. Ghidini et al. (Eds.): AI*IA 2018, LNAI 11298, pp. 460–473, 2018.
https://doi.org/10.1007/978-3-030-03840-3_34

of information while acting in the environment [11]. The structure of this information depends on the particular scenario and the application objectives, but also on the particular behavior a robot aims to achieve [1,13]. The knowledge can be static if a robot performs always the same task in the same environment. The knowledge must be dynamic instead, if a robot must be capable of learning from experience and adapt its behaviors.

A uniform approach capable of "closing the loop" between the representation capabilities and the acting capabilities of an autonomous robot in a general and uniform way is less explored and mostly still open as a problem. Such a capability would be particularly helpful for assistive robots taking care of senior users in different daily life situations. There is a high number of situations that an assistive robot may deal with as well as a high number of tasks that it may perform to support/help older adults. The aim of defining a comprehensive planning domain for all such possible situations is a sort of "unsupported desiderata" that contributed to trigger the research line topic of this paper. More in general, we are pursuing the long-term research objective to provide an assistive robot with the ability to take autonomous decisions for both supporting senior persons in their living environments and having effective and safe interactions with them. Specifically, we focus on scenarios where a senior user with mild cognitive and/or physical impairments lives in her home with the need of a continuous assistance from a personal robotic assistant. In such a scenario, a robot should (i) acquire information about the user and the environment via a sensor network, (ii) analyze and reason over such information and (iii) *proactively* take decisions to (effectively and safely) support with continuity the user in her daily home-living activities. Thus, we are investigating the integration of knowledge representation and reasoning with automated planning and execution techniques with the aim of creating the cognitive capabilities needed to reason about the status of the environment and dynamically decide assistive tasks to perform.

As a case study, we leverage our past experience by defining a realistic scenario derived from the GiraffPlus project [9]. The project was aimed at creating an integrated environment to support seniors in their living environments. That project represents an interesting testbed for continuous monitoring integrating a sensor network, software services and a telepresence robot. In this context, a robot must be capable of interpreting data coming from the sensor network according to a well defined semantics and build *knowledge* characterizing the state of the environment and the monitored user. Then, a robot must process such knowledge in order to recognize particular *situations* that require the proactive execution of some *tasks* to support the daily-home living. Although the project was successfully completed as well as all scientific and technological objectives achieved, the outcomes of the evaluation process highlighted that the system functionalities still need to be further developed and deployed to more properly respond to user needs [6]. Then, additional work has been done, e.g., for increasing the HRI capabilities of the Giraff robot [10]. Furthermore, a new research initiative called KOaLa (*Knowledge-based cOntinuous Loop*) has been started recently with the aim of realizing a cognitive architecture for the synthesis of a continuous "sense-plan-act" cycle. In [5], an initial description of the overall cognitive architecture of KOaLa is provided, in terms of high level modules that create a dialogue between sensor data gathering, the ontological approach to create background texture for a knowledge processing mechanism, and identified a path toward planning and acting. This paper adds specific details to the ontological approach of KOaLa and describes the goal recognition and triggering mechanism needed to dynamically generate *planning goals* to enable the use of a planning and acting module in a proactive way.

2   KOaLa: A Cognitive Architecture for Autonomy

KOaLa propose a innovative cognitive architecture for autonomy capable of integrating knowledge representation and reasoning with automated planning and execution. As Fig. 1 shows, the envisaged architecture realizes an hybrid control process by integrating two different types of knowledge. A knowledge about the environment allows an artificial agent to interpret sensor data coming from the "external world" and dynamically recognize events and/or activities. A Knowledge Base (KB) and a dedicated Ontology provide the internal structures needed to represent and maintain the KB. A knowledge about the capabilities of an artificial agent characterizes the operations and actions it can perform to interact with the entities of the environment and change the state of the environment (i.e. *act*).

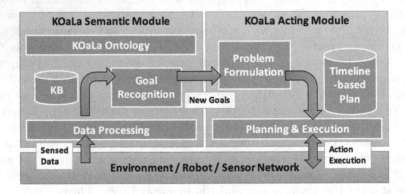

Fig. 1. The envisaged cognitive architecture for autonomy

As Fig. 1 shows, the KOaLa (hybrid) control process leverages the tight integration of two distinct *intelligent modules*. The *semantic module* is responsible for managing knowledge processing in order to internally represent the status of the environment and the available capabilities. It receives data from the environment through some sensing devices like e.g., sensors, IoT devices or robot actuators. Sensed data is then interpreted and processed to build and update a KB. Data processing relies on the KOaLa ontology which formally defines a *semantics* for concepts and properties an agent is supposed to deal with. The resulting KB is continuously analyzed by a *goal recognition* process which is in charge of detecting particular *situations* that require an agent to proactively perform some high-level *tasks*.

The synthesis and the execution of these tasks is then managed by the *acting module* which leverages the timeline-based approach to synthesize and execute the set of actions needed. Specifically, it relies on PLATINUm [18,19] which represents a novel planning and execution software framework successfully applied in realistic manufacturing scenarios [15]. PLATINUm complies with the formal characterization of the timeline-based approach give in [7] and therefore, it is capable of dealing with temporal uncertainty at both planning and execution time.

2.1 Context-Based Ontological Approach

The semantic module of the envisaged architecture must be capable of interpreting data coming from the environment and process such data to generate knowledge. A common language to uniformly represent and reason on sensor data is necessary. The KOaLa ontology has been defined to specify a clear semantics of the information a robot is supposed to manage. It leverages the Web Ontology Language (OWL) [3] and relies on the Semantic Sensor Network Ontology (SSN) [8] and the DOLCE Ultra Light ontology (DUL). The ontology provides a general description of the entities and properties that may compose the environment a robot operates in. This general knowledge is characterized by following a *context-based approach* which takes into account different perspectives. Namely, each context characterizes the knowledge of a robot with respect to three particular points of view: (i) the *sensor context*; (ii) the *environment context*; (iii) the *observation context*.

The sensor context characterizes the knowledge about the sensors that compose the environment. It formally describes the deployment of the sensors and the properties they may observe. This context extends the SSN ontology with the aim of providing a more detailed representation of the different sensing devices that can compose the environment as well as the different types of property that can be observed. This detailed description allows a robot to dynamically recognize the actual set of sensing capabilities and therefore the type of information it can deal with. As an example, the class `SSN:Property` which is a sub-class of `DUL:Quality`, models the qualities of an event or an object a sensor can observe according to the SSN ontology. The class `SSN:Property` has been extended as show in Fig. 2 in order to model the specific types of property a particular sensing device is capable of observing over time.

The proposed ontology distinguishes between two particular types of property. The class `HealthProperty` models physiological parameters of a person like e.g., `BloodPressure`, `BodyWeight`, a robot may monitor over time. The class `EnvironmentProperty` models parameters concerning the state of the environment like e.g., `Luminosity`, `Temperature`. Similarly, different types of sensor have different capabilities and can observe different types of property. Thus, also

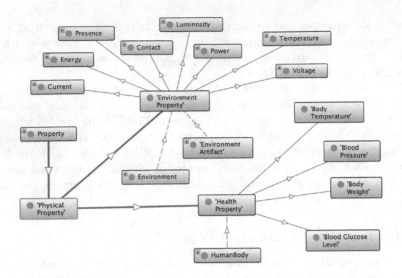

Fig. 2. The KOaLa extension of the class `SSN:Property`

the class `SSN:Sensor` has been extended to model the particular types of sensing device available and the associated sensing capabilities. The class `Pir` and the class `Switch` are two examples of sensors used that can be formally defined as follows:

```
Pir ⊑ SSN:Sensor ⊓
      ∃ SSN:observes.Luminosity ⊓
      ∃ SSN:observes.Temperature ⊓
      ∃ SSN:observes.Presence
```

```
Switch ⊑ SSN:Sensor ⊓
         ∃ SSN:observes.Energy ⊓
         ∃ SSN:observes.Voltage ⊓
         ∃ SSN:observes.Power ⊓
         ∃ SSN:observes.Current
```

The environment context enriches the sensor context by taking into account the physical environment data comes from. Sensor data always represents a measurement of a particular physical element of the environment, according to their deployment. This context introduces the ontological elements needed to model the physical objects that can be part of an environment, the properties that characterize their states and the deployment of sensors. This context leverages the DUL ontology by extending the classes `DUL:PhysicalAgent`, `DUL:PhysicalArtifcat` and `DUL:PhysicalPlace`. According to DUL semantics, a `DUL:PhysicalAgent` is a `DUL:PhysicalObject` capable of self-representing a `DUL:Description` in order to plan a `DUL:Action`. This interpretation is well suited to model the *agents* that can be part of the envisaged application scenarios. Considering an assistive robotics scenario, the types of agent that can be taken into account are (i) *assistive robots* and (ii) *patients*.

The class `AssistiveRobot` has been introduced to model an assistive robot as a `DUL:PhysicalAgent` capable of performing some `Activity`. Similarly, the class `Patient` has been introduced to model a `DUL:NaturalPerson` which is a `DUL:PhysicalAgent` living inside his/her home environment and capable of performing some `Activity`. However a `Patient` is also an element of the environment whose properties can be observed through dedicated sensors. There-fore a `Patient` is associated to some `HealthProperty` that can be observed.

```
Patient ⊑ DUL:NaturalPerson ⊓
          ∃ performs.Activity ⊓          AssistiveRobot ⊑ DUL:PhysicalAgent ⊓
          ∃ SSN:hasProperty.HealthProperty          ∃ performs.Activity
```

The class `DUL:PhysicalPlace` has been extended to introduce the differ-ent types of structural part that can compose an environment together with the related properties. The individuals of these classes are associated with a `DUL:SpaceRegion` which localizes them in space. Each `Place` can be associated to a set of sensors deployed on through some `SSN:Platform`, and to a set of `DUL:Property` characterizing its state.

Given, the physical elements that can compose an environment, their proper-ties and the available sensors, their deployment and the related sensing capabili-ties, the observation context characterizes the knowledge about the features that can actually produce information and the resulting events and the activities that can be observed. This context introduces the concepts of `ObservableFeature` and `ObservableProperty` by leveraging concepts like `SSN:FeatureOfInterest` and `DUL:Role`. It revises the concept of `SSN:FeatureOfInterest` by interpret-ing it as a `DUL:Role` an object can play according to sensor deployment. The individuals of the class `ObservableFeature` model physical elements of the envi-ronment that *play the role* of "being observable" through a set of associated sensing devices. According to this interpretation, an object is *interesting* with respect to an agent, if and only if there is at least one sensing device that allow an agent to gather information about the properties of the object. In such a case the object is said to be *observable* and can be formally defined as follows:

```
ObservableFeature ⊑ DUL:Role ⊓
          SSN:FeatureOfInterest ⊓
          ∃ isObservableThrough.SSN:Sensor ⊓
          ∃ isRoleOf.DUL:Object ⊓
          ∃ hasObservableProperty.SSN:Property
```

The key point of the proposed semantics is that, a reasoner can dynamically infer the actual set of observable features composing an environment by analyzing the available sensors and their deployment. The information that observable features produce, is modeled by leveraging the SSN ontology which complies with the Stimulus Sensor Observation ontology design pattern (SSO) [12]. Figure 3 shows the structure of the information concerning sensor observations in the SSN ontology.

The KOaLa ontology extends `SSN:Observation` and `SSN:SensorOutput` to model the specific type of information produced by sensors according to their capabilities. The observation context also introduces the classes `DUL:Event` and `DUL:Action` needed to represent the outcome of data processing. The class `ObservedEvent` has been introduced as extension of the class `DUL:Event` to model any type of event or state concerning a physical object of the environment. The class `Activity` has been introduced as extension of the class `DUL:Action` to model any `DUL:Event` that can be performed by an agent and concerns a physi-cal object of the environment. Both these classes have been further specialized to

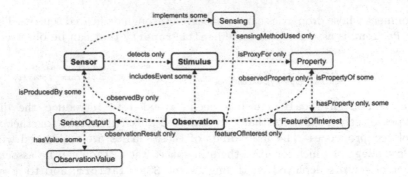

Fig. 3. SSN structure of observations according to the SSO ontology design pattern

model the specific types of event like e.g., `HighTemperature`, `HighLuminosity`, and activity like e.g., `Sleeping`, `Cooking`, that are relevant for a particular application scenario.

```
Activity ⊑ DUL:Event ⊓                          ObservedEvent ⊑ DUL:Event ⊓
         ∃ concerns.DUL:Object ⊓                               ∃ concerns.DUL:Object ⊓
         ∃ DUL:hasParticipant.DUL:PhysicalAgent ⊓
```

These three contexts characterize the knowledge of an agent in three different levels of abstraction, organized in a hierarchical way. The resulting structure defines increasingly complex concepts that allow a *stratified knowledge reasoning process* to incrementally abstract sensor data and build the Knowledge Base (KB) of the agent.

2.2   Stratified Knowledge Reasoning Through Contexts

Observations are elaborated by a knowledge processing mechanism capable of interpreting sensor data according to the semantics proposed by KOaLa. This mechanism consists of a *stratified* set of *inference rules* that increasingly abstract and add semantics to sensor data. Each subset of inference rules i.e., a stratum/layer of the knowledge processing mechanism, processes observations by taking into account a particular ontological context. This process can be seen as a *semantic pipeline* which iteratively refines the KB of the agent every time an observation is received.

Figure 4 shows the main steps of the envisaged knowledge processing mechanism and the ontological contexts each step refers to. The *Configuration Detection and Data Interpretation* step of the pipeline generates an initial KB by analyzing the "static" information concerning the configuration of the environment. It analyzes the structure of the environment, the types of sensor available, their capabilities and deployment. The *Feature Extraction* step further analyzes the configuration of the environment in order to determine the *observable features* and the associated *observable properties*. It identifies the set of elements that can actually produce information about the environment and the resulting types of information they can produce (i.e., the properties that can be observed).

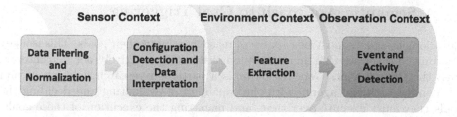

Fig. 4. The KOaLa knowledge processing pipeline

These two steps of the pipeline realize a sort of *self-diagnosis procedure* which allows an agent to determine the available "sensing capabilities".

An `ObservableFeature` characterizes a `DUL:Object` of the environment capable of playing the `DUL:Role` of "being observable". According to the KOaLa semantics, an object can be observed if and only if there are some sensors deployed on it. This interpretation of an observable feature can be formally described by the rule below:

$$
\begin{aligned}
\texttt{DUL:Object(o)} \wedge \texttt{SSN:Platform(p)} \wedge \\
\texttt{SSN:Deployment(d)} \wedge \texttt{DUL:hasPart(o, p)} \wedge \\
\texttt{SSN:hasDeployment(s, d)} \wedge \texttt{SSN:deployedOn(d, p)} \rightarrow \texttt{ObservableFeature(x)} \wedge \\
\texttt{hasObservableFeature(o, x)} \wedge \\
\texttt{isObservableThrough(x, s)}
\end{aligned}
$$

If a sensor s is deployed on a platform p which is part of an object o then the object o is an observable feature of the environment. Similarly, a property of an observable feature can be actually observed if and only if one of the associated sensor is capable of observing that particular property. Thus, properties can play the `DUL:Role` of "being observable" also (i.e., `ObservableProperty`) and, therefore given a set of observable features, the formula below is needed to infer the set of properties a robot is actually capable of observing:

$$
\begin{aligned}
\texttt{ObservableFeature(f)} \wedge \texttt{DUL:Object(o)} \wedge \\
\texttt{DUL:Property(p)} \wedge \texttt{SSN:Sensor(s)} \wedge \\
\texttt{hasObservableFeature(o, f)} \wedge \texttt{DUL:hasProperty(o, p)} \wedge \\
\texttt{isObservableThrough(f, s)} \wedge \texttt{SSN:observes(s, p)} \rightarrow \texttt{ObservableProperty(x)} \wedge \\
\texttt{hasObservableProperty(f, x)} \wedge \\
\texttt{SSN:observes(x, p)}
\end{aligned}
$$

The sets of detected observable features and properties determine the particular types of `Event` and `Activity` a robot is actually capable of recognizing from the observations. The *Event and Activity Detection* step refines the KB by processing observations received by sensors. It encapsulates a set of rules that contextualize observations by taking into account known parameters and features about the environment. For example a rule can analyze the temperature of a room of the environment and detected whether the temperature is *high* or *low* as follows:

$$
\begin{aligned}
\texttt{SSN:Observation(o)} \wedge \texttt{SSN:FeatureOfInterest(f)} \wedge \\
\texttt{SSN:featureOfInterest(o, f)} \wedge \texttt{Room(r)} \wedge \\
\texttt{hasObservableFeature(r, f)} \wedge \texttt{SSN:SensorOutput(d)} \wedge \\
\texttt{SSN:hasOutput(o, d)} \wedge \texttt{SSN:ObservedValue(v)} \wedge \\
\texttt{SSN:hasValue(d, v)} \wedge v < tempLowerBound \rightarrow \texttt{LowTemperature(x)} \wedge \\
\texttt{concerns(x, r)} \wedge \texttt{SSN:isProducedBy(x, o)}
\end{aligned}
$$

3   A Semantic Approach to Goal Triggering

Autonomous agents must be capable of reasoning about their goals. This is a key capability for robots that must autonomously and proactively act and interact with the environment. *Goal reasoning* is a particular research field whose aim is to endow artificial agents with the capability of evaluating and deciding the goals they must execute over time, and managing the execution of these goals. The work [16] formally defines the goal reasoning problem by characterizing the different phases that compose the lifecycle of a goal and their management. The proposed KOaLa cognitive architecture partially addresses the goal reasoning problem by focusing on *goal triggering* or *goal recognition* which enables *proactivity* by linking the semantic module to the acting module of Fig. 1. Specifically, KOaLa proposes a semantic approach to goal triggering by extending the rule-based inference mechanism described in the previous section. An ontological approach defines the semantics of the basic concepts needed to analyze "expected" *situations* and the associated tasks a robot must deal with. Then, a background running process continuously analyzes the KB and leverages the ontological model to dynamically recognize and trigger goals.

3.1   Situations, Supporting Tasks and Goals

The KB provides a complete characterization of the environment, but it is not sufficient to allow an agent to dynamically generate planning goals. Additional semantics is needed to represent *situations* and *tasks* that can be performed within the environment. Situations represent combinations of detected events and/or activities that are relevant in the considered application context. Tasks represent high-level operations an agent can perform when one or more situations are recognized (i.e., preconditions). Tasks usually entail the execution of some actions that may affect the status of the environment and therefore they may have some effects (i.e., postconditions) that must be taken into account. Thus, KOaLa introduces the concepts of `ObservedSituation` and `Task` in order to allow an agent to further analyze detected events and activities, and autonomously determine the tasks that can be performed. Specifically, the ontology defines types of task an agent can perform and link these tasks to the situations that may determine their execution.

According to DUL, a `DUL:Situation` can be seen as a "relational context" created by an observer on the basis of a description. The relationships between situations and events can be expressed by the property `DUL:includesEvent`. An `ObservedSituation` can be seen as a particular `DUL:Situation` associated to some events of type `Activity` and/or some events of type `ObservedEvent`.

$$
\begin{aligned}
\texttt{ObservedSituation} \sqsubseteq\ &\texttt{DUL:Situation}\ \sqcap \\
&\exists\ \texttt{DUL:includesEvent.Activity}\ \sqcap \\
&\exists\ \texttt{DUL:includesEvent.ObservedEvent}
\end{aligned}
$$

Situations may enable the execution of a number of high-level tasks that allow an agent to interact with and change the status of the environment. Thus, a `Task` can be seen as a DUL:Process "transforming" the environment from a starting ObservedSituation (i.e., the preconditions) to an ending ObservedSituation (i.e., postconditions) and can be formally defined as follows:

```
Task ⊑ DUL:Process ⊓
        ∃ hasPrecondition.ObservedSituation ⊓
        ∃ hasPostcondition.ObservedSituation
```

ObservedSituation and Task characterize the capabilities of an agent with respect to the set of events and activities that can be actually detected. These concepts formally model the causality of a particular application scenario and therefore, this knowledge can be used to dynamically configure the planning and execution model of the acting module. Such a dynamic configuration mechanism enforces an higher level of flexibility and adaptability of the overall cognitive architecture. This is particularly needed in highly dynamic environments to automatically handle system reconfigurations without interruptions. The work [4] represents a example of such a dynamic configuration process successfully applied in a real manufacturing scenario.

3.2 Goal Recognition and Triggering

The goal recognition and triggering process leverages the ontology to identify relevant situations occurring inside the environment, determine the needed supportive tasks and trigger goal signals accordingly. This process represents a "semantic bridge" between the representation side and the acting side of the cognitive architecture shown in Fig. 1. The goal recognition process endows a robot with the capability of reasoning on its internal knowledge about the environment and dynamically making decisions. Algorithm 1 shows the procedure of the process which allows a robot to bridge the gap between knowledge representation ($\mathcal{K}$) and planning and execution ($\mathcal{A}$).

Algorithm 1. Description of the goal recognition and triggering process

```
1:  function GOALRECOGNITIONANDTRIGGERING(K, A)
2:      // initialize observation, situation and goal sets
3:      O, S, G ← ∅
4:      // the process continuously waits for observations
5:      while waitObservations (K) do
6:          O ← retrieveObservations (K)
7:          for o ∈ O do
8:              // detect observed events and/or activities
9:              S ← detectSituations (o, K)
10:             for s ∈ S do
11:                 // detect supporting tasks for each situation
12:                 T ← detectSupportingTasks (s, K)
13:                 // prepare goal descriptions
14:                 for t ∈ T do
15:                     // analyze task effects
16:                     e ← checkPostconditions (t, K)
17:                     // make a planning goal description
18:                     G ← prepareGoalSignal (t, s, e)
19:                 // trigger goal signals
20:                 trigger (G, A)
```

The goal recognition and triggering process is always listening for incoming observations (row 5). Every time a new observation is notified from the knowledge $\mathcal{K}$, the process executes the procedure to detect and trigger goal signals to the acting module $\mathcal{A}$ (rows 6–23). Specifically, when an observation is notified, the process retrieves the set of received observations $\mathcal{O}$ from the knowledge (row 6). Then, it analyzes the events and activities associated to the received observations and leverages the ontological model to recognize relevant situations $\mathcal{S}$ (row 9). These situations may represent preconditions for a set of supporting tasks an agent can perform. The set of detected situations $\mathcal{S}$ and the ontological model $\mathcal{K}$ are further analyzed to detect the supported tasks that can be performed (row 12). For each supporting task found, the process must prepare a goal description (rows 14–19) in order to properly trigger goal signals (row 21) to the acting module $\mathcal{A}$. A goal description is characterized by the task t an agent is supposed to perform, an *initial situation* s representing preconditions for task execution and a *final situation* e representing effects of task execution (row 18). Similarly to task detection, the situations and therefore the events and/or activities composing the effects of a task t are found by leveraging the ontological model of the goal recognition process (row 16). Once a set of goal signals $\mathcal{G}$ have been triggered, the acting module $\mathcal{A}$ of the KOaLa architecture leverages PLATINUm to synthesize and execute timeline-based plans and therefore the set of actions needed to carry out desired supporting tasks.

4   KOaLa Meets Giraff

The envisaged cognitive architecture and the related knowledge processing mechanisms can endow an assistive robot with the capabilities needed to better support the daily-home living of seniors through proactive and autonomous interactions. The GiraffPlus application context [9] which consists of a telepresence robot (Robin) living with a senior person inside a sensorized home environment, is well suited to show the capabilities of KOaLa. The typical application scenario of the GiraffPlus project is a single floor apartment composed by a living room, a kitchen, a bathroom, a bedroom and a central corridor connecting all the rooms with the entrance. There are many sensors installed to track activities and events inside the house. Windows and the entrance door have been endowed with a `Gap` sensor to check whether they are open or close. There is one multisensor device like e.g. `Pir`, for each room to track temperature and luminosity and detect motions. There are additional sensors like e.g. `Switch`, to track the usage and energy consumption of electronic devices like a TV, an oven or a microwave. Finally, there could be additional sensors to track physiological parameters of a senior person like e.g., blood pressure or heart rate. All these sensing devices provide a rich and heterogeneous set of data that Robin can analize through KOaLa to recognize situations that require the execution of some tasks and proactively support the home-living. Let us consider an ordinary life scenario showing the role that Robin with the help of KOaLa can play to support senior users. In particular, this scenario aim at concretely describing the inference steps of the "stratified reasoning" mechanism of KOaLa and the increasingly complex information inferred starting from raw sensor data.

Robin can support a senior user during the preparation of his/her meal by reminding dietary restrictions and the pills for the therapy. To do so, Robin must be capable of recognizing that a senior user is cooking and plan supporting tasks accordingly. Considering the available sensors and their deployment, there are several events that Robin can recognize for this purpose. Leveraging the sensor and environment contexts, Robin knows that the sensor pir15 and pir18 have been deployed on the Kitchen of the house and that they are producing observations about the properties Presence, Luminosity and Temperature. The sensor switch8 instead is producing observations about the energy consumption of the TV inside the Kitchen. Robin can further analyze this information by leveraging the observation context. It can infer the events HighLuminosity and Presence concerning the Kitchen according to the data gathered from pir15 (see the rules in Sect. 2.2) and the event WatchingTV as follows:

```
SSN:Observation(o) ∧ SSN:observableFeature(o, f) ∧
  TV(x) ∧ hasObservableFeature(x, f) ∧ SSN:Output(d)
    SSN:hasOutput(o, d) ∧ SSN:hasValue(f, v) ∧
                          Energy(v) → WatchingTV(e) ∧
                          concerns(e, x) ∧ isProducedBy(e, o)
```

These events can be contextualized and further analyzed to recognize activities. In this specific case, Robin can recognize that a senior user is performing an activity a of type Cooking at time t through the following rule:

```
HighLuminosity(e1) ∧ concerns(e1, k) ∧
        Presence(e2) ∧ concerns(e2, k) ∧
HighTemperature(e3) ∧ concerns(e3, k) ∧
isProducedBy(e3, o) ∧ observedBy(o, pir18) ∧
    Kitchen(k) ∧ WatchingTV(e4) → Cooking(a, t) ∧ time(t)
```

The goal recognition process can leverage the inferred knowledge and the ontology to identify relevant Situation and the associated supporting Task to perform. The activity Cooking and the time at which the user is performing it, allow Robin to recognize a PreparingLunch situation to which the task SupportLunch can be associated through the following rule:

```
Cooking(a, t1) ∧ isLunchTime(t) → SupportLunch(t) ∧
                        PreparingLunch(s1, t1) ∧ LunchComplete(s2, t2) ∧
                        hasPrecondition(t, s1) ∧ hasPostcondition(t, s2)
```

According to the detected situation and the associated task, the goal recognition process can trigger a new planning goal $\mathcal{G}$ for the task SupportLunch. Then, Robin synthesizes and executes the set of actions needed to achieve the generated goal by leveraging the acting module of KOaLa. A timeline-based planning model specifies the task decomposition rules needed to synthesize the set of actions needed to reach the kitchen when the user is cooking, remind his/her dietary restrictions, and remind the pills for the therapy right after lunch.

What planning has to do with this? Before closing it is worth presenting a comment of the use of planning that can result somehow as superimposed in this specific paper. Partially the current examples reinforce this idea and different ways exist to obtain similar behavior given their relative simplicity. Indeed our research line is strongly grounded on the use of temporal planning because very important is to achieve a continuity of effects and particularly a continuous adaptation of a pre-existing plan according to sensed information. This can be done by combining a planner like PLATINUm and its integration with both goal triggering described here and *plan domain update* techniques described for example in [4]. Hence given the goal triggering mechanism (this paper) the feasibility of the whole cognitive loop is somehow guaranteed by combining existing homogeneous research results.

5   Conclusions

This paper aims is the natural continuation of an initial work [5] that first introduced KOaLa, a cognitive architecture focused on the integration of knowledge reasoning with planning and acting within a unified control process. This paper blows up a part of the general KOaLA architecture focusing on the ontological approach and the goal recognition and triggering mechanisms to dynamically generate planning goals. A simple but realistic domestic scenario was taken into account to concretely describe the enhanced cognitive approach in action and show how goals can be actually triggered to achieve proactivity. Further work is ongoing to enable extensive integrated laboratory tests to better assess performance and capabilities of the overall system.

References

1. Alirezaie, M., Loutfi, A.: Reasoning for improved sensor data interpretation in a smart home. CoRR abs/1412.7961 (2014). http://arxiv.org/abs/1412.7961
2. Awaad, I., Kraetzschmar, G.K., Hertzberg, J.: The role of functional affordances in socializing robots. Int. J. Soc. Robot. **7**(4), 421–438 (2015)
3. Bechhofer, S., Özsu, M., Liu, L.: OWL: Web Ontology Language. Encyclopedia of Database Systems, Germany (2009)
4. Borgo, S., Cesta, A., Orlandini, A., Umbrico, A.: A planning-based architecture for a reconfigurable manufacturing system. In: The 26th International Conference on Automated Planning and Scheduling (ICAPS) (2016)
5. Cesta, A., Cortellessa, G., Orlandini, A., Umbrico, A.: A cognitive loop for assistive robots - connecting on sensed data to acting. In: IEEE RO-MAN The 27TH IEEE International Symposium on Robot and Human Interactive Communication (2018)
6. Cesta, A., Cortellessa, G., Fracasso, F., Orlandini, A., Turno, M.: User needs and preferences on AAL systems that support older adults and their carers. J. Ambient Intell. Smart Environ. **10**(1), 49–70 (2018)
7. Cialdea Mayer, M., Orlandini, A., Umbrico, A.: Planning and execution with flexible timelines: a formal account. Acta Inf. **53**(6–8), 649–680 (2016)
8. Compton, M., et al.: The SSN ontology of the W3C semantic sensor network incubator group. Web Seman:. Sci. Serv. Agents World Wide Web 17((Supplement C),) 25–32 (2012)

9. Coradeschi, S., et al.: GiraffPlus: combining social interaction and long term monitoring for promoting independent living. In: The 6th International Conference on Human System Interactions (HSI), pp. 578–585 (2013)
10. Cortellessa, G., et al.: ROBIN, a telepresence robot to support older users monitoring and social inclusion: development and evaluation. Telemedicine E-Health **24**(2), 145–154 (2018)
11. Ghallab, M., Nau, D., Traverso, P.: The actors view of automated planning and acting: a position paper. Artif. Intell. **208**, 1–17 (2014). https://doi.org/10.1016/j.artint.2013.11.002. http://www.sciencedirect.com/science/article/pii/S0004370213001173
12. Janowicz, K., Compton, M.: The stimulus-sensor-observation ontology design pattern and its integration into the semantic sensor network ontology. In: Proceedings of the 3rd International Conference on Semantic Sensor Networks, SSN 2010, vol. 668, pp. 64–78. CEUR-WS.org, Aachen (2010)
13. Köeckemann, U., Pecora, F., Karlsson, L.: Inferring context and goals for online human-aware planning. In: 2015 IEEE 27th International Conference on Tools with Artificial Intelligence (ICTAI), pp. 550–557 (2015)
14. Lemaignan, S., Ros, R., Mosenlechner, L., Alami, R., Beetz, M.: ORO, a knowledge management platform for cognitive architectures in robotics. In: 2010 IEEE/RSJ International Conference on Intelligent Robots and Systems (IROS), pp. 3548–3553 October 2010. https://doi.org/10.1109/IROS.2010.5649547
15. Pellegrinelli, S., Orlandini, A., Pedrocchi, N., Umbrico, A., Tolio, T.: Motion planning and scheduling for human and industrial-robot collaboration. CIRP Ann. Manufact. Technol. **66**, 1–4 (2017)
16. Roberts, M., Shivashankar, V., Alford, R., Leece, M., Gupta, S., Aha, D.W.: Goal reasoning, planning, and acting with actorsim, the actor simulator. In: Conference on Advances in Cognitive Systems (2016)
17. Tenorth, M., Beetz, M.: Representations for robot knowledge in the KnowRob framework. Artif. Intell. **247**, 151–169 (2017). https://doi.org/10.1016/j.artint.2015.05.010. special Issue on AI and Robotics
18. Umbrico, A., Cesta, A., Cialdea Mayer, M., Orlandini, A.: Integrating resource management and timeline-based planning. In: The 28th International Conference on Automated Planning and Scheduling (ICAPS) (2018)
19. Umbrico, A., Cesta, A., Cialdea Mayer, M., Orlandini, A.: Platinum: a new framework for planning and acting. In: Esposito, F., Basili, R., Ferilli, S., Lisi, F.A. (eds.) AI*IA 2017 Advances in Artificial Intelligence, pp. 498–512. Springer International Publishing, Cham (2017). https://doi.org/10.1007/978-3-319-70169-1_37

Energy-Aware Multiple State Machine Scheduling for Multiobjective Optimization

Angelo Oddi[1](✉), Riccardo Rasconi[1], and Miguel A. González[2]

[1] Institute of Cognitive Sciences and Technologies, ISTC-CNR, Rome, Italy
{angelo.oddi,riccardo.rasconi}@istc.cnr.it
[2] Department of Computing, University of Oviedo, Oviedo, Spain
mig@uniovi.es

Abstract. Optimising the energy consumption is one of the most important issues in scheduling nowadays. In this work we consider a multi-objective optimisation for the well-known job-shop scheduling problem. In particular, we minimise the makespan and the energy consumption at the same time. We consider a realistic energy model where each machine can be in *Off*, *Stand-by*, *Idle* or *Working* state. We design an effective constraint-programming approach to optimise both the energy consumption and the makespan of the solutions. Experimental results illustrate the potential of the proposed method, outperforming the results of the current state of the art in this problem.

Keywords: Constraint-programming · Job-shop scheduling
Energy considerations · Multi-objective optimisation

1 Introduction

The job shop is a scheduling problem widely studied in the literature due to the fact that it is a model which is close to many real production environments. It is proven that the job shop is NP-hard, and so its resolution is very complex. In the literature we can find many different solving approaches for the job shop, from exact methods to all kinds of meta-heuristic algorithms.

Although the makespan is the most studied objective function, energy considerations are increasingly important nowadays, mainly for economical and environmental reasons. In fact, we can find a number of papers addressing the energy-efficient job shop. For example, Zhang and Chiong [12] try to minimise both the weighted tardiness and the energy consumption in a job shop where the processing mode of operations can be modified. Another approach is that of Liu et al. [7], where it is considered a simple energy model where the machines can only be in

This research has been supported by the Spanish Government under research project TIN2016-79190-R. ISTC-CNR authors were supported by the ESA Contract No. 4000112300/14/D/MRP "Mars Express Data Planning Tool MEXAR2 Maintenance".

© Springer Nature Switzerland AG 2018
C. Ghidini et al. (Eds.): AI*IA 2018, LNAI 11298, pp. 474–486, 2018.
https://doi.org/10.1007/978-3-030-03840-3_35

Working or in *Idle* state. González et al. [4] improve the results reported in [7] by using a hybrid evolutionary meta-heuristic and also a constraint-programming approach. One problem with the last two papers is that the considered energy model is not too realistic. The model proposed by May et al. [8] is much more interesting, as the machines can be either in the *Idle*, *Working*, *Off*, or switched to a *Stand-by* state.

In this paper we consider this last energy model and try to minimize at the same time the makespan and the energy consumption in a job shop. Although some multi-objective works consider weighted or lexicographical approaches, probably the most interesting approaches are those based on the Pareto Front.

In particular, we have designed a constraint-based procedure to minimise both the makespan and the energy consumption, within a well-studied multi-objective optimisation method to generate the whole Pareto (i.e., the ϵ-constraint method [9]). The contribution of the paper is the following. We propose a constraint-based model where: (i) we add as decision variables the states of the machines during the no-working periods (i.e., *Idle*, *Off*, or *Stand-by* states); (ii) we introduce energy aware constraints that exploit the total order of activities on each machine, as well as the lower bound on each machine's total execution time, ultimately implementing a new propagation rule. We show that this new model exhibits interesting performances, outperforming both the results obtained in [8], and the more recent results obtained in [10].

This paper is organised as follows: Sect. 2 formulates the problem at hand and Sect. 3 describes the solving methods. Then, in Sect. 4 we analyse our proposals and we compare them with the state-of-the-art algorithms [8,10], and finally in Sect. 5 we report some conclusions and ideas for future work.

2   Problem Formulation

The job shop scheduling problem (JSP) consists on scheduling a set of N jobs, $J = \{J_1, \ldots, J_N\}$ in a set of M machines or resources, $R = \{R_1, \ldots, R_M\}$. Each of the jobs J_i consists of n_i tasks $(\theta_{i1}, \ldots, \theta_{in_i})$ that must be scheduled exactly in that particular order. Each task requires a given resource during all its processing time. Additionally, no preemption is allowed, so when a resource starts processing a task, it cannot be interrupted until it ends. Moreover, resources can at most process one task at a time. The objective of the problem is to minimise some objective functions subject to the described precedence and capacity constraints. Although we have denoted the tasks as θ_{ij} in this problem definition, in the following we will denote them by a single letter, if possible, in order to simplify the expressions. We denote by Ω the set of tasks, by p_u the processing time of task u, by r_u the resource required by task u, and by s_u the starting time of task u (which needs to be determined).

As we have seen, the JSP has precedence constraints, defined by the routing of the tasks within the jobs, that translate into linear inequalities: $s_u + p_u \leq s_v$, where v is the next task to u in the job sequence. The problem has also capacity constraints, as the resources can only process one task at a time, and they translate into disjunctive constraints: $(s_u + p_u \leq s_v) \vee (s_v + p_v \leq s_u)$, where u and v are tasks requiring the same resource. The objective is to build a feasible schedule, i.e. determine a starting time for each task such that all constraints are fulfilled. In the following, given a feasible schedule, we will denote with PJ_v and SJ_v the predecessor and successor of v, respectively, in the job sequence, and with PM_v and SM_v the predecessor and successor of v, respectively, in its resource sequence. In addition, we will denote with α_k and ω_k the first and last operations respectively on machine R_k in the considered schedule.

The goal of the present analysis is the minimisation of both the energy consumption and the overall completion time, or *makespan*. In general, for a minimization problem with two objective functions f_i ($i = 1, 2$), a solution S is said to be *dominated* by another solution S', denoted $S' \prec S$, if and only if for each objective function f_i, $f_i(S') \leq f_i(S)$ and there exists at least one i such that $f_i(S') < f_i(S)$. However, the possibly conflicting nature of these two objectives may prevent the existence of a unique solution S^* that is optimal w.r.t. both the objectives. Therefore, in this work we are interested in the set of all optimal "tradeoffs", which are known as the *Pareto optimal* solutions, i.e. solutions such that the improvement of one objective necessarily implies the worsening of the other objective. The Pareto front PS^* is the set of solutions S, such that for each $S \in PS^*$ there is no solution S' which dominates S ($S' \prec S$).

The makespan is the first objective function and corresponds to the maximum completion time of the schedule, that is $\max_{u \in \Omega}\{s_u + p_u\}$. About the second objective the energy model is taken from [8], where it is supposed that a resource can be in five different states: *Off*, *Stand-by*, *Idle*, *Setup* or *Working*. However, May et al. in their experiments from [8] consider together the times and energy consumption of the *Working* and *Setup* states; as a consequence, we can consider a total of four possible states (see Fig. 1). The power consumption in each state for a given resource R_k is denoted by P_k^{idle}, $P_k^{stand-by}$ and $P_k^{working}$, whereas if the machine is *Off* it consumes no power. Additionally, we assume that the machine can instantly switch from *Idle* to *Stand-by*, *Off* or *Working*, consuming no power. On the other hand, switching from *Off* to *Idle* requires an amount of $T_k^{ramp-up-off}$ time units, whereas switching from *Stand-by* to *Idle* requires $T_k^{ramp-up-stand-by}$ time units. In both cases, the power consumed when ramping up is denoted by $P_k^{ramp-up}$. In Fig. 1 we show the considered state diagram, which is the same for each machine. Also, we assume that all machines do not consume any energy before the processing of its first task assigned. It is easy to see that in the job shop scheduling problem, each resource must always process the same set of tasks, and so the working energy consumption is the same in every possible schedule. Therefore, following [8], in order to reduce the energy consumption we consider the WEC (Worthless Energy Consumption) measure as the second objective function to minimize, which is defined as follows:

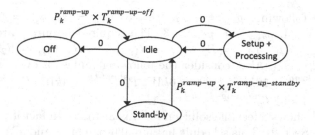

Fig. 1. State diagram for a machine, indicating the energy consumed in each transition

$$WEC = \sum_{k=1,...,M} (P_k^{idle}\, t_k^{idle} + P_k^{stand\text{-}by}\, t_k^{stand\text{-}by}) +$$
$$\sum_{k=1,...,M} P_k^{ramp\text{-}up} (n_k^{standby}\, T_k^{ramp\text{-}up\text{-}standby} + n_k^{off}\, T_k^{ramp\text{-}up\text{-}off}) \quad (1)$$

where t_k^{idle} is the total amount of time spent by R_k in *Idle* state, $t_k^{stand\text{-}by}$ is the total amount of time spent by R_k in *Stand-by* state, $n_k^{standby}$ is the number of times that resource R_k transitions from *Stand-by* to *Idle* state, and finally n_k^{off} is the number of transitions from *Off* to *Idle*.

To the aim of assessing how the power consumption of the machines may vary depending on the different states to which they are allowed to transition, we follow the analysis performed in [8], taking into account two different machine behavior *policies*, which we will respectively call *P3* and *P4* as described in the following. The *P3* policy is implemented by switching the machines on at their first operation and switching them off at their last, with the possibility to switch them on and off from the *Idle* state, between any pair of consecutive tasks belonging to the production batch (see Fig. 1). The *P4* policy is similar to the previous one, with the addition of the *Stand-by* state. According to the *P4* policy, each machine can transition from the *Idle* state to the *Stand-by* state during the production batch, whenever such transition is energetically convenient over both switching the machine on and off again, and leaving it in the *Idle* state. In [8] two more policies called *P1* and *P2* are investigated, but such policies are not taken into account in this work because they are very simple and hence not of great interest for our purposes.

According to Baker [2], the makespan is a regular performance measure, which means that it can be increased only by increasing at least one of the completion times in a given schedule. To optimize regular measures it is enough to consider "left-shift schedules", i.e. schedules that are built from a given ordering of the tasks, in such a way that each operation starts in the earliest possible time after all the preceding tasks in the ordering. As opposed to the makespan, the WEC is a non-regular measure, and it can sometimes be decreased by increasing the completion time of some tasks while leaving the other tasks unmodified.

To better illustrate the problem we present a small toy example. Consider an instance with 3 jobs (with 3 tasks for each job) and 3 resources. The processing times are the following: $p_{\theta_{11}} = 4$, $p_{\theta_{12}} = 5$, $p_{\theta_{13}} = 2$, $p_{\theta_{21}} = 2$, $p_{\theta_{22}} = 5$, $p_{\theta_{23}} = 3$, $p_{\theta_{31}} = 4$, $p_{\theta_{32}} = 7$, $p_{\theta_{33}} = 3$. The required resources are as follows: $r_{\theta_{11}} = R_1$, $r_{\theta_{12}} = R_2$, $r_{\theta_{13}} = R_3$, $r_{\theta_{21}} = R_1$, $r_{\theta_{22}} = R_3$, $r_{\theta_{23}} = R_2$, $r_{\theta_{31}} = R_2$, $r_{\theta_{32}} = R_1$, $r_{\theta_{33}} = R_3$. Also, consider the following values for every machine $k \in \{1, 2, 3\}$: $P_k^{working} = 10kW$, $P_k^{idle} = 6kW$, $P_k^{stand-by} = 4kW$, $P_k^{ramp-up} = 8kW$, $T_k^{ramp-up-off} = 3$ and $T_k^{ramp-up-stand-by} = 1$.

Figure 2(a) shows a feasible solution for this instance. In fact it is a "left-shift schedule" (see Sect. 2). This schedule has a makespan of 18 and a WEC of 40 (16 from R_2 plus 24 from R_3). In resource R_2 we have decided to switch the machine to *Stand-by* state between the end of θ_{31} and the beginning of θ_{23}, because in this case it adds 16 units to the WEC, whereas if switched *Off* it would add 24 units and if it remained *Idle* it would add 18 units. Using the same reasoning we switch R_3 off between the end of θ_{22} and the beginning of θ_{33}.

This "left-shift schedule" can be improved by delaying some tasks. As an example, Fig. 2(b) shows the same solution after delaying task θ_{31}. Now there is only one time unit between the end of θ_{31} and the beginning of θ_{23}, and so the best option is to leave the machine in *Idle* state. The makespan is still 18 but the WEC is reduced from 40 to 30.

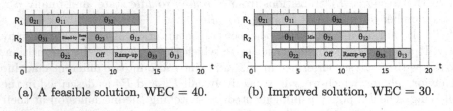

(a) A feasible solution, WEC = 40.   (b) Improved solution, WEC = 30.

Fig. 2. Improving a solution by delaying one task.

3   The Proposed Solving Method

As we have seen in the previous section, the WEC is a non-regular performance measure. Moreover, the work [8] only considers "left-shift schedules", while we have seen that they can be improved by delaying some tasks, in order to reduce the total energy consumption. In this section we describe a procedure that takes into account the non-regularity of the WEC objective such that an approximation of the Pareto front is generated by a Constraint Programming (CP) procedure. It is worth noting that the proposed CP approach is in principle able to find an optimal WEC value if given sufficient computational time (we do not provide any formal proof about this property).

3.1   Energy Optimisation: A Constraint Programming Approach

Constraint Programming (CP) is a declarative programming paradigm [1]. A constraint program is defined as a set of *decision variables*, each ranging on a discrete domain of values, and a set of *constraints* that limit the possible combination of variable-value assignments. After a *model* of the problem is created, the solver interleaves two main steps: *constraint propagation*, where inconsistent values are removed from variable domains, and *search*. CP is particularly suited for solving scheduling problems where the decision variables are associated to the problem operations. In particular, each operation variable a is characterised at least by two features: s_a representing its start time, and p_a representing its duration. For scheduling problems, a number of different *global constraints* have been developed, the most important being the `unary-resource` constraint [11] for modelling simple machines, the `cumulative` resource constraint [6] for modelling cumulative resources (e.g., a pool of workers), and the `reservoir` [5] for modelling consumable resources (e.g., a fuel tank). In particular, given `unary-resource`(A), the constraint holds if and only if all the operations in the set A never overlap at any time point. A number of propagation algorithms are embedded in the `unary-resource` constraint for removing provably inconsistent assignments of operation start-time variables.

We describe a Constraint Programming (CP) model based on the problem defined in Sect. 2, where the main *decision variables* are the start times s_a of the operations $a \in \Omega$ characterized by a processing time p_a. Each start time s_a ranges in the interval $[0, H - p_a]$, where H is the problem's horizon. The set of decision variables is then extended with the start times s_{OnOff_k} of the $OnOff_k$ intervals, where each $OnOff_k$ interval is defined as spanning over all the operations executed on machine k. Hence, the s_{OnOff_k} variable represents the first instant when machine k is turned on. The model, whose utilisation will be described in the experimental section (Sect. 4), is built on top of the IBM-ILOG CPLEX Optimization Studio CP Optimizer and its details are as follows.

Let O_k be the set of problem operations assigned to machine $k = 1, \ldots, M$ and U_k be a set of auxiliary *unit-duration operations*, assigned to a dummy unary machine mirroring k (it is worth noting that the two sets O_k and U_k represent separate processing orders of activities). The introduction of the auxiliary set of operations U_k[1] is necessary to represent the position of each activity $a \in O_k$ in the processing orders imposed among the operations assigned to each machine $k \in R$. More concretely, the auxiliary unit-duration operations indirectly implement the definition of a *successor function* SM_a (returning the successor of each operation a for each total order imposed on the set of operations O_k assigned to a machine k). To the best of our knowledge, this workaround is necessary because we want to use the native OPL construct to implement the global constraints `unary-resource`(O_k) for efficiency reasons, and the successor function is not natively present in the OPL language (see IBM ILOG CPLEX Optimization Studio OPL Language Reference Manual, Version 12 Release 7.1).

Operationally, the set of *unit-duration* operations $u \in U_k$ can be assigned to the dummy machine k (in the same fashion of the operations a) so that, for

---

[1] We were inspired to adopt this solution by a post on a discussion board on the website www.or-exchange.com about the explicit representation of an interval position in a OPL `sequence`. This discussion board does not seem available anymore.

each processing order imposed on a machine k, $a_0 \prec a_1 \prec \ldots \prec a_i \prec \ldots \prec a_M$, an identical order is imposed on the unit-duration operations $u_0 \prec u_1 \prec \ldots \prec u_i \prec \ldots \prec u_M$. In this manner, the position i of the operation a_i coincides with the start-time value of the unit-duration operation u_i. For the reasons above, the starting times s_u of the operations $u \in U_k$ must be added to the model as additional set of *decision variables*. In addition, a specific global constraint is added in the CP model given below to impose the same order among the activities in the sets O_k and U_k, see constraints (3i).

The definition (2a) represents the successor function SM_p, such that the position of the operation $p \in O_k$ coincides with the start-time value $s_{u(p)}$ of its corresponding unit-duration operation $u^{(p)} \in U_k$, and the successor q (if exists) corresponds to the unary activity $u^{(q)} \in U_k$, such that $s_{u(q)} = s_{u(p)} + 1$. Whereas, according to Sect. 2, the energy objective WEC (2c) is the sum of the unload energy consumption E_{pq}^k (i.e., when a machine is *Idle*, switched *Off*, or switched to a *Stand-by* state) of each pair of contiguous operations (p, q) assigned on the same machine k (2b), where $d_{pq} = s_q - e_p$ is the difference between q's start time and p's end time. The makespan objective C_{max} is described at line (2d).

$$SM_p = \begin{cases} q & \exists u^{(q)} \in U_k : s_{u(q)} = s_{u(p)} + 1 \\ nil & \text{otherwise} \end{cases} \tag{2a}$$

$$E_{pq}^k = min\{P_k^{idle} d_{pq}, \\ P_k^{stand-by}(d_{pq} - T_k^{ramp-up-standby}) + P_k^{ramp-up} T_k^{ramp-up-standby}, \\ P_k^{ramp-up} T_k^{ramp-up-off}\} \tag{2b}$$

$$WEC = \sum_{k=1,\ldots,M} \sum_{\substack{p \in O_k, \\ q = SM_p, q \neq nil}} E_{pq}^k \tag{2c}$$

$$C_{max} = \max_{a \in \Omega}\{s_a + p_a\} \tag{2d}$$

Once all the necessary definitions have been provided and all the variables have been introduced, we present the CP model (optimisation criteria and constraints). Line (3a) represents the lexicographic minimisation of the objective pair WEC and C_{max} with the energy WEC as primary objective. According to the implemented ϵ-constraint method [9] for calculating the Pareto set, we optimise the energy WEC, while we impose an upper bound to the other objective C_{max} in the form $C_{max} \leq C_\epsilon$ (see (3b)). The constraints in (3c) represent the linear orderings imposed on the set of operations Ω by the set of jobs J. Constraints (3d) impose to the set O_k of operations requiring machine k to be contained in the *spanning* operations $OnOff_k$, $k = 1, \ldots, M$. More specifically, for each operation $v \in O_k$, the following constraints $s_{OnOff_k} \leq s_v$ and $s_v + p_v \leq s_{OnOff_k} + p_{OnOff_k}$ hold, such that operation $OnOff_k$ starts together with the *first* present operation in O_k according to the order imposed on the k-th machine, and ends together with the *last* present operation.

Constraints (3f), (3g), and (3h) impose that the minimal energy is consumed between the end of the first and the beginning of the second task, for each pair of contiguous activities (p, q) on a resource k. These constraints rely on the assumption that $P_k^{stand-by} \leq P_k^{idle} \leq P_k^{ramp-up}$ and $T_k^{ramp-up-standby} \leq T_k^{ramp-up-off}$, under such assumptions, there are two cutoff values, $T_k^{idle\text{-}standby}$ and $T_k^{standby\text{-}off}$ (depicted in Fig. 3), such that if $s_v - e_u \in [0, T_k^{idle\text{-}standby}]$ the minimal energy state is *Idle*, when $s_v - e_u \in (T_k^{idle\text{-}standby}, T_k^{standby\text{-}off}]$ the minimal energy state is *Stand-by*, otherwise the minimal energy state is *Off*.

$$\text{lex min}\,(WEC, C_{max}) \tag{3a}$$

s.t. :

$$C_{max} \leq C_\epsilon \tag{3b}$$

$$s_v + p_v \leq s_{SJ_v} \quad v \in \Omega \setminus \{\theta_{1n_1}, .., \theta_{Nn_N}\} \tag{3c}$$

$$\textbf{span}(OnOff_k, O_k) \quad k = 1, .., M \tag{3d}$$

$$ed_p \in \{0, 1, 2\}\ p \in \Omega \tag{3e}$$

$$SM_p = q \wedge (ed_p = 0) \Rightarrow s_q - e_p \leq T_k^{idle\text{-}standby} \tag{3f}$$

$$SM_p = q \wedge (ed_p = 1) \Rightarrow s_q - e_p > T_k^{idle\text{-}standby} \wedge s_q - e_p \leq T_k^{standby\text{-}off} \tag{3g}$$

$$SM_p = q \wedge (ed_p = 2) \Rightarrow s_q - e_p > T_k^{standby\text{-}off} \tag{3h}$$

$$\textbf{same-sequence}(O_k, U_k) \quad k = 1, \ldots, M \tag{3i}$$

$$s_u \leq (|O_k| - 1)\ u \in U_k;\ k = 1, \ldots, M \tag{3j}$$

$$\textbf{unary-resource}(O_k)\ k = 1, \ldots, M \tag{3k}$$

$$\textbf{unary-resource}(U_k)\ k = 1, \ldots, M \tag{3l}$$

$$\Delta t_k^{proc} + \Delta t_k^{standby} + \Delta t_k^{off} \leq C_{max}\ k = 1, \ldots, M \tag{3m}$$

We introduce a set of decision variables $ed_p \in \{0, 1, 2\}$, $p \in \Omega$ (constraint (3e)) representing the unload state (i.e., 0 when machine is *Idle*, 1 when it is switched to a *Stand-by* state, and 2 when switched *Off*) imposed on every pair of contiguous activities (p, q) on the same machine. The constraints in (3i) impose the same order between the activities in the two sets O_k and U_k by means of the global constraints $\textbf{same-sequence}(O_k, U_k)$. The constraints in (3j) bound the start-time value of each unit-duration operation u to $|O_k| - 1$ operations assigned to the machine k. (3k) and (3l) represents the non-overlapping constraints imposed by the machines M to the operations in O_k and U_k, through the global constraints $\textbf{unary-resource}(O_k)$ and $\textbf{unary-resource}(U_k)$, respectively.

Finally, (3m) represents the so-called *energy aware constraints* imposed on the subset of (energy) decision variables cd_p associated to each subset of operations O_k, $k = 1, \ldots, M$. The rational behind this constraints is the following: for each machine k, the set of operations U_k requiring that machine must be totally ordered. In addition, according to the values of the decision variables ed_u, with $u \in O_k$, a minimum (non zero) delay equal to $T_k^{ramp\text{-}up\text{-}standby}$ (when $ed_u = 1$) or $T_k^{ramp\text{-}up\text{-}off}$ (when $ed_u = 2$), must be inserted between the operation u and its successor (if it exists). Hence, each machine's total order has a lower-bound of the total execution time (from the start-time of the first operation to the end-time of the last one) which can be calculated as the sum of the three terms $\Delta t_k^{proc} + \Delta t_k^{stand\text{-}by} + \Delta t_k^{off}$, such that: $\Delta t_k^{proc} = \sum_{u \in O_k} p_u$ is the sum of the operation processing times in machine

k; $\Delta t_k^{standby} = \sum_{u \in O_k, ed_u = 1} T_k^{ramp-up-standby}$ is the minimum total delay due to *Stand-by* states; $\Delta t_k^{off} = \sum_{u \in O_k, ed_u = 2} T_k^{ramp-up-off}$ is the minimum total delay due to *Off* states. Such lower-bound cannot be greater than the solution makespan C_{max}, hence decisions on the variables ed_u can be pruned according to the constraints (3m). This new propagation rule is the main innovation with respect to work [10], and we evaluate it in Sect. 4.

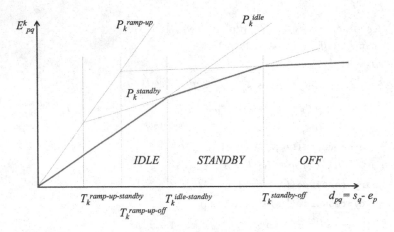

Fig. 3. Minimal energy consumption E_{pq}^k between two consecutive operations (p, q).

3.2   The Bi-criterion ϵ-Constraint Method

A well-known multi-objective optimization method to generate the Pareto front is the ϵ-constraint method [9]. It works by choosing one objective function as the only objective and properly constraining the remaining objective functions during the optimisation process. Through a systematic variation of the constraint bounds, different elements of the Pareto front can be obtained.

Algorithm 1 presents the ϵ-constraint method for the case of a bi-criterion objective function $\mathbf{f} = (f^{(1)}, f^{(2)})$. The algorithm is used in the experimental section of the work and takes the following inputs: (i) the objective $\mathbf{f}$, (ii) the bounds $f_{min}^{(2)}$ and $f_{max}^{(2)}$ on the second component of the objective, and (iii) the decrement value δ. As previously mentioned, the method iteratively leverages a procedure provided in input to solve constrained optimization problems, i.e., the CP() procedure corresponding to the constraint programming model previously described. Note that we consider a slightly different ϵ-constraint method, such that the given CP procedure considers a lexicographic minimisation instead of single-objective minimisation problem, with $f^{(1)}$ as primary and $f^{(2)}$ as secondary key. The algorithm proceeds as follows: after initializing the constraint bound ϵ to the $f_{max}^{(2)}$ value, a new solution S is computed by calling CP() at each step of the *while* solving cycle. If S is not dominated by any of the existing solutions in the current Pareto front approximation P, then S is inserted

---

Algorithm 1. Bi-criterion ϵ-constraint method

Require: The objective $\mathbf{f}$, the bounds $f_{min}^{(2)}$ and $f_{max}^{(2)}$, and the decrement value δ

    $P \leftarrow \emptyset$;

    $\epsilon \leftarrow f_{max}^{(2)}$;

    while $\epsilon \geq f_{min}^{(2)}$ **do**

      $S \leftarrow \mathrm{CP}(\mathbf{f}, \epsilon)$;

      if $(S \neq nil) \wedge (\nexists S' \in P : S' \prec S)$ **then**

        $P \leftarrow (P \cup \{S\}) \setminus \{S' \in P : S \prec S'\}$;

      end if

      $\epsilon \leftarrow \epsilon - \delta$;

    end while

    return P

---

in P, and all the solutions possibly dominated by S are removed from P. The rationale behind this method is to iteratively tighten the constraint bound by a pre-defined constant δ at each step of the solving cycle.

4 Experimental Results

In this section we will analyze the results we have obtained with our CP procedure, and compare such results with the state of the art in [8,10]. In our work, we test our model against three well-known JSP instances called, respectively, FT06, FT10 and FT20 (as considered in [8]). These instances were introduced by Fisher and Thompson [3], and are characterized by different dimensions (*number-of-jobs* × *number-of-machines*): FT06 (6×6), FT10 (10×10), and FT20 (20×5). According to the literature, the optimal makespan of these instances is 55, 930 and 1165, respectively. The energy values for the machines are those described in the toy example of Sect. 2. In our tests, we have compared our results with those present in two recent works [8,10] and related to the machine behavior policies $P3$ and $P4$ introduced in Sect. 2, as these are the most interesting from the energy minimization standpoint. From the analysis performed in Sect. 2, it is certain that the solutions obtained with the $P4$ policy will exhibit energy consumptions lower than or equal to those obtained with the $P3$ policy, due to the additional possibility of switching machines to *Stand-by* state.

Figure 4 graphically presents a comparison of the obtained results in instances FT10 and FT20 (results for FT06 instance can only be found in Tables 1 and 2) using policies P3 and P4. In particular, the plots labelled *"MayEtAl-2015"* and *"OddiEtAl-2017"* describe the Pareto front approximations reported in [8] and [10], respectively, whereas the plots labelled *"CP"* describe the Pareto front approximations obtained with our new constraint programming model using the set of *energy-aware constraints* described in Sect. 3.1.

In these tests, for the CP model we allowed for a maximum 5 minutes for each FT06 solution and a maximum 15 minutes for each FT10 and FT20 solutions. The proposed CP model has been implemented on the IBM-ILOG CPLEX

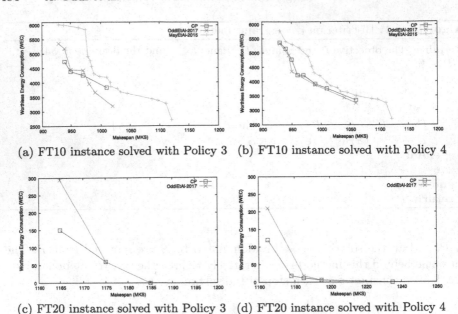

(a) FT10 instance solved with Policy 3   (b) FT10 instance solved with Policy 4

(c) FT20 instance solved with Policy 3   (d) FT20 instance solved with Policy 4

Fig. 4. Pareto set approximations: instances FT10 and FT20 using policies 3 and 4

Table 1. Pareto set approximations data relative to Fig. 4 (Policy P3)

Problem	Pareto set approximation - set of pairs (MKS, WEC)
FT06	MayEtAl-2015: { (60, 146), (59, 152), (57, 176), (56, 180), (55, 192) }
	OddiEtAl-2017: { (55, 126) }
	CP: { (55, 126) }
FT10	MayEtAl-2015: { (1121, 2708), (1111, 3270), (1097, 3378), (1087, 3430), (1045, 3626), (1034, 3678), (1028, 3792), (1017, 3864), (1016, 4008), (1010, 4188), (998, 4208), (988, 4310), (984, 4570), (982, 4758), (978, 4908), (974, 5840), (963, 5912), (939, 6001), (930, 6013) }
	OddiEtAl-2017: { (1020, 3188), (990, 3658), (980, 3950), (970, 4424), (950, 4446), (940, 5178), (930, 5354) }
	CP: { (1010, 3826), (970, 4252), (950, 4378), (940, 4726) }
FT20	OddiEtAl-2017: { (1185, 0), (1175, 60), (1165, 294) }
	CP: { (1185, 0), (1175, 60), (1165, 150) }

Optimization Studio V. 12.7.1.0, a state-of-the-art commercial CP development toolkit, and executed on a Core(TM)2 Duo CPU, 3.33 GHz under Windows 10. Therefore, we used the same running times and the same machine as in [10].

As the Fig. 4 shows, our new CP model demonstrates a further improvement over the existing results, especially for the FT20 instance. Relatively to the FT06 instance, the new *energy-aware constraints* do not produce any improvement, most likely because the solutions obtained in [10] are already optimal. The energy-aware propagation rule is less effective on the FT10 instance, as the "short" activity chains that characterize each machine (note that the

Table 2. Pareto set approximations data relative to Fig. 4 (Policy P4)

Problem	Pareto set approximation - set of pairs (MKS, WEC)
FT06	MayEtAl-2015: { (60, 146), (59, 152), (58, 174), (57, 176), (56, 178), (55, 192) }
	OddiEtAl-2017: { (55, 124) }
	CP: { (55, 124) }
FT10	MayEtAl-2015: { (1121, 2708), (1111, 3268), (1097, 3378), (1087, 3406), (1060, 3512), (1045, 3626), (1034, 3658), (1028, 3792), (1017, 3852), (1010, 3972), (998, 4208), (988, 4310), (984, 4538), (978, 4886), (963, 5182), (951, 5307), (940, 5402), (930, 5786) }
	OddiEtAl-2017: { (1060, 3258), (1040, 3440), (990, 3880), (950, 4356), (945, 4922), (930, 5332) }
	CP: { (1060, 3356), (1010, 3764), (990, 3918), (970, 4226), (960, 4228), (950, 4772), (940, 5150), (930, 5370) }
FT20	OddiEtAl-2017: { (1195, 6), (1185, 18), (1165, 210) }
	CP: { (1235, 0), (1195, 6), (1185, 12), (1178, 18), (1165, 120) }

jobs/machines ratio is 1) do not allow the propagation rule to efficiently evaluate the impact of each state decision on the ed_u variables (see the CP model in Sect. 3.1). On the FT20 instance, the new CP model provides interesting results, further improving on the solutions obtained in [10] for both the P3 and the P4 policies, confirming that the proposed propagation rule is more effective on instances characterized by a higher *jobs/machines* ratio. The exact numerical figures related to the Pareto front approximations shown in Fig. 4 are reported in Tables 1 and 2, respectively for the P3 and P4 policies. Overall, if we compare policies 3 and 4, we can observe that the latter usually obtains solutions with lower energy consumption. This means that, as expected, the additional possibility of switching the machine to *Stand-by* state is indeed beneficial. For example, in the FT06 instance we were able to reduce the WEC from 126 to 124, while maintaining the optimal makespan of 55. Also, in the solution with the optimal makespan (1165) of FT20, the WEC is reduced from 150 to 120.

5 Conclusions

In this paper we have considered a bi-objective optimization in the job shop scheduling problem. We minimise at the same time the makespan and the energy consumption. To this end, we consider an energy model in which each machine can be *Off, Stand-by, Idle* or *Working*. To solve this complex problem we designed a constraint-programming approach based on a model that exploits energy aware constraints. Our proposal is analyzed and compared against the current state-of-the-art algorithms, obtaining better results. For future work we plan to consider even more realistic energy models. For example if we do not consider the setup and working states together, or also if we consider a flexible environment, i.e. a task can be performed by several machines, each one with different energy consumptions and/or processing times. On the other hand, we can also consider less rich models, for example not quantifying costs but dividing them in costly and non-costly. In this case we expect worse results overall, but it can be a viable approach in some settings where quantifying costs can be difficult.

References

1. Apt, K.: Principles of Constraint Programming. Cambridge University Press, New York (2003)
2. Baker, K.: Introduction to Sequencing and Scheduling. Wiley, London (1974)
3. Fisher, H., Thomson, G.L.: Probabilistic learning combinations of local job-shop scheduling rules. In: Muth, J.F., Thomson, G.L. (eds.) Industrial Scheduling, pp. 225–251. Prentice Hall, Englewood Cliffs (1963)
4. González, M.A., Oddi, A., Rasconi, R.: Multi-objective optimization in a job shop with energy costs through hybrid evolutionary techniques. In: Proceedings of the Twenty-Seventh International Conference on Automated Planning and Scheduling (ICAPS-2017), pp. 140–148. AAAI Press, Pittsburgh (2017)
5. Laborie, P.: Algorithms for propagating resource constraints in AI planning and scheduling: existing approaches and new results. Artif. Intell. **143**(2), 151–188 (2003)
6. Le Pape, C., Baptiste, P., Nuijten, W.: Constraint-Based Scheduling: Applying Constraint Programming to Scheduling Problems. Springer, New York (2001). https://doi.org/10.1007/978-1-4615-1479-4
7. Liu, Y., Dong, H., Lohse, N., Petrovic, S., Gindy, N.: An investigation into minimising total energy consumption and total weighted tardiness in job shops. J. Clean. Prod. **65**, 87–96 (2014)
8. May, G., Stahl, B., Taisch, M., Prabhu, V.: Multi-objective genetic algorithm for energy-efficient job shop scheduling. Int. J. Prod. Res. **53**(23), 7071–7089 (2015)
9. Miettinen, K.: Nonlinear Multiobjective Optimization. International Series in Operations Research & Management Science. Springer, New York (2012). https://doi.org/10.1007/978-1-4615-5563-6.   https://books.google.it/books?id=bnzjBwA AQBAJ
10. Oddi, A., Rasconi, R., González, M.: A constraint programming approach for the energy-efficient job shop scheduling problem. In: Gunawan, A., Kendall, G., Soon, L., McCollum, B., Seow, H.V. (eds.) Proceedings of the 8th Multidisciplinary International Conference on Scheduling : Theory and Applications (MISTA 2017), 05–08 December 2017, Kuala Lumpur, Malaysia, pp. 158–172 (2017)
11. Vilím, P., Barták, R., Čepek, O.: Unary resource constraint with optional activities. In: Wallace, M. (ed.) CP 2004. LNCS, vol. 3258, pp. 62–76. Springer, Heidelberg (2004). https://doi.org/10.1007/978-3-540-30201-8_8
12. Zhang, R., Chiong, R.: Solving the energy-efficient job shop scheduling problem: a multi-objective genetic algorithm with enhanced local search for minimizing the total weighted tardiness and total energy consumption. J. Clean. Prod. **112**, 3361–3375 (2016)

Recommendation Systems and Decision Making

Modeling the Changing of the Individual Satisfaction in a Group Context: A Study on Two Sized Groups

Francesco Barile[1]([⊠]), Judith Masthoff[2,3], and Silvia Rossi[4]

[1] Free University of Bozen-Bolzano, Bolzano, Italy
francesco.barile@unibz.it
[2] University of Aberdeen, Aberdeen, UK
[3] Utrecht University, Utrecht, Netherlands
j.f.m.masthoff@uu.nl
[4] University of Naples Federico II, Naples, Italy
silvia.rossi@unina.it

Abstract. General approaches for Group Recommendation Systems start from the individual recommendations and merge them in a way to determine the best choice for the whole group. The results presented in the literature showed that traditional aggregation techniques do not seem to capture all the features of real-world scenarios. Furthermore, recent studies in Behavioral Economics evidence the necessity to define utility models that are not compatible with the self-interested utility-maximizing behavior of the traditional economic paradigm. In this work, starting from Other-Regarding Preference models that characterize the utility of an individual considering his/her own behavioral characteristics and the utility of another individual, we aim at obtaining a general model where such characteristics are described in terms of interpersonal relationships, such as, tie strength and conflict. We started by performing an analysis on opinion shifts based on a two sized groups user study, with the aim to empirically determine the extent of the considered parameters on a possible model. The results show that the opinion shifting on the evaluation of an activity to be performed in a group is related to the two considered factors.

Keywords: Group Recommendation Systems · Social dynamics Other Regarding Preferences

1 Introduction

Recommendation Systems (RSs) are software systems supporting users in a decision-making process. Such systems can be applied in several domains, as touristic applications that provide suggestions to plan a vacation, or systems that help users in choosing movies to watch, music to listen, and so on. In many of these cases, there is the possibility that not a single user, but a group of people,

© Springer Nature Switzerland AG 2018
C. Ghidini et al. (Eds.): AI*IA 2018, LNAI 11298, pp. 489–501, 2018.
https://doi.org/10.1007/978-3-030-03840-3_36

has to choose an activity to perform together. In this case, Group Recommendation Systems (GRSs) give a support to group decision-making by trying to suggest items that can be of interest for all considering the preference of each group member. General approaches for GRSs start from the individual recommendations, provided by an individual RS, and merge them in a way to determine the best choice for the whole group. Such a merging of recommendations approach has been widely analyzed in Mathematics, Economics and Multi-agent systems (MAS) with the definition of different Social Choice functions [21] where there is an agent acting on behalf of each group member, modeled in way that the agent's utilities, computed on the items in the domain of the system, reflect the satisfaction of the user in relation to such items. This approach assumes that the satisfaction of the users w.r.t an item does not change if the users have to use the item within a group. However, as evidenced by psychological studies on *Emotional Contagion* and *Social Influence*, a person or a group influences the emotions and the behavior of the other people through the conscious or unconscious induction of emotion states and behavioral attitudes, hence the satisfaction of an individual is influenced by the satisfaction of the other people in the group [9,16].

The basic idea of this work is that agents' utilities should be related not only on the users individual satisfactions, but also to the specific group in which the users must perform the recommended items. Hence, the individual utilities must be adapted to the group context. To perform such adaptations, Behavioral Economics studies represent an interesting option. Behavioral Economics regard the necessity to define utility models that are not compatible with the self-interested utility maximizing behavior of the traditional economic paradigm [4, 7,22]. Even if this seems to be in contrast with the Rationality Assumption used in the modeling of Rational Agents, there is much evidence of such behaviors in the observation of human beings [22]. In this field, the term Other-Regarding Preferences (ORP), also sometimes referred to as Social Preferences, is used to indicate a model where the evaluation of the utility of an outcome depends not only on the agent evaluation but also considers the evaluation of the other members, and their losses and gains in utility. The rationality element, in the classical sense, is therefore lacking as some agents would, for example, be willing to receive a smaller gain, even to satisfy some feelings of justice or punishment against other members of their own group [11]. In this context, new ways of analyzing agent interactions have been introduced [22] in order to provide a more accurate prediction of outcomes in cases where ORPs play an important role.

Starting from these considerations, in the present work, we introduce ORP models that can be used to perform the adaptation of the individual utilities to the group context. These models characterize the utility of an individual with respect to his/her own behavioral characteristics and the utility of the other individuals. On the contrary, our long-term goal is the definition of a general model to be used for group recommender systems for small groups of people, where such characteristics are described in terms of interpersonal relationships.

In order to determine the group context parameters to consider in the model, a study on two sized groups is presented where we evaluate the impact of the tie strength and the presence of conflicts. Such factors have been showed to be crucial in the individual satisfactions variation for two-sized groups [3]. Hence, we conducted an experiment on the Amazon Mechanical Turk platform using the results to determine the extent of such parameters in a possible model. The results show that the opinion shifting is indeed related to the two factors, but, as we expected, these two alone are not enough to fully model the opinion shifting process.

2   Other-Regarding Preferences

Recently, Behavioral Economics studies have been highlighted for their role in recognizing the need for explicit models considering the possibility that an agent will bear a personal cost in terms of payoff to increase that of another one [6]. There are many aspects that can have an impact on this phenomenon. In particular, there is evidence that the status of the relationship can have an impact and even the possibility of reciprocity, that means that an agent can concede to another if there is the possibility that the favor will be returned in the future. There is, also, the possibility of Negative reciprocity, since an agent can be glad in decreasing another agent's payoff if it is viewed as an enemy [6].

Other-Regarding Preferences (ORP) models try to consider these possibilities, modeling agents that do not maximizes their own utilities in a way to give a greater (or, in some cases, lower) payoff to some other agents. The Inequality Aversion model is the simplest ORP model. A first version of the model, known as Fehr-Schmidt model [10] is in Eq. 1. For simplicity, we refer to the two agent version.

$$U(m, y) = \begin{cases} m - \alpha * (y - m) & \text{if } m < y \\ m - \beta * (m - y) & \text{if } m \geq y \end{cases} \tag{1}$$

where $U(m, y)$ indicates the ORP utility for the agent, when m is the payoff of the agent (m stands for "my payoff") and y is the payoff of the other agent (y stands for "your payoff"). The parameters α and β are denoted as *marginal rate of substitution*, are specific for each individual agent, and must satisfy $0 \leq \beta \leq \alpha$ and $\beta < 1$. In this model, the considered agent is interested in its own income, and the sign of the marginal rate of substitution between its income and that of the other agent depends on which has the higher income.

An alternative model is the Bolton-Ockenfels two-player model [5], that also assumes that an agent likes its own income and dislikes income inequality. Here, the utility function is defined as in Eq. 2:

$$u(m, y) = v(m, m/(m + y)) \tag{2}$$

Again, m is the agent's payoff, and y is the payoff of another agent. The equation presents a non-linear form and assumes that the function v is globally non-decreasing and concave in the first argument, strictly concave in the second argument, that is the *relative income* $(m/(m + y))$.

The Interdependent Preferences model can be viewed as a generalization of inequality aversion models [22]. Supposing to have a set $A = \{a_1, ..., a_n\}$ of agents. Indicating with $\Omega(s) = \{x_1, ..., x_n\}$ the payoff of each agent, the utility is defined as in Eq. 3:

$$U_i(s) = x_i + \sum_{i \neq j} \lambda_{i,j}(x_i - x_j) * x_j \tag{3}$$

Here, the parameter $\lambda_{i,j}$ can define altruistic or, on the contrary, spiteful behaviors, assigning to it a positive or a negative constant value. Other variants can give a non-constant value to the parameter $\lambda_{i,j}$ [22]. In his work [22], Sobel specifies the relation between this model and the Inequality Aversion models seen before. In the Fehr-Schmidt model, $\lambda_{i,j}$ is positive if $x_i > x_j$ and negative if $x_i < x_j$, in way to have an agent that cares about his payoff but, at the same time, would like to reduce the inequality in payoffs between the two players. On the contrary, in the Bolton-Ockenfels model the utility of the agent a_i is a non-linear function of is payoff x_i and its relative income.

In the context of GRS, very few approaches deal with ORP models. Examples are Salehi and Boutilier [20] that explored the consensus decision-making in social networks, by introducing the concept of empathetic utility on social networks: the satisfaction of an individual depends from both his intrinsic utility and his empathetic utility deriving from the happiness of his neighbors in the social network [20]. In [19], the model of Rabin was used to develop a GRS that deals with fairness by introducing a factor representing the altruistic behavior of a user in the evaluation of the utility that depends on the other member's utility weighted with respect to the user agreeableness personality trait. In [1], authors introduce an approach to generate group recommendations which considers social factors extracted from the social network, while in [14] a model integrating the influences of personality, expertise factor, interpersonal relationships, and preference similarities is described.

3   Toward an ORP Model for Group Recommendation

The ORP models considered in the previous section have the common characteristic of defining the utility of an individual, when in the presence of other agents, starting from the utility of the same individual, computed when considered alone, and the utilities of the other members of the group. They mainly differ in the way to combine such utilities and on the parameters specifying the individual behavioral characteristics of the considered agent. Contrary to these approaches, we aim at modeling such changes in utility focusing not on the individual characteristics, but more on the possible state of relationship among the pairs. We suppose that such characteristics can be automatically determined analyzing the interactions between the group's members, as, for example, in a social network [17].

We define:

- $A = \{a_1, a_1, ..., a_n\}$ as the set of the n agents, one for each user of the system;
- $\Omega = \{\omega_1, \omega_2, ...\omega_m\}$ as the set of the m items of the system;
- $U(a_i, \omega_j) = U_{i,j}$ is the utility of the agent a_i for the item ω_j.

Our long term goal is to define a model to predict the adapted utility, that we denote as $U_{i,j}^G$, representing the utility of the agent a_i for the object ω_j with respect to the context related to the group $G \subset A$ of agents. Hence, we consider the starting utility $U_{i,j}$, and the utilities of the other people in the group (the set $\{U_{t,j} | i \neq t \wedge a_t \in G \wedge \omega_j \in \Omega\}$).

While our long-term goal is to derive a general model that can be used for small groups, we start focusing on two-sized group to analyze the dynamics related to the interpersonal relationships that can have an impact on the changing in the individual utility. In a second step, we will generalize the results for groups with more than 2 people.

In Eq. 6, we define the *shift* of the utility of the agent a_i on a object ω_j related to the presence of a second agent a_k. As we can see, the shift is computed as the difference between the initial difference among the utility of the agent a_i and another agent a_k, defined in Eq. 4, and the final difference, computed as in the Eq. 5. Hence, if the difference increases, we have a positive shift. On the contrary, if the difference decreases, we have a negative shift.

$$\Delta_{i,k,j}^{init} = |U_{k,j} - U_{i,j}| \tag{4}$$

$$\Delta_{i,k,j}^{final} = |U_{k,j} - U_{i,j}^G| \tag{5}$$

$$\Gamma_{i,k,j} = \Delta_{i,k,j}^{init} - \Delta_{i,k,j}^{final} \tag{6}$$

Many studies analyze the problem of how to model social influence between people, especially in the social dynamics field, and, in recent years, theories of opinion dynamics assume the possibility of positive and negative interpersonal influence [23]:

- *Positive influence* occurs when the initial opinion of an individual shifts towards the opinion of another person, when the individual is exposed to it;
- When *Negative influence* happens, the individual shifts his opinion increasing the difference with the opinion of another person [23].

In the case of Negative influence, there is the possibility that opinion differences between groups intensify, leading groups to positions that are the two extremes of an opinion spectrum, in the phenomenon known as Bi-polarization [15]. Bi-polarization can be amplified if the model supports homophily, the process with whom people like similar people, and heterophobia, that, on the contrary, is the disliking of dissimilar others [23].

3.1   Tie Strength

The concept of ties strength was introduced in [13] as a combination of the amount of time, the emotional intensity, the intimacy (mutual confiding), and the reciprocal services which characterize the ties. It can be viewed as the importance of a social relationship between two individuals [2], and, despite there being a great amount of research in this field, the evaluation of this concept still results in being a great research problem. Recent studies try to estimate the strength of the tie using information derived from Online Social Networks [17,18]. In [12], an approach to distinguish between strong and weak ties is proposed. A similar classification was proposed in [13], where tie strength is distinguished between *weak*, *intermediate* and *strong*.

It appears reasonable that the variation in individuals' utilities can be influenced by the strength of the tie between them. Our starting hypothesis is that the tie strength directly impacts on the variation in the individuals' utility, determining how the individuals can be influenced by each other in a pair. We start from the assumption that the "perceived tie strength" is not bidirectional, hence the same tie could have a different "strength value" for each person in the pair.

3.2   The State of a Relationship

A factor that can influence the opinion shift between two individuals is the type of relationship between them and the state of this relationship [16]. The literature on Social Influence highlights that in presence of a peaceful and friendly relationship, Positive Influence, usually, occurs. Unfortunately, no studies show a robust explanation of how Negative Influence works.

Hence, an objective of the study conducted in this work focuses in particular on the analysis of the impact of the presence of conflicts in the variation of an individual's utility. It is clear that the problem is close to the Opinion Shifting problem, but not exactly the same. Hence, it is reasonable to expect that, in case of peaceful relationships, a positive variation of utility should occur, as in the Positive Opinion Shifting phenomenon. On the contrary, a Negative variation may take place when there is a conflict between people. Hence, a second objective of this study is trying to underline such considerations.

4   A Case Study on Two-Sized Groups

In our previous works [3], we presented a first qualitative analysis of an experiment conducted to determine if the tie strength and the presence of conflicts can influence the direction and the magnitude of emotional contagion towards a positive and a negative influence. Here, we extend such analysis try to determine the extent of the influence of such parameters on a possible model to predict the user's satisfactions related to the group.

The experiment was focused on two-sized groups and was conducted with an online questionnaire, using the Amazon Mechanical Turk platform. In the previous works, we showed that the tie strength has an impact with Positive influence, that increases when the strength becomes stronger, and that the presence of conflict can lead to a Negative influence, mostly in the case of weak ties. In particular, there is a general positive shifting in the case of good relationships, i.e. when the participant likes the other person, and, as we expected, this shifting increases when the strength of the ties became stronger. Furthermore, in the case of a small initial difference between initial evaluations, when, hence, there is an initial agreement between the participant in the study and the hypothetical other one, we can notice a substantial absence of shifting in the case of a good relationship, so we can observe that people that have similar ideas and like each other tend to keep the same position, and not change their evaluations. Instead, in the indifferent and conflict relationships, we noticed a Negative influence.

Here, we use these results to estimate the possible parameters of an ORP model.

4.1   Description of the Experiment

In a first step, we verified that the participants could understand the scenarios given in the experiment. Since the questionnaire is provided in English language, an English test was taken by each participant, and only those who passed the test were included. After that initial step, the questionnaire starts providing a detailed explanation of the experiment, explaining to the users that the ties strength may be weak, intermediate or strong, according to the definition provided in [13]. The different tie strength are defined as follows:

- Weak: indicates a person with whom the participant has a weak relationship, with occasional interactions;
- Intermediate: is for a person with whom the participant has regular interactions;
- Strong: means that the interaction of the participant with this person occurs every day, many times a day, so their relationship can be defined as strong.

Regarding conflicts, we were inspired by [23] and decided to distinguish between:

- Like: People with whom the participants are in a peaceful relationship, namely, at this moment, they like them and they are on good terms;
- Indifferent: People with whom the participants are neither in a conflict nor in a peaceful relationship, and therefore, they are indifferent to them;
- Dislike: People with whom they are in a conflict situation, namely, at this moment, they dislike and with whom they are on bad terms.

After the explanation of these concepts to the users, we presented the view shown in Fig. 1, containing two evaluations for the same eight activities, one supposed to be made by the user in the past, and the other by another agent. Here, we must specify that the users are not provided with information about the context and on the real items. We choose to not propose concrete activities to avoid that such knowledge could influence participants' answers. For this reason,

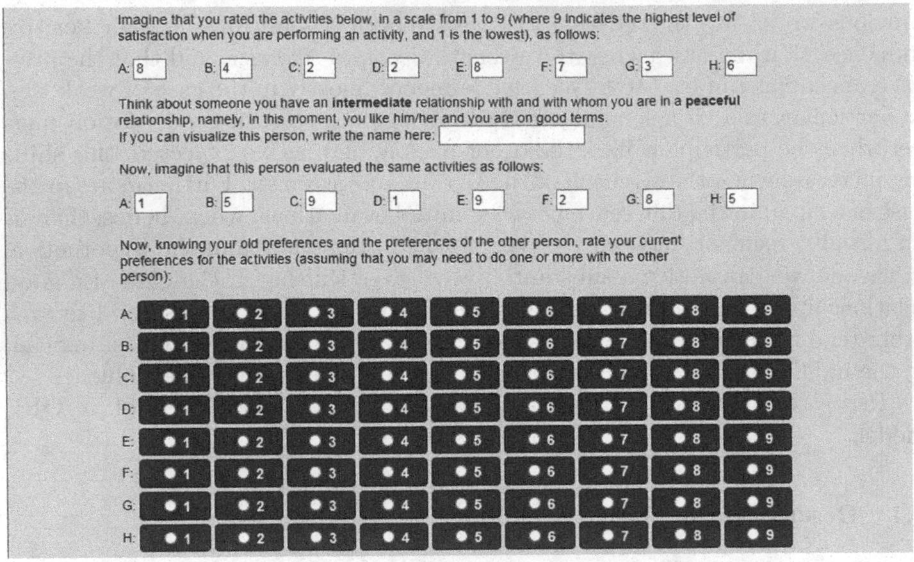

Fig. 1. Screenshot of the online questionnaire.

we cannot ask for user's evaluations of their satisfactions. On the contrary, the first set of evaluations is presented as a previous evaluation, made by the user in the past. The evaluations are on a scale from 1 to 9, where 9 indicates the highest level of satisfaction when the users are performing an activity, and 1 is the lowest.

After that, a second set of evaluations, for the same activities, is presented. Here, we asked the participants a stretch of the imagination; in fact, they are asked to think about someone with whom they have a relationship with determinate characteristics, given by the possible combinations of the type of tie strength and conflicts explained before. To help the participant to view the scenario more accurately as possible and to better identify himself into the proposed scenario, we asked to write the name of the person that they are thinking about. Obviously, we do not store this information. Then, we ask the participants to imagine that the second evaluations have been provided by the person they are visualizing.

Finally, we ask the participants to rate their satisfaction for the proposed activities, knowing their old satisfaction and the satisfaction of the other person and assuming that they have to perform the activities together. Again, all the evaluations are requested on a scale between 1 and 9 included. Each participant was asked to perform the test three times, answering for only 3 different configurations out of the 9 possible combinations, keeping the tie strength the same but varying the conflict. This choice is made to guarantee that the test occupies only few minutes, since, as suggested in [8], questionnaires that take more than a few minutes to complete may produce a loss of concentration in participants.

Hence, the designed questionnaire has been designed to require only 5 min to be completed.

We recruited 60 participants, collecting more than 1,400 evaluations. Each participant was paid $ 0.50 for the participation in the study.

4.2   Initial Evaluations Configurations

The two sets of initial evaluations have been designed in order to cover different situations. Namely, the differences between the participant's initial ratings and other person's ratings are set to present cases of agreement on the evaluation of the activity and cases of disagreement. Furthermore, the given ratings are set in order to have in half of the cases that the participant's rating is greater than the rating by the other person, and in the other half of the cases, the opposite. Firstly, we distinguish between *Large* and *Small* initial differences, and even between *Positive* and *Negative* differences. A large difference maps an initial disagreement between the two people, while a small difference indicates an initial agreement in the evaluations. On the other hand, a positive difference indicates that participant's initial rating is lower than the other person's one and, on the contrary, a negative difference is the case of a participant's initial rating being higher than the other person's one.

Focusing on the large initial difference, since we use a rating scale between 1 and 9, we can notice that such configurations give more chances to positive

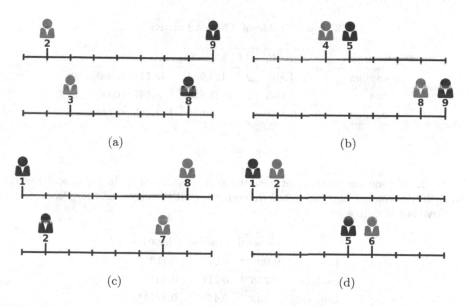

Fig. 2. Initial preferences for the participant (in green) and for the other person (in blue): (left) for large initial difference configuration, (right) for small initial difference configuration, for negative (a and b) and positive (c and d) initial difference. (Color figure online)

shifting, while possibilities of a negative shifting are very limited because the initial participant's rating is very near the boundaries of the scale. We decided to set four configurations with large difference, two positive and two negative, as shown in Fig. 2 (left). Regarding small initial differences, we have an initial agreement between people. Here, we have a very small possibility for positive shifting, since the initial ratings are very similar, with a difference of one value. Also in this case, we have four configurations, two positive and two negative, see Fig. 2 (right).

4.3   Result Analysis

According to a two-way Anova analysis, there are statistically significant changes in the shift considering the variation in the tie strength and in the conflict state. Results are showed in Table 1, where the interaction term is represented by the conflict * ties row. Results show that there are not interaction between the two fixed factors, in fact the $p\_value = 0.129$. Hence, we have an ordinal interaction.

Then, we perform a correlation analysis to quantify the impact of each individual factor, using the Pearson correlation. Also, following the models presented in the literature, we evaluate the correlation between the shift and the initial difference in the utilities, and we perform the analysis comparing two cases, i.e., the case with a positive initial difference (where the user's initial evaluation is greater then the other person's initial evaluation), and the case with negative initial difference (in the opposite case). Results are reported in Table 2.

Table 1. Table of ANOVA2 analysis.

Source	Sum Sq.	d.f.	Mean Sq.	F	p-value
conflict	251.807	2	125.904	39.715	0.000
ties	51.656	2	25.828	8.147	0.000
conflict * ties	22.631	4	5.658	1.785	0.129

Table 2. Pearson correlation between the shift, computed as in Eq. 6, and the tie strength, the conflict and the initial difference for all the cases, and for Positive and Negative initial difference.

	General	Positive	Negative
ties	0.091**	0.071	0.113**
conflict	0.226**	0.211**	0.241**
Init. Diff.	0.432**	0.437**	0.427**

We can see that the conflict factor has a great correlation, while the tie strength seems not to have a great impact, mostly in the case of a negative initial difference. Furthermore, the initial difference also has an high correlation with the shift. We evaluate also the correlation between the initial utility U_{ij} and the adapted utility $U_{i,j}^G$ evaluation. In this case, we have a general positive Pearson strong correlation (0.657), and the $p-value < 0.001$ confirming a statistical significance.

Finally, we perform a multiple regression analysis using conflict and initial difference as predictors and the shift as dependent variable. Results are reported in Table 3. As we can see there are not great differences between the two cases of negative and positive initial difference. However, the values of R^2 suggest that the two variables are not enough to explain all the variations of the shift variable.

Table 3. Multiple regression analysis with conflict and initial difference as predictors and shift as dependent variable, for the two cases of positive and negative initial difference.

	R^2	Constant	Conflict	Init. Diff.
Negative	0.240**	−1.215	0.540**	0.300**
Positive	0.236**	−1.048	0.477**	0.310**

5   Conclusions and Future Work

In the context of recommendation systems, it is well known that people tend to influence each other, hence the utility of each person related to a particular item can change with respect to the utilities of the individuals which whom he/she has to use the item. Hence, in GRS it is necessary to consider this influence in the process of generation of the group's recommendations.

The work presented here is trying to address the problem to use an ORP model in the recommendation context, trying to adapt the individual utilities estimated by an individual RS to the specific context of the group in which the item will be used. In order to do so, we presented a study performed to explore the factors that should be considered in the ORP parameters setting, and, in particular, to analyze the impact of tie strength and the status of the relationship in two-sized groups. The study deepens the analysis of an experiment showed in a previous work [3] where we showed a clear impact of the tie strength and the status of the relationships on the phenomenon.

Here, we firstly show that the two factors have an ordinal interaction on the shift, while the correlation analysis suggests that the status of the relationship is the most influencing factor, together with the size of the initial difference between the initial utility of the user and the utility of the other member of the group. These results are confirmed by the results of the multiple regression analysis, that also suggests that other factors should be considered in the general model.

Such results can be used as starting point for the definition of a general model applicable to small groups of more than two members. However, in this study, we decided to not provide the users with contextual information about the items of the system to obtain information not influenced from this knowledge, but we plan to confirm these results in experiments that consider more concrete scenario. Then, we will also analyze the impact of such contextual information comparing the results to the one presented here.

Furthermore, in future work, we aim to analyze the performance of such other-regarding preferences model both at the aggregate and individual level. At the individual level, it will be necessary to perform further studies on the fitting performances of the model, in which we generate the adapted utilities with our model and compare them with the evaluation provided from the real users and, also, asking the participants to give a feedback on the computed utilities. At the aggregate level, instead, we will integrate the model in a Group Recommendation System evaluating the performances comparing them with classical baselines. Furthermore, it will be interesting to investigate other social factors, such as user personality that could be integrated into the functions to provide more accurate recommendations.

References

1. Alina Christensen, I., Schiaffino, S.: Social influence in group recommender systems. Online Inf. Rev. **38**(4), 524–542 (2014)
2. Arnaboldi, V., Guazzini, A., Passarella, A.: Egocentric online social networks: analysis of key features and prediction of tie strength in Facebook. Comput. Commun. **36**(10), 1130–1144 (2013)
3. Barile, F., Masthoff, J., Rossi, S.: The adaptation of an individual's satisfaction to group context: the role of ties strength and conflicts. In: Proceedings of the 25th Conference on User Modeling, Adaptation and Personalization, UMAP 2017, pp. 357–358. ACM (2017)
4. Blanco, M., Engelmann, D., Normann, H.T.: A within-subject analysis of other-regarding preferences. Games Econ. Behav. **72**(2), 321–338 (2011)
5. Bolton, G.E., Ockenfels, A.: Erc: a theory of equity, reciprocity, and competition. Am. Econ. Rev. **90**, 166–193 (2000)
6. Cox, J.C., Friedman, D., Gjerstad, S.: A tractable model of reciprocity and fairness. Games Econ. Behav. **59**(1), 17–45 (2007)
7. Dufwenberg, M., Heidhues, P., Kirchsteiger, G., Riedel, F., Sobel, J.: Other-regarding preferences in general equilibrium. Rev. Econ. Stud. **78**(2), 613–639 (2011)
8. Dunbar, R.I., Spoors, M.: Social networks, support cliques, and kinship. Hum. Nat. **6**(3), 273–290 (1995)
9. Elfenbein, H.A.: The many faces of emotional contagion: an affective process theory of affective linkage. Organ. Psychol. Rev. **4**(4), 326–362 (2014)
10. Fehr, E., Schmidt, K.M.: A theory of fairness, competition, and cooperation. Q. J. Econ. **114**(3), 817–868 (1999)
11. Fehr, E., Schmidt, K.M.: Chapter 8 the economics of fairness, reciprocity and altruism - experimental evidence and new theories. In: Kolm, S.C., Ythier, J.M. (eds.) Foundations, Handbook of the Economics of Giving, Altruism and Reciprocity, vol. 1, pp. 615–691. Elsevier (2006)

12. Gilbert, E., Karahalios, K.: Predicting tie strength with social media. In: Proceedings of the SIGCHI Conference on Human Factors in Computing Systems, pp. 211–220. ACM (2009)
13. Granovetter, M.S.: The strength of weak ties. Am. J. Sociol. **78**(6), 1360–1380 (1973)
14. Guo, J., Zhu, Y., Li, A., Wang, Q., Han, W.: A social influence approach for group user modeling in group recommendation systems. IEEE Intell. Syst. **31**(5), 40–48 (2017)
15. Mäs, M., Flache, A.: Differentiation without distancing. Explaining bi-polarization of opinions without negative influence. PloS One **8**(11), e74516 (2013)
16. Masthoff, J., Gatt, A.: In pursuit of satisfaction and the prevention of embarrassment: affective state in group recommender systems. User Model. User-Adapt. Interact. **16**(3–4), 281–319 (2006)
17. Rossi, S., Barile, F., Caso, A., Rossi, A.: Pre-trip ratings and social networks user behaviors for recommendations in touristic web portals. In: Monfort, V., Krempels, K.-H., Majchrzak, T.A., Turk, Ž. (eds.) WEBIST 2015. LNBIP, vol. 246, pp. 297–317. Springer, Cham (2016). https://doi.org/10.1007/978-3-319-30996-5_15
18. Rossi, S., Caso, A., Barile, F.: Combining users and items rankings for group decision support. In: Bajo, J., et al. (eds.) Trends in Practical Applications of Agents, Multi-Agent Systems and Sustainability. AISC, vol. 372, pp. 151–158. Springer, Cham (2015). https://doi.org/10.1007/978-3-319-19629-9_17
19. Rossi, S., Cervone, F.: Social utilities and personality traits for group recommendation: a pilot user study. In: Proceedings of the 8th International Conference on Agents and Artificial Intelligence, pp. 38–46 (2016)
20. Salehi-Abari, A., Boutilier, C.: Empathetic social choice on social networks. In: 13th International Conference on Autonomous Agents and Multiagent Systems, pp. 693–700 (2014)
21. Senot, C., Kostadinov, D., Bouzid, M., Picault, J., Aghasaryan, A., Bernier, C.: Analysis of strategies for building group profiles. In: De Bra, P., Kobsa, A., Chin, D. (eds.) UMAP 2010. LNCS, vol. 6075, pp. 40–51. Springer, Heidelberg (2010). https://doi.org/10.1007/978-3-642-13470-8_6
22. Sobel, J.: Interdependent preferences and reciprocity. J. Econ. Lit. **43**(2), 392–436 (2005)
23. Takács, K., Flache, A., Mäs, M.: Discrepancy and disliking do not induce negative opinion shifts. PLOS One **11**(6), e0157948 (2016). https://doi.org/10.1371/journal.pone.0157948

Learning Fuzzy User Models for News Recommender Systems

Mauro Dragoni[✉]

Fondazione Bruno Kessler, Trento, Italy
dragoni@fbk.eu

Abstract. Online news reading has become a widely popular way to read news articles from news sources around the globe. With the enormous amount of news articles available, users are easily overwhelmed by information of little interest to them. News recommender systems help users manage this flood by recommending articles based on user interests rather than presenting articles in order of their occurrence. In this paper, we propose an approach using evolutionary algorithm to learn fuzzy models of user interests used for recommending news articles gathered from RSS feeds. These models are dynamically updated by track the interactions between the users and the system. The system is ontology-based, in the sense that it considers concepts behind terms instead of simple terms. The approach has been implemented in a real-world prototype newsfeed aggregator with search facilities called iFeed. Experimental results show that our system learns user models effectively by improving the quality of the recommended articles.

1 Introduction

Owing largely to the ever-increasing volume and sophistication of information on the web, we are able to access an enormous amount of data from around the globe. The downside of this information explosion is that users are often overwhelmed by information of little interest to them. The key challenge for the users is to find relevant information based on their interests. This problem has led to the evolution of recommender systems that help users find the information they need, based on their interests. Recommender systems pro-actively present users with information related to their interests rather than requiring the user to search for, and then filter through, information based on explicit queries. Many organizations use recommender systems to recommend various types of products to the user. For example, Netflix recommends movies to its users based on the user's movie ratings compared to other similar users' ratings. Amazon recommends various types of products such as gadgets, books, or movies and Pandora Radio recommends music based on a user's past history and preferences. In addition, news recommender systems that recommend news articles from around the globe have become popular. There are many online news services such as Google News and Yahoo News. However, with plenty of news available,

© Springer Nature Switzerland AG 2018
C. Ghidini et al. (Eds.): AI*IA 2018, LNAI 11298, pp. 502–515, 2018.
https://doi.org/10.1007/978-3-030-03840-3_37

the driving problem is to identify and recommend the most interesting articles to each user so that they are not swamped by irrelevant information. These articles should be related to each user interests but also include those news stories that are generating a lot of interest around the globe.

In this paper, we present an approach based on the exploitation of fuzzy user models for recommending news article that are interesting with respect to both the history of the interactions between users and the system and the explicit information provided by users during the creation of their profile. The approach is based on the use of fuzzy logic for expressing the uncertainty associated with the interest degree of a user with respect to a given topic and on the application of evolutionary algorithms for performing a validation of a broad set of profiles with the aim of learning the one better fitting with users' interests.

The paper is organized as follows: Sect. 2 begins with an overview of strategies adopted for news recommendation. Section 3 presents the evolutionary algorithm used for evolving the users' models implemented into the system. Then, Sect. 4 shows the experiments that we have carried out and discusses their results. Finally, Sect. 5 concludes the paper.

2   Related Work

News recommender systems are widely used and are a promising research direction. With so many information sources, the Web provides fast access to the millions of news articles around the globe. However, users need recommendations to help them find the most interesting articles from this flood of information. News recommender systems can be broadly classified into two types based on the type of recommendations made to the user. Some recommender systems take advantage of online social networking sites to provide interesting news articles to the user. Such recommendations are called popularity-based news recommendations since the articles are ranked based on their popularity identified from the social networking websites. Other recommender systems recommend interesting news articles to the user solely based on the user's interests. Such recommendations are called profile-based news recommendations since they rank the news articles based on the user's interests. The following two sections explore the applications based on the popularity based recommendation and profile-based recommendation techniques.

Popularity Based News Recommender Systems. News recommender systems are widely used to help readers filter through an ever-growing flood of information. Many researchers focus on using real-time social networking sites such as Facebook, Google Plus, and Twitter to identify the most popular current news stories. Because they are instant and widely available, they provide a massive source of information on current events. However, because they are unmoderated, the quality of the information is variable. [1] discuss a method to determine which Twitter users are posting reliable information and which posts are interesting.

Micro-blog posts can also be used as a way of identifying the popularity of certain events. [2] represent users and items based on micro-blogging reviews of movies and used this technique with various movie recommendation strategies on live-user data. [3] focus on using micro-blogging activity to recommend news stories. Their recommender system, Buzzer, is applied to RSS feeds to which the users have subscribed. Buzzer mines terms from RSS and Twitter feeds and uses them to rank articles. [4,5], they extended their work by considering the public-rank and the friends-rank strategy rather than just considering the articles from the users? index.

Profile-Based News Recommender Systems. Profile-based, or personalized, news recommender systems recommend articles to the user based solely on his/her interests. A user profile is built based on the preferences or interests of the user. In one of the earliest news recommendation systems, [6] created News Dude, a personal news-recommending agent that uses TF-IDF in combination with a Nearest Neighbor algorithm in order to recommend news stories to users [7]. They developed a hybrid user model that considers both long-term and short-term interests and found out that this model outperformed the models that consider either of these interests.

Similarly, [8] described a content-based recommender system that recommends news articles to a user based upon the user's short-term and long-term reading preferences. The work from [9] presents a good correlation between user profile features and its relative efficiency for recommendations. They evaluate and compare three different strategies for building user profile upon Tweeter stream. The three types of user profile are: entity-based user profiles, hashtag-based user profiles, and topic-based user profiles. They concluded that entity-based user profiles are the most valuable profiles and that they are a better fit for recommendation purposes. They then used this type of profile in their personalized news recommender system. Recently, [10] proposed an innovative recommender system to recommend personalized news stories using content-based analysis of tweets in Twitter. In their work, they first build a user profile by extracting keywords from the content of tweets, re-tweets and hashtags. A keyword classifier based on deep neural network analysis is being used to classify interesting keywords. Then, they recommend news articles to the user using topic modeling techniques as well as TF-IDF.

Our news recommender system falls in the second category of approaches by implementing an algorithm based on the analysis and evolution of conceptual user profiles.

3   The Approach

Evolutionary algorithms (EAs) [11,12] are a broad class of stochastic optimization algorithms, inspired by biology and in particular by those biological processes that allow populations of organisms to adapt to their surrounding environment: genetic inheritance and survival of the fittest. An EA maintains a population of candidate solutions for the problem at hand, and makes it evolve by iteratively applying a (usually quite small) set of stochastic operators, known as *mutation*, *recombination*, and *selection*.

Mutation randomly perturbs a candidate solution; recombination decomposes two distinct solutions and then randomly mixes their parts to form novel solutions; and selection replicates the most successful solutions found in a population at a rate proportional to their relative quality. The initial population may be either a random sample of the solution space or may be seeded with solutions found by simple local search procedures, if these are available. The resulting process tends to find, given enough time, globally optimal solutions to the problem much in the same way as in nature populations of organisms tend to adapt to their surrounding environment.

In the proposed system, an individual of the population is a vector of as many components as the document clusters in the repository; each component is the fuzzy degree to which the user is interested in the relevant cluster ($0 =$ not interested at all, $1 =$ absolutely interested).

3.1   Fitness Function

By definition, the quality of a model should be measured as the degree to which the relevant user is satisfied, overall, with the answers to his queries. However, such overall user satisfaction cannot be measured in a single interaction. The only thing that can be indirectly estimated is user satisfaction with respect to an actual query. Therefore, the fitness of a user model can only be estimated incrementally, by subsequent refinements, every time an answered filtered by it is given feedback by the user. At each moment, the fitness of a user model is known with imprecision, which, by its nature, may be represented as a fuzzy interval [13] in the interval $[0, 1]$, where 0 represents complete user dissatisfaction and 1 indicates complete user satisfaction, which would occur if all queries were answered with the desired set of documents ordered by decreasing user interest.

This fuzzy interval can be represented by means of a trapezoid (a, b, c, d) where (a, d) is the support interval and (b, c) the core interval.

When a random user model is created, there is complete ignorance on its fitness; this is represented by a fuzzy fitness of $(0, 0, 1, 1)$, i.e., the whole $[0, 1]$ interval.

Every time a user submits a query, a model is selected from the relevant population and used to filter the answer; then an implicit feedback is calculated based on the actions the user takes: these are reading a document and spending time on a document. The fuzzy fitness of the model is then updated based on two coefficients:

$r \in [0, 1]$: the rating (implicitly) given by the user ($0 =$ completely negative, $1 =$ completely positive);

$w \in [0, 1]$: the confidence of the rating.

The updated trapezoid is calculated as follows:

$$a' = (a + wr)/(1 + w);$$ (1)
$$b' = (b + wr)/(1 + w);$$ (2)
$$c' = (c + wr)/(1 + w);$$ (3)
$$d' = (d + wr)/(1 + w).$$ (4)

A positive rating moves the trapezoid to the right, a negative rating to the left, and both shrink it, i.e., make it less uncertain. In addition, also the recombination and mutation operators, as explained below, change the fuzzy interval of fitness.

3.2 Recombination

The recombination operator is implemented by means of uniform crossover, whereby the new individual is created by selecting, for each cluster interest, the corresponding interest from either parent with $\frac{1}{2}$ probability.

Following recombination, the fitness of the offspring is calculated from those of the two parents (a_1, b_1, c_1, d_1) and (a_2, b_2, c_2, d_2) as follows:

$$a = b - (b_1 + b_2 - a_1 - a_2)/2;$$ (5)
$$b = \min\{0.95b_1, 0.95b_2\};$$ (6)
$$c = \max\{1.05c_1, 1.05c_2\};$$ (7)
$$d = c + (d_1 + d_2 - c_1 - c_2)/2.$$ (8)

The rationale behind these formulas is that the fitness of the offspring can be anything in between the fitness of the parents, or even slightly better or worse. The 1.05 and 0.95 factors represent a 5% expansion of the core of the fitness of the parents, which models a slight decrease of precision. The actual value of these factors is not critical, as previous experiments revealed.

3.3 Mutation

The mutation operator perturbs every cluster interest in a user model. In addition, to speed up convergence, an *intelligent* mutation has been used, that has already been applied with success to a similar problem [14]. The main idea behind intelligent mutation is to inject single, larger perturbations and observe the improvement they bring about: if the fitness increases, the perturbation is maintained, otherwise it is discarded.

In this case, intelligent mutation uses user feedback directly to modify the interest of the cluster whose centroid is closest to the query results.

Following mutation, the trapezoid of fitness is updated as follows:

$$a' = \max\{0, b' - (b - a)(1 + s)\};$$ (9)
$$b' = b(1 - s);$$ (10)
$$c' = c(1 + s);$$ (11)
$$d' = \min\{1, c' + (d - c)(1 + s)\},$$ (12)

where $0 \leq s < 1$ is the strength of the perturbations undergone by the mutated user model. The idea is that the fitness of a mutated model is more uncertain than the fitness of the original model.

3.4   Selection

Probabilistic tournament selection is used to select individuals for reproduction. A number of individuals are picked at random to play a tournament. A deviate from a probability distribution obtained by normalizing the fuzzy fitness interval of each individual is extracted and the individual whose deviate is greatest wins the tournament and is inserted in the population for the next generation.

Elitism is implemented: the best individual in the population is passed on unchanged to the next generation. Another slot in the new population is taken by the last individual used for filtering a query answer; the rationale for this choice is that the fitness of that individual incorporates the most recent information on user interests.

4   Experiments and Results

To validate the proposed approach, we have implemented a small but working real-world prototype newsfeed aggregator with search facilities, called iFeed. iFeed is a web-based newsfeed aggregator that is able to crawl news from RSS feeds, to monitor the user's activities (such as queries, clicks, etc.) in order to estimate implicit feedbacks, and to learn user profiles without requesting explicit interactions from users. iFeed is composed of the modules briefly described below.

1. Crawler: this module fetches RSS feeds from the web, extracts news from the XML file containing them, translates them into a conceptual document representation, and stores the news in the database. Documents are represented by means of the conceptual representation described in [15].
2. User Profile Reader (UPR): when a user logs into the system, the UPR loads the models associated with the logged user, selects one of such models, composes a set of 20 documents that are most interesting with respect to the selected model, and recommends them to the user.
3. User Profile Analyzer (UPA): this module updates the user models based on the implicit feedbacks stored in the database. The UPA implements the evolutionary algorithm explained in Sect. 3.
4. Web Interface: this is the interface used by the users to interact with the system through their browser.

iFeed is implemented by using two different programming languages: the crawler, the UPR, and the web interface have been implemented in PHP, while the UPA has been developed in Java. Documents and other data are stored into a MySQL database.

The experiments have focused on three different aspects:

- convergence of the algorithm: we measure the distance between the user models in the population and we show that this distance decreases; this is indicative of how the system learns the real user interests.
- learning the user models: we analyze the correlation between the evolution of the user models and the activities performed by the users of the system.
- quality of the recommended documents: the main aim of the proposed approach is that the more the users interact with the system, the more the quality of the documents recommended by the system increases. We have analyzed this aspect by investigating if the documents read by the users have been recommended by the UPR module or not.

iFeed was launched on April 1st, 2016. Since then, it has been running 24 hours a day and, as of August 10th, more than 1500 users had been involved into this project. Not all the registered users have performed the same amount of activity. Therefore, for the purpose of evaluation, we have considered only the 100 most active users. For each user, we have considered his or her first 100 sessions. In each session, a user generally reads more than one document. A brief statistic analysis related to the users activities illustrates that the total number of documents read by users is 32,578, the average documents per user is 251.56 with a standard deviation of 120.79.

The feeds are grouped in 9 different categories based on different topics (*Politics*, *Economics*, *Science*, *Sports*, etc.). The considered users have been assigned to each category by observing their activities and by asking them which were explicit interests. For each category, we have computed the graphs related to the users' activities in order to study the correlation between the behavior of the evolutionary algorithm and the way the users interact with the system. Moreover, we have analyzed the ability of the system to recommend interesting documents to the users. Due to lack of space, in this paper we present and discuss the results obtained for one of the categories, namely *Politics*. However, the considerations below hold for the other categories as well. We will show details about five of the users who have been assigned to the considered category. Nonetheless, the graphs presented represent the convergence of the algorithm with respect to all of the 100 most active users.

4.1   Creation of the Recommended Document Set

In this section, we describe in more detail how the UPR module works. This module is executed each time a user logs into the system. It aims at retrieving information about the user's profile and at creating a set of 20 documents to recommend to the user. Here, for illustrative purpose, we consider a simple example. We assume to have a user with the models shown in Table 1.

When the user logs into the system, the UPR module chooses randomly one among the models associated to the user, for example Model 2. Then, the interest of each feed in the model is normalized with respect to the sum of all interests of the chosen model. Subsequently, the feeds are ranked in descending order with respect to the feed interests. In order to recommend the user with documents

Table 1. Examples of user models.

Model 1		Model 2		Model 3	
Feed	Interest	Feed	Interest	Feed	Interest
1	0.79	1	0.60	1	0.32
2	0.24	2	0.90	2	0.09
3	0.55	3	0.33	3	0.21
4	0.12	4	0.01	4	0.49
5	0.89	5	0.77	5	0.94

Table 2. Normalization and document publishing.

Model 2 Norm.		Documents published	
Feed	Int. Norm	Coarse value	Published
2	0.34	6.8	7
5	0.30	6.0	6
1	0.23	4.6	5
3	0.13	2.6	$3 \rightarrow_{pub} 2$
4	0.00	0.0	0

distributed in a way to be proportional to the user's interests, we then calculate the number of such documents by multiplying the normalized interests by 20. Finally, the UPR module extracts and recommends documents until the limit of 20 documents has been reached. All the above considerations are illustrated in Table 2.

We can notice that only two among the tree documents coming from Feed 3 will be published by the UPR module, because the limit of 20 documents has already been reached.

4.2 Learning Curve

In this section, the results related to the convergence of the system are presented. The system was set with a population of 30 individuals, the selection of individuals uses a tournament strategy with size 3, and the probabilities of crossover and mutation were respectively 0.75 and 0.10.

The value of 3 for the tournament size is to keep the selective pressure very low and to avoid premature convergence; with a probability of 0.75 for the crossover operator, we favor the exchange of user interests between the models and, finally, with a mutation probability of 0.10 we allow the system to explore more possible solutions. As said above, we have considered only the first 100 sessions for each user, each session corresponds to a generation of the evolutionary algorithm.

The formula used to calculate the sum of all the distances between all models is:

$$\text{Dist} = \sum_{k=1}^{m-1} \sum_{j=k+1}^{m} \sum_{i=1}^{n} |I_{F_i}^k - I_{F_i}^j|, \tag{13}$$

where n is the number of feeds in the system, m is the population size, $I_{F_i}^k$ is the interest in feed F_i of the model k, and $I_{F_i}^j$ is the interest in feed F_i of the model j. Thus, Dist represents the "overall distance" between the evolved user models present in the population and should be interpreted as an index of population diversity.

Figure 1 illustrates the learning curve obtained by analyzing the system's logs for the 50 users considered. We can notice that, for the first 30 generations, the algorithm converges quickly, then, after the 50th generation, the distance between models tends to remain constant. The value of zero is never reached due to the mutation operator. Indeed, the mutation operator introduces perturbations that maintain a small diversity even between individuals with similar interest degrees. Instead, a possible reason for the fact that the graph does not change after 50 generations is that we have supposed that the considered users are only interested in one category.

The models that have high interest degrees receive positive feedback. Therefore, such models have a higher probability of being chosen during the selection phase. After a given number generations the population is composed by similar individuals, therefore, the distance between the models is hardly conditioned by the perturbations applied by the mutation operator.

In general, since the interest for each feed is encoded as a separate gene in the genotype of a model, learning user interests gets harder as the number of feeds available to the users increase. If a user is interested in a restricted subset of feeds, however, it is relatively easy for the evolutionary algorithm to set the genes of the uninteresting feeds to zero and to focus on the few interesting feeds. This is why, when the number of feeds associated to each category is small, as it is the case with the *Politics* category here, the number of generations required by the system to learn satisfactory interest degrees is small too.

On the contrary, when users are interested in different categories, the convergence speed is slower than the situation described above, because the evolutionary algorithm needs to search a larger space of candidate user models.

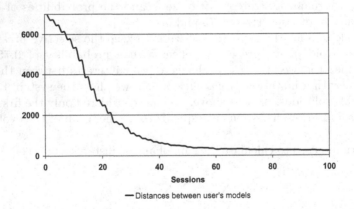

Fig. 1. System's learning curve.

4.3 Statistics of User Activity

In this section we present some statistical data about the user models. This data represents the correlation between the way the users interact with the system and how the user models evolve as a result of these interactions. The presented values correspond to the average of the results obtained for the five users associated to the chosen category. In addition, for completeness, we illustrate in each graph the standard deviation of such results.

Figures 2, 3, and 4 show, respectively, the average, the maximum, and the minimum of the following values:

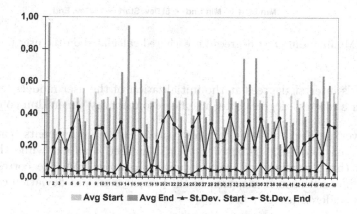

Fig. 2. Average interest degrees for each feed calculated on the user profiles.

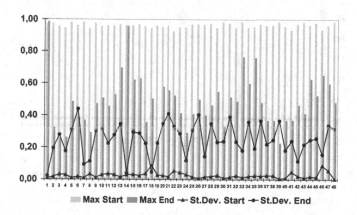

Fig. 3. Maximum interest degrees for each feed calculated on the user profiles.

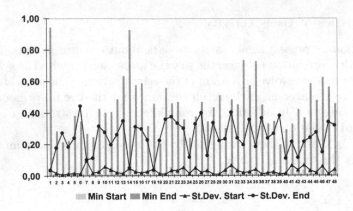

Fig. 4. Minimum interest degrees for each feed calculated on the user profiles.

- the user's interest degrees at the initialization of the user models;
- the user's interest degrees after the last evolutionary generation considered;

Moreover, in Fig. 5 we present the statistics of the documents read by the users for each feed. The x-axis represents the feed number, while the y-axis represents the percentage of read documents coming from the corresponding feed. The lines with markers represent the percent standard deviation calculated over the considered users.

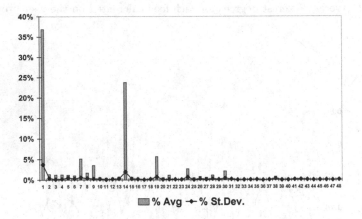

Fig. 5. Statistics about the percentage of documents read for each feed.

We can notice that most of the read documents come from Feeds 1 and 14, which are the feeds associated with the *Politics* category considered in this example. However, the users also read, in a lesser proportion, documents coming from different categories, although we do not study this aspect in depth. We can observe that the average, the minimum, and the maximum value of the interest degrees related to those feeds are very similar. This is due to the ability of the system to learn the user's profiles. Indeed, when a user reads documents coming always from the same two or more sources alike, the models associated with the user's profile tend to assume similar interest degrees for those sources.

Moreover, we can observe that the more a user reads documents coming from a given feed, the less is the standard deviation associated with that feed. Indeed, for Feeds 1 and 14, the standard deviation is very small in every graph. The interest degrees of the other feeds exhibit a higher standard deviation than the two feeds cited above do. This happens for two reasons. The first is that a small number of documents coming from those feeds has been read, so that the system does not have enough information to learn the exact interest degrees. The second is that the genetic operators constantly apply perturbations on all genes, thereby causing the seldom used interest degrees, which are less sensitive to the pressure of selection, to drift away from their optimal values in time. Surprisingly, Feed 18 too presents a small standard deviation. However, after a more in-depth analysis of the results we concluded that this case must be just a coincidence.

4.4   System Evaluation

In this section we discuss how the system improves the quality of the document set recommended to the users. As explained previously, every time a user logs into the system, the UPR module presents the user with a set of 20 documents. The aim of our approach is to recommend the users with documents that are as much as possible in line with their interests. To evaluate this aspect we have considered how many documents, out of those recommended to the user by the system, have been read by users with respect to the total number of documents read. To compare the five users considered above, we have taken the first 200 documents read by each user into account.

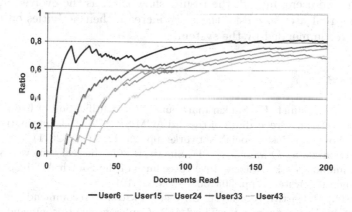

Fig. 6. Trend of the quality of the set of the documents recommended by the system.

The results are shown in Fig. 6. The graph represents the ratio between the number of documents read belonging to the set of the documents recommended by the system and the total number of documents read. Each point is calculated as follows:

$$R_j = DRP_j/j, \tag{14}$$

where DRP_j is the number of documents recommended by the system read when the jth document has been read and R_j is the value of the ratio after the user has read the jth document. We can observe that the more the users interact with the system, the more this ratio increases. This means that the system is able to recommend an increasing number of documents that are interesting to the users. We can also notice that the system's behavior is not the same for all users. The reason behind that is quite obvious: the implicit feedbacks received by the system for each document read are not the same for all users; therefore, for each user, the time required by the system to learn the user's profile may vary.

5   Conclusions

This paper describes an approach to profile-based news recommender systems which exploits a concept-based representation and a machine learning technique, namely evolutionary algorithms, to evolve models of user interests. The evolved models are used to recommend documents to users, that are in line with their interests. The approach is also capable of dynamically tracking changing user interests.

Experiments have been performed on a real-world prototype newsfeed aggregator with search facilities called iFeed, to validate the approach with respect to two criteria. The first is the capability of learning user interests: the results show that the distance between the evolved models decreases as the user interacts with the system. The second is the increase of precision of the set of documents proposed to the users, indeed, the results show that, as the evolved models get closer to the real user interests, the users increase their activities on the set of documents recommended by the system.

References

1. Jackoway, A., Samet, H., Sankaranarayanan, J.: Identification of live news events using Twitter. In: Proceedings of the 3rd ACM SIGSPATIAL International Workshop on Location-Based Social Networks, pp. 25–32. ACM (2011)
2. Garcia Esparza, S., O'Mahony, M.P., Smyth, B.: On the real-time web as a source of recommendation knowledge. In: Proceedings of the Fourth ACM Conference on Recommender Systems, pp. 305–308. ACM (2010)
3. Phelan, O., McCarthy, K., Smyth, B.: Using Twitter to recommend real-time topical news. In: Proceedings of the Third ACM Conference on Recommender Systems, pp. 385–388. ACM (2009)

4. Phelan, O., McCarthy, K., Bennett, M., Smyth, B.: On using the real-time web for news recommendation & discovery. In: Proceedings of the 20th International Conference Companion on World Wide Web, pp. 103–104. ACM (2011)
5. Phelan, O., McCarthy, K., Bennett, M., Smyth, B.: Terms of a feather: content-based news recommendation and discovery using Twitter. In: Clough, P., et al. (eds.) ECIR 2011. LNCS, vol. 6611, pp. 448–459. Springer, Heidelberg (2011). https://doi.org/10.1007/978-3-642-20161-5_44
6. Pazzani, M.J., Muramatsu, J., Billsus, D., et al.: Syskill & webert: identifying interesting web sites. In: AAAI/IAAI, vol. 1, pp. 54–61 (1996)
7. Billsus, D., Pazzani, M.J.: A personal news agent that talks, learns and explains. In: Proceedings of the Third Annual Conference on Autonomous Agents, pp. 268–275. ACM (1999)
8. Li, L., Zheng, L., Yang, F., Li, T.: Modeling and broadening temporal user interest in personalized news recommendation. Expert Syst. Appl. 41(7), 3168–3177 (2014)
9. Abel, F., Gao, Q., Houben, G.-J., Tao, K.: Analyzing user modeling on Twitter for personalized news recommendations. In: Konstan, J.A., Conejo, R., Marzo, J.L., Oliver, N. (eds.) UMAP 2011. LNCS, vol. 6787, pp. 1–12. Springer, Heidelberg (2011). https://doi.org/10.1007/978-3-642-22362-4_1
10. Oh, K.J., Lee, W.J., Lim, C.G., Choi, H.J.: Personalized news recommendation using classified keywords to capture user preference. In: 16th International Conference on Advanced Communication Technology, pp. 1283–1287. IEEE (2014)
11. DeJong, K.A.: Evolutionary Computation: A Unified Approach. MIT Press, Cambridge (2002)
12. Eiben, A.E., Smith, J.E.: Introduction to Evolutionary Computing. Springer, Berlin (2003). https://doi.org/10.1007/978-3-662-44874-8
13. Zadeh, L.A., Klir, G.J., Yuan, B.: Fuzzy Sets, Fuzzy Logic and Fuzzy Systems: Selected Papers by A. L. Zadeh. World Scientific, Singapore (1996)
14. Dragoni, M., Tettamanzi, A.: Evolutionary algorithms for reasoning in fuzzy description logics with fuzzy quantifiers. In: Proceedings of GECCO 2007, London, UK, vol ?, pp 1067–1074 (2007)
15. Dragoni, M., da Costa Pereira, C., Tettamanzi, A.: A conceptual representation of documents and queries for information retrieval systems by using light ontologies. Expert Syst. Appl. 39(12), 10376–10388 (2012)

Novelty-Aware Matrix Factorization
Based on Items' Popularity

Ludovik Coba[✉], Panagiotis Symeonidis, and Markus Zanker

Free University of Bozen-Bolzano, 39100 Bozen-Bolzano, Italy
{lucoba,psymeonidis,Markus.Zanker}@unibz.it

Abstract. The search for unfamiliar experiences and novelty is one of the main drivers behind all human activities, equally important with harm avoidance and reward dependence. A recommender system personalizes suggestions to individuals to help them in their exploration tasks. In the ideal case, these recommendations, except of being accurate, should be also novel. However, up to now most platforms fail to provide both novel and accurate recommendations. For example, a well-known recommendation algorithm, such as matrix factorization (MF), tries to optimize only the accuracy criterion, while disregards the novelty of recommended items. In this paper, we propose a new model, denoted as popularity-based NMF, that allows to trade-off the MF performance with respect to the criteria of novelty, while only minimally compromising on accuracy. Our experimental results demonstrate that we attain high accuracy by recommending also novel items.

Keywords: Recommendation algorithms · Evaluation
Novelty · Collaborative filtering · Matrix factorization

1 Introduction

Recommender systems aim primarily at providing accurate item recommendations while ignoring many times additional quality criteria such as the novelty of a recommended item [2]. There are many definitions of item novelty [2]. For example, the popularity-based novelty focuses on discovering non-popular products that match the crowd's interest. In terms of MF for providing novel item recommendations, related work [5,23] observed that by raising the dimensionality of the MF model (i.e., by increasing the number of latent factors), we can recommend items coming from the long tail (i.e. more novel items), but with big losses in terms of accuracy. In addition, an increased number of latent factors directly affects the efficiency of MF models.

In this paper, we provide novel item recommendations based on matrix factorization. We propose a MF method that simultaneously recommends accurate and novel items. Our proposed method, denoted as NMF, has the advantage of controlling through a regularization term how novel items will be recommended,

© Springer Nature Switzerland AG 2018
C. Ghidini et al. (Eds.): AI*IA 2018, LNAI 11298, pp. 516–527, 2018.
https://doi.org/10.1007/978-3-030-03840-3_38

without increasing the number of latent factors of MF [5, 23]. Moreover, we introduce an integrated way to evaluate novelty, denoted as Novelty-nDCG, which is
based on the well-known nDCG [3], but adjusted for our case-scenario in recommender systems, and distinguishes a more novel item from a less novel item.
N-nDCG also can be used with different definitions [2, 22] of item novelty, as will
be described later. However, item novelty should not be considered equal to the
diversity of a recommendation list.

In the remainder of this paper, Sect. 2 discusses the related work. In Sect. 3,
we define item novelty, and the evaluation of a recommendation list of items.
Then, we propose a framework for novel MF. Section 4 presents our experimental results on two well-known datasets. Finally, Sect. 5 concludes and describes
future work.

2   Related Work

Recommender systems' effectiveness cannot be measured by considering only the
accuracy of recommendations. Jannach et al. [13], noticed that researchers are
increasingly aware of this problem, and that aspects related to the users' experience like explanations, novelty and serendipity have to receive more attention.

Furnas et al. [8] proposed Singular Value Decomposition (SVD) to factor a
matrix into three matrices. An instance of SVD, known as classic matrix factorization (MF), searches for two matrices (U and V), whose their multiplication
gives an approximation of the original matrix A. That is, if we have a matrix A
with n rows and m columns, we can find two matrices, one U with n rows and k
columns and one V with m rows and k columns, such that $UV^{\top}$ produces A with
the blank entries filled and a small deflection of the initial values. Another MF
method is known as *CUR Matrix Decomposition*[17], because the initial matrix
is factorized to 3 matrices (C, U and R). One quick observation about CUR
decomposition is that row and column that are used to construct matrices C
and R are randomly selected from matrix A. It is obvious that this selection will
affect CUR-approximation.

Several methods have been proposed to compute matrices U and V. For
example, Lee and Seung [15] proposed the definition of a cost function (i.e.,
$\|A - UV\|^2$), which can be minimised either by using multiplicative update rules
or by using additive update rules of the well-known gradient descent method. In
addition, Dhillon and Sra [7] proposed multiplicative update rules that incorpo
rate weights for the importance of each element of the approximation predicted
matrix $\hat{A}$. Please notice that the objective function $\|A - UV\|^2$ is convex either
in U only or V only. However, since it is not convex in both variables together,
we can only guarantee finding a local minimum solution, rather than a global
minimum of the cost function. Thus, since in general the problem has not an
exact solution, the computation of U and V is commonly approximated numerically with methods, such as gradient descent or alternating least squares (ALS).
Recently, Lin [16] proposed an algorithm to resolve the convergence issues of

the optimization procedure. His algorithm guarantees the convergence to a stationary point. However, Lin's algorithm requires even more execution time per iteration than the slow in execution time of Lee and Seung [15] MF algorithm.

As far as item novelty is concerned, Jannach et al. [12] mention in their research that recommender systems aim at boosting recommendations from the long tail of the item popularity distribution, as it increases sales of novel items. There are several works that try to provide both accurate and novel [2,3,22] or diversified item recommendations [3,4], where a diversified item recommendation list tries to capture more aspects of the user's interest. In terms of MF, related work [5,23] has claimed that by increasing the number of latent factors of the basic MF model [14], we can more accurately recommend novel items. A different research direction in MF formulates the item recommendation problem not as a classification problem, but as a ranking problem using pairs of positive items (in the train set) and negative items (not in the train set) as pairwise input. For example, Bayesian Personalized Ranking (BPR) [20] optimises a simple ranking loss such as AUC (the area under the ROC-curve) and uses matrix factorization as the ranking function, that can be directly optimized using a stochastic gradient algorithm. Similarly to BPR, Ning and Karypis [18,19] proposed a set of Sparse LInear Methods (SSLIM), which involve an optimization process to learn a sparse aggregation coefficient matrix based on both a user-item purchase matrix and side information on items.

In contrast to the aforementioned work of Cremonesi et al. [5], and Yin et al. [23], our proposed method incorporates an additional constraint term for novelty into the basic MF formula. This additional information is taken from an external resource of a user-item novelty matrix, which will be defined in the next section. While novelty and accuracy of recommended items are seen as a key feature of the recommendation utility in real scenarios, to our knowledge, there is not much work relating them and systematically measuring trade-offs.

It is useful to make a clear distinction between novelty, diversity and serendipity. Vargas et al. [22] explain that the novelty of an item refers to how different an item is with respect to what has already been experienced by a user or the community. While diversity refers to a set of items, and it is related to how different items are with each other. While serendipity [6] refers to how surprising and interesting is an item for a user. Tomeo et al. [21] extended the regression tree to generate diversified recommendations lists in a multi-attribute setting. Wasilewski and Hurley [11] have proposed a matrix factorization framework to trade-off between the accuracy of item recommendations and the diversity of the items in the recommendation list. In the following, we argue why there is very small overlap between their and our work, by identifying two important differences. The first is that similar to the previous approaches, their MF model computes the pair-wise ranking loss of the objective function (not the element-wise square loss like our methodology). In other words, our MF model is element-wise and predicts the missing values of the user-item rating matrix, whereas their model tries to optimize items' pairwise ranking. The second difference is that we are exploring the trade-off between item recommendation accuracy and item novelty, whereas they explored the trade off between item recommendation accuracy and item diversity. This difference is discussed further in the discussion section. De Gemmis et al. [6] proposed a methodology to propose non-obvious items and to measure their serendipity by measuring via web-cam the facial expression of the users.

3   Popularity-Based Novelty of Recommended Items

In this Section, we will define the novelty of an item for a target user. We want to be able to measure if an algorithm will recommend more novel items to the users. Table 1 summarizes the symbols used in the following sections.

Table 1. Symbols and definitions.

Symbol	Definition
k	Number of nearest neighbors
L_u	Recommendation list for user u
N	Size of recommendation list
$NN(u)$	Nearest neighbors of user u
P_τ	Threshold for positive ratings
I	Domain of all items
U	Domain of all users
R	Domain of the rating scale
u, v	Some users
i, j	Some items
I_u	Set of items rated by user u
U_i	Set of users rated item i
$r_{u,i}$	The rating of user u on item i
$|T|$	Size of the test set
N_i	Novelty of item i

The premise of recommender systems is to suggest to users non-popular items that match their interest, i.e. to make *novel* item recommendations. By doing this, businesses can increase their profits, since these novel items usually might have higher profit margins. Moreover, users will not get bored and disappointed by just getting trivial recommendations of popular items. In the following, we will define the *novelty* of a recommended item and how to measure the novelty of a recommendation list.

Figure 1 depicts the item popularity distribution of a well-known dataset, MovieLens 1ML [9], where items are ranked depending on how frequently they have been rated by users. As it is shown in Fig. 1, the ratings of items follow a long-tailed distribution and the novel items correspond to the long-tail items of this item popularity distribution, where few users have rated or interacted with, whereas items of low novelty correspond to popular items.

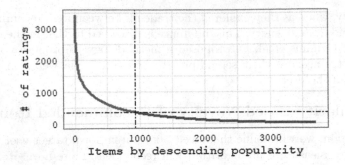

Fig. 1. Popularity distribution of items.

3.1 Defining How Novel Is a Recommended Item

Related work [2] in recommender systems has proposed a lot of definitions of item novelty. However, for a recommender system that consists only from a user-item rating matrix (without any other information about categories of items, domains of users' interests, etc.), it is more suitable the simple popularity-based novelty definition [2], also known as global long-tail novelty, which focuses on discovering relatively unknown items (coming from the long-tail of the item popularity distribution).

Based on the aforementioned arguments, novelty can be defined as the opposite of popularity, which means that an item is novel if few people are aware of it. Thus, we adopt the notion of user inverse frequency [2,22] to measure the novelty N_i of a recommended item i, by taking the inverse of its popularity, as can be shown by Eq. 2:

$$Novelty(i) = -Popularity(i) \tag{1}$$

where Popularity(i) corresponds to the probability that an item is rated or observed or had any other type of an interaction with a user.

$$Novelty(i) = N_i = -\frac{|U_i|}{|U|} \tag{2}$$

where U_i is is the set of users that rated item i, and U is the set of all users.

Based on Eq. 2, an item can be considered as more novel, if the users have less interacted with it (i.e., it took less ratings, or it is not enough purchased or it is less observed/viewed). In order to highlight the existence of highly novel items (favoring few very novel items and penalizing many less novel items), we can consider the logarithm of the novelty, as it is shown in Eq. 3 [2]:

$$N_i = -log_2 \frac{|U_i|}{|U|} \tag{3}$$

3.2   Novelty of Recommendation List

For a user u who is recommended N items, we define as novelty of the L_u recommendation list of items, as follows:

$$N_{L_u} = -\frac{1}{N} \sum_{\forall i \in L_u} log_2 \frac{|U_i|}{|U|}, \tag{4}$$

where U_i is the number of ratings that were given from users on item i, and U is the set of all users. We have to mention that the aforementioned definition of Novelty can not penalize the fact that an item that is less novel is ranked in the recommendation list L_u, above another item that is more novel. To do this, we will define in the following the N-nDCG.

Thus, to obtain a more fine-grained level of granularity we adopt the notion of Novel - normalized Discounted Cumulative Gain ($N - DCG_u$) [3], which also takes under consideration the relative position of the recommended items inside L_u.

The first step in the computation of $N - DCG_u$ is the creation of the gain vector. In our case, the gain vector for each item 1 in Lu, consists of its Novelty (N_l), as it is defined in Eq. 3.

The second step in the computation of $N - DCG_u$ applies the *Discounted Cumulative Gain* to the aforementioned gain vector, as shown in Eq. 5.

$$N\text{-}DCG_u = N_{l_1} + \sum_{i=2}^{N} \frac{N_{l_i}}{log_2 i} \tag{5}$$

Based on Eq. 5, we discount the gain at each rank inside L_u to penalize items, which are recommended lower in the ranking, reflecting the additional user effort in order to reach them and take the corresponding explanation [22].

The third step is to normalize the N-DCGu against the "ideal" gain vector. In our case, the "ideal" gain vector considers all recommended items in L_u as having maximum Novelty, N_{max}. That is, all recommended items in L_u are considered as never seen by any user. Thus, the ideal N-IDCG is calculated as:

$$N\text{-}IDCG = N_{max} + \sum_{i=2}^{N} \frac{N_{max}}{log_2 i}, \tag{6}$$

$$N_{max} = -log_2 \frac{1}{|U|}, \tag{7}$$

where U is the set of users, $|U_i|$, from Eq. 3, the number of times item i was rated is considered to be null. Finally, the $N\text{-}nDCG_u$ is the ratio between $N\text{-}DCG_u$ to N-IDCG:

$$N\text{-}nDCG_u = \frac{N\text{-}DCG_u}{N\text{-}IDCG} \tag{8}$$

3.3 Matrix Factorization

Matrix factorization methods are used in recommender systems to derive a set of latent factors, from the user × item rating matrix, to characterize both users and items by this vector of factors. The user-item interaction are modeled as inner product of the latent factors space [14]. Accordingly each item j will be associated with a vector of factors v_j, and each user i is associated with a vector of factors u_i. An approximation of the rating of a user i on an item j can be derived as the inner product of their factor vectors:

$$\hat{r}_{ui} = u_i v_j^T \qquad (9)$$

The u(user) and v(item) factor matrices are cropped to k features and initialized at small values. Each feature is trained until convergence (where convergence specifying the number of updates to be computed on a feature before considering it converged, it can be either chosen by the user or calculated automatically by the package). On each loop the algorithm predicts $\hat{r}_{ij}$, calculates the error and the factors are updated as follows:

$$v_{jk} \leftarrow v_{jk} + \lambda * ((r_{ij} - u_i v_j^T) * u_{ik} - \gamma * v_{jk}) \qquad (10)$$

$$u_{ik} \leftarrow u_{ik} + \lambda * ((r_{ij} - u_i v_j^T) * v_{jk} - \gamma * u_{jk}) \qquad (11)$$

The attribute λ represents the learning rate, while γ corresponds to the regularization term.

3.4 Novel Matrix Factorization

In this Section, we propose an algorithmic framework to trade-off between accuracy and novelty in matrix factorisation.

For popularity-based novelty, to provide more novel item recommendations, we add an additional soft constraint for novelty into the classic regularized matrix factorization formula as shown in Eq. 12:

$$G_{Novel} = \sum_{i,j \in R} (r_{ij} - u_i v_j^T)^2 + \frac{\beta}{2}(\|u_j\|^2 + \|v_j\|^2) + \delta\|u_i - v_j\|N_{ij}, \qquad (12)$$

where δ controls the novelty vector and N_{ij} holds the information of how novel is for user i item j, and β weights the effect of the L2 regularization term. Please notice that $\|u_i - v_j\|$ constraints the representations of the user/item vectors in the latent space, in such a way so that they are close to each other (i.e., their difference is close to zero), in order to minimise the objective function. In other words, we want to bring the user closer to the novel items in the latent space. To do this, we use the Manhattan distance, which overcomes the problem of Euclidean distance's metric over high dimensional spaces, since it does not place more emphasis on outliers, which may dominate other smaller weights computed for other normal data points [1]. Then, to minimize the objective function G_{novel}, we compute the error of the difference among the real and the predicted rating values of items by using a numerical method, such as *Gradient Descent*, and by applying the following update rules:

$$u_i' \leftarrow u_i + \eta(2(r_{ij} - u_i v_j^T)v_j - \beta u_i - \delta N_{ij})$$
$$v_j' \leftarrow v_j + \eta(2(r_{ij} - u_i v_j^T)u_i - \beta v_j + \delta N_{ij}) \tag{13}$$

Henceforth, we call this method Novel Matrix Factorization (NMF). Please notice that MF now becomes just a simplified special case of NMF and can be easily derived from it.

4 Experimental Results

In this Section, we compare experimentally our approach NMF with the Matrix Factorization [14] algorithm (MF).

4.1 Data Sets

Our experiments are performed with two datasets, MovieLens 100K (ML100K) and MovieLens 1ML (ML1M) [10]. ML100K consists of 100,000 ratings assigned by 943 users on 1,682 movies. ML1M contains 1,000,209 anonymous ratings of approximately 3,900 movies made by 6,040 users. The range of ratings is between 1(bad)-5(excellent).

4.2 Experimental Protocol and Evaluation

Our evaluation considers the division of items of each target user into two sets: (i) the training set E^T is treated as known information and, (ii) the test set E^P is used for testing and no information in the test set is allowed to be used for prediction. It is obvious that, $E = E^T \cup E^P$ and $E^T \cap E^P = \oslash$. Therefore, for a target user we generate the recommendations based only on the items in E^T (Table 2).

Except the metric N-nDCG, that was introduced in Sect. 3.2, we use the classic precision, and nDCG metrics as accuracy performance measures for item recommendations.

We perform all experiments with 4-fold double-cross validation, with a training-test split percentage, 75%–25%. The default size of the recommendation list N is set to 10, except to the cases where it is written differently. The presented measurements, based on a two-tailed t-test, are statistically significant at the 0.05 level. All algorithms predict the items of the target users' in the test set.

For both data sets, we have run experiments with a different number of latent factors and values of the hyper-parameters, but we fix them to the value that attained the best accuracy. In particular, for ML100K, the number of latent

Table 2. MovieLens 100K and 1M dataset

Characteristic	ML-100K	ML-1M
# of ratings	100,000	1,000,209
# of users	943	6,040
# of items	1,682	3,952
# of genres	19	18
Average # of genres per item	1.7	1.6
Rating's domain	[1, 5]	[1, 5]

factors, the regularization term β, the learning rate η for MF algorithm is set to 80, 0.001 and 0.001, respectively. For the NMF, we set, in addition, the novelty regularization term δ equal to 0.1 and 1, because, we have run experiments with two NMF variations, whereas the one variation attains high novelty with low accuracy and the other variation attains low accuracy with high novelty. For ML1ML, the number of latent factors for MF algorithm is set to 50, parameters η and β are set to 0.001. For the NMF, we set the novelty regularization term δ again equal to 0.1 and 1.

4.3   Sensitivity Analysis of NMF

In this Section, we want to explore how the performance of NMF in terms of providing novel and accurate recommendations is affected, as we increase the impact of the regularization term δ, which controls novelty in Eq. 12. Both Figs. 2a and b show that as we increase δ, N-nDCG increases till a point and remains then stable, whereas nDCG decreases very drastically even with small values of δ.

That is, as we increase δ, NMF recommends more novel items but the recommendation accuracy drops drastically, which means that novelty and precision accuracy are correlated negatively. To balance the effectiveness of NMF between novelty and accuracy, we set parameter δ equal to 0.1, which is before the point where accuracy starts to drop drastically.

4.4   Comparison with MF

In this Section, we compare NMF algorithm against MF in terms of their accuracy (with precision and nDCG), and novelty (with N-nDCG) performance. For NMF, we have two variations: NMF with the best attained novelty, where $\delta = 1$, and NMF with the balanced trade-off between novelty and accuracy, based on our findings from the previous section, by setting parameter $\delta = 0.1$. Tables 3 and 4 show the performance results for both algorithms on the ML100K and the ML1M datasets, respectively, when we provide top-10 item recommendations. As expected, the best novelty is attained by NMF($\delta = 1$), but with severe losses in terms of precision/nDCG. As it is shown, in the last row of both Tables 3 and 4, NMF($\delta = 0.1$) is able to recommend with minor losses in terms of accuracy

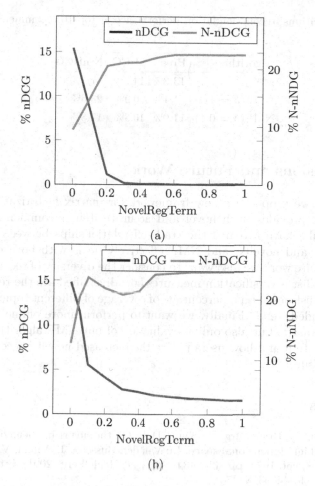

Fig. 2. Sensitivity analysis of NMF for (a) the ML100K and (b) the ML1M data sets.

very novel items. For example, N-nDCG is 15.6% and 17.8%, for ML100K and ML1M, respectively, which is a very impressive improvement over those attained by MF.

Table 3. Algorithms' recommendation performance at top-10 recommended items on ML100K.

Algorithm	Prec	nDCG	N-nDCG
MF	7.6%	7.8%	11.1%
NMF($\delta = 1$)	0.1%	0.1%	22.2%
NMF($\delta = 0.1$)	9.1%	8.9%	15.6%

Table 4. Algorithms' recommendation performance at top-10 recommended items on ML1M.

Algorithm	Prec	nDCG	N-nDCG
MF	13.3%	14.7%	7.1%
NMF($\delta = 1$)	1.1%	0.9%	23.6%
NMF($\delta = 0.1$)	11.9%	10.8%	17.8%

5   Conclusions and Future Work

In this paper, we proposed a new framework for matrix factorization, denoted as NMF, that provides both novel and accurate item recommendations. Our empirical results have revealed the trade-off relationships between algorithmic item accuracy and novelty, and NMF effectively deals with both of these two aspects. In future work we also want to consider the diversity of recommendation list. The intra-list diversification measures how diversified are the recommended items inside a list based on a percentage of coverage of different topics covered by the recommended items. Finally, we want to perform more offline experiments with other datasets, but also online evaluation of our NMF algorithm with real users to evaluate if and how users notice the increased novelty according to our proposed measure.

References

1. Aggarwal, C.C., Hinneburg, A., Keim, D.A.: On the surprising behavior of distance metrics in high dimensional space. In: Van den Bussche, J., Vianu, V. (eds.) ICDT 2001. LNCS, vol. 1973, pp. 420–434. Springer, Heidelberg (2001). https://doi.org/10.1007/3-540-44503-X_27
2. Castells, P., Hurley, N.J., Vargas, S.: Novelty and diversity in recommender systems. In: Ricci, F., Rokach, L., Shapira, B. (eds.) Recommender Systems Handbook, pp. 881–918. Springer, Boston, MA (2015). https://doi.org/10.1007/978-1-4899-7637-6_26
3. Charles, C., et al.: Novelty and diversity in information retrieval evaluation. In: SIGIR Conference, SIGIR 2008, pp. 659–666 (2008)
4. Cheng, P., Wang, S., Ma, J., Sun, J., Xiong, H.: Learning to recommend accurate and diverse items. In: Proceedings of the 26th International Conference on World Wide Web, WWW 2017, pp. 183–192 (2017). https://doi.org/10.1145/3038912.3052585
5. Cremonesi, P., Koren, Y., Turrin, R.: Performance of recommender algorithms on top-n recommendation tasks. In: Proceedings of the Fourth ACM Conference on Recommender Systems, RecSys 2010, pp. 39–46. ACM, New York (2010). https://doi.org/10.1145/1864708.1864721
6. De Gemmis, M., Lops, P., Semeraro, G., Musto, C.: An investigation on the serendipity problem in recommender systems. Inf. Process. Manag. **51**(5), 695–717 (2015). https://doi.org/10.1016/j.ipm.2015.06.008. https://www.sciencedirect.com/science/article/pii/S0306457315000837

7. Dhillon, I.S., Sra, S.: Generalized nonnegative matrix approximations with Bregman divergences. In: NIPS, pp. 283–290 (2005)
8. Furnas, G., Deerwester, S., Dumais, S.T.: Information retrieval using a singular value decomposition model of latent semantic structure. In: Proccedings ACM SIGIR Conference, pp. 465–480 (1988)
9. Harper, F.M., Konstan, J.A.: The movielens datasets: history and context. ACM Trans. Interact. Intell. Syst. **5**(4), 19:1–19:19 (2015). https://doi.org/10.1145/2827872
10. Harper, F.M., Konstan, J.A.: The MovieLens datasets. ACM Trans. Interact. Intell. Syst. **5**(4), 1–19 (2015)
11. Hurley, N.J.: Personalised ranking with diversity. Proceedings of the 7th ACM Conference on Recommender Systems - RecSys 2013, vol. 2, no. 1, pp. 379–382 (2013). https://doi.org/10.1145/2507157.2507226. http://dl.acm.org/citation.cfm?doid=2507157.2507226
12. Jannach, D., Lerche, L., Kamehkhosh, I., Jugovac, M.: What recommenders recommend: an analysis of recommendation biases and possible countermeasures. User Model. User-Adap. Inter. **25**(5), 427–491 (2015)
13. Jannach, D., Resnick, P., Tuzhilin, A., Zanker, M.: Recommender systems - beyond matrix completion. Commun. ACM **59**(11), 94–102 (2016). https://doi.org/10.1145/2891406
14. Koren, Y., Bell, R., Volinsky, C.: Matrix factorization techniques for recommender systems. Computer **42**(8), 42–49 (2009). https://doi.org/10.1109/MC.2009.263
15. Lee, D.D., Seung, H.S.: Learning the parts of objects by nonnegative matrix factorization. Nature **401**, 788–791 (1999)
16. Lin, C.J.: On the convergence of multiplicative update algorithms for nonnegative matrix factorization. IEEE Trans. Neural Netw. **18**(6), 1589–1596 (2007)
17. Mahoney, M.W., Drineas, P.: Cur matrix decompositions for improved data analysis. Proc. Nat. Acad. Sci. **106**(3), 697–702 (2009). https://doi.org/10.1073/pnas.0803205106. http://www.pnas.org/content/106/3/697.abstract
18. Ning, X., Karypis, G.: SLIM: Sparse linear methods for top N recommender systems. In: 2011 IEEE 11th International Conference on Data Mining (ICDM), pp. 497–506. IEEE (2011)
19. Ning, X., Karypis, G.: Sparse linear methods with side information for top-n recommendations. In: Proceedings of the Sixth ACM Conference on Recommender Systems, pp. 155–162. ACM (2012)
20. Rendle, S., Freudenthaler, C., Gantner, Z., Lars, S.T.: BPR: Bayesian personalized ranking from implicit feedback. In: Proceedings of the Twenty-Fifth Conference on Uncertainty in Artificial Intelligence, UAI 2009, pp. 452–461. AUAI Press, Arlington (2009). http://portal.acm.org/citation.cfm?id=1795114.1795167
21. Tomeo, P., Di Noia, T., De Gemmis, M., Lops, P., Semeraro, G., Sciascio, E.D.: Exploiting regression trees as user models for intent-aware multi-attribute diversity. Technical report. http://grouplens.org/datasets/movielens
22. Vargas, S., Castells, P.: Rank and relevance in novelty and diversity metrics for recommender systems. In: Proceedings of the Fifth ACM Conference on Recommender Systems, RecSys 2011, pp. 109–116. ACM, New York (2011). https://doi.org/10.1145/2043932.2043955
23. Yin, H., Cui, B., Li, J., Yao, J., Chen, C.: Challenging the long tail recommendation. Proc. VLDB Endowment **5**(9), 896–907 (2012)

Improving the User Experience with a Conversational Recommender System

Fedelucio Narducci(✉), Marco de Gemmis, Pasquale Lops,
and Giovanni Semeraro

Department of Computer Science, University of Bari Aldo Moro,
Via E. Orabona, 4, Bari, Italy
{fedelucio.narducci,marcode.gemmis,pasquale.lops,
giovanni.semeraro}@uniba.it

Abstract. Chatbots are becoming more and more popular for several applications like customer care, health care, medical diagnoses. Generally, they have an interaction with users based on natural language, buttons, or both. In this paper we study the user interaction with a content-based recommender system implemented as a Telegram chatbot. More specifically, we investigate on one hand what are the best strategies for reducing the cost of interaction for the users and, on the other hand how to improve their experience. Our chatbot is able to provide personalized recommendations in the movie domain and implements critiquing strategies for improving the recommendation accuracy as well. In a preliminary experimental evaluation, carried out through a user study, interesting results emerged.

Keywords: Conversational recommender system · Chatbot
User experience

1 Background and Motivations

The peculiarity of a conversational recommender system is its capability of interacting with the user during the recommendation process [1]. The user can provide feedback that the recommender can use for improving the next recommendation cycles. Accordingly, the acquisition of the preferences is an incremental process that might not be necessarily finalized in a single step. In fact, a cycle of interactions between the conversational recommender system and the user is repeated as long as some liked items are recommended. Hence, the goal of these systems is not only to improve the accuracy of the recommendations, but also to provide an effective user-recommender interaction.

In this paper we propose a movie recommender system implemented as Telegram chatbot[1]. Chatbots are a kind of bots which emulate user conversations.

---

[1] The chatbot can be tested by searching for @MovieRecSysBot in Telegram list of contacts.

© Springer Nature Switzerland AG 2018
C. Ghidini et al. (Eds.): AI*IA 2018, LNAI 11298, pp. 528–538, 2018.
https://doi.org/10.1007/978-3-030-03840-3_39

We implemented a Telegram chatbot since users can interact with the system through a clean and well-known user interface daily used on their smartphone. However, our application can be easily moved to other applications (e.g. Facebook Messenger).

The entities and properties the chatbot deals with (e.g. movies, directors, actors, genres, etc.) are extracted from DBpedia[2]. The chatbot uses these properties for eliciting user preferences, for providing recommendations as well as for generating personalized explanations in natural language. The system is also capable of adapting its behavior to the user feedback by implementing a critiquing strategy proposed in [2].

The main contribution of this work is to investigate the user experience with a conversational recommender system under two points of view: the reduction of the cost of interaction for the users and the improvement of their experience. In this work the conversational recommender system adopts a user interface based on buttons.

The rest of the paper is organized as follows: the relevant literature is analyzed in Sect. 2; Sect. 3 describes how the chatbot works and its interaction with the user, and finally, the experimental evaluation and the discussion of results are reported in Sect. 4. Section 5 draws the conclusion and the future work.

2   Related Work

There is a renewed interest in conversational recommender systems in the literature. So far, the research in the field of recommender systems has been mainly focused on algorithms for improving the accuracy of rating predictions on top-n recommendations [3–5], while the presentation of recommendations to the users [6] and their interaction with the recommender have not been widely investigated.

This work is mainly focused on the analysis of strategies for improving the experience of the user with a conversational recommender. Several work analyzed the interaction between users and recommender systems under different aspects [7]. In [8], Chen and Pu argue that an easy-to-use interface is paramount in critique-based recommender systems. Berkovsky et al. [9] demonstrated that explanation and persuasion are two important characteristics for convincing users to follow the recommendations. This result is also confirmed in [10], where the highest user satisfaction is achieved by personalized explanations using item features. In [11], Kveton and Berkovsky focus their attention to devise a method that simplifies content discovery and minimizes the cost of reaching an item of interest by proposing a generalized linear search. Mahmoud and Ricci [1] demonstrate that effective conversational systems can be built by adapting the strategy for assisting online users in acquiring their goals. Similarly, in [12] the authors propose a system capable of learning how to interact with users. Christakopoulou et al. [13] develop a preference elicitation framework to identify which questions

---

[2] http://wiki.dbpedia.org/.

should be asked to a new user to quickly learn her preferences. In [14], the user iteratively refines a query by providing critiques like *more like item I, but smaller* for improving the recommendations.

The goal of this work, compared to the prior researches, is to study the user experience with a conversational recommender under a broader perspective that analyzes how the user interaction can be influenced by different aspects like the initial user ratings (i.e. on popular items or not), the interaction mode (i.e. by buttons or by typing), the object of preference (i.e. items or item properties), and how the users enjoy critiquing and explanation functions.

3   Description of the Chatbot

The chatbot designed in this work implements the workflow depicted in Fig. 1. In the *Preference Acquisition* step, the chatbot asks the user to express her interests. It asks questions related to entities (e.g, movies and persons) and their properties in DBpedia (e.g, genre, role, director, actors). When the user starts the interaction, her profile is empty, so the recommender system needs to address a classical cold-start problem. The system offers two different strategies to allow users express their preferences: (i) rating a set of *items* or *properties* proposed by the system; (ii) typing the entities or properties she is willing to rate. The first option allows the user to express the preferences by tapping buttons, while the second one implements an entity recognizer based on the Levenshtein distance [15] by means of a *Did you mean* function (Fig. 3(a)).

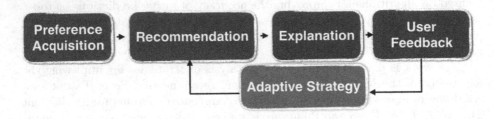

Fig. 1. The Bot workflow

The second step is the *Recommendation*. The Bot currently implements the PageRank with Priors [16], also known as Personalized PageRank. The Personalized PageRank works on a graph composed of items and properties extracted from DBpedia. In our system the nodes of the graph are entities in the movie domain like *American Beauty, Brad Pitt, Quentin Tarantino*, and the edges are the relations that connect these entities like *director, producer, actor*. The Personalized PageRank assigns different weights to different nodes to get a bias towards some nodes (in this case, the preferences of a specific user). The algorithm has been effectively used in other recommendation environments [4].

Figure 2 shows how the user preferences and the DBpedia properties are represented in a single graph. The algorithm is run for each user and the assignment of the probabilities to the nodes has been inspired by the model proposed in [17]: 80% of the total weight is evenly distributed among items and properties liked by the user (0% assigned to items disliked by the user), while 20% is evenly distributed among the remaining nodes. The algorithm generates a ranking of the items potentially interesting for a given user.

The chatbot also implements an *Explanation* component. Tintarev and Masthoff [10] point out that explaining a recommendation is generally intended as *justifying the suggestion*, but it might be also intended as *providing a detailed description* that allows the user to understand the qualities of the recommended item. The chatbot is able to provide both types of explanation. Details about an item can be obtained by tapping on the *Details* button (Fig. 3(b)) which shows information extracted from IMDB on a specific movie. The *Why?* button implements the explanation algorithm described in [18]. The idea is to use the connections in the DBpedia-based graph between the user preferences and the recommended items for explaining why a given item has been recommended.

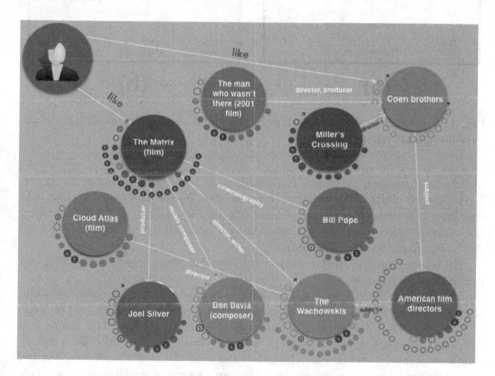

Fig. 2. Example graph which connects users, items and entities in DBpedia

An example of natural-language explanation provided by the system is: "I suggest you *Duplex* because you like movies where: the actor is *Ben Stiller* as

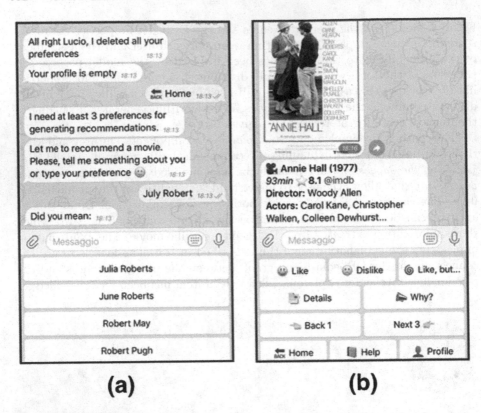

(a)   **(b)**

Fig. 3. A screenshot of the Bot during the training phase in typing mode (a), and the recommendation phase (b)

in *Meet the Fockers*, the genre is *Comedy* as in *American Reunion*. Moreover, I recommend *Duplex* because the actor is *Ben Stiller* and you like him". In this case the system used the connections, extracted from DBpedia, between the recommended movie *Duplex* and the user preferences (i.e.*Meet the Fockers*, *American Reunion*, and *Ben Stiller*).

By tapping on the *Profile* button the user can also explore her profile, and update her preferences.

Finally, the Bot allows the user to give a feedback on a recommendation. It implements the *Adaptive Strategy* proposed in [2]. By tapping on the *Like, but...* button (Fig. 3(b)) the user activates the *Refine* process. The *Refine* is a critiquing strategy which allows the user to express a preference on a movie, but to separately evaluate its characteristics (e.g, *I like Pulp Fiction, but not Quentin Tarantino*). Therefore, the user can express a preference on a single property of a movie. The node associated to the property the user does not like (e.g., Quentin Tarantino) will be removed from the graph used by the PageRank and the recommendation process starts again on the new updated graph. The Algorithm 1 formalizes the process for leading the conversation. For the sake of simplicity, the algorithm does not report the functions for exploring and updating the profile. These are two functionalities the Bot offers to the user. Through these functions the user can view the preferences stored in her profile and change them. At the end, when the profile has been updated, the system will run again the PageRank and generate a new set of recommendations.

Data: *Recommendations* = top-5 recommendations, *Profile* = set of user
   preferences, *Graph* = graph representation of user preferences, items,
   entities, properties
Profile ← Profile + new preferences (items, entities, properties);
Recommendations ← PageRank (Graph, Profile);
Show Recommendations;
while *User does not accept Recommendations* **do**
   Feedback ← User feedback;
   Refine(Feedback);
   Recommendations ← PageRank (Graph, Profile);
   Show Recommendations;
end

Algorithm 1. Algorithm for Conversational Recommender

begin
   for *each liked characteristics* ∈ *Feedback* **do**
   | Profile ← Profile + liked characteristics
   end
   for *each disliked characteristics* ∈ *Feedback* **do**
   | remove disliked characteristic from Graph
   end
   return Graph, Profile
end

Procedure Refine(Feedback)

4   Experimental Evaluation

We designed a user study by involving 415 subjects (female $= 36.1\%$, master degree or PhD $= 37.9\%$, medium-high interest in movies $= 93.2\%$). The subjects were recruited by sharing on Facebook, LinkedIn, and some mailing lists, the invitation to take part in the experiment. The goal of our experiment is to define the best strategies for reducing the user interaction cost and improving her experience. Our experiment has three variables:

– *the selection of the items proposed to the user in cold-start situation.* There are two different strategies: (i) the selection based on the *most popular items*, and

(ii) the selection based on the *most diverse items*[3]. Strategy (i) proposes items that the user likely knows by reducing the time for acquiring the preferences, while the strategy (ii) proposes items that are different among them (e.g. different director, or genre, or actors) in order to build a more accurate profile.

- *the interaction mode.* The user can (i) *tap* the button corresponding to the chosen answer (she must choose among the answers proposed by the system), or (ii) *type* the name of the entity or property for which she wants to express a preference (e.g. a movie, an actor, a director, a genre).
- *the preference elicitation.* There are two possibilities for eliciting preferences: (i) to express a preference on a movie (e.g. *American Beauty*), and (ii) to express a preference on a movie property (e.g. *Quentin Tarantino, Julia Roberts, comedy movies*).

By combining these variables, we obtained the four configurations reported in Table 1. Each user was randomly assigned to one of the four configurations. It is worth noting that when the user expresses her preferences on movies and properties (i.e. conf # 4) she has to type her preferences. Indeed, to make available all the possible choices by buttons was complicated. Conversely, when the user can choose only movie properties (i.e. conf # 3) the interaction through buttons is available by categorizing the properties (e.g. Actor, Director, Music Composer, etc.) and by proposing only the most popular entities for each category. This is the reason why we have four configurations instead of six.

According to the experimental protocols designed in [11,13] we adopted the following metrics for evaluating the cost of interaction: *number of questions (NQ)*, i.e. the number of questions the chatbot asked before and after the recommendation, *question-answering time (QT)*, i.e. the time (in seconds) to answer to the chatbot questions, the *interaction time (IT)* (in seconds) i.e. the time from the preference acquisition to the recommendation acceptance. In order to evaluate the accuracy of the recommender we calculated the percentage of recommended lists where at least a liked movie appears in *Liked Lists (LL)*, and the *average precision (AP@k)* computed as follows:

$$AP@k = \frac{\sum_{l=1}^{k} P@l \cdot rel(l)}{k}, \qquad (1)$$

where $P@l$ is the precision considering the first l positions in the recommended list, $rel(l)$ is an indicator function equal to 1 if the item at rank l is liked, 0 otherwise. In our experiment, $k = 5$.

Experimental Protocol. We deployed a chatbot[4] designed to run a *between-subject* experiment, i.e., we tested four different configurations and each user was randomly assigned to one of them. When the user starts the experiment, her profile is empty.

---

[3] The diversity is computed by the Jaccard index on the movie properties between the items in the user profile and the items not rated yet.

[4] @MovieRecBot.

We asked the user to provide some basic demographic data. Then, each user follows the workflow depicted in Fig. 1. First, the user expresses her preferences according to the assigned configuration. Then the chatbot shows a set of five recommendations and for each recommended item the user can choose among 'like', 'dislike', 'like, but...', 'skip to the next movie'. Furthermore, for each movie she can look at more details extracted from IMDB or can obtain a personalized explanation. At the end of the experiment the user gives an overall rating on her general satisfaction of the interaction with the system on a 5-point Likert scale. The recommender works on a graph composed of 42,583 nodes of which 7,672 are movies. We collected 153 users for conf #1, 131 users for conf #2, 118 users for conf #3, and 127 users for conf #4. As stated in [19], the minimum acceptable sample size for each experimental condition was set as 73, thus our experiment guaranteed the significance of the results.

Results and Discussion. Table 2 shows the results for the accuracy metrics, and Table 3 shows the results for the interaction-cost metrics. The best overall results in term of LL and AP@k is achieved by configuration #4, which is the only one where the user can type her preferences. Hence, this interaction leads to more accurate user profiles and, consequently, more accurate recommendations. Configuration #4 has also a low interaction time (IT) (i.e. 388 s). As regards the different selection mode in cold start situations, results show that when the selection is based on popularity (i.e. conf #1), a higher accuracy is achieved compared to the selection based on diverse items (i.e. conf #2). Furthermore, conf #1 has also a lower interaction time than conf #2. So, the selection based on popularity should be preferred to a selection based on diversity. The comparison between the configurations based on the preferences expressed on the items (i.e. conf # 1, 2) or on the item properties (i.e. conf # 3) shows that the latter achieves a lower accuracy as well as a larger cost of interaction. Hence, the preference elicitation based on the item properties is generally more tiring for the user and less effective. Finally, the comparison between the interactions based on buttons (i.e. conf # 1, 2, 3) and the interaction based on typing the user preferences (i.e. conf # 4) shows that the latter mode is better both in terms of accuracy and interaction cost.

By analyzing the configurations in terms of NQ and QT emerged that the number of questions is generally very similar among the different configurations. This is likely due to a quite standard procedure in the training phase. An interesting outcome emerged by analyzing the correlation between question time and interaction time: the largest time for providing answer did not imply an equally largest interaction time (i.e. conf #4), probably because the interaction mode (i.e. typing) is effective.

Other interesting statistics extracted from the analysis of the system logs shows that the critiquing strategy leads to an improvement up to +9.41% in terms of LL and up to +31.04% in terms of Ap@k. The explanation function has been used for ~13% of recommended movies, and ~50% of the users explored their profile during the interaction.

Table 1. The four configurations of the Bot

conf #	Rated objects	Selection	Interaction
1	Movies	Popularity	Buttons
2	Movies	Diversity	Buttons
3	Properties	–	Buttons
4	Movies/Properties	–	Typing

Table 2. Accuracy metrics - in bold the best result for each metric

conf #	LL	AP@k	Overall rating
1	0.9038	0.5662	4.14
2	0.8971	0.4958	**4.20**
3	0.8793	0.5149	3.69
4	**0.9140**	**0.5853**	4.11

Table 3. Interaction-cost metrics

conf #	NQ	QT	IT
1	20.22	**11.75**	**352**
2	21.00	14.05	390
3	21.08	14.34	412
4	**19.90**	16.76	388

Finally, the overall rating on the experience with the Bot is greater than 4 for all the configurations with the exception of conf #3 so, the users have been generally satisfied by the experience with the chatbot.

5 Conclusion and Future Work

In this paper we proposed a movie recommender system implemented as Telegram chatbot. We evaluated different interaction modes in terms of interaction cost and recommendation accuracy. We implemented a critiquing strategy which adapts the recommendations to the user feedback. Results obtained by carrying out a user study demonstrated that when the user can type her preferences, the recommender shows the best trade off between accuracy and cost of interaction. An interaction based on buttons should propose popular items for reducing the interaction cost and improving the recommendation accuracy. Furthermore, the preferences given on the items are generally more effective than the preferences given on the item properties. Other interesting outcomes are that the critiquing strategies can lead to very significant improvements in terms of recommendation accuracy, and that the explanation and the profile-exploration functions are features liked by the users.

As future work, we will investigate an interaction completely based on natural language and we will test the recommender on other domains like music and book.

Acknowledgment. This work has been funded by the projects UNIFIED WEALTH MANAGEMENT PLATFORM - OBJECTWAY SpA - Via Giovanni Da Procida nr. 24, 20149 MILANO - c.f., P. IVA 07114250967, and PON01 00850 ASK-Health (Advanced system for the interpretations and sharing of knowledge in health care).

References

1. Mahmood, T., Ricci, F.: Improving recommender systems with adaptive conversational strategies. In: Proceedings of the 20th ACM Conference on Hypertext and Hypermedia, pp. 73–82. ACM (2009)
2. Mcginty, L., Smyth, B.: Adaptive selection: an analysis of critiquing and preference-based feedback in conversational recommender systems. Int. J. Electron. Commer. **11**(2), 35–57 (2006)
3. Lops, P., De Gemmis, M., Semeraro, G., Narducci, F., Musto, C.: Leveraging the LinkedIn social network data for extracting content-based user profiles. In: RecSys 2011 - Proceedings of the 5th ACM Conference on Recommender Systems, pp. 293–296 (2011)
4. Basile, P., Musto, C., de Gemmis, M., Lops, P., Narducci, F., Semeraro, G.: Content-based recommender systems + DBpedia knowledge = semantics-aware recommender systems. In: Presutti, V., et al. (eds.) SemWebEval 2014. CCIS, vol. 475, pp. 163–169. Springer, Cham (2014). https://doi.org/10.1007/978-3-319-12024-9_21
5. Musto, C., Narducci, F., Lops, P., de Gemmis, M.: Combining collaborative and content-based techniques for tag recommendation. In: Buccafurri, F., Semeraro, G. (eds.) EC-Web 2010. LNBIP, vol. 61, pp. 13–23. Springer, Heidelberg (2010). https://doi.org/10.1007/978-3-642-15208-5_2
6. Felfernig, A., Burke, R., Pu, P.: Preface to the special issue on user interfaces for recommender systems. User Model. User-Adapt. Interact. **22**(4), 313–316 (2012)
7. Narducci, F., Musto, C., Semeraro, G., Lops, P., de Gemmis, M.: Leveraging encyclopedic knowledge for transparent and serendipitous user profiles. In: Carberry, S., Weibelzahl, S., Micarelli, A., Semeraro, G. (eds.) UMAP 2013. LNCS, vol. 7899, pp. 350–352. Springer, Heidelberg (2013). https://doi.org/10.1007/978-3-642-38844-6_36
8. Chen, L., Pu, P.: Critiquing-based recommenders: survey and emerging trends. User Model. User-Adapt. Interact. **22**(1–2), 125–150 (2012)
9. Berkovsky, S., Freyne, J., Oinas-Kukkonen, H.: Influencing individually: fusing personalization and persuasion. ACM Trans. Interact. Intell. Syst. (TiiS) **2**(2), 9 (2012)
10. Tintarev, N., Masthoff, J.: Evaluating the effectiveness of explanations for recommender systems. User Model. User-Adapt. Interact. **22**(4–5), 399–439 (2012)
11. Kveton, B., Berkovsky, S.: Minimal interaction content discovery in recommender systems. ACM Trans. Interact. Intell. Syst. (TiiS) **6**(2), 15 (2016)
12. Sun, Y., Zhang, Y., Chen, Y., Jin, R.: Conversational recommendation system with unsupervised learning. In: Proceedings of the 10th ACM Conference on Recommender Systems, pp. 397–398. ACM (2016)

13. Christakopoulou, K., Radlinski, F., Hofmann, K.: Towards conversational recommender systems. In: Proceedings of the 22nd ACM SIGKDD International Conference on Knowledge Discovery and Data Mining, pp. 815–824. ACM (2016)

14. Smyth, B., McGinty, L., Reilly, J., McCarthy, K.: Compound critiques for conversational recommender systems. In: Proceedings of the 2004 IEEE/WIC/ACM International Conference on Web Intelligence, WI 2004, pp. 145–151. IEEE Computer Society, Washington, DC (2004). https://doi.org/10.1109/WI.2004.45

15. Yujian, L., Bo, L.: A normalized levenshtein distance metric. IEEE Trans. Pattern Anal. Mach. Intell. **29**(6), 1091–1095 (2007)

16. Haveliwala, T.H.: Topic-sensitive pagerank: a context-sensitive ranking algorithm for web search. IEEE Trans. Knowl. Data Eng. **15**(4), 784–796 (2003)

17. Musto, C., Lops, P., Basile, P., de Gemmis, M., Semeraro, G.: Semantics-aware graph-based recommender systems exploiting linked open data. In: Proceedings of the 2016 Conference on User Modeling Adaptation and Personalization, pp. 229–237. ACM (2016)

18. Musto, C., Narducci, F., Lops, P., De Gemmis, M., Semeraro, G.: ExpLOD: a framework for explaining recommendations based on the linked open data cloud. In: Proceedings of the 10th ACM Conference on Recommender Systems, pp. 151–154. ACM (2016)

19. Knijnenburg, B.P., Willemsen, M.C.: Evaluating recommender systems with user experiments. In: Ricci, F., Rokach, L., Shapira, B. (eds.) Recommender Systems Handbook, pp. 309–352. Springer, Boston (2015). https://doi.org/10.1007/978-1-4899-7637-6_9

Twitter User Recommendation
for Gaining Followers

Francesco Corcoglioniti[1]([⊠]) [iD], Yaroslav Nechaev[1,2] [iD], Claudio Giuliano[1] [iD],
and Roberto Zanoli[1]

[1] Fondazione Bruno Kessler, Via Sommarive 18, 38123 Trento, Italy
[2] University of Trento, Via Sommarive 14, 38123 Trento, Italy
{corcoglio,nechaev,giuliano,zanoli}@fbk.eu

Abstract. While social media presence is increasingly important for businesses, growing a social media account and improving its reputation by gathering followers are time-consuming tasks, especially for professionals and small businesses lacking the necessary skills and resources. With the broader goal of providing automatic tool support for social media account automation, in this paper we consider the problem of recommending a Twitter account manager a top-K list of Twitter users that, if approached—e.g., followed, mentioned, or otherwise targeted on social media—are likely to follow the account and interact with it, this way improving its reputation. We propose a recommendation system tackling this problem that leverages features ranging from basic social media attributes to specialized, domain-relevant user profile attributes predicted from data using machine learning techniques, and we report on a preliminary analysis of its performance in gathering new followers in a Twitter scenario where the account manager follows recommended users to trigger their follow-back.

Keywords: Social media · Recommendation systems
Machine learning

1 Introduction

Social media presence is recognized as an important factor for businesses, as it provides a channel for reaching potential customers, enabling for instance to gather their preferences and feedback, increase revenues through social marketing, and in general improve brand awareness and reputation [19]. However, maintaining a social media account and growing it by acquiring and engaging followers—the potential customers—are not for free. On the one hand, a successful account must provide some value to its followers, e.g., in terms of posted contents, conversation, and engagement. On the other hand, unless there is a reputation capital to leverage (e.g., a famous brand) and excluding the questionable practice of buying fake followers, gathering valuable followers that may interact and provide value to the account (differently from fake followers) may

© Springer Nature Switzerland AG 2018
C. Ghidini et al. (Eds.): AI*IA 2018, LNAI 11298, pp. 539–552, 2018.
https://doi.org/10.1007/978-3-030-03840-3_40

not be easy: these users have to discover the account first, so they must be actively searched, engaged and converted into followers by the account manager. All these activities require time and skills, and may be economically non-viable for professionals and small businesses lacking the required resources. While social media account automation tools exist to help account managers, they typically cover only the most basic tasks, like scheduling and optimizing posts for different social networks, and the feasibility and potential of further account automation targeting followers' engagement and account growth are still largely unexplored.

With the long term goal of investigating complex forms of social media account automation, in this paper we consider the problem of automatically identifying the social media users that are most likely to follow a given target account if approached by the account manager—e.g., followed, mentioned, or otherwise targeted in a social media message—to make them aware of the account existence. This is a form of *recommendation problem* where: (i) the target/active user is the social media account manager; (ii) the system has to provide a top-K list of potential followers ranked by the estimated likelihood that they will follow the target account, if engaged; (iii) the system may leverage data about users already following the target account (content-based view) or users following accounts similar to the target one (collaborative-filtering view); and (iv) the feedback about a recommendation is not provided directly by the account manager, but depends on the decision of the recommended user to convert into a follower.[1] The considered problem can be also related to *microtargeting* [4], as users are selected according to their characteristics and, based on that, engaged to stimulate a certain response: to follow the target account.

As it is known that rich profiling is crucial for microtargeting, as well as for content-based recommendation techniques, to address the considered problem we propose a *content-based recommendation system* [13] where recommended items are social media users, described with a rich profile that includes both domain-independent *basic user attributes* directly extracted from social media, and more computationally expensive, possibly domain-specific *specialized user attributes* derived from social media data using state-of-the-art classification techniques. We select Twitter and the (popular) Italian football domain for our experiments, thus considering specialized attributes such as a user's supported team. We performed a preliminary evaluation of the performance levels—conversion, interaction, and follower growth rates—achieved using the proposed system on a real Twitter account in the football domain, where the account manager follows the users recommended by the system to trigger their follow-back. We find that the use of specialized attributes significantly improves the performance when compared to baseline recommendation strategies not using them. At the same time, the daily use of the system allows achieving follower growth rates on par or even better than the rates of "competing" accounts in the same domain.

---

[1] The decision has to occur in a reasonable time window after the user has been engaged (causality). For simplicity, we assume also that the account manager trusts the system and engages all recommended users. If not, then also the feedback by the account manager about whether or not to engage a user should be accounted for.

The follow recommendation strategies discussed in this paper were implemented as part of our social media account automation system—Pokedem [6]. In addition to recommending users to follow, Pokedem also recommends the original content to post to engage the followers after their acquisition. Even though the posting strategies are out of the scope of this paper, they are undoubtedly a vital follower retention mechanism and will be briefly discussed in the paper.

The remainder of this paper is organized as follows. Section 2 summarizes related works. Section 3 describes the proposed recommendation system and the considered user attributes. Section 4 reports on the implementation of the approach within Pokedem. Section 5 reports on the use of the system on a real Twitter account, evaluating its performance against simpler recommendation baselines and similar Twitter accounts. Section 6 concludes.

2   Background and Related Work

Many social media, like Twitter, Facebook, Instagram, Pinterest, and LinkedIn, provide for a unidirectional *follow* relation between a *follower* and a *followee* users (using Twitter terminology). The relation is established by the follower, which then receives and may interact (e.g., share, reply, like) with all the contents posted by the followee. Therefore, increasing the number of followers allows a user to engage and broadcast his own contents to a larger audience, making his account more popular, reputable, and influential. This is clearly a goal for any business use of social media.

Many strategies are used to acquire followers on social media. Ignoring the paid promotion of one's account via the social media platform, and the purchase of fake followers [8] that generally violates terms of use and brings no interaction (acquired followers are fake "zombie" accounts), these strategies generally sum up to (i) providing original contents and other value that may attract users, and (ii) actively engaging users, e.g., by following or mentioning them, to convert them into followers. For the latter strategies, the choice of the users to engage is crucial. Mass follow strategies typically (and controversially) pick random users, but even if they convert into followers they may not be interested in interacting with the account, making them of limited value from a social and business points of view. On the other hand, manually picking users is time-consuming and does not scale.[2] A *recommendation system* suggesting potential followers to engage would thus be an invaluable asset for social media account managers.

The use of recommendation techniques to suggest the users to follow on social media has already been studied in the literature. However, the proposed approaches focus on recommending followees that a target/active user may find interesting. These approaches typically leverage either the social network topology via collaborative filtering techniques [1,11,23], the topics and features of

---

[2] In our tests, we spent 3 min per user if visual clues (e.g., profile picture and banner) could be exploited to assess a user's relevancy, and up to 15 min if the full profile had to be checked to determine if the user might be a potential follower.

user-generated contents via content-based techniques [2], or both kinds of features [3,10]; some approaches also consider the user sentiment [22] and personality traits [21]. The task solved by these approaches differ from our task as they do not aim at recommending users that may follow-back the target account, although in principle one may apply such systems *indirectly* by providing a ranked list of recommendations for *every* user in the social network (which may be millions) and then rank those users based on how high our target account looking for followers appears in those lists or how high it is scored (a ranking that we may assume to correlate with the follow-back likelihood). This is however an impractical solution if the goal is to provide recommendation to a single (or few) target account(s), and we are thus not investigating it further in this paper.

Other approaches in the literature take a network-centric view in recommending followees, e.g., by aiming at maximizing the content spread on the network [5], and thus address a task different from ours. Twitter itself provides a followee recommendation service [9] that operates by default on each user homepage and is accountable for a large fraction of the follow relations on Twitter. A survey of recommendation tasks and systems on Twitter is provided by Kywe et al. [12].

3   Proposed Approach

We propose a follower recommendation system that employs a simple *content-based recommendation algorithm* [13] (Sect. 3.1) together with a rich user representation featuring both *basic user attributes* directly obtained from social media (Sect. 3.2) and *specialized user attributes* estimated via supervised or rule-based classification techniques (Sect. 3.3).

3.1   Recommendation Algorithm

We denote with U the set of social media users (or a relevant sample of them if all users cannot be obtained) and with $a \in U$ the target/active user for which follower recommendations have to be produced. For this problem, the users are also the items to recommend. Each user $u \in U$ is represented with a profile vector $\boldsymbol{u}$ built based on different attributes derived from social media data. Given the set F_a of followers of target user a, we average the vectors of his/her followers to derive a preference vector $\boldsymbol{p}_a = \frac{1}{|F_a|} \sum_{u \in F_a} \boldsymbol{u}$. For each user $u \in U \setminus F_a$ that is a candidate for recommendation, we compute the cosine similarity $s_{a,u} = \frac{\boldsymbol{p}_a \boldsymbol{u}}{|\boldsymbol{p}_a||\boldsymbol{u}|}$ between $\boldsymbol{p}_a$ and $\boldsymbol{u}$. Based on the computed similarities, a top-k list $L_a = (u_1, \ldots, u_k)$ of recommended users $u_i \in U \setminus F_a$ is returned by the system so that $s_{a,u_i} \geq s_{a,u_j}$ for all $i < j \leq k$, and $s_{a,u_i} \geq s_{a,u}$ for all $u \in U \setminus L_{a,k}$.

3.2   Basic User Attributes

We collect the following cross-social media, domain-general *basic user attributes*, each one encoded as one or more binary elements in our user vectors and altogether capturing the information directly obtainable from raw social media data:

– *Activity level.* This binary attribute states whether the user did some posts in the last 6 months, and is motivated by the assumption that inactive users are unlikely to convert into followers if engaged.
– *Languages.* These are the languages associated to the user and his/her messages on social media, each one encoded as a binary vector element. This attribute accounts for the intuition that users whose language(s) differ from the one(s) of the target account may be unlikely to follow it.
– *Number of followers.* Often, users with more followers than the target account are less likely to follow it. We divide this attribute by the number of followers of the target account and discretize the result in binary classes.
– *Followees.* These are the accounts followed by the user, each represented as a binary vector element.[3] This attribute approximates a user's interests [14,20] and we may assume that users following the same accounts are similar.[4]
– *Influence score.* This attribute consists of a h-index like influence measure based on the number of posts and the interactions they obtained, computed as the maximum number h such that there are at least h user posts that obtained at least h interactions (likes, retweets) each. We encode it with a set of "lower than k" binary elements, and we intuitively assume users with large scores to be less likely to follow accounts with lower scores.

3.3 Specialized User Attributes

We consider the following *specialized user attributes*, each one represented with binary elements in our user vector and obtained indirectly using classification techniques on top of available social media data:

– *User type.* This attribute classifies users as either *persons*, *organizations*, or *bots*, based on a hard-coded rule-based classifier that looks for certain clues (e.g., specific keywords such as person names from a gazetteer) in the user social media profile. We expect these user categories to have different follow behaviors and the attribute permits to capture such differences, if any.
– *Gender.* We estimate this attribute using a rule-based strategy that compares the first name of the user (taken from his Twitter account) with two gazetteers of male and female names; the attribute accounts for gender-based differences, e.g., related to user interests, that may impact on the decision of following an account in a certain domain (e.g., the considered football one).
– *Location.* We estimate a user's location using a distant supervision technique where first we extract location data from Twitter user profiles explicitly stating it, using the Pelias[5] geo-coder system to normalize user-supplied location strings with respect to the GeoNames[6] geographic database. This data is

---

[3] An alternative TF/IDF representation is possible, where the IDF is computed on U and the TF may reflect the level of interaction between user and followed account.
[4] This assumption corresponds to a collaborative filtering hypothesis for the related but different task of providing recommendations to the potential followers.
[5] https://github.com/pelias/pelias.
[6] http://www.geonames.org/.

then used as ground truth together with the users' vector representations for training a supervised machine learning classifier (decision tree), which is then applied to predict the location of other Twitter users not declaring it.

- *Favorite Team.* We derive this attribute using a hard-coded rule-based strategy that considers: the football teams followed by a user (if just one it is likely it is his/her favourite team); the football players followed by a user together with the teams they play for; and the occurrence of certain team names or related keywords (e.g., mottos) in a user description. This *domain-specific* attribute accounts for the intuition that a target account biased towards a team is more likely to be followed by supporters of that team.

With the exception of the favorite team, which is specific to the Italian football domain where we evaluate our system, the remaining attributes are domain-general and usually available in any social media and not just Twitter. Note that the attribute classifiers may depend on the specific language considered (in our case, Italian), thus requiring specific adaptation or training for new languages.

4   Implementation

We implemented the approach in our Pokedem social media automation system[7] [6]. The goal of Pokedem is to automate the daily activities of social media account managers, reducing the burden, required time and skills needed for this job and allowing them to focus on activities needing human judgment and creativity. Focusing on Twitter, Pokedem provides an account manager with comprehensive data analytics about the performance of the account as well as the profiling of the target audience. The main feature of Pokedem, however, is its recommendation system implementing (for follow recommendations) the approach of Sect. 3. This system suggests possible actions to perform on the account (tweet/retweet, follow/unfollow, like), with the business-relevant goal [19] of improving account popularity—measured as number of followers—and audience engagement, rather than suggesting people and contents that the user may like as typically considered in Twitter recommendation literature [12].

Pokedem is available as a web application for social media account managers, through which they can manage and operate on a Twitter account. It consists of three components corresponding to distinct tabs in the web UI (Fig. 1):

- *Recommendations.* This tab (excerpt in Fig. 1a) provides a ranked, always up-to-date list of recommended social media actions, with explanations of why they are recommended. The account manager may reject, execute immediately, or schedule a recommended action for later execution at an optimal time chosen by the system. The execute/reject feedback of the account manager for past actions is currently ignored, although it is recorded and may be exploited in the future for further tuning the recommendations.

---

[7] Demonstration video at https://pokedem.futuro.media/.

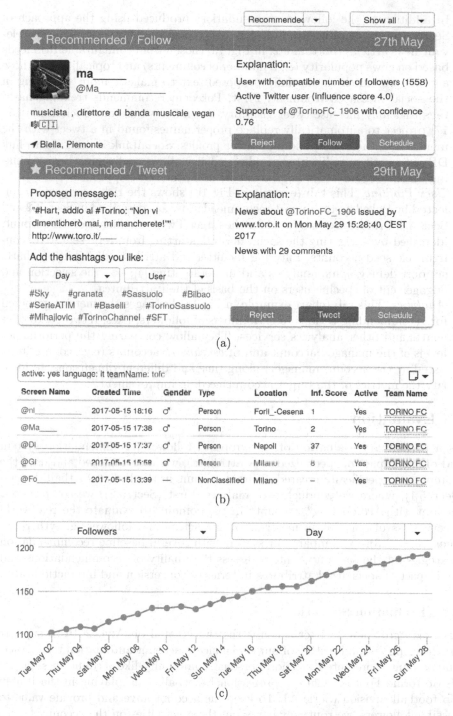

Fig. 1. Pokedem web UI (exemplified for the @esseredeltoro Twitter account): (a) Recommendations tab, (b) User Profiling tab, (c) Analytics tab.

In addition to the follow recommendations produced using the approach of Sect. 3 (top box in Fig. 1a), Pokedem also recommends tweeting links to relevant news articles (bottom box in Fig. 1a) chosen from configurable RSS feeds based on news popularity (e.g., number of comments) and topicality. For those actions, we enrich the initially proposed text to make it more appealing in the social media environment. First, Pokedem recommends trending hashtags that may increase tweet visibility. Secondly, we use our SocialLink [15–17] project to automatically replace proper names found in a tweet with the mentions of the corresponding twitter profiles. SocialLink is designed to link DBpedia entities to Twitter profiles and also allows performing Entity Linking on an arbitrary text (e.g., a tweet) using the same approach [7].

- *User Profiling.* This tab (excerpt in Fig. 1b) shows the rich user profiles collected by Pokedem to support recommendations, as described in Sect. 3.2 and Sect. 3.3. Profiles are computed for the target Twitter audience of the account, identified by navigating the social network starting from representative, configurable seed accounts. Filtering facilities and attribute distribution charts support demographic analyses and microtargeting [4], i.e., the selection and engagement of specific users on the basis of their attributes.

- *Analytics.* This tab (chart example in Fig. 1c) leverages the metrics gathered for recommending actions (e.g., numbers of followers, likes, retweets) to offer charts and other analytics services. They allow comparing the performance levels of the managed account and of *benchmark* accounts (e.g., competitors, listed by the account manager) along time and different dimensions, to identify the metrics of the target account needing improvement.

5 Evaluation

As a preliminary evaluation of the proposed follower recommendation system and of the impact of specialized user attributes, we have deployed and used the system on a specifically created Twitter account in the Italian football domain (Sect. 5.1), where we conduct two analyses. First (Sect. 5.2), we compare our account with "competing" accounts in the domain, to evaluate the real-world effectiveness of our system in terms of interaction and followers growth rates. Then (Sect. 5.3), we compare our system with several baseline recommendation strategies on the same account, to assess the quality of recommendations and the impact of specialized attributes in terms of conversion and interaction rates.

5.1 Evaluation Scenario

@esseredeltoro[8] is a Twitter account that we created on Aug. 2016 to support the development and testing of our social media account automation techniques. The account is presented as a non-personal, community-like account for supporters of Torino Football Club, a professional football team playing in the Italian top football division (Serie A). To keep the account alive and provide value to possible followers, we routinely carry out three activities on the account:

---

[8] https://twitter.com/esseredeltoro.

- *News posting.* Semi-automatically and on a daily basis, we post tweets linking to online news articles about Torino that may be of interest to its supporters. These tweets are drawn from the suggestions in the *Recommendations* tab of Pokedem, as discussed above.
- *Chart posting.* Semi-automatically and after each match, we post charts ranking the Twitter users most active in tweeting about Torino before and during the match, divided by category (e.g., supporters, journalists, fan clubs) and leveraging the user profiling techniques we employ for our recommendations.[9]
- *Conversation.* Manually and when contacted or mentioned, we reply to users' messages and engage them in conversation, also to avoid being seen as a bot.

After an initial two weeks bootstrap period, where we set up the account with its semi-automatic posting of contents and reached ~100 followers, we deployed our follower recommendation system and started following the users suggested by it, giving them a chance to discover our account and follow us back if interested. Apart a two weeks period where we experimented with different recommendation strategies, the system has been always active, permitting the account to reach 1000 followers on April 03, 2017 and 2067 followers as of today (June 11, 2018), overall suggesting that recommended users are actually interested in our account.

5.2 Comparison with Competing Accounts

We compare here the followers growth rates obtained by our account and by the competing accounts here used as baselines, to assess the effectiveness of the proposed recommendation system when used to grow a real account. As interacting with followers is important on social media, we also comment on the number of interactions—replies, retweets, and likes—obtained by @esseredeltoro and the baselines, to see how valuable are the acquired followers.

Experimental Setting. We consider a monitoring period of 6 months from Sept. 15, 2016 to March 15, 2017 where the proposed recommendation system was continuously used on @esseredeltoro, growing the number of followers from 138 to 920 and fostering interaction on the account. To put these effects into context, we identified two groups of competing accounts that serve as baselines, and we compare them with our account in terms of (i) the follower growth rate (avg. new followers per day) they experienced for a similar increase of followers from 100 to 1000 approximately,[10] and (ii) the interaction rates (avg. interactions per user per day) during the last month of this period—Feb. 15, 2017 to March 16, 2017—for which we have data for all the involved accounts.

Baselines. As baselines for this comparison, we identified two groups of Twitter accounts that similarly to @esseredeltoro present themselves as fan accounts supporting Torino Football Club:

---

[9] Examples of posted charts: https://bit.ly/2LXz1kK, https://bit.ly/2PGq4P5, https://bit.ly/2oIIvXS.

[10] Note that the growth from 100 to 1000 followers occurred in different periods for each account. As the growth rate depends on the number of followers previously accumulated, a comparison is possible only for the same growth range.

- *"Follow" accounts.* This group consists of 12 accounts (86 to 3008 followers, avg. 1052) exhibiting a strategy similar to @esseredeltoro, as they appear (by checking number and overlapping of followees and followers) to actively engage users by following them to trigger a possible follow-back.
- *"Post" accounts.* This group consists of 10 accounts (288 to 12800 followers, avg. 3842) that rarely engage users directly but rather focus on posting original content that may attract new followers. Many of these accounts are linked to online blogs and news providers for Torino Football Club.

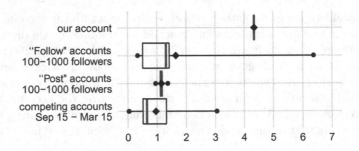

Fig. 2. Growth rates (avg. new followers per day) on our account and the baselines for growing from 100 to 1000 followers and for period Sept. 15, 2016 – March 15, 2017.

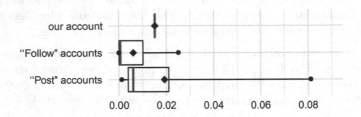

Fig. 3. Interaction rates (avg. interactions per user per day) on our account and the baseline groups of competing accounts for the period Feb. 15, 2017 – March 15, 2017.

Results. The box plot in Fig. 2 compares the growth rates of @esseredeltoro and the two baselines for the 100–1000 followers range, and also shows the growth rate of all competing accounts in the considered Sep 15 – Mar 15 period, which is similar to the other growth rates of these accounts and thus shows that no special event occurred in that period that may have favored @esseredeltoro. Our account maps to a single data point (4.34), while each baseline maps to a box with whiskers extending from minimum to maximum rates observed for the considered competing accounts. Using our recommendation system, @esseredeltoro performed better than any "Post" account in the 100 – 1000 followers range, meaning that our system is more effective at increasing followers than the expensive strategy of posting valuable contents. Compared to the "Follow" accounts distribution, @esseredeltoro performs over the upper quartile, meaning that engaging the users recommended by our system is more effective than following (almost) random users as typically done by "Follow" accounts.

The box plot in Fig. 3 compares the interaction rates on our account and the two baselines, in the Feb. 15, 2017 – March 16, 2017 period. Although "Post" accounts perform better than @esseredeltoro due to the high number of retweets and likes obtained by their original posts, we argue that using the proposed recommendation system helps narrowing the gap as it allows acquiring followers that are more interested in the target account and are thus more likely to interact with it than followers acquired by "Follow" accounts.

5.3 Comparison with Baseline Strategies

We compare here the recommendations by the proposed system with the ones produced by simpler baselines not using specialized user attributes, to assess their impact on followers conversion rates.

Experimental Setting. We simultaneously ran our system and different recommendation baselines on @esseredeltoro for two weeks. During this period, we selected and followed the top 135 users recommended by each strategy (our system, the baselines). Given that Twitter limits the number of people one may follow per day (to oppose mass following), we followed only a few dozen of new people at a time and then waited for some days giving those people a chance to follow us back. After this period, for each strategy we measured the conversion rate, i.e., the fraction of recommended and followed users that followed us back, as well as the number of interactions we had with those users.

Baselines. We chose the following baselines, considering only candidate users that were active (i.e., tweeted) in the last 6 months:

- *Simple Content Based.* This is a simpler version of the proposed approach that only includes followee information in user vectors, using 250 followers acquired before the experiment to compute the preference vector.
- *Torino FC.* Recommended users are randomly taken from the 220 K followers of @TorinoFC_1906,[11] the official account of Torino Football Club followed by passionate Torino supporters that may also be interested in our account.
- *Serie A.* Recommended users are randomly picked from the followers of @SerieA_TIM,[12] the official account of the top Italian football division, followed by 850 K people interested in Italian football and possibly in our account.
- *Twitter.* Twitter account suggestions [9] are based on several factors, including the social connections, posted tweets, and past interactions of the target

---

[11] https://twitter.com/TorinoFC_1906.
[12] https://twitter.com/SerieA_TIM.

account. As these suggestions are provided to any Twitter user and allow finding similar accounts, they represent an obvious baseline.

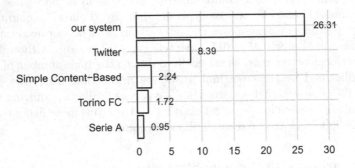

Fig. 4. Conversion rates (percentage of recommended users converted into followers) for the compared strategies.

Results. Figure 4 shows the conversion rates measured for our system and the considered baselines. We observe a large difference between the system and the Simple Content-Based baseline using only followee information, and a much greater difference with Torino FC, and Serie A baselines, confirming that a rich user characterization in terms of domain-specific attributes is important to target the right users and achieve high conversion rates. All the interactions observed during the experiment period were only with users recommended by the proposed system, suggesting that followers obtained with the considered baselines are less interested in the contents of our account and/or in interacting with it, and are thus of less value from a social media strategy point of view.

6   Conclusions and Future Work

We presented a recommendation system that, leveraging specialized user attributes learned from social media data, suggests users that are likely to convert into followers of a target/active user account. A preliminary evaluation on a real Twitter account shows that specialized attributes greatly improve conversion rates, and that using the system leads to interaction and follower growth rates that are competitive if compared to similar, "competing" accounts in the same domain. These results originate from ongoing work in investigating forms of social media automation for supporting account managers in their daily activities.

In future, we plan to recommend other action types, to improve the recommendations using feedback from similar accounts, and to expand the evaluation by testing the system on more Twitter accounts and domains. We also plan to improve the accuracy of attribute classifiers by leveraging the vector representation of Twitter users developed for SocialLink [17], and to increase the number of classified attributes by leveraging the alignment of Twitter users to DBpedia entities whose RDF properties can be used as training data for the classifiers [18].

Acknowledgments. This work was partially supported by the EC Commission through EIT Digital's High Impact Initiative Street Smart Retail (HII SSR).

References

1. Armentano, M.G., Godoy, D., Amandi, A.: Topology-based recommendation of users in micro-blogging communities. J. Comput. Sci. Tech. **27**(3), 624–634 (2012)
2. Armentano, M., Godoy, D., Amandi, A.: Followee recommendation based on text analysis of micro-blogging activity. Inf. Syst. **38**(8), 1116–1127 (2013)
3. Barbieri, N., Bonchi, F., Manco, G.: Who to follow and why: link prediction with explanations. In: Proceedings of KDD, pp. 1266–1275 (2014)
4. Barbu, O.: Advertising, microtargeting and social media. Procedia - Soc. Behav. Sci. **163**, 44–49 (2014)
5. Chaoji, V., Ranu, S., Rastogi, R., Bhatt, R.: Recommendations to boost content spread in social networks. In: Proceedings of WWW, pp. 529–538 (2012)
6. Corcoglioniti, F., Giuliano, C., Nechaev, Y., Zanoli, R.: Pokedem: an automatic social media management application. In: Proceedings of RecSys, pp. 358–359 (2017)
7. Corcoglioniti, F., Palmero Aprosio, A., Nechaev, Y., Giuliano, C.: MicroNeel: Combining NLP tools to perform named entity detection and linking on microposts. In: Proceedings of EVALITA (2016)
8. Cresci, S., Di Pietro, R., Petrocchi, M., Spognardi, A., Tesconi, M.: Fame for sale: efficient detection of fake Twitter followers. Decis. Support Syst. **80**, 56–71 (2015)
9. Gupta, P., Goel, A., Lin, J., Sharma, A., Wang, D., Zadeh, R.: WTF: The who to follow service at Twitter. In: Proceedings of WWW, pp. 505–514 (2013)
10. Hannon, J., Bennett, M., Smyth, B.: Recommending Twitter users to follow using content and collaborative filtering approaches. In: Proceedings of RecSys, pp. 199–206 (2010)
11. Kim, Y., Shim, K.: TWILITE: a recommendation system for Twitter using a probabilistic model based on latent Dirichlet allocation. Inf. Syst. **42**, 59–77 (2014)
12. Kywe, S.M., Lim, E.P., Zhu, F.: A survey of recommender systems in Twitter. In: Proceedings of SocInfo, pp. 420–433 (2012)
13. Lops, P., de Gemmis, M., Semeraro, G.: Content-based recommender systems: state of the art and trends. In: Ricci, F., Rokach, L., Shapira, B., Kantor, P.B. (eds.) Recommender Systems Handbook, pp. 73–105. Springer, Boston (2011). https://doi.org/10.1007/978-0-387-85820-3_3
14. Nechaev, Y., Corcoglioniti, F., Giuliano, C.: Concealing interests of passive users in social media. In: Proceedings of Re-coding Black Mirror ISWC Workshop (2017)
15. Nechaev, Y., Corcoglioniti, F., Giuliano, C.: Linking knowledge bases to social media profiles. In: Proceedings of SAC, pp. 145–150 (2017)
16. Nechaev, Y., Corcoglioniti, F., Giuliano, C.: SocialLink: linking DBpedia entities to corresponding Twitter accounts. In: Proceedings of ISWC, pp. 165–174 (2017)
17. Nechaev, Y., Corcoglioniti, F., Giuliano, C.: SocialLink: exploiting graph embeddings to link DBpedia entities to Twitter profiles. Prog. Artif. Intell. (2018, to appear)

18. Nechaev, Y., Corcoglioniti, F., Giuliano, C.: Type prediction combining linked open data and social media. In: Proceedings of CIKM (2018, to appear)
19. Paniagua, J., Sapena, J.: Business performance and social media: love or hate? Bus. Horiz. **57**(6), 719–728 (2014)
20. Piao, G., Breslin, J.G.: Inferring user interests in microblogging social networks: a survey. User Model. User-Adapt. Interact. **28**, 277–329 (2018)
21. Tommasel, A., Corbellini, A., Godoy, D., Schiaffino, S.: Personality-aware followee recommendation algorithms: an empirical analysis. Eng. Appl. Artif. Intell. **51**, 24–36 (2016)
22. Yuan, G., Murukannaiah, P.K., Zhang, Z., Singh, M.P.: Exploiting sentiment homophily for link prediction. In: Proceedings of RecSys, pp. 17–24 (2014)
23. Zhao, G., Lee, M.L., Hsu, W., Chen, W., Hu, H.: Community-based user recommendation in uni-directional social networks. In: Proceedings of CIKM, pp. 189–198 (2013)

Analytical Network Process Method Under the Belief Function Framework

Amel Ennaceur[1,2(✉)], Zied Elouedi[1], and Eric Lefevre[3]

[1] Institut Supérieur de Gestion, LARODEC, Université de Tunis, Tunis, Tunisia
amel_naceur@yahoo.fr, zied.elouedi@gmx.fr
[2] Faculté des Sciences Juridiques, Economiques et de Gestion de Jendouba,
Université de Jendouba, Jendouba, Tunisie
[3] Univ. Artois, EA 3926 LGI2A Béthune, LGI2A, 62400 Arras, France
eric.lefevre@univ-artois.fr

Abstract. This paper describes a belief extension of the analytic network process (ANP), a multi-criteria prioritization method to model decision making under uncertain context. The approach accommodates the use of qualitative preference relations as input information in the pairwise comparison matrices. Instead of applying the Saaty scale in the prioritization process, a new method, based on the belief function theory, is applied. The proposed approach is illustrated by examples.

1 Introduction

The Analytic Hierarchy Process (AHP) [13,14] is one of the most widely used multi-criteria decision making (MCDM) methods. This approach assumes that the decision making problem can be structured hierarchically, where each element is independent from all the others.

However, in some situations, strong dependencies between inter-level or intra-level elements may exist. To solve this problem, a supermatrix approach [15] was proposed by Saaty, named the Analytic Network Process (ANP). Its main aim is to extend the AHP method to model interactions and feedback.

Like AHP method, the pairwise comparison technique is used to compute ANP method priorities. Each element is then paired and compared using the Saaty's scale. However, due to the uncertainty on the expert assessments, the crisp pairwise comparison technique in the standard AHP and ANP approaches seems insufficient and imprecise to capture the right assessments of decision makers.

As a way to handle this uncertainty, using of fuzzy set theory has been largely suggested in the literature. Accordingly, several fuzzy ANP methods [1,9,10] and fuzzy AHP [8] have been introduced.

In the same way, under the belief function framework, the AHP method has been extended to handle imperfection. Many AHP extensions were introduced [3,4,7]. Therefore, we propose, in this paper, to combine the ANP method and the belief function theory. A new multicriteria decision making technique that is able to represent decision making under uncertain context.

© Springer Nature Switzerland AG 2018
C. Ghidini et al. (Eds.): AI*IA 2018, LNAI 11298, pp. 553–563, 2018.
https://doi.org/10.1007/978-3-030-03840-3_41

This paper is aimed at presenting a Qualitative ANP approach. The proposed method suggests the use of belief preference relations in the supermatrix [4,5]. We propose to derive meaningful priorities from qualitative decision structures. Instead of applying the Eigenvector method in the prioritization process, a new model, which obtains crisp priorities from qualitative assessments is applied.

In what follows, we first present some definitions needed for belief function theory. Next, we describe the ANP method in Sect. 3. Then, Sect. 4 details our new multicriteria method, and gives an example to show its application. Finally, Sect. 5 concludes the paper.

2   Belief Function Theory

In this section, we briefly introduce the belief function theory as interpreted by the Transferable Belief Model (TBM). More Details can be found in [16–18].

2.1   Basic Concepts

Let Θ be the frame of discernment representing a finite set of elementary hypotheses related to a problem domain, where 2^{Θ} is the set of all the subsets of Θ [16].

The belief assignment (bba), denoted by m, represent the impact of a piece of evidence on the different subsets of Θ.

$$\sum_{A \subseteq \Theta} m(A) = 1. \tag{1}$$

The basic belief mass (bbm), denoted $m(A)$, models the part of belief committed exactly to A. The events having positive bbm's are called focal elements, where $\mathcal{F}(m) \subseteq 2^{\Theta}$ is the set of all focal elements of the bba m.

Accordantly, a belief function is defined for $A \subseteq \Theta$ and $A \neq \emptyset$ as:

$$bel(A) = \sum_{\emptyset \neq B \subseteq A} m(B) \text{ and } bel(\emptyset) = 0. \tag{2}$$

2.2   Decision Making

The TBM proposes two level models. First, the credal level where beliefs are entertained and represented by belief functions. Second, the pignistic level where beliefs are used to make decisions and represented by the so called pignistic probabilities, $BetP$ [17]:

$$BetP(A) = \sum_{B \subseteq \Theta} \frac{|A \cap B|}{|B|} \frac{m(B)}{(1 - m(\emptyset))}, \forall A \in \Theta. \tag{3}$$

2.3   Uncertainty Measures

In the case of the belief function framework, different uncertainty measures (UM) have been defined, such as [11, 12]:

$$H(m) = \sum_{A \in \mathcal{F}(m)} m(A) \log_2(\frac{|A|}{m(A)}).$$ (4)

The measure H is aimed at assessing the total uncertainty arising in a body of evidence due to both randomness (ignorance and inconsistency) and nonspecificity associated with a bba.

The measure H attains its global maximum when the bba distributes both randomness and nonspecificity uniformly over the largest possible set of focal elements.

3   Analytical Network Process Method

One of the most known multi-criteria decision making approach is the Analytical Network Process (ANP). The originality of ANP lies in its ability to represent complex decision making problems and to involve dependencies and feedbacks between decision elements.

Unlike AHP, ANP makes no assumptions about the independence of higher level elements from lower level elements and about the independence of the elements within a level (see Fig. 1). An AHP hierarchy is based on a main objective, a selected criteria, sub-criteria and decision alternatives, but a network model has cycles connecting its clusters of elements (outer dependence) and loops that connect a cluster to itself (inner dependence).

The main steps of ANP are described in what follows [15].

3.1   Constructing of the Network Structure

The ANP process starts by constructing the group of elements and clusters that would best model the problem. Indeed, the elements in terms of criteria, sub-criteria and alternatives are defined and clusters of these elements are respectively formed. So, a network is developed based on the relationships between and within these clusters.

3.2   Building Pairwise Comparison

Like AHP, the pairwise comparison process is used to model the expert preferences and to estimate the local priorities of the selected criteria, sub-criteria and alternatives.

To represent his assessments, the decision maker has to respond to the following question: Given an element (in the same cluster or in another cluster) or a cluster, how much more does a given element (cluster) of a pair influence that element (cluster) with respect to a criterion?

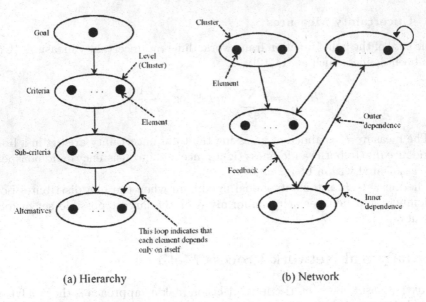

(a) Hierarchy   (b) Network

Fig. 1. The difference between a hierarchy and a network models [15]

The responses to these questions, the expert use the Saaty scale, where 1 indicates indifference between the two elements and 9 indicates a strong preference of the element under consideration over the comparison element (see Table 1).

Table 1. The Saaty rating scale

Saaty's scale	Definition
1	Equal importance
3	Somewhat more important
5	Much more important
7	Very much more important
9	Absolutely more important
2, 4, 6, 8	Intermediate values

Once the pairwise comparisons are completed, a local priority vector is derived for all comparison matrices.

To validate the expert judgments', a consistency index is calculated to check the consistency of the pairwise comparisons matrices.

3.3 Construction the Supermatrix

When all the local priorities are calculated, these are used to form the super-matrix. In this method, each local priority vectors is entered as a part of some column of a matrix (see Fig. 2),

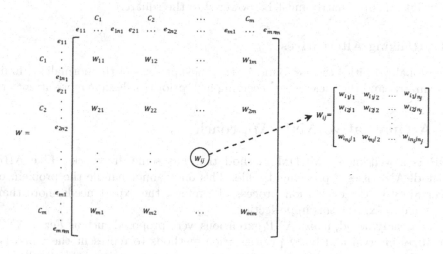

Fig. 2. An example of one of the supermatrix block matrices [15]

where C_m denotes the mth cluster with n_m elements $(e_{m1}, e_{m2}, ..., e_{n_m}$, where e_{n_m} represents the nth element in the mth cluster).

W_{ij} is a priority vector representing the impact of the elements in the ith cluster on the elements in the jth cluster ($W_{ij} = 0$ if there is no influence between the clusters). Figure 3 illustrates a sample example [20].

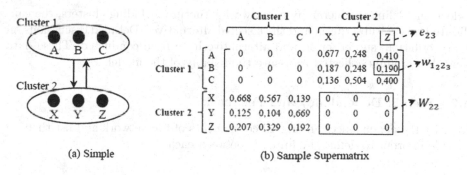

(a) Simple   (b) Sample Supermatrix

Fig. 3. An illustrative example of a network

The next step, according to Saaty methodology, is to construct the weighted supermatrix using the component matrix to weight the supermatrix previously assembled.

To calculate the weighted supermatrix is a need to make the matrix stochastic. This condition is necessary for obtaining the resulting limit supermatrix. This matrix is calculated elevating the weighted supermatrix to the nth power. This procedure allows capturing the transmission of influences from all the paths of the network. For example, to obtain indirect influences through a third element, the weighted supermatrix must be powered to the square.

3.4   Ranking Alternatives

The global priorities can be found in the relevant rows of the normalized limit supermatrix and those elements receiving high priorities deserve more attention.

4   A Qualitative ANP Approach

ANP is a well-known MCDM method that has some drawbacks. Like AHP method, ANP uses a predefined scale. This one cannot handle the problem of uncertainty in the evaluation process. Therefore, the expert needs more than $1-9$ scale to express this imperfection.

As already noted, many ANP extensions were proposed such as Fuzzy ANP. It utilizes interval and fuzzy prioritization methods to represent the pair-wise comparisons matrix and to derive interval or fuzzy local priorities [1,9,10].

However, our proposed method, which derives belief priorities from qualitative assessments, can be easily applied to increase the capabilities of the ANP for dealing with inconsistent and uncertain judgments.

In the following, we present a new way of comparisons under the ANP approach and we introduce our suggested solution.

4.1   Step 1: Network Model

Select and define the hierarchy or network structure including clusters, the candidate criteria, sub-criteria and the selected alternatives. Detailed discussions on every criterion, sub-criterion and alternative have been conducted. These data must be carefully collected to assure the reliably of the model.

4.2   Step 2: Dependency and Feedback

Identify the dependences among all components of the network and list them in a table in order to define the impacts between each.

4.3   Step 3: Pairwise Comparison Matrices

Construct pairwise comparison matrices of the elements with preference relations.

Like standard ANP, the comparison of elements connected to others follows the same principal and method as in AHP. So, each two elements are compared in terms of dominance with respect to a common aspect. Therefore, instead of using Saaty's scale, the responses to the pairwise comparison questions are scaled on the basis of a flexible way using binary preference relations [5].

For example, to compare criteria to the main objective, the corresponding matrix is shown in Table 2 [7].

Table 2. An example of the pairwise comparison matrix

	e_{11}	e_{12}	$\ldots$	e_{mn}
e_{11}	-	P_{12}	$\ldots$	P_{1n}
e_{12}	-	-	$\ldots$	P_{2n}
$\ldots$	-	-	-	$\ldots$
e_{mn}	-	-	-	-

In this Table, P_{ij} is a binary relation. It may be:

1. a strong preference relation $\succ$
2. a weak preference relation $\succeq$
3. an indifference relation $\sim$
4. an unknown relation.

4.4   Step 4: Local Priorities

Derive relative importance weights (local priorities) from the constructed pairwise comparison matrix using the belief prioritizing method.

Transforming belief functions from qualitative assessments and generating quantitative beliefs have been handled by many works [2, 6, 10]. In this study, we consider approaches presented in [2] and [6].

As we have mentioned, to express his assessments, an expert may use the strict preference ($\succ$) or the indifference ($\sim$) or the weak-preference ($\succeq$) or unknown relations.

Based on [6], these relations are transformed into constraints as follows:

$$e_{11} \succ e_{12} \Leftrightarrow bel(e_{11}) - bel(e_{12}) \geq \gamma \tag{5}$$

$$e_{11} \succeq e_{12} \Leftrightarrow \varepsilon \leq bel(e_{11}) - bel(e_{12}) \leq \gamma \tag{6}$$

$$e_{11} \sim e_{12} \Leftrightarrow |bel(e_{11}) - bel(e_{12})| \leq \varepsilon \tag{7}$$

where ε is the smallest gap between two degrees of belief. Its value is a constant defined by the decision maker. Similarly to the preference index ε, γ is the indifference threshold.

After modeling the different preference relations, we introduce the preference relations as an optimization problem whose resolution, according to some uncertainty measures (nonspecificity measures, conflict measures, composite measures), allows the generation of the least informative or the most uncertain belief functions. Therefore, each preference relation is transformed into its corresponding constraint as follows.

$$Max_m UM(m)$$
$$s.t.$$
$$bel(e_{11}) - bel(e_{12}) \geq \gamma \quad \forall(e_{11}, e_{12}) \text{ for which } e_{11} \succ e_{12}$$
$$bel(e_{11}) - bel(e_{12}) \leq \gamma \quad \forall(e_{11}, b) \text{ for which } e_{11} \succeq e_{12}$$
$$bel(e_{11}) - bel(e_{12}) \geq \varepsilon \quad \forall(e_{11}, e_{12}) \text{ for which } e_{11} \succeq e_{12} \quad (8)$$
$$bel(e_{11}) - bel(e_{12}) \leq \varepsilon \quad \forall(e_{11}, e_{12}) \text{ for which } e_{11} \sim e_{12}$$
$$bel(e_{11}) - bel(e_{12}) \geq -\varepsilon \quad \forall(e_{11}, e_{12}) \text{ for which } e_{11} \sim e_{12}$$
$$\sum_{e_{1i} \in \mathcal{F}(m)} m(e_{1i}) = 1; m(a) \geq 0; \forall e_{1i} \subseteq \Theta; m(\emptyset) = 0.$$

where UM is a measure of uncertainty. In this case, we take the measure of uncertainty H as defined in Eq. 4.

The first constraint models the strict preference. The second and third ones represent the weak preference relation. The fourth and fifth constraints are derived from the indifference relation. ε and γ are a constant specified by the decision maker.

The choice of ε and γ affects whether a binary relationship holds. While selecting an appropriate value is not an easy task, because in most cases there are good reasons for choosing non-zero.

Consequently, the obtained bba provide an estimate of the local priorities for the decision elements being compared. Then, the obtained vector has to be transformed into pignistic probabilities (see Eq. 3).

Example. Let us consider the following preference relation matrix (see Table 3).

Table 3. Comparison matrix

Criteria	e_{11}	e_{12}	e_{13}
e_{11}	-	$\succ$	$\succ$
e_{12}	-	-	$\succ$
e_{13}	-	-	-

The expert has identified the following assignments:

- He assume that the preference threshold is $\gamma = 0.02$.
- each preference relation is transformed into a constraint.
  1. $e_{11} \succ e_{12} \Leftrightarrow bel(e_{11}) - bel(e_{12}) \geq 0.02$
  2. $e_{11} \succ e_{13} \Leftrightarrow bel(e_{11}) - bel(e_{13}) \geq 0.02$
  3. $e_{12} \succ e_{13} \Leftrightarrow bel(e_{12}) - bel(e_{13}) \geq 0.02$

- The following step is to transform the obtained constraints into an optimization problem.

$$Max_m H(m) = m(e_{11}) * log_2(1/m(e_{11})) + m(e_{12}) * log_2(1/m(e_{12}))$$
$$+ m(e_{13}) * log_2(1/m(e_{13})) + m(\Theta) * log_2(3/m(\Theta));$$

s.t.

$$bel(e_{11}) - bel(e_{12}) \geq 0.02$$
$$bel(e_{11}) - bel(e_{13}) \geq 0.02 \tag{9}$$
$$bel(e_{12}) - bel(e_{13}) \geq 0.02$$
$$\sum_{e_{ij} \in \mathcal{F}(m)} m(e_{ij}) = 1, m(e_{ij}) \geq 0, \forall e_{ij} \subseteq \Theta; m(\emptyset) = 0,$$

- By solving this optimization problem, we obtain the result defined in Table 4.

Table 4. Weights assigned to the selected criteria

Criteria	$\{e_{11}\}$	$\{e_{12}\}$	$\{e_{13}\}$	Θ
m^Θ	0.228	0.208	0.188	0.376

Criteria	$\{e_{11}\}$	$\{e_{12}\}$	$\{e_{13}\}$
$BetP^\Theta$	0.352	0.333	0.315

- Then, the obtained bba is transformed into pignistic probabilities as shown in Table 4.

4.5   Step 5: Consistency

The quality of the estimation of local priorities highly depends on the consistency of judgments that the decision makers performed throughout the pairwise comparisons. At this level, expert has to evaluate the obtained bba. Thus, the proposed method addresses this problem. In fact, if the preference relations are consistent, then the optimization problem is feasible. Otherwise no solutions will be found. Thus, the expert may be guided to reformulate his assessments.

4.6   Step 6: Build Supermatrix

Construct the supermatrix with the obtained priorities in order to form an unweighted supermatrix. In this step, each pignistic probabilities (local priority vectors) computed in the step 4 is entered as a part of a relevant column of the supermatrix.

Then, we follow the same steps as standard ANP. We have to normalize the supermatrix to column stochastic to get the sum of the elements in each column is equal to one.

After that, we limit the weighted supermatrix by raising it to a sufficiently large power (where is an arbitrarily large number) until it converges into a stable supermatrix.

Finally, we aggregate the weights of criteria and the scores of alternatives into final priorities by multiplying the scores by the weights of the control criteria.

5   Conclusion

This paper presents a new method which combines both the AHP approach and the belief function theory to deal with complex decision making problems. Our solution proposes to handle uncertain pairwise comparison judgments. Thus, using preference relations in all pair-wise comparison matrices has facilitated the elicitation process. In fact, our approach suggests an easier elicitation of expert assessments through the reduction of necessary information and using qualitative information rather than exact numbers. At the same time, our approach handles uncertainty by adopting each obtained priority as a basic belief assignment.

As a further work, we propose to consider uncertainty in the supermatrix calculations to represent the uncertainty associated with the cumulative influence of each element on every other element with which it interacts in the network.

References

1. Asan, U., Serdarasan, A.S.S.: A fuzzy analytic network process approach. In: Computational Intelligence Systems in Industrial Engineering, Atlantis Computational Intelligence Systems, pp. 155–179 (2012)
2. Ben Yaghlane, A., Denoeux, T., Mellouli, K.: Constructing belief functions from expert opinions. In: Proceedings of the 2nd International Conference on Information and Communication Technologies: from Theory to Applications (ICTTA 2006), Damascus, Syria, pp. 75–89 (2006)
3. Beynon, M., Xu, D.C., Marshall, D.: An expert system for multi-criteria decision making using dempster shafer theory. Expert. Syst. Appl. **20**, 357–367 (2001)
4. Ennaceur, A., Elouedi, Z., Lefevre, E.: Handling partial preferences in the belief AHP method: application to life cycle assessment. In: Pirrone, R., Sorbello, F. (eds.) AI*IA 2011. LNCS (LNAI), vol. 6934, pp. 395–400. Springer, Heidelberg (2011). https://doi.org/10.1007/978-3-642-23954-0_37
5. Ennaceur, A., Elouedi, Z., Lefevre, E.: Multicriteria decision making based on qualitative assessments and relational belief. In: Baldoni, M., Baroglio, C., Boella, G., Micalizio, R. (eds.) AI*IA 2013. LNCS (LNAI), vol. 8249, pp. 48–59. Springer, Cham (2013). https://doi.org/10.1007/978-3-319-03524-6_5
6. Ennaceur, A., Elouedi, Z., Lefevre, E.: Modeling qualitative assessments under the belief function framework. In: Cuzzolin, F. (ed.) BELIEF 2014. LNCS (LNAI), vol. 8764, pp. 171–179. Springer, Cham (2014). https://doi.org/10.1007/978-3-319-11191-9_19
7. Ennaceur, A., Elouedi, Z., Lefevre, E.: Multi-criteria decision making method with belief preference relations. Int. J. Uncertain. Fuzziness Knowl.-Based Syst. **22**(4), 573–590 (2014)
8. Laarhoven, P.V., Pedrycz, W.: A fuzzy extension of Saaty's priority theory. Fuzzy Sets Syst. **11**, 199–227 (1983)
9. Mikhailov, L.: Deriving priorities from fuzzy pairwise comparison judgments. Fuzzy Sets Syst. **134**(3), 365–385 (2003)
10. Mikhailov, L., Singh, M.G.: Fuzzy analytic network process and its application to the development of decision support systems. IEEE Trans. Syst. Man Cybern. **33**(1), 33–41 (2003)

11. Pal, N., Bezdek, J., Hemasinha, R.: Uncertainty measures for evidential reasoning I: a review. Int. J. Approx. Reason. **7**, 165–183 (1992)
12. Pal, N., Bezdek, J., Hemasinha, R.: Uncertainty measures for evidential reasoning II: a review. Int. J. Approx. Reason. **8**, 1–16 (1993)
13. Saaty, T.: A scaling method for priorities in hierarchical structures. J. Math. Psychol. **15**, 234–281 (1977)
14. Saaty, T.: The Analytic Hierarchy Process. McGraw-Hill, New-York (1980)
15. Saaty, T.: Decision making with dependence and feedback: The Analytic Network Process. RWS, Pittsburgh (1996)
16. Shafer, G.: A Mathematical Theory of Evidence. Princeton University Press, Princeton (1976)
17. Smets, P.: The application of the transferable belief model to diagnostic problems. Int. J. Intell. Syst. **13**, 127–158 (1998)
18. Smets, P., Kennes, R.: The transferable belief model. Artif. Intell. **66**, 191–234 (1994)
19. Wong, S., Lingras, P.: Representation of qualitative user preference by quantitative belief functions. IEEE Trans. Knowl. Data Eng. **6**, 72–78 (1994)
20. Yu, R., Tzeng, G.H.: A soft computing method for multi-criteria decision making with dependence and feedback. Appl. Math. Comput. **180**, 63–75 (2006)

Author Index

Printed in the United States
By Bookmasters